JAPAN

BUSINESS

**World Trade Press
Country Business Guides**

CHINA Business
HONG KONG Business
JAPAN Business
KOREA Business
MEXICO Business
SINGAPORE Business
TAIWAN Business

JAPAN
BUSINESS

The Portable Encyclopedia
For Doing Business With Japan

Christine A. Genzberger   Edward G. Hinkelman

David E. Horovitz   William T. LeGro

Jonathan W. Libbey   Charles Smithson Mills

James L. Nolan   Stacey S. Padrick

Karla C. Shippey, J.D.   Kelly X. Wang

Chansonette Buck Wedemeyer   Alexandra Woznick

Auerbach International • CIGNA Property and Casualty
Ernst & Young • Foreign Trade • Far Eastern Economic Review
Japan External Trade Organization (JETRO)
Reed Publishing (USA) Inc.

Series Editor: Edward G. Hinkelman

WORLD TRADE PRESS ®

Resources for International Trade

1505 Fifth Avenue
San Rafael, California 94901
USA

Published by World Trade Press
1505 Fifth Avenue
San Rafael, CA 94901
USA

Cover and book design: Brad Greene
Illustrations: Eli Africa
Color Maps: Gracie Artemis
B&W maps: David Baker
Desktop Publishing: Kelly R. Krill and Gail R. Weisman
Charts and Graphs: David Baker and Kelly R. Krill
Publication Reviewer: Aanel Victoria

Library of Congress Cataloging-in-Publication Data
Japan business : the portable encyclopedia for doing business with
    Japan / Christine Genzberger . . . [et al.].
        p.   cm. – (World Trade Press country business guides)
    Includes bibliographical references and index.
    ISBN 0-9631864-2-6 : $24.95
    1. Japan—Commerce—Handbooks, manuals, etc.   2. Japan—Commerce—
Encyclopedias.   I. Genzberger, Christine.   II. Series.
HF3827.J37 1994   93-45974
658.8'48'0952–dc20   CIP

Printed in the United States of America

ACKNOWLEDGMENTS

The contributions of hundreds of trade and reference experts have made this book possible.

We are indebted to numerous international business consultants, reference librarians, travel advisors, consulate, embassy, and trade mission officers, bank officers, attorneys, global shippers and insurers, and multinational investment brokers who answered our incessant inquiries and volunteered facts, figures, and expert opinions.

A special note of gratitude is due to those at the U.S. Department of Commerce, the Japan External Trade Organization (JETRO), and the Singapore Trade Development Board.

We relied heavily on the reference librarians and resources available at the Marin County Civic Center Library, Marin County Law Library, San Rafael Public Library, San Francisco Public Library, University of California at Berkeley libraries, and U.S. Department of Commerce Library in San Francisco.

Thank you to attorneys John Kakinuki, Robert T. Yahng, and Anne M. Kelleher, with Baker & McKenzie, San Francisco, Roger Fleischman, Fleischman & Fleischman, San Francisco, and Alexander Calhoun, Grahm & James, San Francisco, who spent precious time in assisting us with the law section. We also extend our sincere appreciation to Barry Tarnef, with CIGNA Property and Casualty Co., who graciously supplied information on world ports.

We also acknowledge the valuable contributions of Philip B. Auerbach of Auerbach International, San Francisco, for translations; all the patient folks at Desktop Publishing of Larkspur, California; and Leslie Endicott and Susan August for reviewing, proofing, and correcting down to the smallest detail.

Thanks go to Elizabeth Karolczak for establishing the World Trade Press Intern Program, and to the Monterey Institute of International Studies for its assistance.

To Jerry and Kathleen Fletcher, we express our deep appreciation for their immeasurable support during this project.

Very special thanks to Mela Hinkelman whose patience, understanding, generosity, and support made this project possible.

DISCLAIMER

We have diligently tried to ensure the accuracy of all of the information in this publication and to present as comprehensive a reference work as space would permit. In determining the contents, we were guided by many experts in the field, extensive hours of research, and our own experience. We did have to make choices in coverage, however, because the inclusion of everything one could ever want to know about international trade would be impossible. The fluidity and fast pace of today's business world makes the task of keeping data current and accurate an extremely difficult one. This publication is intended to give you the information that you need in order to discover the information that is most useful for your particular business. As you contact the resources within this book, you will no doubt learn of new and exciting business opportunities and of additional international trading requirements that have arisen even within the short time since we published this edition. If errors are found, we will strive to correct them in preparing future editions. The publishers take no responsibility for inaccurate or incomplete information that may have been submitted to them in the course of research for this publication. The facts published indicate the result of those inquiries and no warranty as to their accuracy is given.

Contents

Introduction

Japan, the world's second-largest economy, occupies an important position in virtually every industry and business activity worldwide. An isolated, island-based feudal nation with relatively few natural resources, Japan has had to rely on trade to drive its modern rise, developing an international outlook that has not come naturally to its inwardly-focused people. The conclusion of the Pacific War in 1945 left Japan's economy in ruins, forcing it to start over again the process it had painfully begun less than a century before.

Since the late 1940s Japan has built a dominant, modern, internationally-oriented industrial economy. This economy is based on product innovation, high-quality production, advanced services, and, increasingly, domestic consumption. Japan's economy grew at an average rate of more than 10 percent per year between 1981 and 1992, although that rate has slowed sharply in recent years. Japan is also the second-largest trading economy in the world, yet trade represents only about 15 percent of its total economy. Its trade has doubled since 1982, growing at an annual rate of more than 7 percent.

Japan is a market well worth investigating from a number of perspectives. For buyers, Japan can provide a wide range of quality goods at virtually any level of sophistication. It is a dominant producer of automobiles, trucks, buses, and parts; ships; computers; electronics, particularly consumer and office electronic devices, and components such as integrated circuits and semiconductors; steel products; and organic chemicals, among many other items. Its businesses can handle anything from the smallest to the largest orders.

From the seller's standpoint Japan needs a wide range of agricultural and industrial raw materials, intermediate components, and specialty items to feed its voracious industries. Both the upgrading of its industrial base and its large public- and private-sector development projects require materials, capital goods, and service inputs. And rising demand from Japan's affluent, cosmopolitan, and knowledge-able consumers offers opportunities to place goods in the island's rapidly growing consumer markets.

For manufacturers Japan has a pool of well-educated, semiskilled to highly skilled labor experienced in the areas already noted as well as in many others. In addition to its advanced industrial plant, Japan has built a variety of specialized production facilities and its production infrastructure offers a base for a variety of outsourcing needs.

For investors, Japan is in the process of opening up additional areas of its economy that had previously been off-limits to foreigners, including many areas of its growing domestic markets and service and financial sectors. It particularly encourages foreign participation in its high-technology industries for the development of key technologies.

The Japanese miracle is showing signs of both maturity and age. Japan's economy is so large that it can no longer grow at rates and in ways that were feasible earlier. And its population is aging, presenting new problems and opportunities. Japan is in the process of refocusing its economy on high- and mid-level technologies and high-value-added, clean, capital-intensive products as it gives up its edge in low-cost, low-technology production. It is concentrating on original research and development rather than applications as it has in the past. The power of its large business and financial organizations and trading companies as well as the adaptability of its small- and medium-sized businesses argue that it will successfully make the transition to a new economy.

Although Japan's political face is changing, the country maintains a core of stability within its pro-business government. The overall level of change is expected to accelerate over the near term, making Japan an even more complex and challenging—as well as compelling—place in which to do business.

JAPAN Business was designed by business-people experienced in international markets to give you an overview of how things actually work and what current conditions are in Japan. It will give you the head start you need as a buyer, seller, manufacturer, or investor to be able to evaluate and operate in Japanese markets. Further, it tells you where to go to get more specific information in greater depth.

The first chapter discusses the main elements of the country's **Economy**, including its development, present situation, and the forces determining its future prospects. **Current Issues** explains the top four concerns affecting the country and its next stage of development. The **Opportunities** chapter presents 11 major areas of interest to importers and 10 additional hot prospects and 13 major areas for exporters plus 15 more hot opportunities. Discussions of 12 major sectoral growth areas and a section on special foreign access zones and industrial parks follows. The chapter also clarifies the nature of the government procurement that will drive Japan's multibillion-dollar development plans, including the 23 major projects that have been opened to foreign bidding under the Major Products Arrangement. **Foreign Investment** details policies, incentives, regulations, procedures, and restrictions, with particular reference to Japan's high technology, research and development, services, and infrastructural development thrust.

Although Japan is banking on high technology, services, and consumer spending to fuel its economy in the future, it remains a highly diversified industrial economy with many thriving low- and medium-technology operations. The **Foreign Trade**, **Import Policy & Procedures**, and **Export Policy & Procedures** chapters delineate the nature of Japan's trade: what and with whom it trades, trade policy, and the practical information, including nuts-and-bolts procedural requirements, necessary to trade with it. The **Industry Reviews** chapter outlines Japan's 16 most prominent industries and their competitive position from the standpoint of a businessperson interested in taking advantage of these industries' strengths or in exploiting their competitive weaknesses. **Trade Fairs** provides a comprehensive listing of trade fairs in Japan, complete with contact information, and spells out the best ways to maximize the benefits offered by these chances to see and be seen.

Business Travel offers practical information on how to travel in Japan including travel requirements, resources, internal travel, local customs, and ambiance, as well as comparative information on accommodations and dining in Tokyo, Fukuoka, Nagoya, and Osaka, the main business markets in Japan. **Business Culture** provides a user-friendly primer on local business style, mind-set, negotiating practices, and numerous other tips designed to improve your effectiveness, avoid inadvertent gaffes, and generally smooth the way in doing business with the Japanese. **Demographics** presents the basic statistical data needed to assess the Japanese market, while **Marketing** outlines resources, approaches, and specific markets in the country, including five ways to build a good business relationship, seven ways to sell your product, and five ways to help your local agent.

Business Entities & Formation discusses recognized business entities and registration procedures for setting up operations in Japan. **Labor** assembles information on the availability, capabilities, and costs of labor in Japan, as well as terms of employment and business-labor relations. **Business Law** interprets the structure of the Japanese legal system, giving a digest of substantive points of commercial law prepared from Martindale-Hubbell with additional material from the international law firm of Baker & McKenzie. **Financial Institutions** outlines the workings of the financial system, including banking and financial markets, and the availability of financing and services needed by foreign businesses. **Currency & Foreign Exchange** explains the workings of Japan's complex foreign exchange market operations. **International Payments** is an illustrated step-by-step guide to using documentary collections and letters of credit in trade with Japan. Ernst and Young's **Corporate Taxation** and **Personal Taxation** provide the information on tax rates, provisions, and status of foreign operations and individuals needed to evaluate a venture in the country.

Ports & Airports, prepared with the help of CIGNA Property and Casualty Company, gives current information on how to physically access the country. The **Business Dictionary**, a unique resource prepared especially for this volume in conjunction with Auerbach International, consists of more than 425 entries focusing specifically on Japanese business and idiomatic usages to provide the businessperson with the basic means for conducting business in Japan. **Important Addresses** lists more than 1,100 Japanese government agencies and international and foreign official representatives; local and international business associations; trade and industry associations; financial, professional, and service firms; transportation and shipping agencies; media outlets; and sources of additional information to enable businesspeople to locate the offices and the help they need to operate in Japan. Full-color, detailed, up-to-date **Maps** aid the business traveler in getting around the major business venues in Japan.

JAPAN Business gives you the information you need both to evaluate the prospect of doing business in Japan and to actually begin doing it. It is your invitation to this fascinating society and market. Welcome.

Economy

In less than 150 years, Japan has transformed itself from an isolated feudal nation into the second largest economic power in the modern world, with most of its growth coming in the years since World War II. The country consists of more than 6,850 volcanic islands located southeast of the Asian mainland. Only Japan's four main islands, which make up 98 percent of its land area, are economically significant. With an area of 377,740 square km (145,846 square miles), Japan is one-and-a-half times larger than the United Kingdom and slightly smaller than California.

Some 77 percent of Japan's nearly 125 million people reside in urban areas. Although overall population density in this seventh most populous country is on the order of nearly 330 persons per square km (857 per square mile), about 70 percent of Japan's inhabitants live on the narrow coastal plain that runs down the eastern side of Japan's main islands, which means that population density in the Tokyo area approaches 12,000 people per square mile, among the densest on earth.

About 75 percent of Japan's surface is mountainous. Some 67 percent is forested, 19 percent is arable, 1 percent is grasslands, and 10 percent is residential; the remaining 3 percent represents water, bare rock, and other waste land. Japan is extremely poor in natural resources; its only natural resources of economic significance are deposits of low-grade coal and its coastal fisheries. From the beginning of its existence as a modern nation, Japan has focused on imports of raw materials and exports of high-value-added manufactures to secure and maintain its preeminent place in the world.

HISTORY OF THE ECONOMY

Japan dates its beginnings to the legendary Emperor Jimmu who in 660 BC founded the Yamato imperial line. Japan was not organized as a coherent state with a permanent capital until AD 710. In AD 1192 local military governors, the *shoguns*, seized power from the court and reduced the emperor to a figurehead. The feudal period lasted until 1868. Except for relatively limited contacts with neighboring China and Korea, Japan remained isolated. The first Westerners to reach Japan were Portuguese traders who arrived in 1542. Traders and missionaries from other European nations tried to establish beachheads in Japan until the Tokugawa shogunate expelled all foreigners in 1639.

The Opening of Japan and the Beginning of the Modern Era

Japan remained isolated from the *gaijin* or outside persons until 1854, when a military expedition from the United States opened relations with the country under threat of force. In 1868 the Tokugawa shogunate collapsed and power returned to the Emperor Meiji. A forward-looking individual, the emperor set about studying foreign developments with a view to moving his country into a position of importance in the international sphere.

Japan began an intensive campaign to modernize its industrial, military, educational, and political systems. The feudal system was abolished, and a quasi-parliamentary government with a Western-style legal system was put in place through a constitution adopted in 1889.

During this period of rapid modernization, Japan came to grips with its lack of resources and vulnerability in the modern world as well as its resentment of the bullying of foreign powers. Japan's nationalistic military, raised in the tradition of the *samurai* warrior class and newly organized along authoritarian lines imported from Prussia, acquired substantial influence over the nascent civilian government. The militarists promoted expansion as a means of gaining resources and establishing Japan as a major power in its own right.

The country went to war with China (1894-1895) and with Russia (1904-1905), gaining the island of Formosa, concessions in Manchuria, and the Korean peninsula which it annexed as a colony in 1910. Japan fought against Germany in World War I, but felt that Western nations unfairly deprived it of Germany's Far Eastern territories in treaty negotiations after the war.

The military began a major buildup in the 1920s and 1930s. During the Depression of the 1930s, Japan made an explicit policy decision to deal with its domestic economic problems through territorial expansion. It seized Manchuria outright in 1931, invading China in 1937. Increased tensions between Japan and Western powers over economic and political control in the Far East led Japan into war with the United States and other countries in 1941.

Japan was ultimately defeated in a devastating war that ended in 1945 with the emperor's capitulation. Japan lost all its overseas possessions as well as some domestic islands, and it was occupied by US forces until 1952. In 1947 Japan adopted a modern constitution that included additional Western elements, placed tight controls on its military forces, and demoted the emperor to figurehead status once again.

The Postwar Rise

Japan's work force was decimated and its infrastructure demolished during World War II, so it had to rebuild its economy from scratch. Japan also lost control of overseas resources. The first tasks that it faced after the war were to satisfy domestic demand for basic necessities and reconstruct the country's infrastructure and industry. Stringent restrictions on imports kept demand under tight control. By foregoing consumer spending, the Japanese were able to develop the highest savings rate in the world.

To generate the funds and foreign exchange needed for rebuilding, Japan developed its export-oriented light manufacturing industry. Close cooperation between government and industry, a strong work ethic, a conscious decision to concentrate on quality control, and a small defense budget (at a time when other major economies were involved in an expensive arms race), coupled with substantial foreign aid credits and the opportunity to replace obsolescent plant with state-of-the-art facilities, enabled the Japanese to move quickly beyond recovery into a period of major economic development. Driven by high rates of saving, heavy government investment, and high growth in productivity, Japan's economy expanded rapidly from the 1950s through the 1980s, despite the recessionary impact of oil embargoes in the 1970s.

Japan's postwar government has been very business-oriented, creating a structure in which it uses regulations and support services to help private industry. The country is managed by the "iron triangle," the coalition of businesses, bureaucrats, and politicians, all of whom generally work toward the same goal.

The conservative Liberal Democratic Party (LDP) held power from its formation in 1955 until it was replaced by a coalition administration in mid-1993. Although Japan has had several established opposition parties, its tradition of consensus politics has kept them largely subservient to the majority party and allowed a web of interrelationships to build up that have advanced Japan's economic interests but also have confined it to a rigid bureaucratic straitjacket of managerial rules that inhibit unsponsored innovation even as they promote approved mainstream activity. The Japanese political system is entering a period of transition.

Until the 1970s Japan did not possess the resources needed to support basic research and development activity on its own. Instead, its industries became highly adept at developing applications for technology that had been created elsewhere. The first examples of Japanese skill in this area included cameras and consumer electronics based on the transistor, which led Japan into electronic and technical product innovation. Japan also had the advantage of a large enough domestic population that manufacturers could develop products and markets internally, perfect them at home, and then export the proved items. Because it had limited land area and limited consumer budgets, Japan was forced to focus on efficiency and low-cost production both in manufacturing process and finished product. These skills enabled it to perfect leading-edge products for sale at competitive prices that have been warmly received abroad.

Since the early 1980s Japan has amassed increasingly large trade surpluses, which have become a sensitive issue with its trading partners. In recent years, these trade imbalances have kept the yen high, making Japanese goods less attractive in depressed and saturated world markets. Japan has been fighting a global economic slowdown since 1990, one complicated by the collapse of its overheated financial and real estate markets, which its surpluses had driven to speculative highs. Although Japan remains a high-quality producer, it also has become a high-cost producer, a fact that is forcing it to look for different ways of shoring up its position.

SIZE OF THE ECONOMY

Japan's gross domestic product (GDP) was ¥424.7 trillion (US$3.674 trillion) in 1992, up from ¥421.3 trillion (US$3.383 trillion) in 1991. By comparison, US GDP in 1992 was US$5.954 trillion—nearly 40 percent higher. However, the United States has twice as many people as Japan, so per capita GDP was higher for the Japanese. In fact, at US$29,560 it was the highest in the world among major nations, up from US$27,255 in 1991, an increase of 8.5 percent in dollar terms.

Japan's Gross National Product (GNP)

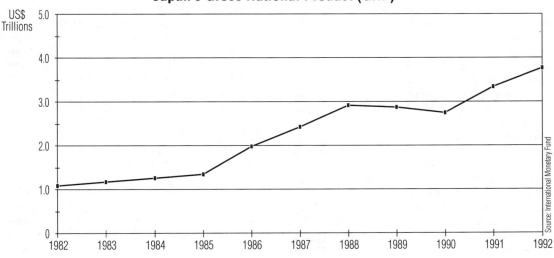

Source: International Monetary Fund

However, the growing strength of the yen kept the real value of this gain to less than half of what it was in nominal terms. In comparison, per capita GDP in the United States was US$23,300 in 1992 and US$20,528 in 1991.

As is the case in many areas, Japan does things differently when it comes to economic reporting. It operates using an April fiscal year so that figures must be adjusted to get comparable calendar-year figures. And because it is usually necessary to wait until well after the close of the fiscal year and the various revisions to get final figures, there is often a significant lag in data availability.

During the 1950s and 1960s Japan's GDP grew at an average annual rate of 10 percent. Growth slowed to an annual average rate of 4.5 percent during the 1970s, due primarily to increases in oil prices which sent shock waves through Japan's economy, dependent as it was on imported energy. In fact, Japan's GDP actually shrank by 0.2 percent in 1975. However, even at this slower average rate, Japan still grew faster than most Western industrial nations during the 1970s.

Growth picked up again during the early 1980s, but the strengthening yen slowed it down to 2.5 percent in 1986. Growth reached a recent high of 6.2 percent in 1988, and it has been easing ever since. Real growth was a minuscule 0.8 percent in 1992, and figures for the first quarter of the 1993 fiscal year show that the economy actually contracted by 0.5 percent, an annualized rate of –2 percent and far below the 3.5 percent that officials had predicted. Forecasters are hoping for break-even performance in 1993 and predict only anemic recovery in 1994, between 0.25 and 1.5 percent.

Japan's Position in the World

In 1971 Japan became the third largest economy in the world after the United States and the USSR. Since that time, Japan has not only maintained its advanced economic position but improved it. By the mid-1980s, Japan had tied or passed the United States as the world's primary financial power by such measures as the market value of its stock market and net exports of capital. By 1988 Japan's GDP was 25 percent of the combined total of the Organization for Economic Cooperation and Development (OECD) countries, whereas it had been only 5 percent in 1960.

By decade's end, Japan had become the world's leading creditor nation, and its high international reserve position not only gave it added weight in international economic affairs but made it a lightning rod for the concerns of trading partners. In the late 1980s Japan passed the former Soviet Union in the overall size of its economy to move into the number two spot, and many observers have predicted that Japan's economy will pass that of the United States by the end of the 1990s if not sooner.

CONTEXT OF THE ECONOMY

Although Japan is best known for its high-profile exports, it depends primarily on its immense domestic economy. In 1992 exports represented 9 percent of Japan's gross national product (GNP), while they accounted for 21.6 percent in Britain, 33.8 percent in Germany, and 8 percent in the United States. Japan's enormous trade surpluses result not so much from its predatory mercantilism, as critics argue, as they do from tight limits on imports other than necessary raw materials.

The Domestic Economy

One reason why Japan's domestic economy is so large is that consumer prices are kept artificially high by import restrictions and arcane, rigid internal distribution arrangements which pyramid middlemen on top of middlemen. The scarcity of land means that real estate and housing costs are high, and a protected and subsidized agricultural sector means that food prices are also high. A 3 percent consumption tax, similar to a value-added tax, levied in 1989 also helps boost consumer costs.

The Japanese traditionally have worked long hours, forgone consumer purchases, and saved a large percentage of their incomes as part of their concept of *gaman*, or endurance, which they see as making them special. The government is now trying to encourage people to ease up somewhat on the number of hours worked and to spend more money on themselves as a means of reducing Japan's immense trade surplus and placating its trade partners. But the government is fighting an ethic of sacrifice and a fear that lessening the amount of work done will cause the individual to become soft and the country to lose its position among nations. Despite its long-standing success, the Japanese still consider Japan to be a poor underdog country, and they are loath to change habits that they see as having kept the wolf from the door.

Japan is primarily a nation of small businesses. Small-scale retailers account for the vast majority of sales in its domestic economy, and they in turn support a huge hierarchy of intermediaries. The Japanese system is efficient in terms of output but inefficient in cost and far from elegant in design. Between 1979 and 1985 Japanese labor productivity rose at an annual rate of 3.9 percent, while real labor costs fell at an annual average rate of 0.8 percent. Since the mid-1980s both output and cost measures have dropped, until in 1992 the hourly output of Japan's industrial workers dropped by 6.2 percent and cost per unit of output rose by a stunning 18.3 percent. Even allowing for the effect of the appreciated yen, Japan's productivity and cost-efficiency currently rank relatively low in comparison with those of other industrialized nations.

Big Business

During Japan's industrial buildup in the late nineteenth and early twentieth centuries, large integrated trading houses with government connections became the dominant heavy industrial, commercial, and financial powers in Japan. These *zaibatsu* were conglomerates active in a whole range of vertically integrated and self-dealing businesses. Because of their role in providing materiel for Japan's war effort, the Allies broke them up after the country's defeat. However, the Japanese have reconstituted them and they play a major role in directing Japan's contemporary economy. The big six—Mitsui, Fuyo, Sanwa, Mitsubishi, Sumitomo, and Ichikan—and their myriad subsidiaries produce the consumer brand names familiar around the world.

The hallmark of the homogeneous Japanese social ethos is consensus, a concept that also defines many of its business arrangements. Although Japan is a strongly competitive capitalist country, it is inbred to a remarkable degree through *keiretsu*, or holding companies. Even though the individual giants and their multitude of subsidiaries compete directly, they all maintain elaborate crosscutting ties and mutual controls via stock holdings, interlocking directorates, and joint ventures, joint research and development, and joint marketing and distribution arrangements.

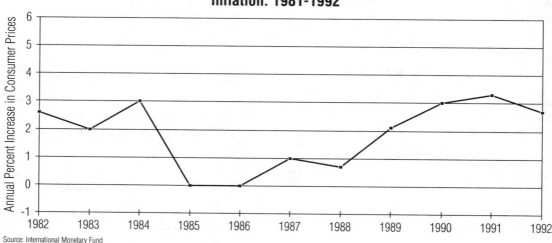

**Japan
Inflation: 1981-1992**

Source: International Monetary Fund

Government Role in the Economy

Japanese business is regulated—overregulated, many would say—by 10,717 types of necessary permits, licenses, and approvals as well as by less formal procedures, known as *administrative guidance.* Although Western business would characterize such "guidance" as blatant interference, the Japanese express horror at the idea of a managed economy, arguing that they are only helping companies and enforcing regulations. Japan is also extremely hierarchical and bureaucrats wield enormous and largely independent power over day-to-day operations.

The Japanese see one of government's most important functions as setting industrial policy, determining where the economy should go, and providing the means for it to get there. The powerful Ministry of International Trade and Industry (MITI) fulfills this major role. Government also acts as a referee among Sumo-like *keiretsu* members by providing a level domestic playing field in which it directs and finances research, nurses developing technologies along, makes sure that all players have initial equal access to the results, and generally sees that all parties behave in an appropriately harmonious Japanese manner.

THE UNDERGROUND ECONOMY

Japan has little of what is traditionally thought of as an underground economy. Because it is so ethnically homogeneous, there is little room for an informal economy within outsider enclaves, because there are no outsider enclaves (with the exception of a large Korean minority, consisting primarily of Japanese born well-acculturated businesspeople). The bureaucracy is so all-pervasive, and the various levels and sectors of the economy are so intertwined

that evasion of regulation and taxation is difficult.

Although street crime hit a postwar high in 1992, it is still negligible when compared to other developed countries. However, organized crime is well developed, operating a parallel economy dealing in illegal goods and services. The *yakuza,* or Japanese mafia, is attempting to diversify and invest its profits in legitimate business, and scandals linking payoffs by *yakuza* godfathers to politicians often surface.

The Japanese system is rigid, and there is a high degree of bureaucratic control. However, there is relatively little corruption in the operation of the system from the bottom up. Those inside the system generally benefit from it, and those outside the system have few opportunities to manipulate or evade it. It is not without its abuses, most of which occur from the top down. For instance, bid rigging and kickbacks are considered to be rampant. The importance placed on consensus means that collusive practices, which in the West are considered gross offenses, tend to be viewed far more leniently in Japan because they help to even out the process that divides the pie and keep everyone on the inside happy.

As elsewhere, business offers lucrative positions to bureaucrats when they leave the government. Former bureaucrats serve on the boards of 23 percent of the major companies in Japan despite restrictions on accepting positions in the industries that they regulated. Japanese politicians depend heavily on business for campaign contributions, a dependence that leaves them open to charges of influence peddling and favoritism.

In the 1970s a scandal involving payoffs and influence peddling in a major procurement deal with the Lockheed company brought down the government. This pattern has been repeated since, most recently in the late 1980s, by the Recruit scandal, in

Japan
Consumer Price Index (CPI)

Sources: International Monetary Fund, International Financial Statistics

which a number of political insiders were caught receiving illegal gifts of stock in return for favors. In the early 1990s large securities firms were found to have reimbursed certain large customers extralegally for investment losses at the expense of small investors and the firms' shareholders. In mid-1993 the status quo was disrupted again when payments to leading politicians by construction firms contributed to the election of an outsider as prime minister.

Given the degree of crosscutting holdings and high-level business cooperation, insider trading, market manipulation, and price-fixing are suspected to be relatively common, as is industrial espionage. However, the system as a whole can be said to operate in a generally clean, if hardly transparent, fashion, and many of the points of dispute can be attributed to different cultural perceptions of certain activities.

INFLATION

Given the virtually uninterrupted headlong growth that the Japanese economy experienced over the last 40 years, inflation has been negligible, although government manipulation of conditions has helped keep it that way. Between 1978 and 1982, inflation, as measured by consumer prices, grew at an annual average rate of 2.9 percent, and the average annual rate shrank to 1.25 percent between 1983 and 1989. Essentially break-even in 1985 and 1986, inflation reached a high of 3.3 percent in 1991 and eased to 2.7 percent in 1992. Forecasters estimate that it may rise by 1 percent for all of 1993, courtesy of the recession, and pick up slightly to 1.2 percent in 1994. As measured by wholesale price increases, inflation averaged 1 percent between 1987 and 1991 and never topped 1.8 percent during that period.

Much of this restrained growth in the rate of inflation results from the growing strength of the yen since the mid-1980s, which has boosted Japanese purchasing power. The introduction of a national consumption tax in 1989 offset its impact only slightly. In fact, the continued climb in the value of the yen against the dollar (its value surged 20 percent in the first six months of 1993, and the exchange rate hit a record high of ¥100 to US$1 at midyear) as well as against other major currencies has effectively canceled its inflationary impact.

LABOR

In 1992 Japan's labor force totaled 67.75 million, just over half of the population. Of this number, 7.9 percent was employed in agriculture, 33.6 percent in industry, and 58.5 percent in the service sector. The labor force is highly motivated and highly educated. Education is compulsory for nine years, and 90 percent of those who go on finish high school or trade school, while almost 60 percent of these graduates receive additional education and training. The current labor shortage in Japan has prompted the government to allow the importation of skilled foreign labor. However, both the government and organized labor have so far resisted attempts to import unskilled workers, and 40 percent of the small- to medium-sized businesses—the types most likely to need unskilled and semiskilled workers—state that a shortage of labor is their greatest management problem.

Lifetime Employment

Japan has been known erroneously as the land of lifetime employment. In the past, large companies provided workers with extensive training and sought to amortize the investment by encouraging them to stay with the company until retirement. The guaranteed job was an effort to build loyalty. Training and worker development are still strong in Japanese firms, but two new trends have been noted: an increase in labor mobility between companies and a decreased reluctance to dismiss surplus employees. Some large firms are moving toward greater reliance on temporary contract workers as opposed to permanent workers.

Firings, which are still frowned upon, require extensive documentation. Few firms lay workers off without overwhelming cause, because downturns have traditionally been of short duration, and employers have been willing to carry excess workers in order to have them available when things pick up. Estimates place the number of surplus employees with no duties or make-work jobs on corporate payrolls at more than one million. In sharp contrast with small firms, 46 percent of large Japanese companies feel that they have too many employees and are looking for ways to trim their work force. As the recession drags on, more large firms are offering thinly disguised early retirement incentives and resorting to outright dismissals. Another tactic is to make surplus workers' lives so boring or unpleasant that they will quit of their own accord, saving the company the embarrassment of having to actually fire them. Some large firms are also lowering their retirement age, a move that is being resisted by the government, which needs the continued revenues from taxes.

Unemployment

Given Japan's labor shortage, unemployment has been a relatively minor consideration. It averaged 2.5 percent between 1978 and 1988, peaked at 3 percent in 1989, and retreated to 2.1 percent in 1992. Predictions call for 2.3 percent unemployment in 1993 and 2.5 percent in 1994, although a growing minority of forecasters suggests that unemployment is headed for the 3 percent to 3.5 percent range in 1993 and 1994 based on the weakness of the economy. Some extreme views predict a 5 percent unemployment rate by 1995.

The Role of Unions

Unions have been relatively unimportant in Japan. Union membership is declining, and in 1992 fewer than one-quarter of Japan's workers belonged to a union. Union militancy, which was never very strident, peaked in the mid-1970s, and has since faded. The time lost due to work stoppages dropped by 98 percent between 1974 and 1990, and the number of disputes fell by 35 percent between 1986 and 1991.

Despite a reorganization of Japanese unions in 1989 to form the supposedly stronger and more militant Japanese Trade Union Confederation, labor-management relations in Japan remain generally amicable. Most unions are company-specific. That is, they are linked to their firms, not to a trade or industry at large. In keeping with the ideal of consensus and avoidance of conflict, unions see their main role as negotiating side issues, such as length of the workweek. In fact, salary negotiations are kept separate from the main labor negotiations.

Wages

In 1991 the average weekly wage in Japan was US$590, plus mandated benefits—workers' compensation, unemployment insurance, pension, and health insurance—amounting to 19.5 percent of the wage rate, an additional US$115. The total—US$705—is the highest in Asia; the comparable figures are US$245 in Taiwan, US$295 in South Korea, and US$4.90 in China. Moreover, the figure excludes the customary position, family, and housing allowances; the semiannual bonuses which amount to 25 percent to 35 percent of salary; and all of the additional benefits that employ-ers commonly provide in Japan. Legal minimum wages in 1993 are on a sliding scale from US$5.64 to US$4.84 per hour. The labor shortage means that actual wages paid are considerably higher.

Traditionally wage increases have been a set percentage granted across the board in the spring to all employees regardless of merit. This policy was designed to promote company loyalty and discourage individual differences. Individual circumstances traditionally have been accommodated by manipulating allowances. This situation is changing as individual merit increases become increasingly accepted in Japan.

Workweek

The Japanese have the longest workweek in the industrialized world: Japanese workers spend 11.5 percent more time on the job than US workers, 21.8 percent more than French workers, and 26.4 percent more than German workers. Labor laws were revised in 1987 to cap the regular work week at 46 hours, institute mandatory overtime pay, and guarantee a minimum six days a year of paid vacation.

Factory personnel have an average workweek of 41 hours, while the general work population puts in 39.5 hours per week. These figures are down from a nominal 43.6 hour workweek and an actual 56 hour workweek as recently as 1985. At 47.9 hours, South Korean factory workers have the longest workweek in Asia; the average workweek is 46.9 hours in Singapore and 45.4 hours in Taiwan.

Until recently, three-quarters of the Japanese work force worked on weekends, and workers usually took only half of their average 15 days of annual vacation. The government is trying to reduce hours worked. It now closes its own offices on Saturdays,

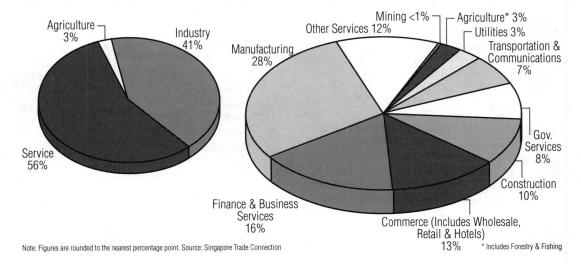

Structure of the Japanese Economy - 1990

Agriculture 3%
Industry 41%
Service 56%

Other Services 12%
Manufacturing 28%
Mining <1%
Agriculture* 3%
Utilities 3%
Transportation & Communications 7%
Gov. Services 8%
Construction 10%
Commerce (Includes Wholesale, Retail & Hotels) 13%
Finance & Business Services 16%

Note: Figures are rounded to the nearest percentage point. Source: Singapore Trade Connection   * Includes Forestry & Fishing

and it requires banks to do the same. However, it will take time for the rest of the country's employers to fall into line.

ELEMENTS OF THE ECONOMY

Although Japan is best known for its export-oriented manufacturing sector, the service sector provides the largest share of Japan's output, 55.7 percent. Some 41.8 percent of the country's domestic output comes from the industrial sector; most of that output is directed at the domestic market. A shrinking 2.5 percent comes from agriculture, fishing, and forestry. The service sector is expected to grow in importance at the expense of the industrial and agricultural sectors during the next few years as the Japanese population and economy continue to mature.

Between 1988 and 1992 the average annual fixed investment in Japan was around 33 percent of GDP, compared with 15 percent for the US and 25 percent for the newly industrialized economies (NIEs) of Asia. Japan's domestic savings rate, which for years has averaged 15 percent, has funded much of this investment. A significant portion also has been funded by government debt, but as part of its program to realign the economy structurally, the government hopes to reduce its borrowing significantly over the next few years. Its success will depend on whether it yields to the temptation to prime the pump with stimulus spending. However, in September 1993 the new government announced a US$57.4 billion stimulus package, the third such multibillion dollar package in a year, following it with plans for a fourth multibillion dollar tax cut stimulus package in early 1994.

AGRICULTURE

Japan has traditionally been an agricultural country, and although only 2.5 percent of GNP is now derived from agriculture, fisheries, and forestry combined, the sector employs an outsized 7.9 percent of the work force. Some 19 percent of Japan's land area is cultivable. About 9 percent of all land is irrigated while 1 percent is under permanent cultivation. Family farms, which account for the majority of agricultural holdings, are extremely small, and cultivation is labor-intensive. Output per unit is among the highest in the world, but Japanese agriculture is also among the most costly and inefficient. Major crops are rice, sugar beets, sugar cane, wheat, barley, soybeans, potatoes, sweet potatoes, cabbages, melons, citrus fruits, and tea. Animal products include pork, poultry, beef, milk, eggs, and silkworms. Major imports include soybeans, wheat, and fodder crops, such as maize.

The Japanese revere their agricultural heritage, and the emperor's few remaining ceremonial functions include participating in planting and harvest rituals. Agriculture still receives the 13 percent share of Japan's public works budget that it had in 1980, although the number of households engaged in farming has fallen by 30 percent to less than 5 percent of all households. Agriculture is heavily subsidized and protected by import restrictions and quotas, and foreign investment in agricultural is prohibited. Japan produces about 50 percent of its food needs and relies on imports for the remainder.

Although the Japanese would be better off buying virtually all their food abroad, self-sufficiency in food production, especially rice, is a politically sensitive issue. The dominating LDP party also has a strong support base in agricultural areas, which years of gerrymandering to strengthen the effect of the agricultural constituency have reinforced, so that it is unlikely that the status quo regarding agriculture will change in the near future, despite international pressures, high prices, and recurrent shortfalls in Japan's production, particularly rice. Political reforms passed in early 1994 call for redistricting to address this disproportionate agricultural influence, but it remains to be seen how this will play out.

Japan is the leading fishing nation in the world, producing 15 percent of the world's total catch. The fishing industry employs less than 1 percent of the work force, but its contribution to Japan's domestic food supply and export earnings is substantial. Depletion of fish stocks and exclusion from other nations' maritime economic zones will cause this industry to shrink in future years, although aquaculture is a growing subsector. Because of its close connection with subsistence issues, the fishing industry is also a politically powerful lobby.

Forestry is of minor importance in Japan. Although two-thirds of Japan is wooded and 37 percent of the wooded area consists of tree farms, domestic supply can fill only about 30 percent of domestic demand. Japan is the world's largest importer of forest products.

MANUFACTURING AND INDUSTRY

Manufacturing and industry, which includes mining, construction, and utilities, has driven Japan's postwar economic miracle. In 1990 manufacturing and industry accounted for 41.8 percent of domestic output and employed 34 percent of the work force. Manufacturing alone contributed 28.9 percent, making it the largest single subsector in the economy.

Although Japan's manufacturing sector is perhaps the best in the world in terms of equipment and process, it faces some severe problems, including substantial overcapacity; lack of price competitiveness, particularly with respect to other Asian economies; and contraction of domestic and international demand due to worldwide recession.

Heavy industries predominate because of the massive investment that they have received and their impressive economies of scale. During the 1950s and 1960s average annual investment in plant and equipment was 22 percent, and in 1992 capital spending was still 20.5 percent of GNP. The automobile industry, which in 1990 produced a record 13.9 million units of all types, is the world leader, although high prices are eroding its market share. Japan is number one in the production of steel, and, despite capacity cutbacks, it still produces half of the world's tonnage in ships. The country's industry is also important in the areas of metallurgy, machine tools, electronics and electrical equipment, construction equipment, and chemicals.

Because of the labor component involved in heavy industry and much medium industry, Japan has for several years been shifting away from such areas as steel, shipbuilding, bulk chemicals, and lower-end consumer electronics to cleaner, high-technology, high-value-added industries, such as semiconductors, office equipment, telecommunications equipment and networks, robotics, computers, aerospace, and biotechnology as well as other research-oriented areas, such as materials science. Between 1986 and 1991 Japan spent US$3.5 trillion on new high-tech plant and equipment. Public and private sources annually spend close to 3 percent of GNP on applied research and development, the highest proportion in the world. During the late 1980s Japan had more personnel devoted to R&D than Germany, Britain, and France combined.

Japan still has a 95 percent share of the worldwide market in videocassette recorders (VCRs), 85 percent in copiers, and 70 percent each in facsimile machines and industrial robots. Market saturation is a growing concern because, particularly in Japan but also in the United States, most households already have a full complement of consumer electronics, and future sales in these primary markets will depend on replacement units, upgrades, and new technology. Large Japanese producers of consumer electronics and other goods are implementing plans that will move 40 to 50 percent of production in such labor-intensive functions as textiles and electronics assembly overseas, especially for goods destined for export.

The Japanese are worried about what they call the *hollowing out* of the economy. This phenomenon involves moving well-paying manufacturing jobs overseas to take advantage of cheaper labor costs. The concern is not so much for lower-end factory workers, who are already in short supply as it is, but for the small- and medium-sized subcontractors and suppliers who will be left in the lurch as their big company customers follow the multinational route. (Refer to "Opportunities" and "Industry Reviews" chapters.)

SERVICES

Japan has already become a service nation, with 58.7 percent of the work force employed in and 55.7 percent of the domestic output coming from the service sector, which includes wholesale and retail trade; financial services such as banking, insurance, and real estate; transportation and communications; and government services. The sector grew from roughly 50 percent of the economy in 1970 to close to 60 percent

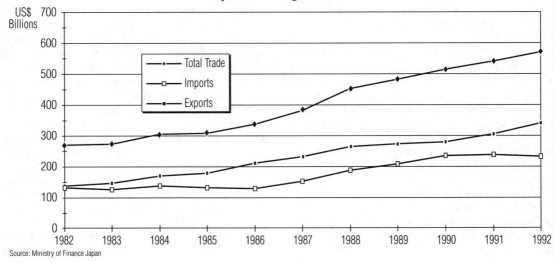

Japan's Foreign Trade

US$ Billions

— Total Trade
— Imports
— Exports

Source: Ministry of Finance Japan

Japan's Leading Exports By Commodity - 1991

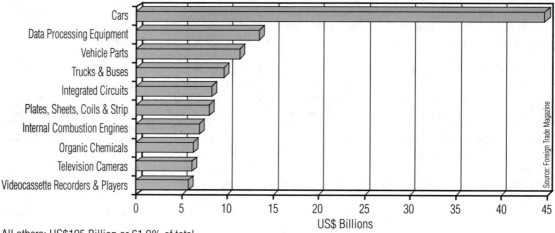

Cars
Data Processing Equipment
Vehicle Parts
Trucks & Buses
Integrated Circuits
Plates, Sheets, Coils & Strip
Internal Combustion Engines
Organic Chemicals
Television Cameras
Videocassette Recorders & Players

0   5   10   15   20   25   30   35   40   45
US$ Billions

Source: Foreign Trade Magazine

All others: US$195 Billion or 61.9% of total
Total 1991 Exports: US$314.9 Billion

in the early 1990s. Growth in this sector is expected to accelerate in the future as production moves offshore and the Japanese economy matures.

Japan is a world financial center, and finance is the largest subsector. The market value of Japan's stock exchange surpassed that of the United States during the mid-1980s, although it has fallen by nearly 50 percent from its 1987 high to a market value of US$1.9 trillion in mid-1993, compared to the mid-1993 US market value of US$2.4 trillion. Even at reduced levels, many issues traded on the Tokyo exchange are generally considered to be overvalued, with prices far out of balance with respect to earnings. *Mochiai* or crosscutting stock holdings among large companies have restricted the float, which is estimated at around only 20 percent of total shares listed on the market. However, as the recession continues, many firms are making plans to sell assets, including permanent stock holdings in other companies, to raise cash which could ultimately make the market more efficient.

Banking is fairly highly developed, but it remains relationship oriented to the point that firms deal only with their own banks regardless of costs or service. And because Japanese firms tend to have very high proportions of debt to equity, their banks often effectively become partners in their operations. Bank lending has shrunk substantially, and Japan's once-dominant banks are looking at an estimated US$500 billion in questionable loans worldwide.

Most interest rates are still controlled to a certain extent by the Bank of Japan, the central bank. In late 1993 the discount rate in Japan stood at 1.75 percent, a postwar low. At the same time the prime rate stood at 4 percent. (Refer to "Financial Institutions" chapter.)

Japanese wholesale and retail business still operates on an archaic model with many layers of middlemen, with each adding a markup, and thousands of mom-and-pop stores catering to consumers. This inefficient distribution system is regulated by laws designed to protect small businesspeople from predatory competition. However, their main effect is to protect the ruling party, which counts on the votes of those protected. Vertical integration between manufacturer and seller, plus agreements among nominal competitors dividing up territories, further restrict consumer choice and keep prices artificially high. Recently, large discounters have begun to make some inroads in the traditional system, especially in apparel, electronics, and furniture.

TRADE

Japan is one of the premier trading nations in the world, surpassed by only the United States and Germany in terms of total value of exports and imports combined. In 1991 Japan reported total trade of US$572.6 billion, up 3.9 percent from the US$551.2 billion recorded in 1991. Exports rose by 10.75 percent to US$339.6 billion, while imports registered a slight drop of 1.5 percent to US$233 billion. As of mid-1993, exports were running at an annualized level of US$350 billion, up 8.9 percent from the corresponding figure for the preceding year. Imports were estimated at US$235 billion, up 5.8 percent from the year-earlier quarterly figure. Preliminary estimates for 1993 suggest that total trade should reach at least US$575 billion and that it could hit US$600 billion.

Japan's total trade has grown at an average annual rate of 14.4 percent since 1960. Between 1960 and 1980 its exports grew at 18.9 percent, and its

Japan's Leading Imports By Commodity - 1991

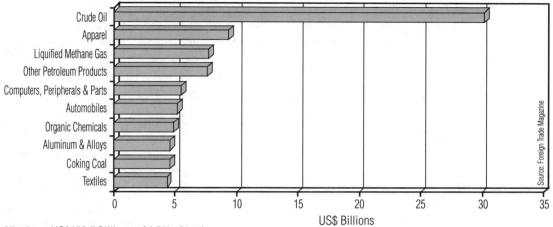

Crude Oil
Apparel
Liquified Methane Gas
Other Petroleum Products
Computers, Peripherals & Parts
Automobiles
Organic Chemicals
Aluminum & Alloys
Coking Coal
Textiles

0   5   10   15   20   25   30   35

US$ Billions

Source: Foreign Trade Magazine

All others: US$152.7 Billion or 64.5% of total
Total 1991 Imports: US$236.6 Billion

imports at 18.8 percent. Since 1980 annual growth in exports has slowed by more than half to 8.3 percent. Annual growth in imports has slowed even more to 4.8 percent annually, one-quarter of the earlier rate. Despite the government campaign to boost consumption and imports, the growth rate of imports is off noticeably. This is due primarily to the collapse of oil prices and from the fact that the yen is strong and Japan uses cheap dollars to pay for most of its petroleum imports.

In 1960 when Japan's economy was still getting off the ground, imports represented 52.3 percent of its total trade. In 1975 and 1980 when Japan was suffering from the sudden jump in oil prices, imports again exceeded exports. However, the balance of trade was firmly fixed in the positive column by 1985, when exports represented 57.6 percent of total trade. In 1991 exports accounted for 57.1 percent of Japan's total trade, down slightly from the 57.5 percent average maintained since 1985. Observers are concerned that the current recessionary climate may lead Japanese firms to dump unsold domestic goods into overseas markets, a move that would only increase its already bloated trade surplus.

Japan's huge balance of trade surplus has caused concern both in Japan and elsewhere since it started to grow in the 1980s. Japan's balance of trade has climbed steadily since the mid-1980s, hitting US$107 billion in 1992. Its balance of trade was US$57.6 billion for the first six months of 1993. For the month of August alone, Japan's trade surplus was US$7.5 billion, up 7.5 percent from the year-earlier period in dollar terms, although the strength of the yen meant that it was actually off by 11 percent for the same period in yen terms. Preliminary year-end figures for calendar 1993 placed Japan's trade surplus at

US$120.4 billion, an all-time high.

International reserves stood at US$82.5 billion in May 1993, up from US$71 billion a year earlier and second only to Taiwan's reserves of US$84.9 billion, the largest in the world. Japan is in the ambivalent position of having been too successful: it faces the threat that irate trading partners will gang up on it to block its still important export sales. Even without such concerted action, the high-priced yen could still choke off Japanese exports.

EXPORTS

Japan's main exports are manufactured goods for developed countries, although shipments of parts and components for assembly at low-cost production sites, primarily in Southeast Asia, for reshipment back to Japan where they are finished and reexported is a growing element of its export focus.

In 1992 Japan's leading exports were transportation products (25.7 percent of total exports), electronics products (22.8 percent), and machinery (22.5 percent). Together these three categories accounted for 71 percent of total exports. The next five largest categories—metals (6.3 percent), chemicals (5.6 percent), precision instruments (4.7 percent), textiles (2.5 percent), and non-metallic minerals products (1.1 percent)—represented an additional 20.2 percent. Remaining exports by category accounted for less than 1 percent of the total.

Mid-year figures for 1993 indicate that the dollar value of Japan's exports remained high but that the strength of the yen was eating into unit sales. Exports of autos were down 17.2 percent, and video equipment was down 15.2 percent on a unit volume basis. However, sales of semiconductors were up 29.6

percent, again on a unit basis.

Japan has long since outgrown its major dependence on such labor-intensive light industrial manufactures as textiles, although all categories of textiles and textile products continue to account for 2.5 percent of its total exports. It also has shifted away from assembly, which provided its export strength up until about ten years ago, now that far cheaper outsourcing sites are available offshore. Japan holds the lead, certainly in Asia, in ;high-tech, high-value-added manufactures, but as its overall competitive advantage plateaus, it can be expected to shift increasingly to management of production elsewhere and other service exports. This process will be long and gradual.

IMPORTS

Japan's main imports were mineral fuels, machinery and equipment, foodstuffs, raw materials, chemicals, and textiles. Together, these six categories account for 81.3 percent of Japan's total imports.

Energy accounts for almost one-quarter of all Japan's imports, while raw and intermediate inputs account for at least another quarter. Food and production machinery represent one-third, leaving only about 15 percent of all imports to be classed as nonessential or final consumer products. Statistics from August 1993 showed imports rising, and observers speculated that firms were taking advantage of the strong yen to stock up on cheap raw materials so they could cut production costs and price products attractively for the domestic market.

TRADING PARTNERS

Developed countries are the primary markets for Japan's exports. The United States is by far the biggest buyer of Japanese goods, taking 29.3 percent of its total exports. Germany and the United Kingdom together take just over 10 percent, while the developing Asian economies—South Korea, Taiwan, and Hong Kong—account for slightly more than 17 percent. The remaining 43.3 percent of Japan's exports are spread around the world, with countries in Southeast Asia, Europe, and Latin America representing substantial and growing markets, although as of 1991 none of these countries accounted individually for more than 3.5 percent of its exports.

Japan buys almost half of its imports from developing countries, mainly oil suppliers, such as Saudi Arabia, the United Arab Emirates and other Persian Gulf states, and Indonesia. An additional third of its imports come from developed countries; the United States, with 22.7 percent, is Japan's largest import source. Other Pacific Rim countries are important in Japan's economic sphere, supplying raw materials, intermediate components, and some finished goods. China is Japan's second largest source of imports at 6 percent of the total, trailed by Australia, Indonesia, and South Korea; Germany is Japan's next largest supplier with a 4.5 percent share.

FOREIGN PARTICIPATION IN THE ECONOMY

Japan traditionally has sought outside technology and expertise and it has paid close attention to the outside experts it selects on its own. It is less accepting of unsolicited advice, and it always modifies imported concepts to suit its own needs and ideas. The economy's handlers are looking increasingly to replace heavy government borrowing with investment capital from external sources, although it remains difficult for outsiders to break into the system. Japan is not so much xenophobic as it is ethnocentric, and it is difficult to convince the Japanese to do things differently. Most official barriers to foreign investment have been removed, and in fairness locals have to deal with most of the same maddening regulations that foreigners complain about. Nevertheless, it is difficult to participate in Japan's relatively closed economy, where the prevailing attitude is do it our way, and it better be good.

Size of Foreign Participation

Japan is one of the world's great foreign investors. Its net foreign assets rose from US$11.5 billion in 1980 to US$380 billion in 1991. In contrast, cumulative foreign investment in Japan between 1951 and 1991 was only US$22.8 billion and the sum was divided among 47,347 separate investments. The United States has accounted for 43.5 percent of the total; European countries made 25 percent of these investments, Asian countries 14.5 percent, and other countries 17 percent.

In 1991 direct foreign investment was US$4.3 billion, nearly one-fifth of all foreign investment since 1950. Asian and European investment was up, while US investment was down. In the first six months of 1992 direct foreign investment was up by 62 percent over the same period in 1991. However, the deepening recession and the sky-high yen are expected to result in a substantial easing of foreign investment during 1993. There has also been a trend toward fewer but larger foreign investments. In 1991 the number of investments fell by 29 percent, while the value of those investments increased by 56 percent.

Areas of Foreign Investment

Since 1987 55 percent of all foreign investments have been in manufacturing, while much of the remaining investment has gone into trade and services. The recent trend has been toward increased investment in services. In 1991 56.3 percent of foreign investments were in financial services, trade, and other services.

Foreigners have been active in manufacturing in Japan where the chemicals and electronics industries have been primary targets. Foreign banking and financial services, such as brokerage, and business services, such as consulting and accounting, are reasonably well established, although there have been few available licenses and many barriers to market penetration. There are still restrictions on the operations of foreign law firms, although Japan is talking about relaxing some restrictions and allowing foreign attorneys, of which there were only 79 in the entire country in mid-1993, to operate somewhat more freely. Self-dealing with captive insurers has limited foreign penetration of the Japanese insurance market. Some large retailers have gained a foothold, although wholesale and retail distribution is still effectively closed to outsiders.

Japan is currently gearing up to make major investments in infrastructure, with new construction and upgrading of such facilities as roads, bridges, ports, airports, and commercial and industrial facilities as well as recreational, health care, and retirement facilities. Officials have offered to allow foreign construction firms to bid under slightly relaxed but still restrictive rules, however observers say the new rules will extend eligibility to only a very few firms. The government is spearheading these projects, but private business is expected to take the lead in developing hundreds of thousands of new housing units.

Pros and Cons of Investing in Japan

The high cost of entry is a significant barrier to foreign investment in Japan. However, the search for outside capital, the 50 percent drop in local share prices, and the 20 to 50 percent drop in real estate values since 1990 have helped to a limited extent to offset the strength of the yen for foreign investors. Labor, capital, and land remain expensive, and strong local relationships that tend to limit availability of these and other inputs can make it difficult to obtain necessary commodities in satisfactory amounts. Intimate government involvement in business affairs is another drawback.

The government does make tax incentives, loan guarantees, and preferential treatment available to foreign investors. Japan's other attractions include its modern infrastructure, skilled labor force, an affluent and increasingly sophisticated consumer population, and proximity to other countries on the thriving Pacific Rim. Japan has extensive licensing requirements and maintains specific restrictions against foreign participation in such areas as agriculture, forestry, fisheries, mining, petroleum refining, telecommunications, munitions and defense, and

leather products. It also reserves the right to restrict technology transfers.

Although Japanese approval and licensing procedures are onerous, it is usually possible to navigate through them and gain the necessary official approvals. Customer acceptance is less assured, as Japanese businesses and consumers continue to prefer known products and relationships. (Refer to "Foreign Investment" chapter.)

GOVERNMENT ECONOMIC DEVELOPMENT STRATEGY

Japan is a free market capitalist economy, but the government plays a major role in setting economic policy and in regulating the activities of participants. Although the government has little direct involvement in the ownership or operation of economic entities, as is the case in much of the rest of Asia, it maintains the tightest oversight of any of the developed nations via regulation and informal but mandatory administrative guidance of firms through often overlapping ministerial bureaucracies. The government does not set specific five-year plans, as do many Asian governments, but it does determine industrial policy, directing its sectors into suggested areas of endeavor and facilitating their entry by providing seed money and research, technical, and regulatory support. Currently Japan is concentrating its efforts on the high-technology, high-valued-added arena.

Basic Japanese policy calls for stable growth in the economy driven by consumer demand and for using reduced dependence on exports and increased purchases of imports to reduce its trade surplus and maintain harmonious relations with its trading partners. These goals depend on deregulation and a more open market policy. Officials also want to make investments in infrastructure and in research and development while at the same time reducing government borrowing. As outlined in the Law on Multi-Centered Nation Building, the government is calling for a decentralization of control over industry and services. Under the law the central government gives local authorities increased autonomy to plan and implement development.

Planning Versus Change

In the past Japan has been highly effective in planning and establishing the consensus needed for implementing its plans. But that past was a time of rapid growth, and the government was only required to direct a relatively small stream into well-agreed upon channels. Japan's planners have been less successful in adapting to its maturing economy and managing structural change, which can be likened to changing the course of a large river in full flood.

Japan has been formally committed to deregulation and restructuring since the mid-1980s, but results to date have been minimal. Observers note that the government's plans are weak on specifics, including target numbers and deadlines. Government representatives shy away from setting specific numbers on the grounds that they don't want to overmanage their free market economy, but even insiders scoff at this explanation, noting that leaving the setting of specifics to the bureaucrats—vested interests who are opposed to virtually any change in the status quo—amounts to abandoning all hope of achieving any results at the outset.

POLITICAL OUTLOOK FOR THE ECONOMY

In 1994 Japan is entering its fourth year of recession. The victim of a worldwide slowdown, its problems have been worsened by structural problems unique to its situation. In August 1993 voters elected a new prime minister, Morihiro Hosokawa, who had run as an outsider. A provincial governor who was not considered to be a member of the ruling elite, and had broken away from the reigning LDP, Hosokawa has espoused relatively liberal views on restructuring. One of his first acts was to draw up a list of rules and regulations to be altered or dropped in order to streamline the doing of business in Japan. The list was broadened and incorporated into Hosokawa's ¥6.2 trillion (about US$56 billion) stimulus package. He also proposed striking changes in Japan's electoral system that would shift it from proportional to direct election of legislators in an attempt to make its operation more transparent and less prone to corruption and manipulation.

Despite his call for deep and dramatic change, Hosokawa did not come to office with a ringing mandate or a ready-made program, and he must go slowly while he tries to craft programs and line up support. The new prime minister was elected basically because he kept his head down during the most recent round of political scandals, and he is not considered to be an influential leader. Despite his high popular approval ratings his position is considered so tenuous that a defeat on any of the issues before the Diet, Japan's legislature, could result in his losing power. This would throw the system into turmoil while politicians look for another yet candidate for prime minister. The only ones without taint are equally lacking in influence to undertake major reform, and the crucial task of realigning Japan's economic and political system will be delayed even longer.

Governmental policy is implemented by a large, entrenched, conservative civil service bureaucracy that has been known to drag its collective feet. The resulting environment is highly stable but extremely slow to react. Although the government has pushed—sometimes aggressively, but more often tentatively—for a restructuring of the economy and what amounts to a sea change in the way in which the Japanese view themselves, such policies face slow going because they depend not only on a shift in the fundamental attitudes of the people at large but also on enthusiastic support from the bureaucracy. Observers characterize Japanese politicians as lobbyists to the powerful bureaucracy rather than policymakers, and the collusive network of intersecting interests both inside and outside the public sector will make change a gradual and hard-fought process.

There are some signs that Japan's business community is taking the initiative in some areas of reform. Some in the private sector are even beginning to question the validity of the traditional system in which their enterprises relied on and deferred to the government. These skeptics now say that although the government has helped them, it has also overprotected and limited them so that they now find themselves at a disadvantage in the increasingly competitive world markets.

The export market is running on momentum alone, and Japanese business recognizes that the country will not be able to export its way out of recession this time. Of even greater concern as the economy tries to rely more on home markets, domestic demand is down by 0.1 percent, and it would be down much more if the government had not increased its spending by 22.5 percent in 1993. The downturn is extending from the manufacturing sector into the service sector, and bankruptcies are growing at an alarming rate.

Large firms, facing a drop in profits for 1993 estimated at an average 17 percent, are doing the unthinkable: they are laying off workers and selling assets. They also are sending production overseas to low-cost sites, which will take its toll on consumer confidence and future domestic job growth. Corporate bigwigs who normally defer to the government are beginning to make increasingly pointed public comments and suggestions. No matter how radical the cuts in employment and expenses are by Japanese standards, domestic firms have yet to make the level of cuts necessary to rationalize their operations and reverse declines in their profitability.

Japanese corporations have concentrated, admirably, on the long term, developing relationships and gaining market share at the expense of near-term profitability. Shareholders have long been considered to be an unimportant constituency, but firms are now recognizing that they must move away from a focus on gaining market share to one of increasing profits and satisfying shareholders if they are to adapt successfully to the new world economy in which investors and consumers have choices that previously had been denied them in Japan.

Government Plans

The government is considering a range of measures to deal with the extended economic slump. Some, such as stimulus packages, amounting to US$260 billion over an 18 month period have already been enacted, although they may be modified along the way. The September stimulus package included funds for expanded public works projects, low-cost loans for small business and home purchases, and minimal tax breaks for families with dependent children. Some 94 business rules were slated for either easing or outright abolition, and the plan called vaguely for cutting government regulation of business in half. Other possibilities include more rapid deregulation, import promotion, and tax cuts. Many both inside and outside Japan are focusing on the need for a sharp tax cut to free up consumer spending and investment funds.

In an attempt to reduce public spending in the early 1980s, the government raised income taxes. Marginal rates can go as high as 65 percent and fall unevenly on 90 percent of salary income, 60 percent of small business income, and 40 percent of farm income. Politicians have lacked the strength to rationalize this preferential tax structure, and the government has relied on bracket creep to reduce its borrowings. As a result consumption as a percentage of GDP has been falling since 1984. Economists argue that it will take a major tax cut to generate the domestic spending that Japan's economy needs to dig itself out of its current problems. The government has justified retention of the existing tax system and maintenance of a 3 percent budget surplus in recent years as hedges against the future social security needs of a population that is rapidly aging, even though the Japanese social security system has a substantial surplus.

The aging population will represent a major drain on the economy at a point in the not too distant future. The lack of housing is another important public policy concern. However, these issues have diverted policymakers from more fundamental concerns. It is increasingly clear that the Japanese economy is changing in structurally significant ways and that it will need stronger leadership as it adjusts. (Refer to "Current Issues" chapter.)

JAPAN'S INTERNATIONAL ROLE

Japan is a member of many international organizations, including the United Nations and most of its agencies, the International Monetary Fund (IMF), the General Agreement on Tariffs and Trade (GATT), and the Organization for Economic Cooperation and Development (OECD), as well as numerous other international and regional bodies, including the increasingly influential organization for Asia Pacific Economic Cooperation (APEC).

Japan's Official Development Assistance (ODA) program makes it the world's second largest overseas aid donor, although complaints have been heard in the international community that Japan's aid is tied by requirements that recipients must spend it with Japanese firms and that it amounts to an exclusionary domestic subsidy.

Despite Japan's standing as the world's second largest economy, it has so far declined to take a leading political role. The Japanese have argued that they must remain unaligned because of their need to maintain neutrality and trade relations across the board and that their constitution prohibits them from military involvement and thus prevents them from taking political action that might need to be backed up by force. These arguments are viewed as disingenuous in many circles. As its system and its position in the world change further, Japan can be expected to accept an increasingly large and more vocal role in world affairs.

Current Issues

RING OUT THE OLD, RING IN THE NEW: POLITICS IN JAPAN

The Liberal Democratic Party (LDP), a misnomer for this only marginally democratic and decidedly conservative political machine, was the ruling party in Japan from its founding in 1955 until mid-1993. In 1993 a historic election resulted in the removal of the LDP prime minister and the loss of the LDP's majority in the Japanese legislature or Diet. Defections by 39 of the LDP's 274 Diet members were instrumental in bringing down their party's leader, Kiichi Miyazawa. In June 1993 the lower house voted a motion of no confidence, ending thirty-eight years of what was effectively single-party rule in Japan.

Before the Fall

Historically the Japanese people have generally been viewed as passive and rather uninterested where politics are concerned, finding it easier to tend to other business and stick with the familiar regardless of problems. That may no longer be the case. Japan has changed dramatically during the last thirty years, and the Japanese have been increasingly influenced by Western fashions, values, and even attitudes regarding political activism. Now the Japanese do not appear to be willing to stand idly by as the latest round of scandals break among their political leaders. The stubborn recession, which has dragged on without them seeing their leaders take any effective action to invigorate the becalmed economy, has proved to be the last straw. In March 1993, when a high-ranking LDP leader was convicted of tax evasion and receiving bribes (and, in addition, was found to be holding more than US$51 million), the apathy of the electorate metamorphosed into outrage. The traditional practice of forcing corrupt fallen leaders to resign in quiet but affluent disgrace, meanwhile making way for the next clone was not enough to pacify the electorate this time.

Certain LDP leaders, similarly enraged by the party's manifest inability to clean up its act, began splintering away from the ruling party and setting up new reform-minded groups, notably the New Harbinger Party, the Japan New Party, and the Japan Renewal Party. Recognizing how tenuous its hold on power had become, the LDP promised a massive spring cleaning. It presented a package of four political reform bills designed to wean itself away from traditional sources of graft and transform Japan's outmoded electoral system. More than half of the members of the Diet agreed to sign a petition in support of such political reforms.

For months prior to the final June blowup, Miyazawa had been arguing that his party had to actually pass its reform bills or risk losing public confidence. However, his arguments apparently fell on deaf ears within the go-slow establishment. Partly because of Miyazawa's lack of boldness in following through on his promises to push through reform, the LDP leadership had temporized, failing to reach agreement regarding the electoral-reform proposal. On July 18, 1993, discontent snowballed, resulting in a motion of no confidence in the lower house, booting the veteran Miyazawa out of office, who was then forced to call general elections. It finally appeared that the people of Japan would no longer settle for promises, and the country began the journey into a brave new world.

What Brought About the Change in the Electorate?

Japan's more cosmopolitan electorate, influenced by extensive contact with the West through foreign visitors, overseas travel, education, international business experience, and global communications availability, now appears to want leaders who are more like those of Western powers. They appear to want leaders who can overcome traditional Japanese conservatism and indirectness and stand up and be effective both at home and abroad. Empowered leaders competent in the international realm are of increasing importance as Japan's role in the world community grows through participation in the United Nations.

G-7 summits, and other international political forums as well as in international trade. Thus, the Japanese electorate is interested in less parochial, more internationally minded leaders who will be able to negotiate directly and on an equal footing with their Western counterparts. They want leaders to deal resolutely with increased foreign pressures regarding access to Japanese markets and expectations for Japan's participation in the world community.

The Japanese electorate has also been influenced by the Western trend toward less deliberative, younger leaders such as US President Bill Clinton, who won over Japanese citizens during his 1993 trip to Japan. The electorate wants to see its leaders as able to act decisively, taking personal initiative and responsibility rather than relying on the glacial, consensus-building traditional Japanese decision-making process in which nothing is often decided for fear of upsetting the system and in which real responsibility is often diffused. Voters also want more open policy debate with less deference to the old guard leadership, and they are hoping for new leaders to make bold moves to lift the economy and put Japan back on top.

Foreigners also welcome the changed atmosphere. In the minds of most Western leaders, Japan should take more initiative in global affairs, especially issues involving trade, United Nations mandated activities, aid to needy and newly democratic nations (particularly Russia), environmental concerns, and international conflict resolution. Basically, Western powers want Japan to assume not only the title of a superpower, but also the global responsibilities of superpowerdom. Provided, of course, that Japan decides to see things their way. Even so, many would be willing to put up with a feisty Japan if that Japan would just assume some real responsibility, which they see Japan as having evaded for entirely too long.

Moreover, with the United States retreating in the post-Cold War era from the strong role it has played in Asia during the past 50 years, Japan is being pushed to fill the leadership vacuum that has been created. And with its US military security umbrella shrinking, Japan must also be alert to increasing threats in the region, including a resurgent China and a volatile North Korea.

A Bite to Match its Bark

Many observers of the Japanese political scene had questioned whether public outrage would really be enough to kick the entrenched old guard out of the Diet and, having seen it actually happen, whether the newfound public activism would be enough to make it stick. In July 1993 the electorate's bite proved to be at least as big as its bark. The LDP lost its controlling majority in the 511-member parliament by 33 votes, although it continued to be the largest party

in the Diet. The party also lost 52 seats in the lower house, leaving it with a total of 223 seats. Meanwhile, the three new centrist parties won a significant 103 seats. As part of the post election reshuffling, Miyazawa was replaced as leader of the LDP by Yohei Kono, a young reformer with a cleaner image.

However, as a tainted party insider Kono proved not to be clean enough, nor could he rally enough internal support to successfully consolidate his hold within the LDP. However, outsider Morihiro Hosokawa, a relatively young and unknown provincial governor, had distanced himself convincingly from corruption and scandals through his defection from the LDP in 1991 and the formation of the Japan New Party. Almost by default, Hosokawa was chosen to run for prime minister by a coalition of seven parties, including the largest opposition party, the Socialists, campaigning on a change platform. This basically anti-LDP plan called for the Diet to dismantle the overly centralized, outmoded system of government. Although views among the coalition party members range widely from center right to hard left (or as hard as it gets within mainstream Japanese politics), the members set aside their more divergent ideological differences, drafted a joint manifesto, and took the unheard of step of ganging up to openly challenge the LDP.

And amazingly it worked. When the dust settled, the newly formed coalition controlled 245 seats to the LDP's 223, allowing Hosokawa to come to power by a small but better than razor thin 22 seat margin. Hosokawa immediately set about espousing a program calling for change in electoral rules and campaign financing, deregulation and freer markets, and close ties with the United States in the context of a more globally involved Japan.

The Bureaucratic Straitjacket

Japan's new leaders claim to favor open political debate over the old back room consensus-building pattern of decision making that has allowed politics to be dominated by deal-making pols and unelected bureaucrats. Because bureaucrats have traditionally been the real decision makers in domestic and international policy in Japan, true parliamentary debate has been lacking. Politicians, who were mainly involved in internal party maneuvering and securing campaign funds for the next round, often merely parroted the debate script crafted by the bureaucrats who exercised true administrative control in the context of the system.

The amount of actual change a new prime minister, no matter how motivated or how popular, can effect is still an unknown. The bureaucracy has extensive leeway in setting policy, much more actual power than the politicians. And even if the politicians seize the reins and dictate sweeping policy changes, those changes must still be implemented by the bureaucracy, which can hamstring the mandated changes through foot-dragging and the drafting of implementing regulations that emasculate the new rules. Although the new political leaders may control the steering wheel, the bureaucrats still have firm control over the throttle, the brake pedal, and the gearshift.

The other element is business, which has a large say in what goes into the gas tank. In the past politicians have acted primarily as brokers between the business interests that funded them and the bureaucrats that ran the country. Businesspeople funneled money to politicians for reelection campaigns and other expenses. In return politicians interpreted laws and other regulations to the advantage of business interests. Cynics see the LDP-led government primarily as having served as a self-important messenger and mediator between the bureaucrats and business. A more functional analysis would see a delicately balanced but highly stable and extremely focused symbiotic system, the so-called "iron triangle."

It was this frozen and inadequately adaptive situation that finally led the Japanese to vote for change. With a long-running recession gouging deeper holes into their psyches and their pocketbooks, Japanese voters were ready to do something about a system that was perceived as too comfortable for the inside members and because of this unable to deal effectively with the flailing economy. Deals that protected the status quo had too often been seen as squelching innovation and responsiveness, and the system was suffocating under the weight of prevailing political favors and payoffs.

The Inauguration of a New Era?

In his uncharacteristically bold and direct inaugural speech, Hosokawa pledged to reshape the electoral system, clean up corruption, and reduce Japan's embarrassingly high trade surplus to restore peace between itself and its increasingly restive allies. He proclaimed that it was time to take firm action to reinvigorate the economy, expand domestic demand, and develop more consumer oriented policies.

Now it was the LDP's turn to criticize, and criticize it did. The party leadership, still smarting from their stinging defeat and adjusting to the unaccustomed role of a loyal opposition, claimed that Hosokawa was vague, unrealistic, and that, besides, they had already said it all before. Hosokawa was also taken to task for being "fascistic" in his directness, ignoring time-honored Japanese canons of harmony while failing to defer to his elders and betters. Although the still potent LDP has been able to slow the reformers, to date it has not been able to dethrone them, and Hosokawa's popularity—an stunning approval rating of 79 percent in at least one early 1994 poll—gives them pause in their attempts to do so.

Despite an acknowledged need for immediate action on economic issues, Hosokawa made political reform the centerpiece of his new administration, anteing up virtually all his political chips in a bid to push his reform measures. Six months after his election, Hosokawa still had not developed a coherent economic policy, largely because he had been unable to put the political reform issue to bed. Although the reform package made it through the lower house of the Diet, it was rejected in the upper house in mid-January 1994. This failure was due largely to defections by Socialist members of the ruling coalition, who analysts say lost their nerve and voted against the measure in fear of losing their newfound influence.

The Perils of Morihiro

Hosokawa had originally said that he would resign and call new elections if the reform bill failed to pass. However, he postponed such drastic action, saying that he would do so only if some reform package failed to pass by the end of the legislative session on January 29. Hosokawa and the LDP—which recognized that it ultimately had much to lose by appearing to be unwilling to accept popular demands for reform—hammered out a last minute face-saving compromise.

The Japanese drew a collective sigh of relief at the passage of some reform—any reform—package. It appeared to allow them to get beyond the fratricidal diversions and on to the overriding issue of the economy. All parties finally tacitly acknowledged that a defeat for Hosokawa, no matter delicious it would be for the LDP and a few others in the short-run, would instigate a prolonged period of infighting during which the politicians would be exposed to the wrath of the populace and during which no progress could be expected to be made on critical economic matters.

The resulting reform plan was a much-watered down version of the original. It was also incomplete, requiring the Diet to set details and pass implementing legislation in its next session. However, the plan did call for the phasing out of corporate political contributions in five years (but not immediately as had the original) and for a massive redistricting designed to take disproportionate influence away from rural constituencies, which have favored status quo politicians, and augment that of the more numerous and generally more progressive urban voters. Observers expect real change to be slow but inexorable, with party politics as Japan has known them for the past 40 years to be forever altered. It is still possible that the politicians could lose their resolve and try to get by with cosmetic changes while protecting their customary position. However, most understand that they would do so at their peril.

There is a great deal of speculation that existing parties may collapse under the weight of all this change in their traditional way of doing business. The LDP and the Socialists, as the largest and best established parties, have the most to lose from such an outcome. However, the more forward-looking leaders among their ranks are arguing that they will lose everything if they try to hang onto the past and fail to move into the future. The likely outcome is that the parties will re-form, ultimately purging themselves of their antireformist old guards, and take on an at least somewhat more open character. However, there will be considerable confusion and uncertainty as these changes are sorted out over the next few years and the Japanese body politic gropes for a new *modus operandi*.

One of the main reasons that the various factions finally came together to agree on a reform package was that they felt the ire of the people who were growing increasingly impatient for an economic program. Having dodged the political reform bullet, the Hosokawa government promised to announce such a program within a week. However, having narrowly avoided destruction over political reform, the coalition was immediately threatened over the terms of the proposed stimulus package. As widely anticipated, the package was to include an income tax cut of more than US$55 billion, but to pay for this largesse, the government slipped in a deferred hike in the consumption tax from the current 3 percent to 7 percent to take effect after three years. The Socialists, who adamantly opposed any rise in taxes, threatened to pull out of the government, causing its fall. And Prime Minister Hosokawa was due in Washington, DC in less than a week's time, where the Clinton administration was putting additional pressure on him to whip his bureaucrats into line and agree to numerical quotas for a US share of the Japanese domestic market under the threat of retaliatory measures if Japan failed to agree to this modest proposal. Poor Morihiro.

The Hosokawa government quickly withdrew its tax cut and its consumption tax—which had been included at the insistence of the powerful Ministry of Finance which opposes any deficit financing—and went back to the drawing board to try to come up with an alternate proposal.

JAPANESE TRADE SURPLUSES, UNITED STATES TRADE DEFICITS, AND INTERNATIONAL TRADE HEADACHES

Envied, often resented, and sometimes feared throughout the world, Japan holds the highest trade surplus of all the industrialized economies in the world, about 3.5 percent of its gross domestic product (GDP) in 1992 and US$120.4 billion in actual (preliminary) numbers in 1993. Its surplus with the United States alone now runs in the neighborhood of US$50 billion. The US and the Clinton administration have had enough of this trade imbalance and have vowed to get tough. But just how tough to get in this no-more-mister-nice-guy scenario remains an open question.

US Frustrations

The United States has accused Japan of unfairly obstructing the entry of its products to Japanese markets, particularly in sectors such as automobiles

and technology, among others, and in foreign investment in general. It is further angered but what it sees as Japan's failure to enforce past agreements designed to improve US trade access and lower the deficit. US trade negotiators are tired of what they see as separate sets of rules that result in open markets for Japanese products in the US but restrict the penetration of US products into Japanese markets.

Japan's trade surplus shrank somewhat from 1987 to 1990, giving the parties involved some breathing room. However, it began rising again in 1992, quickly reaching uncomfortable heights. In 1992 the increase in the US trade deficit resulted largely from a 10 percent increase in imports of Japanese goods into the US while Japanese imports of US goods remained about the same, adding insult to injury. The Organization for Economic Cooperation and Development (OECD) estimated that Japan's current-account surplus would reach US$130 billion in 1993—with a growing portion of that surplus representing trade with the United States. Japan's record trade surplus of US$120.4 billion was bad but not as bad as earlier predicted. However, despite official efforts to boost consumption, Japanese imports showed no real change from the previous year. And the problem is further exacerbated by the strong yen that earns the Japanese more on their exports while at the same time dropping the value in dollars of their augmented imports and boosting the surplus.

As a general goal, the United States is pushing for the rapid deregulation of Japan's financial system and the liberalization of direct foreign investment, both areas which authorities argue have been obstructed in the past and continue to be restricted in the present. The United States further wants to see actual improvement in the numbers. It wants Japan to contract to reduce its trade surplus by more than half, from 1992's 3.5 percent of GDP to 1.5 percent over the near term. The Clinton administration also wants to increase US imports to Japan by one-third over a three year period. It wants to see guarantees of increased government procurement of foreign goods, increased access—what it calls "comparable access," or equal access to be measured by a set percentage of market share—to Japanese markets for foreign firms, particularly for financial institutions and other service firms, high technology concerns, and manufacturers, such as those of automobiles and parts.

Japanese "Intransigence"

The Japanese have responded with several arguments. First, they deny that they are guilty as charged, insisting that their markets are as open as they can be and that outsiders simply fail to understand their special needs and provide the goods and services that can make it in Japan. A somewhat belligerent subset of this argument has been the recurrent theme that the US should stop being such a whiner. If US exporters aren't successful, maybe the problem originates at home rather than in Tokyo. The prevailing viewpoint in Japan has long been that the US should clean up its own messy house instead of blaming Japan for its own problems. In the past top Japanese leaders have accused US workers of being lazy and incompetent and producing shoddy goods as the true reason for poor US international trade performance. However, as Japan's economy has drifted steadily downward during the recession that is now entering its fourth year, such smug superiority is fading. Especially as US worker productivity now substantially surpasses that of Japanese workers. Welcome as any reduction in such finger-pointing is, it risks triggering a resurgence in Japan of the opposite underdog syndrome. Nevertheless, despite such swings in the Japanese collective psyche during which they see themselves as either supermen or 98-pound weaklings, the Japanese are likely to continue to see themselves as different, with the rest of the world being not quite so blessed as they are.

In the second place, the Japanese have resisted US demands that trade imbalances be rectified, arguing that that is just the way things are. In particular, they have balked at setting specific numerical targets for trade, accusing the United States of tinkering with truly free trade and trying to manage it unfairly to its own advantage. Even when US and Japanese negotiators have been able to agree in principle that there is a problem and on what should be done about it, they have been unable to agree on an appropriate means of measuring the results. US trade negotiators have argued that Japan should commit to taking foreign imports to an extent that allows foreigners to gain a percentage of the Japanese domestic market equivalent to that held by foreigners in other developed economies worldwide (the foreign share of the Japanese market is currently well below that held by foreigners—especially Japanese—elsewhere).

The Problems with Getting Tough

Getting tough with Japan would mean pursuing aggressive trade policies that restrict or exclude Japanese goods from the US market should Japan fail to agree to plans to open its own protected markets in a manner that would guarantee a rise in sales by US firms and a reduction in the existing trade imbalance as called for in current US policy. As the United States attempts to push the Japanese to open their markets, the Japanese government, particularly its Ministry of Finance, has been digging in its heels.

The US also incurs additional risks in playing the get-tough card. To retain its credibility, it must be willing to follow through by actually cutting off one of its largest and closest trade partners and political allies should the Japanese fail to respond in a satisfactory manner. Yet in doing so the United States would legitimize the protectionist viewpoint, the very position it criticizes in Japan, losing the moral high ground that it has worked so hard to establish.

From the historical perspective it is well to remember that according to the Japanese viewpoint, the incident that precipitated World War II was the United States government's placing of a trade embargo on Japan, preventing it from importing US scrap steel. This action—essentially a retaliatory trade action—deprived it of its main source of a critical strategic resource. There is considerable evidence that the United States failed to understand the seriousness with which Japan viewed this gesture: it was interpreted by the militarist Japanese government as an outright act of war. Communications, understanding, interdependence, and the military interests and belligerency of both parties have all changed since that time. However, it is well to remember that trade ultimatums can escalate tensions, allowing things to get out of hand.

Some economists and policymakers contend that the best strategy is to keep one's own markets open regardless. This should allow a high level of competition, leading to lower prices for consumers and increased efficiency among domestic manufacturers. Should the United States stoop to retaliatory protectionist measures, they argue, it will be opening a Pandora's box of escalating counterpunches. Protectionists in the United States would be expected to have a field day, particularly those in the automotive industry: automotive imports account for 70 percent of America's total merchandise trade deficit with Japan, and auto workers have long urged foreign car owners to park their Japanese cars in Tokyo. Protectionists in Congress, having already rallied against the North American Free Trade Agreement (NAFTA), would be expected to be quick to add their voices to the case against Japan, although the issues and personalities rapidly become complex and clouded. For example, veteran Japan-basher Lee Iacocca, formerly of Chrysler, was quick to sign on as a NAFTA promoter.

New Leaders, New Strategies?

Shortly after coming to power himself and formulating a policy with respect to Japan, Clinton had to rethink it when the new Japanese coalition government gained power in July 1993. Clinton had thrown down the gauntlet to then Prime Minister Miyazawa as recently as April 1993. Although Miyazawa promised at the time to open Japan's rice market to international suppliers, he failed to take any action and was rapidly in no position to do so.

However, when Morihiro Hosokawa, a new young Japanese leader committed to promoting a variety of reforms and to maintaining close ties with the United States came to power in August 1993, it seemed like an opportune time for the United States to conciliate rather than to challenge, and the two administrations enjoyed a honeymoon for a period of months. By year-end with no appreciable change in the Japanese position, the honeymoon was beginning to wear somewhat thin, and the US was once more pushing the Japanese to show results.

The Culprit of the Latest Round of the Case of the Rising Surplus

Weakness in domestic demand is in large part responsible for the resurgence of Japan's external trade surplus. In the 1980s a growing appetite for consumer goods, especially brand name foreign imports, took on a significantly greater role in Japan's economy. Now with a lingering recession that is forcing Japan to take a hard look at the way it operates, consumer confidence is down and consumers have tightened the purse strings. This reluctance to buy disproportionately affects foreign imports. Conversely, as the US economy begins to show signs of emerging from its own comatose state, consumers are more hopeful and more willing to spend money on consumer goods, often foreign imports. As a result both the US deficit and the Japanese surplus are growing, adding fuel to the fire.

A Look on the Bright Side

Although bilateral trade tensions continue interminably, the US-Japanese relationship involves more than trade. Since the 1950s the United States and Japan have had a generally cooperative relationship, which has provided one of the few certainties which both could use to base policy in Asia. Similarly, all Japanese governments in the postwar period have acknowledged a close relationship with the United States as a given in their foreign policy. Despite substantial cultural and historic differences, both point to several important commonalties: a basic business orientation, a democratic political structure, high literacy rates, freedom of expression, and universal suffrage. The United States and Japan have also developed a close global partnership in support of shared values and concerns such as antiterrorist and antidrug initiatives, development assistance, aspects of foreign policy, and elements of environmental protectionism.

Because of the two nations' combined economic and technological clout—together they account for 40 percent of world's GNP and 60 percent of that of the industrialized nations—the relationship between the US and Japan has become global in scope. Although in the past the partnership has been measured primarily in economic and technological terms, in the future it can be expected to have a larger political dimension as Japan assumes a greater international role and associates itself more actively and closely with Western political and security goals. The overall Japanese-US relationship is mutually beneficial, and it is in the best interests of both nations to persevere in their attempts to keep trade relations both in perspective and as free and open as possible. Nevertheless, the issues are important to both and both will be sorely tempted to rise to the bait which is virtually guaranteed to provoke the other.

JAPAN'S NEW ROLE IN ASIA: CAN WE TALK?

While the United States steams over its rising trade deficit with Japan, which grew by 14 percent to US$44 billion in 1992, it can draw cold comfort from the fact that things could be worse. Japan's surplus with its Asian neighbors surged 32 percent—more than double the rate of the US deficit—to US$42 billion during the same period.

Overall the percentage of Japan's exports destined for the United States is falling, while its exports to Asian countries are soaring. Japanese exports shipped to the United States dropped from 40 percent of its total exports during the mid-1980s to 28 percent in 1992. During the same period, exports to Southeast Asia jumped from 20 percent of the total to 31 percent. Japan's trade surplus with Southeast Asian countries has nearly tripled from US$12 billion in 1986 to US$47 billion in 1993. The dollar value of Japanese exports to China alone has doubled over the last two years.

Spending Time in the Western Camp

These figures are symbolic of Japan's growing role in Asia as it returns to its historically neglected Asian roots. In the 19th century, as Western powers horned in on Asia, the Japanese were able to learn from the experience of the Chinese. The lessons learned included the observation that to resist change and the Western barbarians was to risk losing not merely face but sovereignty as well. Besides, the barbarians had a lot of interesting things that Japan lacked and going along with them provided the only avenue available for obtaining such goods. The Japanese shrewdly aligned themselves with and instituted reforms that were pleasing to the Western powers. And although they resented having to take a back seat to the Western interlopers, they were able to spare themselves the unpleasantness of actually being forced into submission. The Japanese were quick to transcend Asian isolationism and latch onto the possibilities offered by the newcomers, no matter how uncultured they might be.

Associating itself with the West to gain access to

what it could bring them—following the main chance, as it were—caused some loss of face and crisis of conscience within Japan. However, it did not pose particular problems with respect to what the neighbors might think. The ethnocentric Japanese had relatively little solidarity with their Asian neighbors. In fact, they historically had tended to look down on their weaker, poorer, and—from their own viewpoint—less cultured Asian neighbors.

This attitude of separateness was reinforced by Japan's development as a rapidly modernizing world-class military and industrial power. Japan proved its mettle by trouncing Russia, a quasi-European nation, in 1905, and gaining the basis of a colonial empire of its own. Japan played a peripheral role in World War I, siding with the Allies and gaining recognition by being included among the so-called Big Five Allied signatories of the Treaty of Versailles in 1919. Although this acknowledged Japan's status as an emerging world power and made it an honorary "Western" nation, it turned out to be unfortunate because the treaty served to deprive Japan of what it considered to be its rightful spoils: Germany's Far Eastern possessions. Nevertheless, despite its subsequent conflict with and defeat by the United States and other Western allies, Japan remained separate but firmly oriented toward the larger world dominated by the West.

Changes in the Wind?

However, as the century in which Japan considered itself as belonging basically to the Western camp draws to a close, things are shifting significantly. Now that Japan's economic power is not merely on a par with that of the Western nations but has far surpassed that of virtually all of them, Japan has begun casting hungry and, some fear, entirely too proprietary looks at the emerging economies of Asia. Moreover, as the domestic problems of its main ally and rival, the United States, mount, Japan's post-war reliance on the US is waning. Japan's investment in the United States peaked in the late 1980s. Today the Japanese are eyeing trade and investment opportunities to be found closer to home. Many of these Asian countries have raw materials, cheap labor, and growing domestic business and consumer markets, that are growing at 8 to 9 percent or more per year.

Now that the economic heavyweights—Germany, Britain, and the United States—have become less of a challenge, Japan is beginning to spar with the lightweights that are swiftly building up their economic muscles. Japan's hope is that its own economic muscles, weakened by a global recession, will regain strength from working out with these up-and-coming stars of Asia.

The Japanese are also showing renewed interest in their Asian cousins that goes beyond the strictly economic. Twice as many Japanese are traveling to Asia as made such trips ten years ago. Increasing numbers of Japanese are working in other Asian countries, and an estimated 200,000 Asian foreigners are working in Japan. As a result, Japan's attitude toward its Asian neighbors is changing, although the Japanese still have a somewhat superior attitude toward their neighbors, particularly the less wealthy, lesser developed ones.

This increased Japanese presence and economic maneuvering in Asia is beginning to worry the Western economic powers. Although no formal trade agreements have been established between Japan and its Southeast and East Asian neighbors, the Japanese are insinuating themselves into Asian markets in ways beyond what any formal agreement would attempt to establish. Some foresee Japan's economic moves in Asia as forming a de facto trade and investment group that ties up the Asian markets for Japan's exclusive use. Intraregional trade within the East Asia region, including Japan, is responsible for about 10 percent of total world trade and is increasing annually. Observers note several tactics in the Japanese expansion.

Inroads Through Investment During the five years between 1984 and 1989, Japanese annual direct investment in Asia increased five-fold, placing it ahead of even expansive US investment in Asia. The US share of foreign direct investment in Asia declined from 48.2 percent in 1990 to 43.3 percent in 1992. Japan's share increased during that same period from 12.2 percent to 14.3 percent, notwithstanding an overall worldwide slowdown in Japanese foreign investment during that time frame. While Japanese direct investment in 1991 declined most significantly in North America and Europe—down 30.8 percent and 34.4 percent, respectively—Japanese investment in China in both the manufacturing and nonmanufacturing sectors grew significantly, rising by 91.8 percent and 24 percent, respectively. In 1990 the United States put US$233 billion in direct investment into Asia's newly industrialized countries (NICs)—Hong Kong, Korea, Singapore, Taiwan—and the Association of Southeast Asian Nations (ASEAN)—Philippines, Malaysia, Indonesia, and Thailand. Japan's share was US$441.7 billion, almost double the amount invested by the US.

Inroads Through Trade Currently suffering from low domestic demand and stagnant growth in its domestic economy, Japan is eyeing the lucrative Asian consumer market as a means to reinvigorate its own economy. For example, Japan's Toyota was expected to secure a 30 percent share of the car market in the ASEAN nations in 1993. With an anticipated doubling of consumer demand—from one million to two million units—for cars and light trucks during the 1990s in these markets alone, Japanese

businesses hope for unprecedented growth and financial returns.

Japan has also become a big import market for products from East Asia, further strengthening its ties with the region. Japan's imports of manufactured goods from the NIEs, ASEAN, and China grew threefold from US$8.8 billion in 1985 to US$36.1 billion in 1991. While Japan's imports of low grade manufactured goods such as garments and other sundry items from the NIEs peaked in 1981 and has declined ever since, its imports of higher grade products, such as office equipment, audio equipment, semiconductors and other electronic components, scientific and optical equipment, and other machinery, have been increasing at an accelerating clip. Since 1989 numerous products have appeared in the Japanese market, such as air conditioners, refrigerators, and telephones from Thailand and the Philippines; radios and parts and computer parts from Malaysia; and textile products from Indonesia, that previously had never been imported.

This growing symbiosis provides a market for Japanese exports, while Japanese imports of their goods gives their Asian neighbors the wherewithal to afford them. And the buildup of the Japanese trade surplus with these countries serves to place them in thrall to the Japanese by soaking up their liquidity. Competitors from elsewhere worry that the relationship is becoming not merely habitual but exclusive.

Inroads through Foreign Aid In recent years Japan, after World War II one of the world's largest recipients of economic assistance, has become one of the largest providers of foreign aid worldwide, operating on a level comparable to that of the United States. The forms of aid include grants in aid, "soft" loans, and technical cooperation. This technical cooperation has enabled Japan to become the supplier for many of the projects financed by its Official Development Assistance program. The program aims to focus spending on infrastructure from which Japanese companies can profit. This benefit explains why more aid is targeted toward Asia with its booming growth rates than toward Africa, which is unlikely to offer a payback in future business. Some argue that Japan, which supplies more than half of all aid to ASEAN nations and China, has tended to use its foreign aid program as a front to subsidize trade by national firms.

Money Talks

Given Japan's dominant position, its economic maneuvering, and not-too-distant memories of World War II, the image of the Ugly Japanese is replacing that of the Ugly American. Many Asians harbor unpleasant memories of Japanese behavior before and especially during World War II and of the Greater East

Asian Co-Prosperity Sphere, the Japanese name for the colonial economic unit that they tried to impose on their Asian neighbors at the time. Many are uncomfortable that the renewed Japanese economic thrust represents an attempt to establish a similar dominance using only somewhat less coercive means. Now many Asians are beginning to lament their previous strident criticisms and calls for the Yankees to "go home," for that is just what Yankees have begun to do.

Whoever controls the purse strings tends to call the tune. For Asia that purse holder is increasingly speaking with a Japanese accent. Still, the United States remains Asia's most lucrative export market, and most Asian countries would welcome greater US investment and involvement, but it has been slow to come in recent years. Thus, Japan's influence continues to grow and the siren song of the yen is drowning out that of the dollar.

THE JAPANESE ECONOMY: IS THERE LIGHT AT THE END OF THE TUNNEL, OR IS IT JUST AN ONCOMING TRAIN?

Many both in Japan and abroad have begun to speculate that if what goes up truly must come down, the sun is beginning to set on the economy in the land of the rising sun. Could this be the end of Japan's glorious growth during the last 40 years? Or is it merely taking time out to recharge its batteries in an economy that has set the example for most other economies around the world? Economists speculate and differ, but the Japanese are staying worried, at least for now.

More Gloomy Numbers

The woes that have stubbornly hung on and in many cases steadily worsened in Japan since the economic downturn that began in early 1990 are producing symptoms in numerous parts of its economic body. There have been a record number of bankruptcies, particularly among small- and medium-sized firms, although many of these firms may have been poorly capitalized and marginal to begin with. Bankruptcies peaked in 1992 and fell somewhat in 1993, but this has provided little reassurance because the remaining failures have been among larger firms, leaving open the prospect that more downstream firms will be shaken out further down the line.

Real GDP growth rate shrank to an anemic 1.7 percent in calendar 1992 from 4.1 percent a year earlier, and preliminary estimates expect no more than break-even performance for 1993. Growth was actually negative during mid-1993. Observers hold out little hope for a robust recovery, although many expect the Japanese economy to finally bottom out

during the first six months of 1994. Many estimates for real growth in 1994 range from 0.25 percent to around 1.5 percent, with a rebound of less than 2 percent in 1995.

There has been no growth in bank lending to corporations, indicating a stagnant economy with little new investment. Industrial production slid by 8.2 percent from January to December 1992, registering no improvement during 1993. Japan also experienced a drop in retail sales of 5.7 percent during 1992 as consumer confidence withered. Despite some recent strength, attributed mainly to foreign bargain hunters, the Japanese stock market remains stalled at a level nearly 50 percent below that reached in 1989. Japanese industry suffers from substantial overcapacity, major firms are beginning to shift significant amounts of production overseas because of high domestic costs, conservative estimates peg the number of redundant and at risk workers at a minimum of one million, and the yen, which recovered above the 110 level with respect to the dollar at the end of 1993, is eroding again to the 107-109 danger zone again in early 1994. The list goes on in a seemingly endless manner.

Japanese Corporations Corporate profits have declined for three straight years, the first time since World War II that such a thing has happened, and are expected to continue to decline in 1994. Although few employees have actually been laid off to date, they are feeling the crunch in other ways. Companies have cut back on overtime pay and bonuses (these two items normally account for around 40 percent of a worker's total compensation), are forcing more employees to take early retirement or dropping the retirement age to reduce head count, have frozen promotions and the hiring of new employees, and, in what is perhaps the most psychologically significant move, are beginning to dismantle the sacred *saraiiman* or lifetime white-collar employment.

Companies have resisted taking action for as long as they possibly could, but now many calculate that they will be unable to weather the continued recession unless they take draconian measures. If they are to be able to survive they will have to radically improve profitability, and this means slashing expenses, mainly labor costs. This does not encourage consumer confidence.

Japanese Consumers As corporate Japan rethinks its policy of virtually unconditional loyalty to its employees, those employees are similarly beginning to shift their allegiances. Tired of hard work and high earnings that fail to translate into high purchasing power because of artificially high prices on consumer goods, the Japanese want to see the benefits of their superpower status and begin enjoying the same rewards they see accruing in other advanced nations. These rights of success include more lei-sure time, larger and more sumptuous living spaces, and cheaper consumer prices, especially for im-ported goods. As employees, they are starting to realize there is more to life than what happens at the office and that loyalty may be a two-way street. As consumers, they are demanding lower-priced goods, making discount and bargain items the hot new fashion in Japan.

At the same time, they are ambivalent. Old hab-its die hard, and in tough economic times they won-der if they have already lost their chance. Govern-ment policy makers have been calling for a massive tax cut to prime the consumer spending pump. How-ever, indications are that most consumers would bank such excess income because of fears about their future, meaning that the economy probably would not receive enough of a jolt to revive it and could even suffer more due to the shortfall in rev-enue. This, of course would drive interest rates up as the government would have to either cut back on programs or issue more debt, which would in turn make consumers more likely to cut back on pur-chases and save even more, and so on.

Getting to the Heart of the Matter

Just as economists of all schools of thought speculate about the reasons behind Japan's eco-nomic miracle over the past twenty years, so they speculate about its ailments and possible antidotes today. One thing is clear: Japan's economy is highly overregulated in areas where competition should be at its fiercest. With protectionism and strict regula-tion, Japanese companies in the service sector have been able to cruise placidly along below an artifi-cially low speed limit, resulting in productivity far below that of many firms in the same industries else-where. In other industries, corruption, bribery, and other under-the-table allocation procedures have often determined which firms receive choice con-tracts, often without regard to economic consider-ations. The lack of transparency in this thicket of regulations and web of arcane operating procedures has been a continuing bone of contention between the Japanese and foreigners.

The Land of the Rising Yen

On top of its domestic financial problems, heavy regulations further aggravate Japan's trade surplus and have placed increasing upward pressure on its appreciating yen. The surging yen has begun to cripple various Japanese exporters. The rate of the yen (about ¥108 to the US$ in early February 1994) is deemed unprofitable by Japanese firms involved in export markets. This rate is adding to the rush by domestic firms to cut their costs by outsourcing pro-duction abroad.

The government is proposing to remedy the eco-nomic downturn by introducing a stimulus package of increased government spending and tax cuts. However, many observers argue that previous stimu-lus packages haven't had the desired result and that the government needs to look to freeing up its fiscal policy and relax its regulations and restrictions.

Groggy But Still Standing

Although no nation has escaped unscathed dur-ing the rolling global recession of the early 1990s, Japan is taking things especially hard. With its virtu-ally unbroken postwar economic prosperity and numerous consecutive years of significantly rising incomes, the Japanese were not psychologically pre-pared for such an economic jolt.

Regardless of the weight of the blow, most would argue that Japan, with its wealth of riches in both capital and labor, cannot be kept down indefinitely. The Japanese, with one of the highest literacy rates in the world, have a very well educated hard work-ing labor force. Known for their strong entrepreneur-ial spirit, the Japanese have proportionally more small businesses than are found in the United States, the proverbial home of individual garage enterprises, or the United Kingdom, the proverbial nation of shop-keepers. Moreover, the Japanese people have dem-onstrated their willingness to sacrifice present ben-efits for future stability and security.

Opportunities

OPPORTUNITIES FOR IMPORTING FROM JAPAN

In Japan, as in most countries, a relatively small number of industries dominate in the international trade and investment arena. Japan's major export industries include automobiles, consumer electronics, computers, semiconductors, and iron and steel. Other key industries in Japan's economy are mining, nonferrous metals, petrochemicals, pharmaceuticals, biotechnology, shipbuilding, aerospace, textiles, and processed foods. While Japan still offers ample opportunity for foreign importers, rising competition from the newly industrialized countries (NICs) in Asia, accompanied by appreciation of the yen, indicates that economic growth within these key industries will become more moderate in the future. The following section describes Japan's most important industries and the opportunities they offer to foreign importers.

AUTOMOBILES AND AUTO PARTS

Japan is one of the top producers of automobiles in the world, with passenger cars, other motor vehicles, and automotive parts comprising its primary output. Total production has declined since 1991, but automobiles still account for approximately one-fifth of Japan's exports. Vehicle exports to Asia, Oceania, the Middle East, and Latin America continue to increase, though exports to Europe and North America are falling, mirroring the sluggish economic conditions in those regions and increased offshore auto production by Japanese-owned facilities. Yet motorcycle and other two-wheeler production in Japan has risen for three consecutive years, reaching 3.16 million units in 1992, an increase of 4.3 percent over the previous year.

Automobile parts also represent a substantial segment of total sales. Major production items include engine parts, chassis and drive train parts, car body parts, electrical and electronic parts, and accessories.

Some of the HOT items:
- auto accessories
- body parts
- buses
- electrical parts
- engine parts
- intermediate and full-sized passenger automobiles
- motorcycles and other two-wheel vehicles
- trucks

SHIPBUILDING

Japan is the world's largest shipbuilding nation and largest merchant shipbuilder. In mid-1992 the Japanese shipbuilding industry, fueled by a two-year backlog of orders, received more than 35 percent of global merchant ship orders as measured by gross tonnage. Mitsubishi Heavy Industries, Ishikawajima-Harima Heavy Industries, and Hitachi Zosen are Japan's primary shipbuilders. Production orders for very large crude carriers (VLCCs) have increased the fastest, followed by tankers, bulk carriers, and such high value-added vessels as liquefied natural gas (LNG) and liquefied petroleum (LPG) carriers.

Some of the HOT items:

- bulk carriers
- floating structures
- large tankers
- LNG and LPG carriers
- very large crude carriers (VLCCs)

ELECTRONICS

Japan's electronics industry is expected to continue to expand steadily through the 1990s in response to rising world demand for sophisticated electronic consumer and industrial products. Japan's top electronics companies—Matsushita Electric, Sony, Toshiba, Hitachi, and Mitsubishi Electric—play a dominant role in the world electronics market. Key manufacturing strengths and technology innovation are other indicators of Japan's leading status in this field. Primary industry sectors include consumer and industrial electronics as well as electrical parts and components.

Consumer and Industrial Electronics

Japan is likely to continue to play a leading role in the global market for consumer electronics goods. To maintain their market share, Japanese manufacturers place strong emphasis on value-added products, quality improvements, and new areas of consumer demand. They are also increasing offshore production as a means of reducing Japan's trade surplus and cutting production costs.

Japanese firms produce a wide range of products, from personal stereos to household appliances. Color televisions, video equipment, and hi-fi systems have been the leading products, but a new generation of digital technology will in all likelihood sustain new products through the 1990s. New technologies are expected to result in a strong market in the future for audiovisual products.

In addition, manufacturers of electrical goods are gradually switching their production from consumer items to industrial products. Office communications, office automation equipment, and robotic devices continue to offer high growth opportunities. Products include plain paper fax (PPF) machines, electronic copiers, and compact digital telephones.

Electronic Parts and Components

Japan's production of electronic components captures over 50 percent of the global market for such items as passive components, functional components, mechanical components, active devices, and liquid crystal displays (LCDs). The Japanese market for electronic components is expected to grow at an average annual rate of 5 to 7 percent. According to Nikkei industry forecasts, a significant driving force behind this growth is an expected recovery in integrated circuit sales and increased sales of LCDs and other products.

Some of the HOT items:

- air conditioners
- cameras, parts, and accessories
- cellular telephones
- coupling parts
- digital tape recorders and cassettes
- electronic copiers
- high-definition television (HDTV) sets
- industrial robots
- liquid crystal displays (LCDs)
- passive components
- plain paper fax (PPF) machines
- printed circuit boards
- small power transceivers
- video cassette recorders (VCRs)

SEMICONDUCTORS

Semiconductor devices are the key components of computers and a wide variety of other electronic equipment. In 1992 Japan's semiconductor exports increased, primarily due to a recovery in the US personal computer market. However, Japanese semiconductor producers are currently faced with increased capital costs, declining profits, and increased competition from other Asian suppliers. An overcapacity of direct random access memory chips (DRAMs), in particular, has hurt the profitability of Japanese semiconductor producers.

This downturn has caused Japanese semiconductor divisions to move toward such higher value-added product sectors as microprocessing, digital signal processing (DSPs), and application-specific integrated circuitry (ASICs). At the same time, foreign strategic alliances have focused on such sectors as HDTV chip development, microprocessor development, ASIC development, and computer-aided design (CAD) projects. As for future opportunities, product development of metal oxide silicon (MOS) microcomponents, logic, and memory devices offers the greatest potential within the semiconductor industry.

Some of the HOT items:

- application-specific integrated circuits (ASICs)
- digital signal processors (DSPs)
- flash memories
- logic devices
- memory devices
- metal oxide silicon (MOS) microcomponents
- microprocessors

COMPUTERS AND PERIPHERALS

International trends toward computer downsizing and open systems have led Japanese manufacturers to shift from large mainframes to smaller computers. There are 10 mainframe and more than 30 small and medium-sized computer manufacturers in Japan, including NEC, Fujitsu, Toshiba, Apple Japan, and IBM Japan. Key products include mainframe, general and personal computers, terminals, printers, memory devices, and auxiliary equipment.

Although the economic recession has cut into overseas exports of some items, innovative developments in digitized audio and video data suggest areas for future growth. Multimedia computing, applied to products such as CD-ROM (read-only memory) players, is a rapidly growing market.

Some of the HOT items:

- external memory storage devices
- flat panel displays
- general computers
- input and output devices
- laptop and notebook computers
- multimedia products
- printers
- terminal devices
- thin-film transistor color screens
- workstations

IRON AND STEEL

Japan ranks among the world's top producers of iron and crude steel. Economic downturns in the steel industry have curtailed output, but iron and steel exports still surpassed one million unit tons in 1992, up 5.5 percent from the previous year. Exports include crude steel, sheet metal, plate steel, steel pipe, and secondary products. Exported metal products include construction-grade steel as well as stainless and other steel-based alloys.

Some of the HOT items:

- cast and die-cast products
- coils
- metal goods and tools
- plate steel
- reinforcing bars •
- rolled products
- sheet metal
- stainless steel
- steel pipe
- wire rods

NONFERROUS METALS

In order to compete against Korean and Taiwanese steel exports, Japanese manufacturers are diversifying into lightweight structural products made from both steel and nonferrous metal composites, particularly aluminum. End-user export items that make extensive use of nonferrous metals include automobiles, telecommunications equipment, electric machines, and construction materials.

Some of the HOT items:

- aluminum automobile parts and components
- aluminum cast and die-cast products
- copper and brass products
- metal products
- rolled aluminum products
- titanium aerospace materials
- zinc-plated steel sheets

CHEMICALS

Chemicals form one of the building blocks for Japan's automotive, electronics, agricultural, and pharmaceutical industries. Organic, inorganic, and agricultural chemicals as well as allied chemical products are the main outputs. Export demand for these chemicals and related goods is sensitive to developments in other major industries and overall economic health.

Organic chemicals (including petrochemicals) represent the largest sector within the global chemical industry. Of these, petrochemicals account for more than 20 percent of all world trade. The large share of petrochemicals in the global chemical industry is due to the high value of pharmaceutical and drug products. (*See* Opportunities for Growth.) Japan is one of the leading producers of such primary chemicals as methanol, ethylene, propylene, butadiene, benzene, toluene, and xylene. These products may then be refined into such petrochemicals as styrene monomers, polystyrene, and vinyl chloride resin, which are themselves the precursors to a variety of plastics, fibers, elastomers, and fertilizers.

Some of the HOT items:

- adhesives and sealants
- fat products and soaps
- fertilizers and pesticides
- heavy chemicals
- paints and coatings
- petrochemicals
- plastics

PHARMACEUTICALS

Until recently, Japanese pharmaceutical companies focused exclusively on the domestic market. But declining domestic sales have prompted these companies to aggressively expand into European and US markets. These companies have also substantially increased R&D spending in an effort to develop new products for the international market. Drugs developed in Japan that are now used abroad include Herbesser, Gaster, and Mevalotin. Herbesser is used to treat angina pectoris, Gaster is effective against ulcers, and Mevalotin treats hypercholesterolemia. A Japanese drug called FK-508, which is used to prevent transplant rejections, is also sold internationally.

Some of the HOT items:
- FK-508
- Gaster
- Herbesser
- Mevalotin

MACHINERY AND EQUIPMENT

Japan's machine industry has progressed in tandem with the electronics and automobile industries. The introduction of mechatronics and advances in machine tool making have substantially enhanced the competitiveness of Japanese products.

Japanese manufacturers produce a full range of machinery, including turbines, earth-moving equipment, and numerically controlled machine centers. However, production tends to focus on more sophisticated, higher value-added items, such as power generation equipment, civil engineering and mining equipment, metalworking machines, measuring instruments, and precision machinery parts.

Demand for industrial robots is expected to grow in step with the trend toward flexible manufacturing systems. The development and application of artificial intelligence technology and micromachines will create numerous opportunities for foreign importers.

Some of the HOT items:
- boilers
- conveyer equipment
- electrical equipment
- electrostatic machines
- industrial robots
- machining centers
- measuring instruments
- mechanical handling equipment and parts
- metal processing machinery
- mining machines
- numerically controlled machine tools
- power generation motors
- rotary electrical machines
- steam turbine generators

- switch gear and control equipment
- vending machines

ARTS AND HANDICRAFTS

Arts and handicrafts have a long and established history in Japan. Japanese artisans produce sculpture, ceramics, calligraphy, wood block, charcoal, and ink artwork. Natural and seasonal symbols and motifs predominate, and respect for nature is also expressed in the creation of lacquer, wood and paper art, and handicraft items.

Some of the HOT items:
- bamboo products
- Buddhist sculptures
- calligraphy artworks
- ceramics
- handmade paper products
- ink paintings
- lacquer ware
- masks
- netsuke
- screen and wall paintings
- wood block prints

TEN EXTRA PROSPECTS FOR IMPORTING FROM JAPAN

- advanced materials
- aviation electronics
- clocks and watches
- foods
- medical equipment
- paper products
- radio broadcast receivers
- scientific and optical products
- telecommunications equipment
- textile products

OPPORTUNITIES FOR EXPORTING TO JAPAN

In November 1991 Japan's Ministry of Trade and Industry (MITI) established the Business Global Partnership with 40 of Japan's automobile, electronics, machinery, steel, nonferrous metal, chemical, and trading companies. These 40 firms together annually import US$120 million in goods, amounting to 51 percent of Japan's imports. These companies, along with another 160 companies in key industries (for example, machine tools, manufacturing equipment, and glass), are expected to draw up and implement voluntary import plans. Targets for import expansion include parts, components, and capital goods. Foreign firms offering competitive pricing and quality service can take advantage of lucrative prospects ranging from advanced ceramic components and industrial plastics to refrigeration equipment, commercial art, cosmetics, and sporting goods. The following sectors are considered to be the best prospects for foreign companies exporting to Japan.

REFRIGERATION EQUIPMENT

Despite the recession, demand for refrigeration equipment has been increasing in line with the high volume of building construction and orders for new residential housing supplies. Industry analysts predict that shipments of refrigeration equipment will grow by 5 percent annually through 1995. Import items currently in demand are commercial refrigeration equipment, ice-making machines, freezers, prefabricated refrigeration and cold storage, refrigerating display cases (freshness control equipment), and refrigeration units for transportation systems.

Some of the HOT items:
- customized (freshness control) refrigeration machines
- customized refrigerator cabinets and counters
- refrigerating and freezing display cases
- refrigerating and freezing equipment and heat pumps
- refrigerating and freezing equipment parts
- refrigeration units (with non-chlorofluorocarbon refrigerants)

INTERIOR AND COMMERCIAL ART

A softening in prices at the high end of the art market has allowed amateur collectors to enter the lower end of the market. Japanese households are showing more interest in prints, posters, photographs, and other forms of commercial art that can be used in interior decorating. For most of these purchasers, the primary criterion in selection is personal taste; only a small number buy art for investment purposes.

Retailers and other commercial entities are seeking high-quality art to decorate their facilities. Corporations are purchasing art to enliven the workplace environment, as well as to enhance corporate public relations through the contribution of art works for social and philanthropic purposes. Over the next several years, projected annual growth for interior and commercial art in Japan is a healthy 50 percent.

Some of the HOT items:
- crafts
- stamps and reprints of expensive originals
- original prints (lithographs, serigraphs, and etchings)
- photographs
- posters

COSMETICS AND TOILETRIES

Japanese consumers are extremely receptive to quality cosmetics imported from Europe and the United States. While European, particularly French, cosmetics, have long been admired, US cosmetics are increasingly well regarded among Japanese consumers. As price-consciousness continues to spread, opportunities improve for intermediate-priced foreign cosmetics.

In general, though, the Japanese cosmetics market is a mature one, in which consumers are willing to pay high prices for high-quality products. Women under the age of 40 make over 40 percent of cosmetics purchases, with the greatest number of purchases being made by women in their 20s. Environmentally sound products, time-saving cosmetics for working women, and products specially designed for women over 40 offer the greatest potential sales. Promising items include perfumes and body fragrances, hair care products, natural foundations, eye makeup, lipsticks, and skin care products.

Some of the HOT items:
- bath preparations
- face powder
- hair care preparations
- natural cosmetics
- skin care products
- sun screen products

ADVANCED CERAMICS COMPONENTS

Advanced ceramics components are used in fields ranging from electronics, energy, aviation, and space to medical and marine equipment. By the year 2000 the Japanese market for advanced ceramic components is expected to reach US$40 billion, approximately five times the present volume.

The Japanese market for advanced ceramics, in particular for electronic applications, is expected to grow rapidly. Opportunities for foreign exporters can be found in the electromagnetic components industry, which includes such products as integrated circuit (IC) substrates, semiconductors, magnetic materials, capacitors, piezoelectric elements, and insulators.

Some of the HOT items:

- capacitors
- discs and tapes
- electromagnetic insulators
- IC substrates and packages
- magnetic materials
- piezoelectric elements and vibrators
- spark plugs
- thermistors, varistors, and compound semiconductors

FRAME RELAY EQUIPMENT

Nippon Telegraph and Telephone (NTT) has announced that asynchronous transport mode (ATM), an advanced telecommunications technology capable of transporting enormous volumes of data, will be installed in the late 1990s. However, many industry experts believe that frame relay technology should first be introduced as a transition technology, but NTT adopted frame relay technology in 1993. In the future, frame relay and ATM are likely to coexist.

Thus there is a growing interest in frame relay among manufacturers, common carriers, and end users. Potential key Japanese users such as NTT, Integrated Communications Systems Sector (ICS), NTT Data Communications Systems Corporation, and Kokusai Denshin Denwa want to learn how frame relay can reduce costs for leased circuits services and provide multivendor connectivity. An important application is the transmission of data among local area networks (LANs).

Japan is at least two years behind in the development of frame relay technology and commercial applications. Enormous market potential exists for frame relay equipment, including switches, routers, servers, analyzers, and hardware and software network systems.

Some of the HOT items:

- frame relay multi-protocol routers
- frame relay network management systems
- frame relay portable software
- frame relay protocol analyzers
- frame relay servers
- frame relay switches
- frame relay terminal adapters

OFFICE AND INSTITUTIONAL FURNITURE

Metal furniture accounts for 80 to 85 percent of the office furniture market in Japan. The development of office automation equipment introduces an additional prospect for growth in the office and institutional furniture market.

The office furniture market in Japan began to expand after MITI announced the Proposal on Promotion of New Offices in 1986. According to the proposal, the new offices are intended to be more comfortable and functional so that employers and employees can be more creative and productive. A local trade journal recently reported that the new offices account for 5 to 10 percent of total offices in Japan. These offices need furniture that can accommodate office automation equipment, office systems furniture, panels and partitions, ergonomic chairs, and desks for workstations.

According to industry sources, the Japanese office and institutional furniture market has not yet reached maturity, and potential for growth looks strong.

Some of the HOT items:

- desks and tables equipped with office automation equipment
- ergonomic chairs
- filing and storing cabinets
- furniture for executive offices
- low partitions and panels
- modular furniture

MEDICAL EQUIPMENT

The gradual introduction of the Regional Medical Care Plan in Japan during the late 1980s has fostered an emphasis on renovating existing hospitals and acquiring technologically advanced and cost-effective medical equipment. This trend is expected to contribute to a steady expansion of Japan's medical equipment market. Products for the elderly (refer to the following section on nursing home equipment) as well as diagnostic and therapeutic products—imaging equipment, sports medicine products, implantable devices, and emergency medical equipment—have the greatest potential for growth.

Some of the HOT items:

- anesthesia instruments
- artificial limbs, hips, knees, and joints
- automated blood and chemical analyzers, blood gas analyzers
- automated blood cell counters and sorters
- breathing devices
- cardiac catheters and other catheters
- cardiac output analyzers
- cardiac pacemakers
- centrifuge equipment
- defibrillators
- electro-surgical instruments
- emission computer tomographs (CTs)
- hypothermia equipment
- intensive care monitors for infants
- laser photo-coagulators
- laser surgical instruments
- magnetic resonance image (MRI) scanners
- medical and dental x-ray equipment and films
- monitoring and telemetry systems
- nuclear medicine equipment
- orthopedic appliances
- orthopedic instruments
- pulmonary function analyzers
- pulse oximeters
- renal dialysis devices and disposable products
- resuscitators
- surgical and ophthalmological instruments
- ultrasonic CTs
- x-ray CTs

NURSING HOME EQUIPMENT

The graying of the Japanese population is proceeding faster than in any other country in the world. Today, 12.3 percent of the Japanese population is over age 65. By the year 2025, this segment will increase to 25.7 percent.

Japan's growing senior population and the rising cost of geriatric health care portend a shift from the expensive health care provided in hospitals to the less expensive health delivery systems typified by nursing homes. (According to a recent newspaper report, about 75 percent of Japanese hospitals are operating at a loss.) In sum, the demand for nursing home equipment in Japan should expand rapidly in the coming years.

Some nursing home equipment is available in Japan, but almost all of it is single-purpose. Therefore, foreign suppliers of integrated nursing home equipment that covers a series of actions are likely to have a significant competitive advantage. The best opportunities in this subsector include toilet and personal hygiene equipment, bathroom-related equipment, equipment used to lift patients, and specialty bedding. (*See* Opportunities for Growth, Home Health Care.)

Some of the HOT items:

- automatic carrying machines
- automatic rollover beds
- automatic ventilators
- beds equipped with lavatory facilities
- bedsore-prevention beds
- chairs for bathtubs
- electrical patient detectors (location sensors)
- fully automatic patient dryers
- fully automatic patient washers
- machines enabling patients to step into bathtubs
- patient lifters
- small in-house wheelchairs
- step-saving gadgets (including simple in-house escalators)
- sterilizers and deodorants
- voice printers

LABORATORY SCIENTIFIC INSTRUMENTS

Japan's relatively high level of spending on R&D and on capital investment in quality control manufacturing continues to support a comparatively high growth rate for laboratory scientific instruments. Foreign suppliers have already established themselves in this market in Japan. Industry sources project that the Japan market for laboratory scientific instruments will grow at an average rate of 3 to 6 percent during the next two years, depending on the speed of economic recovery. Analytical instruments and electric test and measuring instruments represent two leading areas of opportunity for foreign exporters.

Some of the HOT items:

electric test and measuring instruments
- digital/analog convertible IC testers
- handheld digital multimeters
- logic analyzers with high-speed sampling capability
- multi-channeled digital oscilloscopes
- portable and compact FFT analyzers
- protocol analyzers for ISDN, LAN, and WAN
- protocol analyzers with expert systems
- spectrum analyzers for mobile communication
- VXI standardized oscilloscopes

analytical instruments
- automated atomic absorption emission analyzers
- electro-kinetic chromatographs (EKC)
- Fourier transform infrared spectrophotometers (FTIR)
- FT nuclear magnetic resonance spectrometers
- "hyphenated" instruments (GC-FTIR, LC-MS, LC-ICP-MS)

- infrared laser diode spectrometers
- laboratory application software (LAS)
- laboratory automation systems and equipment
- laser counters for particles suspended in liquid (especially for the IC manufacturing industry)
- robotics
- secondary ion mass spectrometers (SIMS)
- supercritical fluid chromatographs (SFC)
- total reflection x-ray analyzers
- trace element analyzers

FOOD PROCESSING MACHINES

The traditional Japanese diet of rice and fish is undergoing great change, as consumption of meat and prepared foods as well as dining out gain in popularity. As a result, there is an emerging market for specialized food processing machinery.

Japan's food processing technology lags behind that of the Western countries except in specialized areas such as rice-cleaning machines and instant Chinese noodle (ramen)-making machines. Thus Japan's food processing machinery industry depends largely on imported technology from North America and Western Europe.

Demand for meat processing machinery is expected to grow by 8 to 10 percent a year over the next three to four years. Japanese consumers are interested in specialized meat processing machinery that is hygienic, easy to maintain, and capable of processing foods new to their diet.

Some of the HOT items:
- compact and lightweight machinery
- machinery that can be operated without specialized skills
- machinery that can be used in fast-food establishments
- machines that are easy to maintain, repair, and clean
- machines that can be fitted into production lines and systems
- machines that can produce processed or pre-cooked foods

ADVANCED INDUSTRIAL PLASTICS

Plastics production seems to have already matured in most of Japan's industrial sectors, but the application of plastic in industrial engineering is now approaching its growth stage. For the past three years, demand for industrial plastic resins has experienced double-digit increases. These resins, of course, are used extensively in those industries in which Japan excels: automobiles, electronics, office automation equipment, and precision machinery. Demand for plastics should keep pace with overall industrial production.

Some of the HOT items:
- glass fiber reinforced polyethylene terephthalate (GF-PET)
- liquid crystal polymer (LCP)
- modified polyphenylene ether (M-PPE)
- polyacetal (POC)
- polyamide (PA)
- polyamide imide (PAI)
- polyarylate (PAR)
- polybutylene terephthalate (PBT)
- polycarbonate (PC)
- polyether ether ketone (PEEK)
- polyether sulphone (PES)
- polyetherimide (PEI)
- polyimide (PI)
- polyphenylene sulfide (PPS)

SPORTING GOODS

There are almost no tariffs, import quotas, or regulations in the Japanese sporting goods market, which has grown by 6 percent annually for the last several years. Factors driving this growth include increased resort development, an increase in leisure time, the development of new lightweight materials, and the announcement that Japan will host the Winter Olympics in 1998. The growing popularity of golf, skiing, and other outdoor recreational activities promise a lucrative market for foreign exporters of sporting goods and equipment.

Some of the HOT items:
- camping equipment
- fitness equipment
- golf balls
- golf clubs
- golf equipment
- hiking equipment
- pleasure boats
- ski boots
- ski equipment
- skis
- sports shoes

WORKSTATIONS

The market for application-specific workstations has been growing very rapidly in Japan. High-demand products include graphic, sigma, and intelligent workstations. In addition to UNIX-based workstations, high-performance and low-priced workstations have created opportunities within the super computing and personal computer markets.

According to recent market surveys, the trends in workstation utilization entail greater networking, the use of packaged software, and the desire for more user-friendly equipment.

Network computing, a new trend in engineering applications, is certain to expand into other business areas. Local area networks (LANs) and wide area networks (WANs) are two major areas in which increasing numbers of workstations are needed. Reduced instruction set computing (RISC) workstations are currently being used by Yamaichi Securities. Workstations are also important in network management systems and mainframe decision support systems.

Some of the HOT items:
- high-end PC workstations
- LAN/WAN operating systems
- RISC architecture workstations
- UNIX-based workstations

FIFTEEN EXTRA PROSPECTS FOR EXPORTING TO JAPAN

- air conditioning equipment
- aircraft and parts
- apparel
- computer and peripherals
- computer software
- diamonds and diamond jewelry
- drugs and pharmaceuticals
- electronic components
- giftware
- industrial chemicals
- industrial process control
- pollution control equipment
- printing and graphic arts equipment
- seafood
- security and safety equipment

OPPORTUNITIES FOR GROWTH

As a leading economic, financial, and industrial nation, Japan offers abundant business opportunities. No company can ignore the Japanese market and remain competitive against its Japanese counterparts in today's global market. To enter and succeed in this highly lucrative market, firms must make a long-term commitment and offer quality and price-competitive products or services.

INFORMATION SERVICES

The Japanese market for information services has been rapidly expanding since 1985. Three principal factors account for this remarkable growth. The first is the development of new technologies, represented by application of optical disks to computer memory fields and the commercialization of more integrated on-line network systems. Second, the on-line ratio in domestic databases has been growing year by year. Some suppliers of on-line database systems have started gateway services to make their on-line database services more accessible and further expand the market. Third, the liberalization of telecommunications lines has opened up the value-added network (VAN) market in Japan. The internationalization of VAN services is also likely to propel expansion of the Japanese database market, as access costs to foreign databases decline.

TELECOMMUNICATIONS

Japan's telecommunications market is expected to reach US$14 billion in 1993, with an annual growth rate of about 3 percent. The Ministry of Posts and Telecommunications is considering deregulation of subscriber terminals effective April 1994. Currently, terminals of mobile communications services (including cellular and paging) are owned by service providers. Subscribers then rent the units from the carriers. When full deregulation takes place, the market for mobile communications in Japan should expand significantly, providing more business opportunities for foreign vendors. For foreign companies that do not have a presence in the Japanese market, digital cordless telephone equipment and services represent an upcoming opportunity. It should be noted, however, that foreign firms need to establish nationwide distribution channels in order to compete against Japanese vendors. Strategic alliances with Japanese manufacturers or trading firms on a nonexclusive basis may provide the best opportunities.

WASTE MANAGEMENT

Concerns about the global environment are steadily increasing in Japan. Although imports of recycling equipment are minimal, there are other means for overseas suppliers of recycling equipment and services to enter the Japanese market. Foreign companies, however, should not regard Japan as a market in which to bring entire recycling or waste processing systems. Rather, foreign equipment and system suppliers should introduce practical systems and software for integrated or partial waste management in collection, sorting, processing, and disposal, as well as focusing on the importation and sales of equipment.

PHARMACEUTICALS

Although Japan's pharmaceutical makers maintain a dominant position in their huge domestic market, none of then has yet broken into the top ranks of the world's dominant pharmaceutical companies. However, US and European firms appear to be speculating that the top Japanese companies will eventually make the transition to world-class competitors. As a result, many foreign firms are rushing to tap into Japan's aggressive R&D efforts by forming strategic alliances. Others are establishing independent R&D operations in Japan. While prospects are bright for the larger Japanese firms, a shakeout appears to be looming for Japan's myriad small and medium-sized pharmaceutical makers. This may present opportunities to foreign firms not yet in this market or for those looking to expand into manufacturing or distribution.

BIOTECHNOLOGY

A recent industry report projects a US$27 billion market by the year 2000 for Japan's biotechnology industry. As a result, an odd conglomeration of pharmaceutical, electronics, food, chemical, distillery, and even textile companies are competing to develop capabilities in biotechnology. Despite diverse interests, the Japanese market for biotechnology is in fact developing from a relatively small base in all areas except pharmaceuticals. Prospects for spectacular growth exist, however, in chemicals, agribusiness (including forestry and fisheries), and pollution control. In looking for near-term opportunities, Japanese firms will likely give priority to alliances or the acquisition of small firms specializing in biotechnology and biological modeling. Such technology includes bioengineering techniques and computer models of human physiology and receptor sites for designing tailor-made drugs.

HOME HEALTH CARE

Japan's rapidly aging population and rising health care costs are expected to spur future growth in the demand for economical home health care products and services. Sales of home health care products and services are projected to increase by 10 to 12 percent annually through the next decade. Although some major areas of Japan's home health care service market are largely dominated by government agencies, specialized niches can be competitively served by foreign companies. Promising products include wheelchairs and walking supports, hospital-type beds adapted for home use, bathing equipment, sensory aids, physical therapy equipment, monitoring and communications systems, self-diagnostic kits, and medical waste management equipment.

EXERCISE AND STRESS MANAGEMENT

Stress management is not a new concept in Japan. However, the methods used the Japanese to reduce stress are changing, creating markets for goods and services. It is worth noting that some experts rate stress levels in Japan among the highest in the world. Stress management products that could be successfully marketed in Japan by foreign suppliers include exercise equipment, whirlpools, massage equipment, biofeedback machines, vitamins, nourishment drinks, stress management training services, and alcohol rehabilitation programs.

MAIL ORDER SHOPPING

In the past several years Japanese consumers have become more interested in mail order from abroad as a way to buy inexpensive foreign goods directly from overseas manufacturers. The Japanese government promotes the mail order import business through such measures as the publication of Mail Order Shopping Guide by the Japan External Trade Organization (JETRO). In addition, the Manufactured Imports Promotion Organization (MIPRO) displays mail order catalogs at the World Import Mart in Ikebukuro in Tokyo. Bookstores such as Sports Train Books also sell mail order catalogs.

FRANCHISES

Domestic demand for convenience services makes Japan one of the most attractive markets for foreign franchisers. Companies with the greatest potential for success are those that provide specialized products or services; for example, home delivery systems and high-quality services for the elderly. Demand for gourmet, health, and natural foods as well as sports and leisure facilities is also likely to remain strong. Foreign service-oriented franchises should also be able to expand in the Japanese market. To do so, they need to pay particular attention to marketing strategies, especially for such services as nursing schools and childcare centers.

LEISURE

Leisure represents a new wave of commercial opportunity in Japan. In addition to promoting the development of leisure facilities and tourism, the Japanese government is actively planning to build or encourage the building of resorts, retirement communities, and other leisure-related facilities. The Ministry of Transport has begun a ten-year project (1989-1999) to build some 370 marinas and 800 mooring spots for yachts and motor boats.

TOURISM

Tourist travel, mainly to international destinations, remains one of the fastest-growing industries in Japan. This trend coincides with efforts by government and businesses to enhance the overall quality of life in Japan. Shorter working hours and greater interest in leisure portend continued growth in the travel market. Specialized tour packages and smaller tour groups for Japanese overseas travelers are two key trends worth following. Popular destinations include the United States, Canada, Europe, and Oceania.

TAILOR-MADE SERVICES

Personalized services for sophisticated consumer tastes make up a small, but growing part of Japan's service industry. Examples of these new services include Glamour Shot KK and Cut Ups Japan KK, both of which offer personal photographic mementos. In addition to catering to customers' needs, successful services make efficient use of telecommunications to provide quick, accessible information. Some of the most promising new ventures are consulting services for women who are returning to the workplace.

PUBLIC PROCUREMENT OPPORTUNITIES

A massive infrastructure buildup is under way in Japan. Trillions of dollars are being spent on airports, bridges, roads, port development projects, heliports, intelligent buildings, telecommunications systems, conference centers, medical cities, and science cities. In short, there are abundant opportunities for foreign companies to sell to Japanese government entities. Computers, construction services, telecommunications, and medical equipment are among the most promising fields.

Major Procurement Projects

Major projects scheduled for the 1990s include:

Immediate projects:
- New Chitose Airport expansion, Phase III
- Sendai Airport Building for International Passengers
- Import Integrated Terminal, Yokohama Daikoku Pier
- Kyoto Station Building
- Ueno Station Building
- Rinku Gate Tower Building
- Kurushima Suspension Bridge
- Makuhari high-rise apartment
- New National Theater
- Kansai National MOC Government Building
- National Olympic Memorial Center
- Social Insurance Hospital
- Research Center for Aging and Health
- Tokyo University of Foreign Studies
- Ministry of Education Facilities
- Postal Savings Nikko Kirifuri Resort
- Synchrotron Radiation Facilities

Future projects:
- Fukuoka Airport Terminal Building (West)
- Saitama YOU & I
- Second National Diet Library
- Minami-Aoyama NTT project
- Chubu International Airport
- Fukushima International Airport

All these projects are part of an official US-Japan agreement known as the Major Projects Arrangements (MPA). The purpose of MPA is to enable US firms to familiarize themselves with Japanese bidding procedures for major public works. While bias toward Japanese firms may exist within certain areas, final selection is supposed to be based upon overall candidate qualifications and open bidding.

New Chitose Airport expansion, Phase III

Hokkaido. 1992-1997. Estimated cost: ¥20 billion.

The Ministry of Transport (MOT) will commission construction works for a 3,000-meter runway, an apron, and taxiway. A third-sector entity will commission a terminal building construction project, inclusive of architectural design, construction, and goods procurement.

For information regarding status or procurement procedures, contact:

Contract Division, Sapporo Development
Construction Department
Hokkaido Development Bureau
West 19, North 2, Chuo-ku
Sapporo, Hokkaido 060, Japan
Tel: [81] (11) 611-0111 Fax: [81] (11) 621-3513

Sendai Airport Terminal Building for International Passengers

Miyagi Prefecture. 1991-1996. Estimated cost: ¥4 to ¥5 billion.

The MOT will commission construction works for a total floor area estimated at 10,000 square meters. In addition to architectural design and construction work (1992-1993), the Sendai Airport Terminal Company (SATC) will tender procurement of airport equipment and supplies.

For information regarding status or procurement procedures, contact:

Mr. Yoshio Yamazaki, Chief of General Affairs Section
Sendai Airport Terminal Co., Ltd.
Aza-Minamihara, Shimomasuda
Natori City, Miyagi Prefecture 989-24, Japan
Tel: [81] (22) 322-4301 Fax: [81] (22) 322-0145

Import Integrated Terminal, Yokohama Daikoku Pier

Yokohama City, Kanagawa Prefecture. 1991-1996. Estimated cost: ¥90 billion.

A third-sector entity will commission a construction project, which will include a warehouse as well as storage, distribution, and processing facilities. Estimated total floor space will be 370,000 square meters.

For information, contact:

Mr. Akira Shimizu, Deputy Manager
Import Integrated Terminal Yokohama Daikoku Pier
Port Bureau, Yokohama City Government
Sangyo Boeki Center Bldg.
2 Yamashita-cho Naka-ku
Yokohama City 231, Japan
Tel: [81] (45) 671-7330 Fax: [81] (45) 671-7158

Kyoto Station Building

Karasuma-Shiokoji, Shimogyo-ku, Kyoto. 1991-1994. Estimated cost: ¥100 billion.

The project includes construction of a new terminal building at the JR Kyoto station. The terminal building will house a hotel, a department store, restaurants, shops, and other facilities. Construction will take place on the site of the present JR Kyoto station building (approximately 38,000 square meters).

For information regarding status or procurement procedures, contact:

Mr. Tetsuhisa Shima, Manager of Planning Division
Kyoto Station Building Development Co., Ltd.
JR Kyoto Station Karasuma
Shiokoji, Shimogyo-ku, Kyoto 600, Japan
Tel: [81] (75) 361-4394 Fax: [81] (75) 361-4395

Ueno Station Building

Tokyo. 1990-2000: architectural design (1990-1995), coordination work with residents (1990-1991), coordination work with related governmental agencies (1990-1991), environmental assessment (1992-1993), construction work (1994-2000). Estimated cost: ¥80 billion.

A third-sector entity will commission a multiple-use facility, including hotel and commercial facilities, as an annex of the JR Ueno Station. Conceptual plans call for a high-rise structure that will include a subway station, commercial offices, retail space, department stores, hotel facilities, health club, observatory, art museum, theater, and parking facilities. Opportunities for foreign firms will be in architectural design, consulting, building construction, and goods procurement.

East Japan Railway Company (JR East) is conducting preliminary planning. For information regarding status or procurement procedures, contact:

Mr. Masataka Nagahama, Director
Ueno Kaihatsu Project, Kaihatsu Jigyo Honbu
East Japan Railway Company
2-10-1, Yurakucho, Chiyoda-ku
Tokyo 100, Japan
Tel: [81] (3) 3217-0240 Fax: [81] (3) 321-21973

Rinku Gate Tower Building

Osaka. 1990-1994. Estimated cost: ¥100 billion.

A third-sector entity will commission construction of twin-tower buildings for an international conference center. The center will include offices and a 57-story hotel. Total floor space will be 150,000 square meters.

For information regarding status or procurement procedures, contact:

Mr. Kazuo Morichika, Senior Associate Advisor
Construction Contact
Rinku Gate Tower Building Co., Ltd.
Kitahama Center Bldg.
1-12, Higashi Korai Bashi, Chuo-ku
Osaka 540, Japan
Tel: [81] (6) 949-2888 Fax: [81] (6) 949-1232

Kurushima Suspension Bridge

Shikoku. 1988-1999. Estimated cost: ¥210 billion.

A Ministry of Construction-related public corporation, Honshu-Shikoku Bridge Authority, will commission a construction project (civil engineering work and goods procurement) of a 4.1-km suspension bridge. The Kurushima Bridge is part of a project that will connect Onomichi (on Honshu island in Hiroshima Prefecture) to Imabari (on Shikoku island in Ehime Prefecture). This will be one of three routes connecting Honshu and Shikoku islands.

For information regarding status or procurement procedures, contact:

Mr. Makoto Kitagawa
Manager, Planning and Development Department
Honshu-Shikoku Bridge Authority
5-1-5, Toranomon, Minato-ku
Tokyo 105, Japan
Tel: [81] (3) 3434-7281 x3115
Fax: [81] (3) 3578-9298

Makuhari high-rise apartment

Chiba Prefecture. 1992-1994. Estimated cost: ¥10 billion.

The Makuhari high-rise apartment building project is one of several buildings to be constructed in the residential zone of the Makuhari development area. The 40-story building is projected to include 300 to 400 units. Disagreements between government organizations and developers may affect the overall design and size of the units.

For information regarding status or procurement procedures, contact:

Mr. Katsumi Suzuki, Director
Contract Administration Division, Finance Dept.
Housing and Urban Development Cooperation
1-14-6, Kudan-kita, Chiyoda-ku
Tokyo 102, Japan
Tel: [81] (3) 3263-8309 Fax: [81] (3) 3263-8180

New National Theater

Tokyo. 1992-1996 (delayed). Estimated cost: ¥65 billion.

The Ministry of Construction (MOC) has been entrusted with construction of the New National Theater (tentative name) by the Promotion Agency for Japanese art and culture (PAJ), a corporation having special status under the Ministry of Education, Culture, and Science. This building will have five stories above ground, four stories underground, and a tower. Total floor area will be 68,879 square meters, including a main theater, a medium-sized theater, and a small theater—all to be used for opera, ballet, musicals, and other cultural performances.

For information regarding status or procurement procedures, contact:

Mr. Shuichi Okuda, Director; or Mr. Nagano, Planning, First Division,
Government Building Department
Kanto Regional Construction Bureau
Ministry of Construction
1-3-1 Otemachi, Chiyoda-ku
Tokyo 100 Japan
Tel: [81] (3) 3211-6261 x5151
Fax: [81] (3) 3285-0519

Kansai National Ministry of Construction (MOC) Government Building

Osaka. 1992-1994. Estimated cost: ¥5 billion.

Japan's first 24-hour airport, the Kansai International Airport (KIA), is being constructed on an artificial island five kilometers offshore, south of Osaka in the Senshu area. The Kansai National MOC Government Building will be built adjacent to the International Cargo Terminal buildings at the southwest end of the KIA island. MOC will commission a construction project (construction and goods procurement) for a customs building, which will also serve as a quarantine station for plants and animals. The facilities will have five floors of 11,600 square meters.

Although many of the procurement tenders have already been awarded, for status information contact the Kinki Regional Office of MOC in Osaka.

National Olympic Memorial Center

Tokyo. 1992-1995. Estimated cost: ¥54 billion.

The current Olympic center, which consists of over 20 small structures, was built in 1954 as residences for US military personnel. The new Olympic center will be located on the same site and will consist of seven structures. Four will provide lodging, and the other three will house a gymnasium, a cultural center, and other facilities. The Olympic center will be owned and operated under the jurisdiction of the Ministry of Education (MOE), but construction has been entrusted to the Ministry of Construction (MOC).

For information regarding status or procurement procedures, contact:

Mr. Takafumi Kondo, Deputy Director
Planning Section A,
Government Building Planning Division
Government Building Department
Ministry of Construction
2-1-3, Kasumigaseki, Chiyoda-ku
Tokyo 100, Japan
Tel: [81] (3) 3211-6261 Fax: [81] (3) 3285-0519

Social Insurance Hospital

Tokyo. 1991-1994. Estimated cost: ¥5 to ¥6 billion.

Joto Social Insurance Hospital will be built in the area designated by the Tokyo Metropolitan Government (TMG) as Kameido-Ohshima-Komatsubara redevelopment area PK-10. The new hospital, to be located in Kameido 9-chome in downtown Tokyo's Koto ward, will not be far from the existing hospital. The new hospital complex will include a steel-frame reinforced concrete building consisting of two wings connected by a low-rise extension. Business opportunities lie in construction, goods procurement, and gerontological and other basic hospital needs.

For information regarding status or procurement procedures, contact:

National Property Section, Management Division
Social Insurance Administration Department
Welfare Bureau, Tokyo Metropolitan Government
2-8-1 Nishi-Shinjuku Shinjuku-ku
Tokyo 163-10, Japan
Tel: [81] (3) 5321-1111 x33-585
Fax: [81] (3) 5388-1410

or contact:

Accounting Division, General Administration Dept.
Social Insurance Agency
Ministry of Health and Welfare
1-2-2, Kasumigaseki, Chiyoda-ku
Tokyo 100, Japan
Tel: [81] (3) 3501-1711 x3549
Fax: [81] (3) 3504-1250

Research Center for Aging and Health

Ofu City, Aichi Prefecture. 1992-1995. Estimated cost: not available.

The Ministry of Health and Welfare (MHW) will commission (pending feasibility) a project for the construction of various public health facilities, all of which will be an annex of the national sanitarium in Aichi Prefecture.

For information regarding status or procurement procedures, contact:

Mr. Natsuki Furukawa, Assistant Director
International Affairs Division
Ministry of Health and Welfare
1-2-2, Kasumigaseki, Chiyoda-ku
Tokyo 100, Japan
Tel: [81] (3) 3591-8983 Fax: [81] (3) 3501-2532

Tokyo University of Foreign Studies

Tokyo. To be scheduled. Estimated cost: ¥14 billion.

The Ministry of Education will commission a construction project for a new university building. This is to be one of the government's public building relocation projects. The facilities (60,000 square meters) will be relocated in the suburbs of Tokyo.

For information regarding status or procurement procedures, contact:

Mr. Haruo Yonehara, Specialist of Facility
Administration Office
Facilities Planning Division
Facilities Planning and Administration Department
Ministry of Education, Science and Culture
3-2-2, Kasumigaseki, Chiyoda-ku
Tokyo 100 Japan
Tel: [81] (3) 3581-4211 Fax: [81] (3) 3593-7783

Ministry of Education Facilities

Tokyo. 1994. Estimated cost: ¥14 billion.

The Ministry of Education will commission construction of three laboratory buildings: the National Institute of Polar Research, the Institute of Statistical Mathematics, and the National Institute of Japanese Literature. These are also three of the Japanese government's public building relocation projects. The facilities will be relocated to the suburbs of Tokyo. The three buildings will have a combined area of 60,000 square meters.

For information regarding status or procurement procedures, contact:

Mr. Haruo Yonehara, Specialist of Facility
Administration Office, Facilities Planning Division,
Facilities and Planning and Administration Dept.
Ministry of Education, Science and Culture
3-2-2, Kasumigaseki, Chiyoda-ku
Tokyo 100, Japan
Tel: [81] (3) 3581-4211 Fax: [81] (3) 3593-7783

Postal Savings Nikko Kirifuri Resort

Nikko City, Tochigi Prefecture. 1991-1996. Estimated cost: ¥10 billion.

The Ministry of Post and Telecommunication will commission a construction project for resort facilities. The Kirifuri resort is only a small part of the 170,000-hectare conceptual plan, and participation in the Kirifuri resort may lead to greater opportunities in the area.

For information regarding status or procurement procedures, contact:

Mr. Takahiro Iwasa, General Affairs Division
Building Department, Ministry of Posts and
Telecommunications
1-3-2, Kasumigaseki, Chiyoda-ku
Tokyo 100-90, Japan
Tel: [81] (03) 3504-4293 Fax: [81] (3) 3580-6657

Synchrotron Radiation Facilities

Harima Science Park, Hyogo Prefecture. To be scheduled. Estimated cost: ¥44 billion.

The Science and Technology Agency (STA) and two related public agencies, the Japan Atomic Energy Research Institute (JAERI) and the Institute of Physical and Chemical Research (RIKEN), will commission a construction project for the world's largest synchrotron radiation facility.

For information regarding status or procurement procedures, contact:

JAERI-RIKEN Spring-8, Project Team
2-28-8, Hon-komagome, Bunkyo-ku
Tokyo 113, Japan
Tel: [81] (3) 5395-2800 Fax: [81] (3) 3941-3169

Future Projects

Fukuoka Airport Terminal Building (West)
Fukuoka.

An official decision on the construction of this project has been delayed due to local concern over the potential environmental impact.

Saitama YOU/I

Saitama Prefecture.

YOU/I is an acronym for the four cities in which the projects will be located: Yono City, Ohmiya City, Urawa City, and Ina Town. The YOU/I project will offer diverse business opportunities to foreign firms in such fields as urban development consulting, architectural design, general contracting, and building supplies manufacturing. Saitama YOU/I will have 15 building projects and related civil engineering work. Projects include Saitama Coliseum, Saitama Messe Exhibition Hall, and a Japanese government building. For information, contact:

The YOU/I Plan Promotion Office
3-15-1, Takasago, Urawa-shi
Saitama 336, Japan
Tel: [81] (48) 824-2111 Fax: [81] (48) 824-6381

Second National Diet Library

Aichi Prefecture.

A decision of the Diet is required to initiate this project. A preliminary study has been conducted to determine the need for this library and a possible site.

Minami-Aoyama NTT Project

Aoyama, Tokyo.

It is difficult to anticipate if and when this project will move forward in the face of neighborhood objections.

Chubu International Airport

Chubu.

Although the local community has agreed to the project in principle, issues that remain to be settled include the need for an airport, use of the airspace, the appropriate manner of cost-sharing, and assessments of profitability.

Fukushima International Airport

Fukushima.

Foreign procurement pending local and/or national government ruling on whether to proceed with the project.

For information on all the projects, contact:

Mr. Shuichi Machida, Director,
Construction Market Access Promotion Office
Ministry of Construction
2-1-3, Kasumigaseki, Chiyoda-ku
Tokyo 100, Japan
Tel: [81] (3) 3580-4311, x2765
Fax: [81] (3) 5251-1935

Market Access Promotion
Office of the Ministry of Transport
Mr. Makoto Takahashi, Director
Japan Civil Aviation Bureau, Ministry of Transport
2-1-3, Kasumigaseki, Chiyoda-ku
Tokyo 100, Japan
Tel: [81] (3) 3580-3111, x8362
Fax: [81] (3) 3580-7963

PUBLIC PROCUREMENT PROCESS

OFFICIAL DEVELOPMENT ASSISTANCE (ODA)

Japan's foreign aid programs present a unique opportunity for foreign suppliers. In recent years, Japan, once one of the largest recipients of economic assistance, has become one of the largest providers of foreign aid in the world. Yen loans to less developed countries are being made through the Overseas Economic Cooperation Fund (OECF), the Export-Import Bank of Japan, and other Japanese government organizations. A large percentage of official development assistance (ODA) will be going to projects in Asia and Latin America.

There are several ways to obtain business through Japan's ODA: working with trading houses, joint ventures with Japanese or developing country-based firms, and competitive bidding. Whatever the choice, foreign firms must make a concerted effort to understand and adhere to ODA procedures.

STATUTES AND CODES

Government procurement in Japan conforms to the GATT Procurement Code. Uruguay Round negotiations are seeking to significantly expand the coverage of the code, including in Japan. Foreign suppliers would benefit from the extension of GATT Procurement Code coverage to prefectural and local governments. They would also benefit from greater access to government purchasing plans, a streamlining of the pre-bid qualifications process, and a bid protest system. At this time, the Japanese government has plans to simplify the procurement of foreign goods and services through at least 100,000 special drawing rights (SDRs) which will be administered by the government and 34 quasi-governmental agencies.

GENERAL PROCEDURES

Foreign bidders who wish to sell under the government procurement program should appoint a local agent or representative. Local representation, though not mandatory, is strongly recommended because of short deadlines and the necessity of submitting bids and other documentation in Japanese (bidding through Nippon Telegraph and Telephone is one of the few exceptions). After obtaining approval from the appropriate government agency, bidders may compete for contracts. Under the provisions of the GATT Procurement Code, foreign companies are permitted to bid on specific invitations prior to qualification if there is sufficient time to complete the qualification procedures.

Most Japanese government agencies use permanent lists of qualified suppliers under a selective tendering system. Between December and February of each year, an announcement appears in the Japanese government gazette, *Kampo*, with information on procedures and criteria for becoming a prequalified bidder for a particular agency. In order to be placed on the lists, suppliers or their agents are required to apply during a specified period prior to the beginning of the fiscal year, which runs from April 1 through March 31. Foreign suppliers are permitted to apply through the end of the Japanese fiscal year. Bidders should understand that it is often essential to participate in specification development before the bid proposal is published. New companies may face difficulties because the procurement officials tend to be biased against new suppliers.

Foreign Access Zones

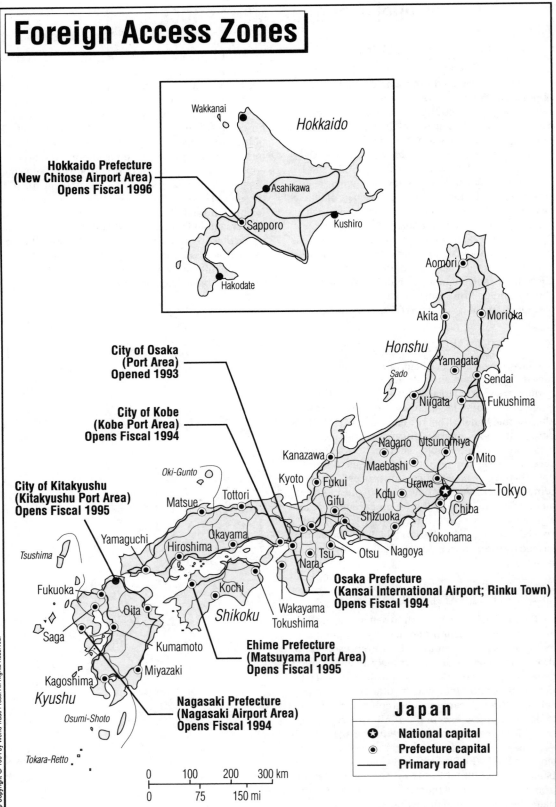

Hokkaido Prefecture
(New Chitose Airport Area)
Opens Fiscal 1996

Wakkanai

Hokkaido

Asahikawa

Sapporo   Kushiro

Hakodate

Aomori

Honshu

Akita   Morioka

Sado   Yamagata

Niigata   Sendai
Fukushima

City of Osaka
(Port Area)
Opened 1993

City of Kobe
(Kobe Port Area)
Opens Fiscal 1994

Nagano   Utsunomiya

Kanazawa   Maebashi   Mito

Kyoto   Fukui   Urawa   Tokyo
Gifu   Kofu
Kofu   Chiba
Shizuoka
Yokohama

City of Kitakyushu
(Kitakyushu Port Area)
Opens Fiscal 1995

Oki-Gunto   Tottori

Matsue

Yamaguchi   Okayama
Hiroshima

Tsu   Otsu   Nagoya
Nara

Tsushima

Fukuoka

Oita

Osaka Prefecture
(Kansai International Airport; Rinku Town)
Opens Fiscal 1994

Saga

Kochi

Shikoku

Wakayama
Tokushima

Ehime Prefecture
(Matsuyama Port Area)
Opens Fiscal 1995

Kumamoto

Miyazaki

Kagoshima

Kyushu

Nagasaki Prefecture
(Nagasaki Airport Area)
Opens Fiscal 1994

Osumi-Shoto

Tokara-Retto

Japan	
✪	National capital
⊙	Prefecture capital
—	Primary road

0   100   200   300 km

0   75   150 mi

SPECIAL TRADE ZONES

FOREIGN ACCESS ZONES

Background

In early 1993 the government of Japan officially approved seven foreign access zones (FAZs) at port areas, including airports. The designations were intended to promote imports and foreign investment. The FAZs provide various preferential measures, and they integrate cargo handling facilities, bonded warehouses, and other import facilities in one location. Foreign companies may also have an opportunity to participate in the construction of the facilities.

Incentives

By law, each FAZ is required to have "basic facilities for import promotion." Such facilities must include at least one of the following: a distribution center, exhibition hall, imported goods processing site, wholesale mart, or an import information center.

Several supporting measures are called for under the FAZ law:

- Credit guarantees and payment of 5 percent of the construction costs of facilities by the Industry Base Development Foundation;
- Preferential tax treatment includes a special accelerated depreciation period for designated buildings and facilities;
- Low-interest loans will be available from the Japanese government or Hokkaido Tohoku Development Finance Corporation;
- Supplemental measures include real estate taxes and consideration of special allowances for local government bonds for construction of international commercial facilities;
- Low-interest loans to private companies and other special incentives for small businesses will be available from the Japan Development Bank;
- The Japan External Trade Organization (JETRO) will establish support center(s) to provide import information and counseling as well as to house exhibitions and trade meetings; and
- Simplified measures are currently underway for FAZs to be designated as bonded areas.

Locations and Timetables

If the development of the FAZs progresses smoothly, the facilities will be in operation during the following fiscal years:

- City of Osaka (Osaka Port Area), 1993;
- Osaka Prefecture (Kansai International Airport, Rinku Town), 1994;
- Nagasaki Prefecture (Nagasaki Airport Area), 1994;
- City of Kobe (Kobe Port Area), 1994;
- Ehime Prefecture (Matsuyama Port Area), 1995;
- City of Kitakyushu (Kitakyushu Port Area), 1995;
- Hokkaido Prefecture (New Chitose Airport Area), 1996.

Future Plans

Studies will be carried out in 10 other prefectures in 1993-1994 to assist local officials in their plans to establish FAZs. They are Ibaraki, Shizuoka, Toyama, Ishikawa, Fukui, Kyoto, Hiroshima, Yamaguchi, Kumamoto, and Oita.

INDUSTRIAL PARKS

There are over 200 industrial parks in Japan's 47 prefectures. Many of these industrial parks are designed to attract R&D investment in advanced technologies. Foreign companies may also establish manufacturing plants. Each prefecture has its own rules and incentives. The most common incentives given at the prefectural level are low-interest loans and tax breaks.

For information regarding special trade zones, contact:

Mr. Hirobumi Arai, Investment Promotion Div.
Information Service Department
Japan External Trade Organization
2-5 Toranomon 2-Chome, Minato ku
Tokyo 105, Japan
Tel: [81] (3) 3582-5571 Fax: [81] (3) 3585-3628

Foreign Investment

INVESTMENT CLIMATE AND TRENDS

As an island country with few natural resources, Japan has long used foreign trade and investment as its principal tools for national development. This trend seems to be accelerating, especially since the mid-1980s, as the volume of trade and investment among the European Community, the United States, and Japan has grown exponentially. As the global economy has become increasingly interdependent, Japanese investment abroad has surged. In contrast, foreign direct investment in Japan since 1990 has amounted to about US$10 billion—very low given the magnitude of Japan's economy. In 1990 foreign investment in Japan was less than half the value of Japan's investment overseas.

Japan Under Pressure to Reform The imbalance just noted has been a source of friction between Japan and its major trade partners, especially the United States. Other countries have repeatedly called on Japan to remove import barriers, eliminate restrictions on foreign investment, and simplify investment procedures. Officials of foreign governments and investors have identified numerous formal and informal barriers to entry in the Japanese market: high relative costs of capital and labor, long-standing ties between the Japanese government and local businesses, the reluctance of Japanese firms to alter existing personal and supplier relationships, difficulty in locating and recruiting qualified personnel, crosscutting stock holdings among allied companies, the low percentage of publicly traded common stock in many companies, and the general unwillingness of the parties to a *keiretsu* (industrial grouping) to allow a member to come under foreign control.

Another barrier is the extent of business regulation in Japan. Foreign nationals often complain about the number of licenses, permits, and approvals required for almost any type of commercial activity. Administrative edicts, collectively referred to as *administrative guidance*, are sometimes issued with seeming disregard for such concepts as constitutional limits on government power or due process.

Perhaps due both to pressure from outside and to recession at home, Japan has taken steps in recent months to improve the investment climate. These steps include new tax incentives, loan guarantees, and additional preferential treatment for foreign companies and individuals planning to invest in Japan. Moreover, Japan's new prime minister, Morihiro Hosokawa, appears committed to increased openness and market deregulation.

Attractive Aspects of the Japanese Market Although there are difficulties associated with investment in Japan, there are also a number of positive aspects. They include a diligent and highly skilled work force, harmonious labor-management relations, one of the world's most modern infrastructures, proximity to the growing markets of China and other Asian countries, and wealthy and increasingly sophisticated consumers.

Another factor is that, since the mid-1980s, the growth of the Japanese economy has become increasingly dependent on domestic demand for goods and services. Domestic demand is the greatest in such high-tech industries as electronic technology, biotechnology, and materials science, and such service industries as advertising, information and communication technology, and financial services. As these industries play an increasingly important role in Japan's economy, they present potentially lucrative investment opportunities.

Finally, in keeping with its penchant for capital investment, Japan is spending heavily on major infrastructure projects, including airports, bridges, roads, high-speed railways, marinas, resorts, retirement communities, conference centers, and medical facilities. The decision to hold the 1998 Winter Olympics in Nagano creates numerous opportunities in the areas of transportation, consulting, engineering, and construction.

What it Takes to Invest in Japan Although Japan is a challenging place in which to do business, it is not the closed market that it was even a decade ago. For those who have a quality product or service and a willingness to shoulder the high initial cost of market entry, it is possible to achieve a respectable market share and make a reasonable or even a large profit.

The commitment required to succeed in Japan has four main elements:

- Sufficient financial resources and personnel, especially staff who can speak and read Japanese and provide excellent customer service;
- A willingness to modify products to meet the needs of Japanese customers and to provide technical manuals and sales literature in Japanese;
- Patience and a long-term view toward maximizing market share at a reasonable profit; and
- Careful monitoring of Japanese government regulations and the activities of Japanese competitors.

LEADING FOREIGN INVESTORS

During the forty years between 1950 and 1990, a total of US$18.4 billion of investment flowed into Japan. The United States accounted for 46.5 percent of this figure, European nations for 27 percent, and other Asian countries for most of the remaining 26.5 percent. As an indication of the dramatic increase in global investment in recent years, more than 60 percent of the investment just cited occurred between 1987 and 1990.

INVESTMENT POLICY

Inward and outward investment to and from Japan is officially unrestricted. Nevertheless, foreign investment in Japan requires careful consideration, especially with respect to marketing, manufacturing, distribution, and taxation. Numerous informal barriers still exist. However, Japan has been active in promoting foreign investment since the 1980s by providing incentives of various kinds, reducing regulations, and encouraging the importation of goods.

Prior to World War II, industrial development in Japan was centered three areas: Tokyo, Osaka, and Nagoya. Prolonged economic growth around these cities has led to an excessive concentration of population and industries. In contrast, such outlying regions as Hokkaido, Tohoku, Shikoku, and Kyushu have experienced significantly less development and have traditionally been less attractive to investors.

By the late 1960s extensive migration to major urban centers had created severe regional imbalances. Pollution and overcrowding became important social issues. The Japanese government responded by initiating programs restricting factory construction in the major metropolitan areas and modernizing transportation networks in the rural regions.

In the 1970s the government enacted a series of measures, including both financial and tax incentives, to attract businesses to underdeveloped regions, and the government-sponsored Japan Regional Development Corporation began construction of several industrial parks.

But many of the Japanese government's goals for industrial relocation had not been met by the mid-1980s. Moreover, many industries in Japan had changed from labor-intensive manufacturing to capital-intensive activities based on advanced technologies. And pressure from Japan's major trading partners to deregulate the economy and open it up to foreign investment was increasing.

The government enacted new measures in the late 1980s to accelerate regional development of high-technology industries. The Ministry of International Trade and Industry (MITI) coined the term Technopolis for high-technology industrial parks. The aim was to create attractive towns in less-developed regions of Japan where industry, academia, and residents could coexist.

While it is still possible to establish business operations in Japan's major metropolitan areas, land and factory and office space are scarce and expensive. In the less-developed regions where Technopolis parks have been located, land and building space are more plentiful and less costly. Moreover, wage rates are estimated to be 10 to 30 percent lower in these regions than they are in large urban areas.

By early 1993 26 areas throughout Japan had been designated Technopolis development areas. In all these areas, research institutions have been established or expanded, universities and colleges have been created or enlarged, and companies in such high-tech industries as computer hardware and software, biotechnology, and new materials have opened for business.

Definition of *Foreign Investor* Under the Foreign Exchange and Foreign Trade Control Law (FEFTCL), a foreign investor is any nonresident individual, any company incorporated in or with a principal office in a foreign country, any company or other organization with a majority of nonresident directors, and any Japanese company that is at least 50 percent owned by a foreign national. (However, a resident foreigner is not classed as a foreign investor.)

An investor in any of the four categories just defined is required to provide advance notification of a direct investment in Japan.

Definition of *Investment* A direct inward investment in Japan is any of the following seven actions:

- Establishment of a branch, plant, or sales office in Japan (excluding banks, insurance companies, securities companies, and liaison offices engaged in market research and the collection of information);
- Acquisition of any amount of stock in a privately held Japanese company. This does not include the transfer of stock from one foreign investor to another;
- Acquisition of 10 percent of the stock in a publicly traded Japanese company;
- Transfer to a foreign investor by any individual nonresident of shares in a private company acquired during the nonresident's stay in Japan;
- Alteration of a company's objectives by a foreign investor who holds more than one-third of the shares;
- Any loan to a Japanese company (excluding financial institutions) of more than ¥200 million (about US$1.8 million) for a period of five years or less or ¥100 million (about US$900,000) for a period in excess of five years; or
- Acquisition of privately traded bonds.

Notification Procedures No formal advance approval is required for foreign investment in Japan. However, no matter how or where a foreign national invests, the individual or company must notify the Ministry of Finance and the government minister who has jurisdiction over the industry concerned. Investors who are not residents of Japan must file their official notification through a resident agent. The information requested usually includes the names and addresses of the parties to the transaction as well as business descriptions and information about the financial status of the entities involved. The forms should be submitted to the International Department of the Bank of Japan, which acts as an intermediary between investors and government ministries. The International Department should receive the forms three months before the expected date of the transaction. (Refer to "Business Entities & Formation" chapter for a discussion of procedures.)

The majority of foreign investment cases are processed by the Bank of Japan on the same day that an application is filed. In certain cases, as with investments in restricted activities, the notification is forwarded to the MITI, which has 20 to 30 days in which to suspend or request modifications in the proposed investment. In a few cases, the review period can be extended to four to five months. Restricted activities include agriculture, forestry, fisheries, petroleum refining, mining, and manufacturing of leather products.

Foreign investors who establish joint ventures are required to file a joint company agreement with the Japan Fair Trade Commission (JFTC) within 30 days

of completing such an agreement. The FTC reviews whether the proposed joint venture violates the Anti-Monopoly Law. Notification of the joint venture should be sent to the Fair Trade Commission.

Repatriation of Capital and Earnings Japan places no limits on the repatriation of capital, earnings, or the proceeds from sales of imported goods providing the transaction is proper and legal. Under extraordinary circumstances repatriation can be delayed. There is no legal mechanism for denying it.

INVESTMENT INCENTIVES

Many kinds of incentives are available specifically to foreign investors, including tax incentives, financial incentives, and government loan guarantees. Foreign investors may also take advantage of the general incentives offered to Japanese investors. These include additional tax incentives and subsidies. While the national and local governments in virtually all areas of Japan offer some incentives, the incentives available in industrial and designated Technopolis parks are the most attractive.

Tax Incentives Three types of tax incentives are offered to foreign investors. First, foreign investors are eligible for special depreciation allowances on buildings and equipment for up to five years. Second, the carryover period for net loss after the start of a business operation can be extended from three to seven years. However, when a foreign investor takes advantage of the depreciation allowance, the carryover period may not be extended beyond three years. Third, the local landholding tax is not levied on a foreign investor who begins building a manufacturing facility on it within one year after acquiring the site.

Financial Incentives The Japan Development Bank (JDB) was established in 1951 to supplement private sources of finance and to help carry out the government's development plans. The JDB has a loan division for eligible foreign-owned companies with a foreign capital share of 50 percent or greater.

Eligible foreign investors are those who invest in high-technology fields, including R&D facilities; who promote the exchange of advanced technology; or who expand imports significantly. In February 1993 the rate on loans for investors in these categories was 5 percent. Foreign investors who do not meet these qualifications may still be eligible for loans at an interest rate of 5.2 percent.

Loan periods in Japan can last anywhere from 12 months to 25 years. The upper limit on a loan is approximately 40 percent of the total investment, but the percentage may change according to the JDB's available resources. On average, it takes one month from the time the loan application is filed for the loan to be disbursed.

Like the JDB, the Hokkaido Development Agency was established in the 1950s, but its special financial incentives are restricted to foreign investors in Japan's northeast region. Its loan conditions are identical to those of the JDB, except that they will lend up to 70 percent of the total investment amount.

Of particular interest to small businesses wishing to receive a low-interest loan is the Small and Medium Enterprises Agency. With the help of a government subsidy, small business investors can obtain loans at rates 0.7 percent under the usual lending rates.

Government Loan Guarantees Foreign investors can obtain government loan guarantees of up to 95 percent of the loan amount, provided they use the loans to acquire buildings and equipment or as working capital. Foreign investors should contact the Ministry of Finance.

General Incentives The Japanese government offers a variety of general incentives to foreign and Japanese investors. Tax incentives for the establishment of manufacturing facilities are based on 11 different regional development laws and acts. Incentives involve the special depreciation of both buildings and equipment and reductions in five kinds of local taxes, including an enterprise tax, a fixed asset tax, a property acquisition tax, a special landholding tax, and an enterprise establishment tax. Foreign investors should obtain the services of a locally based accountant or tax consultant to be sure that they file tax forms correctly.

Japanese and foreign investors can qualify for three types of subsidies: an industrial relocation subsidy, a regional employment promotion subsidy, and factory inducement subsidies that are offered by prefectural and municipal governments. Investors who relocate a factory to an area in which the government is promoting industry receive subsidies for the installation of environmental and welfare facilities. Installation of environmental facilities includes the planting of trees and other vegetation on a factory or building site; welfare facilities refers to such things as employee lounge areas and cafeterias. Employers are required to provide such facilities in Japan.

Investors who create employment opportunities by constructing or expanding manufacturing facilities in areas where jobs are scarce qualify for a national subsidy. The amount of the subsidy is based on the actual wage and investment expenditures for the manufacturing facilities.

Many local governments provide subsidies for the construction of a factory in designated areas. The subsidies are often more generous than those offered by national entities.

REGULATORY AGENCIES

All foreign investment into Japan is governed by the FEFTCL. The Ministry of Finance (MOF) has ultimate jurisdiction over exchange control, which in Japan covers most types of direct inward investment, registration of foreign capital and technology, capital transactions, currency accounts, and repatriation of capital and earnings.

Most foreign investors will need to work through either the Foreign Investment Section of the MOF's International Finance Bureau or the International Department of the Bank of Japan. The Ministry of International Trade and Industry (MITI) also handles issues relating to foreign investment.

LOANS AND CREDIT

Japanese corporate finance has traditionally been characterized by a high dependence on external funding, especially bank loans. But as the Japanese financial and stock markets have been liberalized and internationalized during the last decade, investors in Japan have become increasingly dependent on such internal funding as bonds and equities. Loans and credit from a variety of private and public financial institutions, including city banks, regional banks, national banks, long-term credit banks, trust banks, and securities companies, are readily available to qualified investors.

Public financial institutions supply various kinds of loans at favorable interest rates when an investor's intended use meets specific policy requirements. Moreover, a foreign investor eligible for public finance will find it easy to obtain private finance. Foreign investors will generally have little difficulty receiving loans from a public financial institution for any of the following industrial activities: establishing a factory in a location that contributes to regional development; application of new technologies, such as amorphous silicon, solar batteries, and ceramic condensers; use of energy-saving or alternative energy equipment; and establishment of pollution prevention facilities, such as water recycling systems, and industrial waste disposal or recycling systems. (Refer to "Important Addresses" chapter for a list of banks and their addresses.)

COMMERCIAL AND INDUSTRIAL SPACE

Land and commercial facilities in Japan tend to be expensive. Rental and purchase prices in major metropolitan areas can be astronomically high. The general lack of space, especially in urban centers, and intensive speculation during the 1980s helped to drive up costs. Moreover, most industrial sites are developed under the direction of public sector agencies, which makes it difficult for private companies to construct facilities on their own. Local governments usually work together with one of two national government agencies, the Japan Regional Development Corporation or the Ministry of Home Affairs.

Industrial Parks Japan is making a considerable effort to promote commercial growth in its less developed areas. Most commercial and industrial space in Japan is confined to designated industrial parks. There are almost 2,000 such parks at the present time. Some are Technopolis parks, which attempt to create entire planned communities. The MITI has identified almost 1,000 additional sites throughout Japan that it feels are suitable for industrial development.

Commercial Land Prices Land prices vary widely by prefecture and location (coastal and inland). In 1990 the average price for land in coastal industrial parks was ¥77,780 (about US$581) per square meter, and in inland parks the average price was ¥25,650 (about US$192) per square meter. The following table reviews average land prices in coastal and inland industrial parks by district.

Average Land Prices for Industrial Sites in Japan by District

(per square meter, 1990 prices)

district	coastal	inland
Chugoku	¥37,660 (US$359)	¥15,380 (US$146)
Hokkaido	¥15,940 (US$152)	¥7,940 (US$76)
Hokuriku	¥27,140 (US$258)	¥16,460 (US$157)
Kanto	¥551,910 (US$5,256)	¥44,030 (US$419)
Kinki	¥124,200 (US$1,183)	¥62,040 (US$591)
Kyushu	¥21,840 (US$208)	¥10,370 (US$99)
Okinawa	¥21,900 (US$209)	¥24,450 (US$233)
Shikoku	¥33,340 (US$318)	¥21,160 (US$202)
Tohoku	¥16,240 (US$155)	¥1,920 (US$18)
Tokai	¥29,950 (US$285)	¥25,030 (US$238)

Source: Japan Ministry of International Trade and Industry.
Note: Real estate prices have fluctuated widely during recent years and investors will need to consult local agents to get an idea of current prices.

The Kanto and Kinki districts are by far the most expensive places in which to purchase commercial land, while prices are lowest in the Hokkaido and Tohoku districts.

Locating and Leasing Office Space The usual way to search for office space is with the assistance of a real estate agent. In the large cities, you will find real estate agents who specialize in serving foreign clients. They can often provide a good deal of useful information, such as where specific industries are located in a given city, and they can also answer questions about daily life in Japan. An agent can also be helpful in overcoming the anxiety that Japanese owner may have in leasing an office to a foreign tenant. English-language newspapers advertise available office space. Many new real estate openings appear on the market in spring and fall. However, prices tend to be somewhat higher during these seasons.

Once the prospective tenant has located and inspected office space, he or she must conclude a provisional contract with the owner. The provisional contract usually involves paying the owner about one-tenth the amount of the security deposit. This so-called *shikikin* is a good faith deposit that helps to guarantee that the lease will be signed. The prospective tenant forfeits the *shikikin* if the lease is not signed. After deciding to rent an office, the tenant and owner conclude a formal lease contract, which typically requires the tenant to pay the owner a security fee equivalent to about 24 months of rent. The owner returns the fee at the end of the lease. Rent is usually paid at the end of each month. A tenant is often required to pay an additional monthly maintenance fee, which may or may not include utilities. This needs to be settled during lease negotiations.

Office prices in the Tokyo area vary widely. According to a survey of newly constructed office buildings conducted by the *Nikkei-Shinbun* newspaper in late 1991, office space was renting for ¥20,000 to ¥90,000 (US$155 to US$698) per *tubo*. A *tubo* is approximately 3.3 square meters.

INVESTMENT ASSISTANCE

Foreigners who are considering investing in Japan can draw on a variety of resources, both in Japan and overseas. The main Japanese public and semipublic organizations offering basic information and consulting services are the Industrial Location Bureau of the International Trade Administration Bureau of the MITI, the Japan Regional Development Corporation, the Japan External Trade Organization (JETRO), and the Japan Development Bank (JDB). The JETRO and the JDB have offices in many major cities throughout the world.

The Center for Development of Power Supply Regions (CPR) is another useful source of information. Established in 1990 as a semipublic organization under the direction of the MITI, the CPR offers a free factory site retrieval service, which includes current data on land prices, water supply, transportation, and so on for more than 5,000 factory sites.

Each of Japan's 47 prefectures now has a Local Internationalization Center, which provides information on investment procedures and the investment climate in the region.

Moreover, numerous private organizations offer basic information and consulting services for virtually every aspect of investment in Japan. These organizations include management consulting firms, accounting firms, law firms, commercial banks, trading houses, and real estate agencies.

USEFUL ADDRESSES

Listed below are the address of many of the agencies and organizations mentioned in this chapter. In addition, chambers of commerce, embassies, other banks and government agencies may be worth contacting. (Refer to "Important Addresses" chapters for a detailed listing.)

Bank of Japan
1-1, Hongoku-cho 2-chome
Nihonbashi, Chuo-ku
Tokyo 103, Japan
Tel: [81] (3) 3279-1111 Fax: [81] (3) 3245-0358
Tlx: 22763

Center for Development of Power Supply Regions
107 Ark Mori Building
1-12-32 Akasaka, Minato-ku
Tokyo, Japan
Tel: [81] (3) 5562-9711 Fax: [81] (3) 5562-9802

Hokkaido Development Agency
1-1, Kasumigaseki 3-chome, Chiyoda-ku
Tokyo 100, Japan
Tel: [81] (3) 3581-9111

Japan Development Bank
9-1, Ohtemachi 1-chome, Chiyoda-ku
Tokyo 100, Japan
Tel: [81] (3) 3244-1770 Fax: [81] (3) 3245-1938
Tlx: 24343

Japan External Trade Organization
2-5, Toranomon 2-chome, Minato-ku
Tokyo 105, Japan
Tel: [81] (3) 3582-5570 Fax: [81] (3) 3505-6248
Tlx: 24378

Japan Fair Trade Commission
International Affairs Division
2-2-1 Kasumigaseki, Chiyoda-ku
Tokyo 100, Japan
Tel: [81] (3) 3581-5481 x574/5

Ministry of International Trade and Industry
3-1, Kasumigaseki 1-chome, Chiyoda-ku
Tokyo 100, Japan
Tel: [81] (3) 3501-1511

Ministry of Finance
1-1, Kasumigaseki 3-chome, Chiyoda-ku
Tokyo 100, Japan
Tel: [81] (3) 3581-4111, 3508-7324

Ministry of Home Affairs
1-2, Kasumigaski 2-chome, Chiyoda-ku
Tokyo 100, Japan
Tel: [81] (3) 3581-5311

Small and Medium Enterprises Agency
1-3-1, Kasumigaseki, Chiyoda-ku
Tokyo 100, Japan
Tel: [81] (3) 3501-1511

Foreign Trade

Although it is relatively large in terms of territory and population, Japan is a nation of islands with few natural resources. In 1991 it imported nearly three-quarters of its food and nearly all of its energy needs (it is dependent on the Middle East for about 75 percent of its oil and is soon to rely on imported rice, as well, much to its chagrin). Japan must also import most raw and many intermediate materials to produce for its huge domestic economy as well as to fuel its high-value-added export manufactures.

Japan is the third-largest trading economy in the world, surpassed only by Germany and the United States. Contrary to the popularly held image, however, Japan is no longer an export-driven economy. In 1992 exports accounted for only about 9 percent of Japan's gross national product (GNP). By comparison, exports represent about 8 percent of the economy of the United States, 21.6 percent of that of Great Britain, 26 percent of South Korea's, 33.8 percent of Germany's, 41.5 percent of Taiwan's, and 121 percent of that of Hong Kong. Although Japan is known for high-profile, big-name goods that dominate product categories and markets worldwide, its large, albeit artificially inflated, domestic market is far and away the engine that drives its economy.

But the Japanese economy is facing problems of major proportions that cannot be ameliorated simply by increasing its exports, the favored response in the past. Its growth can no longer support the vast redundancy and inefficiency in either its small business or large corporate sectors. Japan has become a high-cost producer, and its leading edge position and high quality are rapidly losing the ability to sustain the price points necessary to maintain its economic preponderance in international markets. Japan's industry suffers from overcapacity in what is an increasingly globalized economy. Although it holds the lead in numerous product categories worldwide, Japan is facing renewed competition and market saturation in the primary markets for its main export goods, while up-and-coming secondary markets are still underdeveloped and unable to take up the slack by buying its

high-end goods. And its lower-range commodity goods are becoming increasingly uncompetitive as well. Japan is rapidly becoming a service-based economy. Its service sector already accounts for 58.7 percent of the economy and is growing rapidly at the expense of the industrial sector.

Japanese firms are finally reaching the point at which they must restructure. The watchword, especially as it regards Japan's participation in international markets, has been market share. Now even the giants are having to worry about profitability. Sheer numbers helped when getting business at any cost and servicing the relationship was the primary intent. However, now operations will have to become "lean and mean" to deliver profitability. The whole set of complex interrelationships upon which Japanese business and society have been built is beginning to unravel, and no clear blueprint for what the successor structure will look like has emerged.

THE EXPORT-IMPORT DILEMMA

Japan managed to be basically self-sufficient for centuries, largely by doing without. However, once it began the push to upgrade its economy to world standards in the late 19th century, it was forced to become a major importer of technology and materials as well as a major exporter to pay for its purchases. It succeeded largely by doing without imported consumer goods, forming a deeply engrained habit. The export orientation got an added boost when Japan was forced to look outward for the funds and inputs necessary to rebuild its economy following World War II. As recently as the 1970s, after it had become well established as an industrial power but still had worries about supplies of energy and other raw materials, Japan continued to focus on trade to a great degree. However, its huge domestic market began to take precedence not only in size but also in emphasis, during the 1980s, when domestic growth and affluence reduced external markets to a secondary position.

Japanese Imports by Country (in US$ billions)			
Country	1991	1990	% change
United States	$53.3	$52.4	2%
China	14.2	12.1	17
Australia	13.0	12.4	5
Indonesia	12.7	12.7	0
South Korea	12.3	11.7	5
Germany	10.7	11.5	-7
United Arab Emirates	10.5	9.1	15
Saudi Arabia	10.0	10.5	-5
Taiwan	9.5	8.5	12
Canada	7.7	8.4	-8
Malaysia	6.5	5.4	20
France	5.8	7.6	-24
Thailand	5.3	4.1	30
United Kingdom	5.0	5.2	-4
Italy	4.5	5.0	-10

Source: Foreign Trade Magazine

Japanese Exports by Country (in US$ billions)			
Country	1991	1990	% change
United States	$91.5	$90.3	1%
Germany	20.6	17.8	16
South Korea	20.0	17.5	14
Taiwan	18.3	15.4	19
Hong Kong	16.3	13.1	24
Singapore	12.2	10.7	14
United Kingdom	11.0	10.8	2
Thailand	9.4	9.1	3
China	8.6	6.1	41
Malaysia	7.6	5.5	38
Canada	7.3	6.7	9
Netherlands	7.2	6.2	16
Australia	6.5	6.9	-6
France	6.1	6.1	0
Indonesia	5.6	5.0	12

Source: Foreign Trade Magazine

Japan's exports are characterized by heavy industrial products and mass-produced consumer goods. In 1992 the largest category of exports were transportation related (25.7 percent of total exports, 17.8 percent of which represented auto exports). Electronics products were next (22.8 percent, 5.1 percent of which were components as opposed to finished products), followed by machinery (22.5 percent). Together, these three categories accounted for 71 percent of total exports. The next five largest categories—metals (6.3 percent, 3.9 percent of which represented exports of iron and steel), chemicals (5.6 percent), precision instruments (4.7 percent), textiles (2.5 percent), and non-metallic mineral products (1.1 percent)—accounted for an additional 20.2 percent. Remaining items each accounted for less than 1 percent of the total by category.

Automobiles, computers, and electronics components are the primary exports of the Japanese economy. Much of the growth in exports of equipment and semiconductors and other similar components represents shipments to offshore Japanese subsidiaries involved in outsourced production, primarily for the export market but also to provide cheaper goods for domestic consumption.

In 1992 Japan's imports were dominated by fossil fuels (22.6 percent of total imports, 12.9 percent of which represented crude oil), machinery and equipment (18.4 percent), food (16 percent, including fish which accounted for 5.4 percent of the to-

tal), raw materials (10.3 percent), chemicals (7.4 percent), and textiles (6.6 percent). Together these six categories accounted for 81.3 percent of imports. In 1991 the top imports were energy (23.1 percent) and raw materials (11.5 percent). Capital goods accounted for 15 percent and food for 14.6 percent. Consumer goods represented about 13.8 percent of 1991 imports. Growth in total spending was restrained due to a harsh continuing recession and lack of consumer confidence, but the habitual suspicion of foreign goods remains a disproportionately important factor.

Imports will continue to be a fact of life in Japan, as will be the exports needed to earn foreign exchange. But Japan's economic success has been so great that its economy can generally command the resources it needs, making trade a less pressing consideration in recent years. Because of its ability to create leading edge applications products from technology developed elsewhere, Japanese industry has been able since the 1960s to lead rather than merely follow world market demand.

By the end of the 1980s the Japanese economy had reached a level of development that not only allowed it to focus on its vast and robust domestic sector but actually required it to do so. This new focus is being promoted by official policy encouraging the Japanese to reduce their reliance on exports while increasing their consumption of both foreign and domestically produced goods. This policy has been prompted largely by the complaints of trading partners regarding Japan's large, persistent, and growing trade surpluses.

These surpluses are the legacy of years of restrictions designed to hold down imports and the outflow of scarce foreign exchange, that have continued to restrain imports long after the need to do so has passed. Although most official import barriers have fallen, and tariffs are now relatively low and in line with those in other industrialized countries, Japan does not subscribe to harmonized international standards and its import procedures are still idiosyncratic and far from transparent. Moreover, more than 40 percent of all Japanese exports and nearly 80 percent of all imports into Japan are handled by the roughly 7,700 Japanese trading companies. The largest 158 such firms are responsible for 80 percent of all of Japan's trade. Dominated by the Big Nine *sogo sosha*—C. Itoh, Marubeni, Sumitomo, Mitsui, Nissho Iwai, Mitsubishi, Nichimen, Tomen, and Kanematsu—trading companies act as an unofficial filter determining what goods get into the country and get shelf space and promotion.

Foreign complaints about exclusionary Japanese markets are justified, although less justified than disgruntled foreigners often claim. Many foreign sellers have failed to adapt their products for Japanese markets, provide the necessary follow-through and service, or exercise the requisite patience needed to succeed in Japanese markets. Still, official Japan remains at best ambivalent toward imports, and the Japanese market system—with its heavy regulation, high overheads, and exclusionary and collusive operating agreements—has effectively kept many foreign goods from achieving adequate distribution even when official barriers have been grudgingly

Top 10 Japanese Exports by Percent Increase – 1991

Commodity	% change
Cargo ships	76%
Television cameras	33
Heating & cooling machinery	25
Radios	25
Motorcycles & parts	21
Tubes, pipes & fittings	19
Discrete devices	16
Watches & clocks	13
Textiles machinery	13
Audio-visual equipment & parts	12

Source: Foreign Trade Magazine

removed. The ultimate arbiter, the ethnocentric Japanese consumer, continues to spend in a restrained fashion, especially on foreign goods, although a sustained rise in spending on consumer goods can certainly be predicted for the future.

Even though imports recently have been growing at a greater rate than exports—58.3 percent for imports as opposed to 37.2 percent for exports between 1987 and 1991—they do so from a much smaller base, and exports continue to represent a much greater absolute figure as well as a larger percentage of total trade. In 1987 imports made up roughly 40 percent of total trade, while exports were 60 percent. In 1991, the gap had narrowed to 43 percent for imports and 57 percent for exports, although exports continue to dominate. Even at an increased growth rate for imports, they won't reach parity with exports until well into the 21st century.

Between 1960 and 1980, the growth rate of exports roughly paced that of imports (18.9 percent versus 18.8 percent, respectively). However, from 1980 through 1990 exports grew at an average annual rate of 8.3 percent while imports grew at only 4.8 percent. Despite efforts to rein in exports and boost imports, the disparity between the two seems to be growing. Oil prices have remained basically weak since the mid-1980s, and Japan pays for its oil in cheap dollars, not expensive yen. Many of the same considerations apply to its food imports, oil being a significant component of the cost of food production.

The strength of the yen, which has become an international currency, has further affected the disjunction between imports and exports. A study conducted in late 1993 showed that only 4 percent, 21 of 527 surveyed, of companies involved in export op-

Top 10 Japanese Imports by Percent Increase – 1991

Commodity	% change
Audio-visual equipment & parts	38%
Plates, sheets, coils & strip	35
Electronic tubes & semiconductors	18
Fresh & frozen pork	18
Scientific, medical & optical equipment	16
Integrated circuits	15
Electronic measuring & controlling instruments	15
Liquefied methane gas	15
Fruits	14
Plastics materials	13

Source: Foreign Trade Magazine

erations figured that they could made a profit at an exchange rate of ¥110 to the US dollar or below, and the yen remained below that level for much of 1993.

Even as the strong yen reduces the competitiveness of Japanese goods, the goods that are sold bring in more dollars, which has so far more than offset the drop in unit volume and exacerbated the situation when figured on a dollar basis. By the same token, the cheapness of key imports, such as oil and food, has reduced import costs. For the month of October 1993, Japanese exports were down by 12 percent in yen terms, although they still posted a 1.2 percent rise in dollar terms. For the same period, imports rose by 0.9 percent in dollar terms but were down by 12 percent in yen terms. The resulting merchandise balance of trade registered as an 11 percent fall into deficit territory in yen terms but still showed a 1.7 percent rise in dollar terms, even though it was worth considerably less to the Japanese. Even when they restrain their exports and boost import consumption, the Japanese may not get any credit.

BALANCE OF TRADE

Since the 1970s the disparity between exports and imports has led to growing merchandise trade surpluses. And unlike the situation in several other Asian countries that offset a structural merchandise trade surplus (or deficit) by a corresponding deficit (or surplus) in intangibles, Japan, as the world's leading creditor nation, derives a large and growing foreign exchange revenue stream from financial dealings and sales of other services which adds to its overall current account surplus. Japan's trade surplus has risen steadily since the mid-1980s, reaching US$107 billion in 1992. Preliminary figures for 1993 place Japan's trade deficit at US$120.4 billion, up 12.5 percent from 1992.

Japan's trade surplus has become an international issue of major proportions. It is a stumbling block in relations between Japan and its biggest trading partner and closest ally, the United States. Other trading partners, as well, have threatened or instituted protectionist measures in retaliation.

Japan's international reserves stood at US$82.5 billion in May 1993. This figure represents a rise of 16 percent from US$71 billion a year earlier. These reserves are second only to the outsized US$84.9 billion in reserves boasted by Taiwan. Japan has a substantial public debt, but the majority is held internally, and the Japanese hold quantities of foreign securities and other overseas assets that could be liquidated—albeit not without cost to the world financial system—to shore up its position at home if necessary.

Japan has announced a series of substantial stimulus packages, plans a massive investment program, and may well institute a huge income tax cut in 1994 to jump-start its economy, all measures expected to be very costly for the government. In addition, Japan is looking at a rapidly aging population that will require expanding expenditures on social services. Nevertheless, Japan has one of the world's highest savings rates—in 1992 the average Japanese household maintained total savings equal to more

Top 10 Japanese Imports (in US$ billions)

Commodity	1991	1990	% change
Crude oil	$30.2	$31.6	-4%
Apparel	9.3	8.7	7
Liquified methane gas	7.7	6.7	15
Other petroleum products	7.6	9.7	-22
Computers, peripherals & parts	5.5	5.1	8
Automobiles	5.2	6.2	-16
Organic chemicals	4.9	4.5	9
Coking coal	4.6	4.5	2
Aluminum & alloys	4.6	4.7	-2
Textiles	4.3	4.1	5

Source: Foreign Trade Magazine

Top 10 Japanese Exports (in US$ billions)

Commodity	1991	1990	% change
Cars	$44.7	$41.3	8%
ADP equipment	13.4	12.1	11
Vehicle parts	11.3	10.9	4
Trucks & buses	9.5	9.1	4
Integrated circuits	8.2	7.6	8
Plates, sheets, coils & strip	7.9	7.4	7
Internal combustion engines	6.9	6.5	6
Organic chemicals	6.2	5.6	11
Television cameras	6.1	4.6	33
Videocassette recorders & players	5.7	6.4	-11

Source: Foreign Trade Magazine

Japan's Leading Trade Partners

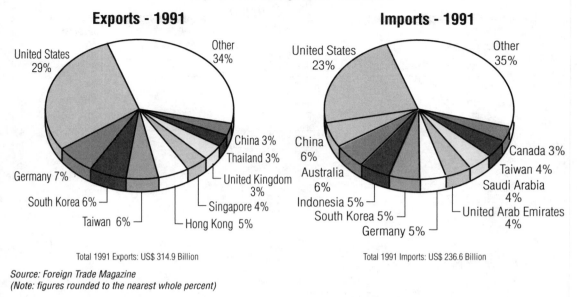

Exports - 1991

United States 29%
Germany 7%
South Korea 6%
Taiwan 6%
Hong Kong 5%
Singapore 4%
United Kingdom 3%
Thailand 3%
China 3%
Other 34%

Total 1991 Exports: US$ 314.9 Billion

Imports - 1991

United States 23%
China 6%
Australia 6%
Indonesia 5%
South Korea 5%
Germany 5%
United Arab Emirates 4%
Saudi Arabia 4%
Taiwan 4%
Canada 3%
Other 35%

Total 1991 Imports: US$ 236.6 Billion

Source: Foreign Trade Magazine
(Note: figures rounded to the nearest whole percent)

than 2.25 times its disposable income—meaning that an immense reservoir of assets potentially available to finance national programs exists.

TRADING PARTNERS

Japan continues to focus its trade on major markets. Developed countries are the main customers for its products, although it buys about half of its imports—mostly energy and raw materials—from developing countries. Even Japan's moves into smaller developing markets have been made primarily in order to indirectly gain access to major markets. Such was the case with its entry into the Mexican market in the late 1980s, when its goal was not to serve that market so much as it was to gain another entree into the US market. This situation is changing as developing markets grow large enough to be of interest to Japanese businesses on their own merits.

The United States is Japan's largest trading partner, taking 29.1 percent of its exports and providing 22.5 percent of its imports in 1991 (28.2 percent and 22.4 percent respectively in 1992). However, once the United States is out of consideration the picture changes rapidly. Japan's next-largest customer is Germany, which takes only 6.5 percent of its exports, followed by South Korea with a 6.4 percent share, Taiwan (5.8 percent), Hong Kong (5.2 percent), Singapore (3.9 percent), the United Kingdom (3.5 percent), Thailand (3 percent), and China (2.7 percent). Together, these top nine customers take 66.1 percent of total exports, leaving the remaining third for other buyers, none of which takes more than a 2.75 percent share of the total. The fastest-growing area

of trade lies within Asia. Although Japan is a nearby quality supplier for rapidly growing Asian economies, its goods are meeting resistance due to suspicion and high prices.

Following the United States with its 22.5 percent share, China (with a 6 percent share) is the next-largest source of imports to Japan. Other sources include Australia (5.5 percent), Indonesia (5.4 percent), South Korea (5.2 percent), Germany (4.5 percent), the United Arab Emirates (4.4 percent), Saudi Arabia (4.2 percent), Taiwan (4 percent), and Canada (3.3 percent). Together, these top ten countries provide 65 percent of all imports, with remaining countries each providing less than 3.25 percent of total imports. Asian countries provide nearly one-quarter of all imports, mostly of raw materials. Japan buys at low bulk commodity prices and offers in return expensive high value-added items which few can afford. The complaint of Japan's trading partners all along has been that Japan does not maintain any kind of parity with its trading partners, leading to large imbalances.

OFFICIAL DEVELOPMENT POLICY

Japan does not issue official plans along the lines of the documents prepared by many other Asian nations. However, it does promote (and enforce) distinct strategies, all the while denying that it engages in any form of management of its free-market economy. Broad policy calls for continued but controlled and stable growth driven by increased domestic consumption and for reduced export dependence. Japan is also calling for increased deregula-

Japanese Imports by Commodity
(in US$ billions)

Commodity	1991	1990	% change
Food & Live Animals			
Fresh & frozen shrimp and lobster	$3.1	$2.8	11%
Fruits	2.5	2.2	14
Fresh & frozen pork	2.0	1.7	18
Vegetables	1.9	1.7	12
Alcoholic beverages	1.9	1.7	12
Crude Materials			
Logs	$4.1	$4.5	-9
Lumber	3.0	3.0	0
Copper	2.2	2.4	-8
Mineral Fuels			
Crude petroleum	$30.2	$31.6	-4
Liquefied methane gas	7.7	6.7	15
Petroleum products	7.6	9.7	-22
Coking coal	4.6	4.5	2
Liquefied petroleum gas	2.8	2.5	12
Chemicals			
Organic chemicals	$4.9	$4.5	9
Pharmaceuticals	3.1	2.8	11
Plastic materials	1.8	1.6	13
Manufactured Goods Classified by Material			
Aluminum & alloys	$4.6	$4.7	-2
Textiles	4.3	4.1	5
Plates, sheets, coils & strip	2.7	2.0	35
Diamonds	2.1	2.5	-16
Metal manufactures	2.0	1.8	11
Machinery & Transport Equipment			
Computers, peripherals & parts	$5.5	$5.1	8
Cars	5.2	6.2	-16
Electronic tubes & semiconductors	3.9	3.3	18
Aircraft	3.2	3.2	0
Integrated circuits	3.0	2.6	15
Electronic measuring & controlling instruments	3.0	2.6	15
Miscellaneous Manufactured Goods			
Clothing	$9.3	$8.7	7
Nonmonetary gold	2.6	3.6	-28
Audio-visual equipment & parts	2.2	1.6	38
Scientific, medical & optical instruments	2.2	1.9	16
Total, including Others	**$236.7**	**$234.8**	**1%**

Source: Foreign Trade Magazine

Japanese Exports by Commodity
(in US$ billions)

Commodity	1991	1990	% change
Chemicals			
Organic chemicals	$6.2	$5.6	11%
Plastic materials	4.7	4.4	7
Manufactured Goods Classified by Material			
Plates, sheets, coils & strip	$7.9	$7.4	7
Woven fabrics	4.3	3.9	10
Tubes, pipes & fittings	3.8	3.2	19
Paper & paper products	2.2	2.0	10
Machinery & Transport Equipment			
Cars	$44.7	$41.3	8
ADP equipment	13.4	12.1	11
Vehicle parts	11.3	10.9	4
Trucks & buses	9.5	9.1	4
Integrated circuits	8.2	7.6	8
Internal combustion engines	6.9	6.5	6
Heating & cooling machinery	3.5	2.8	25
Textile machinery	3.4	3.0	13
Motorcycles & parts	3.4	2.8	21
Mechanical handling equipment	3.3	3.0	10
Electronic measuring & controlling instruments	3.0	2.7	11
Tankers	3.0	1.7	76
Cargo ships	2.4	2.5	-4
Discrete devices	2.2	1.9	16
Electronic Goods & Parts			
Television cameras	$6.1	$4.6	33
Videocassette recorders & players	5.7	6.4	-11
Audio-visual equipment parts	3.7	3.3	12
Radios	3.1	2.5	24
Televisions	2.2	2.1	5
Facsimile machines	2.0	2.0	0
Miscellaneous Manufactured Goods			
Copying machines	$2.6	$2.4	8
Watches & clocks	2.6	2.3	13
Phonographic records & tapes	2.3	2.3	0
Total, including Others	**$314.5**	**$286.9**	**10%**

Source: Foreign Trade Magazine

tion and more decentralization, extending responsibility for economic decisions to lower levels of government that currently must refer and defer to the national level.

Observers note that this call for change in the status quo suffers from excessive gradualism and dependence on Japan's entrenched bureaucrats. Bureaucrats have high status in Japan and are given credit for much of Japan's past success through their stewardship and management of public-private-sector cooperation. However, the conservative bureaucracy is considered a roadblock to progress rather than an effective agent of change. The current coalition reformist government is also considered too weak to force the issue with the powerful bureaucrats, so the effectiveness of any government initiatives designed to redirect the stumbling economy remains in doubt.

The government has plans to promote a variety of major infrastructural projects, including massive construction programs designed to increase the housing stock and provide recreational and health-care facilities to deal with a population that is enjoying more leisure time and is also aging rapidly. In addition, the government wants to increase spending on research and development to allow its industry to stay at the top of the technology curve and simultaneously to reduce government borrowing.

Many observers both in and out of government consider these goals to be both overly ambitious and mutually contradictory, and there is concern that Japan could fall back on its old expedient of simply boosting its exports to pull itself out of the current slump without dealing with underlying structural problems.

INTERNATIONAL ORGANIZATION MEMBERSHIPS

Japan has joined a variety of international organizations, although it has tended to hold itself aloof from participating in binding decisions taken in such forums. Unlike some smaller economies that rely on such memberships to legitimize themselves and open doors to larger trading partners, Japan has always maintained its separateness. It has now reached a size, prominence, and dominant position that allow it to remain separate and effectively dictate terms to a certain extent. However, Japan is finding that in an increasingly interconnected global economy, its size and specialness alone are no longer enough to successfully manipulate situations to its own advantage.

Japan is a member of the United Nations and most of its agencies, the General Agreement on Tariffs and Trade (GATT)—which has led it to drop many of its official trade barriers—the Organization for Eco-

Top Japanese Imports from US (in US$ billions)			
United States	**1991**	**1990**	**% change**
Computer peripherals & parts	$2.4	$2.2	9%
Logs, lumber & veneers	2.0	2.3	-13
Civilian aircraft	1.9	2.2	-14
Fish & fish products	1.9	1.8	6
Source: Foreign Trade Magazine			

nomic Cooperation and Development, and the Asia Pacific Economic Cooperation group, among others.

The Official Development Assistance program doles out Japan's foreign aid in its role as the world's second-largest aid donor. Trading partners have protested that requirements that such aid be spent with Japanese firms amount to an unfair export trade subsidy for domestic firms.

Import Policy & Procedures

INTRODUCTION

Japan places few formal restrictions on imported goods, and its average tariff rates are among the lowest in the world, in line with other industrialized nations. In response to complaints by trading partners that Japan has discouraged the consumption of foreign products, the government and businesses have launched campaigns in recent years to promote imports. Nevertheless, tariff rates on many imported agricultural products remain high. Moreover, many imports face a wide and complex range of standards, certifications, and other informal and technical barriers, including health and sanitary regulations. (Refer to the "Foreign Investment" and "Economy" chapters.) Thus, the import process is at times slow and difficult. But the fact remains that Japan offers an enormous market of sophisticated and affluent consumers.

The following chapter discusses Japan's import policy and procedures. This information is useful for people who want to sell goods and services to Japan, for those who establish manufacturing facilities or other operations in Japan, and for foreign investors. (Refer to "Marketing" chapter for information on selling in Japan.)

REGULATORY AUTHORITIES

Foreign trade in Japan is regulated primarily by the Ministry of International Trade and Industry (MITI), the Ministry of Finance (MOF), and the Bank of Japan. Various foreign exchange banks are responsible for verifying import and export payments. The MITI handles most import and export reporting requirements (although foreign exchange banks issue import licenses following approval by MITI), and the MOF has jurisdiction over customs and tariff control and regulation.

Ministry of International Trade and Industry (MITI)
3-1, Kasumigaseki 1-chome, Chiyoda-ku
Tokyo 100, Japan
Tel: [81] (3) 3501-1511

Ministry of Finance (MOF)
1-1, Kasumigaseki 3-chome, Chiyoda-ku
Tokyo 100, Japan
Tel: [81] (3) 3581-4111 Fax: [81] (3) 3508-7324

Customs and Tariff Bureau
Ministry of Finance
1-1 Kasumigaseki 3-chome, Chiyoda-ku
Tokyo 100, Japan
Tel: [81] (3) 3581-2852
Fax: [81] (3) 3593-1223, 3581-0460 Tlx: 24980 MOFJ

Bank of Japan
1-1, Hongoku-cho 2-chome
Nihonbashi, Chuo-ku
Tokyo 103, Japan
Tel: [81] (3) 3279-1111 Fax: [81] (3) 3245-0358
Tlx: 22763

Export-Import Bank of Japan
4-1, Otemachi 1-chome, Chiyoda-ku
Tokyo 100, Japan
Tel: [81] (3) 3287-1221 Fax: [81] (3) 3287-9540
Tlx: 23728

IMPORT POLICY

In principle, imports are unrestricted, except for designated items that fall under the state-trading, national security, public health, and moral protection provisions of the General Agreement on Tariffs and Trade (GATT). In all, Japan's Import Restriction System covers 81 items. Other restrictions apply to goods from specific countries, although many of these are gradually being lifted. Among the few items that are prohibited to import are rice and an endangered species of sea turtle. (In 1991, Japan agreed to ban importation of a species of sea turtle in order to avert trade sanctions by the United States).

Comprehensive Trading Companies

The majority of Japan's imports and exports are handled by several trading companies called comprehensive trading companies. This two-tiered system can cause delays in payment, as many imports and exports must first go through the trading companies before reaching the importing company or other end user. Generally, delays are no longer than 30 days on secured terms.

The trading companies were originally wholesalers, but today their operations concentrate on domestic exports, imports, and trade between third-party countries. The companies also assist their customers and suppliers by providing financing and business information; coordinating large projects, such as the construction of petrochemical plants; developing sources of natural resources; and by facilitating the exchange of goods and services between domestic and international parties. Most of the comprehensive trading companies have established extensive worldwide organizations to carry out these responsibilities. The top nine companies are Mitsubishi Shoji, Mitsui Bussan, C. Itho, Marubeni, Sumitomo Shoji, Niddho-Iwa, Tomen, Nichimen, and Kanematsu-Gosho.

Import Licenses

Restricted items can be imported with authorization from the MITI and an import license from a foreign exchange bank. To receive the import license, the importer must present a bank with an authorized quota certificate from the MITI. The certificate is usually valid for four months from the date of issuance. Import licenses, which guarantee a right to foreign exchange, are generally valid for six months.

The importation of certain goods from specified countries or shipping areas requires individual authorization from the MITI. At one time, imports of most fruits and vegetables were banned for health reasons, but controls are gradually being lifted on the importation of 53 fruits and vegetables from 24 countries. Among the agricultural products that will be admitted are tomatoes and sweet peppers from the Netherlands, mangoes from Thailand, apples from Australia, Canada, the United States, and New Zealand, grapefruits and lemons from Turkey, oranges from Italy, and squash from Taiwan.

In 1990, Japan agreed to ease restrictions on liquor licensing, pharmaceutical sales, and the importation of wood products. However, Japan maintains an almost complete prohibition on rice imports and has rejected a GATT recommendation to convert all non-tariff barriers on agricultural products to tariffs.

Quotas

Japan applies quota limits to imports, most of which are agricultural commodities. For items subject to an import quota, a lower primary tariff rate is applied until the quantity exceeds the quota threshold, at which time a higher duty is assessed. To receive the primary duty rate on restricted products, an importer must obtain a quota certificate in advance from the MITI.

Between 1988 and 1990, the government reduced or eliminated quotas on several food products, including non-citrus fruit juices; fruit pastes and purees; tomato ketchup, sauce and juice; frozen yogurt; ice cream; whipped cream; processed cheese; chickpeas; and lentils.

Customs Tariffs

In January 1988, Japan adopted the Harmonized Commodity Description and Coding System (HS) of tariff classification. Customs tariffs are administered by the Customs and Tariff Bureau of the Ministry of Finance. As a member of GATT, Japan accords most-favored-nation tariff treatment to most of its trading partners.

Although Japan maintains one of the lowest average tariff rates in the world, rates on agricultural products remain high, averaging about 12 percent. The highest tariffs are imposed on animal feed, bakery goods, beef, confectionery sugar, corn grits, dairy products, dried egg products, fruit juices, grain products, oranges, pork, potato flakes, poultry, processed foods, sweet corn, tomato products, vegetable oil, wine, and wood products. However, Japan has agreed to lower the tariff rate on some of these products. For example, in 1993 the import tariff on beef was lowered by 50 percent.

Tariff duties are usually assessed based on the cost of an imported product plus any insurance and freight charges that may be incurred in transporting the goods to Japan (such as CIF). Most duties are levied on an ad valorem basis. For a few items, a specific rate, based on the number of units imported, applies. Still other items are assessed on an ad valorem basis or at a specific rate, at the discretion the customs official.

Countertrade

There is no record of countertrade involving the Japanese government or other public enterprises in Japan during the last 10 years.

Environmental Protection and Pollution Control

Manufacturers in Japan are being urged to promote recycling of by-products generated in the manufacturing process and to redesign products and parts to be more recyclable. Although Japan's first recycling law (enacted in October 1991) does not contain mandatory provisions, products containing recyclable materials are becoming more popular.

In November 1992, the Environment Agency designated special zones in the Kanto and Kansai areas where strict limitations are to be placed on total emissions of nitrogen oxides. This regulation will have the greatest impact on owners of vehicles that use diesel fuel. The special zones cover 196 local communities in Chiba, Hyogo, Kanagawa, Osaka, Saitama, and Tokyo Prefectures. As of December 1993, vehicle inspection clearance will be refused to motor vehicles in these zones that do not meet emission standards.

Environmental concern is growing in Japan, and the domestic market for pollution control, environmental protection equipment, and waste cleanup is expected to increase dramatically in the coming years. The most important agencies responsible for environmental management and protection are:

Environmental Policy Division
Industrial Location and Environmental Protection Bureau
Ministry of International Trade and Industry
1-3-1 Kasumigaseki, Chiyoda-ku
Tokyo 100-45, Japan
Tel: [81] (3) 3501-1679 Fax: [81] (3) 3580-6379

Office of Industrial Waste Management
Water Supply and Environmental Sanitation Department
Ministry of Health and Welfare
1-2-2 Kasumigaseki, Chiyoda-ku
Tokyo 100-45, Japan
Tel: [81] (3) 3501-0040 Fax: [81] (3) 3502-6879

Global Environment Department
Environmental Agency
1-2-2 Kasumigaseki, Chiyoda-ku
Tokyo 100, Japan
Tel: [81] (3) 3580-4982 Fax: [81] (3) 3504-1634

IMPORT PROCEDURES

Import License

Most goods entering Japan now qualify as "freely importable" and do not require an import license. For restricted items, the importer must obtain authorization and an import quota certificate from the MITI, and then apply for an import license from an authorized foreign exchange bank.

Import Declaration

The import declaration requirements are complicated and subject to frequent change. Firms should follow their importer's instructions with regard to special certificates and other documents. The import declaration must be prepared and filed by the importer in Japan. It must include the mark, shipping number, description, quantity, and value of the goods; the place of origin, purchase, and shipment of the goods; and the name or registered mark and nationality of the vessel or aircraft that transported the merchandise. Once customs accepts the import declaration, it may not be altered without special approval of customs.

Method of Payment

All standard international methods of credit and payment apply in Japan. 90- to 100-day promissory notes and letters of credit are some of the most common terms of payment. (Refer to "International Payments" chapter for more information.)

Health and Sanitary Requirements

Japanese health and sanitary regulations are strictly enforced. All imported plants and soils, animals, meat, and viscera of animals must be accompanied by a phytosanitary inspection certificate, issued by the government of the exporting country, attesting that the shipment is free from infectious materials or diseases.

The Food Sanitation Law requires that an Import Notification Form be submitted for all food products at the time of importation. The use of chemicals and additives in foods is severely restricted in Japan. Additive regulations follow a "positive list" approach, which indicates those additives that are permitted, the maximum tolerable amount, and the foods in which the additives may be used. Cosmetics are governed by similar regulations.

Packaging, Marking, Labeling, and Testing Standards

Knowledge of Japanese standards is extremely important for businesses that plan to introduce products or services in this market. Standards are highly regulated, both by official rules and by voluntary private standards (for example, industrial standards). Many of the industrial standards have been modified to conform to international practices but, in general, businesses are best advised to follow Japan's published standards to ensure acceptance of imports. However, standards change periodically, and it is important to obtain the most recent information.

The Measurement Law requires that all imported products and shipping documents show metric weights and measurements. There is no requirement that products display the place of origin. However, if labels indicating origin are determined to be false or misleading, they must be removed or corrected; otherwise, the goods will be returned.

There are no generic regulations for the marking of packages, but certain goods—including food, drugs, cosmetics, clothing, and electrical appliances—are covered by specific regulations outlined, respectively, in the Food Sanitation Law, the Pharmaceutical Affairs Law (ordinances of the Ministry of Health), and the Electrical Appliance and Material Control Law. A product may be controlled by more than one law, or different laws may apply to products of the same group. Businesses should consult with their importer or agent to ensure that products meet the requirements.

Much of the information on standards is available only through government ministries, and most of their written materials are available only in Japanese. Regulations govern the technical specifications of a product, as well as packaging, marking, labeling, testing, transportation and storage, and installation.

The principal agency that establishes standards is the Industrial Standards Committee of the MITI. The Japanese Standards Association (JSA) is also part of the MITI and is responsible for publishing the industrial standards. The JSA has published all of the 8,593 standards now in force.

Over 90 percent of the industrial standards have been translated into English, with new translations issued each July. The *JIS Yearbook* contains general information on Japanese standards, application procedures, and listings of all JSA publications with prices. If a standard has not yet been translated, JSA will translate it at a per-page cost. To obtain the *JIS Yearbook* or to request a translation, contact:

Sales Department, Japanese Standards Association
4-1-24 Akasaka, Minato-ku
Tokyo 107, Japan
Tel: [81] (3) 3583-8003, Fax: [81] (3) 3586-2029

JSA also operates three libraries in Tokyo, Osaka, and Nagoya that are open to the public. The main library in Tokyo has a collection of over 700,000 Japanese and foreign standards. The libraries are open 9:30 am to 5:00 pm, Monday through Friday.

Japanese Standards Association (JSA) Library
4-1-24 Akasaka, Minato-ku
Tokyo 107, Japan
Tel: [81] (3) 3583-8001

To provide electronic information on both domestic and foreign standards, JSA sponsors *Kikaku Net*, an on-line, dial-up database offered through such database vendors as Japan Information Processing Service Co., Ltd. and Nikkei Telecom. Database entries include standard number, name, and date of approval. The network contains 13,000 domestic standards—including the industrial standards and agricultural standards—as well as 235,000 foreign standards, including those from the International Standards Organization and the International Electrotechnical Commission.

Businesses in the United States can connect to *Kikaku Net* by modem in New York, Los Angeles, and Washington, D.C., through Nikkei Telecom's *Needs* network. While much of the information is in English, Japanese-language Telecom software is required to navigate *Needs*; appropriate MS-DOS and Macintosh software are commercially available. Information about *Needs* can be obtained from Mr. Miyagi or Mr. Duff at:

Nikkei Telecom
1325 Avenue of the Americas, Suite 2500
New York, NY 10019
Tel: (212) 261-6243 Fax: (212) 261-6249

Access to *Kikaku Net* through *Tymnet* is also available. *Kikaku Net* is very expensive, charging US$400.00 a month plus US$2.00 a minute. For further information about *Kikaku Net*, contact:

Database Information Processing Service Co., Ltd.
2-4-24 Toyo, Koto-ku
Tokyo 135, Japan
Tel: [81] (3) 5690-3202 Fax: [81] (3) 5690-3227

Information about current standards for packaging, marking, and labeling can also be obtained by contacting:

Standards Information Center
Information Service Department
Japan External Trade Organization (JETRO)
2-2-5, Toranomon, Minato-ku
Tokyo 105, Japan
Tel: [81] (3) 3582-5511 Fax: [81] (3) 3589-4179

Although the JSA's main task is to internationalize Japanese standards, its International Standardization Cooperation Center answers questions raised by foreigners about Japanese standards. This center will also refer inquiries to Japanese industrial organizations and translate the responses into English. For further information, contact the International Standardization Cooperation Center. To facilitate acceptance of their products in Japan's domestic market, foreign producers can qualify to receive an official Japanese industrial standards mark, which indicates that the imported product meets Japanese specifications. Some 1,100 foreign products now carry the Japanese industrial standards mark, including electric appliances, textiles, and construction machinery.

Japan Standards Association
Olumu Building, 3rd Floor
4-6-11 Akasaka, Minato-ku
Tokyo 107, Japan
Tel: [81] (3) 3583-8073 Fax: [81] (3) 3582-2390

An application for a Japanese industrial standards mark must be made through a local Japanese representative. The fee per application is ¥120,000 (US$1,165). The applicant must also pay the costs, including travel expenses, for an inspection of the manufacturing facility by a MITI official. A guide to the application process and an application form are available from the MITI. The application must be filled out in Japanese.

Samples and Advertising Matter

Japan is a member of the International Convention to Facilitate the Importation of Commercial Samples and Advertising Material. Samples of merchandise and printed advertising matter may enter Japan duty free. Particularly valuable samples may be temporarily admitted duty free under deposit or bond for the amount of the duty. All samples must be accompanied by the following documents and sent to the consignee: commercial invoice showing the CIF value (in US dollars), a complete description of the goods, a bill of lading (or air waybill), and a letter of authority if a broker is used. A statement declaring that the goods are samples must also be given at customs.

ATA Carnet

Japan is a signatory to the ATA Carnet Convention, and accepts carnets under the ATA carnet scheme established by the Customs Cooperation Council in conjunction with the International Bureau of Chambers of Commerce. Under this convention, a single customs document allows expeditious, duty-free entry of articles having commercial value that are intended for display at trade fairs, exhibitions, seminars, or similar events. Such goods may be brought into Japan by travelers or shipped to them separately by air or sea, and may remain in Japan up to six months. Customs officials at the port of entry set the time limit based on information provided by the shipper.

For information on obtaining an ATA carnet in Japan, contact:

Japan Commercial Arbitration Association
6th Fl., Tokyo Kotsu Kaikan 10-1
Yuraku-cho, Chiyoda-ku
Tokyo 100, Japan
Tel: [81] (3) 3214-0641/3 Fax: [81] (3) 3201-1336

Entry and Warehousing

When goods arrive at a Japanese port or bonded airport, they are transferred to a bonded area until cleared through customs. Under special circumstances, and with the approval of customs, a shipment can be inspected at a place other than the usual bonded area. Once goods enter Japan, they may be transported in bond only between ports of entry, customs airports, bonded areas, customs offices, or other places specified by the Director of Customs. The Director of Customs may require a security deposit equivalent to the amount of the customs duty payable. The deposit is returned upon arrival of the goods at a designated location.

There are five types of bonded areas in Japan: designated bonded areas, bonded sheds, bonded warehouses, bonded factories, and bonded exhibit sites. For additional information, contact the Chief Inspector of the Customs and Tariff Bureau.

Ministry of Finance
3-1-1 Kasumigaseki, Chiyoda-ku
Tokyo 100, Japan
Tel: [81] (3) 3581-4111/2852
Fax: [81] (3) 3593-1223/3581-0460 Tlx: 24980 MOFJ

Electric Current

Japan: AC 50 and 60 cycles (varies), 100/200 volts, 1,3 phases, 2, 3 wires. *Okinawa*: AC 60 cycles, 100/200 volts in nonmilitary facilities; 120/240 volts in military facilities, 1 phase, 2, 3 wires.

In 1988 MITI transferred 73 electrical appliances and materials from Category A to Category B. Category B products do not require factory inspection, type approval, or laboratory testing by the MITI. However, the products must still conform to Japan's Electrical Appliance and Material Control Law and have markings similar to those in Category A. This reclassification has reduced the paperwork, testing fees, and time required for foreign manufacturers to market products in Japan. The products include conduits, under-floor ducts, cable wiring switch boxes, electric heating appliances (toasters, ovens, etc.), and electric motor-operated or magnetically driven appliances (food processors, routers, power tools, etc.)

DOCUMENTATION

Customs procedures have been simplified in recent years, but a number of documents are still required. For commercial shipments to Japan, irrespective of value or mode of transport, these documents include a commercial invoice, bill of lading or air waybill, a certificate of origin (for certain articles), packing list, and insurance certificate (may be required). Depending on the nature of the goods being shipped or as requested by the importer, bank, or letter of credit clause, other special certificates (for example, sanitary, veterinary, free sale, and testing), may also be required. The importer is responsible for obtaining and presenting to customs an import license, when necessary, and for filling out and presenting to customs an import declaration. Facsimile signatures are not permitted on documents. To be certain that all required documentation is provided at the time a shipment arrives in Japan, firms should consult with their agent or importer.

Commercial Invoice

Customs officials require a commercial invoice, but there is no special form for this document. A minimum of two to three copies of the invoice should be issued on the shipper's letterhead and signed by the exporter or an approved representative of the exporter. The invoice should either precede or accompany the shipment; otherwise, clearance of the shipment is likely to be delayed.

The invoice must contain the following information: marks, numbers, name, tariff classification, and an accurate description of the goods; quantities, gross and net metric weights; unit value of the goods, and total value; itemized expenses (including freight, insurance, and shipping charges); place and date of preparation of the invoice; destination and consignee; and the conditions of the contract that relate to the determination of value of the goods. Additional information may be required by the importer, by the importer's bank, or due to the nature of a particular commodity.

Packing List

Two copies of the packing list should be forwarded with the commercial invoice and other shipping documents to assist in customs clearance. The packing list should provide an exact description of all items in the shipment, the gross and net weight of each package, the exterior measurements of the each package, the total number of shipping containers, and the gross weight and measurement. All measurements, both on the documents and the goods, must be in metric units.

Bill of Lading

Bills of lading for shipment by water and air waybills for transport by air are used to designate title to specific merchandise. Three signed original bills of lading should be sent through banking channels, and two unsigned copies should be forwarded to the consignee. For goods sent by air, a standard set of 10 (one original and nine copies) should be provided. The information that must be included on the bill of lading (or air waybill) is usually specified in the letter of credit. Information that may be required includes the name of the ship; the name of the shipper; the ultimate consignee and, when applicable, intermediate consignee(s); the number of packages and their markings; and a description of the goods, including gross metric weights and measurements.

Certificate of Origin

A certificate of origin is required only for goods granted duty concessions by Japan under GATT. Such a certificate must be notarized by a local chamber of commerce or by a Japanese consular or diplomatic official. Suppliers and shippers should follow the advice of their principals, as the importer in Japan can easily obtain the latest rulings for goods that can be cleared through customs without a certificate of origin.

There is no standard form for the certificate of origin. Shippers can use either the general form available from commercial stationers or submit a document with the following information: place of origin, marks and/or numbers of the commodities, commodity description, number of packages, quantities of the merchandise, total value, port of shipment, and destination. The certificate should also include a statement that the commodities listed were produced or manufactured in the place of origin shown on the document. The document must be signed and dated by the applicant and the certifying officer. Usually, two copies of the certificate of origin are needed.

Pro Forma Invoice

A pro forma invoice may be requested by the importer. There are no official requirements for the form or content of this document; follow the instructions of the importer or agent.

Insurance Certificate

Normal practices pertain to the insurance certificate. Exporters and other suppliers are advised to follow the instructions of the importer or insurance company.

FOREIGN TRADE ZONES

There are no free trade zones or free ports in Japan. However, customs officials do allow the bonding of some warehouses and processing facilities in certain areas adjacent to ports on a case-by-case basis.

A law enacted in early 1992 calls for the creation of at least seven foreign access zones (FAZs) by 1996, with an additional five FAZs under consideration. Officials at the MITI say that the FAZs will provide support facilities for import procedures, such as disinfecting and fumigation; exhibition halls and information centers for import businesses; facilities for distribution of imports, including storage and handling; and facilities for wholesalers of imports and processing of imports. Customs officials will treat each FAZ as a bonded area.

The Kitakyushu FAZ will have an international general distribution center and other supporting facilities. In Nagasaki, the FAZ will be located on reclaimed land on the north side of the international airport. It will be managed by the present international cargo terminal company, and will include a new cargo terminal, a dispatch center, and exhibition and marketing facilities. (Refer to "Opportunities" chapter for more information on FAZs.)

Export Policy & Procedures

INTRODUCTION

Exporting from Japan is generally easier than importing into the country. Some categories of products require an export license, and certain types of products must be inspected prior to export in order to ensure compliance with Japanese standards of product design and manufacture. Most other restrictions are the result of voluntary export controls adopted in response to pressure from trading partners to limit exports. Several thousand Japanese trading companies handle the majority of the country's exports and imports. In addition to acting as a liaison between buyer and seller, many trading companies also provide trade consulting and other business services.

The following chapter discusses Japan's export policy and procedures. This information is useful for people who want to purchase goods and services from Japan, for those who establish manufacturing facilities or other operations in Japan, and for foreign investors.

REGULATORY AUTHORITIES

Foreign trade is regulated primarily by the Ministry of International Trade and Industry (MITI), the Ministry of Finance (MOF), and the Bank of Japan. Various foreign exchange banks are responsible for verifying import and export payments. The MITI handles most import and export reporting requirements, and it issues export licenses. The MOF has jurisdiction over customs and tariff control and regulation.

Ministry of International Trade and Industry (MITI)
3-1, Kasumigaseki 1-chome, Chiyoda-ku
Tokyo 100, Japan
Tel: [81] (3) 3501-1511

Ministry of Finance (MOF)
1-1, Kasumigaseki 3-chome, Chiyoda-ku
Tokyo 100, Japan
Tel: [81] (3) 3581-4111 Fax: [81] (3) 3508-7324

Customs and Tariff Bureau
Ministry of Finance
1-1 Kasumigaseki 3-chome, Chiyoda-ku
Tokyo 100, Japan
Tel: [81] (3) 3581-4111, 3581-2852
Fax: [81] (3) 3593-1223, 3581-0460 Tlx: 24980 MOFJ

Bank of Japan
1-1, Hongoku-cho 2-chome
Nihonbashi, Chuo-ku
Tokyo 103, Japan
Tel: [81] (3) 3279-1111 Fax: [81] (3) 3245-0358
Tlx: 22763

Export-Import Bank of Japan
4-1, Otemachi 1-chome, Chiyoda-ku
Tokyo 100, Japan
Tel: [81] (3) 3287-1221 Fax: [81] (3) 3287-9540
Tlx: 23728

EXPORT POLICY

Export Restrictions and Licensing

In principle, the exportation of most products from Japan is free from constraints. However, certain restrictions are imposed for various reasons. Over 330 categories of products must be examined prior to shipment abroad, including bearings, bicycles, cameras, chinaware, tape recorders, and watches. The Export Articles Design Law stipulates that 20 categories of products, among them fountain pens and furniture, must be registered and their designs approved prior to export. An export license issued by the MITI is required in the following circumstances:

- When exporting to designated countries specific items, including strategic goods, goods affecting the domestic balance of supply and demand, goods that may force the recipient country to impose import quotas or to increase import duties, goods subject to excessive competition in the international market, goods on which the United Nations has placed an embargo, and goods that require approval by the Japanese customs authorities.

- When exporting under specific contract arrangements, such as processing or consignment; only certain goods may be exported for processing.
- Exports for which there are unusual methods of settlement, such as settlement after one year or more, or settlement by offset against amounts payable.

Voluntary Export Controls

From time to time, Japan exercises voluntary export controls on certain products destined for designated countries. Consistent trade surpluses with most of its largest trading partners (especially with the United States) have led Japan to develop a series of voluntary controls. The most notable of these limits concerns the export of motor vehicles to the United States, Canada, and the United Kingdom. Certain electronic products are also subject to voluntary export control.

The export controls are based on the Export and Import Transactions Law, which also provides for the creation of export unions and export/import associations. Export unions are organized by area and allow small and medium-size trading companies to combine and function as one large organization. At present, there are eight export unions in Japan. The associations are organized by product; 31 currently deal with exports and 13 with imports. With approval from the MITI, these associations may collectively agree on the pricing, quality, and quantity of exports or imports, without violating the Anti-Monopoly Law.

Comprehensive Trading Companies

The majority of imports and exports are handled by several trading companies called comprehensive trading companies. This two-tiered system can cause delays in payment, as many imports and exports must first go through the trading companies before reaching the importing company or other end user. Generally, delays are no longer than 30 days on secured terms.

The trading companies were originally wholesalers, but today their operations concentrate on domestic exports, imports, and trade between third-party countries. The companies also assist their customers and suppliers by providing financing and business information; coordinating large projects, such as the construction of petrochemical plants; developing sources of natural resources; and by facilitating the exchange of goods and services between domestic and international parties. Most of the comprehensive trading companies have established extensive worldwide organizations to carry out these responsibilities. The top nine companies are Mitsubishi Shoji, Mitsui Bussan, C. Itho, Marubeni, Sumitomo Shoji, Niddho-Iwa, Tomen, Nichimen, and Kanematsu-Gosho.

DOCUMENTATION

Although customs procedures in Japan have been simplified in recent years, a number of documents are still required for goods that leave the country. For commercial shipments by air or sea out of Japan these documents include a commercial invoice, bill of lading or air waybill, a certificate of origin (for certain articles), packing list, and insurance certificate (may be required). Special documents may be requested by the importer, bank, or letter of credit clause. The exporter is responsible for obtaining and presenting to the inspection officials an export license and registration approval, as required. Facsimile signatures are not permitted on documents. To be certain that all required documentation is accounted for at the time a shipment leaves Japan, firms should consult with their shipper or export agent.

Commercial Invoice

There is no special form for the commercial invoice. A minimum of two to three copies of the invoice should be issued on the shipper's letterhead and signed by the exporter or an approved representative of the exporter. The invoice should either precede or accompany the shipment; otherwise, clearance of the shipment is likely to be delayed.

The invoice must contain at least the following information: marks, numbers, name, tariff classification, and an accurate description of the goods; quantities, gross and net metric weights; unit value of the goods, and total value; itemized expenses (including freight, insurance, and shipping charges); place and date of preparation of the invoice; destination and consignee; and the conditions of the contract that relate to the determination of value of the goods. Additional information may be required by the importer, by the importer's bank, or due to the requirements of a particular commodity.

Bill of Lading

The bill of lading (or, for air shipments, the air waybill) constitutes the document of title to the merchandise. It must conform strictly with the terms in the letter of credit. For shipments under cost, insurance, and freight (CIF), cost, freight/carriage and insurance paid (CIP), or other related methods, the supplier contracts and pays for the freight. However, many buyers prefer to arrange for the shipment themselves in cooperation with a local freight forwarder, consolidator, or shipping line. In this case, payment is made under such terms as free alongside ship (FAS), free on board (FOB), free on board airport (FOA), or other related methods. Buyers should make certain that the shipping agent is aware of the correct terms and how the freight charges will be paid. This information will help the carrier prepare the bill of lading in accordance with the conditions of the letter of credit, purchase contract, and other documents.

The bill of lading lists the port of departure, port of discharge, name of the carrying vessel, and date of issue. The date of issue is very important because it indicates whether goods have been shipped within the time period required in the letter of credit. Suppliers must submit all required documents on time to receive payment under the terms of the credit.

Bills of lading can be either negotiable or nonnegotiable. A negotiable bill of lading is made to the order of the shipper, who makes a blank endorsement on the back, or it is endorsed to the order of the bank that issues the letter of credit. A nonnegotiable bill of lading is consigned to a specific party (to the buyer or buyer's representative) and endorsement by the shipper is not required. In this case, the consignee must produce the original bill of lading in order to take delivery.

Packing List

A packing list is recommended and should be forwarded with the commercial invoice and other shipping documents to assist in customs clearance. The following information should be included in the packing list: an exact description of all items in the shipment, the gross and net metric weight of each package, the exterior measurements of the each package, the total number of shipping containers, and the gross metric weight and measurement. There should be two copies of the packing list.

Export Declaration

If the value of an export item exceeds ¥3 million (about US$27,000), an export declaration must be submitted to the Customs and Tariff Bureau of the Ministry of Finance and to an authorized foreign exchange bank.

Certificate of Origin

A certificate of origin is sometimes required by certain countries for specific products. Such a certificate must be notarized by a local chamber of commerce, or by a consular or other diplomatic official. Suppliers and shippers should follow the advice of their principals in determining whether a certificate of origin is necessary.

Generally, there is no standard form for a certificate of origin. Shippers can use either the form available from commercial stationers or submit a document with the following information: place of origin, marks and/or numbers of the commodities, commodity description, number of packages, quantities of the merchandise, total value, port of shipment, and destination. The certificate should also include a statement that the commodities listed were produced or manufactured in the place of origin shown on the document. The document must be signed and dated by the applicant and the certifying officer. In most cases, there should be two copies of the certificate of origin.

Insurance Certificate

Normal practices pertain to the insurance certificate. Exporters and other suppliers are advised to follow the instructions of the importer and insurance company.

Industry Reviews

This chapter describes the status of and trends in major Japan industries. It also lists key contacts for finding sources of supply, developing sales leads and conducting economic research. We have grouped industries into 16 categories, which are listed below. Some smaller sectors of commerce are not detailed here, while others may overlap into more than one area. If your business even remotely fits into a category don't hesitate to contact several of the organizations listed; they should be able to assist you further in gathering the information you need. We have included industry-specific contacts only. General trade organizations, which may also be very helpful, particularly if your business is in an

industry not covered here, are listed in the "Important Addresses" chapter at the end of this book.

Each section has two segments: an industry summary and a list of useful contacts. The summary gives an overview of the range of products available in a certain industry and that industry's ability to compete in worldwide markets. The contacts listed are government departments, trade associations, publications, and trade fairs which can provide information specific to the industry. An entire volume could likely be devoted to each area, but such in-depth coverage is beyond the scope of this book. Our intent is to give you a basis for your own research.

All addresses and telephone numbers given are located in Japan, unless otherwise noted. The telephone country code for Japan is [81]; other telephone country codes are shown in square brackets where appropriate. Telephone city codes, if needed, appear in parentheses.

We highly recommend that you peruse the chapters on "Trade Fairs" and "Important Addresses" chapters, where you will find additional resources including a variety of trade promotion organizations, chambers of commerce, business services, and media.

AEROSPACE, AIRCRAFT, AND AIRCRAFT PARTS

Japan is among the world's leaders in developing high-tech aircraft and aircraft equipment. Although Japan's military defense establishment accounts for over 70 percent of orders, about half of Japan's production of aircraft and aircraft parts is exported, mainly to Europe and the United States. In contrast, Japan's aerospace industry is a weak competitor in global markets. The Chubu region is a leading center in Japan's aerospace and aircraft industries.

Products For the civilian sector, Japanese aircraft manufacturers produce parts of B737s, 747s, 757s, and 767s for foreign companies. Firms are also manufacturing fuselage extension panels for airbus aircraft. For the military sector, Japan's aircraft industry manufactures anti-submarine aircraft, jet fighters, and parts for missiles, other weaponry, and tanks. Japan's aerospace industry is focusing on production of communications satellites and rockets for launching them.

Competitive Situation

With declining orders from Japan's military establishment, aircraft manufacturers in Japan are expanding their production of civilian equipment and are actively seeking orders for civilian aircraft parts. Some R&D funds have been devoted to developing a mid-size passenger jet. Major Japanese airplane manufacturers have entered into joint ventures with overseas companies for design and production of new jumbo and supersonic passenger planes. In preparation for production of these advanced craft, capital investments are now being made in new plant construction and expansion of existing facilities in Japan. To exploit increasing civilian demand for aircraft engines, several Japanese manufacturers have formed joint projects with foreign companies to develop innovations in jet and other aircraft engines and to supply high-tech engine parts.

Japan's National Space Development Agency, which has been primarily responsible for developing technology for Japan's aerospace program, has transferred that technology to a private company that was formed to procure and launch payloads. In addition to launching Japanese communications satellites, this company is negotiating to launch satellites for Korea.

Government Agencies

Defense Agency
7-45, Akasaka 9-chome, Chiyoda-ku
Tokyo 100
Tel: (3) 3408-5211

Ministry of Transport
1-3, Kasumigaseki 2-chome, Chiyoda-ku
Tokyo 100
Tel: (3) 3580-3111

Trade Organizations

Japan Association of Defense Industries
2nd Fl., Le Dond Building 21-3,
Akasaka 2-chome, Minato-ku
Tokyo 107
Tel: (3) 3584-6755 Fax: (3) 3584-7363

The Society of Japan Aerospace Companies, Inc.
Hibiya Park Building
8-1, Yuraku-cho 1-chome, Chiyoda-ku
Tokyo 100
Tel: (3) 3211-5678 Fax: (3) 3211-5018

Directories/Publications

Asian Aviation
(Monthly)
Asian Aviation Publications
2 Leng Kee Rd., #04-01 Thye Hong Centre
Singapore 0315
Tel: [65] 4747088 Fax: [65] 4796668

Japan Aviation Directory
(Annual)
Wings Aviation Press Inc.
Kanda Kitamura Building
1302 Kanda Higashi Konya-cho
Tokyo 101
Tel: (3) 3258-0880 Fax: (3) 3258-5004

Trade Fairs

Refer to the Trade Fair chapter for complete listings including contact information, dates, and venues. Trade fairs with particular relevance to this industry include the following, which are listed in that chapter under the heading given below:

Aerospace & Oceanic
- Airport Systems International Show Tokyo
- International Exhibition & Symposium– "Airport, Communication & Environment"

For other trade fairs that may be of interest, we recommend that you also consult the headings Computer & Information Industries; Electronic, Electric, & Communication Equipment; Factory Automation; and Transportation.

COMPUTER AND OTHER INFORMATION PRODUCTS

Japan holds nearly a 30 percent share of worldwide revenues for computers and related equipment. Production is focused on hardware, but software firms are developing an increasing number of exportable products. Japan's major export markets for computer products are in Europe and the United States.

Four major firms produce most of Japan's computer-related products. Key centers of Japan's computer industry are in Kyushu and Miyazaki.

Computer Hardware

Mainframes Japan's computer firms have gradually increased their share of world markets for mainframe computers to about 25 percent. Japanese-produced mainframe computers for high-volume general-purpose business applications are available in water-cooled and air-cooled models. Demand for mainframes has decreased as consumers shift to workstations and personal computers, but Japan's mainframe computer makers are remaining competitive by providing systems that work as networks for strategic information systems (SIS), which allow information exchange with other companies. In addition, mainframe markets are supported by consumer demand for replacement, new, and expansion equipment.

Midrange Multiuser Systems Demand for Japan's multiuser computer systems is growing steadily, particularly for use in factories, laboratories, and other businesses that depend on computer networking. This type of computer system can perform a wide range of tasks, including machine control, calculation, communication, and design functions. These systems are sold in various components and can be easily expanded or integrated into existing systems. Japan's computer firms are focusing on creating high bit machines for this market, and on improving controller and server technology for computer networking.

Workstations Japan's computer firms hold about 10 percent of the worldwide workstation market. Some Japanese workstation production has been on an original equipment manufacturer (OEM) basis for US companies. However, the Japanese computer firms have not matched the prices and performance offered by US workstation suppliers. To increase their competitiveness, Japanese firms have invested in, and formed joint ventures with, US firms that produce workstations.

Personal Computers Worldwide market demand for personal computers (PCs) has risen rapidly, and most of Japan's PC production output is exported. These computers are being used for an ever-increasing number of business and home applications. As market trends shift toward higher-bit PCs, Japan's computer manufacturers are concentrating R&D in this area. Japan's PC makers offer competitively priced models with such advanced features as CD-ROM players.

Portable Computers Global demand for portable computers is rising dramatically. Japan's computer firms manufacture competitively priced quality components for laptop, notebook, and personal digital devices. The most significant exports are active matrix liquid crystal displays (AM-LCDs). Japanese computer firms are developing pen-based technology for portable computers, which is expected to replace the track ball now used in many models.

In an effort to maximize profits from portable computer sales while demand is high, Japanese computer manufacturers have entered into engineering, design, and manufacturing joint ventures with US companies. R&D for notebooks and laptops focuses on the production of compact, lightweight machines with fast processing and high-bit capacity.

Storage Hardware Japan holds less than 20 percent of the worldwide market for disk drives but supplies significant quantities of components and materials (such as spindle motors, bearings, neodymium magnets, and high-quality aluminum substrate materials) to US hard disk drive manufacturers for assembly. Most Japanese-made floppy and hard disk drives are sold to domestic computer manufacturers for incorporation into word processors, PCs, and workstations. Japanese computer manufacturers have begun investing heavily in US firms that produce thin-film disks and other advanced technology products.

Monitors Monochrome and color monitors are produced in Japan, although color monitors account for the largest percentage of output. Japanese computer firms are the largest producers of thin-film transistor color screens, popular for notebook and laptop computers. To produce competitively priced monitors, Japan's computer makers have moved many of their production facilities to Southeast Asia.

Printers Japan's computer manufacturers offer an array of line and serial printers. High-speed impact and nonimpact line printers are mostly sold to mainframe consumers. Impact and nonimpact serial printers, which include thermal transfer, ink jet, and laser printers, are used with PCs and other word processing units. Several Japanese computer manufacturers produce printers on an original equipment manufacturer (OEM) basis for domestic and foreign companies with established brand names.

Software

Japan's software companies are top world suppliers of game software. However, the worldwide recession and slumps in global consumer electronic markets have severely hurt Japan's software developers, and many firms have declared bankruptcy since 1991. Japan's surviving software firms are diversifying into higher technology products through joint arrangements with US software producers.

CAD/CAM/CAE Systems Japan's activities in computer-aided design, computer-aided manufacturing, and computer-aided engineering (CAD/CAM/CAE) software and workstations primarily consist of assembling these systems from parts produced by US companies. Several US firms supply Japan's CAD/CAM/CAE makers with central processing units (CPUs) on an OEM basis. US computer manufacturers have also begun to enter into license and royalty agreements with Japanese computer producers for domestic production of CAD/CAM/CAE systems. Through such agreements, new technologies can be developed while capacity to manufacture high-quality products can be expanded. The US manufacturers can concentrate on R&D, and their Japanese partners can focus on production engineering.

Virtual Reality Programs Several Japanese companies are exploring applications of virtual reality software, which has been primarily used by the US film and entertainment industry. Japanese firms are considering such applications as theme park attractions, video games, sports simulators, visual automobile design, and architectural and construction planning. They are also investigating potential applications in the educational, medical, and transportation fields. Although US technology for virtual reality software is more sophisticated and advanced than Japanese-made programs, Japanese manufacturers can produce high-quality hardware for these programs. To improve the technology of their virtual reality software, some Japanese computer companies are considering joint ventures and licensing agreements with US firms.

Competitive Situation

Japan's computer industry has seen several years of declining worldwide computer markets. Faced with economic recession and low profits, businesses throughout the world have reduced their capital expenditures for computer systems. In addition, mainframe consumers are downsizing to PC networks and workstations, markets in which Japan's firms face stiff price competition from other Asian countries.

Nevertheless, Japan's computer industry appears to be slowly growing, spurred in particular by the continuing recovery of the US economy, aggressive R&D investment, and increasing international cooperation among computer companies. Japan ranks first in the world in creation and production of advanced semiconductor devices, digital imaging technology, high-density data storage, and optoelectronics. The Japanese government and computer firms are continuing to invest heavily in R&D in massive parallel processing, optical and neural computing, virtual reality programming, speech and voice recognition systems, and fuzzy logic projects. Large-scale computer systems and supercomputers have been targeted for improvements in performance, which has led to an increase in exports. Japan's computer manufacturers are also developing memory laminated magnetic heads, which are expected to facilitate production of smaller laptop computers with greater memory capacity. In addition, Japanese firms continue to invest domestically and abroad to acquire high-tech computer production facilities.

Government Agencies

Patent Office
4-3, Kasumigaseki 3-chome, Chiyoda-ku
Tokyo 100
Tel: (3) 3581-1101

Science & Technology Agency
2-1, Kasumigaseki 2-chome, Chiyoda-ku
Tokyo 100
Tel: (3) 3581-5271

Trade Organizations

Japan Business Machine Makers Association
Dai-Ichi Mori Building
12-1, Nishi-Shombashi 1-chome, Minato-ku
Tokyo 105
Tel: (3) 3503-9821 Fax: (3) 3591-3646

Japan Information Service Industry Association
Yusei Gojokai Kotohiro Building
14-1, Toranomon 1-chome, Minato-ku
Tokyo 105
Tel: (3) 3595-4051 Fax: (3) 3595-4055

Directories/Publications

Asian Computer Directory
(Monthly)
Washington Plaza
1st Fl., 230 Wanchai Rd.
Wanchai, Hong Kong
Tel: [852] 8327123 Fax: [852] 8329208

Asia Computer Weekly
(Bimonthly)
Asian Business Press Pte. Ltd.
100 Beach Rd., #26-00 Shaw Towers
Singapore 0718
Tel: [65] 2943366 Fax: [65] 2985534

Asian Computer Monthly
(Monthly)
Computer Publications Ltd.
Washington Plaza, 1st Fl.
230 Wanchai Road
Wanchai, Hong Kong
Tel: [852] 9327123 Fax: [852] 8329208

Asian Sources: Computer Products
(Monthly)
Asian Sources Media Group
22nd Fl., Vita Tower
29 Wong Chuk Hang Road
Wong Chuk Hang, Hong Kong
Tel: [852] 5554777 Fax: [852] 8730488

OEP: Office Equipment & Products
(Monthly)
Dempa Publications
1-11-15, Higashi Gotanda, Shinagawa-ku
Tokyo 141
Tel: (3) 3445-6111

Science & Technology in Japan
(Quarterly)
Three "I" Publications
Yamaguchi Building
5-16, Uchikanda 1-chome, Chiyoda-ku
Tokyo 101
Tel: (3) 3291-3161 Fax: (3) 3291-3764

What's New in Computing
(Monthly)
Asian Business Press Pte. Ltd.
100 Beach Rd., #26-00 Shaw Towers
Singapore 0718
Tel: [65] 2943366 Fax: [65] 2985534

Trade Fairs

Refer to the Trade Fair chapter for complete listings, including contact information, dates, and venues. Trade fairs with particular relevance to this industry include the following, which are listed in that chapter under the headings given below:

Computer & Information Industries

- BOARD COMPUTER Japan Add-on Boards for Small Computer Exhibition
- CASE JAPAN Computer Aided Software Engineering Japan
- Computer Chemistry System Exhibition
- Data Show
- Factory Automation Hiroshima
- Hi-Tech Kyushu
- Hitech Hamamatsu
- Kurume-Tosu Techno Fair
- Kyushu International Techno Fair
- MACWORLD Expo Tokyo
- Micro Computer Show
- Microcomputer System & Tool Fair
- Scan-Tech Japan
- Software Show Tokyo
- Software Systems USA
- WINDOWS World Tokyo

Computer Graphics

- Automotive CAD/CAM/CAE Show (Automotive Design & Development Show)
- Computer Graphics Osaka
- International Technical Exhibition on Image Technology and Equipment
- NICOGRAPH
- CADMEC
- West Japan CAD CAM CAE System Exhibition
- DATABASES
- DATABASE TOKYO

Factory Automation

- CAD/CAM/CAE System Show (High Technology Tokyo)
- CAD/CAM/CAE System Show Nagoya (Factory Automation Nagoya)
- CAD/CAM/CAE System Show Osaka (Osaka Mechatronics Fair)
- CAE 8 CAD/CAM Systems Show (Technology Japan)
- CIM JAPAN-Computer Integrated Manufacturing Systems
- FA Computer & Network System (Factory Automation Nagoya)
- FA Computer & Network System (Osaka Mechatronics Fair)
- FA INTELLIGENT NETWORK System Show (Technology Japan)
- Imagetech

For other trade fairs that may be of interest, we recommend that you also consult the headings Electronic & Electric Equipment; and Office Automation.

ELECTRONIC CONSUMER AND COMPONENT PRODUCTS

Japan is the world's largest producer of consumer electronics and the second largest producer of electronic components. Five of the world's top ten electronic companies are Japanese, and Japan dominates world markets for many electronic products. Primary export markets for Japanese-produced electronic products are in Europe and the United States. Japan's major electronic consumer and component producers are located in Chubu.

Electronic Consumer Products

Over half of Japan's consumer electronic production is exported. Products include stereos and other audio equipment, car audio systems, tape recorders, televisions, compact disc players, video cameras, and videocassette recorders.

Japan's production and sales of electronic consumer products have slowed, primarily because of market saturation and worldwide recession. To retain a competitive edge in global markets and to reduce trade friction, Japan's electronic firms have moved some consumer appliance production facilities to export-destination countries and to countries with lower labor costs. Firms are also exploring new markets, especially in Southeast Asia and Eastern Europe. In addition, the firms are promoting products with high-tech features, such as digital recording equipment, high-definition televisions, digital compact cassettes, and mini-disc players.

Active Electronic Components

Active components made in Japan include assorted semiconductors, diodes, tubes, and transistors. Of these, semiconductors and liquid crystal displays (LCDs) are the most significant exports. Most Japanese computer firms are increasing R&D investment in the production of thin-film transistor LCDs, which improve color displays to near-photographic quality.

Semiconductors Japan's electronic firms produce 10 percent of the world's semiconductor chips, and semiconducter components made up over 5 percent of Japan's 1992 total exports. The 11 major Japanese semiconductor manufacturers provide chips for microcomponents; logic devices, such as integrated circuits (ICs); and memory devices. Major exports include dynamic random access memory (DRAM) chips, most of which are shipped to US computer manufacturers.

To remain competitive in global markets, Japanese semiconductor manufacturers are investing heavily in expanding their production and research facilities and in R&D for high-tech products, such as 16-, 64-, and 256-megabit DRAM chips. In addition, firms are focusing on increasing production capacity and improving production and design efficiency. To better coordinate manufacturing and international market needs, one major Japanese semiconductor firm has built a semiconductor design facility near its assembly and inspection plant, reducing the time needed to create semiconductor devices for specific applications.

Passive Electronic Components Japanese-made passive electronic components include resistors, capacitors, transformers, quartz oscillators, connectors, and switches. Production of passive electronic components in Japan is rising steadily, and demands for Japanese-produced composite parts, which consist of several passive components, are increasing. Firms are also developing passive parts that incorporate solid-state microchips, such as aluminum electrolytic capacitors for solid-state chips. Major centers for electronic passive component manufacturing are in Sendai and Kyushu.

Printed Circuit Boards Japanese production of printed circuit boards (PCBs) is soaring. Japanese manufacturers have retained their world status as top PCB suppliers by continuing to make technical innovations for these boards, such as high value-added multilayer boards and lower specific inductive capacity boards.

Superconductive Materials Japan's electronic industry is making heavy R&D investments in superconductive devices. Companies are developing practical applications for such materials as a copper oxide superconductive substance containing carbonate groups, a yttrium-based oxide superconductive thick film, and several types of bismuth-based superconductive substances.

Competitive Situation

Though sensitive to changing market trends, Japan's electronic industry has been depressed since 1991, primarily reflecting worldwide recession. Before 1990, the industry focused on semiconductor production. As global markets for semiconductors became saturated, Japanese firms redirected investments toward liquid crystal display components for high-tech appliances and computer products. When computer sales fell off, the industry shifted to high-tech integrated circuits (ICs), particularly 4-megabit dynamic random access memory (DRAM) chips for US computer firms. Most Japanese electronic component makers are being cautious in expanding IC production, however, citing uncertainties in global markets. Market demand has increased in the United States but not in other countries, perhaps because a dumping dispute between Korean suppliers and US authorities caused US firms to shift to Japanese suppliers. Concerns about IC price instability and overproduction remain.

Japan's electronic industry is undertaking ex-

tensive research into the development of micro-fabrication and nanofabrication technology, with the goal of further miniaturizing electronic components, such as semiconductors. This industry is also investing in research on super-diamond materials to replace silicon. This new technology is expected to revolutionize the semiconductor industry because diamond films are superior to silicon in heat resistance, heat conductivity, electric mobility, and photoemission energy. Applications include industries, such as space and nuclear power, that involve extreme environments.

Government Agency

Science & Technology Agency
2-1, Kasumigaseki 2-chome, Chiyoda-ku
Tokyo 100
Tel: (3) 3581-5271

Trade Organizations

Electronic Industries Association of Japan
Tosho Building
2-2, Marunouchi 3-chome, Chiyoda-ku
Tokyo 100
Tel: (3) 3211-2765, 3213-1073 Fax: (3) 3287-1712

Electronic Materials Manufacturers
Association of Japan
Toranomon Kotohirakaikan Building
2-8, Toranomon 1-chome, Minato-ku
Tokyo 105
Tel: (3) 3504-0351 Fax: (3) 3591-8130

Electronic Products Importers' Association
1-13, Shinjuku 1-chome, Shinjuku-ku
Tokyo 160
Tel: (3) 3225-8910 Fax: (3) 3225-9001

Federation of Electro Plating Industry Association,
Japan
Kikai Shinko Kaikan
5-8, Shibakoen 3-chome, Minato-ku
Tokyo 105
Tel: (3) 3433-3855 Fax: (3) 3433-3915

Japan Electrical Manufacturers' Association
4-15, Nagatacho 2-chome, Chiyoda-ku
Tokyo 100
Tel: (3) 3581-0391, 3581-4841/4 Fax: (3) 3593-3198

Japan Electric Association
7-1, Yurakucho 1-chome, Chiyoda-ku
Tokyo 100
Tel: (3) 3216-0551 Fax: (3) 3214-6005

Japan Electric Wire & Cable Exporters' Association
Konwa Building
12-22, Tsukiji 1-chome, Chuo-ku
Tokyo 104
Tel: (3) 3542-7531 Fax: (3) 3542-7533

Japan Electronic Industry Development
Association
Kikai Shinko Kaikan
5-8, Shibakoen 3-chome, Minato-ku
Tokyo 105
Tel: (3) 3433-6296 Fax: (3) 3433-6350

Japanese Electric Wire & Cable Makers'
Association
12-22, Tsukiji 1-chome, Chuo-ku
Tokyo 104
Tel: (3) 3542-6031 Fax: (3) 3542-6037

Japan Wire Products Exporters' Association
Tekko Kaikan
2-10, Nihombashi Kayaba-cho 3-chome
Chuo-ku
Tokyo 103
Tel: (3) 3669-5311 Fax: (3) 3666-6835

Directories/Publications

AEU : Journal Of Asia Electronics Union
(Bimonthly)
Dempa Publications
1-11-15, Higashi Gotanda, Shinagawa-ku
Tokyo 141
Tel: (3) 3445-6111

Asian Electricity
(11 per year)
Reed Business Publishing Ltd.
5001 Beach Rd., #06-12 Golden Mile Complex
Singapore 0719
Tel: [65] 2913188 Fax: [65] 2913180

Asian Electronics Engineer
(Monthly)
Trade Media Ltd.
29 Wong Chuck Hang Road
Hong Kong
Tel: [852] 5554777 Fax: [852] 8700816

Asian Sources: Electronic Components
(Monthly)
Asian Sources Media Group
22nd Fl., Vita Tower
29 Wong Chuk Hang Road
Wong Chuk Hang, Hong Kong
Tel: [852] 5554777 Fax: [852] 8730488

Electronic Business Asia
(Monthly)
Cahners Publishing Company
275 Washington St.
Newton, MA 02158, USA
Tel: [1] (617) 964-3030 Fax: [1] (617) 558-4506

Japan Electronic Buyers' Guide
(Annual)
Dempa Publications Inc.
11-15, Higashi Gotanda 1-chome
Shinagawa-ku
Tokyo 141
Tel: (3) 3445-6111 Fax: (3) 3445-6101

JEI, Journal of the Electronics Industry
(Monthly)
Dempa Publications, Inc.
1-11-15, Higashi Gotanda, Shinagawa-ku
Tokyo 141
Tel: (3) 3445-6111

Journal of Electronic Engineering
Dempa Publications, Inc.
1-11-15, Higashi Gotanda, Shinagawa-ku
Tokyo 141
Tel: (3) 3445-6111

Trade Fairs

Refer to the Trade Fair chapter for complete listings, including contact information, dates, and venues. Trade fairs with particular relevance to this industry include the following, which are listed in that chapter under the heading given below:

Electronic, Electric & Communication Equipment
- Automotive Electronis Show (Automotive Design & Development Show)
- Chubu Electronics Show
- Communications TOKYO
- DISKCON JAPAN International Exhibition and Symposium on Disk and Disk Drive Manufacturing
- Electrical Construction Exhibition
- EMC JAPAN Exhibition for Solutions on Electromagnetic Interference
- Equipment Exhibition of Motion Picture & Television
- Fineprocess Technology Japan
- Frontier Technology Fair (tentative name)
- Insulation
- International Broadcast Equipment Exhibition (InterBEE)
- Internepcon Japan
- Internepcon Osaka
- Inter Opto
- International Optoelectronics Exhibition
- Japan Electronics Show
- JPCA Show
- Microwave USA
- Power Supply Japan-Japan Switching Power Supply Technology Exhibition
- SEMICON/Japan
- SEMICON/Kansai-Kyoto
- SEMICON/Yokahama
- Supercomputing Japan-International High-Performance Computing Exhibition and Conference
- Telecom Japan
- Tokyo Professional Audio Show

For other trade fairs that may be of interest, we recommend that you also consult the headings Computer & Information Industries; Factory Automation; Furniture & Housewares; Machines & Instruments; and Tools.

FOOD AND BEVERAGES

Agriculture and fishing account for about 2.5 percent of Japan's national income, but both industries are domestically oriented. Japan holds a 15 percent share of the world's total fish catch, with a fleet of over 150,000 boats, and it has one of the world's top five whaling industries. Food processing constitutes one of the country's largest industries, with over 300,000 companies involved. Processed foods are among Japan's top five exports.

Agricultural Products Japanese farms are relatively small and highly labor-intensive, although farm technology and mechanization are advanced. Rice farming is the mainstay of the agricultural industry, but potatoes, cabbages, vegetables, sugar cane and beets, melons, citrus fruits, wheat, barley, soy beans, and tea are also cultivated. Farm populations are declining, with resulting drops in production and in Japan's share of its own markets.

Fisheries

Most of Japan's fresh and processed fish is sold domestically. Major fishing fleets are located in Hachinohe, Hokkaido, and Nagasaki. Processed fish are produced largely in Shizuoka and Aichi Prefectures.

Products Tuna is a significant export of Japan's food processing industry. Japanese-processed tuna exports include fresh, canned, airtight preserved, and frozen yellowfin and albacore. Canned tuna is packed in oil or water. Major export markets for Japanese-processed tuna are in Guam, Puerto Rico, Brazil, China, Taiwan, Hong Kong, Canada, Switzerland, Belgium, and the United States, as well as countries throughout Southeast Asia, Africa, the South Pacific, and the Middle East.

Other significant Japanese-processed fish products include dried, semi-dried, canned, and plastic-sealed mackerel, pollack, pilchards, cod, salmon, sardines, scallops, squid, clams, sea snails, shrimp, eel, and butterfish, some of which is processed using frozen imported fish. Japan's fish processing industry also supplies a substantial amount of dried seaweed, most of which is imported from Chile, Spain, and Portugal and is sold to domestic markets.

Japan's freshwater aquaculture produces primarily rainbow trout and tilapia, which are consumed domestically with only a few exports to Taiwan. Inshore aquaculture fisheries also produce squid, clams, crustaceans, shallow-water fish, and dolphins.

Competitive Situation

Japan's fishing industry is suffering from shrinking resources and catch areas, as well as from high cooperation fees for fishing in Russian waters. Salmon fishing is banned in some coastal waters, and fishing in Russian waters is limited to specific allocations. By international agreement, pollack fishing in the Bering Sea is restricted, and a moratorium exists on drift net fishing and high-seas salmon fishing. Sardines are also in short supply. As a result of fishing cutbacks, Japan's fish processing industry is facing shortages of fish stock, including squid, which are commonly caught by means of drift nets.

Larger fishing vessels continue to operate under joint ventures and agreements in distant waters along Peru's coast, in the Southeast Pacific, in the Indian and Atlantic Oceans, and within the Mediterranean, but smaller fishing vessels are unable to reach these distant fishing grounds. The Japanese government has offered to reimburse boat owners for scrapping their vessels. Those owners who remain in business face high costs for retraining crews and refitting ships to meet international regulations. In an effort to save the fishing economy, some Japanese port areas are developing coastal aquaculture, raising and farming oysters, seaweed, scallops, and coho salmon. Miyagi is one of Japan's leaders in the development of aquaculture.

Processed Foods Japanese food processors offer a broad variety of products, ranging from traditional food items (miso, tofu, soy sauce) to dairy products, frozen foods, and alcoholic beverages. Faced with growing competition from imports into domestic markets, Japan's food processors have shifted to higher-quality exportable products and have become more responsive to both domestic and foreign consumer preferences and dietary trends. Several major food processing companies are building new facilities and expanding existing ones. These firms are also investing in R&D for biotechnology to boost food production and new products aimed at health-conscious consumers. Some firms are experimenting with high-pressure processes that cook and pasteurize foods while preserving flavor and aroma. Other processes under development modify acidity in citrus drinks and other beverages.

Government Agencies

Food Agency
2-1, Kasumigaseki 1-chome, Chiyoda-ku
Tokyo 100
Tel: (3) 3502-8111

Ministry of Agriculture, Forestry and Fisheries
1-2-1, Kasumigaseki 1-chome, Chiyoda-ku
Tokyo 100
Tel: (3) 3502-8111

Ministry of Health & Welfare
2-1, Kasumigaseki 1-chome, Chiyoda-ku
Tokyo 100
Tel: (3) 3502-7111, 3503-1711, 3508-7527

Trade Organizations

All Japan Coffee Association
5th Fl., Kitamura Building
17-15, Nishi Shimbashi 1-chome, Minato-ku
Tokyo 105
Tel: (3) 3580-9870 Fax: (3) 3580-1516

Beer Breweries Foundation of Japan
Showa Building
8-18, Kyobashi 2-chome, Chuo-ku
Tokyo 104
Tel: (3) 3561-8386

Brewing Society of Japan
6-30, Takinogawa 2-chome, Kita-ku
Tokyo 114
Tel: (3) 3910-3853 Fax: (3) 3910-3748

Central Association of Livestock Industry
Zenkoku Choson Kaikan
11-35, Nagata-cho 1-chome, Chiyoda-ku
Tokyo 100
Tel: (3) 3581-6676 Fax: (3) 5511-8205

Coffee Importers' Association of Japan
c/o Marubeni Corp.
4-2, Ote-machi 1-chome, Chiyoda-ku
Tokyo 100-88
Tel: (3) 3282-4775 Fax: (3) 3282-7372

Flour Millers Association
15-6, Nihombashi Kabuto-cho, Chuo-ku
Tokyo 103
Tel: (3) 3667-1011 Fax: (3) 3667-1673

Food and Nutrition Association
Sin Kokusai Building
4-1, Marunouchi 3-chome, Chiyoda-ku
Tokyo 100
Tel: (3) 3211-5628 Fax: (3) 3211-5629

Grain Importers Association
1-16, Nihombashi 2-chome, Chuo-ku
Tokyo 103
Tel: (3) 3274-0172 Fax: (3) 3274-0177

Import Molasses Conference
Toranomon Jitsugyo Kaikan
1-20, Toranomon 1-chome, Minato-ku
Tokyo 105
Tel: (3) 3591-8729 Fax: (3) 3591-8729

Japan Agricultural Products Exporters' Association
Arai Building
10-7, Shimbashi 2-chome, Minato-ku
Tokyo 105
Tel: (3) 3591-8323 Fax: (3) 3508-2335

Japan Banana Importers Association
5th Fl., Zenkyoren Building
7-9, Hirakawa-cho 2-chome, Chiyoda-ku
Tokyo 102
Tel: (3) 3263-0461 Fax: (3) 3263-0463

Japan Brewing Machinery Industry Association
Todoroki Kanda Building
21, Kanda Nishiki-cho 1-chome, Chiyoda-ku
Tokyo 101
Tel: (3) 3291-9383 Fax: (3) 3291-9383

Japan Canned Foods Exporters' Association
Fuji Building, 6 Fl.
5-3, Yaesu 1-chome, Chuo-ku
Tokyo 103
Tel: (3) 3281-5341 Fax: (3) 3281-5344

Japan Citrus Fruits Importers Association
Kinoshita Building
8-10, Kyobashi 2-chome, Chuo-ku
Tokyo 104
Tel: (3) 3561-1366 Fax: (3) 3535-6620

Japan Confectionery Importers Association
c/o Meidiya Co. Ltd.
2-8, Kyobashi 2-chome, Chuo-ku
Tokyo 104
Tel: (3) 3271-9518 Fax: (3) 3274-4890

Japan Convenience Foods Industry Association
Kimura Building
5-5, Alakusabashi 5-chome, Taito-ku
Tokyo 111
Tel: (3) 3865-0811 Fax: (3) 3865-0815

Japan Dairy Products Association
6th Fl., Komodo Kudan Building
14-19, Kudan-Kita 1-chome, Chiyoda-ku
Tokyo 102
Tel: (3) 3264-4131 Fax: (3) 3264-4139

Japan Dried Fruits Importers Association
c/o Shoei Foods Corp.
7, Akihabara 5-chome, Taito-ku
Tokyo 110
Tel: (3) 3253-1231 Fax: (3) 5256-1914

Japan Eel Importers Association
Shuhosha Building
6, Nihombashi Muromachi 1-chome, Chuo-ku
Tokyo 103
Tel: (3) 3279-2501 Fax: (3) 3279-2516

Japan Export Frozen Marine Products Association
Rm. 206, Chuo Mansion
1-5, Arai 1-chome, Nakano-ku
Tokyo 165
Tel: (3) 3386-4358 Fax: (3) 3386-4234

Japan Feed Trade Association
Koizumi Building
3-13, Ginza 4-chome, Chuo-ku
Tokyo 104
Tel: (3) 3563-6441 Fax: (3) 3567-2297

Japan Fisheries Association
Sankaido Building
9-13, Akasaka 1-chome, Minato-ku
Tokyo 107
Tel: (3) 3587-2551, 3585-6681/3
Fax: (3) 3582-2337

Japan Foodstuff Association
c/o Nihon Nogyo Kenhyusho
3, Kioicho, Chiyoda-ku
Tokyo 102
Tel: (3) 3265-4917

Japan Frozen Foods Exporters' Association
Rm. 206, Chuo Mansion
1-5, Arai 1-chome, Nakano-ku
Tokyo 165
Tel: (3) 3386-4116 Fax: (3) 3386-4234

Japan Livestock Dealers Association
Baji Chikusan Kaikan
2, Kanda Surugadai 1-chome, Chiyoda-ku
Tokyo 101
Tel: (3) 3291-9394 Fax: (3) 3291-0126

Japan LiveStock Traders Association
6th Fl., Osakaya Building
1-9, Mita 3-chome, Minato-ku
Tokyo 108
Tel: (3) 3454-1435 Fax: (3) 3453-7095

Japan Marine Products Importers Association
Yurakucho Building
10-1, Yuraku-cho 1-chome, Chiyoda-ku
Tokyo 100
Tel: (3) 3214-3407 Fax: (3) 3214-3408

Japan Oil & Fat Importers & Exporters Association
Kyodo Building (Shin Horidome)
10-12, Nihonbashi, Horidome-cho 1-chome
Chuo-ku
Tokyo 103
Tel: (3) 3662-9821 Fax: (3) 3667-7867

Japan Oil Meal & Vitamin Exporters' Association
Kyodo Building (Shin Horidome)
10-12, Nihombashi, Horidome-cho 1-chome
Chuo-ku
Tokyo 103
Tel: (3) 3662-9823 Fax: (3) 3667-7867

Japan Sake Brewers Association
1-21, Nishi Shimbashi 1-chome, Minato-ku
Tokyo 105
Tel: (3) 3501-0101 Fax: (03) 3501-6018

Japan Sheep Casing Importers Association
Yoshinoya Building
32-6, Nishi Gotanda 1-chome, Shinagawa-ku
Tokyo 141
Tel: (3) 3493-6301 Fax: (3) 3491-1772

Japan Soft Drinks Bottlers Association
4-17, Koishikawa 2-chome, Bunkyo-ku
Tokyo 112
Tel: (3) 3814-0666

Japan Spirits & Liquors Makers Association
Koura Dai 1 Building
1-6, Nihombashi Kayaba-cho 1-chome
Chuo-ku
Tokyo 103
Tel: (3) 3668-4621 Fax: (3) 3668-7077

Japan Sprouting Bean Importers Association
Dai-ichi Suzumaru Building
39-8, Nishishimbashi 2-chome, Minato-ku
Tokyo 105
Tel: (3) 3431-3895 Fax: (3) 3431-3882

Japan Sugar Import & Export Council [The Japan]
Ginza Gas Hall
9-15, Ginza 7-chome, Chuo-ku
Tokyo 104
Tel: (3) 3571-2362 Fax: (3) 3571-2363

Japan Sugar Refiners' Association
5-7, Sambancho, Chiyoda-ku
Tokyo 102
Tel: (3) 3262-0176, 3288-1511 Fax: (3) 3288-3399

Japan Tea Association
2-9-12, Higashi Shinbashi, Minato-ku
Tokyo 105
Tel: (3) 3431-6711 Fax: (3) 3431-6711

Japan Tea Exporters' Association
81, Kitaban-cho
Shizuoka, Shizuoka Pref. 420
Tel: (54) 271-3428 Fax: (54) 252-0331
Tlx: 20331

Japan Wine and Spirits Importers' Association
Dai-ichi Tentoku Building
13-5, Toranomon 1-chome, Minato-ku
Tokyo 105
Tel: (3) 3503-6505 Fax: (3) 3503-6504

National Dairy Association
Nyugyo Kaikan
3, Kioicho, Chiyoda-ku
Tokyo 102
Tel: (3) 3264-4131

Tuna Packers' Association of Japan
3rd Fl., N.P. One Building
5-6, Ueno 3-chome, Taito-ku
Tokyo 110
Tel: (3) 3832-3150 Fax: (3) 3832-3165

Directories/Publications

Asia Pacific Food Industry
(Monthly)
Asia Pacific Food Industry Publications
24 Peck Sea St., #03-00 Nehsons Building
Singapore 0207
Tel: [65] 2223422 Fax: [65] 2225587

Asia Pacific Food Industry Business Report
(Monthly)
Asia Pacific Food Industry Publications
24 Peck Sea St., #03-00 Nehsons Building
Singapore 0207
Tel: [65] 2223422 Fax: [65] 2225587

Food Industry (Shokuhin Kogyo)
(Semimonthly; Japanese)
Korin Publishing Co.
P.O. Box 41, Shitaya
Tokyo 110-91

Gateux/Gatou
(Monthly; Japanese)
Federation of Japan Confectionery Associations
10-26, Ebisu 1-chome, Shibuya-ku
Tokyo 150
Tel: (3) 3444-8711 Fax: (3) 3444-8935

Statistical Yearbook of Ministry of Agriculture, Forestry and Fisheries (Norin Suisansho Tokeihyo) (Annual)
Norin Tokei Kyokai
c/o Otori Building
11-14, Meguro 2-chome, Meguro-ku
Tokyo 153
Tel: (3) 3492-2942

Trade Fairs

Refer to the Trade Fair chapter for complete listings, including contact information, dates, and venues. Trade fairs with particular relevance to this industry include the following, which are listed in that chapter under the headings given below.

Agriculture, Forestry & Fisheries
- Agriculture Technology Exhibition
- HI-TECH HORTI-MATION International Horticultural Exhibition

Food, Beverages & Food Processing
- Beer & Spirits
- Better Confectionery Show
- CATEREX JAPAN: Japan Food Catering & Equipment Exhibition
- International Confectionery Tokyo
- International Food & Beverage Exhibition and Conference for Japan and Asia (FOODEX JAPAN)
- Japan Foodservice Show
- MOBAC SHOW Osaka International Food & Beverage Exhibition
- Supermarket Trade Show
- Tokyo International Sea Food Show
- Wine Japan—International Wine, Spirits, Beers and Beverages Exhibition and Convention

For other trade fairs that may be of interest, we recommend that you also consult the headings Medicine & Pharmaceuticals and Packaging; Printing & Papers.

HOUSEHOLD APPLIANCES AND PHOTOGRAPHIC EQUIPMENT

Japan is a top world supplier of refrigeration and air conditioning equipment. Exports of other household appliances account for less than 25 percent of Japan's appliance production. Japan's camera production and exports dominate world markets, and over 70 percent of Japan's production of photographic equipment is exported.

Household Appliances Of Japanese-made household appliances, significant exports include washing machines, microwave ovens, rice cookers, bread makers, and assorted small consumer appliances.

Japanese firms that produce consumer appliances are attempting to increase sales in an already saturated market by shifting to higher added-value products, improving quality, and discovering new areas of consumer demand. Some manufacturers have moved production facilities offshore to reduce deficit exports and trade friction.

Refrigeration Equipment Japan has approximately 20 refrigeration equipment manufacturers, five of which account for about 70 percent of production. These firms produce household appliances, commercial and industrial refrigeration devices, and vehicle air conditioning equipment. Exports nearly doubled in 1992, accounting for approximately 30 percent of production value. Major export markets are in Asia and the Middle East.

Products include commercial and household freezers and refrigerators, water coolers, ice makers, refrigerating display cases, and freezing, refrigerating, and condensing units. Residential air conditioning units are available in a variety of models, such as window units, small two-piece units, dehumidifiers, and central air conditioning equipment. Large industrial cooling systems include package-type equipment, fan coil units, air cleaners, total heat exchangers, and clean-room coolers for computer rooms and test facilities.

Faced with serious environmental concerns over freon coolants that produce chlorofluorocarbons, Japan's refrigeration manufacturers are producing equipment that uses alternative coolants. To remain competitive in world markets despite rising labor costs and labor shortages, Japan's refrigeration producers are investing in facilities and joint ventures in other Asian countries.

Photographic Equipment Japan's producers of photographic equipment offer a broad array of cameras and related goods: manual cameras, automatic cameras with multiple features, lenses and flash accessories, tripods and other stands, and film. Faced with declining production and exports because of the rising value of the yen, Japanese camera makers have introduced new models with innovative features. Japan's photographic equipment suppliers are diversifying into new product lines and markets to remain competitive with lower-priced cameras produced in other Asian countries.

Trade Organizations

Japan Battery and Appliance Industries Association
No. 9 Mori Building
2-2, Atago 1-chome, Minato-ku
Tokyo 1-5
Tel: (3) 3436-2471 Fax: (3) 3436-2617

Japan Brush Manufacturers Association
10-6, Ebisu Nishi 3-chome, Naniwa-ku
Osaka 556
Tel: (6) 643-1887 Fax: (6) 643-1888

Japan Camera Industry Association
JCII Building
25, Ichiban-cho, Chiyoda-ku
Tokyo 102
Tel: (3) 5276-3891 Fax: (3) 5276-3893

Japan Ceramic Tile Manufacturers' Association
39-18, Daikan-cho, Higashi-ku
Nagoya 461
Tel: (52) 935-7235 Fax: (52) 935-4072

Japan Housing Equipment & System Association
23 Mori Building
23-7, Toranomon 1-chome, Minato-ku
Tokyo 105
Tel: (3) 3503-4546 Fax: (3) 3503-4540

Japan Motion Picture Equipment Industrial
Association
Kikai Shinko Building
5-8, Shiba Koen 3-chome, Minato-ku
Tokyo 105
Tel: (3) 3434-3911 Fax: (3) 3434-3912

Japan Pottery Exporters' Association
Nihon Tojiki Center
39-18, Daikan-cho, Higashi-ku
Nagoya 461
Tel: (52) 935-7232 Fax: (52) 936-8424

Japan Pottery Manufacturers' Federation
Toto Building
1-28, Toranomon 1-chome, Minato-ku
Tokyo
Tel: (3) 3503-6761

Japan Refrigeration and Air-Conditioning Industry
Association
Kikai Shinko Kaikan
5-8, Shibakoen 3-chome, Minato-ku
Tokyo 105
Tel: (3) 3432-1671 Fax: (3) 3438-0308

Japan Stainless Steel Exporters' Association
Tekko Kaikan
16, Nihombashi Kayabacho 3-chome
Chiyoda-ku
Tokyo 103
Tel: (3) 3669-0871, 3669-4431

Publication

Asian Sources: Gifts & Home Products
(Monthly)
Asian Sources Media Group
22nd Fl., Vita Tower
29 Wong Chuk Hang Road
Wong Chuk Hang, Hong Kong
Tel: [852] 5554777 Fax: [852] 8730488

Trade Fairs

Refer to the Trade Fair chapter for complete listings, including contact information, dates, and venues. Trade fairs with particular relevance to this industry include the following, which are listed in that chapter under the headings given below:

Construction & Housing
- JAPAN HOME SHOW International Building Materials & Interiors Exhibition
- Kobe International Home Fair
- Tokyo International Good Living Show
- West Japan Total Living Show

Furniture & Housewares
- Aichi Superior Furniture Exhibition
- International Furniture Fair Tokyo
- International Glassware Show
- International Housewares Show Tokyo
- Internationale Frankfurter Messe Asia
- JAPAN DIY SHOW in OSAKA
- JAPAN DIY-HC SHOW
- JAPANTEX
- Lifestyle

Hobbies, Recreation & Travel
- Photo Accessory & Imaging System Show (Nagoya)
- Photo Accessory & Imaging System Show (Osaka)
- Photo Accessory & Imaging System Show (Tokyo)

Tools: Precision & Optical Equipment
- International Professional Photo Fair

For other trade fairs that may be of interest, we recommend that you also consult the headings Electronic, Electric & Communication Equipment; and Gifts, Jewelry & Stationery.

INDUSTRIAL CHEMICALS, MINERALS, AND MATERIALS

Industrial chemical, mineral, and material products are among Japan's top five exports. The principal exports are iron, steel, and industrial chemicals, a large portion of which are shipped to Southeast Asia, China, Europe, and the United States.

Agrochemicals Japan's agrochemical production is domestically oriented; less than 20 percent of output is shipped overseas. However, declining domestic markets have led manufacturers to boost exports. Agrochemical products made in Japan include insecticides, fungicides, and herbicides. Most of Japan's agrochemical producers are relatively small firms.

The domestic agrochemical market has declined substantially in recent years because Japanese agriculture is facing three major crises. First, the government's liberalization of food imports, including imports of rice, has created stiffer competition in the domestic market. Second, substantial decreases in farm population because of severe labor conditions has resulted in the Japanese government's promotion of larger-scale, more cost-efficient rice farming operations; these policies, in turn, have decreased the number of agrochemical consumers. Third, growing consumer awareness of environmental and health issues related to the use of pesticides has slowed sales of agrochemicals and has made farmers more selective in their purchases.

In response to falling domestic demand, Japanese agrochemical firms have become more aggressive in international markets, and exports are rising rapidly. Producers are also shifting product lines to agrochemicals that are safer and more efficient. Although production has declined, these firms are sustaining their profits by manufacturing specialty chemicals, such as hormone-based insecticides that regulate insect behavior or growth and highly concentrated, lightweight, jumbo-granule herbicides. Profit margins for smaller agrochemical producers have been low because these firms have had to invest substantial funds in R&D for high value-added products and in replacement of a complex and inefficient distribution system. To increase profit margins and to become more competitive in global markets, some Japanese agrochemical firms have entered into joint ventures and technology transfer arrangements with foreign companies. Other manufacturers have focused on developing products to fill market niches that are largely ignored by foreign competitors.

Fine Ceramics Development of high-tech industrial ceramics is being undertaken by a few Japanese firms, primarily centered in Kagoshima. These materials are relatively new, and widespread usage has been impeded by their relatively high cost. However, applications are growing in the vehicle industry for Japanese ceramic materials made of silicon nitride, used in manufacturing engine parts, gas turbine blades, and other parts exposed to high temperatures. Japan's electronic firms are also using domestically produced fine ceramics of aluminum nitride, which help prevent overheating in such densely integrated devices as printed circuit boards.

Petrochemicals Japan's petrochemical industry supplies domestic and foreign markets with such chemical products as polystyrene (mainly used to produce audiovisual equipment), vinyl chloride, and polyvinyl resins for agricultural and plumbing purposes.

Japan's petrochemical industry is suffering a major decline because global markets are oversupplied with one of its major chemical products, ethylene, used in medicine, agricultural chemicals, and organic chemical manufacture. Production has been drastically cut as demand has fallen throughout major industry sectors that consume ethylene-based products. Tight competition in worldwide ethylene markets intensified in 1992 when Korean companies began producing an additional two million tons of ethylene. Some Japanese firms have closed plants, and construction plans for new facilities have been delayed. Increases in plastic exports to China and Southeast Asia have not been sufficient to turn around Japan's petrochemical industry.

Steel The number one country in steel production, Japan has a diversified steel industry which includes both large blast-furnace integrated-steel makers and smaller electric-furnace mini-mills. Mini-mills account for at least 30 percent of Japan's crude steel output. Major steel products include concrete reinforcing bars, H-beams, and hot rolled coils. Exports, which account for only a small percentage of total output, are shipped primarily to China and Southeast Asia.

Declining sales and sharply falling profits have forced Japan's integrated steel producers to slash capital investment plans and to rationalize labor costs. Much of this decline is attributed to shrinking domestic demand for steel from the construction and automobile industries. Japan's integrated steel industry, which is land-intensive, is further burdened by land tax policies, which were initially implemented to discourage land price speculation and increase the supply of land. Moreover, some of Japan's steel producers have faced anti-dumping charges and duties imposed by the United States, resulting in a decline of exports to US firms. Japanese steel companies subsequently diverted much of their exports to Southeast Asia, but profits have been eroded by increased competition from Korean and Taiwanese steel exports. Environmental concerns are also adding to the costs for Japanese integrated steel makers. Several of the major steelmakers are exploring diversification into aluminum, hoping to capture the increasing demands of vehicle manufacturers for lighter weight, easily recyclable materials.

In contrast to integrated-steel producers, Japan's mini-mills have become more competitive because of technological and economic factors that favor electric-furnace manufacturers: ferrous scrap prices have declined steeply since 1992, enabling mini-mills to cut production costs in half. Mini-mills also require less land, smaller workforces, and simpler management structures. When prices fall, these mills have acted to avoid excessive competition and have reduced output, rather than expanding capacity to make up for lower profit margins. In response to import competition from South Korea and China, Japan's mini-mills have adopted technological innovations to reduce production costs.

The Japanese government has instituted programs to stimulate demand for steel, but mini-mills are the main beneficiaries because much of this additional demand will be for relatively low value-added construction materials, most of which are produced by the mini-mills, not the integrated-steel producers.

Government Agencies

Agency of Natural Resources and Energy
3-1, Kasumigaseki 1-chome, Chiyoda-ku
Tokyo 100
Tel: (3) 3501-1511

Environmental Agency
1-2-2, Kasumigaseki 3-chome, Chiyoda-ku
Tokyo 100
Tel: (3) 3581-3351

Trade Organizations

Aluminum Products Association
13-13, Akasaka 2-chome, Minato-ku
Tokyo 107
Tel: (3) 3583-7971 Fax: (3) 3589-4574

Artificial Abrasive Industrial Association
2-6, Kasumigaseki 3-chome, Chiyoda-ku
Tokyo 100
Tel: (3) 3580-0866 Fax: (3) 3580-0867

Asbestos Cement Products Association
Takahashi Building
10-8-7, Ginza, Chuo-ku
Tokyo
Tel: (3) 3571-1359

Association of Petrochemical Industries
Iino Building
1-1, Uchisaiwaicho 2-chome, Chiyoda-ku
Tokyo 100
Tel: (3) 3501-2151

Atomic Energy Commission
2-1, Kasumigaseki 2-chome, Chiyoda-ku
Tokyo 100
Tel: (3) 3581-2585

Ceramic Society of Japan
22-17, Hyakunincho 2-chome, Shinjuku-ku
Tokyo 160
Tel: (3) 3362-5231

Federation of Japan LP-Gas Associations
Sogo No. 6 Building
4-12, Hirakawacho 1-chome, Chiyoda-ku
Tokyo 102
Tel: (3) 3264-3457

Japan Aluminum Federation
Nihombashi Asahi Seimei-kan
1-3, Nihombashi 2-chome, Chuo-ku
Tokyo 103
Tel: (3) 3274-4551 Fax: (3) 3274-3179

Japan Asbestos Products Industrial Association
Tomono Honsha Building
12-4, Ginza 7-chome, Chuo-ku
Tokyo 104
Tel: (3) 3541-4584 Fax: (3) 3541-4958

Japan Asphalt Association
6-7, Toranomon 2-chome, Minato-ku
Tokyo 105
Tel: (3) 3502-3956 Fax: (3) 3502-3376

Japan Brass Makers' Association
12-22, Tsukiji 1-chome, Chuo-ku
Tokyo
Tel: (3) 3542-6551 Fax: (3) 3542-6556

Japan Carbon Association
Tokyo Kaijo Building
Shinkan, 2-1, Marunouchi 1-chome
Chiyoda-ku
Tokyo 100
Tel: (3) 3213-3488 Fax: (3) 3212-4490

Japan Cement Association
Hattori Building
10-3, Kyobashi 1-chome, Chuo-ku
Tokyo 104
Tel: (3) 3561-8632 Fax: (3) 3567-8570

Japan Cement Exporters Association
Hattori Building
1, Kyobashi 1-chome, Chuo-ku
Tokyo 104
Tel: (3) 3561-1030

Japan Chemical Exporters' Association
Nihon Shuzo Kaikan
1-21, Nishi Shimbashi 1-chome, Minato-ku
Tokyo 105
Tel: (3) 3504-1801 Fax: (3) 3595-3344

Japan Chemical Importers' Association
Nihon Shuzo Kaikan
1-21, Nishi Shimbashi 1-chome, Minato-ku
Tokyo 105
Tel: (3) 3501-1304 Fax: (3) 3595-3344

Japan Chemical Industry Association
Tokyo Club Building
2-6, Kasumigaseki 3-chome, Chiyoda-ku
Tokyo 100
Tel: (3) 3580-0751 Fax: (3) 3580-0764

Japan Coal Association
Hibiya Park Building
18-1, Yuraku-cho, Chiyoda-ku
Tokyo 100
Tel: (3) 3214-0581

Japan Coke Association
15-12, Toranomon 1-chome, Minato-ku
Tokyo 105
Tel: (3) 3502-0581 Fax: (3) 3502-0584

Japan Copper Development Association
Konwa Building
12-22, Tsukiji 1-chome, Chuo-ku
Tokyo 104
Tel: (3) 3542-6631

Japan Galvanized Iron Sheet Exporters'
Association
Tekko Kaikan
2-10, Nihombashi Kayaba-cho 3-chome
Chuo-ku
Tokyo 103
Tel: (3) 3669-5331 Fax: (3) 3669-6685

Japan Gas Association
15-12, Toranomon 1-chome, Minato-ku
Tokyo 105
Tel: (3) 3502-0111/6
Fax: (3) 3502-0013, 3502-3676

Japan Inorganic Chemical Industry Association
6th Fl., Haiji Nihonbashi Building
9-9, Nihonbashi Kodenma-cho, Chuo-ku
Tokyo 103
Tel: (3) 5640-1648 Fax: (3) 5640-2368

Japan Iron & Steel Exporters' Association
Tekko Kaikan
2-10, Nihombashi Kayaba-cho 3-chome
Chuo-ku
Tokyo 103
Tel: (3) 3669-4811 Fax: (3) 3667-0245

Japan Iron and Steel Federation
Keidanren Kaikan
9-4, Otemachi 1-chome, Chiyoda-ku
Tokyo 100
Tel: (3) 3279-3611 Fax: (3) 3245-0144

Japan Iron & Steel Scrap Importers Association
Fuji Building
5-3, Yaesu 1-chome, Chuo-ku
Tokyo 103
Tel: (3) 3201-7906 Fax: (3) 3281-3674

Japan Iron and Steel Wholesalers' Association
Tekko Kaikan
16, Nihombashi Kayabacho 3-chome
Chiyoda-ku
Tokyo 103
Tel: (3) 3669-5861

Japan Light Metal Association
Nihombashi Asahi Seimei Building
1-3, Nihombashi 2-chome, Chuo-ku
Tokyo 103
Tel: (3) 3273-3041 Fax: (3) 3213-2918

Japan Mining Industry Association
Shin Hibiya Building
3-6, Uchisaiwaicho 1-chome, Chiyoda-ku
Tokyo 100
Tel: (3) 3502-7451 Fax: (3) 3591-9841

Japan Natural Gas Association
No. 5 Mori Building
17-1, Toranomon 1-chome, Minato-ku
Tokyo 105
Tel: (3) 3501-1396 Fax: (3) 3501-1398

Japan Non-Ferrous Metal Exporters' Association
c/o Nihon Shindo Kyokai
Konwa Building
12-22, Tsukiji 1-chome, Chuo-ku
Tokyo 104
Tel: (3) 3542-6551 Fax: (3) 3542-6556

Japan Petroleum Development Association
Keidanren Kaikan
9-4, Otemachi 1-chome, Chiyoda-ku
Tokyo 100
Tel: (3) 3279-5841 Fax: (3) 3279-5844 Tlx: 29400

Japan Polyethylene Products Industry Association
Kyoei Building
15-17, Nihombashi Kofune-cho, Chuo-ku
Tokyo 103
Tel: (3) 3661-3834 Fax: (3) 3661-3849

Japan P.V.C. Association
Iino Building
1-1, Uchisaiwai-cho 2-chome, Chiyoda-ku
Tokyo 100
Tel: (3) 3506-5481 Fax: (3) 3506-5487

Japan Rubber Importers Association
Tosen Building
10-8, Nihombashi, Horidome-cho 1-chome
Chuo-ku
Tokyo 103
Tel: (3) 3666-1460 Fax: (3) 3668-8462

Japan Steel Constructors Association
2-18, Ginza 2-chome, Chuo-ku
Tokyo 104
Tel: (3) 3535-5078 Fax: (3) 3562-4657

Japan Society of Chemical Engineers
Kyoritsu Kaikan
6-19, Kohinata 4-chome, Bunkyo-ku
Tokyo 112
Tel: (3) 3943-3527

Japan Special Steel Exporters' Association
2-10, Nihombashi Kayaba-cho 3-chome
Chuo-ku
Tokyo 103
Tel: (3) 3669-2631 Fax: (3) 3668-1540

Japan Stainless Steel Exporters' Association
Tekko Kaikan
16, Nihombashi Kayabacho 3-chome
Chiyoda-ku
Tokyo 103
Tel: (3) 3669-0871, 3669-4431

National Agricultural Chemical Wholesalers Union
Zen-Noyaku Building
3-4, Uchikanda 3-chome, Chiyoda-ku
Tokyo 101
Tel: (3) 3254-4171

National Petroleum Dealers Association
Sekiyu Kaikan
17-14, Nagata-cho 2-chome, Chiyoda-ku
Tokyo 100
Tel: (3) 3593-5771 Fax: (3) 3597-1712

Nippon Cast Iron Foundry Association
Kikai Shinko Kaikan
5-8, Shiba Koen 3-chome, Minato-ku
Tokyo 105
Tel: (3) 3432-2991

Petroleum Association of Japan
Keidanren Kaikan
9-4, Otemachi 1-chome, Chiyoda-ku
Tokyo 100
Tel: (3) 3279-3811

Petroleum Producers' Association of Japan
Keidanren Kaikan
9-4, Otemachi 1-chome, Chiyoda-ku
Tokyo 100
Tel: (3) 3279-5841

Society of Agricultural Chemical Industry
Nihombashi Club Kaikan
5-8, Nihombashi Muro-machi, 1-chome
Chuo-ku
Tokyo 103
Tel: (3) 3241-0215 Fax: (3) 3241-3149

Society of Synthetic Organic Chemistry, Japan
Kagaku Kaikan
5, Kanda Surugadai 1-chome, Chiyoda-ku
Tokyo 101
Tel: (3) 3292-7621 Fax: (3) 3294-7622

Steel Castings & Forgings Association of Japan
Tekko Building
8-2, Marunouchi 1-chome, Chiyoda-ku
Tokyo 100
Tel: (3) 3201-0461 Fax: (3) 3211-6903

Directories/Publications

Asian Oil & Gas
(Monthly)
Intercontinental Marketing Corp.
P.O. Box 5056
Tokyo 100-31
Fax: (3) 3667-9646

Asian Plastic News
(Quarterly)
Reed Asian Publishing Pte. Ltd.
5001 Beach Rd.
#06-12 Golden Mile Complex
Singapore 0719
Tel: [65] 2913188 Fax: [65] 2913180

Chemical Industry
(Monthly)
Maruzen Company Ltd.
3-10, Nihonbashi 2-chome, Chuo-ku
Tokyo 103
Tel: (3) 3272-7211 Fax: (3) 3274-3238

Japan Chemical Annual
(Annual)
Chemical Daily Company Ltd.
3-16-8, Nihonbashi Hama-cho, Chuo-ku
Tokyo 103
Tel: (3) 3663-7932 Fax: (3) 3663-2530

Japan Chemical Week
(Weekly)
Chemical Daily Company Ltd.
3-16-8, Nihonbashi, Hama-cho, Chuo-ku
Tokyo 103
Tel: (3) 3663-7932 Fax: (3) 3663-2530

Japan Chemical Directory
(Annual)
Chemical Daily Company Ltd.
3-16-8, Nihonbashi Hama-cho, Chuo-ku
Tokyo 103
Tel: (3) 3663-7932 Fax: (3) 3663-2530

Japan Petroleum & Energy Trends
(Biweekly)
Japan Petroleum & Energy Consultants Ltd.
CPO Box 1185
Tokyo 100-91
Tel: (4) 7573-1931 Fax: (4) 7573-1934

Japan Plastics Age
(Monthly)
Plastics Age Company Ltd.
10-6, Kajicho 1-chome, Chiyoda-ku
Tokyo 101

Journal of the Fuel Society of Japan (Nenryo Kyokaishi)
(Monthly; Japanese, summaries in English)
Maruzen Company Ltd.
3-10, Nihonbashi 2-chome, Chuo-ku
Tokyo 103
Tel: (3) 3272-7211 Fax: (3) 3274-3238

Journal of the Mining And Metallurgical Institute of Japan
(Monthly; Japanese, with titles, summaries in English)
Maruzen Company Ltd.
3-10, Nihonbashi 2-chome, Chuo-ku
Tokyo 103
Tel: (3) 3272-7211 Fax: (3) 3274-3238

Oil & Gas News
(Weekly)
Al Hilal Publishing (FE) Ltd.
50 Jalan Sultan, #20-06, Jalan Sultan Centre
Singapore 0719
Tel: [65] 2939233 Fax: [65] 2970862

Trade Fairs

Refer to the Trade Fair chapter for complete listings, including contact information, dates, and venues. Trade fairs with particular relevance to this industry include the following, which are listed in that chapter under the headings given below:

Industrial Materials & Chemicals
- Advanced Materials & Engineering Exhibition (Osaka Mechatronics Fair)
- Automotive Materials Show (Automotive Design & Development Show)
- Expo Nonwovens Asia
- Fine Ceramics Fair
- High-Tech Materials Exhibition
- INCHEM TOKYO International Trade Fair for Chemical and Process Engineering
- International Plastic Fair (IPF)
- JP-Plastics & Rubber Fair
- TECHTEXTIL ASIA-International Trade Fair & Symposium for Industrial Textiles

Metal & Metal Finishing
- BLECH-JAPAN International Sheet Metal Working Technology Exhibition
- Mould & Die Exhibition (High Technology Tokyo)

- Mould & Die Exhibition (Factory Automation Nagoya)
- Mould & Die Exhibition (Osaka Mechatronics Fair)
- Surface Finishing & Coating Exhibition
- Wire-Tokyo

For other trade fairs that may be of interest, we recommend that you also consult the headings Agriculture, Forestry & Fisheries; Electronic, Electric & Communication Equipment; Environmental Industries & Civil Engineering; and Packaging, Printing & Paper.

INDUSTRIAL MACHINERY

Exports constitute a small but growing share of Japan's total production of industrial machinery. Many Japanese industrial machinery producers have overseas affiliates, particularly in Europe and the United States. Other exports are shipped to the Middle East, Southeast Asia, and China.

Products Industrial machinery produced in Japan includes boilers and power plants; civil engineering, agricultural, mining, and chemical equipment; papermaking, plastic molding, metalworking, and metal processing equipment; pumps, compressors and fans; conveyor equipment; electric power-generating machinery; hydraulic equipment; and sewing, spinning, and knitting machines. Of particular significance are industrial robots, which are being used in automotive, electronic, electrical, construction, distribution, and nonmanufacturing industries. Although large businesses have curtailed capital spending for robots, small to mid-size companies are automating and have increased their orders. Heavy construction machinery, such as hydraulic shovels, cranes, and bulldozers, is also available from Japanese companies and their overseas affiliates.

Japanese suppliers of environmental equipment are also top world competitors. More than 10 major Japanese companies produce and export freon recovery and recycling equipment that uses activated carbons to absorb freon. Other firms have developed equipment with more efficient media for freon absorption.

Competitive Situation

The health of Japan's industrial machinery industry directly reflects that of the country's general manufacturing industries, which are end-users of industrial machinery. To keep products competitively priced despite appreciation of the yen and rising labor and production costs, many Japanese industrial machinery suppliers have moved production facilities offshore. Nevertheless, sales have declined in recent years because of the effect of the worldwide recession on general manufacturing industries. Moreover, sales to leasing and rental companies, which usually account for 30 to 40 percent of total purchases, have slowed because such companies are reluctant to buy when interest rates are high.

Apart from cutting costs and reducing production, Japanese industrial machinery makers are targeting overseas ventures as a way of remaining competitive internationally and creating more stable overseas supply sources. In an attempt to increase sales, a few Japanese manufacturers are adding new models of equipment with high value-added features to their product lines.

Japan's industrial robot sector is an exception to the declining profitability in machinery industries. Demand is intense, but Japanese robot makers have been unable to meet it because of a shortage of system engineers. Japan's robotic firms are developing high-tech precision robots that will make autonomous decisions by recognizing colors or shapes, processing that information, and then operating according to set instructions. In addition, R&D is expanding into mobile robots (such as for hospital cleaning) and into micromachines for application in medical fields and in confined industrial areas (such as nuclear power reactors and plants).

Trade Organizations

Japan Boiler Association
Meiji-Seimei Mita Building
14-10, Mita 3-chome, Minato-ku
Tokyo 108
Tel: (3) 3453-0103 Fax: (3) 3798-0630

Japan Die Casting Association
Kikai Shinko Kaikan
5-8, Shiba-koen 3-chome, Minato-ku
Tokyo 105
Tel: (3) 3434-1885 Fax: (3) 3434-8829

Japan Food Machinery Manufacturers' Association
Window Building, 2nd Fl.
4-8, Roppongi 7-chome, Minato-ku
Tokyo 106
Tel: (3) 3796-0981 Fax: (3) 3796-1655

Japan Forging Industry Association
1-13, Nihombashi Hon-cho 3-chome, Chuo-ku
Tokyo 103
Tel: (3) 3241-7661, 3242-8102
Fax: (3) 3241-7663

Japan Machinery Exporters' Association
Kikai Shinko Kaikan
5-8, Shiba-koen 3-chome, Minato-ku
Tokyo 105
Tel: (3) 3431-9507 Fax: (3) 3436-6455

Japan Machinery Importers' Association
Koyo Building
2-11, Toranomon 1-chome, Minato-ku
Tokyo 105
Tel: (3) 3503-9736 Fax: (3) 3503-9779

Japan Printing Machinery Manufacturers
Association
Kikai Shinko Kaikan
5-8, Shibakoen 3-chome, Minato-ku
Tokyo 105
Tel: (3) 3434-4661 Fax: (3) 3434-0301

Japan Society of Industrial Machinery
Manufacturers
Kikai Shinko Kaikan
5-8, Shiba Koen 3-chome, Minato-ku
Tokyo 105
Tel: (3) 3434-6821 Fax: (3) 3433-4767

Japan Textile Machinery Association
Kikai Shinko Building
5-8, Shiba Koen 3-chome, Minato-ku
Tokyo 105
Tel: (3) 3434-3821 Fax: (3) 3434-3043

Machine Tool Importers Association of Japan
Toranomon Kogyo Building
2-18, Toranomon 1-chome, Minato-ku
Tokyo 105
Tel: (3) 3501-5030 Fax: (3) 3501-5040

Packaging Machinery Manufacturers
Association
7th Fl., Kimura Building
5-5, Asakusabashi 5-chome
Tokyo 111
Tel: (3) 3865-2815 Fax: (3) 3865-2850

Testing Machinery Association of Japan
Nihon Keiryo Kaikan Building
25-1, Nando-cho, Shinjuku-ku
Tokyo 162
Tel: (3) 3268-4849 Fax: (3) 3268-4840

Directories/Publications

Asiamac Journal: The Machine-Building and Metal
Working Journal for the Asia Pacific Region
(Quarterly)
Adsale Publishing Company
21st Fl., Tung Wai Commercial Building
109-111 Gloucester Road
Hong Kong
Tel: [852] 8920511 Fax: [852] 8384119, 8345014
Tlx: 63109 ADSAP HX

Journal of the Textile Machinery Society of Japan
(Monthly)
Textile Machinery Society of Japan
Osaka Science & Technology Building
Utsubo Koen
8-4, Utsubo Hon-machi 1-chome, Nishi-ku
Osaka 550
Tel: (6) 443-4691

Trade Fairs

Refer to the Trade Fair chapter for complete listings, including contact information, dates, and venues. Trade fairs with particular relevance to this industry include the following, which are listed in that chapter under the headings given below:

Factory Automation
- Automatic Machines & Technology Exhibition (Osaka Mechatronics Fair)
- Automatic Machines & Technology Exhibition
- Automatic Machines & Technology Exhibition (Factory Automation Nagoya)
- Automotive Manufacturing Show (Automotive Design & Development Show
- CIM JAPAN-Computer Integrated Manufacturing Systems
- Exhibition of Measurement & Inspection by Image Technology
- International Industrial Robot Exhibition
- Mechatronics Technology Japan
- Robomation (Osaka Mechatronics Fair)

Machines & Instruments
- CERAM JAPAN
- Factory Automation System Exhibition (High Technology Tokyo)
- HVAC & R JAPAN
- IFPEX (International Fluid Power Exhibition)
- Industrial Machine Exhibition Kanazawa
- International Metalworking Machines Exhibition (Osaka Mechatronics Fair)
- International Metalworking Machines Exhibition (Factory Automation Nagoya)
- International Metalworking Machines Exhibition (Intermex Tokyo) (High Technology Tokyo)
- International Vacuum Show
- Interphex Japan
- Japan Glass plus Metal
- Kyushu Scientific Instruments Show
- LOGIS-TECH TOKYO (International Material Handling and Distribution Exhibition)
- Modern Scientific Instruments Show
- MOTION ENGINEERING JAPAN Motion & Power Transmission Exhibition
- Nagoya International Woodworking Machinery Fair
- Osaka Wood Technology Fair
- POWDERTEC OSAKA Osaka International Powder Technology Exhibition
- Scientific Instruments Show Tohoku
- THERMOTEC
- Toyama Techno Fair
- Vending Industry Fair
- West Japan Machine Tool Fair

For other trade fairs that may be of interest, we recommend that you also consult the headings Aerospace & Oceanic; Agriculture, Forestry & Fisheries; Computer & Information Industries; Construction & Housing; Electronic & Electric Equipment; Environmental & Energy Industries; Food, Beverages & Food Processing; Textiles & Apparel; and Tools.

JEWELRY

Japan's jewelry industry is domestically oriented; less than 5 percent of its jewelry is exported.

Products Japan's jewelry makers produce a broad array of items, including rings, necklaces, pendants, earrings, and bracelets. These goods are available as costume jewelry and in precious metal settings of gold, platinum, and silver. Of the gemstones, diamonds and pearls are the most popular, followed by rubies, sapphires, emeralds, and various semi-precious stones, such as moonstones and aquamarines.

Competitive Situation

Domestic sales of Japanese jewelry have dropped since 1992, reflecting the domestic recession. In an effort to appeal to recession-conscious consumers, most Japanese jewelers are concentrating on creating innovative designs and high-quality products. Manufacturers have developed techniques to produce pure gold products at high temperatures, making them as solid as 18-karat gold. Some companies have improved hypo-allergenic products to take advantage of increasing global demands, and others are concentrating on consumer trends in markets such as platinum jewelry.

Trade Organizations

All Japan Diamonds & Precious Stones Importers' Association
Tokyo Biho Kaikan
1-24, Akashi-cho, Chuo-ku
Tokyo 104
Tel: (3) 3542-5023 Fax: (3) 3542-5023

Japan Brass Makers' Association
12-22, Tsukiji 1-chome, Chuo-ku
Tokyo
Tel: (3) 3542-6551 Fax: (3) 3542-6556

Japan Clock and Watch Association
Kudan TS Building
9-16, Kudankita 1-chome, Chiyoda-ku
Tokyo 102
Tel: (3) 5276-3411 Fax: (3) 5276-3414

Japan Imitation Pearl & Glass Beads Exporters' Association
6, Tai-cho
Tzumi-shi, Osaka Pref. 594
Tel: (725) 41-2133 Fax: (725) 41-2135

Japan Import Watch and Jewelry Wholesalers Association
Sakata Higashi Ueno Building
19-6, Higashi Ueno 1-chome, Taito-ku
Tokyo 110
Tel: (3) 3832-7567 Fax: (3) 3834-4040

Japan Pearl Export & Processing Cooperative Association
Shinju Kaikan
6-15, Kyobashi 3-chome, Chuo-ku
Tokyo 104
Tel: (3) 3562-5011

Japan Pearl Exporters' Association
Nihon Shinju Kaikan
122, Higashi-machi, Chuo-ku
Kobe 650
Tel: (78) 331-4031 Fax: (78) 331-4345

Japan Watch Importers Association
Chuokoron Building
8-7, Kyobashi 2-chome, Chuo-ku
Tokyo 104
Tel: (3) 3563-5901 Fax: (3) 3563-1360

Directories/Publications

Asian Sources: Timepieces
(Monthly)
Asian Sources Media Group
22nd Fl., Vita Tower
29 Wong Chuk Hang Road
Wong Chuk Hang, Hong Kong
Tel: [852] 5554777 Fax: [852] 8730488

Jewellery News Asia
(Monthly)
Jewellery News Asia Ltd.
Rooms 601-603, Guardian House
32 Oi Kwan Road
Wanchai, Hong Kong
Tel: [852] 8322011 Fax: [852] 8329208

World Jewelogue
(Annual)
Headway International Publications Co.
907 Great Eagle Center
23 Harbour Rd.
Hong Kong
Tel: [852] 8275121 Fax: [852] 8277064

Trade Fairs

Refer to the Trade Fair chapter for complete listings, including contact information, dates, and venues. Trade fairs with particular relevance to this industry include the following, which are listed in that chapter under the heading given below:

Gifts, Jewelry & Stationery
- Gift & new life goods show Osaka
- International Gift Show All Western Japan
- International Jewelry Tokyo
- Tokyo International Gift Show
- Variety Impex (Import/Export) Fair

RADIO COMMUNICATION EQUIPMENT

Japan is a top world supplier of radio communication equipment. Much of Japan's radio communication equipment, which includes large-scale units, small-scale equipment, and components, is exported to Southeast Asia and China.

Large-Scale Radio Equipment Japanese-made large-scale radio communication equipment includes electric measuring equipment, signal generators, and microwave systems. Fewer than 70 Japanese enterprises manufacture electric measuring equipment for microwave and radio systems. Products include spectrum analyzers, oscilloscopes, and signal generators. Japan's exports of signal generators include domestically manufactured products as well as reexports.

Japanese-made microwave radio systems include fixed and mobile radio communication systems, with the latter accounting for a growing percentage (now 70 percent) of total production. Other microwave radio communication equipment available from Japanese firms include klystrons, microwave waveguides, and transmitting and receiving tubes and amplifiers.

Small-Scale Radio Equipment Japanese-made small-scale radio equipment includes automobile radio communication systems, mobile radio communication systems, and disaster prevention control systems.

Components Only a few Japanese manufacturers of radio communication system components are independent; most are subsidiaries of large companies. Component products made in Japan include radio frequency parts, noise filters, structural parts, microwave and quasi-millimeter wave equipment, transformers, crystal filters, crystal oscillators, monolithic crystal filters, and network stimulators.

Government Agency

Ministry of Posts & Telecommunications
3-2, Kasumigaseki 1-chome, Chiyoda-ku
Tokyo 100
Tel: (3) 3504-4411 Fax: (3) 3592-9157

Trade Organization

Communications Industry Association of Japan (CIA-J)
Sankei Building Annex
1-7-2, Otemachi, Chiyoda-ku
Tokyo 100
Tel: (3) 3231-3156 Fax: (3) 3246-0495

Publication

Asia Pacific Broadcasting & Telecommunications (Monthly)
Asian Business Press Pte. Ltd.
100 Beach Rd.
#26-00 Shaw Towers
Singapore 0718
Tel: [65] 2943366 Fax: [65] 2985534

Trade Fairs

Refer to the Trade Fair chapter for complete listings, including contact information, dates, and venues. Trade fairs with particular relevance to this industry include the following, which are listed in that chapter under the headings given below:

Electronic, Electric & Communication Equipment
- Communications TOKYO
- International Broadcast Equipment Exhibition (InterBEE)
- Internepcon Japan
- Internepcon Osaka
- Microwave USA
- Telecom Japan
- Tokyo Professional Audio Show

Hobbies, Recreation & Travel
- Amateur Radio Festival
- Japan Hobby Show

SHIPS AND MARINE EQUIPMENT

Japan's shipbuilding industry is the world leader, producing half of all the world's tonnage in ships. Seven major shipbuilders operate in Japan, with major centers of shipbuilding in Nagasaki and Sasebo.

Products Japan's shipbuilders have concentrated on oil tankers; very large crude carriers (VLCCs) and liquefied natural gas carriers (LNGs) are the most significant vessel exports. Exports of cargo freighters and container vessels have been rising, and Japan also supplies high-speed hydrofoils.

Competitive Situation

Ship construction remains a major industry in Japan, but the industry has suffered serious declines over the last 15 years as worldwide demand for oil, and therefore oil tankers, has fallen. Two major shipbuilders survived by cutting workforces and closing several shipyards, but many mid-size firms have folded.

Since 1990, the need to replace aging fleets worldwide has spurred global demand for VLCCs, and Japan's shipbuilders are once again making profits. To avoid future economic hardship when demand slows, these shipbuilders are automating production without adding shipyard facilities and are offering higher wages to attract more skilled labor. In addition, to preserve their markets, Japan's shipbuilders are concentrating on delivering vessels of higher gross tonnage but at a slower production rate.

Government Agencies

Kobe Port and Harbor Bureau
5-1, Kano-cho, 6-chome
Kobe
Tel: (78) 331-8181 Tlx: 78548

Ministry of Transport
1-3, Kasumigaseki 2-chome, Chiyoda-ku
Tokyo 100
Tel: (3) 3580-3111

Nagoya Port Authority
8-21, Irifune, 1-chome, Minato-ku
Nagoya 455-91
Tel: (52) 661-4111 Fax: (52) 661-0155
Tlx: 0446 3816 NPA J

Osaka Port Authority
8-24, Chikko, 2-chome, Minato-ku
Osaka
Tel: (6) 572-2121 Tlx: 5356320

Sendai Port Authority
Miyagi Prefectural Government
8-1, Honcho, 3-chome
Sendai
Tel: (22) 221-3211 Fax: (22) 211-3296

Yokohama Port & Harbor Bureau
5th Fl., Sangul Boeki Center Building
2, Yamachia-cho, Naka-ku
Yokohama City
Tel: (45) 671-2880

Trade Organizations

Cooperative Association of Japan Shipbuilders'
Sempaku Shinko Building
15-16, Toranomon 1-chome, Minato-ku
Tokyo 105
Tel: (3) 3502-2061 Fax: (3) 3502-1479

Japanese Marine Equipment Association
Bansui Building
5-16, Toranomon 1-chome, Minato-ku
Tokyo 105
Tel: (3) 3504-0391, 3502-2041
Fax: (3) 3504-0397, 3591-2206

Japan Marine Products Importers Association
Yurakucho Building
10-1, Yuraku-cho 1-chome, Chiyoda-ku
Tokyo 100
Tel: (3) 3214-3407 Fax: (3) 3214-3408

Japan Ship Exporters' Association
Senpaku-Shinko Building
15-16, Toranomon 1-chome, Minato-ku
Tokyo 105
Tel: (3) 3502-2094 Fax: (3) 3508-2058

Japanese Shipowners' Association
Kaiun Building
6-4, Hirakawa-cho 2-chome, Chiyoda-ku
Tokyo
Tel: (3) 3264-7171 Fax: (3) 3262-4760 Tlx: 22148

National Federation of Medium Trawlers
Toranomon Chuo Building
1-16, Toranomon 1, Minato-ku
Tokyo
Tel: (3) 3508-0361 Tlx: 25404

Directories/Publications

Asian Shipping
(Monthly)
Asia Trade Journals Ltd.
7th Fl., Sincere Insurance Building
4 Hennessy Road
Wanchai, Hong Kong
Tel: [852] 5278532 Fax: [852] 5278753

Journal of the Marine Engineering Society in Japan
(Nihon Hakuyo Kikan Gakkai Shi)
(Monthly; Japanese, with summaries in English)
Nihon Hakuyo Kikan Gakkai
c/o Osaoa Building
2-Gokan Chiyoda-ku, 2-2 Uchisaiwaicho 1
Tokyo
Tel: (3) 3503-5518

Lloyd's Maritime Asia
(Monthly)
Lloyd's of London Press (FE)
Rm. 1101 Hollywood Centre
233 Hollywood Road
Hong Kong
Tel: [852] 8543222 Fax: [852] 8541538

Shipping & Transport News
(Monthly)
Al Hilal Publishing (FE) Ltd.
50 Jalan Sultan, #20-06, Jalan Sultan Centre
Singapore 0719
Tel: [65] 2939233 Fax: [65] 2970862

Trade Fairs

Refer to the Trade Fair chapter for complete listings, including contact information, dates, and venues. Trade fairs with particular relevance to this industry include the following, which are listed in that chapter under the heading given below:

Aerospace & Oceanic
- International Ocean and Coastal Development Exhibition and Symposium

Vessels & Parts
- Osaka International Boat Show
- Sea Japan
- Tokyo International Boat Show

For other trade fairs that may be of interest, we recommend that you also consult the heading Sporting Goods.

SPORTING GOODS AND RECREATIONAL EQUIPMENT

Japan's makers of sporting goods and recreational equipment are gradually advancing in worldwide competitiveness, particularly in such areas as golf equipment, fitness machines, and hunting products. This industry has been slow to develop in Japan because of small domestic markets for sports and recreational products. Major export markets are in Europe and the United States.

Golf Equipment Japanese manufacturers of golf products offer assorted irons and woods, course and driving range balls, and various accessories. Five golf club manufacturers account for about 80 percent of production, and two companies dominate the production of golf balls. Most golf club makers in Japan assemble their products from imported and domestically produced shafts and heads.

The quantity of golf clubs produced annually in Japan has been decreasing since 1989, but the value of the golf clubs has risen each year as firms improve their product lines. In contrast, golf ball production has increased every year, despite a worldwide slowdown in the sporting goods industry due to the recession. In an effort to improve overseas and domestic sales, Japanese golf equipment companies have instituted aggressive marketing strategies. Many of these firms have acquired licensing agreements to label their products with brand names of US and European companies.

To become more competitive with US producers and to meet changing worldwide consumer demand, Japan's golf equipment manufacturers are investing in new product designs. Innovations include lightweight equipment, improved club shafts made of ultra-light boron-reinforced graphite, and "carbonex a" irons, which have stainless steel cavity-back heads to increase driving power and silicone-carbide club faces to increase ball spin. A few Japanese manufacturers are introducing computer-aided golf simulators, which are becoming more popular as golfers worldwide face overcrowded courses and high green fees.

Fitness Equipment Japanese companies manufacture various types of high-end fitness equipment, including compact multi-exercise machines and computerized systems with medical checks and individually tailored exercise programs.

Hunting Fewer than five Japanese manufacturers produce shotgun shells for hunting and sports shooting. These firms supply about 65 percent of the domestic market for shotgun shells. Japanese shells are known for high quality and relatively competitive prices, although manufacturers producing lower-priced shells in Korea, China, Germany, and Australia are strong competitors.

Trade Organizations

Japan Bicycle Exporters' Association
25, Karakiyo-cho 8-chome, Tennoji-ku
Osaka 543
Tel: (6) 762-7371 Fax: (6) 762-4102

Japan Bicycle Manufacturers' Association
9-3, Akasaka 1-chome, Minato-ku
Tokyo 107
Tel: (3) 3583-3123 Fax: (3) 3589-3125

Japan Golf Goods Association
4th Fl., Kobayashi Building
6-11-11 Soto-Kanda, Chiyoda-ku
Tokyo 101
Tel: (3) 3832-8589 Fax: (3) 3832-8594

Sporting Goods Importers' Association of Japan
c/o Tyrolia Japan K.K.
3-19, Kanda-Jimbocho, Chiyoda-ku
Tokyo 101
Tel: (3) 3265-0901 Fax: (3) 3265-0805

Trade Fairs

Refer to the Trade Fair chapter for complete listings, including contact information, dates, and venues. Trade fairs with particular relevance to this industry include the following, which are listed in that chapter under the headings given below:

Hobbies, Recreation & Travel
- Amateur Radio Festival
- AOU Amusement EXPO
- Camping & RV Show Nagoya
- Camping & RV Show Osaka
- Camping & RV Show Tokyo
- Camping Car Trade Show
- Event Promotion Show
- Japan Hobby Show
- Japan World Resort & Cruise Fair
- JATA (JATA Travel Trade Show)
- Park & Leisure Exhibition
- TOUR EXPO
- World Travel Fair

Sporting Goods
- Diving Festival
- Golf Fair Osaka
- International Snow Board Collection & Tokyo Surf Magic
- Japan International Golf Goods Fair
- Professional Leisure Management
- Sports Business Fair Osaka

TELECOMMUNICATION EQUIPMENT

Japan's telecommunication equipment exports are growing as Japanese producers bend to consumer trends. Major export markets are in Europe and the United States.

Products A wide array of telecommunication

equipment is available from Japanese manufacturers: corded and cordless phones, facsimile machines, cellular telephones, and wired-circuit and wireless communication equipment.

Competitive Situation

Faced with declines in sales of private branch exchanges and of cordless phones and facsimiles for home use, Japan's telecommunication companies are looking toward global markets and increasing their production of compact cellular and other mobile telephones. To improve sales, Japanese manufacturers have developed more sophisticated products, such as high-speed advanced protocol facsimile and plain paper facsimile machines, compact and water-resistant cordless phones, and multiple function telephones with liquid crystal displays. These firms are also investing heavily in R&D for frame relay technology and its commercial applications. Several major Japanese telecommunication firms are cooperating in a joint venture with US companies to produce telemarketing systems that link computers with digital private branch exchanges.

Government Agency

Ministry of Posts & Telecommunications
3-2, Kasumigaseki 1-chome, Chiyoda-ku
Tokyo 100
Tel: (3) 3504-4411 Fax: (3) 3592-9157

Trade Organizations

Japan Business Machine Makers Association
Dai-Ichi Mori Building
12-1, Nishi-Shombashi 1-chome, Minato-ku
Tokyo 105
Tel: (3) 3503-9821 Fax: (3) 3591-3646

Communications Industry Association
of Japan (CIA-J)
Sankei Building Annex
1-7-2, Otemachi, Chiyoda-ku
Tokyo 100
Tel: (3) 3231-3156 Fax: (3) 3246-0495

Directories/Publications

Asia Pacific Broadcasting & Telecommunications
(Monthly)
Asian Business Press Pte. Ltd.
100 Beach Rd.
#26-00 Shaw Towers
Singapore 0718
Tel: [65] 2943366 Fax: [65] 2985534

Science & Technology in Japan
(Quarterly)
Three "I" Publications
Yamaguchi Building
5-16, Uchikanda 1-chome, Chiyoda-ku
Tokyo 101
Tel: (3) 3291-3161 Fax: (3) 3291-3764

Telecom Asia
(Bimonthly)
CCI Asia-Pacific (HK)
Suite 905, Guardian House
32 Oi Kwan Road
Wanchai, Hong Kong
Tel: [852] 8332181 Fax: [852] 8345620

Trade Fairs

Refer to the Trade Fair chapter for complete listings, including contact information, dates, and venues. Trade fairs with particular relevance to this industry include the following, which are listed in that chapter under the heading given below:

Electronic, Electric & Communication Equipment
- Communications TOKYO
- Equipment Exhibition of Motion Picture & Television
- International Broadcast Equipment Exhibition (InterBEE)
- Internepcon Japan
- Internepcon Osaka
- Microwave USA
- Telecom Japan

For other trade fairs that may be of interest, we recommend that you also consult the headings Aerospace & Oceanic and Office Automation.

TEXTILES AND APPAREL

Approximately 25 percent of Japan's textile output is exported, and textiles are among the country's top 10 exports. Most exports are of fabric, and Japan's textile manufacturers are top world producers of high-quality shingosen long-fiber polyester fabrics. The Chubu area plays a leading role in the country's textile industry.

Fabrics Japan's textile makers primarily produce synthetic fiber fabrics, the most significant of which are polyester filament fiber fabrics. Such fabrics include shingosen fabrics, aramid fiber materials, polyacrylonitrile fiber materials, high-tensile-strength carbon fiber fabrics, and composite fibers. Production of natural fiber fabrics, such as cotton, linen, and silk, has declined substantially, and Japan's textile industry is no longer competitive in world markets for natural fiber fabrics.

Apparel Japan's apparel industry is domestic-oriented, with exports accounting for less than 5 percent of output. Principal exports are women's woven and knitted outerwear, knitted sweaters, and knitted t-shirts; women's outerwear includes raincoats, suits, jackets and blazers, slacks, overcoats, dresses, jumpers, and skirts. Other significant exports are men's suits and shirts.

Japanese apparel makers have diversified their

product lines to design and produce more Western-style clothes, general purpose clothing, uni-sex items, and irregular size wear. Faced with severe labor shortages because of a declining birthrate and increasing migration from rural to urban areas, some Japanese sewing mills have imported labor from joint-venture sewing mills in China. Other Japanese apparel manufacturers operate production facilities in countries where labor is cheaper and more plentiful. Japanese apparel companies also have a number of joint ventures with firms in China and Southeast Asia.

Competitive Situation

Japan's textile industry is facing strong competition from other Asian countries, particularly China, Korea, Taiwan, and Hong Kong. In addition, this industry has been hurt by the appreciation of the yen. To increase global competitiveness, Japan's textile manufacturers are providing more diverse and high-quality products, with an emphasis on luxury and high-fashion designs. Many firms have also moved production facilities offshore to countries where wages are lower.

Trade Organizations

All Japan Leather Association
Toyo Shinyo-Kumiai Honten Building
1-13, Asakusa 6-chome, Taito-ku
Tokyo 111
Tel: (3) 3874-8791

Central Raw Silk Association of Japan
7, 1-chome, Yuraku-cho, Chiyoda-ku
Tokyo
Tel: (3) 3214-5777 Fax: (3) 3214-5778

Cloth Industry Association
Sunshine 60
1-1, Higashi Ikebukuro 3-chome, Toshima-ku
Tokyo 170
Tel: (3) 3986-3503 Fax: (3) 3986-3497

Cotton Traders' Association
7th Fl., Ebisu Building
2-9, Awajimachi 3-chome, Chuo-ku
Osaka 541
Tel: (6) 201-2215 Fax: (6) 231-5122

Japan Chemical Fibers Association
Seni Kaikan, 6 Fl.
1-11, Nihonbashi Honcho 3-chome, Chuo-ku
Tokyo 103
Tel: (3) 3241-2311 Fax: (3) 3246-0823

Japan Cotton and Staple Fiber Weavers'
Association
8-7, Nishi-Azabu 1-chome, Minato-ku
Tokyo
Tel: (3) 3403-9671

Japan Cotton Textile Exporters Association
The Textile Exporters House
4-9, Bingo-machi 3-chome, Chuo-ku
Osaka 541
Tel: (6) 201-0261 Fax: (6) 203-7738

Japan Cotton Waste & General Fiber Exporters
Association
c/o Kansai Orimono Oroshi Shogyo Kyodo Kumiai
3-15, Kawara-machi 1-chome, Chuo-ku
Osaka 541
Tel: (6) 231-3853 Fax: (6) 231-3854

Japan Cotton Yarn Trade Association
16, Uchiawajimachi 1-chome, Higashi-ku
Osaka 540
Tel: (6) 942-5151

Japan Dyestuff Exporters' Association
Senryo Kaikan
18-17, Roppongi 5-chome, Minato-ku
Tokyo 106
Tel: (3) 3585-3372 Fax: (3) 3589-4236

Japan Export Clothing Manufacturers Association
Osaka YM Building
15-26, Fukushima 7-chome, Fukushima-ku
Osaka 553
Tel: (6) 453-9221 Fax: (6) 453-9220

Japan Export Scarf Makers' Industry Association
2, Sumiyoshi-cho 1-chome, Naka-ku
Yokohama 231
Tel: (45) 681-3261 Fax: (45) 681-3264

Japan Felt Association
11-6, Yaesu 2-chome, Chuo-ku
Tokyo 104
Tel: (3) 3281-1906 Fax: (3) 3281-8415

Japan Fur Association
Ginza-Toshin Building
3-11-15, Ginza, Chuo-ku
Tokyo
Tel: (3) 3541-6987 Fax: (3) 3546-2772

Japan Knitting Industry Association
3rd Fl., TKF Kaikan
37-2, Ryogoku 4-chome, Sumida-ku
Tokyo 130
Tel: (3) 5600-2100 Fax: (3) 5600-2101

Japan Leather & Leather Goods Industries
Association
2nd Fl., Meiyu Building
4-9, Kaminarimon 2-chome, Taito-ku
Tokyo 111
Tel: (3) 3847-1451 Fax: (3) 3847-1510

Japan Raw Silk Exporters' Association
Silk Center Building
1, Yamashita-cho, Naka-ku
Yokohama 231
Tel: (45) 641-1953 Fax: (45) 641-1955

Japan Raw Silk Importers' Association
Sanshi Kaikan
9-4, Yuraku-cho 1-chome, Chiyoda-ku
Tokyo 100
Tel: (3) 3214-1526 Fax: (3) 3214-1529

Japan Raw Silk Reelers' Association
Sanshi Kaikan
9-4, Yuraku-cho 1-chome, Chiyoda-ku
Tokyo 100
Tel: (3) 3214-1431 Fax: (3) 3201-6685

Japan Rayon Yarn Traders' Association
Yagi Building
10, Minamikyutaro 2-chome, Higashi-ku
Osaka 541
Tel: (6) 261-9201

Japan Sewing Machine Exporters' Association
Ota Building
11, Sumiyoshi-cho 2-chome, Shinjuku-ku
Tokyo 162
Tel: (3) 3353-8471 Fax: (3) 3341-7919

Japan Sewing Machinery Manufacturers'
Association
Ota Building
2-11, Sumiyoshi-cho, Shinjuki-ku
Tokyo 162
Tel: (3) 3341-7615 Fax: (3) 3341-7919

Japan Silk & Rayon Weavers' Association
15-12, Kudankita 1-chome, Chiyoda-ku
Tokyo 102
Tel: (3) 3262-4101 Fax: (3) 3262-4270

Japan Silk & Synthetic Textiles Exporters'
Association
The Textile Exporters House
4-9, Bingo-machi 3-chome, Chuo-ku
Osaka 541
Tel: (6) 201-1812 Fax: (6) 201-1819

Japan Silk Spinners' Association
4-5, Nihombashi Horidome-cho 2-chome
Chuo-ku
Tokyo 103
Tel: (3) 3661-0235 Fax: (3) 3661-0596

Japan Socks & Stockings Association
27-4, Higashi Nihombashi 2-chome, Chuo-ku
Tokyo 103
Tel: (3) 3851-4848 Fax: (3) 3851-5374

Japan Spinners' Association
Mengyo Kaikan
8, Bingocho 3-chome, Higashi-ku
Osaka 541
Tel: (6) 231-8431 Fax: (6) 229-1590

Japan Textile Council
Seni Kaikan
9, Nihombashi Honcho 3-chome, Chuo-ku
Tokyo 103
Tel: (3) 3241-7801

Japan Textile Products Exporters' Association
The Textile Exporters House
4-9, Bingo-machi 3-chome, Chuo-ku
Osaka 541
Tel: (6) 201-1712 Fax: (6) 201-1719

Japan Textiles Importers Association
Nihombashi Daiwa Building
9-4, Nihombashi Hon-cho 1-chome, Chuo-ku
Tokyo 103
Tel: (3) 3270-0791 Fax: (3) 3243-1088
Yushutsu Sen-i Kaikan
4-9, Bingo-machi 3-chome, Chuo-ku
Osaka 541
Tel: (6) 202-5575 Fax: (6) 202-5585

Japan Towel Industries Association
4-5, Nihonbashi Ningyoucho 3-chome, Chuo-ku
Tokyo 103
Tel: (3) 3663-1087 Fax: (3) 3662-5398

Japan Wool Dyers' & Finishers' Association
Ueno DK Building
15-4, Ueno 1-chome, Taito-ku
Tokyo 110
Tel: (3) 3837-2877

Japan Woolen & Linen Textiles Exporters
Association
The Textile Exporters House
4-9, Bingo-machi 3-chome, Chuo-ku
Osaka 541
Tel: (6) 201-4741 Fax: (6) 231-1045

Japan Woolen Yarn Traders Association
Osaka Keori Kaikan
38, Awajicho 3-chome, Higashi-ku
Osaka 541
Tel: (6) 231-5787

Japan Wool Importers' Association
Mengyo Kaikan
5-8, Bingo-machi 2-chome, Chuo-ku
Osaka 541
Tel: (6) 231-6201 Fax: (6) 231-6276

Japan Wool Spinners' Association
Ueno DK Building
15-4 Ueno 1-chome, Taito-ku
Tokyo
Tel: (3) 3837-7916 Fax: (3) 3837-7918

Nippon Wool Importers' Federation
Takisada Building
3-6, Bingo-machi 2-chome, Chuo-ku
Osaka 541
Tel: (6) 222-9612 Fax: (6) 232-3625

Yarn Twisters Association
5th Fl., Towa Sotokanda Building
10-3, Sotokanda 3-chome, Chiyoda-ku
Tokyo 101
Tel: (3) 3255-0351 Fax: (3) 3255-0380

Directories/Publications

ATA Journal: Journal for Asia on Textile & Apparel
(Bimonthly)
Adsale Publishing Company
Tung Wai Commercial Building, 21st Fl.
109-111 Gloucester Rd.
Wanchai, Hong Kong
Tel: [852] 8920511 Fax: [852] 8384119

Asia Pacific Leather Directory
(Annual)
Asia Pacific Leather Yearbook
(Annual)
Asia Pacific Directories Ltd.
6th Fl., Wah Hen Commercial Centre
381 Hennessy Rd.
Hong Kong
Tel: [852] 8936377 Fax: [852] 8935752

Fashion Accessories
(Monthly)
Asian Sources Media Group
22nd Fl., Vita Tower
29 Wong Chuk Hang Road
Wong Chuk Hang, Hong Kong
Tel: [852] 5554777 Fax: [852] 8730488

Japan Spinners' Association Monthly Report
(Nihon Boseki Geppo)
(Monthly; Japanese)
Japan Institute of Cotton Textile Technology and
Economy
Mengyo Kaikan
5-8, 2-chome, Bingo-machi, Chuo-ku
Osaka
Tel: (6) 203-5161 Fax: (6) 229-1590

JSN International (Textiles)
(Monthly)
JSN International Inc.
4-9 Lidabashi 4-chome, Chiyoda-ku
Tokyo 102
Tel: (3) 3265-6488 Fax: (3) 3263-9078

Textile Asia Index
(Annual)
Business Press Ltd.
30-32 d'Aguilar Street
Tak Yan Commercial Building, 11th Fl.
GPO 185
Central Hong Kong
Tel: [852] 5247441 Tlx: 60275 TEXIA HX

Textile Asia: The Asian Textile and Apparel
Monthly
Business Press Ltd.
1lth Fl., California Tower
30-32 d'Aguilar Street
Central, Hong Kong
Tel: [852] 5247467 Fax: [852] 8106966

Trade Fairs

Refer to the Trade Fair chapter for complete listings, including contact information, dates, and venues. Trade fairs with particular relevance to this industry include the following, which are listed in that chapter under the heading given below:

Textiles & Apparel
- Heimtexil asia
- Japan Grand Shoes Collection
- Japan International Apparel Machinery Trade Show
- New Uniform Messe Japan
- Osaka International Textile Machinery Show (OTEMAS)
- Texture Hi-Tech Ichinomiya
- US Apparel Show
- US Children's Fashion Trade Fair
- World Fashion Trade Fair

For other trade fairs that may be of interest, we recommend that you also consult the headings Furniture & Housewares; Industrial Materials; and Sporting Goods.

TOOLS AND INSTRUMENTS

Japan is one of the world's leaders in global tool and instrument production. Precision instruments accounted for nearly 5 percent of Japan's total exports in 1992. The Chubu area is the center for Japan's tool and instrument industry.

Electric Test and Measuring Instruments Approximately 10 major companies in Japan supply general-purpose electrical test and measuring equipment, such as voltage and power meters. Only about 30 percent, by value, of Japan's electrical test measuring instruments are exported. These products meet applicable international standards, but they are not as technologically advanced as imported instruments, especially those from the United States. Japanese firms also lag in innovative capability for specialized applications. Moreover, Japan's production of electric test and measuring instruments has been decreasing since 1991, reflecting recession-induced cutbacks in capital investment and R&D funds by domestic instrument users.

Machine Tools Japan's machine tool manufacturers primarily produce technologically advanced, low-cost numerically controlled (NC) metal cutting machine tools. Exports account for about 35 percent of domestic production. Japanese-made metal cutting machine tools, which are used to produce other machines, include turning, drilling, boring, milling, grinding, gear cutting, and finishing machines. Many firms focus on the production of NC turning machines and machining centers for mass production, creating extreme competition and price-cutting among Japanese machine tool firms in these areas. Metal cutting machine tools produced in Japan are applied in a broad spectrum of manufacturing enterprises, including the automotive, shipbuilding, general machinery, electric household appliance, watchmaking, aircraft, and camera industries.

Japan's machine tool production is directly affected by business performance in end-user industries. Since 1990, production and sales of Japanese-produced NC machine tools have slowed as a result of reductions in domestic capital investments and overseas sales caused by domestic and worldwide recessions. Accordingly, Japanese machine tool makers have cut production and have adopted various cost-control measures, such as cutting advertisement, entertainment, and travel. They have also postponed capital investment plans, increased unit pricing through added-value products, diversified into other industrial sectors, and focused on production quality rather than quantity.

Demand for NC tools has risen in response to increasing labor shortages and demands for small-lot product manufacturing. To meet consumer trends, Japan's machine tool makers are developing super-high-speed and super-precision processing equipment. In addition, they are shifting their product lines to include machine tools for processing industrial ceramics and other new materials and for automating production, such as flexible manufacturing systems, flexible manufacturing cells, and computer integrated manufacturing. Some producers are also focusing on downsizing equipment for the domestic market, where space is at a premium.

Government Agency

Science & Technology Agency
2-1, Kasumigaseki 2-chome, Chiyoda-ku
Tokyo 100
Tel: (3) 3581-5271

Trade Organizations

All Japan Machinist Hand Tool Manufacturers' Association
Kikai Shinko Kaikan
5-8, Shibakoen 3-chome, Minato-ku
Tokyo 105
Tel: (3) 3432-2007 Fax: (3) 3437-6783

Japan Automotive Machinery and Tool Manufacturers' Association
Kikai Shinko Kaikan
5-8, Shiba Koen 3-chome, Minato-ku
Tokyo 105
Tel: (3) 3431-3773 Fax: (3) 3431-5880

Japan Bench Machine Tool Builders' Association
Kikai Shinko Kaikan
5-8, Shibakoen 3-chome, Minato-ku
Tokyo 105
Tel: (3) 3431-5054 Fax: (3) 3434-6955

Japan Electric Measuring Instruments Manufacturers' Association
9-10, Toranomon 1-chome, Minato-ku
Tokyo 105
Tel: (3) 3502-0601 Fax: (3) 3502-0600

Japan Federation of Scientific Instrument Associations
No. 2 Tomihisa Building
9-7, Nihombashi Hon-cho 3-chome, Chuo-ku
Tokyo 103
Tel: (3) 3661-5131 Fax: (3) 3668-0324

Japan Machine Tool Builders' Association
Kikai Shinko Kaikan
5-8, Shiba Koen 3-chome, Minato-ku
Tokyo 105
Tel: (3) 3434-3961 Fax: (3) 3434-3763

Japan Measuring Instruments Federation
25-1, Nando-cho, Shinjuku-ku
Tokyo 162
Tel: (3) 3268-2121 Fax: (3) 3268-2167

Japan Optical and Precision Instruments Manufacturers' Association
Kikai Shinko Kaikan
5-8, Shiba Koen 3-chome, Minato-ku
Tokyo 105
Tel: (3) 3431-7073

Japan Optical Measuring Instruments Manufacturers' Association
Kikai Shinko Kaikan
5-8, Shiba Koen 3-chome, Minato-ku
Tokyo 105
Tel: (3) 3431-7073

Japan Precision Measuring Instruments Association
Kiuchi Building
7-4, Toranomon 3-chome, Minato-ku
Tokyo 105
Tel: (3) 3434-9557 Fax: (3) 3434-1695

Japan Small Tool Makers' Association
Kikai Shinko Kaikan
5-8, Shibakoen 3-chome, Minato-ku
Tokyo 105
Tel: (3) 3433-6891 Fax: (3) 3432-6947

Japan Surveying Instruments Manufacturers' Association
Kikai Shinko Kaikan
5-8, Shibakoen 3-chome, Minato-ku
Tokyo 105
Tel: (3) 3431-1629

Machine Tool Importers Association of Japan
Toranomon Kogyo Building
2-18, Toranomon 1-chome, Minato-ku
Tokyo 105
Tel: (3) 3501-5030 Fax: (3) 3501-5040

Tokyo Medical Instruments Traders' Association
39-15, Hongo 3-chome, Bunkyo-ku
Tokyo 113
Tel: (3) 3811-6761 Fax: (3) 3818-4144

Tokyo Precision Tool Makers' Association
Parasto Kamata 304
45-6, Kamata 5-chome, Ota-ku
Tokyo 144
Tel: (3) 3730-8585 Fax: (3) 3730-8118

Directories/Publications

Asian Electronics Engineer
(Monthly)
Trade Media Ltd.
29 Wong Chuck Hang Road
Hong Kong
Tel: [852] 5554777 Fax: [852] 8700816

Asian Sources: Hardware
(Monthly)
Asian Sources Media Group
22nd Fl., Vita Tower
29 Wong Chuk Hang Road
Wong Chuk Hang, Hong Kong
Tel: [852] 5554777 Fax: [852] 8730488

Building & Construction News
(Weekly)
Al Hilal Publishing (FE) Ltd.
50 Jalan Sultan, #20-06, Jalan Sultan Centre
Singapore 0719
Tel: [65] 2939233 Fax: [65] 2970862

Electronic Business Asia
(Monthly)
Cahners Publishing Company
275 Washington St.
Newton, MA 02158, USA
Tel: [1] (617) 964-3030 Fax: [1] (617) 558-4506

JEI, Journal Of The Electronics Industry
(Monthly)
Dempa Publications, Inc.
1-11-15, Higashi Gotanda, Shinagawa-ku
Tokyo 141
Tel: (3) 3445-6111

Journal of Electronic Engineering
Dempa Publications, Inc.
1-11-15, Higashi Gotanda, Shinagawa-ku
Tokyo 141
Tel: (3) 3445-6111

Metalworking Engineering and Marketing
(Bimonthly)
News Digest Publishing Company Ltd.
Editorial and Business Office
3-5-3 Uchiyama, Chikusa-ku
Nagoya 464

Science & Technology in Japan
(Quarterly)
Three "I" Publications
Yamaguchi Building
5-16, Uchikanda 1-chome, Chiyoda-ku
Tokyo 101
Tel: (3) 3291-3161 Fax: (3) 3291-3764

Trade Fairs

Refer to the Trade Fair chapter for complete listings, including contact information, dates, and venues. Trade fairs with particular relevance to this industry include the following, which are listed in that chapter under the headings given below:

Tools: Measuring & Testing
- All Japan Optical Measuring Instruments Fair
- AMIEX (Aichi Measuring Instruments Exhibition)
- Electrotest Japan
- INTER MEASURE
- Japan Analytical Instruments Show
- Japan Exhibition Non-Destructive Testing
- JEMIMA T&M
- Maintenance Engineering Show
- Measurement Technology Exhibition Nagoya
- Measuring, Control and Inspection Instruments Show
- Measuring Instruments Show Hokkaido
- MICRO TECH
- Scientific Instrument Show
- Scientific Instrument Show Chugoku, Shikoku Area
- Scientific Instrument Show Japan
- SENSORS EXPO JAPAN (Technology Japan)
- TEST

- Three Dimension Measurement & System Fair (Factory Automation Nagoya)
- West Japan Instrument Exhibition

Tools: Precision & Optical Equipment
- CLEAN Technology Exhibition (Technology Japan)
- Electronic Display Exhibition
- International Optical Fair Tokyo
- International Professional Photo Fair
- IPPF WEST
- MOTORTECH JAPAN
- Japan Small Electric Motor Products & Technology Exhibition
- MST Japan
- Precision Instruments Cleaning Show (Technology Japan)
- Scientific Instruments Show Hokkaido

For other trade fairs that may be of interest, we recommend that you also consult the headings Electronic, Electric & Communication Equipment; Factory Automation, Machines & Instruments; and Medicine & Pharmaceuticals.

TOYS

Approximately 5,000 toy makers operate in Japan. Most are small- to mid-size companies. Japan's major toy export markets are the United States, Germany, Taiwan, Hong Kong, and France. The main toy manufacturing centers are Tokyo, Osaka, and Nagoya.

Products Japan's toy makers produce a broad assortment of toys, games, and models. In worldwide markets, they are best known for electronic games and other electronic toys. Hobby models and electric trains are also significant exports.

Competitive Situation

By 1990, Japan's toy exports began to decrease because of appreciation of the yen. This decline was reversed in 1991, when Japan saturated world markets with electronic games. Japanese toy manufacturers dominate domestic markets for television and electronic games, but are unable to meet domestic market demand for other types of toys, such as radio-controlled gadgets, novelty toys, action figures, and baseball bats.

Trade Organizations

Japan Export Toy Registration Association
22-4, Higashikomagata 4-chome, Sumida-ku
Tokyo 130
Tel: (3) 3829-2518 Fax: (3) 3829-2549

Japan Plastic Toy Manufacturer's Association
22-13, Yanagibashi 2-chome, Taito-ku
Tokyo 111
Tel: (3) 3863-4075 Fax: (3) 3864-9726

The Japan Toy Association
22-4, Higashi-Komagata 4-chome, Sumida-ku
Tokyo 130
Tel: (3) 3829-2513 Fax: (3) 3829-2549

Tokyo Toy Manufacturers' Association
4-16-3, Higashi-Komagata, Sumida-ku
Tokyo 130
Tel: (3) 3624-0461 Fax: (3) 3623-0891

Directories/Publications

Asian Plastic News
(Quarterly)
Reed Asian Publishing Pte. Ltd.
5001 Beach Rd.
#06-12 Golden Mile Complex
Singapore 0719
Tel: [65] 2913188 Fax: [65] 2913180

Asian Sources: Gifts & Home Products
(Monthly)
Asian Sources Media Group
22nd Fl., Vita Tower
29 Wong Chuk Hang Road
Wong Chuk Hang, Hong Kong
Tel: [852] 5554777 Fax: [852] 8730488

Japan Plastics Age
(Monthly)
Plastics Age Company Ltd.
10-6, Kajicho 1-chome, Chiyoda-ku
Tokyo 101

Japan Plastics Industry Annual
(Annual)
Plastics Age Company Ltd.
10-6, Kajicho 1-chome, Chiyoda-ku
Tokyo 101

Trade Fairs

Refer to the Trade Fair chapter for complete listings, including contact information, dates, and venues. Trade fairs with particular relevance to this industry include the following, which are listed in that chapter under the heading given below:

Hobbies, Recreation & Travel
- AOU Amusement EXPO
- Japan Hobby Show
- Tokyo Toy Show

For other trade fairs that may be of interest, we recommend that you also consult the headings Computer & Information Industries; Computer Graphics; Education; Electronic & Electric Equipment; Gifts, Jewelry & Stationery; and Sporting Goods.

VEHICLES AND VEHICLE PARTS

Japan's vehicle and vehicle parts industries are among the top world suppliers of automobiles, trucks, and buses. Over 25 percent of Japan's exports in 1992 were transport products, making them the number one export category. Automobiles alone make up nearly 18 percent of Japan's total exports. Major export markets are in Europe and the United States, although Japan is diversifying into countries in the Middle East, Asia, Oceania, and Latin America, where market demands are growing.

Vehicles Japanese manufacturers are leading world producers of automobiles. Eleven major vehicle makers produce nearly all of Japan's vehicle exports, including subcompact cars, standard-size cars, two-wheel vehicles, trucks, and buses. The Chubu area, particularly around Nagoya, is home to the major vehicle production facilities, including those of Toyota, Mitsubishi, and Honda. At least seven of Japan's major automobile manufacturers also operate production facilities in the United States.

Vehicle Parts Over 500 Japanese firms manufacture vehicle parts; about 50 of these firms produce over 70 percent of the Japanese vehicle parts sold. Less than 20 percent of vehicle parts made in Japan are exported. Japan is among the world's largest producers of catalytic converters, which are primarily sold to domestic and foreign vehicle manufacturers.

A growing portion of exported vehicle parts is made on an original equipment manufacturer (OEM) basis for assembly in overseas plants. In addition, Japanese vehicle parts suppliers have established over 200 production facilities in the United States. These companies supply Japan-invested vehicle facilities built in the United States, as well as US vehicle makers.

Competitive Situation

Since 1990, Japan's vehicle and vehicle parts industries have been hurt by the general economic slowdown in Japan and overseas. Domestic demand for vehicles and vehicle parts has been falling since 1992, and exports have been declining since the late 1980s. Declines in exports to Europe and North America reflect not only the weak economic conditions in those regions, but also the changing relationships between European, North American, and Japanese governments; political unrest in parts of Europe; and increased automobile production by Japanese-owned overseas facilities. The only export category that has increased since 1990 is two-wheel vehicles, but this market is also slowing. Even as global market demand has slowed, vehicle and vehicle parts manufacturers face labor shortages, labor demands for shorter work hours, rising fixed costs, and a continuing need for capital expenditures to improve the efficiency of production lines and to meet increasingly stringent environmental and safety standards.

Japan's vehicle manufacturers are expecting market demand for automobiles to increase as consumers begin to replace vehicles purchased in the 1980s. The industry is also predicting an upturn in domestic automotive markets as a result of government measures to stimulate the domestic economy. In addition, Japan's vehicle makers are hoping to counteract sluggish sales and to increase profitability by (1) expanding exports to Asia, Oceania, Latin America, and the Middle East; (2) decreasing production of automobiles and increasing production of two-wheel vehicles to follow market trends; (3) reducing the number of models introduced, the variety of vehicle parts, and the number of standard features to cut production and R&D costs; (4) improving assembly processes and operational efficiency of all company divisions; and (5) reducing working and overtime hours. As a further cost-cutting measure, most Japanese automotive firms have withdrawn from international car races. In response to foreign protectionist policies, Japan's vehicle makers are stepping up production of vehicles in their overseas factories, particularly in North America.

Japan's vehicle industry still leads the world in productivity, quality, and rapid development of new models. The industry continues to develop innovative safety equipment and is also focusing on environmental features, such as non-freon air conditioners, retrofit non-freon air conditioning units for older cars, fuel-efficient engines with decreased carbon dioxide emissions, recycling systems for vehicle parts, and equipment to reduce nitrous oxide emissions from diesel-powered vehicles. Many Japanese vehicle makers have increased their imports of parts, particularly of high-tech equipment designed for Japanese-made vehicles.

Government Agency

Ministry of Transport
1-3, Kasumigaseki 2-chome, Chiyoda-ku
Tokyo 100
Tel: (3) 3580-3111

Trade Organizations

Japan Auto Body Industries Association Inc.
Kishimoto Building
2-1, Marunouchi 2-chome, Chiyoda-ku
Tokyo 100
Tel: (3) 3213-2031 Fax: (3) 3213-2034

Japan Automobile Dealers Association
7-27, Minami-Aoyama 5-chome, Minato-ku
Tokyo 107
Tel: (3) 3400-8404

Japan Automobile Importers' Association
7th Fl., Akiyama Building
5-3, Kojimachi, Chiyoda-ku
Tokyo 102
Tel: (3) 3222-5421 Fax: (3) 3222-1730

Japan Automobile Manufacturers' Association, Inc.
Otemachi Building
6-1, Otemachi 1-chome, Chiyoda-ku
Tokyo 100
Tel: (3) 3216-5771 Fax: (3) 3287-2072

Japan Automobile Tire Manufacturers' Association
Toranomon Building
1-23, Toranomon 1-chome, Minato-ku
Tokyo 105
Tel: (3) 3503-0191, 3216-5778
Fax: (3) 3287-2072, 3503-0199

Japan Automotive Machinery and Tool Manufacturers' Association
Kikai Shinko Kaikan
5-8, Shiba Koen 3-chome, Minato-ku
Tokyo 105
Tel: (3) 3431-3773 Fax: (3) 3431-5880

Japan Auto Parts Industries Association
Jidosha Buhin Kaikan
16-15, Takanawa 1-chome, Minato-ku
Tokyo 108
Tel: (3) 3445-4211 Fax: (3) 3447-5372
Tlx: 2829

Japan Industrial Vehicles Association
Tobu Building
5-26, Motoakasaka 1-chome, Minato-ku
Tokyo 107
Tel: (3) 3403-5556

Directories/Publications

Guide to the Motor Industry of Japan
(Annual)
Japan Motor Industrial Federation Inc.
Otemachi Building
6-1 Otemachi, Chiyoda-ku
Tokyo 100
Tel: (3) 3216-5771

JSAE Review
(Quarterly)
Society of Automotive Engineers of Japan
10-2, Goban-cho, Chiyoda-ku
Tokyo 102
Tel: (3) 3262-8211 Fax: (3) 3261-2204`

Trade Fairs

Refer to the Trade Fair chapter for complete listings, including contact information, dates, and venues. Trade fairs with particular relevance to this industry include the following, which are listed in that chapter under the heading given below:

Automobiles & Automotive Parts
- Auto Service Show
- Hokkaido Imported Automobile Show
- Kyushu Imported Automobile Show
- Nagoya Imported Automobile Show
- Osaka Auto Service Fair
- Osaka Imported Automobile Show
- Tokyo Imported Automobile Show
- Tokyo Motor Show
- Tokyo 4WD-RV Show

For other trade fairs that may be of interest, we recommend that you also consult the headings Electronic & Electric Equipment; Environmental Industries & Civil Engineering; and Factory Automation.

Trade Fairs

Japan hosts a wide range of trade fairs and expositions that should interest anyone who seeks to do business in this dynamic and expanding economy. Whether you want to buy Japanese goods or exhibit your own goods and services for sale to the Japanese market, you will almost undoubtedly find several trade fairs to suit your purposes.

The listing of trade fairs in this section is designed to acquaint you with the scope, size, frequency, and length of the events held in Taiwan and to give you contact information for the organizers. While every effort has been made to ensure that this information is correct and complete as of press time, the scheduling of such events is in constant flux. Announced exhibitions can be canceled; dates and venues are often shifted. If you are interested in attending or exhibiting at a show listed here, we urge you to contact the organizer well in advance to confirm the venue and dates and to ascertain whether it is appropriate for you. (*See* Tips for Attending a Trade Fair, following this introduction, for further suggestions on selecting, attending, and exhibiting at trade fairs.) The information in this volume will give a significant head start to anyone who has considered participating in a trade fair as an exhibitor or attendee.

In order to make access to this information as easy as possible, fairs have been grouped alphabetically by product category and within product category, alphabetically by name. The names, dates, and frequency of both recent and upcoming events are given along with the site and contact information. Product categories, with cross references, are given following this introduction in a table of contents. Note that the first and last headings listed are out of alphabetical order. Trade fairs listed under *Comprehensive* do not focus on a single type of product but instead show a broad range of goods that may be from one geographic area or centered around a particular theme. The final category, *Others*, is a miscellaneous listing of fairs that do not fit easily into one of the other categories. When appropriate, fairs have been listed in more than one category. The breadth of products on display at a given fair means that you may want to investigate categories that are not immediately obvious. Many exhibits include the machinery, tools, and raw materials used to produce the products associated with the central theme of a fair; anyone interested in such items should consider a wide range of the listings.

As you gather further information on fairs that appeal to you, do not be surprised if the names are slightly different from those listed here. Some large trade fairs include several smaller exhibits, some use short names or acronyms, and Japanese names can be translated in a variety of ways. Dates and venues, of course, are always subject to change.

For further information The Japan External Trade Organization (JETRO) publishes an annual listing of trade fairs held in Japan. This listing organizes fairs primarily by industry type. The list is cross-referenced by name and date. For each event, the listing gives the name, dates, frequency, site, and organizer. For a copy of the calendar, contact the main JETRO office in Tokyo or one of the many JETRO offices throughout Japan and around the world. (Refer to "Important Addresses" chapter for JETRO offices.)

Other valuable sources of information include the commercial sections of Japanese diplomatic missions, chambers of commerce and other business organizations dedicated to assist trade between your country and Japan, and the embassy and consulate of your own country located in Japan. Professional and trade organizations in Japan involved in your area of interest may also be worth contacting. (Refer to "Important Addresses" for Japanese embassies and consulates, Japanese chambers of commerce and business organizations, diplomatic missions located in Japan, and trade organizations.)

While the annual directory *Trade Shows Worldwide* (Gale Research Inc., Detroit, Michigan) is far from comprehensive, it may provide further information on some trade fairs in Japan, and it is worth seeking out at your local business library.

TRADE FAIRS
TABLE OF CONTENTS

Tips for Attending a Trade Fair

Overseas trade fairs can be extremely effective for making face-to-face contacts and sales or purchases, identifying suppliers, checking out the competitors, and finding out how business really works in the host country. However, the cost of attending such fairs can be high. To maximize the return on your investment of time and money, you should be very clear about your goals for the trip and give yourself plenty of time for advance research and preparation. You should also make sure that you are aware of the limitations of trade fairs. The products on display probably do not represent the full range of goods available on the market. In fact, some of the latest product designs may still be under wraps. And while trade fairs give you an opportunity to make face-to-face contact with many people, both exhibitors and buyers are rushed, which makes meaningful discussions and negotiations difficult. These drawbacks can easily be minimized if you have sufficient preparation and background information. Allow at least three months for preparation—more if you also need to identify the fair that you will attend. Under ideal circumstances, you should begin laying the groundwork nine to 12 months in advance.

Tips for Attending a Trade Fair (cont'd.)

Selecting an appropriate trade fair

Consult the listings of trade fairs here to find some that interest you. Note the suggestions for finding the most current calendars of upcoming fairs. Once you have identified some fairs, contact their organizers for literature, including show prospectus, attendee list, and exhibitor list. Ask plenty of questions. Do not neglect trade organizations in the host country, independent show-auditing firms, and recent attendees. Find out whether there are "must attend" fairs for your particular product group. Fairs that concentrate on other but related commodities might also be a good match. Be aware that there may be preferred seasons for trade in certain products. Your research needs to consider a number of points.

Audience • Who is the intended audience? Is the fair open to the public or only to trade professionals? Are the exhibitors primarily foreigners looking for local buyers or locals looking for foreign buyers? Many trade fairs are heavily weighted to one or the other. Decide whether you are looking for an exposition of general merchandise produced in one region, a commodity-specific trade show, or both.

Statistics • How many people attended the fair the last time it was held? What were the demographics? What volume of business was done? How many exhibitors were there? How big is the exhibition space? What was the ratio of foreign to domestic attendees and exhibitors?

Specifics • Who are the major exhibitors? Are particular publications or organizations associated with the fair? On what categories of products does the fair focus? Are there any special programs, and do they require additional fees? Does the fair have particular themes that change each time? How long has the fair been in existence? How often is it held? Is it always in the same location, or does it move each time? How much does it cost to attend? To rent space?

Before you go

- If you have not already spoken with someone who attended the fair in the past, make sure to seek someone out for advice, tips, and general information.
- Make your reservations and travel arrangements well in advance, and figure out how you are going to get around once you get there. Even if the fair takes place in a large city, do not assume that getting around will be easy during a major trade fair. If the site is a small city or less-developed area, the transportation and accommodation systems are likely to be saturated even sooner than they can be in metropolitan areas.
- Will you need an interpreter for face-to-face business negotiations? A translation service to handle documents? Try to line up providers well in advance of your need for their services.
- Do you need hospitality suites and/or conference rooms? Reserve them as soon as you can.
- Contact people you'd like to meet before you go. Organize your appointments around the fair.
- Familiarize yourself with the show hours, locations (if exhibits and events are staged at several different venues), and schedule of events. Then prioritize.

While you are there

- Wear businesslike clothes that are comfortable.
- Immediately after each contact, write down as much information as you can. Do not depend on remembering it.

After the fair

- Within a week after the conclusion of the fair, write letters to new contacts and follow up on requests for literature. If you have press releases and questionnaires, send them out quickly as well.
- Write a report evaluating the experience while it is still fresh in your mind. Even if you don't have to prepare a formal report, spend some time organizing your thoughts on paper for future reference and to quantify the results. Did you meet your goals? Why or why not? What would you do differently? What unforeseen costs arose?
- With your new contacts and your experience in mind, start preparing for your next trade fair.

If you are selling

- Set specific goals for sales leads, developing product awareness, selling and positioning current customers, and gathering industry information; for example, number of contacts made, orders written, leads converted into sales, visitors at presentations, brochures or samples distributed, customers entertained, seminars attended. You can also set goals for total revenue from sales, cost-to-return benefit ratio, amount of media coverage, and amount of competitor information obtained.

- Review your exhibitor kit, paying particular attention to show hours and regulations, payment policies, shipping instructions and dates, telephone installation, security, fire regulations, union regulations, and extra-cost services. Is there a show theme that you can tie into?

- Gear your advertising and product demonstrations to the audience. Should you stress certain aspects of your product line? Will you need brochures and banners in different languages? Even if you do not need to translate the materials currently in use into another language, do you need to re-write them for a different culture? Consider advertising in publications that will be distributed at the fair.

- Plan the display in your booth carefully; you will have only a few seconds to grab the viewer's attention. Secure a location in a high-traffic area—for example, near a door, restroom, refreshment area, or major exhibitor. Use banner copy that is brief and effective. Focus on the product and its benefits. Place promotional materials and giveaways near the back wall so that people have to enter your area, but make sure that they do not feel trapped. If you plan to use videotapes or other multimedia, make sure that you have enough space. Such presentations are often better suited to hospitality suites, because lights are bright and noise levels high in exhibition halls.

- Do not forget about the details. Order office supplies and printed materials that you will need for the booth. If you ordered a telephone line, bring your own telephone or arrange to rent one. Have all your paperwork—order forms, business cards, exhibitor kit and contract, copies of advance orders and checks, travel documents, and so on—in order and at hand. Draw up a schedule for staffing the booth.

- Plan and rehearse your sales pitch in advance, preferably in a space similar to the size of your booth.

- Do not sit, eat, drink, or smoke while you are in the booth.

- If you plan to return to the next show, reserve space while you're still at the fair.

- Familiarize yourself with import regulations for products that you wish to exhibit at the fair.

If you are buying

- Set specific goals for supplier leads and for gathering industry information; for example, number of contacts made, leads converted to purchases, seminars and presentations attended, booths visited. Other goals might be cost-to-return benefit ratio, amount of competitor information gathered, and percentage of projected purchases actually made.

- List all the products that you seek to purchase, their specifications, and the number of units you plan to purchase of each.

- Know the retail and wholesale market prices for the goods in your home country and in the country where you will be buying. List the highest price you can afford to pay for each item and still get a worthwhile return.

- List the established and probable suppliers for each of the products or product lines that you plan to import. Include their addresses and telephone numbers and your source for the information. Contact suppliers before you go to confirm who will attend and to make appointments.

- Familiarize yourself with customs regulations on the products that you seek to purchase and import into your own country or elsewhere. Be sure to include any products that you might be interested in.

Trade Fair	Site	Contact

COMPREHENSIVE Trade fairs exhibiting a wide range of goods

Trade Fair	Site	Contact
ENEX Hiroshima Every 2 years Feb., 1994 (tentative)	Hiroshima Prefecture Industrial Exhibition Hall (tentative)	Energy Conservation Center, Japan (Chungoku Br.) Inoue Bldg. 5F 8-20 Kamihacchobori, Naka-Ku Hiroshima City, Hiroshima Pref. 730 Tel: (82) 221-1961/1975 Fax: (82) 221-1968
ENEX Kitakyusyu Every 2 years Last held: Feb. 26- Mar. 1, 1993	West Japan General Exhibition Center	Energy Conservation Center, Japan (Kyushu Branch) Yoshimi Bldg. 2-8-25 Hakataekimae, Hakata-ku Fukuoka City, Fukuoka Pref. 812 Tel: (92) 431-6402 Fax: (92) 431-6405
ENEX Kobe Every 2 years Last held: Feb. 12-15, 1993	Kobe International Exhibition Hall	Energy Conservation Center, Japan (Kinki Branch) Tel: (6) 364-8965 Fax: (6) 365-8990
ENEX Nagoya Every 2 years Feb., 1994 (tentative)	To be announced	Energy Conservation Center, Japan (Tokai-Hokuriku Branch) Murakami Bldg., 2-13-8 Marunouchi Naka-ku Nagoya 460 Tel: (52) 232-2216/2217 Fax: (52) 232-2218
ENEX Sapporo Every 2 years Last held: Mar. 9-11, 1993	Sapporo Grand Hotel	Energy Conservation Center, Japan (Hokkaido Branch) Hokkaido Keizai Center Bldg., Nishi 2-2 Kita-Ichigo, Chuo-ku, Sapporo City, Hokkaido 060 Tel: (11) 271-4028 Fax: (11) 222-4634
ENEX Tokyo Annual Last held: Feb. 1-5, 1993	Science Museum Exhibition Hall	Energy Conservation Center, Japan SVAX Nishi-Shimbashi Bldg. 7F, 2-39-3 Nishi-Shimbashi, Minato-ku, Tokyo 105 Tel: (3) 3433-0311 Fax: (3) 3433-0393
INTERMAINTECH **International** **Maintenance Technology** **Exhibition** Every 2 years Last held: Nov. 10-13, 1993	Harumi-Tokyo International Fair Ground	Japan Management Association 3-1-22 Shibakoen, Minato-ku, Tokyo 105 Tel: (3) 3434-6211 Fax: (3) 3434-1836/8076 Tlx: J25870
Kobe Import Fair Annual Last held: Oct. 21-24, 1993	Kobe International Exhibition Hall	Kobe Import Fair Council c/o Commerce & Trade Division, Economic Bureau, Kobe City Government, 6-5-1 Kano-cho, Chuo-ku Kobe 650 Tel: (78) 322-5337 Fax: (78) 322-6073
Osaka International **Trade Fair (OITF)** Every 2 years Apr., 1994 (tentative)	International Exhibition Center, Osaka (INTEX Osaka)	Osaka International Trade Fair Commission 1-5-102 Nanko-Kita, Suminoe-ku, Osaka 559 Tel: (6) 612-1042 Fax: (6) 612-8585 Tlx: 526-7660 OITFC J
Sapporo International **Trade Fair** Every 2 years Last held: Jun. 11-16, 1993	AXES Sapporo (Sapporo Exposition Center)	Sapporo International Trade Fair Committee c/o Sapporo City Hall, Nishi 2, Kita-Ichijo, Chuo-ku Sapporo City, Hokkaido 060 Tel: (11) 241-1990 Fax: (11) 251-5130
Tokyo International **Trade Fair** Every 2 years Last held: Apr. 29- May 3, 1993	Harumi-Tokyo International Fair Ground	Tokyo International Trade Fair Commission 4-7-24 Harumi, Chuo-ku, Tokyo 104 Tel: (3) 3531-3371 Fax: (3) 3531-1344 Tlx: 02523935 TITF J
West Japan Import Fair Annual Last held: May 1-5, 1993	West Japan General Exhibition Center	West Japan Industry and Trade Exhibition Association 3-7-1 Asano, Kokurakita-ku Kitakyushu City, Fukuoka Pref. 802 Tel: (93) 511-6848 Fax: (93) 521-8845

Trade Fair	Site	Contact

AEROSPACE & OCEANIC
See also Vessels & Parts

Trade Fair	Site	Contact
Airport Systems International Show Tokyo Annual Last held: Feb. 10-13, 1993	Nippon Convention Center (Makuhari Messe)	Reed Exhibitions Japan, Ltd. Shinjuku Nomura Bldg. 18F, 1-26-2 Nishi-Shinjuku, Shinjuku-ku, Tokyo 163-05 Tel: (3) 3349-8501 Fax: (3) 3345-7929 Tlx: J27280 REC JPN
International Exhibition & Symposium—"Airport, Communication & Environment" Every 2 years Last held: Apr. 21-24, 1993	International Exhibition Center, Osaka (INTEX Osaka)	World Import Mart Co., Ltd. Sunshine City, 3-1-3 Higashi-Ikebukuro, Toshima-ku Tokyo 170 Tel: (3) 3987-3161 Fax: (3) 3981-8371 Tlx: 2723829
International Ocean and Coastal Development Exhibition and Symposium Every 2 years Oct. 26-29, 1994 (tentative)	Kobe International Exhibition Hall	World Import Mart Co., Ltd. Sunshine City, 3-1-3 Higashi-Ikebukuro, Toshima-ku Tokyo 170 Tel: (3) 3987-3161 Fax: (3) 3981-8371 Tlx: 2723829

AGRICULTURE, FORESTRY & FISHERIES
See also Food, Beverages & Food Processing

Trade Fair	Site	Contact
Agriculture Technology Exhibition Every 2 years Last held: Sep. 5-7, 1993	Nagoya International Exhibition Hall	Chemical Daily, Inc. 3-16-8 Nihombashi-Hamacho, Chuo-ku, Tokyo 103 Tel: (3) 3663-7931 Fax: (3) 3663-2330
HI-TECH HORTI-MATION International Horticultural Exhibition Every 2 years Apr. 20-23, 1994 (tentative)	Nippon Convention Center (Makuhari Messe)	Japan Management Association 3-1-22 Shibakoen, Minato-ku, Tokyo 105 Tel: (3) 3434-6211 Fax: (3) 3434-1836/8076 Tlx: JMA J25870

AUTOMOBILES & AUTOMOTIVE PARTS

Trade Fair	Site	Contact
Auto Service Show Every 2 years Last held: Jun. 17-20, 1993	Harumi-Tokyo International Fair Ground	Japan Automotive Service Equipment Association 7-23-5 Shinjuku, Shinjuku-ku, Tokyo 160 Tel: (3) 3203-5131 Fax: (3) 3208-2157
Hokkaido Imported Automobile Show Annual Last held: Feb. 12-14, 1993	Sangyo Kyoshin Kaijo (Tsukisamu Green Dome)	Japan Automobile Importers' Association (Hokkaido Branch) 4-1 Odori-Higashi, Chuo-ku Sapporo City, Hokkaido 060 Tel: (11) 241-2161 Fax: (11) 241-2168
Kyushu Imported Automobile Show Annual Last held: Mar. 18-21, 1993	Fukuoka International Center	Japan Automobile Importers' Association (Kyushu Branch) 3-5-21 Harada, Higashi-ku, Fukuoka City, Fukuoka Pref. 812 Tel: (92) 629-1200 Fax: (92) 622-5837

Note: Country codes for telephone and fax numbers are not displayed unless they are *outside* of Japan. All country codes have square brackets around them, while city codes have parentheses. The country code for Japan is [81].

Trade Fair	Site	Contact
Nagoya Imported Automobile Show Annual Last held: Jan. 22-25, 1993	Nagoya International Exhibition Hall	Japan Automobile Importers' Association (Chubu Branch) YWCA Bldg. 4F, 2-3 Shinsakae-cho, Naka-ku Nagoya 460 Tel: (52) 961-4475 Fax: (52) 961-4751
Osaka Auto Service Fair Every 2 years 1994 (Dates to be announced)	Site information to be announced	Nihon Kogyo Shimbun 2-4-9 Umeda, Kita-ku, Osaka 530 Tel: (6) 343-3222/4 Fax: (6) 341-4773
Osaka Imported Automobile Show Annual Last held: 1993 (Dates not available)	International Exhibition Center, Osaka (INTEX Osaka)	Japan Automobile Importers' Association (Kansai Branch) K & G Kyomachibori Bldg. 5F, 2-6-26 Kyomachibori, Nishi-ku, Osaka 590 Tel: (6) 447-5431 Fax: (6) 447-5461
Tokyo Imported Automobile Show Every 2 years Last held: Jan. 14-17, 1993	Harumi-Tokyo International Fair Ground	Japan Automobile Importers' Association 5-3 Kojimachi, Chiyoda-ku, Tokyo 102 Tel: (3) 3222-5421 Fax: (3) 3222-1730
Tokyo Motor Show Every 2 years Last held: Oct. 22-Nov. 5, 1993	Nippon Convention Center (Makuhari Messe)	Japan Motor Industrial Federation, Inc. Otemachi Bldg., 1-6-1 Otemachi, Chiyoda-ku Tokyo 100 Tel: (3) 3211-8731 Fax: (3) 3211-5798
Tokyo 4WD-RV Show Annual Last held: Feb. 19-21, 1993	Harumi-Tokyo International Fair Ground	Tokyo International Trade Fair Commission 4-7-24 Harumi, Chuo-ku, Tokyo 104 Tel: (3) 3531-3371 Fax: (3) 3531-1344 Tlx: 02523935 TITF J

COMPUTER & INFORMATION INDUSTRIES
See also Computer Graphics; Electronic, Electric & Communication Equipment

BOARD COMPUTER Japan Add-on Boards for Small Computer Exhibition Annual Last held: Feb. 24-26, 1993	Sunshine City Convention Center Tokyo	Japan Management Association 3-1-22 Shibakoen, Minato-ku, Tokyo 105 Tel: (3) 3434-6211 Fax: (3) 3434-1836/8076 Tlx: JMA J25870
Business Show Osaka Annual Last held: Jun. 2-4, 1993	International Exhibition Center, Osaka (INTEX Osaka)	Nippon Omni-Management Association Osaka Kagaku Gijutsu Center Bldg., 1-8-4 Utsubo-Hommachi, Nishi-ku, Osaka 550 Tel: (6) 443-6961 Fax: (6) 441-4319
Business Show Tokyo Annual Last held: May 19-22, 1993	Harumi-Tokyo International Fair Ground	Nippon Omni-Management Association 3-11-8 Sendagaya, Shibuya-ku, Tokyo 151 Tel: (3) 3403-1331 Fax: (3)3403-1710 Tlx: 2422143 NOMAJ
Card Business Fair Annual Last held: Mar. 18-22, 1993	Harumi-Tokyo International Fair Ground	Nihon Keizai Shimbun, Inc. 1-9-5 Otemachi, Chiyoda-ku, Tokyo 100-66 Tel: (3) 3243-9083 Fax: (3) 3243-9086 Tlx: NIKKEI J22308
CASE JAPAN Computer Aided Software Engineering Japan Annual Last held: Jul. 14-16, 1993	Sunshine City Convention Center Tokyo	Reed Exhibitions Japan, Ltd. Shinjuku Nomura Bldg. 18F, 1-26-2 Nishi-Shinjuku, Shinjuku-ku, Tokyo 163-05 Tel: (3) 3349-8501 Fax: (3) 3345-7929 Tlx: J27280 REC JPN

Trade Fair	Site	Contact
Computer Chemistry System Exhibition Annual Last held: May 13-14, 1993	Science Museum Exhibition Hall	Chemical Daily, Inc. 3-16-8 Nihombashi-Hamacho, Chuo-ku, Tokyo 103 Tel: (3) 3663-7931 Fax: (3) 3663-2330
Data Show Annual Last held: Oct. 4-7, 1993	Harumi-Tokyo International Fair Ground	Japan Electronic Industry Development Association Kikai Shinko Kaikan, 3-5-8 Shibakoen, Minato-ku, Tokyo 105 Tel: (3) 3433-4547 Fax: (3) 3433-2003 Tlx: JEIDA J27544
DOWNSIZING JAPAN Annual Last held: Apr. 6-8, 1993	Nippon Convention Center (Makuhari Messe)	Nihon Kogyo Shimbun 1-28-5 Kanda-Jimbocho, Chiyoda-ku, Tokyo 101 Tel: (3) 3292-3561 Fax: (3) 3292-6137
FA Materials Handling & Distribution Systems Exhibition (Osaka Mechatronics Fair) Annual Last held: May 19-22, 1993	International Exhibition Center, Osaka (INTEX Osaka)	Nikkan Kogyo Shimbun, Ltd. (Osaka Branch) 2-16 Kitahama-Higashi, Chuo-ku, Osaka 540 Tel: (6) 946-3384 Fax: (6) 946-3389
Factory Automation Hiroshima Annual Last held: Jul. 2-5, 1993	Hiroshima Prefecture Industrial Exhibition Hall	Nikkan Kogyo Shimbun, Ltd. (Chugoku Branch) 2-3 Matsukawa-cho, Minami-ku Hiroshima City, Hiroshima Pref. 732 Tel: (82) 261-6454 Fax: (82) 263-3070
Hi-Tech Kyushu Annual Last held: Sep. 4-7, 1993	Fukuoka International Center	Nikkan Kogyo Shimbun, Ltd. (Seibu Branch) 1-1 Komondomachi, Hakata-ku, Fukuoka City, Fukuoka Pref 812 Tel: (92) 271-5715 Fax: (92) 271-5743
Hitech Hamamatsu Annual Last held: Jun. 3-5, 1993	Hamamatsu Industrial Exhibition Hall, Hamamatsu Arena	Nihon Kogyo Shimbun 2-4-9 Umeda, Kita-ku, Osaka 530 Tel: (6) 343-3222/4 Fax: (6) 341-4773
Kurume -Tosu Techno Fair Annual Last held: Jul., 1993	Kurume Research Center Bldg.	Nippon Omni-Management Association Nishitetsu Hakataekimae Bldg., 1-6-16 Hakataekimae, Hakata-ku, Fukuoka City, Fukuoka Pref. 812 Tel: (92) 431-3365 Fax: (92) 431-3367
Kyushu Business Show Annual Last held: Oct., 1993	Fukuoka International Center	Nippon Omni-Management Association Nishitetsu Hakataekimae Bldg., 1-6-16 Hakataekimae, Hakata-ku, Fukuoka City, Fukuoka Pref. 812 Tel: (92) 431-3365 Fax: (92) 431-3367
Kyushu International Techno Fair Every 2 years 1994 (Dates to be announced)	Site information to be announced	Kyushu Industrial Technology Center Morimen Bldg. 6F, 2-17-5 Hakataeki-Higashi, Hakata-ku, Fukuoka City, Fukuoka Pref. 812 Tel: (92) 411-7391 Fax: (92) 472-6609
MACWORLD Expo Tokyo Annual Last held: Feb. 10-13, 1993	Nippon Convention Center (Makuhari Messe)	Nihon Kogyo Shimbun 1-28-5 Kanda-Jimbocho, Chiyoda-ku, Tokyo 101 Tel: (3) 3292-3561 Fax: (3) 3292-6137

Note: Country codes for telephone and fax numbers are not displayed unless they are *outside* of Japan.
All country codes have square brackets around them, while city codes have parentheses.
The country code for Japan is [81].

Trade Fair	Site	Contact
Micro Computer Show Annual Last held: Apr. 20-23, 1993	Tokyo Ryutsu Center (TRC)	Japan Electronic Industry Development Association Kikai Shinko Kaikan, 3-5-8 Shibakoen, Minato-ku, Tokyo 105 Tel: (3) 3433-4547 Fax: (3) 3433-2003 Tlx: JEIDA J27544
Microcomputer System & Tool Fair Annual Last held: Nov., 1993	Site information not available	Japan System House Association Nihombashi Mitsuya Bldg. 6F, 18-12 Nihombashi-Hakozakicho, Chuo-ku, Tokyo 104 Tel: (3) 3668-3151 Fax: (3) 3668-2197
Multimedia Annual Last held: Nov., 1993	Site information not available	Nihon Keizai Shimbun, Inc. 1-9-5 Otemachi, Chiyoda-ku, Tokyo 100-66 Tel: (3) 3243-9082 Fax: (3) 3243-9086 Tlx: NIKKEI J22308
Scan-Tech Japan Annual Last held: Sep. 29-Oct. 1, 1993	Tokyo Ryutsu Center (TRC)	AIM Japan Aiosu Gotanda Bldg. 6F, 1-10-7 Higashi-Gotanda, Shinagawa-ku, Tokyo 141 Tel: (3) 3440-9085 Fax: (3) 3440-9086
Software Show Tokyo Annual Last held: Sep., 1993	Sunshine City Convention Center Tokyo (Exhibition Hall A, World Import Mart)	Software Information Center Toto Bldg., 5-1-4 Toranomon, Minato-ku, Tokyo 105 Tel: (3) 3437-3394 Fax: (3) 3437-3398
Software Systems U.S.A. Annual Last held: Sep. 29-Oct. 1, 1993	Sunshine City Convention Center Tokyo (World Import Mart)	U.S. Department of Commerce 14th & Constitution Ave., NW Washington, D.C. 20230, USA Tel: [1] (202) 377-8859 Fax: [1] (202) 377-4324
VME-VXI Futurebus + Japan Annual Last held: Apr. 12-15, 1993	Harumi-Tokyo International Fair Ground	VME Member Landcorp Bldg. 7F, 2-1-1 Arai, Nakano-ku, Tokyo 165 Tel: (3) 5380-5863 Fax: (3) 5380-5862
WINDOWS World Tokyo Annual Last held: Jun. 16-18, 1993	Nippon Convention Center (Makuhari Messe)	Nihon Kogyo Shimbun 1-28-5 Kanda-Jimbocho, Chiyoda-ku, Tokyo 101 Tel: (3) 3292-3561 Fax: (3) 3292-6137

COMPUTER GRAPHICS
See also Computer & Information Industries; Packaging, Paper & Printing

Trade Fair	Site	Contact
Automotive CAD/CAM/CAE Show (Automotive Design & Development Show) Annual Last held: Apr. 7-9, 1993	Sunshine City Convention Center Tokyo (MIPRO Exhibition Hall)	Show Management International, Inc. 1-5-18 Meguro, Meguro-ku, Tokyo 153 Tel: (3) 3493-5871 Fax: (3) 3493-6741
Computer Graphics Osaka Annual Last held: Jun. 9-12, 1993	Mydome Osaka	Japan Management Association Osaka Kokusai Bldg., 2-3-13 Azuchimachi, Chuo-ku, Osaka 541 Tel: (6) 261-7151 Fax: (6) 261-5852
International Technical Exhibition on Image Technology and Equipment Annual Last held: Dec. 8-10, 1993	Tokyo Trade Center	Council of Image Technology and Equipment in Japan 2-16-13 Hyakunin-cho, Shinjuku-ku, Tokyo 169 Tel: (3) 3367-0571 Fax: (3) 3368-1519

Trade Fair	Site	Contact
NICOGRAPH Annual Last held: Nov., 1993	Sunshine City Convention Center Tokyo	Nihon Keizai Shimbun, Inc. 1-9-5 Otemachi, Chiyoda-ku, Tokyo 100-66 Tel: (3) 3243-9082 Fax: (3) 3243-9086 Tlx: NIKKEI J22308
CADMEC **West Japan CAD CAM** **CAE System Exhibition** Annual Last held: May 28-31, 1993	West Japan General Exhibition Center	West Japan Industry and Trade Exhibition Association 3-7-1 Asano, Kokurakita-ku Kitakyushu City, Fukuoka Pref. 802 Tel: (93) 511-6848 Fax: (93) 521-8845
DATABASES **DATABASE TOKYO** Annual Last held: 1993 (Dates not available)	Site information not available	Japan Database Industry Association 2-7 Kagurazaka, Shinjuku-ku, Tokyo 162 Tel: (3) 3235-5966 Fax: (3) 3235-5976

CONSTRUCTION & HOUSING
See also Furniture & Housewares

Trade Fair	Site	Contact
JAPAN HOME SHOW **International Building** **Materials & Interiors** **Exhibition** Annual Last held: Nov. 24-27, 1993	Harumi-Tokyo International Fair Ground	Japan Management Association 3-1-22 Shibakoen, Minato-ku, Tokyo 105 Tel: (3) 3434-6211 Fax: (3) 3434-1836/8076 Tlx: JMA J25870
Kobe International Home Fair Annual Last held: Jun. 3-6, 1993	Kobe International Exhibition Hall	Nikkan Kogyo Shimbun, Ltd. (Osaka Branch) 2-16 Kitahama-Higashi, Chuo-ku, Osaka 540 Tel: (6) 946-3384 Fax: (6) 946-3389
New Building & Business Space Annual Last held: May 19-21, 1993	Mydome Osaka	Japan Management Association Osaka Kokusai Bldg., 2-3-13 Azuchimachi, Chuo-ku, Osaka 541 Tel: (6) 261-7151 Fax: (6) 261-5852
Steel Structural **Technology Show** Every 2 years Last held: Aug. 5-8, 1993	Harumi-Tokyo International Fair Ground	Steel Structure Journal Co., Ltd. Hirano Bldg., 4-8-1 Hacchobori, Chuo-ku, Tokyo 104 Tel: (3) 3553-6961 Fax: (3) 3553-5285
Tokyo International **Good Living Show** Annual Last held: Apr. 20-25, 1993	Harumi-Tokyo International Fair Ground	Tokyo International Trade Fair Commission 4-7-24 Harumi, Chuo-ku, Tokyo 104 Tel: (3) 3531-3371 Fax: (3) 3531-1344 Tlx: 02523935 TITF J
Total Construction **Materials & Equipment** **Fair** Every 2 years Last held: May 26-29, 1993	International Exhibition Center, Osaka (INTEX Osaka)	Nihon Kogyo Shimbun 2-4-9 Umeda, Kita-ku, Osaka 530 Tel: (6) 343-3222/4 Fax: (6) 341-4773
West Japan Total Living **Show** Annual Last held: Mar. 19-22, 1993	West Japan General Exhibition Center	West Japan Industry and Trade Exhibition Association 3-7-1 Asano, Kokurakita-ku Kitakyushu City, Fukuoka Pref. 802 Tel: (93) 511-6848 Fax: (93) 521-8845

Note: Country codes for telephone and fax numbers are not displayed unless they are *outside* of Japan.
All country codes have square brackets around them, while city codes have parentheses.
The country code for Japan is [81].

Trade Fair	Site	Contact

DISTRIBUTION

Trade Fair	Site	Contact
Direct Marketing Exhibition & Symposium Annual Last held: Sep. 20-22, 1993	Sunshine City Convention Center Tokyo	Direct Marketing Exhibition Executive Committee c/o World Import Mart Co., Ltd. Sunshine City, 3-1-3 Higashi-Ikebukuro, Toshima-ku, Tokyo 170 Tel: (3) 3987-3161 Fax: (3) 3981-8371 Tlx: 2723829
Franchise Chain Show Osaka Annual Last held: Nov., 1993	International Exhibition Center, Osaka (INTEX Osaka)	Nihon Keizai Shimbun, Inc. 1-9-5 Otemachi, Chiyoda-ku, Tokyo 100-66 Tel: (3) 3243-9083 Fax: (3) 3243-9086 Tlx: NIKKEI J22308
Franchise Chain Show Tokyo Annual Last held: Aug., 1993	Harumi-Tokyo International Fair Ground	Nihon Keizai Shimbun, Inc. 1-9-5 Otemachi, Chiyoda-ku, Tokyo 100-66 Tel: (3) 3243-9083 Fax: (3) 3243-9086 Tlx: NIKKEI J22308
JAPAN SHOP International Exhibition for Shop Systems and Store Automation Annual Last held: Mar. 18-22, 1993	Harumi-Tokyo International Fair Ground	Nihon Keizai Shimbun, Inc. 1-9-5 Otemachi, Chiyoda-ku, Tokyo 100-66 Tel: (3) 3243-9083 Fax: (3) 3243-9086 Tlx: NIKKEI J22308
Store Automation Show Annual Last held: Mar. 18-22, 1993	Harumi-Tokyo International Fair Ground	Nihon Keizai Shimbun, Inc. 1-9-5 Otemachi, Chiyoda-ku, Tokyo 100-66 Tel: (3) 3243-9083 Fax: (3) 3243-9086 Tlx: NIKKEI J22308

EDUCATION

Trade Fair	Site	Contact
CAI & Educational Media Show (Education Japan) Annual Last held: Apr. 21-24, 1993	Sunshine City Convention Center Tokyo	Nihon Keizai Shimbun, Inc. 1-9-5 Otemachi, Chiyoda-ku, Tokyo 100-66 Tel: (3) 3243-9082 Fax: (3) 3243-9086 Tlx: NIKKEI J22308
Career Management Fair (Education Japan) Annual Last held: Apr. 21-24, 1993	Sunshine City Convention Center Tokyo	Nihon Keizai Shimbun, Inc. 1-9-5 Otemachi, Chiyoda-ku, Tokyo 100-66 Tel: (3) 3243-9082 Fax: (3) 3243-9086 Tlx: NIKKEI J22308
Educational Extensive Event Annual Last held: Jul. 28-30, 1993	Harumi-Tokyo International Fair Ground	Japan Educational Press 1-13-2 Ebisu-Nishi, Shibuya-ku, Tokyo 105 Tel: (3) 3461-7734 Fax: (3) 3780-0080
HRD JAPAN Japan Human Resources Development Exhibition Annual Last held: Feb. 3-6, 1993	Nippon Convention Center (Makuhari Messe)	Japan Management Association 3-1-22 Shibakoen, Minato-ku, Tokyo 105 Tel: (3) 3434-6211 Fax: (3) 3434-1836/8076 Tlx: JMA J25870
Music Education Show (Education Japan) Annual Last held: Apr. 21-24, 1993	Sunshine City Convention Center Tokyo	Nihon Keizai Shimbun, Inc. 1-9-5 Otemachi, Chiyoda-ku, Tokyo 100-66 Tel: (3) 3243-9082 Fax: (3) 3243-9086 Tlx: NIKKEI J22308

Trade Fair	Site	Contact

ELECTRONIC, ELECTRIC & COMMUNICATION EQUIPMENT
See also Computer & Information Industries

Trade Fair	Site	Contact
Automotive Electronis Show (Automotive Design & Development Show) Annual Last held: Nov. 10-12, 1993	Sunshine City Convention Center Tokyo (MIPRO Exhibition Hall)	Show Management International, Inc. 1-5-18 Meguro, Meguro-ku, Tokyo 153 Tel: (3) 3493-5871 Fax: (3) 3493-6741
Chubu Electronics Show Annual Last held: Oct. 27-30, 1993	Nagoya Trade & Industry Center	Chubu Electronics Shinkokai 3-4-41 Rokuban, Atsuta-ku, Nagoya 456 Tel: (52) 661-6476 Fax: (52) 651-5460
Communications TOKYO Annual Last held: Apr. 5-8, 1993	Harumi-Tokyo International Fair Ground	Communications Industry Association of Japan Sankei Bldg. Bekkan, 1-7-2 Otemachi, Chiyoda-ku, Tokyo 100 Tel: (3) 3231-3156 Fax: (3) 3246-0495
DISKCON JAPAN International Exhibition and Symposium on Disk and Disk Drive Manufacturing Annual Last held: Apr. 12-15, 1993	Harumi-Tokyo International Fair Ground	MESAGO Japan Corporation Pare Eteruneru 1004, 4-28-20 Yotsuya, Shinjuku-ku, Tokyo 160 Tel: (3) 3359-0894 Fax: (3) 3359-9328
Electrical Contruction Exhibition Annual Last held: May 26-29, 1993	Harumi-Tokyo International Fair Ground	Japan Electrical Construction Association Inc. 1-7-8 Moto-Akasaka, Minato-ku, Tokyo 107 Tel: (3) 3404-6425 Fax: (3) 3404-6422
EMC JAPAN Exhibition for Solutions on Electromagnetic Interference Annual Last held: Feb. 24-26, 1993	Sunshine City Convention Center Tokyo	Japan Management Association 3-1-22 Shibakoen, Minato-ku, Tokyo 105 Tel: (3) 3434-6211 Fax: (3) 3434-1836/8076 Tlx: JMA J25870
Equipment Exhibition of Motion Picture & Television Annual Last held: May 19-21, 1993	Nippon Convention Center (Makuhari Messe)	Motion Picture and Television Engineering Society of Japan, Inc. Sankei Bldg. Bekkan 9F, 1-7-2 Otemachi, Chiyoda-ku, Tokyo 100 Tel: (3) 3231-7171 Fax: (3) 3241-4284
Fineprocess Technology Japan Annual Last held: Jul. 14-16, 1993	Harumi-Tokyo International Fair Ground	Reed Exhibitions Japan, Ltd. Shinjuku Nomura Bldg. 18F, 1-26-2 Nishi-Shinjuku, Shinjuku-ku, Tokyo 163-05 Tel: (3) 3349-8501 Fax: (3) 3345-7929 Tlx: J27280 REC JPN
Frontier Technology Fair (tentative name) Every 2 years Last held: Nov. 25-27, 1993	Hakata Star Lane	Kyushu Industrial Technology Center Morimen Bldg. 6F, 2-17-5 Hakataeki-Higashi, Hakata-ku, Fukuoka City, Fukuoka Pref. 812 Tel: (92) 411-7391 Fax: (92) 472-6609
Insulation Annual Last held: Nov., 1993	Site information not available	Japan Electrical Insulation Materials Industrial Assn. Iwao Bldg. 2F, 1-16-2 Toranomon, Minato-ku Tokyo 105 Tel: (3) 3591-6371 Fax: (3) 3591-6370

Note: Country codes for telephone and fax numbers are not displayed unless they are *outside* of Japan. All country codes have square brackets around them, while city codes have parentheses. The country code for Japan is [81].

Trade Fair	Site	Contact
International Broadcast Equipment Exhibition (InterBEE) Annual Last held: Nov. 16-18, 1993 (Business Days Only)	Nippon Convention Center (Makuhari Messe)	Electronic Industries Association of Japan Tokyo Shoko Kaigisho Bldg. 7F, 3-2-2 Marunouchi, Chiyoda-ku, Tokyo 100 Tel: (3) 3284-1051 Fax: (3) 3284-0165
Internepcon Japan Annual Last held: Jan. 20-23, 1993	Nippon Convention Center (Makuhari Messe)	Reed Exhibitions Japan, Ltd. Shinjuku Nomura Bldg. 18F, 1-26-2 Nishi-Shinjuku, Shinjuku-ku, Tokyo 163-05 Tel: (3) 3349-8501 Fax: (3) 3345-7929 Tlx: J27280 REC JPN
Internepcon Osaka Annual Last held: Sep. 9-11, 1993	International Exhibition Center, Osaka (INTEX Osaka)	Reed Exhibitions Japan, Ltd. Shinjuku Nomura Bldg. 18F, 1-26-2 Nishi-Shinjuku, Shinjuku-ku, Tokyo 163-05 Tel: (3) 3349-8501 Fax: (3) 3345-7929 Tlx: J27280 REC JPN
Inter Opto International Optoelectronics Exhibition Annual Last held: Jul. 13-16, 1993	Nippon Convention Center (Makuhari Messe)	Optoelectronic Industry and Technology Development Association (OITDA) Toranomon Icchome Mori Bldg. 9F, 1-19-5 Toranomon, Minato-ku, Tokyo 105 Tel: (3) 3508-2091 Fax: (3) 5511-8218
Japan Electronics Show Annual Last held: Oct. 5-9, 1993	Nippon Convention Center (Makuhari Messe)	Electronic Industries Association of Japan Tokyo Shoko Kaigisho Bldg. 7F, 3-2-2 Marunouchi, Chiyoda-ku, Tokyo 100 Tel: (3) 3284-1051 Fax: (3) 3284-0165
JPCA Show Annual Last held: Jun. 8-11, 1993	Harumi-Tokyo International Fair Ground	Japan Printed Circuit Association Toranomon Kiyoshi Bldg. 5F, 4-3-10 Toranomon, Minato-ku, Tokyo 105 Tel: (3) 3436-4970 Fax: (3) 3436-4641
Microwave U.S.A. Annual Last held: Sept., 1993	U.S. Trade Center	U.S. Department of Commerce 14th & Constitution Ave., NW Washington, D.C. 20230, USA Tel: [1] (202) 377-8859 Fax: [1] (202) 377-4324
POWER SUPPLY JAPAN Japan Switching Power Supply Technology Exhibition Annual Last held: Feb. 24-26, 1993	Sunshine City Convention Center Tokyo	Japan Management Association 3-1-22 Shibakoen, Minato-ku, Tokyo 105 Tel: (3) 3434-6211 Fax: (3) 3434-1836/8076 Tlx: JMA J25870
SEMICON/Japan Annual Last held: Dec. 1-3, 1993 (Business Days Only)	Nippon Convention Center (Makuhari Messe)	SEMI Japan Moto-Akasaka Kikutei Bldg. 3F, 1-7-18 Moto-Akasaka, Minato-ku, Tokyo 107 Tel: (3) 5474-0701 Fax: (3) 5474-0705
SEMICON/Kansai -Kyoto Annual Last held: Jun. 9-11, 1993 (Business Days Only)	Kyoto Trade Fair Center (PULSE PLAZA)	SEMI Japan Moto-Akasaka Kikutei Bldg. 3F, 1-7-18 Moto-Akasaka, Minato-ku, Tokyo 107 Tel: (3) 5474-0701 Fax: (3) 5474-0705
SEMICON/Yokohama Annual Last held: Apr. 21-23, 1993 (Business Days Only)	Pacifico Yokohama	SEMI Japan Moto-Akasaka Kikutei Bldg. 3F, 1-7-18 Moto-Akasaka, Minato-ku, Tokyo 107 Tel: (3) 5474-0701 Fax: (3) 5474-0705

Trade Fair	Site	Contact
Supercomputing Japan International High-Performance Computing Exhibition and Conference Annual Last held: Apr. 14-16, 1993	Pacifico Yokohama	Meridian Pacific Group, Inc. 116 East Blithedale Ave., Suite 2 Mill Valley, CA 94941, USA Tel: [1] (415) 381-2255 Fax: [1] (415) 381-1451
Telecom Japan Annual Last held: Jun. 9-11, 1993	Sunshine City Convention Center Tokyo	Nihon Keizai Shimbun, Inc. 1-9-5 Otemachi, Chiyoda-ku, Tokyo 100-66 Tel: (3) 3243-9082 Fax: (3) 3243-9086 Tlx: NIKKEI J22308
Tokyo Professional Audio Show Annual Last held: Jun. 23-25, 1993	Sunshine City Convention Center Tokyo (Exhibition Hall D)	AES/PAS Organizing Committee c/o Japan Audio Society, Mori Bldg., 1-14-34 Jingumae, Shibuya-ku, Tokyo 150 Tel: (3) 3403-6649 Fax: (3) 3403-6545

ENVIRONMENTAL INDUSTRIES & CIVIL ENGINEERING

Trade Fair	Site	Contact
CONET International Construction Equipment Fair Every 2 years Nov. 17-20, 1994	Nippon Convention Center (Makuhari Messe)	Japan Construction Mechanization Association Kikai Shinko Kaikan, 3-5-8 Shibakoen, Minato-ku, Tokyo 105 Tel: (3) 3433-1501 Fax: (3) 3432-0289
GEOTECH Every 2 years Apr. 12-15, 1994	Harumi-Tokyo International Fair Ground	Tokyo International Trade Fair Commission 4-7-24 Harumi, Chuo-ku, Tokyo 104 Tel: (3) 3531-3371 Fax: (3) 3531-1344 Tlx: 02523935 TITF J
International Environment Machinery Fair (tentative name) Annual Last held: Sep. 14-17, 1993	West Japan General Exhibition Center	West Japan Industry and Trade Exhibition Association 3-7-1 Asano, Kokurakita-ku, Kitakyushu City, Fukuoka Pref. 802 Tel: (93) 511-6848 Fax: (93) 521-8845
International Fire Exhibition Every 3 years. Oct. 18-27, 1994	Harumi-Tokyo International Fair Ground	Tokyo International Trade Fair Commission 4-7-24 Harumi, Chuo-ku, Tokyo 104 Tel: (3) 3531-3371 Fax: (3) 3531-1344 Tlx: 02523935 TITF J
INTEROFFICE International Office Environment and Intelligent Building Show Annual Last held: Feb. 3-6, 1993	Nippon Convention Center (Makuhari Messe)	Japan Management Association 3-1-22 Shibakoen, Minato-ku, Tokyo 105 Tel: (3) 3434-6211 Fax: (3) 3434-1836/8076 Tlx: JMA J25870
New Earth (Global Environment Technology Show) Every 2 years Last held: Dec. 7-10, 1993	International Exhibition Center, Osaka (INTEX Osaka)	Osaka International Trade Fair Commission 1-5-102 Nanko-Kita, Suminoe-ku, Osaka 559 Tel: (6) 612-3883 Fax: (6) 612-8585 Tlx: 526-7660 OITFC J
New Factory Exhibition (High Technology Tokyo) Annual Last held: May 28-31, 1993	Harumi-Tokyo International Fair Ground	Nikkan Kogyo Shimbun. Ltd. 1-8-10 Kudan-Kita, Chiyoda-ku, Tokyo 102 Tel: (3) 3222-7232 Fax: (3) 3221-7137 Tlx: NIKKANKO J29687

Note: Country codes for telephone and fax numbers are not displayed unless they are *outside* of Japan. All country codes have square brackets around them, while city codes have parentheses. The country code for Japan is [81].

Trade Fair	Site	Contact
New Factory Exhibition Annual Last held: May 19-22, 1993	International Exhibition Center, Osaka (INTEX Osaka)	Nikkan Kogyo Shimbun, Ltd. (Osaka Branch) 2-16 Kitahama-Higashi, Chuo-ku, Osaka 540 Tel: (6) 946-3384 Fax: (6) 946-3389

FACTORY AUTOMATION
See also Computer & Information Industries, Machines & Instruments

Trade Fair	Site	Contact
Automated Design Engineering for Electonics Annual Last held: Jan. 20-22, 1993	Nippon Convention Center (Makuhari Messe)	Reed Exhibitions Japan, Ltd. Shinjuku Nomura Bldg. 18F, 1-26-2 Nishi-Shinjuku, Shinjuku-ku, Tokyo 163-05 Tel: (3) 3349-8501 Fax: (3) 3345-7929 Tlx: J27280 REC JPN
Automatic Machines & Technology Exhibition (Osaka Mechatronics Fair) Annual Last held: May 19-22, 1993	International Exhibition Center, Osaka (INTEX Osaka)	Nikkan Kogyo Shimbun, Ltd. (Osaka Branch) 2-16 Kitahama-Higashi, Chuo-ku, Osaka 540 Tel: (6) 946-3384 Fax: (6) 946-3389
Automatic Machines & Technology Exhibition Annual Last held: Nov. 2-5, 1993	Harumi-Tokyo International Fair Ground	Nikkan Kogyo Shimbun. Ltd. 1-8-10 Kudan-Kita, Chiyoda-ku, Tokyo 102 Tel: (3) 3222-7239 Fax: (3) 3221-7137 Tlx: NIKKANKO J29687
Automatic Machines & Technology Exhibition (Factory Automation Nagoya) Annual Last held: Jun. 5-8, 1993	Nagoya International Exhibition Hall	Daily Industrial News (Nagoya Branch) 2-21-28 Izumi, Higashi-ku, Nagoya 461 Tel: (52) 931-6151 Fax: (52) 931-6159
Automotive Manufacturing Show (Automotive Design & Development Show Annual Last held: Apr. 7-9, 1993	Sunshine City Convention Center Tokyo (MIPRO Exhibition Hall)	Show Management International, Inc. 1-5-18 Meguro, Meguro-ku, Tokyo 153 Tel: (3) 3493-5871 Fax: (3) 3493-6741
CAD/CAM/CAE System Show (High Technology Tokyo) Annual Last held: May 28-31, 1993	Harumi-Tokyo International Fair Ground	Nikkan Kogyo Shimbun. Ltd. 1-8-10 Kudan-Kita, Chiyoda-ku, Tokyo 102 Tel: (3) 3222-7232 Fax: (3) 3221-7137 Tlx: NIKKANKO J29687
CAD/CAM/CAE System Show Nagoya (Factory Automation Nagoya) Annual Last held: Jun. 5-8, 1993	Nagoya International Exhibition Hall	Daily Industrial News (Nagoya Branch) 2-21-28 Izumi, Higashi-ku, Nagoya 461 Tel: (52) 931-6151 Fax: (52) 931-6159
CAD/CAM/CAE System Show Osaka (Osaka Mechatronics Fair Annual Last held: May 19-22, 1993	International Exhibition Center, Osaka (INTEX Osaka)	Nikkan Kogyo Shimbun, Ltd. (Osaka Branch) 2-16 Kitahama-Higashi, Chuo-ku, Osaka 540 Tel: (6) 946-3384 Fax: (6) 946-3389
CAE 8 CAD/CAM Systems Show (Technology Japan) Annyal Last held: Apr. 12-15, 1993	Harumi-Tokyo International Fair Ground	Nihon Kogyo Shimbun 1-28-5 Kanda-Jimbocho, Chiyoda-ku, Tokyo 101 Tel: (3) 3292-3561 Fax: (3) 3292-6137

Trade Fair	Site	Contact
CIM JAPAN **Computer Integrated Manufacturing Systems** Annual Last held: Jun. 23-26, 1993	Nippon Convention Center (Makuhari Messe)	Reed Exhibitions Japan, Ltd. Shinjuku Nomura Bldg. 18F, 1-26-2 Nishi-Shinjuku, Shinjuku-ku, Tokyo 163-05 Tel: (3) 3349-8501 Fax: (3) 3345-7929 Tlx: J27280 REC JPN
Exhibition of Measurement & Inspection by Image Technology Annual Last held: Jun. 9-11, 1993	Pacifico Yokohama (tentative)	Seiki Tsushin Sha Company, Ltd. 2-16-13 Hyakunin-cho, Shinjuku-ku, Tokyo 169 Tel: (3) 3367-0571 Fax: (3) 3368-1519
FA Computer & Network System (Factory Automation Nagoya) Annual Last held: Jun. 5-8, 1993	Nagoya International Exhibition Hall	Daily Industrial News (Nagoya Branch) 2-21-28 Izumi, Higashi-ku, Nagoya 461 Tel: (52) 931-6151 Fax: (52) 931-6159
FA Computer & Network System (Osaka Mechatronics Fair) Annual Last held: May 19-22, 1993	International Exhibition Center, Osaka (INTEX Osaka)	Nikkan Kogyo Shimbun, Ltd. (Osaka Branch) 2-16 Kitahama-Higashi, Chuo-ku, Osaka 540 Tel: (6) 946-3384 Fax: (6) 946-3389
FA INTELLIGENT NETWORK System Show (Technology Japan) Annual Last held: Apr. 12-15, 1993	Harumi-Tokyo International Fair Ground	Nihon Kogyo Shimbun 1-28-5 Kanda-Jimbocho, Chiyoda-ku, Tokyo 101 Tel: (3) 3292-3561 Fax: (3) 3292-6137
Imagetech Annual Last held: Jun. 9-12, 1993	International Fair Hall	Japan Management Association Osaka Kokusai Bldg., 2-3-13 Azuchimachi, Chuo-ku, Osaka 541 Tel: (6) 261-7151 Fax: (6) 261-5852
International Industrial Robot Exhibition Every 2 years Last held: Nov. 2-5, 1993	Harumi-Tokyo International Fair Ground	Nikkan Kogyo Shimbun. Ltd. 1-8-10 Kudan-Kita, Chiyoda-ku, Tokyo 102 Tel: (3) 3222-7239 Fax: (3) 3221-7137 Tlx: NIKKANKO J29687
Mechatronics Technology Japan Every 2 years Last held: Oct. 15-19, 1993	Nagoya International Exhibition Hall	Nagoya International Trade Fair Commission 2-6-3 Fukiage, Chikusa-ku, Nagoya 464 Tel: (52) 735-2111 Fax: (52) 735-2116
Robomation (Osaka Mechatronics Fair) Annual Last held: May 19-22, 1993	International Exhibition Center, Osaka (INTEX Osaka)	Nikkan Kogyo Shimbun, Ltd. (Osaka Branch) 2-16 Kitahama-Higashi, Chuo-ku, Osaka 540 Tel: (6) 946-3384 Fax: (6) 946-3389
System Control Fair Annual Last held: Oct. 5-8, 1993	International Exhibition Center, Osaka (INTEX Osaka)	Japan Electrical Manufacturers' Association (JEMA) Denki Kogyo Kaikan, 2-4-15 Nagata-cho, Chiyoda-ku Tokyo 100 Tel: (3) 3581-4845 Fax: (3) 3506-0475
Tohoku FA Show Annual Last held: Jun. 24-26, 1993	Sendai Oroshisho Center Sun-Festa	C. N. T., Inc. Hamaso Bldg. 4F, 1-11 Kanda-Ogawamachi, Chiyoda-ku, Tokyo 101 Tel: (3) 3293-2755 Fax: (3) 3293-3520

Note: Country codes for telephone and fax numbers are not displayed unless they are *outside* of Japan.
All country codes have square brackets around them, while city codes have parentheses.
The country code for Japan is [81].

Trade Fair	Site	Contact

FOOD, BEVERAGES & FOOD PROCESSING
See also Agriculture, Forestry & Fisheries

Trade Fair	Site	Contact
Beer & Spirits Annual Last held: May 26-29, 1993	Sunshine City Convention Center Tokyo	JES, Ltd. Seshita Bldg. 301, 2-8-8 Koraku, Bunkyo-ku, Tokyo 112 Tel: (3) 3814-8655 Fax: (3) 3814-8687
Better Confectionery Show Annual Last held: May 8-9, 1993 (Business Days Only)	Osaka Merchandise Mart (OMM)	Weekly Confectionery Journal 1-3-2 Osaka, Tennoji-ku, Osaka 543 Tel: (6) 771-7093 Fax: (6) 771-9435
CATEREX JAPAN: Japan Food Catering & Equipment Exhibition Annual Last held: Dec. 1-4, 1993	Harumi-Tokyo International Fair Ground	Japan Management Association 3-1-22 Shibakoen, Minato-ku, Tokyo 105 Tel: (3) 3434-6211 Fax: (3) 3434-1836/8076 Tlx: JMA J25870
International Confectionery Tokyo Annual Sep. 1-4, 1993 (tentative)	Sunshine City Convention Center Tokyo	JES, Ltd. Seshita Bldg. 301, 2-8-8 Koraku, Bunkyo-ku, Tokyo 112 Tel: (3) 3814-8655 Fax: (3) 3814-8687
International Food & Beverage Exhibition and Conference for Japan and Asia (FOODEX JAPAN) Annual Last held: Mar. 9-13, 1993	Nippon Convention Center (Makuhari Messe)	Japan Management Association 3-1-22 Shibakoen, Minato-ku, Tokyo 105 Tel: (3) 3434-6211 Fax: (3) 3434-1836/8076 Tlx: JMA J25870
International Food Machinery Exhibition Annual Last held: May 25-28, 1993	Nippon Convention Center (Makuhari Messe)	Japan Food Machinery Manufacturers' Association Meiwa Bldg. 5F, 1-15-10 Toranomon, Minato-ku Tokyo 105 Tel: (3) 3503-7661 Fax: (3) 3503-7620
International Hotel and Restaurant Show (HOTERES JAPAN) Annual Last held: Mar. 9-13, 1993	Harumi-Tokyo International Fair Ground	Japan Management Association 3-1-22 Shibakoen, Minato-ku, Tokyo 105 Tel: (3) 3434-6211 Fax: (3) 3434-1836/8076 Tlx: JMA J25870
Japan Foodservice Show Every 2 years Nov. 24-27, 1994	Harumi-Tokyo International Fair Ground	Japan Foodservice Association Ginza Orient Bldg. 5F, 8-9-13 Ginza, Chuo-ku, Tokyo 104 Tel: (3) 3573-3231 Fax: (3) 3572-5099 Tlx: 252-3085 JFSA J
Japan International Food Engineering & Industry Show Every 2 years 1994 (Dates to be announced)	International Exhibition Center, Osaka (INTEX Osaka)	Osaka International Trade Fair Commission 1-5-102 Nanko-Kita, Suminoe-ku, Osaka 559 Tel: (6) 612-1212 Fax: (6) 612-8585 Tlx: 5267660 OITFC J
MOBAC SHOW Every 2 years Last held: Mar. 27-30, 1993	Harumi-Tokyo International Fair Ground	Japan Bakery and Confectionary Machinery Manufacturers' Assocation No. 3 Higashi Bldg., 1 Kanda-Hirakawacho, Chiyoda-ku, Tokyo 101 Tel: (3) 3862-8478 Fax: (3) 3862-8470
Osaka International Food & Beverage Exhibition Every 2 years Last held: Sep. 7-10, 1993	International Exhibition Center, Osaka (INTEX Osaka)	Japan Management Association Osaka Kokusai Bldg., 2-3-13 Azuchimachi, Chuo-ku, Osaka 541 Tel: (6) 261-7151 Fax: (6) 261-5852

Trade Fair	Site	Contact
Osaka International Hotel & Restaurant Show Every 2 years Last held: Sep. 7-10, 1993	International Exhibition Center, Osaka (INTEX Osaka)	Japan Management Association Osaka Kokusai Bldg., 2-3-13 Azuchimachi, Chuo-ku, Osaka 541 Tel: (6) 261-7151 Fax: (6) 261-5852
Supermarket Trade Show Annual Last held: Mar. 17-20, 1993	Nippon Convention Center (Makuhari Messe)	Japan Self-Service Association 7-22-17 Nishi-Gotanda, Shinagawa-ku, Tokyo 141 Tel: (3) 3494-3836 Fax: (3) 3494-3836 Tlx: 2467439 JSSA
Tokyo International Sea Food Show Annual Last held: Jun. 10-12, 1993	Harumi-Tokyo International Fair Ground	JES, Ltd. Seshita Bldg. 301, 2-8-8 Koraku, Bunkyo-ku, Tokyo 112 Tel: (3) 3814-8655 Fax: (3) 3814-8687
West Japan Food Machinery Exhibition Annual Last held: Jun. 11-14, 1993	Fukuoka International Center	Nikkan Kogyo Shimbun, Ltd. (Seibu Branch) 1-1 Komondomachi, Hakata-ku, Fukuoka City, Fukuoka Pref. 812 Tel: (92) 271-5715 Fax: (92) 271-5743
West Japan Kitchen & Cooking Equipment Exhibition Annual Last held: Jun. 11-14, 1993	Fukuoka International Center	Nikkan Kogyo Shimbun, Ltd. (Seibu Branch) 1-1 Komondomachi, Hakata-ku, Fukuoka City, Fukuoka Pref. 812 Tel: (92) 271-5715 Fax: (92) 271-5743
Wine Japan International Wine, Spirits, Beers and Beverages Exhibition and Convention Annual Last held: May 26-29, 1993	Sunshine City Convention Center Tokyo (Exhibition Hall B, Exhibition Hall D, MIPRO Exhibition Hall)	JES, Ltd. Seshita Bldg. 301, 2-8-8 Koraku, Bunkyo-ku, Tokyo 112 Tel: (3) 3814-8655 Fax: (3) 3814-8687

FURNITURE & HOUSEWARES
See also Construction & Housing

Trade Fair	Site	Contact
Aichi Superior Furniture Exhibition Annual Last held: May 20-21, 1993	Nagoya Trade & Industry Center	Aichi Furniture Federative Association 3-13-12 Osu, Naka-ku, Nagoya 460 Tel: (52) 261-5938 Fax. (052) 261-0693
International Furniture Fair Tokyo Annual Last held: Nov. 18-21, 1993	Harumi-Tokyo International Fair Ground	International Development Association of the Furniture Industry of Japan Karukozaka Tanaka Bldg. 3F, 2-16-1 Kagurazaka, Shinjuku-ku, Tokyo 162 Tel: (3) 5261-9401 Fax: (3) 5261-9404 Tlx: IDAFIJ J27924
International Glassware Show Annual Last held: Jan. 21-23, 1993	Sunshine City Convention Center Tokyo (MIPRO Exhibition Hall)	Glass Manufacturers Association of Japan Nippon Garasu Kogyo Center Bldg., 3-1-9 Shimbashi, Minato-ku, Tokyo 105 Tel: (3) 3591-2697 Fax: (3) 3595-2717
International Housewares Show Tokyo Annual Last held: Jun. 10-12, 1993	Nippon Convention Center (Makuhari Messe)	International Housewares Show Conference c/o Japan General Merchandise Promotion Center Sunshine 60 Bldg. 15F, 3-1-1 Higashi-Ikebukuro, Toshima-ku, Tokyo 170 Tel: (3) 3987-1231 Fax: (3) 3987-1238

Note: Country codes for telephone and fax numbers are not displayed unless they are *outside* of Japan. All country codes have square brackets around them, while city codes have parentheses. The country code for Japan is [81].

Trade Fair	Site	Contact
Internationale Frankfurter Messe Asia Annual Last held: Jun. 10-12, 1993	Nippon Convention Center (Makuhari Messe)	Messe Frankfurt, Inc. No. 2 Kiya Bldg. 3F, 4-3-2 Iidabashi, Chiyoda-ku Tokyo 102 Tel: (3) 5275-2851 Fax: (3) 5275-3410
JAPAN DIY SHOW in OSAKA Annual Last held: Mar. 12-14, 1993	International Exhibition Center, Osaka (INTEX Osaka)	Japan DIY Industry Association No. 2 Okano Bldg., 2-16-7 Higashi-Nihombashi, Chuo-ku, Tokyo 103 Tel: (3) 5687-4475 Fax: (3) 5687-4487
JAPAN DIY -HC SHOW Annual Last held: Sep. 3-5, 1993	Nippon Convention Center (Makuhari Messe)	Japan DIY Industry Association No. 2 Okano Bldg., 2-16-7 Higashi-Nihombashi, Chuo-ku, Tokyo 103 Tel: (3) 5687-4475 Fax: (3) 5687-4487
JAPANTEX Annual Last held: Jan. 27-30, 1993	Nippon Convention Center (Makuhari Messe)	Nippon Interior Fabrics Association (NIF) Fukuda Bldg. 6F, 2-3-23 Hamamatsu-cho, Minato-ku, Tokyo 105 Tel: (3) 3433-4521 Fax. (03) 3433-7860
Lifestyle Annual Last held: May 19-22, 1993	Sunshine City Convention Center Tokyo	JES, Ltd. Seshita Bldg. 301, 2-8-8 Koraku, Bunkyo-ku, Tokyo 112 Tel: (3) 3814-8655 Fax: (3) 3814-8687

GIFTS, JEWELRY & STATIONERY

Trade Fair	Site	Contact
Gift & New Life Goods Show Osaka Annual Last held: Jul. 20-21, 1993	Mydome Osaka	Japan General Merchandise Promotion Center Sunshine 60 Bldg. 15F, 3-1-1 Higashi-Ikebukuro, Toshima-ku, Tokyo 170 Tel: (3) 3987-1231 Fax: (3) 3987-1238
International Gift Show All Western Japan 2 times a year Last held: Feb. 3-5, 1993 (Business Days Only)	Kobe International Exhibition Hall	Business Guide, Inc. Nagahori Yachiyo Bldg. 3F, 1-11-9 Minami-Semba, Chuo-ku, Osaka 542 Tel: (6) 263-0075 Fax: (6) 263-0074
International Jewelry Tokyo Annual Last held: Feb. 21-24, 1993	Nippon Convention Center (Makuhari Messe)	Reed Exhibitions Japan, Ltd. Shinjuku Nomura Bldg. 18F, 1-26-2 Nishi-Shinjuku, Shinjuku-ku, Tokyo 163-05 Tel: (3) 3349-8501 Fax: (3) 3345-7929 Tlx: J27280 REC JPN
International Premium Incentive Show 2 times a year. Last held: Apr. 14-16, 1993 (Business Days Only)	Sunshine City Convention Center Tokyo	Business Guide-Sha, Inc. 2-6-2 Kaminarimon, Taito-ku, Tokyo 111 Tel: (3) 3847-9155 Fax: (3) 3843-9850
International Stationery & Office Products Tokyo Show & Conference Annual Last held: Sep. 9-11, 1993	Nippon Convention Center (Makuhari Messe)	All Japan Stationery Association Tokyo Bungu Kyowa Kaikan 6F 1-2-10 Yanagibashi, Taito-ku, Tokyo 111 Tel: (3) 5687-0961 Fax: (3) 5687-0340
Tokyo International Gift Show 2 times a year. Last held: Feb. 18-20, 1993 (Business Days Only)	Harumi-Tokyo International Fair Ground	Business Guide-Sha, Inc. 2-6-2 Kaminarimon, Taito-ku, Tokyo 111 Tel: (3) 3847-9155 Fax: (3) 3843-9850
Tokyo International Stationery Fair Annual Last held: Nov. 9-10, 1993	Tokyo Trade Center	Council of Stationary Industry Cooperative Association 16-2 Kodemma-cho, Chuo-ku, Tokyo 103 Tel: (3) 3667-7853 Fax: (3) 3639-4949

Trade Fair	Site	Contact
Variety Impex (Import/Export) Fair Annual Last held: Aug. 26-27, 1993	Tokyo Trade Center	Boeki Tsushinsha 3-19-2 Kotobuki, Taito-ku, Tokyo 111 Tel: (3) 3841-8817 Fax: (3) 3841-5086

HOBBIES, RECREATION & TRAVEL   Includes art, flower shows, photography, toys
See also Sporting Goods

Trade Fair	Site	Contact
Amateur Radio Festival Annual Last held: Aug. 20-22, 1993	Harumi-Tokyo International Fair Ground	Japan Amateur Radio League, Inc. 1-14-2 Sugamo, Toshima-ku, Tokyo 170 Tel: (3) 5395-3119 Fax. (03) 5395-3130
AOU Amusement EXPO Annual Last held: Feb. 16-17, 1993	Nippon Convention Center (Makuhari Messe)	All Nippon Amusement Machine Operators' Union Riverside Tonakai Bldg. 503, 91 Kanda-Sakumagashi, Chiyoda-ku, Tokyo 101 Tel: (3) 3866-9371 Fax: (3) 3866-9389
Camping & RV Show Nagoya Annual Last held: May 8-9, 1993	Nagoya Trade & Industry Center	Japan Auto Camping Federation Yotsuya Takagi Bldg., 2-9 Yotsuya, Shinjuku-ku Tokyo 160 Tel: (3) 3357-2851 Fax: (3) 3357-2850
Camping & RV Show Osaka Annual Last held: Mar. 6-7, 1993	Twin 21	Japan Auto Camping Federation Yotsuya Takagi Bldg., 2-9 Yotsuya, Shinjuku-ku Tokyo 160 Tel: (3) 3357-2851 Fax: (3) 3357-2850
Camping & RV Show Tokyo Annual Last held: May 14-16, 1993	Yoyogi National Stadium	Japan Auto Camping Federation Yotsuya Takagi Bldg., 2-9 Yotsuya, Shinjuku-ku Tokyo 160 Tel: (3) 3357-2851 Fax: (3) 3357-2850
Camping Car Trade Show Annual Last held: Jan. 30-31, 1993	Tokyo Dome (Big Egg)	Japan Auto Camping Federation Yotsuya Takagi Bldg., 2-9 Yotsuya, Shinjuku-ku Tokyo 160 Tel: (3) 3357-2851 Fax: (3) 3357-2850
Event Promotion Show Annual Last held: Mar. 18-22, 1993	Harumi-Tokyo International Fair Ground	Nihon Keizai Shimbun, Inc. 1-9-5 Otemachi, Chiyoda-ku, Tokyo 100-66 Tel: (3) 3243-9083 Fax: (3) 3243-9086 Tlx: NIKKEI J22308
Japan Hobby Show Annual Last held: May 13-15, 1993	Sunshine City Convention Center Tokyo (All Halls)	Hobby Association of Japan Hori Bldg. 3F, 3-11-1 Asukasabashi, Taito-ku, Tokyo 111 Tel: (3) 3851-6628 Fax: (3) 3864-8535
Japan World Resort & Cruise Fair Annual Last held: Mar. 11-14, 1993	Pacifico Yokohama	World Resort & Cruise Fair Organizing Committee Kotani Bldg. 2F, 1-6-6 Yuraku-cho, Chiyoda-ku, Tokyo 100 Tel: (3) 3580-8255 Fax: (3) 3580-8256
JATA (JATA Travel Trade Show) Every 2 years Last held: Nov. 29-Dec. 2, 1993	New Takanawa Prince Hotel	Japan Association Travel Agents Zennittsu Kasumigaseki Bldg. 3F, 3-3-3 Kasumigaseki, Chiyoda-ku, Tokyo 100 Tel: (3) 3592-1271 Fax: (3) 3592-1268 Tlx: JATAINTL J33822
Park & Leisure Exhibition Annual Last held: Apr. 29- May 3, 1993	Harumi-Tokyo International Fair Ground	System Development Society Akiyama Bldg., 2-24-6 Higashi-Ueno, Taito-ku Tokyo 110 Tel: (3) 3837-5741 Fax: (3) 3837-5743

Note: Country codes for telephone and fax numbers are not displayed unless they are *outside* of Japan.
All country codes have square brackets around them, while city codes have parentheses.
The country code for Japan is [81].

Trade Fair	Site	Contact
Photo Accessory & Imaging System Show (Nagoya) Annual Last held: Apr. 1-6, 1993	Maruei Department Store	Japan Photo & Video Accessory Association JCII Bldg., 25 Ichiban-cho, Chiyoda-ku, Tokyo 102 Tel: (3) 5276-3581 Fax: (3) 5276-3584
Photo Accessory & Imaging System Show (Osaka) Annual Last held: Mar. 19-21, 1993	Mydome Osaka	Japan Photo & Video Accessory Association JCII Bldg., 25 Ichiban-cho, Chiyoda-ku, Tokyo 102 Tel: (3) 5276-3581 Fax: (3) 5276-3584
Photo Accessory & Imaging System Show (Tokyo) Annual Last held: Mar. 5-7, 1993	Science Museum Exhibition Hall	Japan Photo & Video Accessory Association JCII Bldg., 25 Ichiban-cho, Chiyoda-ku, Tokyo 102 Tel: (3) 5276-3581 Fax: (3) 5276-3584
Tokyo Flower Show Annual Last held: Feb. 25-28, 1993	Harumi-Tokyo International Fair Ground	Tokyo International Trade Fair Commission 4-7-24 Harumi, Chuo-ku, Tokyo 104 Tel: (3) 3531-3371 Fax: (3) 3531-1344 Tlx: 02523935 TITF J
Tokyo International Art Show (TIAS) Annual Last held: Jan. 22-24, 1993	Harumi-Tokyo International Fair Ground	Art Press Center, Inc. 2-2-5 Roppongi, Minato-ku, Tokyo 106 Tel: (3) 3505-1221 Fax: (3) 3505 5997
Tokyo Toy Show Annual Last held: Jun. 3-6, 1993	Nippon Convention Center (Makuhari Messe)	Japan International Toy Fair Association 4-22-4 Higashi-Komagata, Sumida-ku, Tokyo 130 Tel: (3) 3829-2521 Fax: (3) 3829-2549
TOUR EXPO Every 2 years Last held: Apr. 22-25, 1993	International Exhibition Center, Osaka (INTEX Osaka)	Osaka International Trade Fair Commission 1-5-102 Nanko-Kita, Suminoe-ku, Osaka 559 Tel: (6) 612-1042 Fax: (6) 612-8585 Tlx: 526-7660 OITFC J
West Japan China Ware Festa Annual Last held: Sep. 23-27, 1993	West Japan General Exhibition Center	West Japan Industry and Trade Exhibition Association 3-7-1 Asano, Kokurakita-ku Kitakyushu City, Fukuoka Pref. 802 Tel: (93) 511-6848 Fax: (93) 521-8845
World Travel Fair Every 2 years Dec., 1994 (tentative)	Site information to be announced	World Travel Fair Organizing Committee 1-5-8 Iidabashi, Chiyoda-ku, Tokyo 102 Tel: (3) 3234-7054 Fax. (03) 3237-9278 Tlx: 2322139

INDUSTRIAL MATERIALS & CHEMICALS
See also Metal & Metal Finishing

Advanced Materials & Engineering Exhibition (Osaka Mechatronics Fair) Annual Last held: May 19-22, 1993	International Exhibition Center, Osaka (INTEX Osaka)	Nikkan Kogyo Shimbun, Ltd. (Osaka Branch) 2-16 Kitahama-Higashi, Chuo-ku, Osaka 540 Tel: (6) 946-3384 Fax: (6) 946-3389
Automotive Materials Show (Automotive Design & Development Show) Annual Last held: Nov. 10-12, 1993	Sunshine City Convention Center Tokyo (MIPRO Exhibition Hall)	Show Management International, Inc. 1-5-18 Meguro, Meguro-ku, Tokyo 153 Tel: (3) 3493-5871 Fax: (3) 3493-6741

Trade Fair	Site	Contact
Expo Nonwovens Asia Every 3 years Mar. 16-18, 1994	Harumi-Tokyo International Fair Ground	Miller Freeman Japan Co., Ltd. 3-11-14-805 Akasaka, Minato-ku, Tokyo 107 Tel: (3) 3584-1560 Fax: (3) 3505-1768
Fine Ceramics Fair Annual Last held: Apr. 22-25, 1993	Nagoya Trade & Industry Center	Japan Fine Ceramics Center 2-4-1 Mutsuno, Atsuta-ku, Nagoya 456 Tel: (52) 871-3500 Fax: (52) 871-3505
High-Tech Materials Exhibition Annual Last held: May 18-21, 1993	Nippon Convention Center (Makuhari Messe)	Nihon Keizai Shimbun, Inc. 1-9-5 Otemachi, Chiyoda-ku, Tokyo 100-66 Tel: (3) 3243-9082 Fax: (3) 3243-9086 Tlx: NIKKEI J22308
INCHEM TOKYO International Trade Fair for Chemical and Process Engineering Every 2 years Last held: Nov. 10-13, 1993	Harumi-Tokyo International Fair Ground	Japan Management Association 3-1-22 Shibakoen, Minato-ku, Tokyo 105 Tel: (3) 3434-6211 Fax: (3) 3434-1836/8076 Tlx: JMA J25870
International Plastic Fair (IPF) Every 3 years Jan. 14-18, 1994	Nippon Convention Center (Makuhari Messe)	Nikkan Kogyo Shimbun, Ltd. 1-8-10 Kudan-Kita, Chiyoda-ku, Tokyo 102 Tel: (3) 3222-7239 Fax: (3) 3221-7137 Tlx: NIKKANKO J29687
JP-Plastics & Rubber Fair Every 1.5 years Last held: Oct. 22-26, 1993	Harumi-Tokyo International Fair Ground	JP Fair Association Ginza Yamagishi Bldg., 2-10-6 Ginza, Chuo-ku Tokyo 104 Tel: (3) 3542-3557 Fax: (3) 3542-3595
TECHTEXTIL ASIA-International Trade Fair & Symposium for Industrial Textiles Every 2 years 1994 (Dates to be announced)	International Exhibition Center, Osaka (INTEX Osaka)	Osaka International Trade Fair Commission 1-5-102 Nanko-Kita, Suminoe-ku, Osaka 559 Tel: (6) 612-1212 Fax: (6) 612-8585 Tlx: 5267660 OITFC J

MACHINES & INSTRUMENTS
See also Tools: Measuring & Testing; Tools: Precision & Optical; other categories which include exhibitions with machines specific to those industries

CERAM JAPAN Last held: Nov. 22-24, 1993	Nippon Convention Center (Makuhari Messe)	MESAGO Japan Corporation Pare Eteruneru 1004, 4-28-20 Yotsuya, Shinjuku-ku, Tokyo 160 Tel: (3) 3359-0894 Fax: (3) 3359-9328
Factory Automation System Exhibition (High Technology Tokyo) Annual Last held: May 28-31, 1993	Harumi-Tokyo International Fair Ground	Nikkan Kogyo Shimbun, Ltd. 1-8-10 Kudan-Kita, Chiyoda-ku, Tokyo 102 Tel: (3) 3222-7232 Fax: (3) 3221-7137 Tlx: NIKKANKO J29687
HVAC & R JAPAN Every 2 years Mar. 1-4, 1994	Harumi-Tokyo International Fair Ground	Japan Refrigeration and Air Conditioning Industry Association Kikai Shinko Kaikan, 3-5-8 Shibakoen Minato-ku Tokyo 105 Tel: (3) 3432-1671 Fax: (3) 3438-0308

Note: Country codes for telephone and fax numbers are not displayed unless they are *outside* of Japan.
All country codes have square brackets around them, while city codes have parentheses.
The country code for Japan is [81].

Trade Fair	Site	Contact
IFPEX (International Fluid Power Exhibition) Every 2 years Last held: Oct. 13-16, 1993	Harumi-Tokyo International Fair Ground	Nihon Kogyo Shimbun 1-28-5 Kanda-Jimbocho, Chiyoda-ku, Tokyo 101 Tel: (3) 3292-3561 Fax: (3) 3292-6137
Industrial Machine Exhibition Kanazawa Annual Last held: Apr. 16-19, 1993	Ishikawa-ken Sangyo Tenjikan	Ishikawa Machinery Association 1-72 Tomizumachi Kanazawa City, Ishikawa Pref. 920-02 Tel: (762) 68-0121 Fax: (762) 68-3577
International Metalworking Machines Exhibition (Osaka Mechatronics Fair) Annual Last held: May 19-22, 1993	International Exhibition Center, Osaka (INTEX Osaka)	Nikkan Kogyo Shimbun, Ltd. (Osaka Branch) 2-16 Kitahama-Higashi, Chuo-ku, Osaka 540 Tel: (6) 946-3384 Fax: (6) 946-3389
International Metalworking Machines Exhibition (Factory Automation Nagoya) Annual Last held: Jun. 5-8, 1993	Nagoya International Exhibition Hall	Daily Industrial News (Nagoya Branch) 2-21-28 Izumi, Higashi-ku, Nagoya 461 Tel: (52) 931-6151 Fax: (52) 931-6159
International Metalworking Machines Exhibition (Intermex Tokyo) (High Technology Tokyo) Annual Last held: May 28-31, 1993	Harumi-Tokyo International Fair Ground	Nikkan Kogyo Shimbun, Ltd. 1-8-10 Kudan-Kita, Chiyoda-ku, Tokyo 102 Tel: (3) 3222-7232 Fax: (3) 3221-7137 Tlx: NIKKANKO J 29687
International Vacuum Show Annual Last held: Sep. 8-10, 1993	Site information not available	Japan Vacuum Industry Association Kikai Shinko Kaikan 512, 3-5-8 Shibakoen Minato-ku, Tokyo 105 Tel: (3) 3459-1228 Fax: (3) 3459-9405
Interphex Japan Every 2 years 1994 (Dates to be announced)	International Exhibition Center, Osaka (INTEX Osaka) (tentative)	Nihon Kogyo Shimbun 2-4-9 Umeda, Kita-ku, Osaka 530 Tel: (6) 343-3222/4 Fax: (6) 341-4773
Japan Glass plus Metal Every 2 years Feb. 17-19, 1994	Nippon Convention Center (Makuhari Messe)	MESAGO Japan Corporation Pare Eteruneru 1004, 4-28-20 Yotsuya, Shinjuku-ku, Tokyo 160 Tel: (3) 3359-0894 Fax: (3) 3359-9328
Kyushu Scientific Instruments Show Every 2 years May, 1994 (tentative)	Site information to be announced	Nihon Kogyo Shimbun 2-4-9 Umeda, Kita-ku, Osaka 530 Tel: (6) 343-3222/4 Fax: (6) 341-4773
LOGIS-TECH TOKYO (International Material Handling and Distribution Exhibition) Every 2 years Oct. 18-22, 1994	Nippon Convention Center (Makuhari Messe)	Japan Institute of Logistics Systems / Japan Material Handling Society Shuwa No. 2 Shiba Park Bldg., 2-12-7 Shibadaimon, Monato-ku, Tokyo 105 Tel: (3) 3432-3291 Fax: (3) 3432-8681
Modern Scientific Instruments Show Every 2 years Apr. 20-23, 1994	Nagoya Trade & Industry Center	Nihon Kogyo Shimbun 1-28-5 Kanda-Jimbocho, Chiyoda-ku, Tokyo 101 Tel: (3) 3292-3561 Fax: (3) 3292-6137

Trade Fair	Site	Contact
MOTION ENGINEERING JAPAN **Motion & Power Transmission Exhibition** Annual Last held: Apr. 14-16, 1993	Nippon Convention Center (Makuhari Messe)	Japan Management Association 3-1-22 Shibakoen, Minato-ku, Tokyo 105 Tel: (3) 3434-6211 Fax: (3) 3434-1836/8076 Tlx: JMA J25870
Nagoya International Woodworking Machinery Fair Every 2 years Last held: Oct. 29-Nov. 2, 1993	Nagoya International Exhibition Hall	Chubu Woodworking Machinery Manufacturers' Association 1-3-33 Kaminaezu, Naka-ku, Nagoya 460 Tel: (52) 321-4470 Fax: (52) 321-4412 Tlx: J 59703
Osaka Wood Technology Fair Every 2 years Sep., 1994 (tentative)	International Exhibition Center, Osaka (INTEX Osaka)	Osaka Woodworking Machinery Cooperative Association 2-1-6 Inari, Naniwa-ku, Osaka 556 Tel: (6) 561-3907 Fax: (6) 568-1897
POWDERTEC OSAKA **Osaka International Powder Technology Exhibition** Every 2 years Last held: Jul. 7-10, 1993	International Exhibition Center, Osaka (INTEX Osaka)	Japan Management Association 3-1-22 Shibakoen, Minato-ku, Tokyo 105 Tel: (3) 3434-6211 Fax: (3) 3434-1836/8076 Tlx: JMA J25870
Scientific Instruments Show Tohoku Every 2 years 1993 (Dates not available)	Sendai Oroshisho Center Sun-Festa	Nihon Kogyo Shimbun 1-28-5 Kanda-Jimbocho, Chiyoda-ku, Tokyo 101 Tel: (3) 3292-3561 Fax: (3) 3292-6137
THERMOTEC Last held: Apr. 12-15, 1993	Harumi-Tokyo International Fair Ground	MESAGO Japan Corporation Pare Eteruneru 1004, 4-28-20 Yotsuya, Shinjuku-ku Tokyo 160 Tel: (3) 3359-0894 Fax: (3) 3359-9328
Toyama Techno Fair Annual Last held: Oct. 1-4, 1993	Toyama Industrial Exhibition Hall	Toyama Prefectural Machinery Industry Association 529 Takada, Toyama City, Toyama Pref. 930 Tel: (764) 42-4021 Fax: (764) 33-6170
Vending Industry Fair Every 2 years 1994 (Dates to be announced)	Site information to be annouced	Japan Vending Machine Manufacturers' Association Shimbashi Tanaka Bldg., 2-37-6 Nishi-Shimbashi, Minato-ku, Tokyo 105 Tel: (3) 3431-7443 Fax: (3) 3431-1967
West Japan Machine Tool Fair Annual Last held: May 28-31, 1993	West Japan General Exhibition Center	West Japan Industry and Trade Exhibition Association 3-7-1 Asano, Kokurakita-ku, Kitakyushu City, Fukuoka Pref. 802 Tel: (93) 511-6848 Fax: (93) 521-8845

MEDICINE & PHARMACEUTICALS

Trade Fair	Site	Contact
Asia Medical Show Every 2 years Last held: May 14-16, 1993	Fukuoka International Center	Nihon Kogyo Shimbun 2-4-9 Umeda, Kita-ku, Osaka 530 Tel: (6) 343-3222/4 Fax: (6) 341-4773
Chemspec Asia Every 1.5 years Last held: Feb. 9-10, 1993	Tokyo Prince Hotel	International Communications, Inc. Kasho Bldg. 2F, 2-14-9 Nihombashi, Chuo-ku, Tokyo 103 Tel: (3) 3273-2441 Fax: (3) 3273-2445

Note: Country codes for telephone and fax numbers are not displayed unless they are *outside* of Japan.
All country codes have square brackets around them, while city codes have parentheses.
The country code for Japan is [81].

Trade Fair	Site	Contact
Exhibition of General Meeting of Japan Society for Clinical Laboratory Automation Annual Last held: Sep. 16-18, 1993 (Business Days Only)	Nippon Convention Center (Makuhari Messe)	Japan Society for Clinical Laboratory Automation Kasai Bldg., 2-31-2 Hongo, Bunkyo-ku, Tokyo 113 Tel: (3) 3818-3205 Fax: (3) 3818-6374
Home Care & Rehabilitation Exhibition Annual Last held: Oct. 26-28, 1993	Harumi-Tokyo International Fair Ground	Health & Welfare Information Association Shin Kasumigaseki Bldg., 3-3-2 Kasumigaseki, Chiyoda-ku, Tokyo 100 Tel: (3) 3581-7851 Fax: (3) 3581-7854
HOSPEX JAPAN International Hospital Engineering Exhibition Annual Last held: Nov. 10-13, 1993	Harumi-Tokyo International Fair Ground	Japan Management Association 3-1-22 Shibakoen, Minato-ku, Tokyo 105 Tel: (3) 3434-6211 Fax: (3) 3434-1836/8076 Tlx: JMA J25870
International Exhibition of Medical Imaging Equipment Annual Last held: Apr. 2-5, 1993	Pacifico Yokohama	Japan Federation of Medical Congress Promotion (JMCP) Omuro Bldg. 5F, 1-6-2 Yushima, Bunkyo-ku, Tokyo 113 Tel: (3) 3816-3450 Fax: (3) 3818-8920
International Modern Hospital Show Annual Last held: Jul. 8-10, 1993	Sunshine City Convention Center Tokyo	Nippon Omni-Management Association 3-11-8 Sendagaya, Shibuya-ku, Tokyo 151 Tel: (3) 3403-1331 Fax: (3) 3403-1710 Tlx: 2422143 NOMA J
Japan Nuclear Medicine Society, General Assembly, Technical Exhibition Annual Last held: Oct. 28-30, 1993	Seaside Hotel Phoenix	Japan Industries Association of Radiation Apparatus Omuro Bldg. 6G, 1-6-2 Yushima, Bunkyo-ku, Tokyo 113 Tel: (3) 3816-3450 Fax: (3) 3818-8920
JETRO IMPORT FAIR : HEALTH CARE Every 2 years Last held: Mar., 1993	Sunshine City Convention Center Tokyo	Japan External Trade Organization (JETRO) 2-2-5 Toranomon, Minato-ku, Tokyo 105 Tel: (3) 3582-5242 Fax: (3) 3505-0450
Osaka International Medical Show Every 2 years 1994 (Dates to be announced)	Site information to be announced.	Nihon Kogyo Shimbun 2-4-9 Umeda, Kita-ku, Osaka 530 Tel: (6) 343-3222/4 Fax: (6) 341-4773

METAL & METAL FINISHING
See also Industrial Materials & Chemicals

Trade Fair	Site	Contact
BLECH-JAPAN International Sheet Metal Working Technology Exhibition Every 2 years Last held: Apr. 14-17, 1993	Nippon Convention Center (Makuhari Messe)	Mack-Brooks Exhibitions, Ltd. Forum Place, Hatfield, Herts. AL10 ORN, U.K. Tel: (44) 0707-275641 Fax: (44) 0707-275544 Tlx: 266350 macbexg
Japan International Machine Tool Fair Every 2 years Oct. 26-Nov. 3, 1994	International Exhibition Center, Osaka (INTEX Osaka)	Osaka International Trade Fair Commission 1-5-102 Nanko-Kita, Suminoe-ku, Osaka 559 Tel: (6) 612-1212 Fax: (6) 612-8585 Tlx: 5267660 OITFC J

Trade Fair	Site	Contact
Japan International Welding Show Every 2 years Apr., 1994 (tentative)	Nippon Convention Center (Makuhari Messe)	Sanpo Pulication, Inc. Sanpo Sakuma Bldg., 1-11 Kanda-Sakumacho, Chiyoda-ku, Tokyo 101 Tel: (3) 3258-6411 Fax: (3) 3258-6430
Mould & Die Exhibition (High Technology Tokyo) Annual Last held: May 28-31, 1993	Harumi-Tokyo International Fair Ground	Nikkan Kogyo Shimbun, Ltd. 1-8-10 Kudan-Kita, Chiyoda-ku, Tokyo 102 Tel: (3) 3222-7232 Fax: (3) 3221-7137 Tlx: NIKKANKO J 29687
Mould & Die Exhibition (Factory Automation Nagoya) Annual Last held: Jun. 5-8, 1993	Nagoya International Exhibition Hall	Daily Industrial News (Nagoya Branch) 2-21-28 Izumi, Higashi-ku, Nagoya 461 Tel: (52) 931-6151 Fax: (52) 931-6159
Mould & Die Exhibition (Osaka Mechatronics Fair) Annual Last held: May 19-22, 1993	International Exhibition Center, Osaka (INTEX Osaka)	Nikkan Kogyo Shimbun, Ltd. (Osaka Branch) 2-16 Kitahama-Higashi, Chuo-ku, Osaka 540 Tel: (6) 946-3384 Fax: (6) 946-3389
Surface Finishing & Coating Exhibition Annual Last held: May 26-29, 1993	Tokyo Ryutsu Center (TRC)	Surface Finishing Society of Japan Kyodo Bldg., 2 Kanda-Iwamotocho, Chiyoda-ku, Tokyo 101 Tel: (3) 3252-3286 Fax: (3) 3252-3288
Wire -Tokyo Every 2 years Last held: Apr. 14-17, 1993	Nippon Convention Center (Makuhari Messe)	Mack-Brooks Exhibitions, Ltd. Forum Place, Hatfield, Herts. AL10 ORN, U.K. Tel: (44) 0707-275641 Fax: (44) 0707-275544 Tlx: 266350 macbexg

OFFICE AUTOMATION

Trade Fair	Site	Contact
Business Machine Show Annual Last held: Jun. 9-11, 1993	Nagoya Trade & Industry Center	Chubu Office Management Association Chukei Bldg., 4-4-12 Meieki, Nakamura-ku, Nagoya 450 Tel: (52) 581-6917 Fax: (52) 581-1928
CEPS (Corporate Electronic Publishing Systems) Japan Annual Last held: Apr. 7-9, 1993	Sunshine City Convention Center Tokyo	Reed Exhibitions Japan, Ltd. Shinjuku Nomura Bldg. 18F, 1-26-2 Nishi-Shinjuku, Shinjuku-ku, Tokyo 163-05 Tel: (3) 3349-8501 Fax: (3) 3345-7929 Tlx: J27280 REC JPN
Japan IM Show Annual Last held: Nov., 1993	Site information not available	Japan Microphotography Association 1-9-15 Kaji-cho, Chiyoda-ku, Tokyo 101 Tel: (3) 3254-4672 Fax: (3) 3256-7038
Kumamoto Business Fair Annual Last held: Oct., 1993	Konan Kaikan	Nippon Omni-Management Association Nishitetsu Hakataekimae Bldg., 1-6-16 Hakataekimae, Hakata-ku, Fukuoka City, Fukuoka Pref. 812 Tel: (92) 431-3365 Fax: (92) 431-3367
Okinawa Business Show Annual Last held: Nov., 1993	Okinawa Convention Center	Nippon Omni-Management Association Nishitetsu Hakataekimae Bldg., 1-6-16 Hakataekimae, Hakata-ku, Fukuoka City, Fukuoka Pref. 812 Tel: (92) 431-3365 Fax: (92) 431-3367
Patent Information Fair Every 2 years Last held: Nov. 10-12, 1993	Science Museum Exhibition Hall	Nihon Kogyo Shimbun 1-28-5 Kanda-Jimbocho, Chiyoda-ku, Tokyo 101 Tel: (3) 3292-3561 Fax: (3) 3292-6137

Note: Country codes for telephone and fax numbers are not displayed unless they are *outside* of Japan. All country codes have square brackets around them, while city codes have parentheses. The country code for Japan is [81].

Trade Fair	Site	Contact
TECHNICAL COMMUNICATION Every 2 years 1994 (Dates to be announced)	Site information to be announced	Japan Management Association 3-1-22 Shibakoen, Minato-ku, Tokyo 105 Tel: (3) 3434-6211 Fax: (3) 3434-1836/8076 Tlx: JMA J25870

PACKAGING, PRINTING & PAPER
See also Computer Graphics, Transportation

CHUBU PACK Every 2 years Apr. 20-24, 1994	Nagoya International Exhibition Hall	Central Packaging & Food Machinery Builder Association Fuji Office Bldg., 2-14-10 Kameshima, Nakamura-ku, Nagoya 453 Tel: (52) 452-3161/2 Fax: (52) 452-7752
(CMM Japan) Converting Machinery/Materials Conference and Exposition in Japan Every 3 years. Apr. 12-15, 1995	Nippon Convention Center (Makuhari Messe)	International Communications, Inc. Kasho Bldg. 2F, 2-14-9 Nihombashi, Chuo-ku, Tokyo 103 Tel: (3) 3273-2441 Fax: (3) 3273-2445 Tlx: 0222-3585 ICSJ
EXPO Paper Asia Every 2 years Last held: May 11-13, 1993	Harumi-Tokyo International Fair Ground	Miller Freeman Japan Co., Ltd. 3-11-14-805 Akasaka, Minato-ku, Tokyo 107 Tel: (3) 3584-1560 Fax: (3) 3505-1768
International Graphic Arts Show Every 2 years Last held: Sep. 24-28, 1993	Harumi-Tokyo International Fair Ground	Japan Graphic Arts Suppliers Committee Tiger Bldg., 3-5-22 Shibakoen, Minato-ku, Tokyo 105 Tel: (3) 3434-4661 Fax: (3) 3434-0301
International Packaging Exhibition Every 2 years Last held: Sep. 16-20, 1993	Harumi-Tokyo International Fair Ground	Japan Packaging Institute Kashikichi Ningyocho Bldg. 7F, 3-10-1 Nihombashi-Ningyocho, Chuo-ku, Tokyo 103 Tel: (3) 3249-6301 Fax: (3) 3249-6305 Tlx: 02522610 PKGINS J
Japan International Packaging Machinery Show Every 2 years Last held: Sep. 13-17, 1993	Harumi-Tokyo International Fair Ground	Japan Packaging Machinery Manufacturers Association Kimura Bldg., 5-5-5 Asakusabashi, Taito-ku, Tokyo 111 Tel: (03) 3865-2815 Fax: (3) 3865-2650
OSAKA PACK Every 2 years Last held: Jun. 9-12, 1993	International Exhibition Center, Osaka (INTEX Osaka)	Nippon Co., Ltd. 1-5-11 Minami-Hommachi, Chuo-ku, Osaka 541 Tel: (6) 262-2401 Fax: (6) 262-2407
Page Annual Last held: Feb. 3-5, 1993	Sunshine City Convention Center Tokyo	JAGAT 1-29-11 Wada, Suginami-ku, Tokyo 166 Tel: (3) 3384-311 Fax: (3) 3384-3116
PRINTEK TOKYO Every 2 years Sep., 1994 (tentative)	Site information to be announced	Tokyo Printing Industry Association 1-16-8 Shintomi, Chuo-ku, Tokyo 104 Tel: (3) 3552-4021 Fax: (3) 3553-2653
Tokyo Light Printing Fair Annual Last held: Jul. 1-3, 1993	Nippon Convention Center (Makuhari Messe)	Tokyo Light Printing Industries Associations Keiinastsu Kaikan, 7-16 Nihombashi-Kodemmacho, Chuo-ku, Tokyo 103 Tel: (3) 3667-3771 Fax: (3) 3249-0377

Trade Fair	Site	Contact

SPORTING GOODS
See also Hobbies, Recreation & Travel; Vessels & Parts

Trade Fair	Site	Contact
Diving Festival Annual Last held: Feb. 19-21, 1993	Sunshine City Convention Center Tokyo	Japan Scuba Association 905 Shake, Ebina City, Kanagawa Pref. 243-04 Tel: (462) 33-4111
Golf Fair Osaka Annual Last held: Mar. 17-18, 1993	Osaka Merchandise Mart (OMM)	Japan Golf Goods Association (Osaka Office) Matsubara Bldg. 3F, 2-1-24 Shinsaibashi-suji, Chuo-ku, Osaka 542 Tel: (6) 211-9363 Fax: (6) 211-9363
International Snow Board Collection & Tokyo Surf Magic Annual Last held: Mar. 18-20, 1993	Sunshine City Convention Center Tokyo	Marine Ad Company, Ltd. Ito Bldg., 3-17-7 Hongo, Bunkyo-ku, Tokyo 113 Tel: (3) 3813-3601 Fax: (3) 3818-3188
Japan International Golf Goods Fair Annual Last held: Feb. 26-28, 1993	Harumi-Tokyo International Fair Ground	Japan Golf Goods Association Kobayashi Bldg. 4F, 6-11-11 Soto-Kanda, Chiyoda-ku Tokyo 101 Tel: (3) 3832-8589 Fax: (3) 3832-8594
Professional Leisure Management Annual Last held: Jan. 31-Feb. 3, 1993	Harumi-Tokyo International Fair Ground	JES, Ltd. Seshita Bldg. 301, 2-8-8 Koraku, Bunkyo-ku, Tokyo 112 Tel: (3) 3814-8655 Fax: (3) 3814-8687
Sports Business Fair Osaka 2 times a year 1993 dates: Apr. 14-15, Sep. 28-29, 1993	International Exhibition Center, Osaka (INTEX Osaka)	Osaka Wholesale Trade Union of Sporting Goods Amano Bldg., 3-5-25 Minami-Semba, Chuo-ku, Osaka 542 Tel: (6) 251-1267 Fax: (6) 251-3125

TEXTILES & APPAREL

Trade Fair	Site	Contact
Heimtexil Asia Annual Last held: Jan. 27-30, 1993	Nippon Convention Center (Makuhari Messe)	Messe Frankfurt, Inc. No. 2 Kiya Bldg. 3F, 4-3-2 Iidabashi, Chiyoda-ku, Tokyo 102 Tel: (3) 5275-2851 Fax: (3) 5275-3410
Japan Grand Shoes Collection 3 times a year 1993 dates: Jan. 21-22, May 26-27, Oct. 13-14, 1993 (Business Days Only)	Kobe International Exhibition Hall	Japan Chemical Shoes Association 3-1-13 Ohashi-cho, Nagata-ku, Kobe 653 Tel: (78) 641-2525 Fax: (78) 641-2529
Japan International Apparel Machinery Trade Show Every 3 years Last held: May 9-12, 1993	Nippon Convention Center (Makuhari Messe)	Japan Sewing Machinery Manufacturers Association Tamagawa Bldg., 1-20 Yotsuya, Shinjuku-ku, Tokyo 160 Tel: (03) 3353-8487 Fax: (3) 3353-5891
New Uniform Messe Japan Every 2 years Sep., 1994 (tentative)	Nippon Convention Center (Makuhari Messe)	Nikkan Kogyo Shimbun. Ltd. 1-8-10 Kudan-Kita, Chiyoda-ku, Tokyo 102 Tel: (3) 3222-7232 Fax: (3) 3221-7137 Tlx: NIKKANKO J29687

Note: Country codes for telephone and fax numbers are not displayed unless they are *outside* of Japan. All country codes have square brackets around them, while city codes have parentheses. The country code for Japan is [81].

Trade Fair	Site	Contact
Osaka International Textile Machinery Show (OTEMAS) Every 4 years Last held: Nov. 11-17, 1993	International Exhibition Center, Osaka (INTEX Osaka)	Osaka International Trade Fair Commission 1-5-102 Nanko-Kita, Suminoe-ku, Osaka 559 Tel: (6) 612-1212 Fax: (6) 612-8585 Tlx: 5267660 OITFC J
Texture Hi-Tech Ichinomiya Annual Last held: Feb. 18-20, 1993	Ichinomiya Sports Culture Center	Nippon Omni-Management Association Kasya Bldg. Minamikan, 5-16-17 Meieki, Nakamura-ku, Nagoya 450 Tel: (52) 581-8291 Fax: (52) 581-8690
U.S. Apparel Show Annual Last h eld: Feb. 8-10, 1993	U.S. Trade Center	U.S. Department of Commerce 14th & Constitution Ave., NW Washington, D.C. 20230, USA Tel: [1] (202) 377-8859 Fax: [1] (202) 377-4324
U.S. Children's Fashion Trade Fair Annual Last held: Feb. 16-18, 1993	U.S. Trade Center	U.S. Department of Commerce 14th & Constitution Ave., NW Washington, D.C. 20230, USA Tel: [1] (202) 377-8859 Fax: [1] (202) 377-4324
World Fashion Trade Fair Annual Last held: Mar. 2-4, 1993	International Exhibition Center, Osaka (INTEX Osaka)	Association of Total Fashion (ATF) Osaka Shoko Kaigisho Bldg., 2-8 Hommachibashi, Chuo-ku, Osaka 540 Tel: (6) 944-6210 Fax: (6) 944-6209 Tlx: c/o OSAKACCI J 65243

TOOLS: MEASURING & TESTING
See also Machines & Instruments; Tools: Precision & Optical; other categories which include exhibitions with tools specific to those industries

Trade Fair	Site	Contact
All Japan Optical Measuring Instruments Fair Annual Last held: Jun. 9-11, 1993	Pacifico Yokohama	Japan Optical Measuring Instruments Manufacturers' Assn. Kikai Shinko Kaikan, 3-5-8 Shibakoen, Minato-ku, Tokyo 105 Tel: (3) 3435-8083 Fax: (3) 3435-8083
AMIEX (Aichi Measuring Instruments Exhibition) Every 2 years Last held: Nov., 1993	Aichi Trade Center (unconfirmed)	Nihon Kogyo Shimbun 1-28-5 Kanda-Jimbocho, Chiyoda-ku, Tokyo 101 Tel: (3) 3292-3561 Fax: (3) 3292-6137
Electrotest Japan Annual Last held: Jan. 20-23, 1993	Nippon Convention Center (Makuhari Messe)	Reed Exhibitions Japan, Ltd. Shinjuku Nomura Bldg. 18F, 1-26-2 Nishi-Shinjuku, Shinjuku-ku, Tokyo 163-05 Tel: (3) 3349-8501 Fax: (3) 3345-7929 Tlx: J27280 REC JPN
INTER MEASURE Every 2 years Jul., 1994 (tentative)	Site information to be announced	Japan Measuring Instruments Federation Nippon Keiryo Kaikan, 25-1 Nando-cho, Shinjuku-ku Tokyo 162 Tel: (3) 3268-2121 Fax: (3) 3268-2167
Japan Analytical Instruments Show Annual Last held: Aug. 31- Sep. 3, 1993	Nippon Convention Center (Makuhari Messe)	Japan Analytical Instruments Manufacturers' Association Taimei Bldg., 3-22 Kanda-Ogawamachi, Chiyoda-ku Tokyo 101 Tel: (03) 3292-0642 Fax: (3) 3292-7157
Japan Exhibition Non -Destructive Testing Every 2 years Oct., 1994 (tentative)	Science Museum Exhibition Hall	Sanpo Pulication, Inc. Sanpo Sakuma Bldg., 1-11 Kanda-Sakumacho, Chiyoda-ku, Tokyo 101 Tel: (3) 3258-6411 Fax: (3) 3258-6430

Trade Fair	Site	Contact
JEMIMA INTERMAC Every 2 years Last held: Oct. 12-15, 1993	Harumi-Tokyo International Fair Ground	Japan Electric Measuring Instruments Manufacturers' Assn. 1-9-10 Toranomon, Minato-ku, Tokyo 105 Tel: (3) 3502-0602/4 Fax: (3) 3502-0600
JEMIMA T&M Annual Last held: Nov., 1993	Site information not available	Japan Electric Measuring Instruments Manufacturers' Association 1-9-10 Toranomon, Minato-ku, Tokyo 105 Tel: (3) 3502-0602 Fax: (3) 3502-0600
Maintenance Engineering Show Annual Last held: Apr. 12-15, 1993	Harumi-Tokyo International Fair Ground	Society of Maintenance Engineers 3-1-24-334 Jingumae, Shibuya-ku, Tokyo 150 Tel: (3) 3404-2974 Fax: (3) 3404-3096
Measurement Technology Exhibition Nagoya Annual Last held: Jul., 1993	Aichi Trade Center	Japan Electric MEasuring Instruments Manufacturers' Association 1-9-10 Toranomon, Minato-ku, Tokyo 105 Tel: (3) 3502-0602 Fax: (3) 3502-0600
Measuring, Control and Inspection Instruments Show Every 2 years Last held: May 20-22, 1993	Hiroshima Prefecture Industrial Exhibition Hall	Nihon Kogyo Shimbun 2-4-9 Umeda, Kita-ku, Osaka 530 Tel: (6) 343-3222/4 Fax: (6) 341-4773
Measuring Intruments Show Hokkaido Every 3 years. Jul., 1995 (tentative)	AXES Sapporo (Sapporo Exposition Center)	Nihon Kogyo Shimbun 1-28-5 Kanda-Jimbocho, Chiyoda-ku, Tokyo 101 Tel: (3) 3292-3561 Fax: (3) 3292-6137
MICRO TECH Every 2 years Last held: Oct. 12-16, 1993	Harumi-Tokyo International Fair Ground	Tokyo International Trade Fair Commission 4-7-24 Harumi, Chuo-ku, Tokyo 104 Tel: (3) 3531-3371 Fax: (3) 3531-1344 Tlx: 02523935 TITF J
Scientific Instrument Show Every 2 years Last held: Oct. 13-16, 1993	International Exhibition Center, Osaka (INTEX Osaka)	Nihon Kogyo Shimbun 2-4-9 Umeda, Kita-ku, Osaka 530 Tel: (6) 343-3222/4 Fax: (6) 341-4773
Scientific Instrument Show Chugoku, Shikoku Area Every 2 years Last held: May 20-22, 1993	Hiroshima Prefecture Industial Exhibition Hall	Nihon Kogyo Shimbun 2-4-9 Umeda, Kita-ku, Osaka 530 Tel: (6) 343-3222/4 Fax: (6) 341-4773
Scientific Instrument Show Japan Every 2 years 1994 (Dates to be announced)	Harumi-Tokyo International Fair Ground	Nihon Kogyo Shimbun 1-28-5 Kanda-Jimbocho, Chiyoda-ku, Tokyo 101 Tel: (3) 3292-3561 Fax: (3) 3292-6137
SENSORS EXPO JAPAN (Technology Japan) Annual Last held: Apr. 12-15, 1993	Harumi-Tokyo International Fair Ground	Nihon Kogyo Shimbun 1-28-5 Kanda-Jimbocho, Chiyoda-ku, Tokyo 101 Tel: (3) 3292-3561 Fax: (3) 3292-6137
TEST Every 2 years Last held: Apr. 12-15, 1993	Harumi-Tokyo International Fair Ground	Testing Machinery Association of Japan (JTM) 25-1 Nando-cho, Shinjuku-ku, Tokyo 162 Tel: (3) 3268-4849 Fax: (3) 3268-4840

Note: Country codes for telephone and fax numbers are not displayed unless they are *outside* of Japan.
All country codes have square brackets around them, while city codes have parentheses.
The country code for Japan is [81].

Trade Fair	Site	Contact
Three Dimension Measurement & System Fair (Factory Automation Nagoya) Annual Last held: Jun. 5-8, 1993	Nagoya International Exhibition Hall	Daily Industrial News (Nagoya Branch) 2-21-28 Izumi, Higashi-ku, Nagoya 461 Tel: (52) 931-6151 Fax: (52) 931-6159
West Japan Intrumentation Exhibition Every 2 years Apr. 20-22, 1994	West Japan General Exhibition Center	West Japan Industry and Trade Exhibition Association 3-7-1 Asano, Kokurakita-ku, Kitakyushu City, Fukuoka Pref. 802 Tel: (93) 511-6848 Fax: (93) 521-8845

TOOLS: PRECISION & OPTICAL EQUIPMENT

See also Machines & Instruments; Tools: Measuring & Testing; other categories which include exhibitions with tools specific to those industries

Trade Fair	Site	Contact
CLEAN Technology Exhibition (Technology Japan) Annual Last held: Apr. 12-15, 1993	Harumi-Tokyo International Fair Ground	Japan Air Cleaning Association Tomoeya Bldg., 1-2-14 Uchi-kanda, Chiyoda-ku, Tokyo 101 Tel: (3) 3233-1486 Fax: (3) 3233-1750
Electronic Display Exhibition Annual Last held: Apr. 21-23, 1993	Pacifico Yokahama	Electronic Industries Association of Japan Tokyo Shoko Kaigisho Bldg. 7F, 3-2-2 Marunouchi, Chiyoda-ku, Tokyo 100 Tel: (3) 3284-1051 Fax: (3) 3284-0165
International Optical Fair Tokyo Annual Last held: Nov., 1993	Nippon Convention Center (Makuhari Messe)	Reed Exhibitions Japan, Ltd. Shinjuku Nomura Bldg. 18F, 1-26-2 Nishi-Shinjuku, Shinjuku-ku, Tokyo 163-05 Tel: (3) 3349-8501 Fax: (3) 3345-7929 Tlx: J27280 REC JPN
International Professional Photo Fair Annual Last held: Mar. 4-6, 1993	Sunshine City Convention Center Tokyo	Nihon Kogyo Shimbun 1-28-5 Kanda-Jimbocho, Chiyoda-ku, Tokyo 101 Tel: (3) 3292-3561 Fax: (3) 3292-6137
IPPF WEST Annual Last held: Sep., 1993	Site information not available	Nihon Kogyo Shimbun 2-4-9 Umeda, Kita-ku, Osaka 530 Tel: (6) 343-3222/4 Fax: (6) 341-4773
MOTORTECH JAPAN Japan Small Electric Motor Products & Technology Exhibition Annual Last held: Apr. 14-16, 1993	Nippon Convention Center (Makuhari Messe)	Japan Management Association 3-1-22 Shibakoen, Minato-ku, Tokyo 105 Tel: (3) 3434-6211 Fax: (3) 3434-1836/8076 Tlx: JMA J25870
MST Japan Annual Last held: Apr. 20-22, 1993	Science Museum Exhibition Hall	MESAGO Japan Corporation Pare Eteruneru 1004, 4-28-20 Yotsuya, Shinjuku-ku Tokyo 160 Tel: (3) 3359-0894 Fax: (3) 3359-9328
Precision Instruments Cleaning Show (Technology Japan) Annual Last held: Apr. 12-15, 1993	Harumi-Tokyo International Fair Ground	Japan Air Cleaning Association Tomoeya Bldg., 1-2-14 Uchi-kanda, Chiyoda-ku, Tokyo 101 Tel: (3) 3233-1486 Fax: (3) 3233-1750
Scientific Instruments Show Hokkaido Every 3 years Jul., 1995 (tentative)	AXES Sapporo (Sapporo Exposition Center)	Nihon Kogyo Shimbun 1-28-5 Kanda-Jimbocho, Chiyoda-ku, Tokyo 101 Tel: (3) 3292-3561 Fax: (3) 3292-6137

Trade Fair	Site	Contact

TRANSPORTATION

Trade Fair	Site	Contact
FA Materials Handling & Distribution System Exhibition (Factory Automation Nagoya) Annual Last held: Jun. 5-8, 1993	Nagoya International Exhibition Hall	Daily Industrial News (Nagoya Branch) 2-21-28 Izumi, Higashi-ku, Nagoya 461 Tel: (52) 931-6151 Fax: (52) 931-6159
FA Materials Handling and Distribution System Exhibition Annual Last held: Nov. 2-5, 1993	Harumi-Tokyo International Fair Ground	Nikkan Kogyo Shimbun. Ltd. 1-8-10 Kudan-Kita, Chiyoda-ku, Tokyo 102 Tel: (3) 3222-7239 Fax: (3) 3221-7137 Tlx: NIKKANKO J29687
INTERMATEX International Materials Handling, Storage and Distribution Every 2 years Last held: Jun. 16-19, 1993	Harumi-Tokyo International Fair Ground	Japan Management Association 3-1-22 Shibakoen, Minato-ku, Tokyo 105 Tel: (3) 3434-6211 Fax: (3) 3434-1836/8076 Tlx: JMA J25870

VESSELS & PARTS
See also Aerospace & Oceanic

Trade Fair	Site	Contact
Osaka International Boat Show Annual Last held: Feb. 19-22, 1993	International Exhibition Center, Osaka (INTEX Osaka)	Japan Boating Industry Association Asano No. 1 Bldg., 2-5-1 Ginza, Chuo-ku, Tokyo 104 Tel: (3) 3567-6707 Fax: (3) 3567-0635
Sea Japan Mar. 9-13, 1994	Pacifico Yokahama	World Import Mart Co., Ltd. Sunshine City, 3-1-3 Higashi-Ikebukuro, Toshima-ku Tokyo 170 Tel: (3) 3987-3161 Fax. (03) 3981-8371 Tlx: 2723829
Tokyo International Boat Show Annual Last held: Feb. 9-14, 1993	Harumi-Tokyo International Fair Ground	Japan Boating Industry Association Asano No. 1 Bldg., 2-5-1 Ginza, Chuo-ku, Tokyo 104 Tel: (3) 3567-6707 Fax: (3) 3567-0635

OTHERS Miscellaneous trade fairs

Trade Fair	Site	Contact
Aqualife Exhibition Annual Last held: Apr. 29- May 3, 1993	Harumi-Tokyo International Fair Ground	System Development Society Akiyama Bldg., 2-24-6 Higashi-Ueno, Taito-ku, Tokyo 110 Tel: (3) 3837-5741 Fax: (3) 3837-5743
Autonomy PR Fair (High Technology Tokyo) Annual Last held: May 28-31, 1993	Harumi-Tokyo International Fair Ground	Nikkan Kogyo Shimbun, Ltd. 1-8-10 Kudan-Kita, Chiyoda-ku, Tokyo 102 Tel: (3) 3222-7232 Fax: (3) 3221-7137 Tlx: NIKKANKO J 29687
Design Engineering Japan Show & Plaza Annual Last held: Jun. 23-26, 1993	Nippon Convention Center (Makuhari Messe)	Reed Exhibitions Japan, Ltd. Shinjuku Nomura Bldg. 18F, 1-26-2 Nishi-Shinjuku, Shinjuku-ku, Tokyo 163-05 Tel: (3) 3349-8501 Fax: (3) 3345-7929 Tlx: J27280 REC JPN
Global Environmental Technology Expo Every 2 years Oct., 1994 (tentative)	Pacifico Yokahama	Nihon Keizai Shimbun, Inc. 1-9-5 Otemachi, Chiyoda-ku, Tokyo 100-66 Tel: (3) 3243-9082 Fax: (3) 3243-9086 Tlx: NIKKEI J22308

Note: Country codes for telephone and fax numbers are not displayed unless they are *outside* of Japan.
All country codes have square brackets around them, while city codes have parentheses.
The country code for Japan is [81].

Trade Fair	Site	Contact
International Salon Tokyo Barber, Beauty, Aesthetic and Bridal Products Annual Last held: Jun., 1993	Nippon Convention Center (Makuhari Messe)	Reed Exhibitions Japan, Ltd. Shinjuku Nomura Bldg. 18F, 1-26-2 Nishi-Shinjuku, Shinjuku-ku, Tokyo 163-05 Tel: (3) 3349-8501 Fax: (3) 3345-7929 Tlx: J27280 REC JPN
Re-Utilization of Resources Exhibition Annual Last held: Apr. 29- May 3, 1993	Harumi-Tokyo International Fair Ground	System Development Society Akiyama Bldg., 2-24-6 Higashi-Ueno, Taito-ku Tokyo 110 Tel: (3) 3837-5741 Fax: (3) 3837-5743

Note: Country codes for telephone and fax numbers are not displayed unless they are *outside* of Japan.
All country codes have square brackets around them, while city codes have parentheses.
The country code for Japan is [81].

Business Travel

Traveling in Japan is as civilized as traveling gets. Trains and planes rank with the most comfortable and efficient in the world. Hotels have refined personal service and solicitude to a degree matched nowhere else. The Japanese people have few equals in health, wealth, intelligence, and drive.

The trappings of Western culture are everywhere in Japan—television, fast food, baseball, movies, traffic jams, telephones, computers—yet somehow the nation has absorbed it all without losing its "Japaneseness." To the Western traveler, Japan is still very foreign, often incomprehensible, sometimes frustrating, completely fascinating—and all the while Japanese hospitality is smoothing the rough edges of business and travel, making it all go down as easily as possible.

NATIONAL TRAVEL OFFICES WORLDWIDE

The Japan National Tourist Organization (JNTO) is as solicitous of the traveler as you might expect in such an hospitable society. Its offices worldwide provide literature and information, and its employees can answer questions or steer you in the right direction. The JNTO is acutely aware of how expensive it is to travel in Japan, and so it publishes *Economical Travel in Japan,* a free source of budget-saving information. JNTO has 16 overseas offices and three in Japan.

JNTO OVERSEAS OFFICES

Australia 115 Pitt Street, Sydney, NSW 2000; Tel: (2) 232-4522.

Brazil Av. Paulista, 509, S/405, 01311-Sao Paulo; Tel: (11) 289-2931.

Canada 165 University Avenue, Toronto, Ontario M5H 3B8; Tel: (416) 366-7140.

France 4-8, rue Sainte-Anne, 75001 Paris; Tel: (1) 42-96-20-29.

Germany Kaiserstrasse 11, 6000 Frankfurt am Main 1; Tel: (69) 20353.

Hong Kong Two Exchange Square, Suite 3606, 8 Connaught Place, Central; Tel: 525-5295.

Korea 10 Da-dong, Chung-ku, Seoul: Tel: (2) 752-7968.

Mexico Temistocles 246-P.B., Col. Reforma Polanco Deleg, Miguel Hidalgo, 11550-Mexico, D.F.; Tel: (5) 254-6666.

Switzerland 13, rue de Berne, 1201 Geneva; Tel: (22) 731-81-40.

Thailand Wall Street Tower Building, 33/61, Suriwong Road, Bangkok 10500; Tel: (2) 233-5108.

United Kingdom 167 Regent Street, London W.1.; Tel: (71) 734-9638.

United States

New York Rockefeller Plaza, 630 Fifth Avenue, Suite 2101, New York, NY 10111; Tel: (212) 757-5640.

Chicago 401 North Michigan Avenue, Suite 770, Chicago, IL 60611; Tel: (312) 222-0874.

Dallas 2121 San Jacinto Street, Suite 980, Dallas, TX 75201; Tel: (214) 754-1820.

San Francisco 360 Post Street, Suite 601, San Francisco, CA 94108; Tel: (415) 989-7140.

Los Angeles 624 South Grand Avenue, Suite 1611, Los Angeles, CA 90017; Tel: (213) 623-1952.

JNTO JAPAN OFFICES

The JNTO headquarters is right next to Yurakucho Rail Station in central Tokyo, but you should visit one of the three JNTO Tourist Information Centers (TICs) in Japan with English-speaking staff.

Narita Airport Airport Terminal Building, 1st Floor Arrival Lobby. Hours: 9 am to 8 pm Monday-Friday; 9 am to noon Saturday. Tel: (476) 32-8711.

Tokyo Kotani Building, 6-6, Yurakucho 1-chome, Chiyoda-ku, near Imperial Palace Moat and two blocks each direction from Yurakucho and Shimbashi Rail Stations. Hours: 9 am to 5 pm Monday-Friday; 9 am to noon Saturday. Tel: (3) 3502-1461.

Kyoto 1st Floor, Kyoto Tower Building, Higashi-Shiokojicho, Simogyo-ku, one block each direction from Higashi Temple and Kyoto Rail Station. Hours: 9 am to 5 pm Monday-Friday; 9 am to noon Saturday. Tel: (75) 371-5649.

Another excellent source of information in Japan is the Japan Travel-Phone, a toll-free, English-speaking service available from 9 am to 5 pm seven days a week. Use it when you can't get to a Tourist Information Center, need travel information, or are having a hard time linguistically. Use your hotel phone or the public yellow, blue or green phones—your ¥10 (about US$0.09) coin will be returned. For information on western Japan, call (0120) 44-4800; for eastern Japan, call (0120) 22-2800. In Tokyo, call (3) 3503-4400; in Kyoto, call (75) 371-5649 (for these two local numbers, the charge is ¥10 for every three minutes).

For help with etiquette and customs, health services, transportation, seminars, classes and entertainment, call the Japan Hotline: (3) 3586-0110.

Another good bet is the Goodwill Guides, 37,000-plus bilingual volunteers scattered throughout every prefecture in the country. They can help you find your way around a city, help with translating, and otherwise relieve your daily grind. Apply at one of the three TICs or at a local tourist information center.

VISA AND PASSPORT REQUIREMENTS

Japan requires a foreigner to have a valid passport, but most foreigners visiting Japan for tourism or business don't need visas if they're staying 90 days or less. You do need proof of sufficient funds and your onward ticket out of Japan. If you plan to work in Japan—at least legally—you need to get a work visa from a Japanese consulate before you arrive. If you stay more than 90 days, you can get an extension for tourism or business, but you'll also need to get an Alien Registration Card and carry it with you at all times.

IMMUNIZATION

You need proof of vaccination only if you're arriving from an infected area. An example would be South America, which is experiencing an epidemic of cholera, or tropical Africa or South America, where yellow fever is endemic.

CLIMATE

Japan stretches 3,000 km (1,875 miles) from Sakhalin to Taiwan—equivalent to the distance between from Kashmir and Colombo, Seville and Stockholm, or Maine and Miami. Add the precipitous mountain ranges that occupy 80 percent of its area and you have a climate of great range and complexity in a nation smaller than France or California. The archipelago's climate is generally temperate, but ranges from the sub-arctic of Hokkaido to the subtropical of Okinawa. The further south you go the warmer each season is.

Most of Honshu has dry, sunny winters. Thanks to cold fronts out of Siberia, Tokyo's January temperatures are about the same as those in London or Washington, DC, and snow soon melts into slush. Shikoku and Kyushu winters are a little milder, while Hokkaido and northern Honshu have severe winters with heavy snows.

Summers are humid, rainy and warm throughout the islands—the standard East Asia monsoon season. The typical Tokyo July high temperature hits 31° C. (88° F.) and torrid spells reach 35° C. (95° F.)—about the same as New York City or Budapest. Like the rest of East Asia, Japan is in the storm track of Pacific summer typhoons, so heed the warnings you hear on radio or television. And as in the rest of East Asia, spring and fall are justifiably celebrated for beautiful weather—warm days, cool nights, fresh breezes.

BUSINESS ATTIRE

Japan follows Confucian standards of etiquette with an English accent. With few exceptions, that means conservative, formal business attire. British style is favored over American and definitely over Italian. Dark suits of fine tailoring and expensive but understated accessories are recommended for both men and women. Women should wear conservative necklines, hemlines, sleeves, and makeup.

There are two exceptions to the formality. If you're in a small-scale business such as fashion, jewelry, or arts and crafts, your contacts would expect you to dress more casually and freely. If you're working in a local concern, you may be expected to dress like your fellow workers—often in a company uniform.

To weather a Tokyo or Osaka winter, you need to dress as warmly as you would in Britain or the Maryland-Virginia area of the United States. For Hokkaido and northern Honshu, think bundling up on a Swedish scale; for Shikoku and Kyushu, think southeastern United States (but definitely not Florida, which is more like Okinawa). Tropical wear and raingear are summertime absolutes everywhere in Japan. (Refer to "Business Culture" chapter.)

AIRLINES

Fukuoka (Fukuoka Airport) This city of 1.2 million is Kyushu Island's commercial, political and cultural center, convenient to the nearby industrial complex of Kita-Kyushu, and an easy jump from Pusan, Korea, and other South and East Asia cities. You can enter Japan through Fukuoka and catch a domestic flight to Tokyo's Haneda Airport, thus avoiding the congestion of Tokyo's Narita Airport. Fukuoka Airport is served by, among others, Air China, All Nippon, Asiana Airlines, British Airways, Cathay Pacific, Continental, Garuda Indonesia, Hawaiian Airlines, Japan Airlines, Japan Air System, Korean Air, Malaysia Airlines, Northwest, Philippine Airlines, Qantas, and Singapore Airlines.

Nagoya (Komaki Airport) This commercial and industrial hub in central Honshu is another alternative to Tokyo for international and domestic flights, especially for flights from South and East Asia. Komaki Airport is an increasingly popular entry point to Japan, and domestic flights can take you to Tokyo's Haneda Airport in the amount of time you'd be standing in customs at Narita Airport. Also convenient to Osaka, Kobe, and Kyoto, Komaki Airport is served by, among others, Air France, Air New Zealand, All Nippon, Asiana Airlines, British Airways, Canadian Airlines International, Cathay Pacific, Continental, Delta, Garuda Indonesia, Japan Airlines, Japan Air System, Korean Air, Lufthansa, Malaysia Airlines, Northwest, Qantas, Singapore Airlines, and Thai Airways.

Osaka (Itami International Airport) This giant industrial center in west-central Honshu is convenient by bus, train, or air to Tokyo, Kyoto, Nagoya, and Kobe, and an easy entry point from South and East Asia. As with Nagoya and Fukuoka airports, Osaka is a convenient way to enter Japan while avoiding the congestion of Narita Airport in Tokyo. ItamiInternational Airport is served by, among others, Air China, Air France, All Nippon, British Airways, Cathay Pacific, Japan Airlines, Japan Air System, Korean Air, Lufthansa, Northwest, Singapore Airlines, Thai Airways, and United.

Tokyo (Narita and Haneda airports) Narita Airport is where most foreigners enter Japan, at least until they know better or have a choice. Narita is served by, among others, Air China, Air France, Air India, Air New Zealand, Alitalia, All Nippon, American, British Airways, Canadian International, Continental, Delta, Garuda Indonesia, Japan Airlines, Japan Air System, KLM, Korean Air, Lufthansa, Malaysia Airlines, Northwest, Philippine Airlines, Qantas, SAS, Singapore Airlines, Swissair, Thai Airways, and United.

Haneda Airport is the other choice. It's much closer to town, with much easier and cheaper access to city center. Taiwan-based China Airlines is the only international carrier serving Haneda: It was relegated there when Mainland China's Air China refused to share Narita, but now it has the last laugh. It may be worth your while to choose China Airlines when you fly to Tokyo.

If you don't have to do business in Tokyo, another strategy is to fly into Osaka, Nagoya, or Fukuoka, instead of the usual convoluted method of flying into Tokyo, taking a train to Haneda and then catching a domestic connecting flight to any of those cities.

AIR TRAVEL TIME

The following is a small sampling of the flights available from cities around the world to Tokyo. All flights arrive at Narita Airport except China Airlines' flights, which land at Haneda Airport.

- From Auckland nonstop on Air New Zealand: 10 hours 55 minutes
- From Bangkok nonstop on Thai Airways: 6 hours
- From Beijing nonstop on Air China: 5 hours
- From Frankfurt nonstop on Lufthansa: 11 hours 10 minutes
- From Hong Kong nonstop on Cathay Pacific: 3 hours 55 minutes
- From Jakarta nonstop on Garuda Indonesia: 8 hours
- From Kuala Lumpur nonstop on Malaysia Airlines: 6 hours 55 minutes
- From London nonstop on British Airways: 11 hours 50 minutes
- From Manila nonstop on Philippine Airlines: 4 hours
- From New York City nonstop on United: 13 hours 50 minutes
- From San Francisco nonstop on United: 10 hours 40 minutes
- From Seoul nonstop on Korean Airlines: 2 hours
- From Singapore nonstop on Singapore Airlines: 6 hours 40 minutes
- From Sydney nonstop on Qantas: 9 hours 25 minutes
- From Taipei nonstop on China Airlines: 3 hours 50 minutes

TIME CHANGES

Japan shares its time zone, nine hours ahead of Greenwich Mean Time, only with Korea and the western half of the island of New Guinea. When you're in Japan, you can determine what time it is in any of the cities listed here by adding or subtracting the number shown to or from Japanese time.

Auckland	+3
Bangkok	-2
Beijing	-1
Frankfurt	-8
Hong Kong	-1
Jakarta	-2
Kuala Lumpur	-1

Time differences (cont'd.)

London ....-9
Manila ....-1
New York .... -14
San Francisco ....-17
Seoul 0
Singapore ....-1
Sydney ....+1
Taipei ....-1

CUSTOMS ENTRY (PERSONAL)

Compared to most East Asian nations, Japan is relaxed about what foreigners bring into the country. You must declare unaccompanied luggage.

Duty-free

- Personal effects you don't plan to sell
- ATA carnet items—professional equipment, commercial samples, and advertising material you don't plan to sell
- Alcohol—three bottles 760 cc each
- Tobacco—100 cigars or 400 cigarettes, or 500 grams total
- Perfume—2 ounces
- Gifts, souvenirs, other—up to ¥200,000 (about US$1,800) worth

Cash—no limit on Japanese or foreign currency

Prohibited or restricted

- Narcotics and other illegal drugs
- Counterfeit or imitation money
- Items that infringe upon copyrights and patents
- Firearms and ammunition
- Pornography that depicts pubic hair

(Refer to "Imports and Importing" chapter for information on commercial imports.)

FOREIGN EXCHANGE

The Japanese yen comes in coin denominations of ¥1, ¥5, ¥10, ¥50, ¥100, and ¥500; and banknotes of ¥1,000, ¥5,000, and ¥10,000. The yen is the only currency accepted in Japan. Most Western currencies are freely negotiable, but Korean won and New Taiwan dollars are virtually impossible to exchange (and there are strict limits on taking them out of their respective countries, anyway). At the end of 1993 the yen was 111.68 to the US dollar. The ¥500 coin was worth about US$4.50.

To buy yen you have to show your passport, fill out some forms, and wait until your number is called—an antiquated system for a self-professed high-tech nation, but a system that's being rapidly updated. The first place to buy yen is at the currency exchange counters in the international airports. You can also buy yen at any number of foreign exchange banks (most large banks) and at hotels and major post offices. Traveler's checks get a better exchange rate than cash, and are also widely accepted as payment at larger hotels, restaurants and stores, as are major international credit cards.

TIPPING

As a general rule, the Japanese neither ask for nor expect tips, and rarely accept them—and even then only with considerable embarrassment. If you hire a driver, it's normal to tip him ¥500 (about US$4.50) for a half day and ¥1,000 (about US$9.00) for a full day. The money that porters demand is a fee—in airports, ¥200 (about US$1.80) per bag, and in railroad stations, ¥300 (about US$2.70) per bag. Full-service hotels and restaurants add a 10 to 15 percent service charge to the bill, so there's no need tip for dining and lodging.

ACCESS TO CITY FROM AIRPORT

Fukuoka Fukuoka Airport is a mere 10 km (6 miles) from city center. The fastest and cheapest way to town is the new subway line—it runs every 3 to 8 minutes, takes 5 to 6 minutes to arrive at Hakata Railway Station in city center, and costs only ¥220 (about US$2.00). A taxi will cost about ¥1,500 (about US$13.50).

Nagoya Komaki International Airport is 18 km (11 miles) north of the city. The shuttle bus leaves every 10 to 15 minutes and takes you to city center in about 40 minutes for ¥700 (about US$6.25). A taxi ride to city center will cost up to ¥5,000 (about US$45), depending on traffic conditions.

Osaka Itami International Airport is 16 km (10 miles) northwest of the city, and easy half-hour ride by bus, train or taxi to city center. The shuttle bus to Osaka Railway Station leaves every 15 minutes and costs ¥340 (about US$3) A taxi to the station will cost about ¥5,000 (about US$45). The new airport, due to open in September 1994, is being built in the bay. It will be even more convenient to Kobe and central Osaka, less so to Kyoto.

Tokyo If Singapore's Changi Airport is a traveler's dream, New Tokyo International Airport at Narita is a nightmare. You know you're in trouble when a city airport doesn't even show up on city maps. It's 66 traffic-choked km (41 miles) from city center. It seems to have been designed by the Mad Hatter. It's too small, chaotically busy, and grindingly slow in customs. In fact, some wags attribute Japan's current recession to the increasing thousands of executives and workers who have become trapped in the terminal or the freeway traffic, or been pushed onto the wrong trains, and never to be seen at their desks again.

Buses, trains, and taxis are plentiful and easy to find—just follow the signs. The shuttle bus takes 90 minutes to two hours to reach various hotels in central city, and charges you at least ¥2,700 (about US$24) for the torture. If you do take a bus, take the nonstop airport limousine bus, which handles big bags and takes you to downtown hotels. It leaves from in front of the arrival lobby.

Trains cost ¥2,800 to ¥4,300 (about US$25 to US$38.50), but at least they deliver you in about 45 minutes to an hour, slightly squished and with diminished lung capacity. If you have a Japan Railways Rail Pass (see Domestic Transportation later in this chapter), you can take the Narita Express Train, which can handle lots of big suitcases and has signs and announcements in English. If you don't have a Rail Pass, you can take the *Keisei* train, somewhat slower than the Express but less than half the price. Both trains leave from beneath the airport terminal.

Taxis are for the truly profligate—¥20,000 (about US$180) for a one- to two-hour-long view of a slowly moving parking lot and of a meter inexorably ticking away while you're sitting still. Take a taxi only after you've arrived near your hotel in a bus or train.

Best bet If you have any choice in the matter, fly China Airlines to Haneda Airport, only 18 km (11 miles) southeast of downtown. The stress and cost factors are logarithmically lower, which could be fundamental in starting your Japan trip off on the right note. The monorail is the best way from Haneda to the Hamamatsu-cho Train Station, which is near the World Trade Center and just 2 km from the Ginza and city center. The ride takes 15 minutes and costs ¥300 (about US$2.70)—considering the horrible alternative, one of the best bargains in Japan. From there you can take a taxi.

ACCOMMODATIONS

In general, Tokyo is so expensive to visit that you may look at your wallet after a couple of days and wonder if you've dropped your money on the ground somewhere or been robbed. Japan as a whole is only slightly cheaper than its chief city. With the Japanese yen so strong against other currencies, you will not lose much face by staying in an affordable hotel instead of the super-deluxe hotels you may have chosen as recently as 1992. Nevertheless, the better your hotel, the more face you gain in the eyes of your status-conscious Japanese contacts—and the more likely the staff are to speak English, provide exquisite service, and offer amenities ranging from same-day laundry to secretarial services (at extra cost, of course).

The typical top-end Tokyo hotel will cost at least ¥20,000 (about US$180) per night. There are only two classes of first-rank hotels: *very* expensive and very, very expensive. Most rooms are Western-style, but Japanese-style rooms are also available, usually in the middle range of the hotel's prices.

Some of the less expensive lodgings, such as business hotels, can cost as little as ¥4,000 (about US$36) per night. They offer little in the way of extra services and amenities—you get a bed in a minuscule room in clean, well-run hotel mostly serving Japanese businessmen, and that's about it, but that may be all you need. The JNTO has a listing of 70 traditional inns—*ryokan*—that specialize in welcoming foreign travelers at rates averaging ¥5,000 (about US$45) per night. The JNTO also has a listing of so-called Welcome Inns, a wide variety of lodgings that cater to foreign visitors—mostly families and groups—at nightly rates averaging ¥8,000 (about US$72). Ask at a JNTO office for information about these budget-saving alternatives.

Most of the hotels listed here are in or near city business or financial centers. If you're on a tight budget, the trick is to stay in the less-expensive hotels away from the center of town and take trains or taxis to your business destinations. Or keep your stay in Tokyo as short as you can; other major Japanese cities are somewhat less expensive. The following list barely scratches the surface. Occupancy rates tend to be high all year-round so book your lodgings well in advance. (Note: The prices quoted here are starting prices for each category of room.)

Tokyo—Top-end

Capitol Tokyu 2-10-3, Nagatacho, Chiyoda-ku 100; Akasaka district, near Imperial Palace, 10-minute taxi ride to Ginza, business district, and Tokyo Station. Two staff per guest; favorite of foreign business travelers. Business center, pool, steam bath, shopping, in-house doctor, travel agency, restaurants. Rates: single ¥24,500 (about US$220); twin ¥33,500 (about US$300); suite ¥90,000 (about US$810). Tel: (3) 3581-4511 Fax: (3) 581-5822 Tlx: 222-3605 THCCAP J.

Imperial Hotel 1-1-1 Uchisaiwaicho, Chiyoda-ku 100; in center of Tokyo, on the edge of the Ginza, in financial district, near the Imperial Palace, 5 minutes by taxi from Tokyo Station. World-famous, prestigious. Business center, health club, 20th-floor indoor pool, shopping, fine restaurants. Rates: twin ¥38,000 (about US$340); suite ¥60,000 (about US$538). Tel: (3) 3504-1111, toll-free (800) 223-6800 in US and Canada Fax: (3) 3581-9146 Tlx: 222-2346 IMPHO J.

Tokyo Hilton 6-6-2 Nishi-Shinjuku, Shinjuku-ku 160; in Shinjuku financial and high-tech district, 4 km from city center, 10-minute walk from Shinjuku Station. Business center, health club, indoor pool, restaurants, shopping. Rates: single ¥27,000 (about US$242); twin ¥34,000 (about US$305); suite ¥75,000 (about US$672). Tel: (3) 3344-3111, US toll-free (800) HILTONS Fax: (3) 3342-6094 Tlx: 232-4515 HILTON J.

Expensive

Dai-Ichi Hotel Annex 1-5-2 Uchisaiwacho, Chiyoda-ku 100; near the Ginza and Imperial Hotel, 3-minute walk to Shinbashi Station. Small (170 rooms). Business center, restaurant, meeting rooms. Rates: single ¥25,000 (about US$224); suite ¥45,000 (about US$403). Tel: (3) 3503-5611 Fax: (3) 3503-5777.

Palace 1-1-1 Marunouchi, Chiyoda-ku 100; across moat from Imperial Palace, 7-minute walk from Tokyo Station. Older, small (405 rooms—try for one on an upper floor facing the Palace). Business center, shopping, restaurants. Rates: single ¥22,000 (about US$197); twin ¥28,000 (about US$250); suite ¥100,000 (about US$895). Tel: (3) 3211-5211 Fax: (3) 3211-6987 Tlx: 222-2580 PALACE J.

Tokyo Renaissance Ginza Tobu 6-14-10 Ginza, Chuo-ku 104; in the Ginza; 1-minute walk to Higashi Station, 4 minutes to Ginza Station. Small (206 rooms), popular with foreigners. Business center, travel center, 24-hour coffeehouse. Rates: single ¥18,000 (about US$161); twin ¥30,000 (about US$269); suite ¥50,000 (about US$448). Tel: (3) 3546-0111, toll-free (800) 228-2828 in US Fax: (3) 3546-8990.

Moderate

Fairmont 2-1-17, Kudan Minami, Chiyoda-ku 102; on east side of Imperial Palace grounds overlooking moat, 15 minutes by taxi to Tokyo Station. Old-fashioned, small (206 rooms—try for one facing the park). Restaurant, bar. Rates: single ¥9,700 (about US$87); twin ¥18,000 (about US$161); suite ¥70,000 (about US$627). Tel: (3) 3262-1151 Fax: (3) 3264-2476 Tlx: 232-2883 FAIRHO J.

Ginza Capital 3-1-5 Tsukiji, Chuo-ku 104. Close to Ginza, 2-minute walk to Shintomicho Station. Restaurants. Rates: single ¥8,200 (about US$73); twin ¥14,300 (about US$128); suite ¥20,500 (about US$184). Tel: (3) 3543-8211 Fax: (3) 3543-7839.

Tokyo YMCA Hotel 7 Mitoshiro-cho, Kanda, Chiyoda-ku 101; few minutes walk from three stations, 2 km from Ginza. 40 small rooms. Laundry, pharmacy, Western restaurant. Rates: single ¥11,000 (about US$98.50); twin ¥16,500 (about US$148). Tel: (3) 3293-1911 Fax: (3) 3293-1926.

Fukuoka—Top-end

Hotel Il Palazzo 3-13, Haruoshi, Chuo-ku 810; near city center. Award-winning architecture, small (62 rooms), exclusive. Restaurants. Rates: ¥20,000 (about US$179) and up. Tel: (92) 716-3333 Fax: (92) 724-3330.

New Otani Hakata 1-1-2 Watanabe-Dori, Chuo-ku 810; near city center, 5-minute taxi ride to Hakata Station. English-speaking staff, convention-transla-

tion facilities, restaurants, shopping, travel agency, pool, meeting rooms. Rates: single ¥17,000 (about US$152); twin ¥24,000 (about US$215); suite ¥35,000 (about US$313). Tel: (92) 714-1111 Fax: (92) 715-5658 Tlx: 726-567.

Expensive

ANA Zenniku Hotel Hakata 3-3-3 Hakata-ekimae, Hakata-ku 812; short walk to Hakata Station. One of the best in town. Health club, shopping, restaurants. Rates: single ¥11,000 (about US$98.50); twin ¥20,000 (about US$179); suite ¥50,000 (about US$448). Tel: (92) 471-7111 Fax: (92) 472-7707 Tlx: 722-288 ANAFUK J.

Fukuoka Yamanoue 1-1-33, Terakuni, Chuo-ku 810; near city center, 10-minute taxi ride to Hakata Station. Spectacular views of city and ocean. Public baths, tennis, restaurants. Rates: ¥10,000 (about US$90) and up. Tel: (92) 771-2131 Fax: (92) 771-8888.

Moderate

Clio Court 5-3, Hakata-eki-chuo-gai, Hakata-ku 812; next to Hakata Station bullet-train exit. Choice of room decor; revolving restaurant with view. Restaurants, sushi bar, gallery. Rates: ¥11,000 (about US$98.50) to ¥23,000 (about US$206). Tel: (92) 472-1111 Fax: (92) 474-3222.

Hakata Miyako 2-1-1, Hakata-eki Higashi, Hakata-ku 812; next to Hakata Station bullet-train exit. Excellent service. Meeting rooms, restaurants, medical clinic. Rates: ¥9,000 to ¥90,000 (about US$81 to US$806). Tel: (92) 441-3111 Fax: (92) 481-1306 Tlx: 724-585.

Nagoya—Top-end

Nagoya Castle 3-19 Hinokuchi-cho, Nishi-ku 451; next to Nagoya Castle, 8-minute taxi ride to Nagoya Station. Try for castle-view rooms. Business center, convention hall, health club, pool, restaurants, shopping, shuttle bus to station. Rates: single ¥11,500 (about US$103); twin ¥20,000 (about US$179); suite ¥70,000 (about US$627). Tel: (52) 521-2121 Fax: (52) 531-3313 Tlx: 59787 CASTLE-J.

Nagoya Hilton 1-3-3 Sakae, Naka-ku 460; in business district, 2-minute walk to Fushimi Station. Large rooms. Business center, conference facilities, health club, tennis, pool, restaurants, shopping, doctor. Rates: single ¥16,500 (about US$148); twin ¥24,000 (about US$215); suite ¥60,000 (about US$537). Tel: (52) 212-1111 Fax: (52) 212-1225 Tlx: HILNGO J.

Expensive

International Hotel Nagoya 3-23-3, Nishiki, Naka-ku 460; in city center, 5-minute taxi ride to Nagoya Station. Favorite of business travelers. Business center, meeting rooms, restaurants, shopping. Rates: single ¥9,000 (about US$81); twin ¥19,000 (about

US$170); suite ¥40,000 (about US$358). Tel: (52) 961-3111 Fax: (52) 962-5937 Tlx: 444-3720 INTERH J.

Nagoya Miyako 4-9-10, Meieki, Nakamura-ku 450; near city center, 5-minute taxi ride to Nagoya Station. Meeting rooms, restaurants, shopping. Rates: single ¥9,000 (about US$81); twin ¥16,000 (about US$143); suite ¥35,000 (about US$313). Tel: (52) 571-3211 Fax: (52) 571-3242 Tlx: 442-2086.

Moderate

Castle Plaza 4-3-25, Meieki, Nakamura-ku 450; near city center, 5-minute walk from Nagoya Station. Convention-translation facilities, health club, pool, sauna, 12 restaurants, shopping. Rates: single ¥8,000 (about US$72); twin ¥14,000 (about US$125); suite ¥37,000 (about US$331). Tel: (52) 582-2121 Fax: (52) 582-8666 Tlx: J59678.

Fitness Hotel 1-2-7, Sakae, Nakamura-ku 450; near city center, 5-minute walk to Nagoya Station. Business hotel, mostly single rooms. Business center, computer workstations, health club, restaurant. Rates: ¥8,000 to ¥11,000 (about US$72 to US$98.50). Tel: (52) 562-0330 Fax: (52) 562-0331.

Osaka

Bear in mind that Osaka is gritty and industrial—even more so than Tokyo. If you can, stay in relatively serene Kyoto and take the 20-minute bullet-train ride to Osaka to do business.

Top-end

New Otani Osaka 1-4, Shiromi, Chuo-ku 540; in Osaka Business Park, near Osaka Castle, 3-minute walk to Osakajo-Koen Station. Business center, health club, pool, tennis, travel agency, restaurants, shopping, medical clinic. Rates: single ¥18,000 (about US$161); twin ¥30,000 (about US$269); suite ¥55,000 (about US$492). Tel: (6) 941-1111 Fax: (6) 941-9769 Tlx: 529-3330 OTNOSK.

Osaka Hilton International 1-8-8, Umeda, Kita-ku 530; in business district, across from Osaka Station. Business center, meeting rooms, health club, pool, tennis, sauna, restaurants, shopping. Rates: single ¥22,000 (about US$197); twin ¥29,000 (about US$260); suite ¥65,000 (about US$582). Tel: (6) 347-7111 Fax: (6) 347-7001 Tlx: 524-2201.

Royal 5-3-68, Nakanoshima, Kita-ku 530; on Nakanoshima Island, in heart of Osaka. Huge. Business center, convention-translation facilities, pools, health club, sauna, steam bath, 24 restaurants, shopping. Rates: single ¥14,000 (about US$125); twin ¥26,000 (about US$233); suite ¥44,000 (about US$394). Tel: (6) 448-1121 Fax: (6) 448-4414 Tlx: J63350 ROYAL HTL.

Expensive

Osaka Grand 2-3-18, Nakanoshima, Kita-ku 530; on Nakanoshima Island, in city center, 5-minute taxi ride to Osaka Station. Meeting rooms, restaurants, shopping. Rates: single ¥11,000 (about US$98.50); twin ¥20,000 (about US$179); suite ¥45,000 (about US$403). Tel: (6) 202-1212 Fax: (6) 227-5054 Tlx: 522-2301 OGRAND J.

Osaka Tokyu 7-20, Chaya-michi, Kita-ku 530; near midtown, 5-minute walk to Osaka Station. Conference facilities, meeting rooms, pool, restaurants, shopping. Rates: single ¥11,000 (about US$98.50); twin ¥20,000 (about US$179); suite ¥50,000 (about US$448). Tel: (6) 373-2411 Fax: (6) 376-0343 Tlx: 523-6751 THCOSA-J.

Toyo 3-16-19, Toyosaki, Kita-ku 531; near city center, 5-minute taxi ride to Osaka or Shin-Osaka stations. Business center, meeting rooms, restaurants, shopping. Rates: single ¥12,000 (about US$108); twin ¥23,000 (about US$206); suite ¥45,000 (about US$403). Tel: (6) 372-8181 Fax: (6) 372-8101 Tlx: 523-3886 TOYOHO J.

Moderate

Hotel California 1-9-30, Nishishinsaibashi, Chuo-ku 542; in city center, 5-minute walk to Shinsaibashi Station. Pure kitsch. Restaurant, bar. Rates: single ¥8,200 (about US$73); twin ¥14,300 (about US$128). Tel: (6) 243-0333 Fax: (6) 243-0148.

Osaka International Community Center Hotel 8-2-6 Uehommachi, Tennoji-ku 543; in Osaka Community Center building, 5-minute walk to Uehommachi Station. Small (50 rooms). Center facilities include library, restaurant, conference facilities, simultaneous interpreting facilities, seminars. Rates: single ¥6,700 (about US$60); twin ¥13,500 (about US$121). Tel: (6) 773-8181 Fax: (6) 773-0777.

Tennoji Miyako 10-48, Hidenincho, Tennoji-ku 543; near city center, in Tennoji Station building. Meeting rooms, restaurant. Rates: single ¥8,500 (about US$76); twin ¥13,000 (about US$116); suite ¥35,000 (about US$313). Tel: (6) 779-1501 Fax: (6) 779-8800 Tlx: 527-8930 MIYAKO J.

EATING

For the Japanese, eating is a way of life. There's much more to Japanese food than you see in Japanese restaurants in foreign countries. There are many regional cuisines, and the Japanese love Italian and French cooking as well—although they add uniquely Japanese touches.

Look for *okonomiyaki*, a kind of pancake or omelet you prepare yourself at the table; *sukiyaki*, thinly sliced beef mixed with vegetables, tofu and noodles; *tempura*, deep-fried prawns, fish, or vegetables; *sushi*, raw fish and vinegared rice, often wrapped in seaweed and sometimes with a surprise dose of wasabi (horseradish) lurking inside; *sashimi*, raw fish eaten with soy sauce; *yakitori*, small pieces of meat on bamboo skewers grilled over a fire; *tonkatsu*, a deep-fried pork cutlet; *shabu-shabu*, slices of tender beef that you hold with chopsticks, swirl in boiling water, then dip in a sauce; *shojin ryori*, Zen Buddhist vegetarian cuisine; and *kaiseki ryori*, Japanese haute cuisine, literally a way of serving and eating incredibly delectable foods in a precise and visually harmonious way that originated in the tea ceremony.

Eating your way through Japan can be expensive, but it can also be reasonable and even cheap. There are almost 200,000 restaurants and bars in Tokyo alone. You can find cheap food in street stalls throughout the country as well as in traditional style noodle and ramen restaurants. You can buy boxed meals, such as *obento*—at ¥600 to ¥1,200 (about US$5.40 to US$10.75) everyone in Japan eats them. And take advantage of the fact that most restaurants serve lunch for less than half the price of dinner for the same food. Keep in mind, too, that some of the best restaurants are in major hotels. You'll find Japan has a great many foreign restaurants—American, French, Chinese, Korean, Italian, Indian, Thai, Indochinese, Russian, even Swedish. However, we've limited our listing to some of the most highly recommended Japanese restaurants.

A note of caution: Japanese of both sexes are heavy-duty drinkers. Few countries publish official tourist guides that devote one-and-a-half pages and three color photos to drinking. Face falls by the wayside; all is forgiven if you do something ridiculous when drunk. Japanese are happy imbibers, too. However, a business traveler is already under enough stress, so it's best to resist the nightly invitations to overindulge in saki and beer.

Tokyo

Gonin Byakusho Hearty, grilled foods. Dinner: ¥4,000 to ¥6,500 (about US$36 to US$58). 3-10-3, Roppongi, Minatoku, 4th floor of Roppongi Square Building, near Roppongi Station. Tel: (3) 3470-1675.

Inakaya *Robatayaki* (charcoal grill) cuisine. Dinner: ¥12,000 (about US$108). 7-8-4, Roppongi, Minatoku, near Roppongi Station. Tel: (3) 3491-9928.

Kisso *Kaiseki* cuisine. Dinner: ¥9,000 to ¥15,000 (about US$81 to US$134). Reservations recommended. 4-6-18, Ginza, near Ginza Station. Tel: (3) 3535-5035.

Takeno Fresh fish. Dinner: ¥3,000 to ¥8,000 (about US$27 to US$72). No reservations. 6-21-2 Tsukiji, Chuo-ku, near fish market and Tsukiji Station. Tel: (3) 3541-8698.

Tonki *Tonkatsu* cuisine. Dinner: to ¥3,000 (about US$27). No reservations. 1-1-2 Shimo-Meguro, Meguro-ku, near Meguro Station. Tel: (3) 3491-9928.

Fukuoka

Gourmet City 12 restaurants with varied menus. Dinner: to ¥2,500 (about US$22.50). No reservations. 4-23, Hakataeki, Chuogai, in basement of Hotel Centraza. Tel: (92) 461-0111.

Gyosai Fresh seafood. Dinner: to ¥4,000 (about US$36). No reservations. 2-2-12, Hakata-ekimae, Hakata-ku, near Hakata Station (sign says "Oki Doki"). Tel: (92) 441-9780.

Ichiki Varied Japanese cuisine, and bar. Dinner: to ¥3,000 (about US$27). No reservations. 1-2-10, Maizara, Chuo-ku. Tel: (92) 751-5591.

Ikesu Kawataro Seafood. Dinner: over ¥10,000 (about US$90). Reservations not required. 1-6-6, Nakasu, Hakata-ku. Tel: (92) 271-2133.

Tsukushino Varied Japanese cuisine, *kaiseki*. Dinner: ¥8,000 to ¥20,000 (about US$72 to US$179). Reservations recommended. 3-3-3, Hakata-ekimae, Hakata-ku, on 15th floor of ANA Zenniku Hotel Hakata, near Hakata Station. Tel: (92) 471-7111.

Nagoya

Kisoji *Shabu-shabu* cuisine. Dinner: ¥6,000 to ¥11,000 (about US$54 to US$98.50). Reservations not necessary. 3-20-15, Nishiki, Naka-ku, near Sakae Station. Tel: (52) 951-3755.

Koraku Varied Japanese cuisine. Dinner: ¥6,000 (about US$54) and above. Reservations required (introduction advised). 3-3, Chikara-machi, Higashi-ku. (52) 931-3472.

Meitetsu Department Store, 9th floor 10 small restaurants with varied menus. Dinner: to ¥2,000 (about US$18). Next to Nagoya Station.

Usquebaugh *Kaiseki* cuisine. Dinner: ¥2,500 to ¥4,500 (about US$22 to US$40). Reservations recommended. 2-4-1, Sakae, Naka-ku. Tel: (52) 201-5811.

Yaegaki *Tempura* cuisine. Dinner: ¥5,000 to ¥7,500 (about US$45 to US$67). Reservations recommended. 3-7, Nishiki, Naka-ku, near Sakae Station. Tel: (52) 951-3250.

Osaka

Ebi Doraku Shrimp cuisine. Dinner: to ¥7,000 (about US$63). Inquire about reservations. 1-6-2, Dotonbori, Chuo-ku (look for big mechanical shrimp in front). Tel: (6) 211-1633.

Fuguhisa *Fugu* (blowfish) cuisine. Dinner: ¥3,000 to ¥4,500 (about US$27 to US40). Inquire about reservations. 3-14-24, Higashi-ohashi, Higashinari-ku. Tel: (6) 972-5029.

Kaen French *kaiseki* (French cuisine in *kaiseki* style). Dinner: ¥11,000 to ¥17,000 (about US$98.50 to US$152). Reservations required. 1-10-2, Sonnezaki-shinchi, Kita-ku, near Yotsubashi and Osaka stations. Tel: (6) 344-2929.

Kani Doraku Crab dishes. Dinner: ¥5,000 to ¥6,500 (about US$45 to US$58). Reservations recommended. 1-6-18, Dotonbori, Chuo-ku (look for huge mechanical crab over door, near big mechanical shrimp restaurant). Tel: (6) 211-8975.

Tako-ume Varied Japanese cuisine; 200-year-old restaurant. Dinner: ¥3,000 to ¥4,500 (about US$27 to US$40). Reservations recommended. 1-1-8, Dotonbori, Chuo-ku. Tel: (6) 211-0321.

LOCAL CUSTOMS OVERVIEW

Japan calls itself the Land of the Rising Sun. Maybe that's the direction everybody was looking in when Confucian social structure and etiquette invaded from the Land of the Setting Sun. In any case, Japan shares with the rest of East Asia some fundamental social attributes: power, status, dignity, integrity, personal connections, patience, patriarchy, obedience to the collective. These are what matter to the Japanese.

- The concept of face is basic to Confucian etiquette. Face is self-respect, status in the eyes of others. Losing face is abhorrent, having it or gaining it is prized. Thus, the open criticism, the disrespect for authority and elders, and the impatience of typical Westerners all cause loss of face in any relationship, personal or business.
- Harmony is key to maintaining face, and so harmony underlies the relationships, work, play, culture, and art of the Japanese. Such reliance on harmony leads to extreme conformity; no one wants to upset the apple cart. All decisions are group decisions; no one wants to say no. Personal responsibility and straight answers are not cherished and not to be found. The buck never stops here—or anywhere else in Japan. Those who expect the Japanese to behave like westerners will be frustrated and confused.
- Confucian society is patriarchal: in business, the boss is father; employees honor and respect him as such. Maybe this patriarchy is the source of Japan's legendary nationalism. The foreigner in Japan on business is both invading the country and insinuating himself or herself into a family. While the Japanese are tolerant of foreigners who don't understand or practice their ways and don't hold their ignorance against them, those ways still erect a formidable barrier. Personal relationships are more important to Japanese than paper contracts.
- However, don't think the contract is unimportant. Once something is in the contract, the Japanese will follow it to the letter. But woe unto anyone who leaves something out of a contract, assuming that it is understood. It may be standard practice where you come from, but you can't count on it being standard practice in Japan.
- Thus, to get your foot in the door of this tightly knit family, you will need formal introductions. You'll also need all the patience, flexibility and respect you can muster.
- Business cards are crucial. Carry plenty of them, always. When you meet a business contact for the first time, shake hands (not too firmly) or bow (be observant; if a bow is offered instead of a handshake, reciprocate). Then exchange cards. Present and receive cards with both hands, and put the card you receive in a pocket above the waist—but only after reading it carefully and respectfully. Your card should have a Japanese translation on the reverse.
- Be prepared to socialize after business—to eat, drink, be merry, drink, sing songs, drink....
- Forget about face in crowds or subways. Everybody loses it in all the pushing and shoving. It's all among strangers, who, after all, are not part of the family and thus undeserving of face.

(Refer to "Business Culture" chapter for an in-depth discussion.)

DOMESTIC TRANSPORTATION

Air There are domestic air flights between more than 65 cities in Japan, via Japan Airlines (JAL), All Nippon Airways, Japan Air Systems, Air Nippon Koku, or South West Airlines. Most flights take less than two hours. The Tokyo-Fukuoka flight takes one hour 45 minutes and costs about ¥26,000 (about US$233) one-way. The Tokyo-Osaka flight takes about one hour and costs about ¥15,000 (about US$134) one-way. The most convenient way to arrange a flight is through a travel agent. Remember to ask about discounts (such as JAL's special fare for husband-and-wife couples whose combined age is at least 88 years!).

Train There's almost no place in Japan you can't get to by train. Japan Railways (JR) has the best coverage and schedule in the world by a substantial margin. JR is a group of six railway companies that cover the entire country, plus several more companies that serve commuters in the big cities. Japanese trains are clean, comfortable, on time, and frequent—at peak hours, its Tokyo commuter trains pass through the stations every 1.5 minutes. Its world-renowned *shinkansen* (bullet trains) hurtle through the countryside at 260 kph (162 mph).

Train travel in Japan has varying levels and cost: super express (*shinkansen*), limited express, express, berth, and reserved-seat, plus coach class and first class within each of these. The *shinkansen* is only slightly cheaper than flying, but still it's more convenient because train terminals are usually in city centers. The Tokyo-Fukuoka bullet train run takes about six hours and costs about ¥22,000 (about US$197). The Tokyo-Osaka trip on the bullet train takes about three hours and costs about ¥14,000 (about US$125). The cheapest way to travel on Japanese trains is with a Japan Rail Pass, which you can buy only outside Japan and only with a tourist visa. It gives you one, two, or three weeks of unlimited first-class or coach travel on JR lines and associated bus and ferry lines at rates ranging from ¥27,800 to ¥78,000 (about US$249 to US$698).

No matter which train you take, be aware that there are always assorted surcharges. For example, Rail Pass holders have to pay a sleeper charge of more than ¥5,000 (about US$45) on the *shinkansen*, even though there are no sleeper cars on the *shinkansen* because none of them run overnight! Don't try to take a large amount of luggage on the *shinkansen*: It's in the station for all of two minutes; your fellow passengers aren't going to wait behind you, and the train isn't going to wait for you. You have just enough time to get yourself on board.

Whenever you travel by train, it's essential to make reservations, because in Japan everybody takes the train everywhere.

Subway All major cities have subways, which run as fast and efficiently as the trains. The 12 Tokyo lines are legendary or notorious, depending on your point of view. The subway is where Confucius's face was surely lost forever during the Japanese rush hours—there is no shame in pushing and shoving your way onto the train, and in fact very large and powerful men are employed to push and shove you. The lines are color coded, signs are in Japanese characters as well as the Roman alphabet, and there are dozens of stops and many interconnections with JR lines. Fares start at ¥140 (about US$1.25).

Bus Bus travel within cities is impractical for foreigners because of language barriers and routes so complex that even the Japanese get confused. The lone exception is Kyoto, where the buses are convenient, easy to use, and have English announcements.

Foreigners can travel with ease on buses between cities. While much slower than the bullet trains, buses are also much cheaper. The express bus from Tokyo to Osaka runs through Nagoya and Kyoto, stopping at the main train station in each city. If you take the night bus to your destination, you also save the considerable cost of a hotel room. The Tokyo-Osaka night run, for example, costs ¥8,450 (about US$76), a little more than half the cost of the *shinkansen* or a first-class hotel room.

Taxi Taxis are the most convenient and most expensive way for foreigners to get around in Japan's cities. An open taxi has a red light in the lower-right corner of the windshield as you face it. The driver opens the left rear door from the inside, and you hop in. Have your destination written down in Japanese characters, and if you're going someplace uncommon—for example, a company office or a friend's house—bring a map with the destination pinpointed. Street addresses often aren't consecutive, very few streets have names, and even when they do the name isn't part of the address (we are not making this up). Even taxi drivers get lost. Pay only the metered fare— unlike certain other East Asian cab drivers, Japanese cabbies are honest. The first 2 km (1.25 miles) cost ¥540 (about US$4.85), and every 370 meters after that cost another ¥80 (about US$0.75). Thankfully, you don't tip the driver!

For assistance with transportation questions, call the Japan Hotline: (3) 3586-0110.

HOLIDAYS/BANK HOLIDAYS

The Japanese have used the Gregorian (Western) calendar since 1873. Paid legal holidays observed in Japan are denoted by * in the following list. If a holiday falls on a Sunday or another normal rest day, the following day is observed as the holiday.

Golden Week begins with Greenery Day on April 29 and ends with Children's Day on May 5, during which time the Japanese travel all over the country and take all the hotel rooms. During the O Bon Festival (August 13-16), many Japanese take the whole week off to return to their home towns for Buddhist ceremonies honoring their ancestors, again jamming the trains and taking all the hotel rooms. In fact, the last week of July and the first three weeks of August

Japanese Holidays

New Year's Day*–January 1
Adults' Day*–January 15
National Foundation Day*–February 11
Spring Equinox*–March 21
Greenery Day*– April 29
Constitution Day*– May 3
National Holiday*–May 4
Children's Day*–May 5
O Bon Festival–August 13-16
Respect-for-the-Aged Day*– September 15
Autumnal Equinox*–September 23
Health-Sports Day*–October 10
Culture Day*–November 3
Labor Thanksgiving Day*–November 23
Emperor's Birthday*–December 23
Christmas–December 25
Osho-Gatsu–December 27
*Paid Legal Holidays

are vacation weeks. On December 27, the Japanese begin the week-long, festive New Year celebrations. Business travelers should abandon all hope of business or travel during these times.

BUSINESS HOURS

Normal business hours are 9 am to 5 pm Monday through Friday with an hour off for lunch from noon to 1 pm. Banks are open from 9 am to 3 pm weekdays. Stores and shops are open from 10 am to 8 pm, although department stores generally close by 7 pm. Most stores take their weekly holiday on Wednesday or Thursday and remain open on Saturday and Sunday.

COMMUNICATIONS

Everybody in Japan is on the phone or the fax. Please hold.

Telephones The Japanese may not have given birth to the telephone, but they certainly have adopted it. Telephone service is first-rate. You can make long-distance and overseas calls from your hotel room, although you should first ask if you can dial direct or must go through an operator and whether there is a surcharge—Japan is also the Land of the Rising Surcharge.

Public telephones are everywhere, color coded, cheap (3 minutes for ¥10—about US$0.09), and best of all, nonvandalized (in Japan, even the handful of vandals need telephones). At press time, there were phones in eight different colors, but some you may never see—pink and light-blue, for example. The ubiquitous public phone is yellow. They can be used to call locally and long-distance and can take ¥10 and sometimes ¥100 (about US$0.90) coins. You can keep feeding the phone coins for as much time as you want; unused coins will be returned, and a warning chime will sound when your time is nearly up. Unless you drop in more money, your call will just end abruptly, causing you to lose face (telephones know nothing of Confucius). Red phones are similar to yellow phones, but are usually privately owned; you find them in stores, restaurants, and shops.

There are two types of green phones, and both take calling cards. The plain green phones can be used to call locally or long-distance and accept both coins and calling cards. Green phones with gold front panels—or some other kind of international-call logo—usually take only cards and can be used to call locally, long-distance, or internationally.

A new dark blue phone accepts coins and credit cards; it has a display of credit card logos on the front. A new gray phone is multiplying in the cities; it takes calling cards and coins, can be used to call internationally, and has a monitor screen that tells

you in English and Japanese what to do and how much time you have left.

You can buy calling cards in stores, souvenir stands, hotels, and vending machines; a ¥1,000 (about US$9) card buys 105 3-minute calls. The green-and-gold phone takes as many cards as you can feed it (international calls cost a pocketful of yen coins); when it's used up one card the phone spits it out and demands another. While calling cards don't save you much money, they are very convenient—and because they are decorated with pictures, they have become popular collectors' items.

Japan has three international call carriers: Kokusai Denshin Denwa (KDD), International Telecom Japan (ITJ) and International Digital Communications (IDC). This makes a difference when you're trying to direct dial internationally because each has its own international access number. (See Direct dialing internationally, below.)

When you call long-distance within Japan, include the 0 with the area code. When you call to Japan from overseas, omit the 0 or the phone will hurl unintelligible Japanese invective at you. Long-distance calls are 40 percent cheaper between 11 pm and 8 am; international rates vary according to carrier. Japan's country code is 81.

To direct dial internationally Dial the international access number—it depends on the carrier—then the country code, then the area code (if there is one), and the phone number. For example, to call World Trade Press direct on a KDD phone, dial 001-1-415-454-9934. The cheapest time to call internationally from Japan is between 11 pm and 5 am Before calling from your hotel room, check to see how vast the hotel surcharges are. Then consider using a pay phone.

Fax, telegram and telex Fax machines are everywhere—in almost every hotel, most businesses, many homes, even in 24-hour convenience stores. Most hotels also have telexes. Your hotel can refer you to a business center or a KDD office, from which you can send faxes, telegrams and telexes. Major post offices can also send telegrams.

Post Office Japan's mail service is typically efficient. Offices are open from 9 am to 5 pm Monday through Friday, but the international branches are open until 7 or 8 pm. Post offices are marked by a bright red T with a line above it, while mailboxes are brilliant orange-red.

The easiest way to mail a letter or package is from your hotel's front desk. Postcards to anywhere in the world cost ¥70 (about US$0.63), and aerograms cost ¥80 (about US$0.72). Letters up to 10 grams cost ¥80 (about US$0.72) to Asia; ¥100 (about US$0.90) to Oceania, the Middle East and North and Central America; and ¥120 (about US$1.07) to Europe, Africa, and South America. If you're expecting mail from abroad, have your correspondents type your name and address to speed delivery.

English-language media Japan has five English-language daily newspapers: *Japan Times* (the best), *Mainichi Daily News, Daily Yomiuri, Asahi Evening News*, and the *International Herald Tribune*. The American magazines *Newsweek* and *Time* are readily available. *Tokyo Journal, Tokyo Time Out,* and *Kansai Time Out* provide information on entertainment and cultural events. *Nihongo Journal* and *Hiranaga Times* are monthly magazines for English-speakers studying the Japanese language. There are several English-language telephone directories.

There's not much in the way of English-language Tokyo radio—J-Wave (81.3 FM) broadcasts music; top-end hotels have KTYO; and then there's the US Armed Forces Far East Network (FEN—810kHz). Hotel cable TV systems receive CNN and some other English-language programming.

Japan Area Codes

Fukuoka	92
Kagoshima	992
Kitakyushu	93
Kobe	78
Kyoto	75
Matsuyama	899
Nagasaki	958
Nagoya	52
Naha	98
Osaka	6
Sapporo	11
Tokyo	3
Toyama	764
Yamagata	236
Yokohama	45

Country Codes of Major Countries

Australia	61
Brazil	55
Canada	1
China	86
France	33
Germany	49
Hong Kong	852
India	91
Indonesia	62
Italy	39
Korea	82
Malaysia	60
Mexico	52
New Zealand	64
Pakistan	92
Philippines	63
Russia	7
Singapore	65
South Africa	27
Spain	34
Taiwan	886
Thailand	66
United Kingdom	44
United States	1

USEFUL TELEPHONE NUMBERS
(*indicates Japanese-speaking personnel only)

- Lost and Found (Tokyo)* (first check at your hotel or at nearest police box)
- Police .... (3) 3814-4151
- Taxi .... (3) 3648-0300
- JR Trains (Tokyo Station) .... (3) 3231-1880
  (Ueno Station) .... (3) 3841-8069
- Subways .... (3) 3834-5577
- Other .... (3) 3814-5760
- Japan Helpline .... (0120) 461-997
- International phone communications services (Kokusai Denshin Denwa Co.) 0057
- Telegrams
  Domestic 115
  Overseas .... (3) 3344-5151
- Calls to the Bullet Train 107
- Information Corner (multilingual)
  .... (45) 671-7209
- Lost or stolen credit cards
  (International collect calls only to US regardless of which country your card was issued in)
  Amex .... (919) 333-3211
  Diners Club .... (303) 799-1504
  MasterCard .... (314) 275-6690
  Visa .... (410) 581-7931
- Japan Hotline .... (3) 3586-0110
- JNTO Tourist Information Centers
  Tokyo .... (3) 3502-1461
  Kyoto .... (75) 371-5649
  Narita .... (476) 32-8711

- Japan Travel-Phone
  Eastern Japan 0088-22-2800
  Western Japan 0088-22-4800
- Subway Information (Tokyo) ...... (3) 3837-7111
- Flight Information
  Narita Airport .... (476) 32-2800
  Haneda Airport .... (3) 3747-8010
- International operator[1] 0051
- International dial access[2] ...... 001, 0041 or 0061
- Home Country Direct[3]
  United States ... 0039-111, 0039-121 or 0039-131
  Hawaii .... 0039-111 or 0039-181
  Australia 0039-611
  Canada 0039-161
  France 0039-331
  Hong Kong 0039-852
  Italy 0039-391
  Korea 0039-821
  New Zealand 0039-641
  Singapore 0039-651
  Thailand 0039-661
  Taiwan 0039-886
  United Kingdom 0039-441

1. You can use the international operator to call certain countries other than your home country that are not part of the Home Country Direct network, but still use your home country calling card. You are charged Japanese rates. The operator will tell you which countries you can call.
2. Which international access number you use depends upon which Japanese phone company your hotel or public phone is tied into. The rates and locations vary. KDD's access number is 001; ITJ's is 0041; IDC's is 0061. The phones don't have any identifying information, so you have to ask at your hotel's front desk, or you have to experiment with the different access numbers. KDD is by far the largest carrier—try 001 first unless you know differently.
3. Home Country Direct enables you to bypass the Japanese telephone system and reach your country directly. A recording offers you the option of using your home country calling card, a credit card (except US), or an operator for collect calls. Avoid using your hotel room phone; there are sizable hotel service charges. Instead, use a pay phone. Narita Airport and most large hotels have special Home Country Direct pay phones with a button for each of the above countries.

COURIER SERVICES

Most of the large international courier services operate in Japan.

Federal Express

Tokyo 3-10, Tatsumi, Koto-ku 135; Tel: (toll-free) (012) 003-200.

Osaka 3-6, Honden 3-chome, Nishi-ku 550; Tel: (6) 584-6565

TNT

Tokyo Number 7 Koike Building, 4th Floor, 3-6 Minami-Shinagawa 2-chome, Shinagawa-ku 140; Tel: (3) 3740-4300 Fax: (3) 3740-4306 Tlx: 2425506 TNTTYO J

Nagoya 1-515, Tokugawa, Higashi-ku 461; Tel: (52) 937-4831 Fax: (52) 937-4796 Tlx: 2425506 TNTTYO J

Osaka 2-6-2, Hotarugaike-Nishimachi, Toyonaka 560; Tel: (6) 843-7562 Fax: (6) 843-5043 Tlx: 2425506 TNTTYO J

UPS

Chiba Unistar Air Cargo (UPS Yamato Co., Ltd.), 717-74, Futamata, Ichikawa City; Tel: (473) 27-1040 Fax: (473) 28-3120.

LOCAL SERVICES

Need a business service in Japan? Just ask. It will be provided. Such services are everywhere. Inquire at your hotel front desk or look in an English-language yellow pages. Here is a list of the basic services you'll need after you arrive.

Business centers

Many first-class and super-luxury hotels have business centers providing secretarial and delivery services, computers, fax machines, and telephones. Among those hotels are:

Tokyo Akasaka Prince, ANA Hotel Tokyo, Capitol Tokyu, Century Hyatt, Dai-Ichi Hotel Annex, Ginza Tokyu, Hilton, Imperial, Mitsui Urban Hotel Ginza, New Otani, New Takanawa Prince, Okura, Pacific Meridien, Palace, Seiyo Ginza, Tokyo Renaissance Ginza Tobu.

Nagoya Castle, Fitness, Nagoya Hilton, International Hotel Nagoya, Kanko.

Osaka ANA Sheraton, Hilton International, Nankai South Tower, Toyo.

Printers

You'll need business cards as soon as you land. If you haven't already had them made, your first-class hotel can usually arrange to have them printed within a couple of days. They should have at least your name and company name in Japanese on the reverse—a translation of your address isn't necessary. Here are three of the many printers in Tokyo who print business cards:

Aoyama Printing Company Tokyo Printing Service, 10-2, Kita Aoyama 3-chome, Minato-ku 107; Tel: (3) 3406-3884 Fax: (3) 3406-6695.

Preseez, Inc. 1-25-20, Shirogane, Minato-ku 108; Tel: (3) 3444-9742 Fax: (3) 5423-7010.

Press Man Basement 1, Tokyo Kotsu Kaikan Building, 2-10-1 Yurakucho, Chiyoda-ku; Tel: (3) 3211-7916 Fax: (3) 3211-7937.

Translators

Japan is awash in information from around the world, and all of it has to be translated into Japanese. Many firms specialize in the field, and many of those all provide secretarial and other business services. Translation firms in Tokyo include:

Business Associates, Inc 1-2-9, Shinjuku, Shinjuku-ku; Tel: (3) 3225-1931 Fax: (3) 3225-1930/1933.

Idea Institute, Inc 1-19-15, Ebisu, Sibuya-ku; Tel: (3) 3446-8660 Fax: 3446-3134.

Japan Translation Center, Ltd 1-21, Kanda Nishiki-cho, Chiyoda-ku; Tel: (3) 3291-0655 Fax: (3) 3294-0657.

Guide-Interpreters

Japan has about 1,200 licensed guide-interpreters. You can hire one through the **Japan Guide Association**, Shin Kokusai Building, 3-4-1, Marunouchi, Chiyoda-ku, Tokyo; Tel: (3) 3213-2706.

STAYING SAFE AND HEALTHY

Japan is probably the safest and healthiest nation on the planet. The thing most likely to pick your pocket or make you sick is the price of everything. Japan's life expectancy is the world's highest, its crime rate one of the world's lowest, and its medical care among the best. Public health standards are high, and tap water is safe to drink. Whatever you need to handle a headache, cold or allergy, or digestive upset is readily available, as are a whole range of personal care products.

If you want to stay in shape but your hotel doesn't have a health club, you can buy a short-term membership at the Clark Hatch Fitness Center, Azabu Towers, 2-1-3, Azabudai, Minato-ku, Tokyo; Tel: (3) 3584-4092.

EMERGENCY INFORMATION

Police officers are available on most major streets. Throughout Japan, the police emergency number is 110; for fire or ambulance, dial 119. The dispatcher, however, may not speak English. If you need a doctor or hospital, ask your hotel to arrange it. Major hotels often have a resident doctor or nurse. Or you can call the 24-hour English-language emergency service Japan Helpline: 0120-461-997.

If your travel in Japan is getting to you and your mental state is not quite what it should be, call the Tokyo English Life Line (TELL) at (3) 3264-4347 or Japan Hotline at (3) 3586-0110. Japan Hotline also offers information and advice on a wide range of topics, from etiquette to health services to transportation.

Hospitals, clinics and dentists (English-speaking)

Tokyo

International Catholic Hospital (Seibo Byoin); 2-5-1, Naka Ochiai, Shinjuku-ku; Tel: (3) 3951-1111.

International Clinic 1-5-9, Azabudai, Roppongi, Minato-ku; Tel: (3) 3582-2646, (3) 3583-7831 (very near Clark Hatch Fitness Center).

Ishikawa Clinic Tel: (3) 3401-6340.

Japan Red Cross Medical Center (Nihon Sekijuji-sha Iryo Center) Tel: (3) 3400-1311.

King's Clinic Tel: (3) 3409-0764.

St. Luke's International Hospital (Seiroka Byoin) 10-1, Akashi-cho, Chuo-ku; Tel: (3) 3541-5151 (member American Hospital Association).

Tokyo Medical and Surgical Clinic 32 Mori building, 3-4-30, Shiba-Koen, Minato-ku; Tel: (3) 3436-3028.

Tokyo Sanitarium Hospital (Tokyo Eisei Byoin) Tel: (3) 3392-6151.

Yamauchi Dental Clinic Shiroganedai Gloria Heights 1F, 3-16-10, Shiroganedai, Minato-ku; Tel: (3) 3441-6377 (member American Dental Association).

Nagoya

Kokusai Central Clinic Nagoya International Center Building; Tel: (521) 201-5311.

National Nagoya Hospital Tel: (521) 951-1111.

Osaka

Osaka University Hospital 1-50, Fukushima, 1-chome, Fukushima; Tel: (6) 451-0051 (emergency patients by ambulance only)

Sumitomo Hospital 2-2, Nakanoshima, 5-chome, Kita-ku; Tel: (6) 443-1261.

Tane General Hospital 1-2-31, Sakaigawa, Nishi-ku; Tel: (6) 581-1071.

Yodogawa Christian Hospital 9-26, Awaji, 2-chome, Higashi Yodogawa-ku; Tel: (6) 322-2250.

DEPARTURE FORMALITIES

If you leave Japan through Narita Airport, you will have to pay a ¥2,000 (about US$18) "Passenger Facility Service Charge." Leaving Japan through customs is simple. You can take up to ¥5 million (about US$45,000) or any amount of foreign cash out of the country without special permission.

If you brought your camera or electronic gear with you to Japan, you should also bring the purchase receipt, or your home country may charge you customs duties when you arrive.

Typical Daily Expenses in Japan

All prices are in Japanese yen (¥) unless otherwise noted. At press time, the exchange rate was US$1 = ¥108.

Expense	LOW Tokyo	LOW Other	MODERATE Tokyo	MODERATE Other	HIGH Tokyo	HIGH Other
Hotel	6,000	5,000	17,000	14,000	30,000	25,000
Local transportation *	350	350	3,000	2,800	7,000	6,500
Food	3,500	2,800	11,000	10,000	20,000	18,000
Local telephone †	50	50	200	200	500	500
Tips	300	300	600	600	2,000	2,000
Personal entertainment **	1,000	1,000	4,000	3,000	10,000	8,000
TOTAL	**¥11,200**	**¥9,500**	**¥35,800**	**¥30,600**	**¥69,500**	**¥60,000**

One-way airport transportation	Public Transit	Taxi
Tokyo	¥2,700-4,000	¥20,000
Fukuoka	¥220	¥1,500
Nagoya	¥700	¥5,000
Osaka	¥400	¥5,000

US Government per diem allowance as of December, 1993	Lodging (US$)	Food & Incidentals (US$)	Total (US$ and ¥)
Tokyo	$235	$108	$343 = ¥37,044
Fukuoka	$165	$139	$304 = ¥32,832
Nagoya	$134	$121	$255 = ¥27,540
Osaka	$166	$166	$332 = ¥35,856

* Based on 2 subway rides for low cost, 2 medium length taxi rides for moderate cost and 4 longer taxi rides for high cost.
† Based on 2 telephone calls from pay phones for low cost, 4 calls from hotel for moderate cost and 6 calls from hotel for high cost
** Based on a visit to a cultural site and coffee shop for low cost, a visit to a disco with a drink for moderate cost and a live floor show or good seats for Kabuki theatre for high cost.

BEST TRAVEL BOOKS

For a Westerner, doing business while traveling in Japan is an intense experience—confusing, frustrating, and tiring on the one hand, exhilarating, fascinating, and rewarding on the other. You would do well to learn as much as possible before setting foot in such an alien culture, especially when your business prospects depend on understanding the people you're dealing with.

That's where travel books come in. Japan itself produces a wealth of travel information, available from the JNTO. And here are three of the most practical and complete travel books published.

Fodor's 93 Japan, New York: Fodor's Travel Publications, 1993. ISBN 0-679-02308-9. 652 pages, US$19.00. Tourist-oriented, so full of sights and sites, explorations and excursions. Strong on hotels, shopping, dining, and nightspots. Includes dozens of excellent maps.

Frommer's Japan '92-'93, by Beth Reiber. New York: Prentice Hall, 1992. ISBN 0-13-333485-6. 585 pages, US$19.00. More traveler- than tourist-oriented; written in the first-person by an experienced Japan-hand. Dozens of good maps; good hotel and dining sections. Helpful "Fast Facts" and traveler's tips sections.

Japan: A travel survival kit, by Robert Strauss, Chris Taylor and Tony Wheeler. Hawthorn, Victoria, Australia: Lonely Planet Publications, 1991. ISBN 0-86442-104-4. 730 pages, US$21.95. Deeply appreciative of the land, the people, and the culture. Also witty, irreverent, and plainspoken. For the independent traveler, especially one on a tight budget: strong on cheap lodging and eating. Like other books, main focus is on Tokyo, but has more than others on rest of the country. Almost twice as many maps as the other two books combined.

Japan

China

Lake Khanka

Russian Federation

Mudanjiang

Jilin

nghun

in

Vladivostok

Nakhodka

Ch'ongjin

North Korea

ongyang

Wonson

Seoul

South Korea

Taejon

Taegu

Pusan

gju

Tsushima

Korea Strait

Ullung do

Tok Do (Liancourt Rocks)

Oki-Gunto

Fukue Jima

Sasebo

Nagasaki

Kagoshima

Osumi-Shoto

Tokara-Retto

Amami Gunto

Okinawa Gunto

Naha

Daito-jima

Philippine Sea

Wakkanai

Kuril Islands
(occupied by Russian Federation, claimed by Japan)

La Perouse Strait

Kunashir-to

12

Asahikawa

Hokkaido

Sapporo

Kushiro

Hakodate

Pacific Ocean

Tsugaru-kaikyo

Aomori

3

2

Akita

Morioka

16

Yamagata

Sado

24

Nilgata

45

Sendai

Fukushima

29

8

Iwaki

Kanazawa

43

Nagano

10

39

Utsunomiya

Fukui

15

Maebashi

35

Mito

Otsu

6

9

47

Urawa

Kyoto

26

Kofu

41

Tokyo

Matsue

Tottori

Gifu

1

19

Chiba

37

31

42

13

22

36

Shizuoka

4

Okayama

11

Kobe

38

Yokohama

Hiroshima

46

33

Hamamatsu

Yamaguchi

17

23

Nagayo

Matsuyama

7

40

28

Tsu

Fukuoka

34

5

Kochi

44

Nara

Saga

30

20

Shikoku

Osaka

Uwajima

Takamatsu

Wakayama

Oita

Tokushima

21

Kumamoto

18

25

Miyazaki

Kyushu

32

Honshu

Sea of Japan

Nampo Islands

Sumisu-jima

Tori-shima

Iwo Jima

Bonin Islands (Ogasawara-Gunto)

Volcano Islands (Kazan-Retto)

40°

30°

130°

140°

Prefectures of Japan
1. Aichi
2. Akita
3. Aomori
4. Chiba
5. Ehime
6. Fukui
7. Fukuoka
8. Fukushima
9. Gifu
10. Gumma
11. Hiroshima
12. Hokkaido
13. Hyogo
14. Ibaraki
15. Ishikawa
16. Iwate
17. Kagawa
18. Kagoshima
19. Kanagawa
20. Kochi
21. Kumamoto
22. Kyoto
23. Mie
24. Miyagi
25. Miyazaki
26. Nagano
27. Nagasaki
28. Nara
29. Niigata
30. Oita
31. Okayama
32. Okinawa
33. Osaka
34. Saga
35. Saitama
36. Shiga
37. Shimane
38. Shizuoka
39. Tochigi
40. Tokushima
41. Tokyo
42. Tottori
43. Toyama
44. Wakayama
45. Yamagata
46. Yamaguchi
47. Yamanashi

National Capital

Prefecture Capital

Secondary City

Prefecture Border

Primary Road

Railroad

0   100   200   300 km

0   75   150 mi

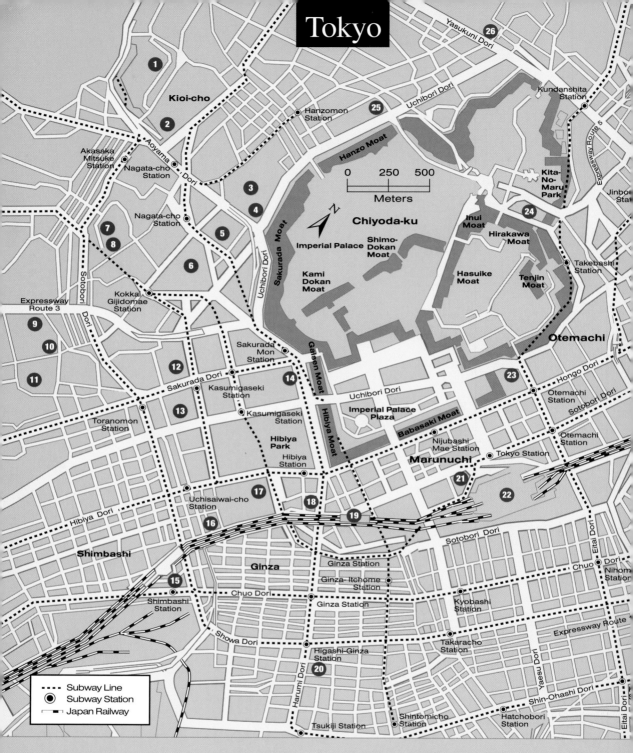

Tokyo

Meters
0 250 500

Kioi-cho

Chiyoda-ku

Imperial Palace

Shimo-Dokan Moat

Kami Dokan Moat

Hanzo Moat

Sakurada Moat

Inui Moat

Hirakawa Moat

Hasuike Moat

Tenjin Moat

Kita-No-Maru Park

Otemachi

Marunuchi

Hibiya Park

Imperial Palace Plaza

Babasaki Moat

Gaisen Moat

Hibiya Moat

Shimbashi

Ginza

Akasaka Mitsuke Station

Nagata-cho Station

Nagata-cho Station

Hanzomon Station

Kokkai Gijidomae Station

Sakurada Mon Station

Kasumigaseki Station

Kasumigaseki Station

Toranomon Station

Hibiya Station

Uchisaiwai-cho Station

Shimbashi Station

Shimbashi Station

Ginza Station

Ginza-Itchome Station

Ginza Station

Higashi-Ginza Station

Tsukiji Station

Shintomicho Station

Hatchobori Station

Takaracho Station

Kyobashi Station

Nihom Station

Otemachi Station

Otemachi Station

Tokyo Station

Nijubashi Mae Station

Takebashi Station

Kundanshita Station

Jinbo Sta

Aoyama Dori

Uchibori Dori

Uchibori Dori

Uchibori Dori

Sotobori

Dori

Sakurada Dori

Hibiya Dori

Chuo Dori

Showa Dori

Harumi Dori

Sotobori Dori

Sotobori Dori

Hongo Dori

Yaesu Dori

Chuo Dori

Eitai Dori

Eitai Dori

Shin-Ohashi Dori

Yasukuni Dori

Expressway Route 5

Expressway Route 3

Expressway Route

Expressway Route

Subway Line
Subway Station
Japan Railway

1	Hotel New Otani	10	American Embassy	18	Tourist Information Center
2	Akasaka Prince Hotel	11	Hotel Okura	19	JR Yurakucho Station
3	National Theater	12	Ministry of Finance	20	Kabukiza Theater
4	Supreme Court	13	Ministry of International Trade and Industry	21	Central Post Office
5	National Diet Library			22	JR Tokyo Station
6	National Diet Building	14	Ministry of Justice	23	Palace Hotel
7	Hie Shrine	15	JR Shimbashi Station	24	National Museum of Modern Art
8	Capitol Tokyu Hotel	16	Dai-ichi Hotel	25	British Embassy
9	Hotel ANA	17	Imperial Hotel	26	Yasukuni Shrine

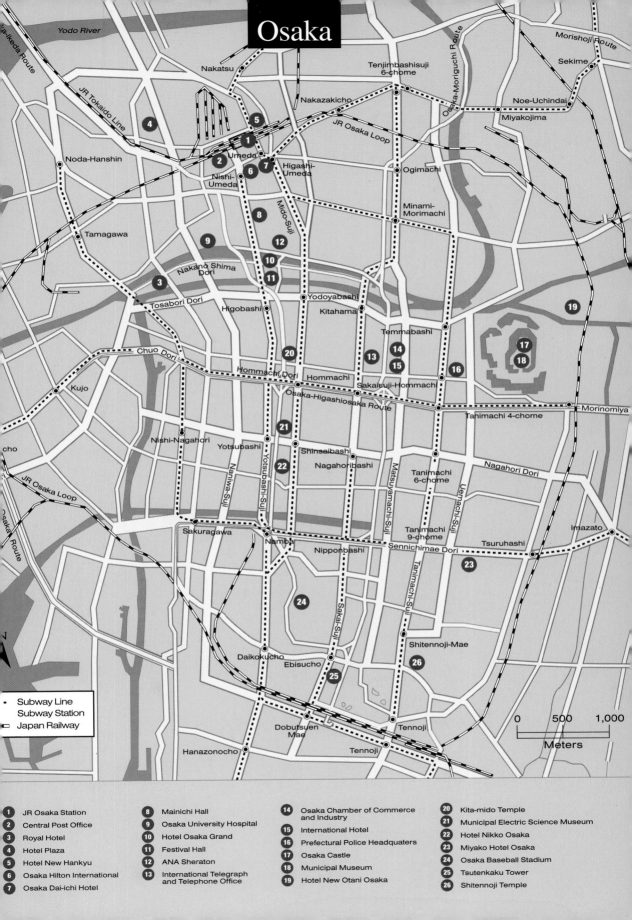

Osaka

1	JR Osaka Station	**8**	Mainichi Hall	**14**	Osaka Chamber of Commerce and Industry	**20**	Kita-mido Temple
2	Central Post Office	**9**	Osaka University Hospital	**15**	International Hotel	**21**	Municipal Electric Science Museum
3	Royal Hotel	**10**	Hotel Osaka Grand	**16**	Prefectural Police Headquaters	**22**	Hotel Nikko Osaka
4	Hotel Plaza	**11**	Festival Hall	**17**	Osaka Castle	**23**	Miyako Hotel Osaka
5	Hotel New Hankyu	**12**	ANA Sheraton	**18**	Municipal Museum	**24**	Osaka Baseball Stadium
6	Osaka Hilton International	**13**	International Telegraph and Telephone Office	**19**	Hotel New Otani Osaka	**25**	Tsutenkaku Tower
7	Osaka Dai-ichi Hotel					**26**	Shitennoji Temple

Subway Line
Subway Station
Japan Railway

0   500   1,000
Meters

Business Culture

Japan is one of the hardest cultures in Asia for Westerners to understand. Although Japanese culture has absorbed many foreign concepts, the Japanese remain enigmatically distinct from other peoples. They are materially more successful than their Asian neighbors and socially more harmonious than modern Western societies. They are a proud, prosperous, diligent, and seemingly selfless people. And while adopting the tools for modern industrial development, they have maintained their cultural integrity in the face of tremendous Western influence.

In a serious attempt to understand Japan, it is necessary to look beyond the Western facade of modern Japan and investigate the centuries-old traditional concepts that continue to guide Japanese society. The philosophical and spiritual history is rich and varied, and many threads are woven into the fabric of Japanese consciousness.

SOURCES OF JAPANESE VALUES AND BELIEFS

Contemporary Japan is a secular society, but many of its values stem from religious practices that emphasize the maintenance of harmonious relations with others (both spiritual beings and other humans) and membership in a family and a community. For most Japanese, the creation of harmonious relations with others through reciprocity and the fulfillment of social obligations is more significant than one's relationship to a higher spiritual being.

At the risk of oversimplifying, Japanese values stem from five great traditions: the indigenous religion of Shinto; Confucianism, Buddhism, and Taoism adopted from China; and Western scientific materialism. All except Shinto originate in foreign cultures. The Japanese have reinterpreted their forms and to some extent their core philosophies to suit them to their own society. The resulting traditions have become so intertwined in Japanese society that they are no longer distinct value systems but rather the sources of what we can call the Japanese ethic.

Shinto

Shinto, which can be translated as the Way of the Gods, is Japan's only indigenous religion. It stresses the harmony of the earth and the spiritual powers of natural features. Mountains, trees, rivers, large rocks, and weather are believed to be imbued with spirits called *kami*. Homage is paid to them in annual rites of fertility, harvest, and the like. In imperial times, the emperor conducted the highest rites, and Shinto was the state religion. Shinto is not widely practiced today, but its traditional teachings still influence Japanese thought.

Perhaps most important to modern Japanese, Shinto holds that the Japanese race is descended from *kami*. Traditionally, Japanese believed themselves to be children of the gods and their origin to be totally different from and superior to that of the rest of humanity. While few Japanese today accept this creed, half a century ago it was used to justify Japan's military invasions of other Asian countries. Some foreign Japan specialists hold that Japanese maintain a belief in their own cultural superiority when they deal with foreigners.

Another important Shinto belief is that the spirit world, mankind, and nature are all bound together and that they should exist in complete peace and harmony. This element is very much alive in the Japanese business environment and Japanese society at large, where the highest premium is placed on maintaining harmony at all costs.

Confucianism

Modern Japanese society is most heavily influenced by the teachings of Confucius, who lived in China more than 2,500 years ago. Confucianism is more a social code for behavior than it is a religion. Its basic tenets are obedience to superiors and paternalistic treatment of subordinates, concepts that form the core of social relations in Japan. Confucius identified five types of relationships, each with very clear duties: ruler to people, husband to wife, parent to child, older to younger, and friend to friend.

Ruler to People In the Confucian view, the ruler commands absolute loyalty and obedience from his people. They are never to question his directives or his motives. In return, the ruler is to be wise and work for the betterment of his people. He should always take their needs and desires into account.

Husband to Wife The Confucian husband rules over his wife as a lord rules over his people. The wife is to be obedient and faithful, and she has a duty to bear her husband sons. The husband has the duty of providing his wife with all the necessities of life.

Parent to Child Children must be loyal to their parents and obey their wishes without question. While the parents must raise and educate their children, the children must care for their parents in old age and always love and respect them.

Older to Younger Respect for age and obedience to all older family members is a key element of the Confucian ethic. Grandparents receive deferential treatment from grandchildren as well as from children.

Friend to Friend The relationship between two friends is the only equal relationship in Confucianism. Friends have a duty to be loyal, trustworthy, and willing to work for each other's benefit. Dishonesty between friends is a social crime and demands punishment.

The Confucian ethic transfers easily into the business environment of Japan, and it is reinforced and modified by several other conditions. Among coworkers, those of greater status and age command the respect of their juniors. Younger people are expected to defer to their elders in speech and manner. In return, elders are expected to reward their juniors for work well done and to assure that their subordinates benefit from any personal successes or promotions that they receive. Seniority is the main criterion for promotions and pay raises.

There is a strong bond among friends in the Japanese business world. Individuals who have established mutual trust and respect with each other will work hard to make each other successful. Favors and gifts between friends must constantly be reciprocated.

Confucianism places women in a distinctly inferior role, and Japanese business observes the Confucian rule. Women of exceptional skill or talent may achieve some success in business, but they are usually relegated to subservient positions, such as secretaries. The result is that women with high levels of education and training are likely to be frustrated in their attempts to find challenging or creative positions in business.

The main effect of Confucianism on Japanese business has been in the development of a strictly hierarchical working environment in which workers are dedicated and industrious. As in most Confucian societies in the Far East, productivity is high, and labor relations are mostly harmonious.

Buddhism and Taoism

Buddhism and Taoism both came to Japan from China more than a thousand years ago, and at one time the Japanese aristocracy embraced a mixture of the two beliefs in what the West knows as Zen Buddhism. Zen reinforces the Shinto belief in harmony, but it is a much more active philosophy than other Asian religions. In ancient times the warrior caste of Japan, called *samurai*, practiced Zen to make themselves better fighters. Zen stresses meditation and concentration. Meditation is not restricted to the kind you do sitting down. Zen practitioners learn to concentrate intensely on every detail of whatever they do, whether it be walking, working, fighting, or negotiating a business deal. Zen is one source of the very intense way in which some Japanese do business, and Japanese businessmen have been referred to as modern-day *samurai*.

Other forms of Buddhism are also present in Japan, the most popular of them being Pure Land Buddhism. Pure Land Buddhism resembles Christianity in its belief that people who are good in this life will go to after they die to a heavenly place where they can live in bliss. Pure Land ensures a degree of ethical considerations in daily affairs, and people are reluctant to be unethical for spiritual as well as for temporal reasons.

Scientific Materialism

Japan was the first Asian country to adopt Western concepts of the natural universe and cause-and-effect relationships that are at the core of scientific materialism. With this knowledge, Japan began to industrialize in the late 1800s, and developed a strong manufacturing base that allowed it to compete in international trade. Japan also used Western military technology to occupy Korea and Taiwan in 1895 and to defeat imperial Russia in 1905. With more than a hundred years of industrialization behind them, the Japanese are well ahead of their Asian neighbors in technology and capitalist business techniques.

The Japanese have an inclusive attitude toward competing philosophies that enables them to accept ideas that many Westerners would find mutually exclusive. Few Japanese have been drawn to exclusivist philosophies that deny the legitimacy of other beliefs. For this reason, they have a remarkable ability to use whatever belief system is appropriate for a particular situation. For instance, a Japanese bioengineer may utilize Western scientific methods at work and at home fervently honor the deceased spirits of his ancestors without seeing any inconsistency between the divergent world views inherent in the two practices. Similarly, a Japanese may be given Shinto rites at birth, a Christian ceremony at his marriage, and a Buddhist funeral at his death.

Japan's early willingness to make use of foreign ideas in its efforts to better its own society points to one paradoxical trait. While the Japanese emphasize cultural homogeneity, they welcome foreign innovations. Perhaps the incomparable social solidarity of the Japanese people, forged over thousands of years, tempers the fear that foreign ideas can weaken the essential qualities that make them Japanese.

ESSENTIALS OF JAPANESE CHARACTER

Japanese are humanists. Japanese business leaders proudly insist that their professional and private lives are centered around the most basic concerns of human beings. They often contrast their own management styles with those in the West, where, they say, managers are overly concerned with impersonal processes and business techniques and pay little attention to the personal needs of their associates and employees.

However, Japanese humanism is different from Western humanism. In the West, individual personalities are the focus of humanist philosophy, and personal liberties are of prime concern. For the Japanese, humanism is concerned not with the rights of individuals but with the relationships between individuals. The harmony of human relationships always takes precedence over the individual desires of the personalities involved. The Japanese take great care to maintain an outward appearance of peace and unity in social situations, even when true feelings are otherwise.

The Importance of Wa

Harmony, peace, and tranquility are the preeminent concerns of Japanese society. This belief is summed up in the traditional concept of *wa*. *Wa* literally means "circle," but it can be understood as the ethic of harmony, unity, peace, and wholeness in a social group. The ethic of *wa* implies a sort of social gestalt where the group is greater than the sum of its individual members. Under this belief, an individual standing alone is incomplete and can find fulfillment only by lending his personal will to the needs of the society in which he lives. Whether stated or implied, *wa* is the guiding philosophy for Japanese in the family, at the company, and even during leisure activities, such as baseball.

Company managers point to *wa* as the secret of Japan's business success. When top executives, middle managers, and production floor employees all embrace *wa*, the result is unparalleled trust, cooperation, loyalty, and even love between all parties involved. Productivity is increased, responsibility is shared, and management-labor relations are smooth.

The Love of Amae

Closely related to *wa* is the concept of *amae*, which can be interpreted to mean unquestioning love between people. In business circles, *amae* means trust and loyalty between associates, and it is the foundation for a working relationship. It is not difficult for foreigners to understand the importance of trust in business, but it may be difficult for them to conceive of the degree of trust implied in *amae*. *Amae* has been likened to the love between a child and its mother. To hold *amae* for another person is to be able to trust him with your life, family, or possessions.

In corporations, managers make a conscientious effort to foster the spirit of *wa* through *amae*. Group-centeredness is supported by company slogans, songs, and philosophies that employees recite in unison every morning before work begins. Workers may also assemble in a yard on the company grounds to engage in group exercises at the start of the day. For those in subordinate positions, *amae* entails a child-like trust and devotion to senior leaders and the company as a whole. A worker may expect the company to take care of all aspects of his life, ranging from housing to health care and salary. A superior in the organization must play the role of a parent to his subordinates and take a deeply personal interest in their well being.

Amae is developed among members of the same sections and departments in the company, and in smaller companies all employees may develop a shared feeling of fraternity and camaraderie. Japanese have a strong desire to belong to a group, and this desire carries over from business into activities. Coworkers routinely spend time together relaxing in bars after work or at company-sponsored picnics on weekends.

The Japanese View of Others

The Japanese define themselves as members of a group, and that definition implies a view of those outside the group. In Japanese language, the terms *uchi* (inside) and *soto* (outside) are relative. In social situations, *uchi* can imply the English word "we" and refers to the individual, the family, a work group, or even all of Japan, depending on the situation. But *uchi* is always defined in opposition to *soto*, or "they." For example, when a foreign businessman meets a Japanese counterpart, the Japanese defines himself as a member of the company with which the foreigner is doing business. However, if the foreigner makes a cultural mistake, such as using his chopsticks incorrectly, the Japanese is likely to define himself as a member of the Japanese race as distinguished from a foreigner.

Although the Japanese inside a group behave harmoniously and subjugate their personal will to the needs of the group, the members of groups often view other groups as enemies or threats. The Japanese are extremely competitive people, and they often work in teams with a goal of outperforming or defeating other teams. This tendency is manifest in the competition between production teams within the same company, in the competition between rival companies, and in the competition among rival nations for global power. In past decades, almost every Japanese citizen subscribed to the competitive goal of Japan's catching up to and surpassing America in economic success.

Japanese management techniques are designed to harness workers' competitive spirits. Workers are organized into teams which try to outproduce each other. On a higher level, the individual subsections within a certain department can gain prestige and recognition by working more efficiently than other subsections.

Keiretsu Kaisha *Corporate Leagues*

At the highest corporate level, corporations are allied in tight coalitions called *keiretsu kaisha* in Japanese. A typical *keiretsu kaisha* includes producers, distributors, suppliers of finished parts and raw materials, financial institutions, and even trade schools. Large megacorporations, such as Mitsubishi and Mitsui, are flagship corporations around which subsidiaries and smaller companies gather for security and profit. Quite often, parts suppliers and banks are locked in to such allegiances and work only with other member corporations. International and foreign businesses often work into such groupings. If the enterprise is successful, these companies gain access to business relations with every other member of the coalition.

On the negative side, the smaller companies in a *keiretsu kaisha* are likely to be virtual prisoners of the demands of the larger companies. If they do not comply with their directives, production orders may be cut, and they may encounter any number of coercive measures. Any attempt to cross over and work with a rival *keiretsu kaisha* invites recrimination and the loss of carefully cultivated relationships.

The Individual and Society

Even Japan has conflicts between the individual and the group. Although a Japanese individual must be a team player and concern himself with the needs of his social group, he also has a deeply personal nature. The needs of the individual and the demands of society are not always compatible. Such incompatibility can cause tension. The Japanese sometimes express the resulting pressures through alcoholism and mild psychosomatic illness.

Social responsibility has dominated over individual desires in Japan for hundreds of years, and transgressions against social norms were punished severely in premodern times. The Japanese have therefore learned to mask their individualism and repress personal desires that could cause social turmoil. Indeed, Japanese consider it a mark of personal strength for an individual to conform to society as closely as he can and not let his selfish desires get out of hand. Self-mastery over antisocial instincts is achieved by overcoming hardship through self-discipline and the personal quest for perfection. In this view, both the self and society can be improved, and their improvement is in fact interrelated, since the Japanese attempt to cultivate a self that is in total harmony with society at large. This picture contrasts sharply with the one that prevails in the West, where each individual strives to express a unique personal character that sets him apart from other people.

Honne *and* Tatamae*:* *Inner Versus Outer Reality*

In the process of protecting group harmony and politeness, Japan has evolved into a society where the visible surface of a situation, the *tatamae*, may be quite different from the true state of affairs, or the *honne*. In business, this means that if you are not very close to a Japanese, he is more likely to tell you the official company policy concerning a subject than to let you know what individuals in the group are really thinking. In Japanese society, both *honne* and *tatamae* are considered to be valid points of view, and you should not interpret misunderstandings as the result of intentional deception.

Saying No

The general reluctance among Japanese to say no to a request or question is one manifestation of the dichotomy between *honne* and *tatamae*. The Japanese believe that declining a request causes embarrassment and loss of face. If a request cannot be met, Japanese may say that it is inconvenient or under consideration. Such expressions generally mean no. Another way of saying no is to ignore a request and pretend that it was not made. Unless a request is really urgent, it is best to respect these signals and not to press the issue.

Sometimes a Japanese will respond to a request by saying, "Yes, but it will be difficult." To a Westerner, this response may seem to be affirmative, but in Japan it may well mean no or probably not. If a person says yes to a question and follows it with a hissing sound made by sucking breath between his teeth, the real answer could be no.

The Japanese also have a habit of telling a person what they believe he or she wants to hear, whether or not it is true. They do this as a courtesy, rarely with malicious intent, although it can be a problem, especially in the workplace. If bad news needs to be told, Japanese will be reluctant to break it. They may use an intermediary to communicate it, or they may imply that the news is bad without ever saying so bluntly. For these reasons, it is best in situations of uncertainty to remain with gentle questions and prolonged discussion in order not to upset the harmonious atmosphere that the Japanese prize so much.

Face

Foreigners must be aware of the importance of face in their social interactions with Japanese. Having face means having a high status in the eyes of one's peers, and it is a mark of personal dignity. Japanese are acutely sensitive to having face in all aspects of social and business life. Face can be likened to a prized commodity; it can be given, lost, taken away, and earned. You should always be aware of the face factor in your dealings with the Japanese and never do or say anything that could cause someone to lose face. Doing so could ruin business prospects and even invite recrimination.

The easiest way to cause someone to lose face is to insult him or criticize him harshly in front of others. Westerners can offend Japanese unintentionally by making fun of them in the good-natured way that is common among friends in the West. Another way to cause someone to lose face is to treat him as an underling when his official status in an organization is high. People must always be treated with proper respect. Failure to do so makes them and the transgressor lose face for all others aware of the situation.

Just as face can be lost, it can also be given by praising someone in front of peers or superiors or by thanking someone for a job well done. Giving someone face earns respect and loyalty, and it should be done whenever the situation warrants.

A person can lose face on his own by not living up to another person's expectations, by failing to keep a promise, or by behaving disreputably. Remember in business interactions that a person's face is not only his own but that of the organization that he represents. Your relationship with the individual and the respect accorded him is probably the key to your business success in Japan.

Social Hierarchies and Status

Japanese society has a hierarchical structure in which most relationships are unequal. This is a direct effect of Confucianism, which describes the natural order of human relations as hierarchical. In ancient Japan, every person was categorized as belonging to a distinct class based on family background and occupation. Classes, ranked from lowest to highest, began with menial laborers and ended with the emperor and his family. Within each class, there was another system of rank, often with the youngest and least skilled people in a particular occupation at the bottom and the oldest, and presumably most skilled and experienced, members at the top. Although modern Japan is officially egalitarian and based on Western concepts of political as well as social equality, it still runs largely on a social system that relies on unequal relationships for harmony and order.

In business environments, seniority within a group is determined more by age and length of service than by individual skill or initiative. The words *kohai* (junior) and *sempai* (senior) are used to express hierarchical relationships in both business and education. The word *doryo* (equal) is seldom used in business circles, because Japanese often find it difficult to work in a personal situation without clearly defined junior-senior roles. A person's educational level and former school are also important in determining status within the group. Family connections are somewhat limited for social leverage at work. Even if a person is from a well-known and powerful family, he will nominally still be junior to any group members who graduated from a more prestigious university or who graduated before him. In the event that two employees in the same work group have nearly identical credentials, their rank may be determined by personal social skills and talents.

Businessmen in Japan are so concerned about status that they cannot be sure of how to behave at their first meeting until their relative status has properly been established. For this reason, they exchange name cards before bowing. If the name cards are too vague, they may ask each other their age, company position, or alma mater. They bow only after they have determined who is the superior. The junior person bows lower. Afterward, they continue to behave as superior and subordinate. The junior person is exceptionally polite.

Style as Substance: The Importance of Etiquette

Courtesy and etiquette are extremely important in Japanese society. Through the centuries, procedures for all kinds of social interactions were codified by intricate rules. The emphasis on etiquette remains so strong that what someone does may be less important than how he does it.

Rules of etiquette largely reflect the superior-subordinate dimension of social interactions. The most telling evidence is found in the language. By most accounts, Japanese is one of the world's hardest languages to learn, not only due to its unusual grammatical structure and difficult writing system but also because it has many rules on how to address parties within a superior and subordinate relationship. For example, there are at least four ways of saying thank you: *domo, domo arigato, domo arigato gozaimasu,* and *domo arigato gozaitashimasu.* The form that you use depends on the relative status of the person to whom you are speaking. In many instances, it is extremely rude to address an individual in a way that does not befit his relative position.

Foreigners visiting Japan for a short time are not expected to know all the details of proper Japanese behavior, but all efforts to be a gracious guest are appreciated. Some knowledge of the Japanese way of doing things demonstrates not only good manners, but also that you have made a sincere effort to get along with your Japanese associates. This section reviews some issues involving body language, politeness, and social conduct.

- Contrary to popular belief, Japanese respect personal space and do not like to be crowded by other people, although crowding can sometimes not be avoided.
- In negotiations, Japanese may suddenly become quiet. This generally means they are thinking very hard, but it can also mean that something has been done to displease them.
- Pointing at a person is considered accusatory, rude or hostile.
- The meaning of laughter and smiles among Japanese depends on the situation. When Japanese are nervous or embarrassed, they often smile or laugh nervously. They may be responding to an inconvenient request or to a sensitive issue that has been brought up in conversation. Another possible explanation is that the smiler or another person nearby has committed a faux pas.
- Japanese set great store in being good listeners, and they often complain that Westerners pay too little attention in conversation and interrupt too often.
- Japanese are taught to avoid direct eye contact, which is seen as intruding on the other party's personal space.
- When Japanese are embarrassed, they cover their faces with their hands.
- When Japanese yawn, cough, or use a toothpick, they cover their mouths.
- It is impolite to point one's feet at another person. Japanese sit upright in chairs with both feet on the floor.
- Good posture is important in Japan. Never slouch in public.
- In some restaurants, men sit cross-legged on the floor. Women sit on their legs or tuck their legs to one side.
- Blowing your nose in public is considered rude.
- In Japanese homes, shoes are removed at the entrance. Be sure to wear clean socks!
- Japanese are not a touchy people, and they rarely hug in public. Lightly touching another person's arm when speaking is a sign of close familiarity. Men and women rarely hold hands in public.
- Public toilets rarely have toilet paper, so bring some along in your pocket or purse.

Women in Society and the Workplace

Though Japan's 1947 constitution includes an equal rights clause for women, gender inequality continues in family life, the workplace, and popular values. The popular phrase "good wife, wise mother" sums up the feminine ideal embraced by men and many women in the country. Women believe that it is in the best interests of themselves, their children, and their country that they stay home and devote themselves to their children, at least while the children are young. In most households, women are responsible for the family budget and make independent decisions about the education, careers, and lifestyles of family members. Women also take the blame for problems that family members have.

In the 1980s, the roles of women in the work force began to change dramatically. An aging population and labor shortages led women to be accepted in production and service industries, and many took this opportunity to begin a career outside the home. Nevertheless, traditional notions of male supremacy persist in business circles. Women earn only about 60 percent as much as their male counterparts. Very few women today hold senior management positions, and this situation is not expected to change soon. Women who work and have a family life carry a double burden, because their husbands do not often share responsibility for raising children and performing household chores.

Japanese Affluence is Still New

The affluence evident in Japan today is a phenomenon only a few decades old. Company executives are often in their forties or fifties, and many come from poor backgrounds. They remember the hardships that their country faced in the aftermath of World War II, and they often remain cautious about their wealth and uncertain about the future. Their attitudes are somewhat similar to those of Americans who grew up in the Great Depression or of Europeans who lived through World War II. Older Japanese enjoy the fruits of economic success, but they are skeptical of the new generation of Japanese who have never experienced real hardship. Elders complain that the young are lazy, selfish, and too influenced by Western culture. Some older people still cannot believe they are really well off, although that mentality may be changing.

Workaholic Lifestyles

Although the Japanese enjoy one of the highest standards of living in the world, on the average they spend more hours at work per year than their counterparts in other developed countries. According to one recent report, the average Japanese employee worked 1,972 hours in 1992, compared to 1,943 hours for Americans, 1,682 hours for the French, and 1,582 hours for Germans.

The official workweek in Japan is 44 hours long, Monday through half of Saturday. Public employees have a 40-hour workweek, with Saturdays and Sundays off. The government has taken steps to reduce work hours, despite protests from industrial and management leaders. A bill passed by parliament reduces the official workweek to 40 hours on April 1, 1994.

DECISION MAKING IN JAPANESE BUSINESS

Decision making in Japanese business is a long, time-consuming process that includes almost every employee involved in the endeavor under discussion. Although the structure of Japanese companies superficially resembles Western businesses, there are some important differences not evident at first glance. In Japanese companies, ideas and suggestions are often initiated by middle or lower-level employees and then passed on via formal and informal channels to higher-ranking managers for review. This upward flow of information is regarded as one major way in which Japanese companies differ from others.

QC Circles

Production-based companies use quality control (QC) circles made up of production floor employees to monitor operations and report back to managers. Management takes seriously suggestions that originate in QC circles on how to improve output. Such participatory decision making helps to identify problems and instills a sense of responsibility in employees. Middle-level managers operate directly with QC circles and assist them in choosing topics to concentrate on. This strengthens top-down management and familiarizes managers with production floor employees.

Two other channels provide information that assists in the decision-making process: sales data from salespeople and a suggestion system. Salespeople give regular debriefings to middle-level managers on product competitiveness and consumer preferences, and this information is then passed on to senior executives. In this way, managers can stay informed about sales and make necessary adjustments. The suggestion system gives employees a means for submitting their ideas directly to the top levels of management.

Foreigners participating in joint ventures need to accept the upward flow of decisions as a fundamental quality of Japanese management. They should participate in the system and not go against the grain simply because they are unfamiliar with the process. Foreigners who try to implement an authoritative management style certain to meet stiff resistance and create ill-will among employees.

The Ringi-sho System

With a few exceptions, decisions are rarely made by a single individual. Usually an important decision begins as a suggestion from a middle-level manager or group of managers that is then circulated in document form among all persons whom it may affect. The written suggestion is called a *ringi-sho*, an expression often translated as "project proposal." Those who approve of the suggestion affix their personal seal to the document as a sign of support and then pass it on to other persons of equal or higher rank in the company. The suggestion gains credibility as seals of approval accumulate. Individuals may suggest modifications of the original proposal, and these may be incorporated into the *ringi-sho*. In the end, if there is sufficient support, the *ringi-sho* will be forwarded up through the management structure to the board of directors. A suggestion that makes it that far is usually authorized for implementation.

There are distinct advantages and disadvantages to the Japanese decision-making system. It allows managers in sections closest to the problem to make key decisions without upsetting the hierarchy of command. However, it would be ineffective if employees at every level were not willing to participate directly in the process by considering the company's problems. Another drawback is that there is very little room for lateral consultation between members of different subsections within the company. In large companies, lateral groups compete for the attention of senior-level managers, and rivalries that impede cooperation can form. Moreover, the *ringi-sho* system is extremely slow compared to a direct top-down decision-making process. However, if a proposal is accepted, it is usually implemented quickly, since all relevant parties are aware of the proposal and have at least nominally approved it.

The preceding description is a generalized view of the decision-making process in Japanese companies, and you should understand that individual companies have different systems. In family-run operations headed by the founder and family patriarch, the *ringi-sho* system may not be used at all. In these companies, the boss often makes all key decisions, and they are implemented at his command.

Middle-Level Managers

The decision-making system in Japanese companies hinges on the role of middle-level managers. Their job is to maintain constant contact with lower-level employees and transmit their needs and desires to top management. They must have a hands-on approach to operations and be familiar with many aspects of the business. And they are usually the prime source for decisions on company policy.

The importance of middle-level managers means that foreign businesspeople must work to establish close relations with many different company employees. They cannot simply meet the top management and assume a solid relationship has been formed. Support from middle-level managers can have decisive importance for the success of a foreign concern.

TIPS FOR FOREIGN BUSINESSPEOPLE

The key to successful business in Japan is personal relationships. Like other Asians, the Japanese make little or no distinction between business and personal relationships. This point cannot be overemphasized. For a foreign businessperson to succeed in Japan, he must cultivate close personal ties with his business associates and earn their respect and trust. Attempts to establish long-term businesses in the country often have failed because foreigners did not recognize that business relationships were also personal.

To be accepted into a network of personal or business relations in Japan is an honor for foreigners, but it entails responsibility and commitment to the members of the network. It is extremely difficult to be accepted as anything but an outsider unless you are introduced to the network by a third party and you also have excellent business credentials.

Gaijin: *The Japanese View of Westerners*

The Japanese word for foreigner is *gaijin*, which means "outside person." No matter how close your relationships with influential Japanese, you must never forget that you are a foreigner. No amount of Japanification or time spent in Japan will change it. Japanese will often identify an expatriate first as a foreigner, then as a businessperson, and only then, if at all, as a friend.

In general, it is extremely difficult for a foreigner to make close friends with Japanese. Japanese may regard the foreigner with a mixture of fear, awe, fascination, and repulsion. Such contradictory and confusing emotions are detrimental to peaceful, harmonious relations, so many Japanese avoid close contact with foreigners. Because personal relations are so important in the conduct of business, such avoidance constitutes an informal but very real trade barrier for foreigners wishing to enter the Japanese market. However, a foreigner with a sincere desire to work in Japan, who can adapt to the culture with relative ease, and who is willing to be patient perhaps for years has a good chance of succeeding in the country.

Some common Japanese perceptions of Westerners are:

- They grow up wealthy and lack the toughness that comes from deprivation.
- They are creative, but do not work well in teams.
- They are motivated, but lack patience.
- They make friends quickly, but their expressions of friendship are often insincere.
- They are selfish and unappreciative of different cultures and ways of doing things
- They, particularly Americans, do not really like Japanese because of World War II.

Networking for Profit

In the business world, Japanese executives work to maintain and expand their networks of contacts. Largely through classmates or family associations, their networks extend to other companies and individuals. While the purpose of such contacts is mutual financial profit, the criteria are the same as those for personal networks. Cultivating friendships in business circles is an art learned through practice and close attention to the needs and expectations of others. You form such relationships by doing favors and demonstrating your integrity and sincerity.

Cultivating Relationships For the foreign businessperson with little or no understanding of Japanese behavior, cultivating solid relationships can be the biggest obstacle to success in Japan. It is therefore extremely useful for a businessperson to familiarize himself with Japanese language and culture before going there to do business. A Japanese who does not already know a potential business associate will hesitate to do business with him until he has had time to get acquainted and size up the potential associate's character and intentions.

Finding Matchmakers The best way to make contact with potential Japanese business associates is to have a mutual friend serve as an intermediary and introducer. If the third party has close relationships with both sides, they alone may constitute sufficiently solid grounds for the conduct of business. Anyone who has worked in Japan or who has cooperated with Japanese in the past could be a key source of business contacts. If you cannot find personal contacts, you can hire a consultant who specializes in bringing Japanese and foreign business interests together.

Sending Delegations

There are a few important points to remember when you send a trade delegation to Japan. First, keep in mind that Japanese are a group-oriented people and that they are more comfortable functioning as members of a group than as individuals. They are confused when members of a visiting group speak as individuals and make statements that are contradictory or inconsistent with the stated views of the group as a whole. Individual opinions are not wanted. Therefore, every trade delegation should have a designated speaker, who is also its most senior member. The Japanese will look to that member for all major communication and accept his words as the words of the entire organization.

Japanese are very concerned about the status that an individual holds in a company or organization. They will evaluate the seriousness of a trade delegation by the rank of its members, and a delegation is not likely to succeed if the Japanese know that its head is a junior executive. Likewise, they will wish to match your delegation with executives of similar status from their own organization. It is wise to send a list of the attending delegates with their ranks in the company, and to request that the Japanese firm do the same.

Arranging the Meeting

Any business meeting, especially one with a larger company, needs to be scheduled weeks in advance. Business meetings in Japan are conducted formally, and Westerners should always prepare thoroughly. Before the meeting, you should mail or fax a detailed document outlining the matter to be discussed. This will give the Japanese time to discuss the matter amongst themselves and to send an appropriate reply. While the Japanese are reluctant to deny a meeting outright, their response may send signals indicating their degree of interest in your offer, and they may send no reply at all if they are not interested. Another way of arranging a meeting is to enlist the aid of a Japanese agent in feeling out potential partners. An experienced agent with the right credentials will already have many contacts in the business world that may be of real use.

Meeting the Company

After finding someone to introduce you to a company in Japan, it is imperative that you meet people on the appropriate levels who can make important decisions. As part of the process you may have to meet the company boss. However, top Japanese executives are often jealously cloistered by a host of vice presidents and junior executives.

When you deal with larger companies, your first meeting may be with young section managers. If your delegation includes more senior-level executives, Japanese section managers may arrange for a superior to meet with you briefly as a courtesy. The absence of a high-level Japanese counterpart in your first few meetings is not necessarily a bad sign. In Japan, a business relationship is usually initiated by junior executives. Higher-ranking executives are in-

troduced as the relationship progresses.

Many foreign businesspeople have been dismayed in meetings with top Japanese executives to find that the boss has very little interest in the details of a particular business project. In Japan, the role of the company leader is quite different from that of leaders in Western companies. Japanese corporate bosses are primarily consensus builders within the organization. They have risen to their positions because of seniority, loyalty, and an ability to get along with others and earn their trust. Rarely does a rugged individualist with a flair for cutting good deals make it into Japanese leadership circles, because that type of person is not well suited to the task of maintaining the unity and spirit of *wa* that is central to Japanese management styles. For this reason, the company head is certainly a good person to meet, but you should not burden him with the intricate technical details of your plan unless he asks for them. Instead, you will probably get farther by being a gracious guest and answering his questions politely, thoroughly and sincerely. Japanese business leaders may ask a few questions about the structure of your company, your experience with the business, and the guiding philosophy of your company's founder.

Whomever you meet first, even if that person is the head of the company, you will need to meet people on many different levels if you want to ensure good relations. Simply going to the top of a company and getting the boss's approval does not mean that all has been taken care of. You must also establish good relations with middle and junior-level managers. If you don't, they may resent you for having bypassed them and feel that their personal integrity has been insulted.

Visiting Etiquette

When you visit a Japanese company, the members of your delegation should remove their coats immediately on entry and put them back on only when they leave. Large companies usually have a reception area where visitors remove their coats. When walking around inside the building, you should drape your coat over your arm.

A functionary will probably escort your group to a conference room or to the office of your principal host. The leader of your delegation should enter the room first, as in all situations, and he should be ready to greet the leader of the Japanese side. Next, your delegation leader should introduce the Japanese leader to the members of your group in descending order of rank. The visitors then exchange name cards, first with the senior Japanese executive, then with his subordinates, in descending order of rank. Sometimes it is difficult to tell whom among the Japanese is the most senior, especially on your first visit. Age and an air of authority will likely give clues to the identity of the Japanese leader, and he should step forward first to make a greeting. Subordinates will then follow in order of seniority. Foreigners seldom outdo the Japanese in formality, but an understanding of the dynamics of introductions will help you to evaluate the relative positions of Japanese representatives.

Bowing and Handshaking When meeting Japanese businesspeople, foreigners should display sincerity and respect. Although the accepted form of salutation between Japanese is the bow, most Japanese with international experience will not expect a bow from a foreigner. Quite often, the Japanese will initiate a handshake. However, some Japanese remain unfamiliar with handshakes and are uncomfortable with the custom of physical contact. If the situation is unclear, you should wait for the Japanese either to offer a hand or to bow, and you should reciprocate accordingly.

Between Japanese, subordinates will bow deeply and their superiors do not. You may be able to determine the relative status between of Japanese associates by observing the depths of their bows. But if bowing is unfamiliar to you and you are in a position where need to bow, pay more attention to making a sincere effort than to matching the depth of the other party's bow. A shallow bow is fine if performed sincerely.

Business Cards Business cards are serious tools for establishing business contacts, and they should not be overlooked. Failure to present a card at the first meeting can indicate to the Japanese that you are unaware of proper business etiquette or that you lack interest. Cards give key information, and without one you risk being forgotten. You should always carry an ample supply of business cards printed in English on one side and Japanese on the other. A business card should include your name, your company's name, and a position title that can give the Japanese some idea of your relative status within the company. It should be approximately 9 cm by 5.5 cm for easy storage in Japanese business card holders.

Large hotels in Japan accustomed to dealing with foreign visitors can have business cards printed for you in one full working day. Count on needing at least a hundred cards for a one-week visit. A Japanese who is familiar with you and your company should check the translation to make sure that you and your company are represented accurately in Japanese. Your name can be transliterated into Japanese.

The proper procedure for exchanging business cards is to give and receive cards with both hands. Hold the card by the corners between the thumb and forefinger. When presenting your card, hold it so that your name faces the recipient. When you receive a card, do not pocket it immediately, but take a few moments to study the card and what it says. The card represents the person who presents it, and it should be given the respect that he is due.

In negotiations, arranging the business cards that you have received in the order in which your Japanese counterparts are seated will help you to identify the current speaker. Of course, you will want to keep the cards together with notes of the meeting.

Letters of Introduction At your first meeting with representatives of a Japanese company, presenting letters of introduction from well-known business leaders, overseas Japanese, or former government officials who have dealt with Japan is an excellent way of showing both that you are a person of high standing and that you mean business. Japanese are very concerned about social standing, and anything that you can do to enhance their regard for you is a plus. But be careful not to appear arrogant or haughty, as Japanese morality condemns such behavior.

Presenting Your Business It is important to present your business early in a relationship. In meetings with middle-level executives and technicians, you will need to explain the details of your business fully if you want the relationship to progress. Japanese are an orderly, thorough people, and the way in which you present yourself is the most important element in successful business at this stage of the relationship. You must be knowledgeable about every detail of your business and able to display this knowledge in a manner that is at once concise and detailed. Most important, your presentation should not neglect the individuals to whom you are speaking. Take their personalities and manners into account throughout your presentation.

Before you give a presentation, you should prepare materials and information that will help to explain your position. You may want to give a presentation kit to each member of the Japanese delegation. As much of the material as possible should be in Japanese. These kits can also be sent to the Japanese company a few days before the meeting. A kit should contain:

- A brochure introducing your company;
- An overview of your company that includes the company's name and address, the names and titles of its top executives, a list of its products, and a short history;
- A short biography of the top executive;
- Information demonstrating that your company's product or service is innovative, different, and better than that of the competition.

Materials presented in Japanese should be written or translated by a Japanese, and the Japanese text should be checked by a third party who is fluent in both Japanese and English. Poorly written Japanese is an embarrassment to your company.

At the meeting, your delegation should open a presentation kit and explain its contents. Kits can be packaged in size A4 folders and enclosed in crisp manila envelopes bearing the company logo. Kits should be packed carefully so that they remain neat during shipment to Japan.

Giving and Receiving Gifts Japanese are inveterate gift givers. Gifts express feelings of friendship and may symbolize hopes for good future business, the conclusion of a successful endeavor, or appreciation for a favor done. Spend some time choosing appropriate gifts before embarking on a trip to Japan. The Japanese consider the Western habit of simply saying thank you for a favor glib and perhaps less than sincere. Favors should be rewarded materially, although gifts can have more symbolic than monetary value. Avoid very expensive gifts unless the recipient is an old associate who has proved to be particularly important in an undertaking. In Japan, gifts are not expected at the first visit, but they may be given if you feel the beginning of a relationship has already been established.

Generally there are two types of gifts in Japan: the personal gift presented to an individual, and the corporate gift, presented to the company as a whole. Personal gifts should presented when others are not around; corporate gifts should be given on the first day of your visit to a Japanese whom you know personally, and that individual should be entrusted with passing it on to the company. You may also give several gifts to many corporate members at a banquet or at the conclusion of negotiations.

In an office or business environment, it is best to present business-related gifts, such as pens or paperweights with your company logo. If only one gift is to be given, it should be presented to the head of the Japanese group at a dinner or on the conclusion of a successful meeting. If gifts are to be given to several individuals, be sure that each person receives a gift of roughly equal value or else that the chief executive receives the gift of greater value. The gifts may be placed on the table at a dinner banquet or presented during an appropriately relaxed time. If you give many gifts, do not omit anyone present or anyone who has shown hospitality during your stay. Bring along extra gifts just in case.

If you are invited to a Japanese person's home, it is courteous to arrive with a small gift. Suitable presents include a basket of fruit, tea, flowers, or any memento from your home country that the Japanese can associate with you. Picture books of your home area make good presents. Presenting a wife with perfume or a child with toys is likely to be appreciated. Such presents show that you are concerned for the family as a whole and not just the business relationship. Foreign liquor is another gift that is much appreciated. French cognac is highly prized, although it can be rather expensive, and it should only be given to those with whom you already have a personal relationship.

As in the case of business cards, the polite way to present and receive a gift is with both hands outstretched. Gifts should be wrapped in paper of a conservative color paper without bows. You should not open a gift that has been presented to you in front of the giver unless he encourages you to do so. Tearing the wrapping off hastily is a sign of greediness.

Patience

During the first several months in Japan, you may accomplish nothing more than getting to know several possible candidates for business relationships. Rushing into business before you have established a sound personal relationship is an invitation to failure. After drawing up a list of potential candidates, take time to evaluate each company carefully and weigh its strengths and weaknesses before you decide who to follow up on. In time, you will learn more about the people in these companies and gain valuable firsthand experience in the country.

After making your first contacts with Japanese businessmen, be prepared to spend a lot of time deepening and strengthening these relationships through visits, dinners, gift giving, and many small favors. While this process is costly and time-consuming, Japanese appreciate all sincere efforts in this area, and no favor done goes unnoticed. Likewise, keep a running account of all favors done for you, all small gifts presented, and the like. The odds are good that you will be expected to reciprocate in the future. Remember this aspect of Japanese business culture whenever someone offers you a favor, dinner, or gift. If you absolutely do not want to be in the person's debt, be creative and find some polite excuse for declining the offer. And decline it only if you have no intention of having a relationship, because declining an offer can be insulting to Japanese.

Maintain Your Perspective

Finally, you will benefit from the process of cultivating personal connections by keeping in mind that it gives you an opportunity to get to know more about the people you are dealing with. Getting to know your business associates is practical regardless of your culture. Learning about the personality of an associate can make communication and understanding smoother, and the resulting knowledge can be critical when it comes time to decide how far to take the business relationship.

THE COMPANY FACE

A foreign business should designate a personable member of the company to act as the face man for the organization in Japan, and that individual should continue to represent the business there on a long-term basis a minimum of three years. Whether they are dealing with a large foreign company or with an individual, Japanese like to deal with the same individual and they will treat every interaction as a personal one. Over time, if the business relationship is a success, Japanese associates may come to regard the face man as a close personal friend. In a joint venture, he may earn the personal allegiance of Japanese employees. Replacing that individual could jeopardize the business relationship unless the current representative introduces the new representative and spends at least several months bringing him closer to the Japanese.

Foreign managers should be older individuals who have at least middle-level executive rank and some experience in working with the Japanese. They should be flexible, patient people who understand that getting things done in a foreign country is not always by the book. Before he arrives in the country, a manager should read up on Asian culture with particular attention to Japanese ethics. Ideally, a foreign manager should have at least an elementary knowledge of the Japanese language.

Foreign Women and Sexism in Japanese Business

Japanese society is dominated by men, and women play supportive roles. Unfortunately for Western businesswomen, this sexual chauvinism is not confined to Japanese nationals. Foreign women have a tough time being taken seriously in the Japanese business environment, and hard work and lots of time spent proving herself may be the only ways in which a woman can force Japanese businessmen to treat her as an equal.

There are exceptions to this rule. However, a woman preparing to do business in Japan must be ready to encounter many difficulties as a result of her sex. She will have to work harder than men, and at the same time she will have to be careful not to upset male egos. She may even have to transfer credit for a job well done to her male colleagues and be willing to take a back seat in negotiations even when she is in fact the most responsible person in a group. Staying calm and cool in the face of prejudice is extremely important.

NEGOTIATING WITH THE JAPANESE

Once you have established a degree of personal understanding with a Japanese company, substantive talks can begin. When arranging for negotiations with Japanese, it is customary to give them as much detail on the issue to be discussed as reasonable, plus notice of all those who will be present. The team leader's name should be listed first. Other members should be listed in order of seniority or importance for the deal. The number of negotiation members can vary widely between two to 10, depending on the nature of the business. The Japanese will try to match their team members with the visitors.

Negotiations are often held in meeting rooms at the Japanese place of business. A functionary escorts the members of the visiting delegation to the meeting room as soon as they arrive. The Japanese team is already there. The head of the visiting delegation should enter the meeting room first. This is Japanese custom, and not to observe it could confuse the Japanese about the identity of the delegation leader. If an interpreter escorts the visiting team, he should enter close behind the leader and remain by the leader's side throughout the negotiations.

After a round of handshakes or bows and smiles, the visitors are seated at the negotiation table. The table is usually rectangular, and teams sit opposite each other, with the heads of delegations sitting eye to eye. Other team members are arrayed next to the delegation heads, often in descending order of importance. Most likely, the guest delegation will be seated facing the door, common Japanese courtesy. Tea or other drinks are provided.

Japanese are patient people and do not expect to jump into substantive negotiations right away. Some small talk is usually necessary in order to get the ball rolling, and this time can also be used to get a feel for those present. The subject of business usually comes up naturally after the participants feel comfortable enough to begin.

After initial courtesies, the head of the host delegation usually delivers a short welcoming speech and then turns the floor over to the head of the guest delegation. Japanese customarily allow visitors to speak first in negotiations. In some ways, this can be to their advantage, but the participants usually know enough about each other's positions through prior communication that there are few surprises. As noted earlier of trade delegations, the senior team leader is looked to for all meaningful dialogue. Conflicting statements from different team members are to be avoided, and team members should speak only when they are asked to do so.

The Japanese do not like surprises in negotiations, so it may be wise to lay out your basic position at this time. It can also be useful to distribute sheets laying out your main points in Japanese. When tackling a business issue at the appropriate time for serious discussion, Japanese appreciate directness. Anything that you can do to clarify their understanding of your position is fine. It may be best to begin your presentation with the big picture, and to wait till later in the talks to move into more detail. However, in some forms of negotiations, the Japanese will expect a very serious and in-depth presentation covering all the major details and answering all foreseeable questions at the very outset of talks. A typical opening statement highlighting the major topics that need to be discussed can last between five and ten minutes.

After the visitor outlines his team's position, the Japanese team leader then takes the floor and answers point by point, remedying any perceived omissions. From this point on, the negotiation process runs with the rhythm of a controlled conversation, not an open-ended chat. The Japanese approach is often to gain a holistic view of the entire proposal, then to break it down into specific chunks, at which time concrete issues and problems can be discussed. Use your own judgment in the talks, and adopt methods that are suitable for your particular subject.

At the end of a meeting, shake the hand of the Japanese team's leader. Only then is it appropriate to shake hands with or nod to the other members of the Japanese team. The head of the foreign delegation should leave the room first, followed by his subordinates. Never leave anything behind, especially the cards exchanged at the beginning of the meeting.

Interpreters

The interpreter is an important member of any trade delegation or negotiating team. While the study of English is mandatory in schools, few Japanese speak much English. Even those who do speak English are not likely to put themselves at the disadvantage of having to speak a foreign language during serious negotiations. One member of the Japanese delegation will probably act as an interpreter, but it is not advisable to depend on that person for communication. There is little risk that he would intentionally try to mislead you, but chances are good that he will not understand all the nuances and inflections that make English so expressive.

Having an interpreter of your own can be expensive, but it is a real advantage, especially in sensitive high-stakes negotiations. Your interpreter should be multicultural as well as multilingual, as able to pick up on feelings and intonations in English as in Japanese. In Tokyo there are several translation services that can provide you with competent service during your visit to Japan.

Tips on Using Interpreters Before a meeting, plan with your interpreter how you will work together, such as how long you should speak before pausing for interpretation. You can help your interpreter by briefing him thoroughly in advance of negotiations and providing him with as much written material as possible.

Look toward the head of the Japanese team, not at the interpreter. Japanese value personal communication. They may understand expressions if not words, and they may even understand more English than they let on. For clarity, speak slowly and do not say too much before allowing the interpreter to speak. A couple of sentences at a time is usually enough. Interpreters need to rest at least every two hours. If negotiations are to continue for more than a day, you may need two interpreters. Using an interpreter can stretch a meeting to three times its normal length, so be patient with the flow of discussion.

After talks or during breaks, review with your interpreter the main points that the two sides have laid. Try to get a feel together for the direction in which negotiations are headed, and anticipate what will need to be said later on. Doing this helps your interpreter to prepare his interpretation so that it will be received in the most favorable way by the Japanese. Understand that very little of substance is directly translatable from English to Japanese, and a quality interpreter tailors his speech to the forms proper for each language.

THE JAPANESE APPROACH TO CONTRACTS

Successful negotiations may result in the signing of a contract, but this is no guarantee that the business relationship is solid. Many Japanese view a written contract as far less meaningful than personal commitments between associates. When Japanese do business with each other, they sometimes do not use contracts at all. Only a verbal agreement between associates who share mutual respect and a close relationship is necessary. If a contract is signed, it is no better than the personal relationship between the signatories. Essentially, the contract is a formal acknowledgment of what the parties have already agreed to. Foreigners should not assume that a contract is binding if it is not backed by a face-to-face personal commitment. However, Japanese who have had experience with the West understand that foreigners insist on contracts and view them as legally binding documents. (Refer to "Business Law " chapter.)

The Japanese often consider a contract to be a loose commitment to do business and not a document outlining every aspect of the business relationship. Some head executives would rather sign a short agreement on the principle of doing business and allow subordinates to work out the details at a later time. It is best to avoid such a contract, because it increases the chance of misunderstanding on both sides and necessitates further negotiations, which can be costly.

Contracts generally have three distinct phases. First, through close personal interaction, foreign and Japanese businesspeople reach a mutual understanding of the goals and obligations entailed in the potential business endeavor. At the same time, they forge ties of mutual trust and respect. Second, the agreement should be put down on paper and signed by the individuals who will be working together and who have already reached a verbal agreement. The written contract should anticipate all future possibilities and state how appropriate adjustments are to be made if they are needed. Third, the contract agreements must be monitored and reviewed during the life of the working relationship to make sure all agreements are implemented and that the situation has not changed to such a degree that the Japanese side finds the contract untenable.

If the associates who sign a contract have a strong relationship, then the contract is usually workable for as long as the two signatories remain in close cooperation. If the foreign signatory for a contract is relocated or if he quits his job, then the Japanese may view the contract the contract as null and void, and it must be renegotiated by new individuals.

While negotiating a detailed contract is important, understand that the Japanese often view any deal with foreigners as only one component of a larger, ongoing relationship. The Japanese see the immediate issue as a sort of building block that allows them to measure and strengthen reliability and cooperation. This is a practical and realistic philosophy that any Westerner who wants to do business in Japan over the long term should appreciate and adopt for his own ventures.

ENTERTAINMENT AND LEISURE IN JAPAN

During the process of cultivating business contacts, or in the evening after negotiations, it is likely that your Japanese hosts will invite you to social gatherings. This element of Japanese business culture is every bit as important as visiting the company or engaging in substantive talks, because leisure time is when personal relationships are formed. This section discusses some entertainment and leisure activities that you may encounter.

Dinner

Japanese executives often invite their guests to dinner at a traditional Japanese restaurant. These restaurants serve elegant meals according to prescribed customs, so it is wise to be familiar with a few key aspects of Japanese table manners.

In traditional restaurants, remove your shoes at the door. Place them neatly in line with the other shoes there, toes facing the exit. A waiter or waitress will then escort your party to a table. Sometimes the table is in a reserved private room with rice paper walls and thick floor mats called *tatami*. There are no chairs in this type of room, and guests sit on the floor. Men should sit cross-legged, and women should kneel or tuck their legs under them to one side. At no point should your knees rise above the edge of the table, which sits quite low, only a couple of feet off the floor.

The head of the visiting delegation is given the place of honor, the position farthest away from and facing the exit. This custom developed in ancient times, when the chief *samurai* was given this place as the best from which to resist attack by assassins. The principal host usually sits next to the place of honor. If interpreters are necessary, they should sit flanking the delegation leaders, and other hosts and guests should alternate around the table.

After you sit down, you will be offered a damp cloth for cleansing the hands. It is impolite to use this cloth to clean the face, neck, or arms, but men sometimes use it to wipe their face on a hot day. After cleansing the hands, replace the cloth on the tray from which it was served. Napkins are not used during the meal.

Before food is served, everyone present drinks a few toasts of sake, Japanese rice wine. Sake is extremely potent, and it is wise to drink slowly. However, tradition calls for the first round of sake to be drunk in unison after the principal host has spoken a few words of welcome and said the traditional *kan pai*, which means dry glass, the Japanee equivalent of "bottoms up." It is proper for the head of a visiting delegation to return the toast. A few appetizers are served along with the sake.

The main dishes are served after these initial courtesies. Japanese food is often served to individuals on square or rectangular trays containing food in dishes or compartments. While Japanese food is delicious and pleasing to the eye, the portions served are smaller than those customary in other countries, such as China and America. Unfortunately for those with large appetites, only second helpings of rice are usually offered, and it is rude to ask for more food.

As a signal to begin eating, your host will pick up his chopsticks and say *itadakimasu*, the Japanese equivalent of the French *bon apetit*. However, no one should begin eating until the principal guest has taken a bite.

Your guest may politely ask if you are able to use chopsticks or if silverware would be more convenient. It is advisable to learn how to use chopsticks before you come to Japan. One good method of learning is to practice picking up peanuts from a bowl. If you are able to pick up a bowlful of peanuts with relative ease, then you should have no trouble at dinner. If you absolutely cannot master chopsticks, silverware will be provided.

If you use chopsticks, here are a few rules that you should observe. First, it is extremely rude to stick chopsticks upright into a bowl of rice. (It reminds Japanese of the incense burned at funerals.) Second, never use chopsticks to point. Third, when taking food from a communal plate, turn your chopsticks around, and pick the food up with the blunt ends to prevent contamination of other people's food. If serving chopsticks are provided, use them. Finally, when you are not using your chopsticks, put them down on the chopstick rest provided, not on a bowl or plate.

Rice is a Japanese staple, and traditionally it was eaten at all meals. Japanese rice is sticky and easy to pick up with chopsticks. When eating rice, it is proper pick it up in lumps. Eat slowly. Japanese do not usually hold a rice bowl to their mouths and shovel it in as the Chinese do. Also, it is normally not appropriate to mix sauces and other food with rice.

If you are nearing the end of the rice in your bowl and you would like more, it is customary to put down your chopsticks and leave a few grains in the bowl as a sign that you would like more. Finishing all your rice is a signal that you have finished eating.

Japanese do not engage in animated conversation during a meal. The main focus is the food, so there often is silence at the table. Westerners sometimes find the silence uncomfortable and will interject words to fill the perceived emptiness. Resist the temptation.

It is probable that your host will offer cigarettes throughout the meal. Many Japanese men smoke, but it is perfectly acceptable to decline the invitation to light up. It is rude to light a cigarette without first offering cigarettes to others. If at all possible, bear with the secondhand smoke; it would be considered quite rude to ask the host not to smoke while enjoying dinner.

In the end of the meal, your Japanese host will ask for the bill. In Japan, it is rude to suggest that you split the bill, and if you have been invited to dinner, do not expect to pay. Also, there s no tipping at Japanese restaurants. Accepting an invitation to dinner puts you in debt to your host, so you should repay the favor later by inviting him out for a meal.

Karaoke

After dinner, hardier Japanese may invite you to go singing at a karaoke club. Karaoke clubs first became popular in Japan in the 1970s, and in recent years the craze has spread to all other countries in East Asia. For the Japanese, the karaoke phenomenon is a technological extension of their natural propensity to sing with close friends.

Karaoke clubs feature a raised platform with a microphone above which is a monitor. The monitor displays preselected music videos with accompanying music, but without vocals. The words to the song are displayed at the bottom of the screen. The designated singer will then sing the words. Many karaoke clubs have English songs, and you may expect to be forced to sing at least one song when you visit a karaoke. For Japanese, being a competent singer enhances face, because one's close friends will be watching. Foreign guests are not expected to sing proficiently, however, and any attempt to sing will be greeted with much praise and applause. In higher-class karaoke clubs, large private rooms with big-screen television sets are the norm. Groups of friends can use these rooms to sing and drink until the sun comes up, attended the while by beautiful hostesses.

Many observers have wondered why karaoke has become so popular in the collectivist cultures of Asia. One answer is that singing in front of one's peers is one of the very few socially acceptable ways in which an individual can display his or her talent without being branded arrogant or self-centered. It fulfills the latent desire to gain credit as an individual without jeopardizing the need to be accepted by the whole group. Of course, no one goes to a karaoke club individually, and it usually is a meeting place for the closest of friends. If you wish to establish close relations with Japanese, going to karaoke is one of the best ways of doing it.

Bars

If you stay in Japan long enough, you will inevitably be invited to accompany coworkers or business associates to a bar. Going to bars is a major form of social interaction, and to be invited along may be a sign that you are accepted as a peer. Refusing to go to a bar can be interpreted as a sign that you are cold and aloof. Friendships are often formed in the course of drinking alcohol.

Japanese are among the heaviest drinkers in Asia. Despite their relatively small size and a slight racial allergy to alcohol, Japanese men can drink a lot. The Japanese affinity for heavy drinking has been attributed to the society's tendency to stifle the individual. Many Japanese find release in alcohol, and they become unusually boisterous and assertive only when they are drunk.

Beer is served in bottles and drunk from small glasses. You should not pour a drink for yourself, but allow others to do it. Likewise, you should pour drinks for others whenever you get the chance. Never ask someone to pour a drink for you but wait for the service to be given freely.

The superior-subordinate nature of relationships in Japan is also evident in drinking etiquette. Normally, subordinates pour drinks for their superiors.

Bring Your Clubs

Besides eating, drinking, and singing, Japanese businessmen also like to get some exercise on the golf course. Golf, a relatively new import from the West, is a high-status game in Japan, as it is in all Asian countries. Visiting foreign businesspeople may be invited to a round of golf, so it can be a definite asset to know how to play and have access to golf clubs. Golfing with a Japanese associate has the advantage of being an activity that can be shared without the need for strong verbal communication. Membership in golf courses is prohibitively expensive in Japan, but urban driving ranges are popping up all over the country. For a reasonable rate, people can go to these ranges in the evening with a few friends and practice driving a bucket or two of balls.

FURTHER READING

The preceding discussion of Japanese business culture and etiquette is only a brief introduction to the complexities of the subject. Before going to Japan, try reading at least one of the books listed here to improve your understanding.

The Japanese Mind: The Goliath Explained, by Robert C. Christopher. New York: Linden Press/Simon & Schuster, 1983. ISBN 0-449-90120-3. $10.00. One of the best books on the market about contemporary Japanese society, its author is an experienced journalist with an in-depth knowledge of Japan. The style is comfortable, and the information is invaluable—a must for those with little understanding of Japan.

Japanese Etiquette and Ethics in Business, by Boye De Menthe. Lincolnwood, Ill.: NTC Business Books, 1991. ISBN 0-8442-8507-2. $14.95. The most popular and well-informed of De Mente's books about business etiquette in Asia, it explains the habits and beliefs that have come to epitomize the Japanese character and business personality.

Culture Shock! Japan, by Rex Shelley. Portland, Ore.: Graphic Arts Center Publishing Company, 1993. ISBN 1-55868-071-3. $10.95. A humorous introduction to many of the seemingly incomprehensible facets of Japanese culture that provides foreigners preparing for a lengthy stay in Japan with helpful tips.

Learning to Bow, by Bruce Feiler. New York: Houghton-Mifflin Company, 1992. ISBN 0-395-647-266. $10.00. A well acclaimed book that examines the Japanese tradition of bowing as a metaphor for Japan's unique culture, concluding that no matter how hard you try, a foreigner will never learn to bow correctly.

Japanese Business Etiquette, by Diana Rowland. New York: Warner Books, 1988. ISBN 0-446-38943-9. $10.95. A short and easy-to-read explanation of the key elements of Japanese business etiquette, this book also provides a woman's view of business and society in Japan.

Do's and Taboos Around the World, edited by Roger Axtell. New York: John Wiley and Sons, 1990. ISBN 0-471-52119-1. $10.95. A humorous and insightful bestseller, compiled by the Parker Pen Company on social customs around the world, that contains a helpful entry on Japan.

Gestures: The Do's and Taboos of Body Language Around the World, by Roger Axtell. New York: John Wiley and Sons, 1991. ISBN 0-471-53672-5. $9.95. A follow-up to the preceding book, focusing on body language in different cultures.

Demographics

AT A GLANCE

The figures given here are the best available, but sources vary in comprehensiveness, in definition of categories, and in reliability. Sources include the United Nations, the World Bank, the International Monetary Fund, and the Japanese government. The value of demographics lies not just in raw numbers but in trends, and the trends illustrated here are accurate.

POPULATION, GROWTH RATE AND PROJECTIONS

Average annual growth rate

1970-80	1.2%
1980-91	0.5%
1991-2000	0.3%

Age structure of population	1991	2025
Under 15 years old	18.1%	15.1%
15 - 64 years old	69.6	59.2
65 or older	12.3	25.7

Urban population (% of total)

1970	71%
1991	77%

Population density per square km (1990): 327.3

1990 POPULATION BY AGE AND SEX

Male: 49.1%
Female: 50.9%

Age	Total	Male	Female
All ages	**123,611,167**	**60,696,724**	**62,914,443**
0 - 1	1,213,685	621,085	592,600
1 - 4	5,279,212	2,704,954	2,574,258
5 - 9	7,466,557	3,821,833	3,644,724
10 - 14	8,526,785	4,369,880	4,156,905
15 - 19	10,007,087	5,122,215	4,884,872
20 - 24	8,800,121	4,468,199	4,331,922
25 - 29	8,070,713	4,078,469	3,992,244
30 - 34	7,787,685	3,925,353	3,862,332
35 - 39	9,003,780	4,524,829	4,478,951
40 - 44	10,658,290	5,349,985	5,308,305
45 - 49	9,018,012	4,482,298	4,535,714
50 - 54	8,088,386	3,997,248	4,091,138
55 - 59	7,724,888	3,783,367	3,941,521
60 - 64	6,745,014	3,236,549	3,508,465
65 - 69	5,103,576	2,194,783	2,908,793
70 - 74	3,817,534	1,559,972	2,257,562
75 - 79	3,018,213	1,197,457	1,820,756
80 - 84	1,832,858	678,385	1,154,473
85 +	1,122,414	357,040	765,374
Unknown	326,357	222,823	103,534

VITAL STATISTICS

Live Births, Marriages and Deaths; Rates per 1,000 persons

Year	Births	Rate	Marriages	Rate	Deaths	Rate
1984	1,489,780	12.5	739,991	6.2	740,247	6.2
1985	1,431,577	11.9	735,850	6.1	752,283	6.3
1986	1,382,946	11.4	710,962	5.9	750,620	6.2
1987	1,346,658	11.1	696,173	5.7	751,172	6.2
1988	1,314,006	10.8	707,716	5.8	793,014	6.5
1989	1,246,802	10.2	708,316	5.8	788,594	6.4
1990	1,221,585	10.0	722,138	5.9	820,305	6.7
1991	1,223,186	9.9	742,281	6.0	829,523	6.7

Child Mortality Rate

1960	37 per 1,000 births
1975	1 per 1,000 births
1990	6 per 1,000 births

Life expectancy at birth **1960** 68
1990 79

Divorces (**1990**): 157,000
 Rate per 1,000 marriages: 1.3

Fertility rate

1970	**1991**	**2000**
2.1	1.5	1.6

POPULATION OF PRINCIPAL CITIES

(1991 estimate)

Tokyo	8,006,386
Yokohama	3,210,607
Osaka	2,512,386
Nagoya	2,097,765
Sapporo	1,663,246
Kobe	1,447,726
Kyoto	1,401,171
Fukuoka	1,192,805
Kawasaki	1,152,639
Hiroshima	1,061,864
Kitakyushu	1,019,501
Sendai	898,173
Chiba	821,003
Sakai	800,331
Kumamoto	615,154
Okayama	587,348
Hamamatsu	530,905
Kagoshima	529,462

POPULATION IN MILLIONS

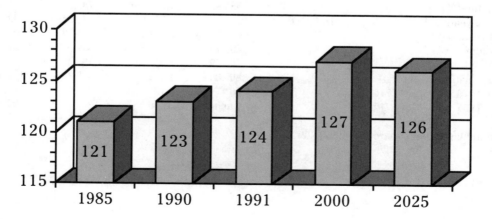

1985	1990	1991	2000	2025
121	123	124	127	126

MANUFACTURING WAGES
Monthly, in thousands of yen

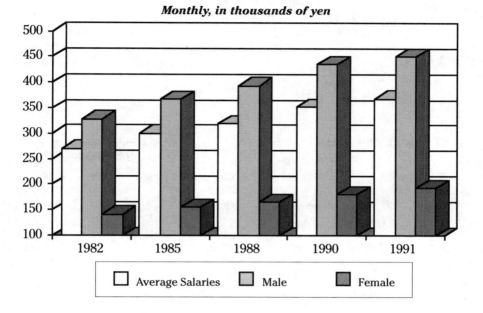

☐ Average Salaries   ▨ Male   ▨ Female

MONTHLY INCOME AND EXPENSES, IN YEN

	1970 ¥	%	1980 ¥	%	1985 ¥	%	1990 ¥	%	1991 ¥	%
Income	112,949		349,686		444,846		521,757		548,769	
Expenses	91,897		282,263		360,642		412,813		430,380	
Living expenses	82,582	100.0	238,126	100.0	289,489	100.0	331,595	100.0	345,473	100.0
Food	26,606	32.2	66,245	27.8	74,369	25.7	79,993	24.1	83,051	24.0
Housing	4,364	5.3	11,297	4.7	13,748	4.7	16,475	5.0	18,234	5.3
Utilities	3,407	4.1	12,693	5.3	17,125	5.9	16,797	5.1	17,642	5.1
Clothing	7,653	9.3	17,914	7.5	20,176	7.0	23,902	7.2	24,451	7.1
Furniture	4,193	5.1	10,092	4.2	12,182	4.2	13,103	4.0	13,944	4.0
Medical care	2,141	2.6	5,771	2.4	6,814	2.4	8,670	2.6	8,776	2.5
Transport & communications	4,550	5.5	20,236	8.5	27,950	9.7	33,499	10.1	34,659	10.0
Education	2,212	2.7	8,637	3.6	12,157	4.2	16,827	5.1	17,129	5.0
Recreation	7,619	9.2	20,135	8.5	25,269	8.7	31,761	9.6	32,861	9.5
Social expenses	6,323	7.7	21,190	8.9	25,224	8.7	28,630	8.6	30,076	8.9
Other	13,514	16.3	43,915	18.6	54,475	18.8	61,939	18.6	64,020	18.6
Non-living expenses:	9,315		44,137		71,153		81,218		84,907	

Net income (income—non-living expenses):

	103,634		305,549		373,693		440,539		463,862	

Balance (net income—living expenses):

	21,052		67,423		84,203		108,844		118,389	
Net savings	13,480		39,714		48,181		74,526		83,104	

Living expenses as **percent** of net income:

	79.7		77.9		77.5		75.3		74.5	
Persons per household:	3.9		3.83		3.79		3.70		3.71	
Earners per household:	1.55		1.50		1.57		1.64		1.66	

Income Distribution

Percent share of GDP (1990)

Lowest 20%	Second 20%	Third 20%	Fourth 20%	Top 20%	Top 10%
8.8	13.2	17.4	23.1	37.5	22.4

NATIONAL INCOME

GNP per capita (1991):	US$26,930
Projected for 2000:	US$59,200
Average annual growth rate 1980-91:	3.6 percent

Average Annual Rate of Inflation

1970-80	8.5%
1980-91	1.5%

Price Index by Category
(1990 = 100)

Category	1989	1990	1991
Food	96	100	105
Housing	97	100	103
Utilities and fuel	98	100	102
Clothing and footwear	95	100	105
Miscellaneous	97	100	103

Net income annual increase rate, after inflation

1984	1985	1986	1987	1988	1989	1990	1991
2.2	1.9	1.2	2.3	4.3	1.5	1.4	1.9

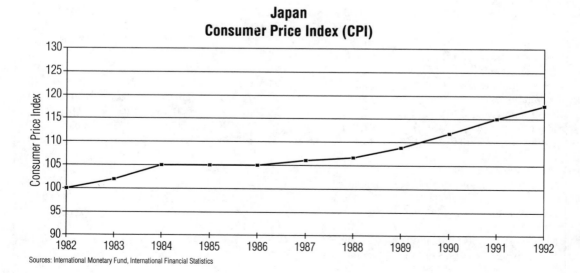

Japan
Consumer Price Index (CPI)

Sources: International Monetary Fund, International Financial Statistics

AVERAGE FAMILY ANNUAL SPENDING ON LEISURE ACTIVITIES

Activity	1965	1975	1985	1989	1990
Eating out	¥14,571	¥64,620	¥127,441	¥146,123	¥153,644
Recreational durable goods*	7,133	25,109	32,968	42,936	38,500
Recreation	23,895	91,262	155,127	181,376	190,085
Sports	1,684	7,752	24,717	28,532	31,230
Tours	10,592	46,205	96,021	118,824	133,141
Other	99,923	174,382	323,107	370,607	363,411
Leisure as percent of living expenses	17.2%	21.6%	23.2%	24.7%	24.4%

* Includes radios, TVs, VCRs, cameras, musical instruments, etc.

JAPANESE RECREATIONAL ACTIVITIES—1990

Activity	Participation (millions)
Eating out	62.2
Driving	57.0
Sightseeing tour (domestic)	54.8
Karaoke	46.6
Watching videos	45.0
Pubs, bars	41.7
Zoos, botanical gardens	41.5
Amusement parks	38.3
Games	36.3
Gardening	35.0

BOOKS

Number of Different Titles Published

Category	1989	1990
Philosophy	1,779	1,762
History	2,561	2,481
Social sciences	9,518	9,798
Natural sciences	2,763	2,970
Technology	3,500	3,346
Business	1,723	1,698
Arts	3,359	3,348
Foreign language study	813	826
Literature	8,354	8,792
Juvenile	2,911	2,986
Reference	795	689
Others	1,622	1,880
TOTAL	39,698	40,576

EDUCATION (1992)

Category	Institutions	Teachers	Enrollment
Primary	24,798	444,903	9,517,429
Lower secondary	11,290	286,965	5,188,314
High schools	5,503	286,092	5,454,929
Junior colleges	592	56,500	504,087
Universities, graduate schools	514	221,311	2,205,516
Technical colleges	63	6,417	53,698

COMMUNICATION CHANNELS

Daily Newspapers

Circulation (millions)			Per 1,000 Persons			Number of dailies		
1979	1986	1990	1979	1986	1990	1979	1986	1988
65.9	68.7	72.5	570	566	591	178	124	158

Televisions and radios

	Number (millions)			Per 1,000 Persons		
	1980	1985	1989	1980	1985	1989
TVs	63.0	70.0	75.0	539	579	610
Radios	79.0	95.0	110.0	678	786	895

Telephones

Number (millions)			Per 100 Persons		
1987	1988	1990	1987	1988	1990
46.3	48.0	52.0	38	39	42

ENERGY CONSUMPTION

(kilograms per capita of coal equivalent)

1980	3,710
1988	3,935
1990	4,164

MOTOR VEHICLES IN USE

(in millions)

	1982	1985	1988	1990	1991
Passenger	25.5	27.8	30.8	34.9	37.1
Commercial	15.0	17.4	20.6	21.6	21.3

NUTRITION

Individual daily average consumption

Calories			% of Calorie Requirements			Protein (grams)		
1980	1986	1990	1980	1984/6	1990	1980	1986	1990
2,778	2,865	2,926	124%	122%	131%	87	91	96

Marketing

HOW TO APPROACH THE JAPAN MARKET

Selling to Japan is easy in theory. However, there are import barriers, obstructive bureaucrats, nontransparent regulations (laws hidden from foreign traders in case they might be thinking of violating them), a huge language barrier, and octopus-like conglomerate monopolies that can stop a less-than-obsessively-committed salesperson dead in their tracks. Nevertheless, all along the way, you'll find knowledgeable, experienced people whose job it is to help you wend your way through the mazes constructed by knowledgeable, experienced people whose job it is to get you lost.

You don't need to spend a fortune on marketing to learn if there is a market; you can find that out in a matter of minutes from a variety of sources—this book is one, and others include your own embassy, trade associations and even Japan's own government trade agency, the Japan External Trade Organization (JETRO). You do need to keep your initial costs as low as possible—probably through direct sales—until you have a toehold. You must also go overboard to service your orders *immediately*, and you must answer your faxes *immediately*. And above all, your company must make the commitment to export, because otherwise your worst problems will come from within, not without. Export sales generate a momentum of their own that is actually hard to stop, and pull along with them repeat business, new accounts, and offers from people eager to be your agent or partner.

Learning the Password

Japan's marketing and distribution system is like no other in the world. How you see it depends on your perspective. It's either needlessly complex or marvelously ingenious. It's incredibly inefficient or remarkably flexible. It's a wall no foreigner can breach or an open border if you know the password.

The password may be "pay attention." A recent survey of Japanese distributors, store managers, and shoppers found that almost 90 percent of the shoppers said there were few stores in their neighborhood selling imported goods. That figure should make many foreign exporters' mouths water.

Because Japanese shoppers increasingly depend on retail stores for information about imported goods, the researchers found that development of more channels for retail sales must be termed a high priority item.

Easier said than done? Observers note that Japan has a complex system of distribution and business practices, which are often seen as exclusionary by foreign parties. Complex and exclusionary are understatements, while to call it a system may be an abuse of the word because the "system" wasn't purposely developed to exclude foreign companies or to be complex. Instead, "byzantine" and "labyrinthine" are more descriptive of the *keiretsu* and their distribution practices. The upshot is that there are many significant barriers to the Japanese market.

- It costs a lot of money to do business in Japan—everything, from rents to salaries to transportation, is expensive. Companies with limited financial resources make up a big part of the 50 percent failure rate for foreign firms operating in Japan.
- Foreign companies often don't understand the Japanese market.
- The *keiretsu* structure tends to make life difficult for foreign exporters: interlocking directorates that include a single large bank that finances all the members; multitiered distribution systems that do little more than create jobs (20 percent of all jobs in Japan are in some level of distribution, twice the rate found in the US); and the practice of members buying only from each other, which excludes even Japanese newcomers.
- Pricing practices ignore the market and inflate prices. While wholesale prices in the US and Germany are slightly more than 1.5 times retail

sales, the ratio is 4 to 1 in Japan, solely because of the huge number of middlemen and the resulting multiplier effect of the profit margins that the middlemen tack on to the products as they flow by, not to mention the consumption tax levied at each step in the process.

- Product testing formalities are complex, needlessly time-consuming, and are not standardized with those of any other country.
- It's often hard for foreign companies to find qualified Japanese employees, partly because Japanese nationalism denigrates employment by foreign firms, and partly because foreign firms have acquired the bad reputation of getting into and out of the market in a short period of time—this in a nation of workers accustomed to lifetime jobs.

Yet there is a certain logic to the system, no matter how convoluted, and so it can be mastered, and even modified to suit you. Not even Japan's legendary, unfair, and arcane trade barriers can account for the dearth of imported products in neighborhood stores. After all, Japan imported more than US$235 billion in foreign products in 1991; measured per capita that nearly equals the US rate. Indeed, the major reasons for foreign failures in Japan have little to do with the Japanese system and much more to do with foreign attitudes.

Yet despite all these barriers—or more accurately, because of them—there's a huge untapped market for imported products and commodities, a market that's been growing 40 percent a year, a market full of high-income, sophisticated buyers yearning to try foreign goods. Leading the field of opportunities are food, chemicals, semiconductors, integrated circuits, audiovisual equipment and parts, scientific instruments, medical and optical instruments, children's clothing, vitamins and other health products, jewelry and accessories, sporting goods, and gardening equipment. In addition, Japan has cut the number and power of its notorious cartels, lowered most of its formal import barriers—although the formidable informal ones remain—and is trying to buy more imported products. (Refer to "Opportunities" chapter for a detailed discussion.)

In this section, you'll learn a variety of ways to enter the US$3 trillion Japanese market, and the strategies many foreign firms have used to succeed in a land of riches.

THE SEVEN-FOLD PATH TO THE JAPANESE MARKET

The key to successful market penetration is matching your product to the distribution system. It's important to do it right the first time, because second chances can be expensive. In Japan it's as difficult to break a business relationship as it is to begin one, and many a foreign firm has been left out in the cold after a disagreement that ended a relationship. Before you decide which channel you'll use to enter the market, consult with JETRO and your country's commerce agency or embassy; both have experts who can guide you to the best decision with manufacturing directories, phone numbers, and contacts. Other valuable resources include the Japan Chamber of Commerce and Industry, various associations for economic cooperation, foreign trade associations, trade fair associations, and sister city organizations. One of your first steps should be to research the market, either on your own or through a major market research company or advertising agency. (Refer to "Important Addresses" chapter as a starting point.)

1. Get an agent

Agents specialize in representing foreign companies. This is an inexpensive way for a small company without the financial resources to set up a Japanese office to get into the market. An agent can be a trading company, a small importer, a wholesaler, a department store, or a consultant.

Japan's 6,000 trading companies are truly varied; they account for US$700 billion in annual sales and handle 60 percent of Japan's imports. Many of the larger trading companies, called *sogo shosha*, have offices worldwide and a finger in every pie in the land. *Sogo shosha* generally handle bulk items such as agricultural products, industrial or raw materials, and textiles. For example, Mitsui—the giant manufacturing, distributing, importing, exporting, shipping, and banking *keiretsu*—alone handles more than 20,000 different products, and its 1989 trade transactions totaled US$126 billion. Its expertise in all areas of business is unsurpassed; it's invaluable to have such power working for you. The immense size of *sogo shosha* firms means that they may not pay close enough attention to the needs of your particular product, but this may be compensated for by their unparalled access to the market.

A step down from the *sogo shosha* are the *senmon shosha*, which are smaller, more specialized trading companies that nonetheless have deep levels of expertise. These smaller companies are better for products requiring after-sales service.

Most agents will want to be the sole agent for the products they handle, from customs to stocking the shelves. This means you have to rely on your agent's reputation, marketing ability, connections in the distribution system, and commitment to you and your product. An agent reduces your risk but also your control over how your product is marketed and sold.

Five Ways to Build a Good Overseas Relationship

1. Be careful in choosing overseas distributors

This is crucial. Whether you choose to go with a sub-sidiary, an agent, an export trading company, an export management company, a dealer, a distributor, or your own setup, you need to investigate the potential and pitfalls of each. Visit potential partners to assure yourself of their long-term commitment to you and your product, as well as their experience, ability, reputation, and financial stability. Do not rely solely on bank or credit sources for information on a prospective distributor's financial stability and resources—hire an independent expert to advise you.

The keys to McDonald's Corporation's success, says company spokesman Brad Trask, is a meticulous search for partners that focuses on "shared philosophies, past business conduct, and dedication. After all, we're asking a businessman to give up two years to be absorbed into the McDonald's way of business. We want to be sure we're right for each other."

2. Treat your overseas distributors equally with their domestic counterparts

Your overseas distributors aren't some poor family relations entitled only to crumbs and handouts. They are part of your company's future success, a division equal to any domestic division. Offer them advertising campaigns, discount programs, sales incentives, special credit terms, warranty deals, and service programs that are equivalent to those you offer your domestic distributors and tailored to meet the special needs of that country.

Also take into account the fact that distributors of export goods need to act more independently of manufacturers and marketers than do domestic distributors because of the differences in trade laws and practices, and the vagaries of international communications and transportation.

McDonald's partners in Japan adhere to the company's overall standards of consistency and quality, Trask says, but in all other ways, the McDonald's restaurants in Japan are thoroughly Japanese—Japanese owned, staffed and operated. "We're not operational police," Trask says. The company knows to leave well enough alone and trust its partners. "Those partners have purchased the rights to a formula for proven success. We've never found anyone foolish enough to fly in the face of success. Instead, they've adapted the formula to suit their needs." Kentucky Fried

Chicken sees things the same way. "We mandate that our partners or licensees have the Colonel up on the logo, and they have to serve original recipe chicken and cole slaw," says Steve Provost, KFC's vice president of International Public Affairs. "Beyond that it's up to them."

3. Learn the do's and taboos

Each country does business in its own way, a process developed over years to match the history, culture and precepts of the people. Ignore these practices and you lose. "McDonald's system has enough leeway in it to allow the local businessmen to do what they have to do to succeed," Trask says. Thus, every new McDonald's in Thailand holds a "staff night" just before the grand opening. The families of the youthful employees descend en masse to be served McDonald's meals in an atmosphere that they can see for themselves is clean and wholesome (Refer to "Business Culture" chapter for a detailed discussion.)

4. Be flexible in forming partnerships

American companies in particular are notoriously obsessed with gaining majority share of a joint venture, the type of partnership most favored by East Asian governments. One reason is accounting: revenue can show up on the books at home only when the stake is more than 50 percent. Another reason is the US Foreign Corrupt Practices Act, which makes US citizens and companies liable for their conduct overseas; the idea, presumptuous at best, is that majority control translates into control of the minority partner.

Ownership is yet another area where the Japanese have succeeded; they see a two-sided relationship where Americans see themselves as the superior partner in knowledge, finances, technology, and culture—in other words, know-it-alls. Westerners, and Americans in particular, have a lot to learn about flexibility in business relationships. McDonald's has chosen the 50-50 joint-venture route, with great profitability—more than half its income now comes from outside the US. KFC is another American company that has found enormous success by being flexible. "We have a philosophy of relying heavily on our joint venture or franchise partners to guide us," says KFC's Trask. "We'd never dream of trying to impose our attitudes on them."

Finally, keep in mind that there is more than one way to do business overseas, and changing laws or market con-

Five Ways (cont'd)

ditions will often force you to consider other options. Where a distributorship worked at first, a joint venture or a licensing agreement may be the way to go later.

5. Concentrate on the relationship

We cannot emphasize this point too greatly. The Confucian culture of East Asia emphasizes personal relationships above all else. Building a good relationship takes time, patience, courtesy, reliability, dignity, honorable conduct, and farsightedness; a poorly developed relationship will doom your best marketing efforts. One US computer maker made a great mistake when it fired its Japanese distributor after a falling-out. The dismissal, handled in a typically abrupt American way, caused the man to lose face, and ruined all the relationships the company had built through this man. For three years afterward, company executives couldn't find another distributor because no one would talk to them. Not only did the company lose untold millions of dollars in sales, but it took $40 million in advertising to create enough consumer-driven demand for Japanese distributors to even consider meeting with the firm.

So do your very best to build a sound, trusting and profitable relationship with your overseas partners. They are putting themselves on the line for you, spending time, money and energy in hopes of future rewards and a solid, long-term relationship.

And by all means, don't expect your foreign distributors to jump through hoops on a moment's notice. For example, they need price protection so they don't lose money on your price changes. If they buy your product for ¥100 and a month later you cut your price to ¥90, you have to give them credit so they don't get stuck with inventory at the higher price. If you raise your price, you have to honor your prior commitment while you give ample notice of the increase.

With their focus on long-term personal relationships and on mutual respect and trust, East Asians, in particular, make honorable partners once you have gained their confidence by showing them they have yours. Give up all short-range thinking.

2. Sell to a Japanese company

Many foreign companies enter licensing agreements with Japanese firms to keep costs down and to tailor the product to Japanese tastes. Look for a company that makes or sells a similar or complementary product. Its distribution system is already in place. But take into consideration the company's distribution coverage, the suitability of its sales staff, its pricing policies, market share, profitability, and image, and whether its long-term marketing strategy includes your product. If there's to be a transfer of technology, you'll want to negotiate for sufficient compensation because the Japanese company may absorb and improve on your technology. Finally, be sure you can supply your product in sufficient quantities and at a high enough level of quality to avoid embarrassing your Japanese buyer.

3. Enter a joint venture

There are many success stories of foreign firms joining established Japanese firms to create a new company. The advantages are several:

- Both partners have a capital investment to protect;
- Costs and risks are shared;
- Plans are mutually agreed upon;
- Expertise is readily available;
- The Japanese partner is already part of a distribution system; and
- Neither partner has undue influence over the new company's daily operations.

Your responsibility includes keeping a close watch on the new company's activities; don't rely totally on your Japanese partner's familiarity with Japan. Joint ventures often end when the Japanese firm buys out the foreign firm, and this prospect should be recognized in the JV agreement.

Britain's Virgin Records entered a 50-50 joint venture with Marui Co., Ltd., a department store chain that specializes in the youth market, which Virgin wanted to target. The result was Virgin's first store in Japan. Opened in 1990, the store follows the standard Virgin foreign operations pattern: a proven overall format with specialized local features. The store's staff is all Japanese. Because of the tie-in with Marui, the store is Japan's first mega-music store, a big contrast to the sometimes intimidating specialized stores more common in Japan. And Marui's location in the Shinjuku section of Tokyo meant access to the young, Western-oriented people Virgin wanted. After only one year of operation, sales had hit the ¥3.3 billion (US$27.5 million) mark.

4. Go it alone

A wholly-owned subsidiary is an expensive, time-consuming prospect, but the rewards can be great.

You've got to have deep pockets for this approach, given Japan's astronomical office rents and the labor shortage, not to mention what amounts to a forced, often painful, education in all aspects of Japanese corporate life, from pension benefits to personnel policies to market intricacies to language. The reward is on the bottom line: you set your own prices and keep all the profits. The biggest multinationals take this approach, and have themselves become members of *keiretsu*.

5. Try a combination approach

There's no reason not to try a variety of market approaches. Lotus Software did it very successfully in Japan. This legendary and innovative US software developer began with intensive market research, and followed up with the development of products that met the market's needs. Lotus set up a wholly owned subsidiary in 1985, and the subsidiary has used several marketing and distribution methods.

But along with the traditional channels, Lotus also sells directly to dealers—both those who specialize in small-lot sales and those who handle large corporate contracts. Lotus holds special seminars to educate its dealers and consumers and also runs a nationwide network of training centers. The company was the first in Japan to contract out software development, allowing outsiders to create special niche-market functions to add to the core product. This means that Lotus products are more than Japanese-language versions of American software: they are actually Japanese products. The company's operating method is 80 percent Japanese, especially in personnel management and in benefits; the US contribution is mainly in fostering the freedom for individuals to create and innovate in technology and marketing. The result of Lotus's commitment to the Japanese market was sales of ¥11 billion (US$92 million) in 1990.

6. Exhibit at a trade fair

This is the premiere, most cost-effective way to introduce your product to Japan. These fairs draw huge crowds, including distributors at all levels. For a small investment, you get to show everyone what you have to offer, present a company image, learn what your prospective customers need and expect, and scout out the competition. (Refer to "Trede Fairs" chapter.)

7. Do it by mail

Catalog sales are enjoying increasing acceptance in Japan, although a major impediment remains the Japanese consumer's desire to inspect a product before buying. Growth in the market is expected to be in the range of 8 to 10 percent annually over the next several years, increasing to US$60 billion and 6 percent of total retail sales by the year 2000. The potential for foreign firms is enormous: they currently account for just over 1 percent of total direct-marketing sales.

With 37 percent of the total, mail order is the fastest-growing piece of the direct-marketing pie and the one most open to foreign firms. Catalog sales make up half the mail-order market. The reasons for the rapid growth include major changes in work habits and lifestyles; a strong yen combined with a strong appetite for foreign goods; toll-free phone numbers; changes in retail credit practices; and improved package delivery systems. Few studies have been done, but the market is generally believed to consist largely of young, upwardly mobile professionals interested in high-quality, fashion-oriented merchandise.

Along with the standard requirements for a successful product in Japan—high quality, fast and on-time delivery, good service, wide selection, and good value—foreign mail-order firms must be prepared to offer:

- convenient credit or payment terms;
- Japanese language catalogs, brochures and order forms;
- Japanese-language customer service; and
- reasonable shipping and handling costs.

Your reward for meeting these requirements is to cut out a host of price-hiking middlemen and the cost of stocking a retailer's shelves.

There are several ways to enter the direct market in Japan. If your company is large enough, an office or showroom is one of the best, providing consumers with a glimpse of your product and giving you a high degree of control over business operations. You can also exhibit at direct-marketing trade fairs. Or you can consider a joint venture with a well-known and established Japanese partner, preferably a retail firm with a strong distribution network. The low-cost alternative is to ship directly from your country to Japanese customers who answer magazine or newspaper ads for catalogs and information. In the time-honored Japanese tradition of innovation and middlemen, several firms have sprung up in recent years to act as agents for foreign mail-order companies. They sell or give away catalogs, take orders, and arrange shipments, all for a fee. These companies have significantly increased opportunities both for Japanese consumers and for foreign companies that wouldn't have been able to establish a presence in this huge and complex market.

The major source of information about the Japanese direct-marketing industry is:

Japan Direct Marketing Association (JDMA)
Mori Building, No. 32
3-4-30 Shibakoen, Minato-ku
Tokyo 105, Japan
Tel: (3) 3434-4700 Fax: (3) 3434-4518.

ADVERTISING

Japan's advertising market is sophisticated, diversified and complex. Consumers get their information from a variety of sources, none of which dominate the market. The accompanying table illustrates the importance of each source, and how there's more to boosting awareness of your product than just advertising.

Japan is awash in advertising, so companies do their best to stand out from the crowd. As a result, ads are entertaining rather than analytical or logical, with wide use of celebrities, graphics, music, and catchy slogans. (Sound familiar?)

Media companies sell or contract much of their space or time to major advertising agencies, which then sell to their clients or to secondary agencies. Japan's largest agencies are in the world's top 30. Several large American firms also play the Japan ad market, including Leo Burnett, Bozell, Young & Rubicam, Saatchi and Saatchi, and McCann-Ericson, either through subsidiaries or through joint ventures with Japanese firms.

Most important source of advertising information *

SOURCE	PERCENT
TV/Radio	76.0
Newspaper/magazine ads	44.8
Flyers inserted into newspapers	34.0
Word of mouth	32.2
Newspaper/magazine articles	28.2
Product catalogs	27.4
Store windows	21.5
Store employees	6.8

* total adds up to more than 100 percent because respondents cited more than one source

Advertisers spent ¥5.7 trillion in 1991, with TV getting the biggest chunk. Japan's current economic slump means that advertisers have cut their budgets, and rates are negotiable for the first time in years, opening the door for new and smaller advertisers. The rates cited in the following paragraphs give a general idea of the costs.

Media Shares of Advertising Expenditures (1991)

TV	29.3%
Newspapers	23.5%
Magazines	6.8%
Radio	4.2%
Transit and other	36.2%

Japan's Top 10 Advertising Agencies (1990) (billings in US$ millions)

1.	Dentsu, Inc.	7,077.4
2.	Hakuhodo, Inc.	3,140.6
3.	Tokyu Agency, Inc.	1,069.6
4.	Daiko Ad, Inc.	1,004,1
5.	Asatsu, Inc.	716.3
6.	I&S Corp.	653.0
7.	Yomiko Ad, Inc.	643.5
8.	Dai-Ichi Kikaku Co., Ltd.	593.2
9.	ME Hakuhodo, Inc.	461.1
10.	Asahi Ad, Inc.	404.4

Sources: US Department of Commerce, HDM/Koukoku Keizai Kenkyuujo

Broadcasting

Japan's TV industry is as concentrated as its newspaper industry, and there are close links between the five private national TV networks and the five private national daily newspapers. TV programs draw huge audiences. More than 15 million viewers tune into Asahi TV's one-hour evening news show, and even a low-rated (1 to 2 percentage points) show can reach 1 to 2 million people. Add such audiences to the insatiable Japanese curiosity about Westerners and Western products, and you have a potentially lucrative marketing outlet.

There are two types of television and radio commercials: time and spot. Time advertisers sponsor a program with three commercials of 30 seconds each, while spot advertising is a simple commercial of 15 seconds on TV and 20 seconds on radio. Time commercials are more expensive, and broadcasters also add production and network fees to the set price. Because broadcasters solicit spot commercials, they charge only for the length of the commercial.

Television rates depend on the time segment, with prime time (called Segment A) lasting from 7 to 11 pm weekdays and from 6 to 11 pm weekends. Segment B is next in cost, covering noontime, early evening and late night on weekdays and Saturdays, and daytime and late night on Sundays. Segment B is less expensive and covers morning and afternoon hours, while Segment C is the cheapest, running from midnight to 7 am.

Segment A time advertising on TV Tokyo costs about US$17,000 for the set of three commercials; in Segment C the cost drops to about US$5,000. Rates for time advertising in Osaka are about 15 percent less. A 15-second spot commercial on TV Tokyo's Segment A costs about US$10,000, while it would cost US$2,800 during Segment C. The same commercial in Osaka would cost about one-third less.

Radio rates are not so segmented; 6 am to midnight is more expensive than midnight to 6 am. On Nippon Bunka Broadcast Radio a three-commercial time advertisement costs about US$2,200 between 6 am and midnight, and about US$1,600 between midnight and 6 am. The Osaka fees are about one-third less. A 20-second spot commercial in Tokyo goes for about US$1,000 between 6 am and midnight, and US$750 between midnight and 6 am. Again, Osaka rates are about one-third less.

The major advertising agencies handle TV advertising. While agency rates are similar, the actual cost depends on the relationships among the agency, the broadcaster and the advertiser. Other factors include the program's popularity, the agency's power and influence, and the advertiser's budget. Broadcasters and agencies expect to sell more time to companies with big advertising budgets, and therefore give them discounts to encourage them to buy some time during non-prime time segments. The bigger the agency, the more likely its client is to get the preferred slots.

The agencies' clout makes it hard for new or smaller businesses to break into prime time, at least with major TV broadcasters. Radio and local TV is less restrictive, and these broadcasters often refer potential advertisers to the right agencies.

Print media

Newspapers Japan's newspapers have the world's largest total circulation, largely because they have a captive audience—millions of commuters trapped on trains with nothing to do for an hour or two but read the paper. The country also has the world's highest literacy rate, and 99 percent of homes have daily newspaper delivery.

Japanese newspapers are classified into three types: national, regional, and local. The five national newspapers are dailies based in Tokyo or Osaka, cover the entire country and have large circulations—more than 50 million total in a country of 125 million people. While *Yomiuri Shimbun* is the biggest, there are also *Asahi, Mainichi, Sankei,* and *Nikkei.* The national dailies publish ads for either national or regional editions, and ads can be further targeted by delivery area, such as Osaka-City, Osaka-North, or Osaka-South. Ad costs vary with the circulation level.

Regional newspapers are based in leading regional cities—for example, Sapporo in the Hokkaido region, Sendai in the Tohoku region, or Nagoya in the Tokai region—and they circulate in each of a region's several prefectures. Local newspapers are usually based in prefecture capitals, with circulation limited to that prefecture. There are 65 regional and local papers.

Japan also has a number of special-interest newspapers, including four business papers: *Nihon Kogyo, Nikkan Kogyo, Nikkei Sangyo,* and *Nikkei Ryutsu.* There are 10 sports newspapers, and six English-language papers: *The Japan Times, The Asian Wall Street Journal, The Asahi Evening News, Mainichi Evening News,* *The Daily Yomiuri,* and *The Japan Economic Journal.* Japan's leading financial newspaper, *Nihon Keizai Shimbun,* outsells the WSJ by more that two to one.

Unlike their colleagues in television, Japanese newspaper advertising divisions deal directly with their advertisers. Not surprisingly, Japanese newspaper advertisements can be a tad costly. A full-page ad in *Yomiuri Shimbun* costs at least US$400,000; add another US$100,000 or so for color and choice of placement. However, you can cut costs by focusing on a particular market, buying a smaller space, and taking advantage of discounts for frequency and space. A one-column ad in the Osaka edition of *Yomiuri Shimbun* costs about US$9,000, compared to US$30,000 for the national edition. A 3-month contract for a one-column ad in *Nikkan Kogyo's* Osaka edition costs US$1,100, compared to US$2,600 for the national edition. Newspaper classified ads are cheaper, of course. Expect to pay more to guarantee a date, page or position for your ad, and for production fees if your ad isn't camera-ready.

Magazines Publishers churn out about 2,250 weekly or monthly magazines, with one for every market niche—including dozens that foreign exporters don't even know exist. By nature, magazines are more likely than electronic media or newspapers to be targeted to specific markets, most notably by sex, income and age group. Magazine ads cost more than newspaper ads, but readers keep their magazines longer, read them more thoroughly, and look at the ads repeatedly. Designers know this and make the ads more colorful and graphic than they do for newspapers.

Back-cover ads are the most expensive. A back-cover color ad in the weekly magazine *Hoseki* (circulation 650,000) costs about US$19,000, while an inside full-page black-and-white ad goes for about US$5,000. The monthly *Bungei Shunju* charges about US$19,000 for a back-cover color ad and about US$6,500 for an inside full-page black-and-white ad. A back-cover color ad in *Nikkei Money* (circulation 380,000) costs about US$20,000, while an inside full-page black-and-white ad costs about US$8,000. Magazine advertising divisions usually deal only with ad agencies, who buy the space in bulk ahead of time and then manage it with their clients or secondary agencies. Thus, new or small businesses are unlikely to get space when and where they want it unless they contract with one large agency. In addition to their hold on priority space, large agencies can offer discounts and marketing and advertising consulting.

Transit advertising Think of it: 21 billion passengers a year, all seeing your ad while they're trapped on the subway or train. (That's when they're not looking at your ad in the newspaper or magazine they're reading.) When they get off the train, there's your ad stuck on the station wall in front of them. They board

Seven Rules for Selling Your Product

1. Respect the individuality of each market

The profit motive generally operates cross-culturally and the nationals of most countries, especially within a given region, will have much in common with one another. However, there will also be substantial differences, enough to cause a generic marketing program to fall flat on its face and even build ill-will in the process. You may have some success with this sort of one-size-fits-all approach, but you won't be able to build a solid operation or maximize profits this way. "Japan proves this point phenomenally," says Steve Provost, KFC's vice president of International Public Affairs. "Our first three restaurants in Tokyo were modeled after our American restaurants, and all three failed within six months. Then we listened to our Japanese partner, who suggested we open smaller restaurants. We've never looked back." However, what works in Japan doesn't necessarily work elsewhere. Other Asian tastes may be more similar to US tastes than to Japanese, or may differ in other ways.

2. Adapt your product to the foreign market

Markets are individual, and you may well need to tailor your products to suit individual needs. As the United States' Big Three automakers have yet to learn, it's hard to sell a left-hand-drive car in a right-hand-drive country. Black may be a popular color in your country, but may also be seen as the color of death in your foreign market. Dress, styles, and designs considered fashionably tasteful at home can cause offense abroad. One major US computer manufacturer endured years of costly marketing miscalculations before it realized that the US is only one-third of its market, and that the other two-thirds required somewhat different products as well as different approaches.

You can avoid this company's multi-million dollar mistakes by avoiding lazy and culturally-biased thinking. A foreign country has official regulations and cultural preferences that differ from those of your own. Learn about these differences, respect them, and adapt your product accordingly. Often it won't even take that much thought, money, or effort. Kentucky Fried Chicken offers a salmon sandwich in Japan, fried plantains in Mexico, and tabouleh in the Middle East—and 450 other locally specific menu items worldwide. And even the highly standardized McDonald's serves pineapple pie in Thailand, teriyaki burgers and tatsuda sandwiches (chicken with ginger and soy) in Japan, spicy sauces with burgers in Malaysia (prepared according to Muslim guidelines), and a seasonal durian fruit shake in Singapore.

3. Don't get greedy

Price your product to match the market you're entering. Don't try to take maximum profits in the first year. Take the long-term view. It's what your competitors are doing, and they're in it for the long haul. The Japanese can be very price-conscious. When you're pricing your product, include in your calculations the demand for spare parts, components, and auxiliary equipment. Add-on profits from these sources can help keep the primary product price down and therefore more competitive.

4. Demand quality

A poor-quality product can ambush the best-laid marketing plans. The Japanese may look at price first, but they also want value and won't buy junk no matter how cheap. And there's just too much competition to make it worth your while to put this adage to the test. Whatever market you gain initially will rapidly fall apart if you have a casual attitude towards quality. And it is hard to come back from an initial quality-based flop. On then other hand, a product with a justified reputation for high quality and good value creates its own potential for market and price expansions.

5. Back up your sales with service

Some products demand more work than others—more sales effort, more after-sales service, more hand-holding of the distributor, and more contact with the end user. The channel you select is crucial here. Paradoxically in this age of ubiquitous and lightning-fast communications and saturation advertising, people rely more than ever on word of mouth to sort out the truth from hyperbole. Nothing will sink your product faster than a reputation for poor or nonexistent service and after-sales support. US firms in particular need to do some serious reputation building for such after-sales service. Although the Japanese see US products as often being superior in quality and performance, they rate their own after-sales service as vastly better. And guess whose products they buy.

Consider setting up your own service facility. If you're looking for a Japanese agent to handle your product, look for one who has qualified maintenance people already familiar with your type of product or who can handle your service needs with a little judicious training. And make sure that this partner understands how important service and support are to you and to your future relationship with him.

6. Notice that foreigners speak a different language

Your sales, service, and warranty information may contain a wealth of information but if it's not in their language, you leave the foreign distributors, sales and service personnel, and consumers out in the cold. It's expensive to translate everything into Japanese, but it's absolutely necessary.

7. Focus on specific geographic areas and markets

To avoid wasteful spending, focus your marketing efforts. A lack of focus means that you're wasting your money, time, and energies. A lack of specificity means that your foreign operations may get too big too fast. Not only does this cost more than the local business can justify or support, it also can translate into an impersonal attitude towards sales and service and the relationships you've working so hard to build. Instead concentrate your time, money, and efforts on a specific market or region, and work on building the all-important business relationships that will carry you over the many obstacles to successful export marketing.

a bus, and what do they see? You guessed it.

Transit ads can be small stickers, framed posters hung for a few days at a local station or in a railway car, or even a huge permanent electrical sign at a major terminal. In Tokyo, you can have 4,940 stickers displayed for a month inside Japan Railway cars for about US$48,000, while 6,000 posters hung inside rail cars for two days costs US$30,000. Or you can put 100 posters in 43 subway stations for a weekly rate of US$22,000. Rates for Osaka and smaller cities are considerably lower.

Because private rail lines are part of large conglomerates that include department stores, entertainment firms, banks, and real estate developers, private transit advertising is pretty well locked up. But public transit companies do have space; they deal only with advertising agencies, assigning spaces by open bids or drawings.

MAJOR MARKETS OF JAPAN

Japan is the second-largest consumer market in the world in terms of purchasing power. Taken independently, several of its regions and cities would each be ranked in the top 20 or so.

SOUTHERN KANTO REGION

Area: 13,549 square km (5,230 square miles)
Population: 31,800,000
Prefectures: Tokyo, Kanagawa, Chiba, Saitama

Centered around Tokyo Bay and including the cities of Tokyo, Yokohama, Kawasaki, and Chiba, Southern Kanto is the financial, political, commercial, and industrial heartland of Japan. More than 40 percent of the nation's factories are in the region, as are nearly 80 percent of foreign affiliates.

Tokyo Prefecture

Land area:	2,183 square km (843 square miles)
Population (1992):	11,634,000
Households (1992):	4,931,735
Gross prefectural product (1990):	¥83.2 trillion
Per capita income (1990):	¥4.5 million
Average monthly wage (1991):	¥475,250
Percentage of owner-occupied housing (1990):	40.4
Passenger car ownership (1991):	0.55 per household
Average commute time (1988):	43 minutes
Number of factories (1991):	40,350
Industrial production (1991):	¥25.37 trillion
Number of retail stores (1988):	147,000
Retail sales (1988):	¥15 trillion

Tokyo is more than just the capital and largest city of Japan. It's also the nation's political, economic and cultural nerve center, the place where change originates and spreads throughout the country and the rest of the world. The gross prefectural product ranks first in the nation, more than double that of second-place Osaka, and its per capita income also leads the country. Yet despite its size and industrial stature, Tokyo's industrial production ranks only fourth among the 47 prefectures.

Japan's (and thus some of the world's) biggest banks are headquartered in Tokyo, including Sumitomo, Dai-ichi and Bank of Tokyo. The world's biggest insurance company (Nippon Insurance), one of the biggest advertising agencies (Dentsu), and four of the six biggest securities firms are also located here, as is Asia's top stock market, the Tokyo Securities and Stock Exchange. Tokyo is the nation's educational center, with Tokyo and Waseda universities, and its citizens are the most highly educated in the country. They are also the best-informed about imported products, make up the country's most accessible and open-minded market, and—with the information, inclination and money to do so—are Japan's biggest buyers of foreign-made goods. The residents of the wards of Chuo, Minato, Shibuya, and Shinjuku lead all Tokyoites in their willingness to buy products not made in Japan.

Chiba Prefecture

Land area:	5,156 square km (1,990 square miles)
Population (1992):	5,614,000
Households (1992):	1,901,524
Gross prefectural product (1990):	¥14.7 trillion
Per capita income (1989):	¥2.8 million
Average monthly wage (1991):	¥388,650
Percentage of owner-occupied housing (1988):	63.4
Passenger car ownership (1991):	0.8 per household
Average commute time (1988):	49 minutes
Number of factories (1991):	9,842
Industrial production (1991):	¥12,546 trillion
Number of retail stores (1988):	52,000
Retail sales (1988):	¥4.5 trillion

Bordering Tokyo on the east and across Tokyo Bay from Yokohama, Chiba is primarily known as the site of Narita Airport—the world's third busiest air cargo handler—but it also has Chiba Harbor, one of the nation's largest ports. The prefecture's industry is more balanced than Tokyo's, with manufacturing, agriculture, forestry, and fisheries all contributing strongly to an economy that ranks ninth in gross prefectural product and seventh in per capita income. Chiba ranks eighth among Japan's 47 prefectures in industrial production, yet it also ranks third in the value of its agricultural production. The Keiyo Industrial Zone sprawls along Tokyo Bay on one of the world's largest reclaimed land areas, churning

out heavy machinery and chemical products that are exported worldwide. Industrial complexes are mushrooming around the airport and the expressways, and many high-tech plants are moving in. The futuristic Nippon Convention Center is the site of international trade fairs.

Kanagawa Prefecture

Land area:	2,412 square km (931 square miles)
Population (1992):	8,002,000
Households (1992):	2,967,625
Gross prefectural product (1990):	Y28.3 trillion
Per capita income (1990):	¥3.2 million
Average monthly wage (1991):	¥413,388
Percentage of owner-occupied housing (1988):	53.7
Passenger car ownership (1991):	0.73 per household
Average commute time (1990):	45 minutes
Number of factories (1991):	17,385
Industrial production (1991):	¥28,846 trillion
Number of retail stores (1988):	73,000
Retail sales (1988):	¥7.1 trillion

Kanagawa is known primarily for its huge city and port of Yokohama. It was through Yokohama Port that Japan became "Westernized" in the late 19th century, but shipping declined precipitously in the 20th century as the prefecture's economy shifted to heavy industry. The city of Kawasaki, wedged in between Tokyo and Yokohama, adds further industrial might to Kanagawa, which now ranks second in industrial production, outstripping even Tokyo and Osaka. Its three main industries are automobiles, shipbuilding and petrochemicals. Aside from its enormous industrial capacity, Kanagawa Prefecture serves mainly as a satellite to Tokyo. Every morning hundreds of thousands of commuters swarm the trains bound for Tokyo. The gross prefectural product is the fourth largest in Japan, and the per capita income ranks third.

Saitama Prefecture

Land area:	3,797 square km (1,466 square miles)
Population (1992):	6,465,000
Households (1992):	2,128,334
Gross Prefectural Product (1989):	¥16.2 trillion
Per capita income (1989):	¥2.85 million
Average monthly wage (1991):	¥354,624
Percentage of owner-occupant housing (1988):	64.8
Passenger car ownership (1992):	0.85 per household
Average commute time (1988):	47 minutes
Number of factories (1991):	24,346
Industrial production (1991):	¥17,811 trillion
Number of retail stores (1988):	60,245
Retail sales (1988):	¥4.9 trillion

Saitama Prefecture borders Tokyo on the north and primarily serves as a bedroom community and industrialized suburb for the capital. Although it lacks cities on the scale of Tokyo or Yokohama, Saitama's industrial production ranks fifth among the prefectures, just below Tokyo itself, with transportation and electrical machinery dominating exports. Many of its residents still commute into Tokyo, 40 minutes away by train, but the rapidly growing economy is allowing increasing numbers to work closer to home. The average age of Saitama's 6.4 million residents is the youngest in Japan, and the prefecture's small cities and suburbs are filling up with young families who want to avoid the long commutes and extreme congestion of their neighbors to the south. The gross prefectural product and per capita income are Japan's eighth largest.

KANSAI REGION

Area: 27,308 square km (10,541 square miles)
Population: 20,474,233
Prefectures: Shiga, Kyoto, Osaka, Hyogo, Nara, Wakayama

Kansai straddles west-central Honshu, from the Pacific Ocean on the south to the Sea of Japan on the north. It ranks second only to the Tokyo region in population, industry, and commerce; on the world stage the region would rank seventh in gross domestic product, just behind the United Kingdom. Kansai includes the giant industrial cities of Osaka and Kobe, as well as the historical and cultural centers of Kyoto and Nara. One of the newest features of Kansai is Kansai Science City, located in the hills of Kyoto, Osaka and Nara prefectures 20 to 30 km from the city centers of Kyoto and Osaka. The totally planned community will have a population of 380,000 working in research and innovation in science, technology and the arts.

Osaka Prefecture

Land area:	1,884 square km (727 square miles)
Population (1992):	8,552,000
Households (1992):	3,148,025
Gross prefectural product (1990):	¥37 trillion
Per capita income (1989):	¥3.4 million
Average monthly wage (1991):	¥421,046
Percentage of owner-occupied housing (1990):	50
Passenger car ownership (1990):	0.63 per household
Average commute time (1988):	38.5 minutes
Number of factories (1991):	42,502
Industrial production (1991):	¥25,375 trillion
Number of retail stores (1988):	116,812
Retail sales (1988):	¥9.2 trillion

Osaka has been a hub of Japan's sea and land transport for hundreds of years, and is now the country's principal distribution center. Located on Osaka Bay, the city served as the national capital many times and exists as a powerful economic and political center independent of Tokyo. Its gross prefectural product and per capita income rank second only to Tokyo's.

The prefecture ranks first in number of factories, with nearly 10 percent of the national total, and third in industrial production. Osaka's industrial production ranges from machinery, electronics, chemicals (26 percent of the national total), and steel to publishing, textiles (45 percent) and apparel (26 percent). Its wholesaling business accounts for more than 15 percent of the national total. Despite this economic power, Osaka is much less expensive than Tokyo, with housing costing about 40 percent less, and commercial and industrial sites going for about half the Tokyo rate.

In search of space for its economic engine, Osaka is literally growing into the sea. Its new Kansai International Airport, being built on an artificial island 5 km offshore in Osaka Bay, is scheduled to open in September 1994 and will be the country's largest. Three more artificial islands are being built to contain Technoport Osaka, scheduled for completion in 2010. Technoport Osaka is to be a futuristic city of 60,000 centered around an international trade fair facility, which is already complete. Rinku Town is being built on 318 hectares (785 acres) of reclaimed land opposite the new airport, to which it will be linked by a bridge. The new town is destined to serve as a distribution and industrial center for the airport, with residences for airport workers, as well as commercial, entertainment and tourism zones.

Hyogo Prefecture

Land area:	8,382 square km (3,235 square miles)
Population (1992):	5,403,000
Households (1992):	1,861,629
Gross prefectural product (1989):	¥17 trillion
Per capita income (1989):	¥2.7 million
Average monthly wage (1991):	¥393,542
Percentage of owner-occupied housing (1991):	70
Passenger car ownership (1991):	1.26 per household
Average commute time (1988):	33.6 minutes
Number of factories (1991):	18,634
Industrial production (1991):	¥16.3 trillion
Number of retail stores (1988):	71,405
Retail sales (1988):	¥4.7 trillion

Hyogo Prefecture, bordering Osaka on the northwest, is best known as the site of Kobe, one of Japan's leading ports and a cosmopolitan city of

1.5 million about 20 km around the bay from Osaka. Hyogo is a center for heavy industry, including chemicals, steel and shipbuilding; its immense Hanshin and Nishi-Harima Technopolis industrial zones spread inland and along the coast into Osaka. The prefecture accounts for 7 percent of Japan's electrical machinery production and 10 percent of its iron and steel output.

Kobe is probably the most Western-oriented city in the country, thanks to its long-term status as an international port. Since the port's opening in 1868, foreign merchants and traders have settled in residential areas in the hills above the harbor, lending great diversity to the city's attractions. The shops, restaurants and nightlife of Kobe are very popular with young Japanese couples and families.

Hyogo is also the northern anchor for the Akashi Straits Bridge, which, when completed in 1998, will be the final link in the 81 km highway linking Shikoku Island with Honshu—and the longest (3.9 km, or 2.4 miles) truss supension bridge in the world.

Kyoto Prefecture

Land area: 4,612 square km (1,780 square miles)	
Population (1992):	2,542,000
Households (1992):	914,787
Gross prefectural product (1990):	¥8.4 trillion
Per capita income (1990):	¥2.8 million
Average monthly wage (1991):	¥387,635
Percentage of owner-occupied housing (1988):	60
Passenger car ownership (1990):	0.7 per household
Average commute time (1990):	32 minutes
Number of factories (1991):	10,502
Industrial production (1991):	¥6.7 trillion
Number of retail stores (1988):	37,849
Retail sales (1988):	¥37.9 trillion

Kyoto is Japan's cultural center—a virtual living museum. The city has more than 600 temples, 20 percent of the country's national treasures, and 15 percent of its important cultural properties. Japan's capital for more than 1,000 years, until the Meiji Restoration in 1868, the city is steeped in history and tradition, which has made it the country's leading tourist destination.

Yet Kyoto is also an industrial power. Glass skyscrapers dominate the central city, and the leading industries are precision machinery, x-ray equipment, office machinery, and textiles. Although its industrial production ranks 17th in the nation, Kyoto's 1.5 million people have Japan's sixth-highest per capita income. Like others in the Kansai region, Kyoto's residents are sophisticated about consumer products and are tuned into Western culture and trends.

TOKAI REGION

Area: 29,406 square km (11,351 square miles)
Population: 14,220,526
Prefectures: Aichi, Shizuoka, Gifu, Mie

While the world regards the Tokyo and Osaka regions as Japan's industrial leaders, the Tokai region has quietly climbed to second place, behind only Southern Kanto Region and surpassing the entire nation of Korea in gross domestic product. Aichi Prefecture, in fact, leads all Japan in industrial production by a considerable margin while still ranking ninth in agricultural production. Meanwhile, Shizuoka Prefecture ranks sixth in industry and 13th in agriculture.

Aichi Prefecture

Land area: 5,147 square km (1,987 square miles)	
Population (1992):	6,650,000
Households (1992):	2,198,000
Gross prefectural product (1989):	¥27.3 trillion
Per capita income (1990):	¥3.2 million
Average monthly wage (1991):	¥411,900
Percentage of owner-occupied housing (1990):	58
Passenger car ownership (1992):	1.1 per household
Average commute time (1988):	26 minutes
Number of factories (1991):	34,911
Industrial production (1991):	¥38.7 trillion
Number of retail stores (1988):	82,043
Retail sales (1988):	¥6.5 trillion

Despite having slightly more than half the population of Tokyo Prefecture, Aichi's industrial production is more than 65 percent greater, and the farms of its Nobi Plain produce 10 times as much. The prefecture's Chukyo Industrial Belt alone is responsible for more than 11 percent of Japan's industrial production. The key to this strength is the city of Nagoya and its suburbs. Here are major seaports on Ise and Mikawa bays, Komaki International Airport, and a maze of railways and highways linking Tokyo and Osaka.

It was the harbor that stimulated Nagoya's industrial growth, which now centers on shipbuilding, food processing, ceramics, automobiles, rail cars, textiles, machine tools, and aircraft. Oil, machinery, wool, cotton, and corn flow into the port from around the world, while every type of Japanese-made product leaves for the nation's far-flung trading partners. Japan's biggest auto maker, Toyota, is headquartered in the suburb of the same name.

Aichi's gross prefectural product is Japan's third largest, while its per capita income ranks fourth. Despite their wealth and the presence of more than 36,000 foreign residents, however, Aichi's citizens are not in forefront of Japanese consumer trends and have a reputation for being hard-sells on foreign-made products and new ideas. Compared to residents of the Tokyo and Osaka areas, they spend little on themselves, instead saving their money for big weddings, big funerals and big festivals.

HELPING YOUR COMPANY LEARN TO LOVE EXPORT MARKETING

Eliminate as much guesswork as you can

Expert export consultation is usually time and money well spent. You need a well thought out marketing plan. You cannot get into successful exporting by accident. It's not a simple matter of saying, "Let's sell our product in Japan." You need to know that your product will, in fact, sell and how you're going to sell it. First, do you need to do anything obvious to your product? Who is your buyer? How are you going to find him? How is he going to find you? Do you need to advertise? Exhibit at a trade fair? How much can you expect to sell? Can you sell more than one product? A plan may be the only way you can begin to uncover hidden traps and costs before you get overly involved in a fiasco. While you may be able to see an opportunity, knowing how to exploit it isn't necessarily a simple matter. You must plot and plan and prepare.

Just go for it

We're not suggesting you throw caution to the winds, but sometimes your "plan" may be to use a shotgun approach—rather than the more tightly targeted rifle approach—and just blast away to see if you hit anything. You can narrow things down later. If your product is new to the market, there may be precious little marketing information, and you may have essentially no other choice. Two scenarios illustrate these points: two companies decide to begin selling similar products in East Asia, which has never seen such products before. Company A hires a market research firm, which spends six months and US$50,000 to come up with a detailed plan. Company Z sends its president to a trade fair—not to exhibit but just to look around and meet people. He follows that trip up with two others. On the last one his new associates present him with his first order. Company Z also spent six months and US$50,000 investigating doing export business, but it has an order to show for it, while Company A only has an unproven plan.

Get your bosses to back you up and stick with the program

Whether your company consists of 10, 50, 500, or 5,000 people—or just you—and whether you're the head of the company, the chief financial officer, or the person leading the exporting charge, there

---

Five Ways to Help Your Local Agent

1. Make frequent visits to Japan to support your agent's efforts. And keep in mind that your competitors are also paying personal visits to their agents and customers. For example, the head office of Arbor Acres Farm, the US chicken broiler breeder, sends representatives to Japan three or four times a year to maintain the strong relationship it has built with its Japanese managers.

2. Hold more demonstrations and exhibits of your products. If you're a supplier to Japanese manufacturers, the value of sales presentations at factories is immeasurable. Factory engineers and managers are directly responsible for the equipment and machinery to be purchased, and they have much influence over the decision to buy.

3. Increase distribution of promotional brochures and technical data to potential buyers, libraries and industry associations so that when your agent makes personal sales calls, the potential customers won't be completely in the dark about your products.

4. Improve follow-up on initial sales leads. Let your agent know you're backing him up with whatever it takes to pursue a lead. Make your agent proud to be associated with you. "All of our foreign partners know that they have the support of a large system behind them," McDonald's spokesman Brad Trask says. "The support system is available on request."

5. Deliver on time. If you don't, you can bet that someone else will. Failure to deliver on time not only makes your agent lose face but jeopardizes your sales. One Tokyo department store manager says that foreign firms have "an extremely spotty record for meeting delivery deadlines." That's a difficult reputation to be saddled with. You can't make ships go faster or make airlines schedule more frequent flights, but you can stockpile your products in Japan to ensure a steady supply to your agent.

must be an explicit commitment to sustain the initial setbacks and financial requirements of export marketing. You must be sure that the firm is committed to the long-term: don't waste money by abandoning the project too early.

International marketing consultants report that because results don't show up in the first few months, the international marketing and advertising budget is *invariably* the first to be cut in any company that doesn't have money to burn. Such short-sighted budgetary decisions are responsible for innumerable premature failures in exporting.

The hard fact is that exports don't bring in money as quickly as domestic sales. It takes time and persistence for an international marketing effort to succeed. There are many hurdles to overcome—personal, political, cultural, and legal, among others. It will be at least six to nine months before you and your overseas associates can even begin to expect to see glimmers of success. And it may be even longer. Be patient, keep a close but not a suffocating watch on your international marketing efforts, and give the venture a chance to develop.

Avoid an internal tug-of-war

Consultants report that one of the biggest obstacles to successful export marketing in larger companies is internal conflict between divisions within a company. Domestic marketing battles international marketing while each is also warring with engineering, and everybody fights with the bean counters. All the complex strategies, relationship building, and legal and cultural accommodations that export marketing requires mean that support and teamwork are crucial to the success of the venture.

Stick with export marketing even when business booms at home

Exporting isn't something to fall back on when your domestic market falters. Nor is it something to put on the back burner when business is booming at home. It is difficult to ease your way into exporting. All the complex strategies, relationship-building, legal and cultural accommodations, and financial and management investment, and blood, sweat, and tears that export marketing requires means that a clear commitment is necessary from the beginning. Any other attitude as good as dooms the venture from the start, and you may as well forget it. We can't overstress this aspect: take the long-range view or don't play at all. Decide that you're going to export and that you're in it for the long haul as a viable money-making full-fledged division within your company.

McDonald's Corporation spokesperson Brad Trask, commenting on his company's overwhelming international success, notes, "We're a very long-term focused company. We do things with patience; we're very deliberate. We're there to stay, not to take the money and run." And Texas Instruments, which has suffered recent losses in its semiconductor business, has made a considered move into long-term joint ventures in East Asia, banking that these investments will provide a big payoff five years down the road.

Business Entities & Formation

FORMS OF BUSINESS ORGANIZATION

Commercial codes in Japan offer Japanese and foreign nationals a variety of recognized options for establishing a business. These options include a variety of companies, partnerships, branches, and representative offices. Investors can also form joint ventures and agent or technical assistance agreements or make equity investments. The specific method of investment and business entity selected will be determined by the objectives, circumstances, the degree of control desired, and the anticipated duration of the investment as well as other business considerations. However, the range of likely solutions to most business needs is fairly narrow.

Of particular interest to foreign investors are the joint stock company, the branch office, and the representative office forms. Although it is legal to structure businesses in other ways, the Japanese most readily accept these forms as vehicles for foreign participation in their large and complicated economy.

Companies

A company is an entity that has been organized and registered for profit-seeking purposes. Companies have legal status as separate juridical persons. The Japanese commercial code recognizes four types of companies: corporations, limited liability companies, unlimited liability companies, and companies with limited and unlimited liability. In practice, the corporation is the business entity of choice for both foreign and domestic operations in Japan.

Corporations The corporation, also known in English as a joint stock company or a company limited by shares, is called *kabushiki kaisha* in Japanese, a term that is often reduced to the shorthand K.K. Not only is the corporation the company structure most often used by both foreign and Japanese firms, but it is also the type most familiar to and preferred by the authorities. The corporation is a separate legal entity, and the liability of its shareholders is limited to the amount of their capital contribution. The le-

gal concepts and regulatory frameworks governing Japanese corporations are similar to those of corporation law found in United States and Germany. Such a company can be 100 percent foreign owned, and both its initial capital and annual net earnings can be repatriated. In principle, a corporation is eligible for any available investment incentives (some other forms of organization might find access to such incentives restricted).

A joint stock company can be formed by one or more founding shareholders, also known as sponsors or promoters. If all initial subscribers are classified as promoters, the courts appoint an outside inspector to attest to the fairness of subscription procedures. To avoid this additional expensive and restrictive step, joint stock companies usually arrange for at least one token outside subscriber. After incorporation, the entity can reduce the total number of shareholders to as few as one through accumulation of outstanding shares. However, legal restrictions prohibit the disenfranchisement of existing shareholders without their approval. There is no legal upper limit on the number of shareholders.

Limited Liability Companies A limited liability company, called in Japanese a *yugan kaisha*, or Y.K., is a closed company with no more than 50 members in which transfer of shares requires agreement among shareholders. Liability is limited by the amount of each participant's capital contribution. Limited liability companies resemble private companies or family corporations in English law. Unlike other types of companies that are formed and regulated under the commercial codes, the limited liability company is governed by a separate specialized body of regulations, the Yugan Kaisha law.

This somewhat simpler form of company is relatively uncommon in Japan, where it is generally perceived as the vehicle of small-time, not very sophisticated operators, an image that few foreign investors will want to project. Although it is perfectly legal for foreigners to use this format, and it could be advantageous in certain circumstances where there

GLOSSARY

Bank of Japan The national central bank of Japan that coordinates approval of foreign investments.

Foreign Exchange and Foreign Trade Control Law (FEFTCL) The statutory framework governing all foreign exchange and international investment and trade activity in Japan.

Japan Fair Trade Commission (JFTC) The official entity that approves contracts between Japanese and foreign entities, including technology transfers and joint ventures. Foreigners have complained that the restrictions placed on contract terms by the JFTC shelter domestic entities and constitute nontariff barriers to firms seeking entry to Japanese markets.

Legal Affairs Bureau The arm of the Ministry of Justice that handles local business registrations. The local offices of this entity operate in lieu of a central commercial registry office.

Ministry of Finance The ministry exercising ultimate legal authority over essentially all areas and aspects of foreign businesses operations and foreign investment in Japan.

Ministry of International Trade and Industry (MITI) The ministry exercising jurisdiction over manufacturing and trade in goods, importing and exporting, and certain areas of technical cooperation in Japan.

are a few shareholders who are interested primarily in control and limitation of liability, the Y.K. form is unlikely to be of interest to foreign investors.

Partnership Companies The remaining two types of companies are known as partnership companies because they resemble general and limited partnerships as they are known in Western law. These companies differ from Western partnerships in that, because they are formed through incorporation instead of by contract, they constitute a separate legal person, and there are limitations on liability that are not usually available to traditional partnerships. However, because they are incorporated entities, partnership companies must pay taxes as corporations, and the resulting net income that is passed on to members is considered taxable income to them. Thus, Japanese partnership companies do not escape the double taxation that makes partnerships popular in many Western systems.

Corporate entities can serve as limited liability

partners, but general partners must be individuals. Because of this restriction, few foreign entities choose this form of organization for business ventures in Japan. There are two forms of partnership company: the unlimited liability company and the company with limited and unlimited liability.

Unlimited Liability Companies An unlimited liability company or *gomei kaisha* requires two or more partners each bearing both unlimited and joint and several liability for company obligations. This structure resembles an incorporated general partnership with a limited number of partner shareholders and a restricted scope of operations. One partner can be elected to serve as general manager, but all members have an obligation to be actively involved in the operations of the partnership. Expulsion is for cause only; it requires the unanimous agreement of the partners; and it must be confirmed by a court. A *gomei kaisha* can convert itself into a *goshi kaisha*—a company with limited and unlimited liability—but the latter type cannot convert itself into the former.

It is legal for foreign individuals to form this type of company, but the possibility of unlimited liability and restrictions on the operations of such a company usually make it an unsuitable vehicle for foreigners seeking to do business in Japan.

Companies with Limited and Unlimited Liability A company with limited and unlimited liability or *goshi kaisha* is similar to an incorporated limited partnership in the United States. It requires one or more partners with unlimited liability for company obligations beyond their capital contribution and one or more whose liability is limited to the amount of capital contributed. Members with limited liability must make their contributions in cash. Limited liability partners cannot serve in managerial or official representative positions, but they may be actively involved in operations, and they may exercise oversight of company affairs. The manager functions more as a trustee than as a managing general partner.

Such businesses are organized primarily as a vehicle to pass tax benefits through to interests that have provided the capital for the venture. Foreign companies can participate in such partnerships only as limited partners, although foreign individuals would be allowed to serve as general partners. These forms are relatively rare, and they usually do not provide a useful means of carrying out regular operations in Japan.

Company Capital Requirements The minimum paid-in capital required to establish a joint stock company is ¥10 million (about US$90,000). The minimum capital for a limited company is ¥3 million (about US$27,000). There are no established maximum amounts for joint stock companies. A minimum 25 percent of the authorized shares must be issued at the time of incorporation, and all issued shares must be fully paid. Shares must have a minimum value of ¥50,000 (about US$450). Many firms incorporated before 1982 (the year when this minimum value went into effect) have shares worth far less. These firms are required to adjust their accounting of shares outstanding over time, and this requirement has led to the existence of fractional shares. Shareholders can hold fractional shares resulting from splits, reverse splits, conversions, and share dividends, but the company cannot issue fractional shares. Fractional shares carry no voting rights, but they can be in bearer form (regular shares must be in registered form). Fractional shares worth less than 1 percent of a full share are not allowed.

Only founding promoters can use assets other than cash to pay for their shares. Such assets are subject to court valuation and approval. However, if the property represents less than 20 percent of the total paid-in capital and less than ¥5 million (about US$45,000) and if it consists of marketable securities or appraised real estate, it can be accepted without court involvement. The difficulty in such cases can usually be avoided by having the promoter sell the property and make the contribution in cash.

Joint stock company shares must be transferable, although the company can set conditions for transfer in its articles of incorporation or bylaws. However, shareholders can transfer shares even without company approval under appeal procedures found in the commercial code that prevent a company from freezing its shares indefinitely. Limited companies require shareholder approval for the transfer of ownership interest. This provision is attractive to some foreign investors who wish to retain tight control over their investment. Under certain limited conditions, share transfers between resident and foreign shareholders and among foreign shareholders can be restricted.

Shares can be issued with par value or no par value. Par value shares can be converted to no par shares and vice versa by action of the board, subject to shareholder approval. Since April 1991 companies have been required to issue all shares except fractional shares in registered form. Companies can issue common, preferred, and various other classes of shares with differential rights regarding voting or distribution of profits. Common shares usually carry voting rights. No more than one-third of the total shares can be nonvoting. Preferred shares are issued infrequently.

A joint stock company can issue domestic straight, convertible, or other debt securities up to an amount equal to its net assets. It can issue foreign securities or secured debt up to an amount equal to twice its net assets. Japanese companies are often highly leveraged, employing far more debt than equity in their financial structures and much more than is common for Western companies.

Joint stock companies must establish legal reserves equal to 10 percent of the annual cash dividends paid until the reserves total 25 percent of the issued capital. Any share premiums are also credited to this reserve. Cash dividends can only be paid out of net earnings, less various reserves and other specified retention accounts, and cannot be paid out of reserves. Payouts are usually made once a year after the end of the fiscal year. Interim dividends can be paid if the corporation attests that it has funds adequate to finish out the year despite having paid the dividend. There is no requirement that dividends be paid at all, and Japanese cash dividends have historically ranged from puny to nonexistent.

Capital can be increased by the sale of additional authorized stock or capitalization of retained earnings, but the sum of such additions may not exceed the corporation's authorized capital without new approvals. Such increases require the approval of shareholders as well as board resolutions. Shareholders have preemptive rights to new shares issued, although these rights can be waived. Authorized capital can be increased by a two-thirds vote of shareholders, but at least 25 percent of the new authorized capital must be issued and paid up at any time.

Capital can be decreased only with the approval of shareholders. Securities can be purchased and retired, although shares may not be bought in and held as treasury stock except in narrowly defined specific instances, such as to fund employee stock purchase plans. Decreases can also be accomplished by using funds available for cash dividends to redeem existing shares, by reducing par values that are above the minimum allowed, or by using capital to offset a deficit.

To prohibit cross-holdings, subsidiaries that are more than 50 percent owned by a parent are barred from acquiring the stock of the parent firm. Corporate holders with over 25 percent of shares in another company are prohibited from voting those shares.

Shareholders, Directors, Officers, and Corporate Governance Corporate governance is the joint responsibility of the board of directors, the shareholders, and the statutory auditor. Specific levels of responsibility can be assigned through the articles of incorporation within the limits established by law.

A general meeting of shareholders must be held at least once every fiscal year within three months of the close of the preceding period. Holders of more than one-third of the voting shares outstanding must be represented to establish a legal quorum for ordinary business. A quorum of greater than 50 percent is required for issues dealing with the alteration of the bylaws and certain financial matters. Companies can write more restrictive quorum rules into their bylaws. Some votes require a two-thirds majority according to statutory rules, but most require only a simple majority of those present to pass. Again, by-laws can specify that larger majorities are required.

A joint stock company must have a board of directors consisting of at least three members—*torishimariyaku*—elected by its shareholders. These directors do not need to be shareholders unless the bylaws require it. A limited company must have at least one but not more than three directors chosen by shareholders from among their number. Individuals must be elected formally by shareholders in order legally to represent a limited company.

Directors serve a maximum term of two years, but they can be reelected for an unlimited number of additional terms. There is no nationality requirement for board membership, but in practice the authorities require a company to have at least one Japanese director before they will register it. Rules state that one or more directors must be designated to serve as executive officers in dealing with operations, business, and legal issues.

Board members are responsible for hiring and firing corporate officers and for undertaking and monitoring company operations. There are no legal provisions for corporate officers other than the board. However, most companies use them to operate. Corporate officers and board members are barred from holding other employment in any similar business without specific authorization from the board, and they must disclose their ongoing interests in such cases.

The board is the ultimate authority for a company. However, it may call special shareholder meetings to decide issues of governance. Special meetings can also be held if shareholders representing 3 percent of the company's stock demand it. Shareholders holding 1 percent of the outstanding shares can propose matters at the annual meeting. Holders of lesser proportions of stock can call special meetings in large corporations with broad ownership.

The Japanese civil code requires a stock company to elect at least one statutory auditor—*kansayaku*—who is not an officer or director to serve for a maximum term of two years. This individual, who functions as an internal auditor and ombudsman for shareholders, is charged with examining the business and financial condition of the company and inspecting the corporate books, records, and documents. Large companies-those with capital greater than ¥100 million (about US$900,000), and liabilities greater than ¥20 billion (about US$18 million), must have two such full-time auditors, one of whom is a certified accountant, responsible for independently auditing the company's books.

Large corporations must publish summary income statements and balance sheets in newspapers or the official gazette immediately after their annual meeting. Smaller companies need only publish a sum-

mary balance sheet. Companies listed on the stock exchange and subject to securities and exchange law must also file financial statements with the Ministry of Finance, where they become part of the public record. There are no other filing requirements. Disclosure is generally weak, although shareholders and creditors have the right to inspect the minutes of shareholder and board meetings and the register of share- and bondholders. Shareholders can gain access to detailed financial data only under extraordinary circumstances.

Dissolution A company can dissolve under any of the following circumstances: the time period specified in the company's articles of incorporation for its existence has expired, the company has merged into a new entity, the company is bankrupt, a court orders its dissolution, or the shareholders and board of directors vote to dissolve it. In cases of merger, the company becomes part of a new entity, with continuity of assets and liabilities specified in the new articles of incorporation. In cases of bankruptcy, the company goes into receivership so that its assets can be disposed of. In other cases, the company liquidates according to specified procedures and the process is overseen by the Legal Affairs Bureau. A director, shareholder, auditor, or creditor can petition for a court-supervised reorganization if insolvency is indicated before the declaration of bankruptcy.

Branch Offices

A branch office—*shiten* in Japanese—is any profit-making office registered and maintained in Japan for which ultimate responsibility is held by the company's principal office. Branch offices are allowed to earn income from direct operations, and they can remit that income to the parent. Although the parent can give the branch a high degree of autonomy, the branch technically must remain under the direct official control of the parent firm.

In general, a branch office gives a foreign entity the same freedom of operation and control as does the establishment of a wholly owned subsidiary corporation. The Japanese see little difference between the two types of entity and one is not felt to be more serious than the other. A foreign firm should consider home country tax advantages when deciding the type of firm to establish in Japan.

Foreign branch offices are resident legal persons. As such they are subject to both the laws and regulations that govern domestic companies and to those governing foreign enterprises. As income-earning entities, they are subject to income and value-added taxes on income earned and operations conducted in Japan. However, capital transfers between parent and branch are considered exempt transactions.

Because the branch is the responsibility of the parent company, there is no minimum working capital requirement, except for specially authorized branches in such areas as financial services. Branches must supply financial information on their own and their parent firm's operations, but this information is not disclosed, except in the case of bank branches. Branches are not required to undergo a statutory audit as are corporations.

Branch offices must appoint a resident official representative to be responsible for local operations and compliance. This individual does not have to be a Japanese national, but must be a legal resident of Japan.

As part of an independent foreign entity, a branch can be closed by its parent at any time provided that such closure does not represent an attempt to evade legal obligations.

A branch office can be established solely to conduct activities that earn no income. If the parent company at a later date expands the scope of branch business operations to encompass direct profit-making activities, it must obtain approval and register with tax authorities before undertaking any income-generating activities.

Foreign entities often use branches when their goal is to minimize the costs of operating in Japan, to conduct a limited-term operation in Japan, or when they do not want to reinvest earnings in Japan. Some firms use a branch office to establish a beachhead in Japan and then convert the branch into a full company at a later date if initial results show that a more ample business presence can be beneficial.

Conversion is a recognized and accepted procedure, but it involves the formation of a new, separate company, not a transformation of the branch into a company. Thus, a branch with losses cannot carry them forward to the new entity. The branch can also be liable for transfer taxes, taxes on gains accruing to the branch during its operations, and additional registration payments, which can make this procedure somewhat expensive. Special provisions allow conversion on a tax free basis if the parent retains 100 percent ownership, the conversion is simultaneous, and the book value of the assets of the successor entity are equal to or less than—but not more than—the assets of the original branch entity.

Representative Offices

A representative office is an entity involved in indirect business activities that do not generate profits for the office. It is only allowed to conduct activities on behalf of its parent company, and it is prohibited from acting on a cooperative basis for other entities, whether they are related or separate. Representative offices have no legal standing as separate legal entities, but they are familiar in practice, being allowed to operate as a courtesy to foreign entities.

The functions of a representative office generally include such activities as advertising, conducting market and competitive research, gathering information for the parent company, providing product and business information, and purchasing and storing goods on behalf of the parent. Representative offices also often monitor the activities of the Japanese distributors and agents that handle their parent company's products in Japan, and they can refer potential customers to the entities that have been authorized to take actual orders. They are limited in the amount of actual customer service and after-sales support that they can provide, but they can supervise local agents who often contract to provide such all-important support as part of their handling of the foreign company's product.

All activities must represent support for parent company operations. A representative office cannot conduct any kind of sales-related activities on its own. Such activities as direct negotiation of contracts, even if the contracts are signed elsewhere, can jeopardize the exempt status of a representative office and leave it open to classification as a permanent establishment, subject to taxation, Japanese regulations, and potential fines for operating without authorization. There are no capital requirements because the head office covers expenses. Because the office generates no income, no taxes are due.

A representative office is easier and generally less expensive to set up than other types of entity. There are no general registration requirements, although representatives of foreign financial services firms must notify the Ministry of Finance of the existence of the office. All foreign representatives and office personnel must obtain commercial visas to operate in Japan.

A representative office offers a degree of flexibility and control for a foreign business wishing to hedge its bets by establishing an immediate if limited market presence without committing to an increased presence in the future or foreclosing any options to expand its scope of activity at a later date.

Liaison Offices

A liaison office is an anomalous entity without legal standing in Japan. In contrast to the representative office, it is not generally acknowledged to be an official representative of a foreign entity. The functions of a liaison office are unofficial and severely limited. Some investors use an informal presence that they call a liaison office to gather information that can help them to decide whether to launch an enterprise in Japan. Others establish liaison offices specifically to monitor the activities of local agents. Because they lack standing, such offices are not viewed as a vehicle for those interested in serious business. Any functions that they might perform are generally undertaken by a more formal representative office.

Commercial Agents and Distributorships

Agents are individuals or firms that provide local representation for a foreign business in the buying of Japanese products or in sales of the business's own products in Japan. Domestic agents can be authorized to conclude contracts on behalf of foreign clients, and they are often responsible for day-to-day transaction functions, some information gathering and market research, and the purchase and delivery of goods, although they cannot serve as a proxy office in Japan.

Thousands of Japanese trading companies, importers, wholesalers, consultants, and individuals operate in this middleman capacity. There are more than 8,000 trading companies, ranging from the huge, big-name *sogo shosha* that account for 50 percent of Japan's exports and 60 percent of its imports to the smaller, more specialized *senmon shosha* that act as intermediaries for most foreign entities. Many maintain offices outside Japan, but entities interested in doing business in Japan will probably want to stay somewhat closer to developments in the country itself and not rely exclusively on long-range intermediaries.

Choosing an appropriate agent is considered to be a critical factor in establishing the all-important initial market presence in Japan. Because the distribution system in Japan is so complicated and dependent on relationships, an agent can either give a foreign entity an edge when breaking into the Japanese market or effectively shut it out from the beginning.

Agency agreements offer the simplest means of establishing a business presence in Japan because they involve a simple contract that can easily be terminated without additional liability provided there is no breach of contract or outstanding liability involved. Termination of such contracts usually requires two months' notice. The low cost of such arrangements is their primary advantage. However, a foreign entity that operates solely through agents sacrifices potential profits and cannot establish direct customer relationships.

An agent should be selected only after a thorough examination of his qualifications and experience. Most foreign entities that anticipate a steady and growing volume of business in Japan find that it is preferable to set up a branch office rather than to rely on agents. However, the use of agents can give a foreign firm a means to gain information and recognition and exploit immediate opportunities in the market while it decides whether it wants to develop a larger presence in Japan.

Licensing and Technology Transfer Agreements

Licensing and technology transfer agreements are contractual agreements by foreign nationals to license or sell rights to specific products, processes, or technologies to Japanese firms or individuals. In exchange for the use of foreign-owned technical expertise or patent or trademark rights and specifications, Japanese entities agree to pay fixed fees or negotiated royalties.

Technology-related agreements must be reported to the Ministry of Finance, which intervenes to stop or alter the terms of the agreements only in extraordinary cases. However, contracts involving specially regulated or designated technologies must be approved by the Ministry of Finance and any other ministries that have jurisdiction over the areas involved. Licensing agreements are also screened by the Japan Fair Trade Commission (JFTC), which can require alterations in or declare the agreement void if it considers that the terms represent restraint of trade or unfair business practice. The US government, among others, has protested this requirement and the operations of the JFTC as constituting a nontariff barrier to trade.

Licensing has several drawbacks. Such arrangements usually allow the licensor to realize only minimal profits, which unexpected costs of administering the contract can reduce to nil. They prevent the licensor from having inputs into marketing of the product or implementation of the process that could have an affect on the success of the agreement, and they result in little market exposure or information being gained. Moreover, underreporting of sales and underremitting of royalties by licensees has been reported.

One additional consideration is that licensing agreements usually give the licensee the right to improve on the processes and technologies that he has licensed and to exploit these improvements in the future. The entity that grants the license can find itself losing market share down the line to the next generation of product that the licensee has developed by improving on the licensor's own system and to which the original licensor has no rights or access.

Joint Ventures

As in much of the rest of Asia, a joint venture in Japan is a vague description that refers to a wide range of mutual agreements between contracting parties, often—but not always—of different nationalities. It is not a specific type of business structure with legal standing, as it is in much Western legal theory and practice.

The Japanese commercial code contains no legal definitions of or provisions for the formation of joint ventures, nor are joint ventures recognized as legal entities in Japan. For this reason, a contractual, unincorporated joint venture without legal standing as a separate entity can cause difficulties for the foreign partner unless it has been carefully structured under the framework of Japanese law. For historical and cultural reasons, most Japanese are reluctant to become involved in such ventures. The only such contractual arrangements in general use are agreements to undertake certain projects in the construction industry.

The vast majority of joint ventures in Japan are set up as a corporation formed by the local and foreign participants to undertake the specific business envisioned. As with any direct foreign investment, a joint venture must be approved by the Ministry of Finance. The contractual arrangements are also subject to review by the Japan Fair Trade Commission (JFTC).

Joint ventures can offer foreign investors the benefits of local knowledge and connections, access to personnel, and risk and cost sharing. However, issues of control and of finances can become points of conflict between foreign and Japanese venture partners. Agendas other than strict profit-making as Westerners understand it are common in Japanese business. For example, Japanese companies often elect not to declare dividends in order to reinvest all earnings in operations even though the foreign partner needs to realize income on current operations in order to make his investment work. Reinvestment can also be motivated by the financial needs of the Japanese parent organization, which may wish to use the financial resources of its downstream partners to bolster its own credit. Financial policy and other governance issues should be worked out in detail before entering into a joint venture agreement. Chemistry is exceptionally important to the success of such cooperative ventures.

Partnerships

Partnerships in Japan are generally organized as incorporated partnership companies: The *gomei kaisha* or *goshi kaisha*. Although it is possible to organize a partnership as a contractual noncorporate entity, it is seldom done in practice, and it would not be recognized as having separate legal standing.

Informal associations resembling partnerships include the *tokumei kumiai* (T.K.) and the *nin-i kumiai* (N.K.). A T.K. is similar to a limited partnership in that it has an operator, similar to the general partner, who has unlimited liability and one or more individuals or corporations serving as limited partners whose liability is limited to their capital contribution. In practice, the limited partners are silent or inactive partners who furnish capital that the general partner needs to undertake the venture.

An N.K. is similar to a general partnership in that each party is active and has full liability. In both cases, the partners participate in the profits and losses according to the terms of the partnership agreement, not in proportion to their inputs. Although these entities are recognized in certain narrow spheres, they have limited legal standing or protection, and they are uncommon in Japan.

The one potential advantage to trying to operate as a partnership is in taxation: Unincorporated partnership-like entities are treated as a conduit rather than as a taxable entity, so income passes directly to the individual partner for tax purposes and double taxation is avoided at the entity level. However, most Japanese shy away from these types of arrangements, and such partnerships are generally not seen as appropriate vehicles for serious foreign investment.

Franchising as a Means of Doing Business in Japan

Franchises are becoming a popular way of doing business in Japan. The ones that have caught on in Japan have been primarily service ventures that often have a short life span. Many have represented fads that flourished until the novelty wears off or local operators copy the essentials of the service offered, often after giving it a customized Japanese twist. Such overseas franchisors as McDonald's are managing to hold their own by playing on name recognition and adapting their offerings to Japanese tastes, adding such items as green tea milkshakes, squid pizza, fried rice, and seaweed sandwiches to their traditional fare.

Foreign investors usually find a Japanese master franchisee, who then recruits the local franchisees. The foreign investor usually earns a lump sum fee plus a royalty on franchise sales.

Foreigners can enter into a joint venture or form a separate company to franchise and manage the businesses in an attempt to gain a larger share of the profits, although local participation is especially critical to the success of such efforts. There are no special requirements for this type of operation other than those associated with the business entity that the franchisor chooses if he elects to become directly involved in Japan. Otherwise, agreements are contractual in nature and covered under the commercial code. They are also subject to review by the Japan Fair Trade Commission.

Sole Proprietorships

Sole proprietorships are not recognized as separate legal entities in Japan, meaning that a proprietor operating in this fashion bears unlimited personal liability. Japanese and in theory foreign nationals may set up sole proprietorships in compliance with relevant Japanese laws. Technically, the smallest commercial ventures undertaken by individuals are exempt from standard registration and reporting requirements. However, there are potential problems with such a course, the main ones involving complications in the way income from such ventures is taxed. In practice, a sole proprietorship is not an accepted or feasible vehicle for a serious foreign investor.

REGISTERING A BUSINESS

In virtually all cases, businesses in Japan must register with the appropriate authorities, and foreign businesses require advance approval before they can begin operations. This section outlines the procedures and documentation required to register a business in Japan. Most entities are formed under Japanese commercial codes, but foreign entities will also need to comply with the separate provisions governing foreign investments.

The complex nature of the regulations governing such procedures makes it highly advisable that, besides conferring with government authorities, individuals or firms wishing to do business in Japan obtain legal and accounting assistance to ensure that they are in compliance with the myriad of regulatory requirements and procedures. In addition, most procedures needed to establish and register a foreign business presence require a Japanese resident to make the actual submissions. (Refer to "Important Addresses" chapter for a partial listing of government agencies and legal and accounting firms.)

Licensing Foreign businesses operating in Japan require foreign investment approval and business licenses from the appropriate authorities. All businesses except representative offices must register with the Legal Affairs Bureau of the Ministry of Justice.

Special Registration for Businesses Besides observing all regulations pertaining to the particular form of enterprise that it has chosen, the foreign business may require additional special authorization or licensing if it operates in certain areas. Businesses can be approved and registered only after such permission has been granted by the ministry that regulates the particular activity.

Businesses involving financial services require special permits and have special eligibility and capital requirements. Businesses related to gas and electric utility operations require special permits and ministerial approval. The operation of a retail business with floor space in excess of 500 square meters (about 5,300 square feet) requires advance approval at the prefecture level, and operation of a retail facility larger than 3,000 square meters (about 33,000 square feet) in provincial areas or 6,000 square meters (about 65,000 square feet) in urban areas requires approvals at both the prefecture and national levels; such approvals can take the better part of a year to process even when no serious problems exist (and local competitors often raise objections).

Businesses that require special authorization include construction, hotels, restaurants, bars, travel agencies, freight forwarding, warehousing, private schools, personal services, real estate management, broadcasting, telecommunications, power generation, domestic transportation, arms and ammunition manufacture and dealing, nuclear energy, aircraft and space industries, pharmaceuticals manufacturing and distribution, security services, agriculture, forestry, fisheries, mining, petroleum refining and marketing, leather and leather products manufacturing, shipbuilding, and banking or other financial services. In practice, it is difficult to receive authorization to operate in most of the areas listed.

These limitations, known as *peacetime controls*, are designed to regulate activities that would interfere with public safety or the maintenance of public order, such as weapons and explosives manufacture; activities that would interfere with key industries, such as fisheries or petroleum processing and distribution; activities in which there is a lack of reciprocity between Japan and the investor's country; or activities that emergency control measures have classified as capital transactions.

Emergency control measures can be brought into play if the Ministry of Finance determines that an imbalance of financial outflows will harm the balance of payments, damage the exchange rate of the yen relative to other currencies, or endanger the smooth functioning of financial and capital markets. Japanese authorities have never put such emergency controls into effect.

If emergency financial controls were to be invoked, foreign entities could expect to have their access to foreign exchange for repatriation of earnings and capital suspended, but not revoked, for a period of time, usually no more than 30 days. The government also retains the right to suspend access to foreign exchange as a means of compelling compliance with treaty obligations.

Restrictions Foreign investors are expressly prohibited from operating in only a few sectors. These include public utilities, such as water supply, postal services, and the manufacture of industrial alcohol. In practice, several areas listed as requiring special authorizations are in effect closed to outsiders. These include the sensitive agricultural sector.

Fees and Expenses Licensing fees vary with the industry, the size and complexity of the business venture proposed, and the type of entity involved. A registration tax of 0.7 percent of paid-in capital is required for joint stock companies. The minimum tax is ¥150,000 (about US$1,350). This tax can be deducted as a corporate expense during the first year of operations.

Professional fees generally run a minimum of ¥10,000 per hour, about US$90. The estimated total costs of establishing a basic corporation are between ¥1 million and ¥2 million (about US$9,000 to US$18,000) for all fees and professional services, but excluding the costs of facilities, equipment, inventory, and staffing. The costs of establishing a branch office are around ¥1 million (around US$9,000).

Registration fees and other associated costs are generally lower for other types of business entities.

Basic Authorizations Needed and Applications Procedures

Japanese commercial codes have specific provisions for the formation and registration of each type of entity. However, every entity must complete the following three basic steps. First, it must obtain foreign investment approval from the Ministry of Finance. Second, it must complete registration procedures with the Legal Affairs Bureau. Third, it must register with local tax and social security and employment authorities in the jurisdiction where it is to operate.

All submissions must be in Japanese and in the requisite numbers of copies, which must be ascertained in each case. Usually, submissions must be made by a local resident agent. Investors can determine the ministries that have jurisdiction and that must be included in submissions by contacting the Foreign Exchange Department of the Bank of Japan.

Summary of Approval and Registration Procedures by Type of Entity

Companies A joint stock company involving foreign investment must receive prior approval from the Ministry of Finance, carry out required incorporation procedures, notify the Ministry of Finance that it has acquired the stock of the Japanese company that it has just formed, file required reports of its incorporation and initial shareholders meeting, register with the Legal Affairs Bureau, and register with the appropriate local tax and employment authorities. All notifications and registrations must be made through an official representative who is a Japanese resident.

Joint Venture Companies A joint venture company—the most common and only recommended type of joint venture structure—follows the procedures just outlined for companies. In addition, joint venture agreements must be submitted to the JFTC for review.

Branch Offices The parent entity must notify the Ministry of Finance of its intention to open a branch office before doing so and register with the Legal Affairs Bureau and with local tax and employment authorities after approval has been received.

Representative Offices A representative office is not required to register with any official body unless it is engaged in a sector, such as financial ser-

Equity Investments: Buying Your Way into a Japanese Company

Some foreign investors seek to buy into Japanese markets by making equity investments in existing companies. In principle, foreigners can buy up to 100 percent of a Japanese entity. In practice, the official Japanese attitude is that entire entities are not sold as such. This attitude is reflected in the domestic business sphere, where mergers and acquisitions have historically been rare. Such business activity would be frowned on to an even greater extent if foreigners attempted to buy a high-profile Japanese firm or one unwilling to be acquired.

The government is likely to withhold approval for acquisitions of substantial portions of most Japanese firms, despite the fact that the government generally encourages the formation of 100 percent foreign-owned new entities and the formation of greater than 50 percent foreign-owned new joint ventures.

Foreigners may acquire up to 10 percent—5 percent for financial firms—of the equity in a public company without official approval, although all acquisitions must be reported to the Ministry of Finance. Any subsequent purchases require prior approval. There is no official limit on the number of separate foreign entities that can acquire a 10 percent interest in a given Japanese entity. However, the authorities can be expected to move to prevent control of high-profile Japanese firms by foreigners in any combination. Lending to a Japanese entity for a term of longer than one year, except by recognized banks, is also subject to approval.

vices, that requires special permits. If it pays employees, it must register with local employment authorities. Representative offices must carefully restrict their operations to allowed activities, and they must immediately file a notification of foreign investment, register as a branch office, and register with tax authorities if they change their function or begin earning income.

Licensing and Technical Assistance Agreements Licensing and technical assistance agreements must be reported to the Ministry of Finance and to the Japan Fair Trade Commission for review of terms.

Unincorporated Partnerships and Sole Proprietorships Unincorporated partnerships and sole proprietorships have no specific registration requirements. They should register with local tax authorities.

Basic Procedures

Foreign Investment Reporting Procedures Formal advance approval of foreign investment is not required in Japan. All foreign entities making what is known as a direct inward investment—that is, all foreigners planning to do business in Japan—all foreign purchases of equity or securities, all private lending of sums in excess of ¥200 million (about US$1.8 million) by foreign to Japanese entities, and all contractual agreements that involve foreign investment must report the investment to Ministry of Finance and other relevant ministries—usually the Ministry of International Trade and Industry (MITI) and ministries overseeing the particular industry—within 15 days of the investment. This report is submitted through the Investment Division of the International Department of the Bank of Japan.

Most such investments will receive automatic, retroactive approval. Authorities are likely to wish to review large investments valued at more than ¥1 billion (about US$9 million). Proposed investments in restricted areas must be submitted three months before the scheduled investment, which must not take place until approval has been received. This approval is supposed to take two weeks, but it may take longer. In practice, investment in restricted areas is usually denied, although financial services have been opened up to significantly greater foreign participation in recent years.

Incorporation Procedures The formation of a corporation or other company type covered by the Japanese commercial code as a new 100 percent foreign-owned venture, a wholly owned subsidiary of a foreign entity, or a Japanese-foreign joint venture involves the following procedures:

- Application to the Ministry of Finance and other ministries governing specific areas of operations via submission to the Bank of Japan for the acquisition of shares under the Foreign Exchange and Foreign Trade Control Law (FEFTCL); such an application is required when a foreigner buys shares in any company organized in Japan even if it is a new entity organized expressly by and for foreign participation; the application must be made by a Japanese national;

- Name search to ascertain that the entity's proposed name is available and allowable;

- Drafting of articles of incorporation;

- Formal meeting of promoters to endorse articles of incorporation; articles and endorsements must be notarized to be considered official;

- Subscription and payment of shares;

- Convening of the initial shareholders' meeting, at which the directors and statutory auditor are appointed;

- Selection by the board of directors of a director to serve as the entity's legal representative;

- Registration of the corporation with the Legal Affairs Bureau of the Ministry of Justice in the prefecture in which the entity will be headquartered within two weeks after the initial shareholders' meeting, at which time the corporation legally comes into existence; and

- Filing of a formal report of the corporation's incorporation with the Bank of Japan.

The articles of incorporation must include the following particulars:

- Name of the corporation;
- Purpose of the corporation;
- Number of shares of authorized capital;
- Par value of shares;
- Number of shares to be issued at time of incorporation;
- Location of the corporation's headquarters;
- Arrangements for making the required public notifications regarding the corporation;
- Name and address of each promoter, plus identification of each promoter as an individual or corporate entity and as a resident or nonresident;
- Specifics of any concessions made to promoters;
- Specifics of payments made to promoters for serving in this capacity;
- Specifics of any contributions of assets made in lieu of cash;
- Specifics of any property to be received upon incorporation; and
- All expenses paid to incorporate the entity.

Actual incorporation procedures can generally be accomplished in a short period of time, but most investors should allow 30 days to complete all arrangements. Overall, the foreign investors should reckon that a minimum of three months will be required to begin doing business in Japan once the decision to do so has been made.

Registration Procedures Once an investment has been approved and an entity has been incorporated, it must then register with the office of the Legal Affairs Bureau of the Ministry of Justice that has jurisdiction in the prefecture in which the operation is to be headquartered as well as with local tax and employment authorities. The entity may also need to register with various other local authorities as determined by the nature of its operations. The primary registration with the Legal Affairs Bureau must occur within two weeks of the initial shareholders meeting. The registration submission must include the following information, which duplicates the material required for incorporation:

- Name and address of the headquarters office of the newly formed Japanese corporation;
- Business objectives of the corporation;
- Total number of shares authorized;
- Par value of shares; and
- Method of public notice for official corporate public communications and notifications.

It must also include the following supplementary information:

- Total number of shares issued and a description and accounting of the classes of shares issued;
- Amount of paid-in capital;
- Names of the directors and statutory auditor; and
- Name and address of the director serving as official representative.

The date of registration is considered to be the date on which the corporation was officially formed. A corporation cannot operate legally until registration procedures have been completed. Once the preliminaries have been taken care of, actual registration can be accomplished in a minimum amount of time.

Grounds for revocation of the company's business registration include failure to begin operations within one year of registration, engaging in illegal businesses, and continuation of business activities that have been determined to constitute a violation in the face of official warnings.

Branch Office Approval and Registration The establishment of a branch office by a foreign entity generally follows the procedure for making an approved foreign inward direct investment. Technically, branches that intend to operate in unrestricted areas do not require prior approval and need only to file a notification that they have begun operations. This document—the Report Concerning the Estab-

lishment of a Branch—must be filed with the Ministry of Finance and the specific ministries governing its areas of operations through the Bank of Japan no more than 14 days after operations have begun. The report must be filed in Japanese by an appointed official resident agent.

In the past, this document had to be filed between three months and 30 days before the intended commencement of operations in order to give authorities time to review it. This advance notice is still required for proposed branches in restricted areas of business. In practice, the authorities allow virtually no operations in restricted activities, except for some financial services activities that are being deregulated.

The report on establishment of a branch includes the following information:

- Identity and address of the foreign investor;
- Particulars on the formation of the parent entity in its home country, size and structure of its capital, and identity of its directors;
- Name of the branch;
- Name and address of the legal agent or representative responsible for branch operations;
- Address of the establishing entity's home office;
- Nationality of the establishing entity;
- Particulars of the proposed business activity, including classification of the branch, reasons for establishing the branch, goals of the branch, and real estate acquisition plans;
- Amount of capital to be supplied; and
- Proposed beginning date for operations.

The branch must register with the prefectural Legal Affairs Bureau within three weeks of receiving Ministry of Finance approval. It must also register with local tax authorities and employment authorities.

The Bank of Japan must be formally notified any time a branch changes the nature of its operations. The Bank of Japan must also be notified if, after applying or receiving approval, the parent decides not to open the branch. Finally, the Bank of Japan must be notified if the parent plans to close the branch.

Technical and Other Licensing Agreements Firms must report technical and other licensing agreements between foreign and Japanese entities to the Ministry of Finance and the ministries that have jurisdiction over the specific industries involved. Usually, agreements involving nonsensitive technologies having a total value of less than ¥100 million (about US$900,000) do not require formal prior approval, and the report serves as an after-the-fact official notification.

The document required—called a Report Concerning Conclusion of License Agreement—must be prepared jointly by the licensor and the licensee and submitted by a resident agent to the Ministry of Finance and other relevant ministries through the Bank of Japan. In the case of agreements involving designated technologies or contracts valued at more than ¥100 million, the parties must file an advance report no more than three months and no less than 30 days prior to the date on which the contract is to go into effect. It is usually assumed that the parties can execute the contract after this report has been submitted. However the authorities can subsequently require changes in the contract or disallow it entirely. The authorities can grant approval in less than the 30 days allotted or take additional time, usually up to five months, to review the contract.

The parties to the agreement are also required jointly to file the contract with the JFTC no more than 30 days after the contract has been executed. The JFTC can require changes or disallow the contract entirely. This review is generally considered more difficult than the initial ministerial review of such contracts, and ministerial approval is no guarantee that subsequent approval will be granted.

Firms must register with local tax authorities regarding fees, royalties, and other income earned on such agreements.

Registration with Local Tax and Other Authorities Registration or notification of business establishment must be filed with local tax authorities. To comply with regulations involving employment, entities must also register with the Labor Standards Office, the Public Employment Security Office, and the Social Insurance Office.

TEN REMINDERS, RECOMMENDATIONS, AND RULES

1. The joint stock company and branch office are the most common types of business entity used by both local and foreign investors. These are also the business formats that Japanese authorities and firms prefer to deal with.
2. The importance of building consensus and of establishing and fostering long-term, person-to-person relationships with individuals in Japanese business organizations should not be underestimated.
3. Although 100 percent foreign ownership of businesses is allowed by Japan, Japanese authorities usually refuse to allow the 100 percent acquisition of an existing business except in extreme circumstances. Authorities also decline to register a corporation than does not have at least one Japanese director as a token of local participation and sensitivity to local business norms.

4. Promoters forming a Japanese corporation do not need to be the actual investors. They are usually nominees of the investors, especially if the investors are foreign corporate entities. If the corporate investor appoints a nominee, both the entity and its nominee count as promoters, making up two of the required seven promoters. The nominee signs with his personal seal as well as with the corporate seal that has been entrusted to him. Certificates of signature and powers of attorney are substituted where foreigners lack actual seals. Promoters must be in Japan to oversee formation processes. An application to purchase shares in a Japanese entity—necessary when a corporation is formed—must be made by a Japanese national. Most foreigners setting up a Japanese corporation use local professionals—attorneys and accountants—as their nominees for these technical procedures. Incorporating entities almost always secure an outside subscriber in addition to the promoters to avoid court supervision of the procedure. This outside subscriber then sells the shares that he has purchased back to a designated buyer.
5. For purposes of registration, branches and any other Japanese offices of foreign firms are considered to be resident entities even if the firm's main office is located abroad.
6. The Foreign Exchange and Foreign Trade Control Law (FEFTCL) defines the legal status and operating regulations for foreign individuals or companies doing business in Japan. The Japanese commercial code contains provisions that govern all business entities, foreign or domestic. Foreign entities are subject to regulation by both.
7. Bylaws are not required for the formation of a Japanese corporation. If supplementary bylaws are not used, as is the case with many Japanese corporations, the articles of incorporation must be extremely detailed to cover all relevant issues of corporate governance. Such provisions are extremely difficult to change once they have been enshrined in the entity's basic charter.
8. The Ministry of Finance can request or demand that specific foreign investment plans be revised or canceled for reasons of national interest. The ministry can take from fewer than 30 days to as long as five months to decide on a proposed investment in restricted sectors that require advance notification. If the government calls for a modification in the proposal, the foreign investor has ten days in which to respond. If the investor has not responded after ten days, the government can declare the requested modification in effect and hold the

foreign investor to its terms or suspend the entire proposal, effectively killing it.

9. Japanese corporations must elect a fiscal year, which can be either a twelve-month or a six-month period. If a six-month fiscal year is established, the corporation must hold meetings and make reports at the close of every fiscal period, that is, twice per calendar year. Entities using a twelve-month fiscal year need only undertake such official reporting once a year.

10. A foreign investor is defined as: an individual who is a nonresident of Japan; a foreign corporation, including the branch of a foreign corporation or the local office of a foreign governmental, quasi-governmental, or international agency; a Japanese domestic corporation with foreign ownership greater than 50 percent; or a Japanese domestic corporation in which foreigners hold more than 50 percent of the directors seats. Resident foreign nationals are not considered foreign investors, and they cannot deal with nonresident foreigners except under the terms of foreign investment regulations.

USEFUL ADDRESSES

In addition to the government agencies listed here, individuals or firms should contact chambers of commerce, embassies, banks and other financial service firms, local consultants, legal and accounting firms, and resident foreign businesses for assistance and information. The information given here is of a general nature. Because Japanese official agencies are very large and have many separate offices, it can be useful to obtain local foreign language directories, which are available at various outlets in Japan, for specific information. (Refer to "Important Addresses" chapter for a more complete listing.)

Bank of Japan
Investment Division, International Department
1-1, Hongoku-cho 2-chome
Nihonbashi, Chuo-ku
Tokyo 103, Japan
Tel: [81] (3) 3279-1111 Fax: [81] (3) 3245-0358
Tlx: 22763

Japan Chamber of Commerce and Industry (JCCI)
2-2 Marunouchi 3-chome, Chiyoda-ku
Tokyo 100, Japan
Tel: [81] (3) 3283-7660, 3283-7500
Fax: [81] (3) 3216-6497

Japan External Trade Organization (JETRO)
Investment Promotion Division
2-5, Toranomon 2-chome, Minato-ku
Tokyo 105, Japan
Tel: [81] (3) 3582-5571 Fax: [81] (3) 3505-6248
Tlx: 24378

Ministry of Finance
3-1-1, Kasumigaseki, Chiyoda-ku
Tokyo 100, Japan
Tel: [81] (3) 3581-4111 Tlx: 24980

Ministry of International Trade and Industry
International Business Affairs Division
1-3-1, Kasumigaseki, Chiyoda-ku
Tokyo 100, Japan
Tel: [81] (3) 3501-6623

Ministry of Justice
Legal Affairs Bureau
1-1, Kasumigaseki 1-chome, Chiyoda-ku
Tokyo 100, Japan
Tel: [81] (3) 3580-4111

FURTHER READING

The preceding discussion is provided as a basic guide for individuals interested in doing business in Japan. The resources described in this section provide additional information on company law, investment, taxation and accounting requirements, and procedural requirements.

Doing Business in Japan, Price Waterhouse. Los Angeles: Price Waterhouse World Firm Limited, 1993. Available in the United States from Price Waterhouse, 400 South Hope Street, Los Angeles, CA 90071-2889; Tel: (213) 236-3000. Available in Japan from Price Waterhouse, Aoyama Building, 7th Floor, 2-3 Kita-Aoyama 1-chome, Minato-ku, Tokyo 107, Japan; Tel: [81] (3) 3404-9351. Covers the investment and business environment in Japan as well as audit, accounting, and taxation requirements.

Establishment of a Representative Office in Japan, A Guide for Foreign Businessmen, Japan External Trade Organization (JETRO) Tokyo: Investment Promotion Division, Japan External Trade Organization, 1992. Available in Japan from Japan External Trade Promotion Organization, 2-5 Toranomon 2-chome, Minato-ku, Tokyo 105, Japan; Tel: [81] (3) 3582-5571. Available in the United States from Japan External Trade Organization, 44th Floor, McGraw-Hill Building, 1221 Avenue of the Americas, New York, NY 10020-1060, USA; Tel: (212) 997-0400. A step-by-step guide for foreign investors interested in establishing a representative office in Japan that covers both practical and official procedures.

Japan International Tax and Business Guide, DRT International. New York: DRT International, 1991. Available in the United States from DRT International, 1633 Broadway, New York, NY 10019-6754, USA; Tel: (212) 489-1600. Available in Japan from Tohmatsu & Co., MS Shibaura Building, 4-13-23 Shibaura, Minato-ku, Tokyo 108, Japan; Tel: [81] (3) 3457-1691, or Katsushima & Co., Mita Kokusai Building, 4-28 Mita 1-chome, Minato-ku, Tokyo 108, Japan; Tel: [81] (3) 3345-41251. An overview of the investment environment, taxation, business organizational structures, business practices, and accounting requirements in Japan.

Q & A Setting Up a Business in Japan: A Guide for Foreign Businessmen, Japan External Trade Organization (JETRO) Tokyo: Investment Promotiom Division, Japan External Trade Organization, 1993. Available in Japan from Japan External Trade Promotion Organization, 2-5 Toranomon 2-chome, Minato-ku, Tokyo 105, Japan; Tel: [81] (3) 3582-5571. Available in the United States from Japan External Trade Organization, 44th Floor, McGraw-Hill Building, 1221 Avenue of the Americas, New York, NY 10020-1060, USA; Tel: (212) 997-0400. A guidebook in question-and-answer format for foreign investors interested in establishing business relations in Japan that covers business formation procedures, foreign investment, taxes, labor, location, and financing options.

Labor

THE LABOR ECONOMY

Japan's economy enjoyed continued growth throughout the 1980s but slowed in the early 1990s due to the worldwide recession and domestic over-extension in such areas as banking and real estate. Unemployment remained low during this period, with small- and medium-sized companies in particular having difficulty finding sufficient skilled labor. Professional and skilled labor is generally scarce, especially in the electronics industry. Under pressure from employers, the government is permitting more skilled foreign workers to enter the country. While there is also a shortage of unskilled workers in some manufacturing industries, the government and labor have been firm in their opposition to importing unskilled foreigners, fearful downward pressure on wages and possible social unrest.

Labor costs in Japan, including wages and salaries, seasonal bonuses, fringe benefits, social security costs, and retirement payments, are high in comparison with other countries in the region and in the world. The cost of labor is often one of the most important considerations of doing business in Japan. High labor costs aside, the Japanese work force is productive and well educated.

Union membership declined steadily during the 1980s, and continued to fall in the 1990s. In 1992, less than one-quarter of the total employed labor force belonged to a union. Even so, organized labor, led by a newly formed confederation (*Rengo*), has successfully negotiated pay increases, reduced working hours, and been responsible for changes in other conditions benefiting workers.

Population

Comprising an area slightly smaller than California, the Japanese islands supported 123.6 million people in 1991. More than 25 percent lived in the greater Tokyo area. Population growth rates have slowed dramatically in recent years. Total population is expected to peak at roughly 133 million early in the 21st century and then begin to decline.

The Japanese have the longest life expectancy in the world—75.9 years for men and 81.2 years for women. The percentage of Japanese 65 years of age and older is expected to double by 2025, at which point it will account for about one-quarter of Japan's total population. With its consequences for the country's economy and social institutions, the aging population is one of the most critical long-term problems facing Japan.

Labor Force

In 1992 Japan's civilian labor force totaled 67.75 million. The number has grown steadily in the last few years—around 3 percent annually. Married women continue to enter the job market, offsetting the slight decline in the number of males. Men make up 59 percent of the work force, and women, 41 percent.

Labor Availability and Distribution by Sector

Prolonged economic growth in Japan has led to labor shortages in many industries and across most skill levels. Small- and medium-sized businesses are having an especially hard time filling positions that require professional and skilled workers. Large firms tend to recruit new personnel directly from the top colleges and universities. As a result, foreigners attempting to establish a business in Japan may find it difficult to recruit employees, especially better-qualified personnel. Foreign businesspeople who form a joint venture company in Japan should expect the Japanese partner to take the lead in recruiting personnel.

Forty percent of the small- and medium-sized firms surveyed in a study conducted by the Ministry of Trade and Industry (MITI) indicated that a labor shortage was the biggest problem facing management. Many employers have pushed for the admission of foreign guest workers, while others have gone ahead and hired unskilled foreign workers illegally despite the existing bans.

The service sector in Japan, measured in terms of employment, at 58.7 percent of the work force in

1990 surpassed industry as the largest sector several years ago. But the service sector is not as prominent as it is in such countries as Great Britain (68.9 percent) and the United States (70.9 percent). Moreover, since government policy maintains large segments of the labor force in export-oriented manufacturing and in protected agriculture, the distribution of workers by sector more closely resembles the distribution in France than it does in the United States. Of the 1992 total employed population, 7.9 percent was employed in agriculture, 33.6 percent in industry, and 58.5 percent in the service sector.

Foreign Workers

Japan has an extremely homogenous society; ethnic Japanese comprise more than 99 percent of the population. Most of the nearly one million foreign residents are Korean nationals born in Japan. In the face of ongoing labor shortages and increasing demands from employers, the government is considering allowing more foreign workers to enter the country on a temporary basis, but progress in this area remains slow.

Unemployment Trends

By virtually any standard, unemployment has not been a significant problem in Japan in recent years. It averaged 2.5 percent from 1978 to 1988, peaking at 3 percent in 1989. Unemployment was 2.1 percent in 1990 and 1991, rising to 2.3 percent in early 1993. However, given the stubborn recession in Japan, some observers suggest that unemployment could reach 3 to 3.5 percent in 1993 and 1994.

However, the unemployment rate differs by age and gender. For example, in 1991 for workers between the ages of 15 and 19, 7.4 percent of the males and 5.7 percent of the females were unemployed, while for persons between the ages of 20 and 24, 3.7 per-

cent of both males and females were out of a job. But the greatest cause for concern is the growing number of unemployed workers over 55; they have become very difficult to place.

There has been some conflict recently between business and government over this issue. Business is allowed to set retirement ages, which average 60 in Japan. However, in an effort to reduce payrolls, many businesses have dropped their retirement ages to as low as 55. Government, on the other hand, needs the revenue from payroll taxes and has been pushing firms to keep workers on their jobs longer.

The tradition of lifetime employment in Japan is no longer assured, at least for employees at large companies. However, this change has less to do with a serious economic crisis than it does with an inevitable slowdown in growth as Japan adjusts to the postindustrial economy.

Lifetime employment became commonplace during the fast growth of the 1960s and 1970s when Japanese firms borrowed technology from abroad, then trained their workers to apply it. To make the training pay off, firms did their best to hold onto employees. The prospect of training gave workers an incentive to stay with their firms over the long term. Now that Japan is one of the world's most technologically advanced countries and growth has slowed, employers' single-minded loyalty to their employees is fading, as is workers' loyalty to their firms.

The use of temporary workers has been common for blue collar jobs, but white collar and technical jobs have been permanent. However, in 1993 Japanese firms boosted their use of temps and contract workers to 19 percent, up from 14 percent in 1989. And conservative Toyota Motor Corp. announced that it was planning to hire a new category of professional contract workers for some jobs that had traditionally been filled by lifetime employees.

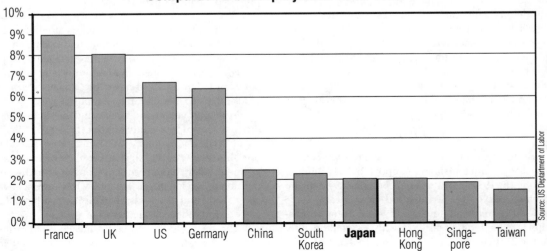

Comparative Unemployment 1990-1991

Source: US Department of Labor

HUMAN RESOURCES

Japan's commitment to investment in human resources via education and training must be counted as one of the main reasons for its economic success and why it will undoubtedly remain competitive despite high costs and the current slowdown. High universal standards in education and constant efforts to upgrade workers' skills give Japan a versatile and productive labor force. By developing its human resources, Japan has more than made up for its lack of natural resources.

The downside of this success is that labor costs have become high. While worker benefits and social security entitlements certainly contribute to these costs, they also include the price of securing the best-qualified university graduates and then training them further.

Education and Attitudes Toward Learning

Established in 1947, Japan's current educational system requires six years of primary school and three years junior high school. Further education is optional. The standard track beyond the minimum level follows three years of high school with two to four years of college or university study. Admission to both private and government-funded schools is highly competitive. An individual's education often plays a major role in determining where he or she ultimately finds a job and what kind of beginning salary he or she receives. Most students graduating from a college or university are between 20 and 22 years of age.

In Japan, students at all levels adhere to a rigorous schedule involving five and a half days of school per week, plus several hours of homework a night and, in many cases, regular attendance at *juku* schools. *Jukus* are private schools that offer tutoring services not only in most academic subjects but also in such subjects as music and fine arts. Nearly half of all ninth-grade students attend a *juku* in the afternoon after school or on weekends. Children often ask to attend since many of their friends are enrolled.

One important consequence of Japan's high educational standards is that students who complete the compulsory nine years are likely to have acquired solid skills in math, reading, writing, natural sciences, history, and foreign languages. These skills are essential not only for those continuing on to higher education but also for those entering the work force.

Training

Vocational and technical schools are common and play an important role in Japan, and they give many young people a reasonable alternative to the extremely competitive colleges and universities. Roughly 400 vocational and technical schools are sponsored by municipalities and the central government. Some 25 percent of all junior high school graduates elect some type of vocational or technical education, while 30 percent enter a college preparatory high school course.

Deciding not to continue beyond junior high school does not necessarily mean the end of one's education. Approximately 40 percent of all students find employment immediately after leaving junior high school. This is possible because many Japanese companies provide new recruits with extensive training. In this way, young Japanese often obtain vocational and technical training outside the formal educational system.

On-the-job training is a fundamental principle in most Japanese companies. Large firms with 1,000 or more employees typically give new recruits full-time training courses lasting anywhere from one week to one year depending on need and experience. Continuous on-the-job training is also a key to advancement. Promotion often depends in part on an individual's achievement in training courses and on written or oral tests.

Japanese managers and other senior-level employees are expected to work closely with lower-level employees, teaching them what they know. In the process of teaching, upper-level employees develop new skills while sharpening existing ones. In turn, managers are often evaluated and promoted on the basis of how well their subordinates learn.

Job rotation is another important feature in nearly every Japanese company, regardless of size. Most workers hold several different positions within their company, thereby learning a variety of skills. (The facts thus belie the common belief that Japanese firms are extremely rigid.) For example, a typical Japanese steelworker is likely to experience about three dozen positions on the shop floor during a lifetime of employment. The benefits of this well-established system of rotation include flexibility among employees, openness to technological change, and relatively little worker specialization.

A look at one Japanese metalworker's progression from handworker to engineer and from student to teacher will illustrate the process of continuous upgrading. During nine years of mostly hands-on work as a metalworker, the employee learned to maintain and service mechanical equipment. He was then promoted to the position of technician and worked for seven years in the company's research laboratory, where engineers informally taught him engineering practices. His promotion to engineer led to 15 years of work in several engineering positions. Finally, he was transferred to the company training center, where he developed curricula and taught courses in factory automation.

Such progression occurs across most industries and firms. By constantly challenging workers to learn new skills and experience a variety of different positions on the shop floor, Japanese industry challenges manual workers to acquire intellectual skills not unlike those of professional-level managers and technicians.

Women in the Work Force

The percentage of women in the work force is rising. In the early 1990s, it stood at 41 percent. In terms of the positions that they occupy within companies and industries, working women in Japan are generally years behind their peers in Europe and the United States. However, in the retail industry, women often reach upper-level management positions, especially in clothing and cosmetic firms.

Women are often viewed as part-time or temporary employees, since it is expected that at some point they will stop working in order to raise a family. Although it has traditionally been somewhat difficult for any workers to come back into the job market, but especially for women, firms are making a greater effort to recruit such reentrants due to the tight labor market.

The Japanese constitution prohibits discrimination on the basis of race, nationality, religion, or sex. Wage levels and benefits are not supposed to differ by gender or any of the other categories just listed. Nevertheless, more often than not, woman are not paid at the same level as men who have equal credentials, not even when they occupy the same position.

The view of women and of women's role in the workplace is changing. Woman are increasingly able to seek legal recourse and improve their situation. In the last couple of years, working women in Japan have filed suits charging sexual harassment and discrimination—and won.

CONDITIONS OF EMPLOYMENT

Japan's constitution authorizes the government to set standards for wages, hours, rest, and other working conditions. The Labor Standards Law stipulates the regulations. Both labor organizations and employers are free to improve upon the minimum regulations set by law. In recent years, unions have focused on reducing total working hours, which are still the longest of all major industrialized countries.

Cost of Living

In 1992 the average annual household income in Japan was ¥6.9 million (about US$55,542). This figure reflects the high cost of living in Japan. Employees can expect to receive various benefits, allowances, and bonuses that help to offset living expenses. Despite the steadily rising cost of everything from housing and education to food and clothing, Japanese living standards are among the highest in the world, as is the Japanese personal savings rate—approximately 15 percent of household income.

Working Hours, Overtime, and Vacations

The legislation affecting working hours, overtime, and vacations was last revised in 1987. Under current rules, the workweek is 46 hours long (a 42-hour workweek is now being considered). Pay for overtime has to be at least one-and-a-quarter times the regular pay rate. Every employee with one or more years of service is entitled to six days of paid vacation per year; the number of days increases with length of service to a maximum of 20 days. In practice, many mid- and upper-level employees do not use all their vacation days. In the last couple of years, employers have begun to order their employees to take time off from work.

Employees in Japan spend more hours per year at work than workers in other industrialized countries—an average of 2,052 hours in 1990, a figure that compares with 1,841 hours in the United States, 1,623 hours in Germany, and 1,685 hours in France. However, there is a growing trend to reduce the number of hours worked; the five-day workweek is becoming increasingly common, especially among office employees. Japanese trade unions and the government have had to lobby hard to implement significant changes.

In its efforts to reduce working hours, the government has had to pay special attention to the concerns of the owners of small- and medium-sized businesses. To encourage firms to cut back hours, the government now closes its own offices on alternate Saturdays, and it requires banking and other financial institutions to close every Saturday. Debate about instituting a five-day week for public schools continues. These measures are expected to have a ripple effect on businesses, and the government hopes that total working hours will eventually decrease to levels similar to those in other industrialized countries.

Special Leave

Employees can receive special leave with pay for such occasions as marriages and funerals. Women are entitled to six weeks of maternity leave before childbirth and eight weeks after childbirth with at least 60 percent of the basic daily wage or salary for the 98 days.

Termination of Employment

The Labor Standards Law dictates the process and conditions under which an employer may dismiss an employee. The law requires the employer to give an employee 30 days notice of his or her dismissal. In the absence of such notice, the employer must pay 30 days' wages or salary. In practice, it is difficult to terminate an employment contract without notice unless an employer reviews the regulations closely and is prepared to make a strong case. Foreign businesses in Japan should hire a Japanese consultant who has experience in labor affairs and who can interpret the law under specific circumstances.

Most companies have lump-sum severance indemnity plans. Employers with ten or more employees are required to establish and file work rules and regulations covering severance allowance with the Labor Standards Inspection Office of the Ministry of Labor. Severance allowances are usually based on length of service, current rate of pay, and the nature of separation (voluntary or involuntary). In general, allowances amount to one month of the employee's current basic salary or wage per year of service. If service years exceed a specified number, the allowance may include an additional percentage. Many companies do not pay for voluntary separation until the employee has worked for at least one to two years.

WAGES AND BENEFITS

Worker benefits in Japan cover four areas: workman's compensation insurance, unemployment insurance, welfare pension insurance, and health insurance. Health and welfare pension insurance are administered by the Ministry of Health and Welfare. Employment and workman's accident compensation insurance are under the direction of the Ministry of Labor. Social security is self-financed by employers and employees. The percentage that each pays depends on the program. The average cost of benefits as a percentage of manufacturing earnings is 19.5 percent.

Ministry of Health & Welfare
Minister, Yuya Niwa,
1-2-2, Kasumigaseki, Chiyoda-ku
Tokyo 100, Japan
Tel: [81] (3) 3502-1711

Ministry of Labor
Minister, Masakuni Murakami
2-2, Kasumigaseki 1-chome, Chiyoda-ku
Tokyo, Japan
Tel: [81] (3) 3593-1211

Every employer must offer the four benefit programs just reviewed, unless he or she has fewer than six employees, in which case unemployment insurance and workman's compensation insurance are optional.

An employee's dependent family members are covered by the employee's health insurance plan. The National Health Insurance *(Kokumin-Kenko-Hoken)* and National Pension *(Kokumin-Nenkin)* Plans guarantee coverage for unemployed Japanese citizens and for those who are not dependents of insured employees. Enterprises that have more than 700 regular employees may form a health insurance association that self-insures its members. Foreign residents of Japan may be included in the National Health Insurance program with permission from a local government authority.

Wages and Salaries

The Labor Standards Law requires employers to pay their employees in cash. Salaries and wages are paid once or twice a month. In many cases, monthly pay also includes allowances, such as a position allowance (based on the employee's position in the firm), a

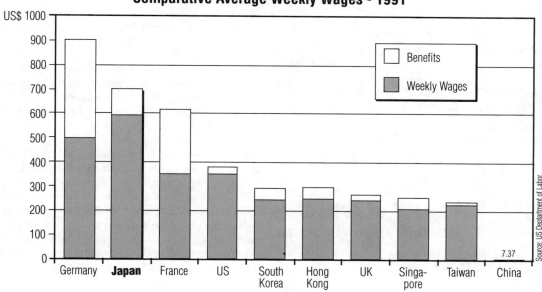

Comparative Average Weekly Wages - 1991

Source: US Department of Labor

family allowance, and a housing allowance. Seasonal bonuses vary by industry and type of business, but most firms pay a minimum of three to four months' basic salary per year. Typically, bonuses are paid twice a year, in the summer and at year's end. Finally, many firms also provide special fringe benefits, such as savings plans and membership in sports clubs.

Compensation at most Japanese companies is based on seniority and current position. Starting pay for new hires is based on the employee's level of education, not on initial job assignment. This sum automatically rises in accordance with a scale established by the company; increases are based on length of service, not on actual job performance. However, employers do tend to consider merit in determining pay. Such factors as performance record, work capabilities, and future potential are increasingly being taken into account. The new focus on contract hires has opened the way to merit pay increases based on individual performance.

The difference in pay between top-, middle-, and lower-level employees tends to be narrower in Japan than it is in other industrialized countries, but pay is less egalitarian from one industry to another.

Average Weekly Earnings by Industry—1990

Industry	¥ (000)	US$*	% Change from 1989
All Industry	85.42	638	3.7
Manufacturing	81.24	607	4.6
Commerce	71.36	533	3.8
Finance	113.08	845	0.8

Source: US Department of Labor
* US$1.00 = ¥133.89

Average Hourly Earnings by Occupation—1990

Occupation	Yen (¥)	US$*	% Change from 1989
Clerical	2,040	15.24	0
Mechanical	2,040	15.24	0
Commercial	5,103	38.11	4.0

Source: US Department of Labor
* US$1.00 = ¥133.89

Average Monthly Earnings Survey

Category	1991		1992	
	¥ (000)	US$*	¥ (000)	US$**
Managerial	559.3	4,335	578.9	4,660
Techinical	307.5	2,383	304.3	2,273

Source: Japan Bureau of Compensation
* US$1.00 = ¥133.89; ** US$1.00 = ¥124.23

Minimum Wage

The Minimum Wages Law stipulates that the Ministry of Labor establishes minimum wages. Minimum wage varies with area, industry, and other specific conditions. For instance, the 1993 minimum wage effective in the Tokyo area for the machine manufacturing industry is ¥4,792 per day or ¥599 (US$5.36) per hour. The highest minimum wage rate in 1993 was ¥630 (US$5.64) per hour, and the lowest was ¥541 (US$4.84) per hour. Prevailing wage rates usually exceed the minimum, because the labor shortage means that few workers are available at minimum wage.

Health Insurance

The health care system consists of eight separate schemes—seven based on occupation plus the catchall National Health Insurance plan mentioned earlier. There are separate programs for private sector employees, seamen, day laborers, employees of the national government, employees of local governments, public enterprises, and school personnel. The occupational programs consist of a general insurance plan administered by the government for small- and medium-sized companies or by health insurance associations in the case of large companies (700 employees or more) or groups of companies.

Health insurance premiums are 8.2 percent of standard regular monthly pay. The maximum is ¥58,220 (about US$521) per month for regular monthly pay of ¥710,000 (about US$6,357) or more. The premium, which is shared equally by employer and employee, is payable monthly. An additional premium equal to 0.8 percent of bonuses is also paid, 0.5 percent by the employer and 0.3 percent by the employee.

The National Health Insurance Plan covers all medical expenses, including dental expenses, resulting from injury or disease not occurring in the course of or due to employment. Employees are required to pay only 10 percent of their own medical expenses. Dependents pay 30 percent of their expenses; for hospitalization, they are required to pay only 20 percent. The national plan also pays 60 percent of an employee's basic average daily wages or salary for the period not paid by the employer to a maximum of 18 months.

Female employees receive a minimum of ¥200,000 (about US$1,790) for giving birth, and at least 60 percent of the basic daily wage or salary for 98 days. Employers may choose to pay a female employee at full rate during maternity leave. Traditionally, Japanese employers have assumed that once a woman has a child she will not return to work for several years if at all. It is now more common for women with children to continue working. Survivors receive ¥100,000 (about US$900) toward the cost of a deceased employee's funeral.

Workman's Compensation Insurance

All firms employing five or more people must provide workman's compensation insurance. Coverage is also available to the self-employed in certain occupations and to workers sent overseas by their employers. Insurance is divided into two categories, depending on whether the injury occurred during actual work time or while commuting to or from work. Under either category, accident victims receive medical benefits, temporary disability compensation, and long-term or permanent disability compensation. There is also a survivor's benefit.

Premiums are calculated as a percentage of total wages or salary, including bonuses. Employers are required to pay the entire premium. The premium varies with industry, ranging from a minimum of 0.6 percent to a maximum of 14.9 percent in the higher-risk construction industry.

The plan covers all medical expenses incurred at designated hospitals for injuries suffered in the course of employment. An employee absent from work due to an accident is paid at the rate of 60 percent of the average daily wage or salary during the preceding three months. Compensation for any remaining disability is paid either as an annuity or as a lump sum in an amount equivalent to the worker's standard daily wage or salary. An employee cannot receive disability pay for a period exceeding 313 days.

In the event of death, the employee's survivors receive a pension calculated using the daily wage or salary of the deceased times a number of days ranging from 153 to 245. The number of days is determined by such factors as the age of the deceased, his or her length of service, and the number of survivors.

Unemployment Insurance

Although the unemployment insurance system is overseen by the Ministry of Labor, it is administered for the most part by local governmental authorities. The system covers all employees other than seasonal workers, seamen, and government employees.

To be eligible for benefits, an individual must have been insured, and he or she must have worked for at least six months before becoming unemployed. Benefits are determined as a percentage of previous earnings; low wage earners receive as much as 80 percent. Duration is based on several factors, including the individual's age, the number of years for which he or she was insured, and the presence of a handicap. Unemployment benefits are paid for up to 300 days, although the maximum can be extended for as long as four years if the person cannot work because of illness. Additional benefits may be granted for training and job search.

The unemployment insurance premium is 1.25 percent of an employee's total compensation including bonuses; it is as much as 1.55 percent in certain industries, such as construction and forestry. Of the 1.25 percent, 0.8 percent is paid by the employer, and 0.45 percent is paid by the employee.

Firms that employ elderly persons, handicapped persons, and widows referred to them by the public employment security office receive a special lump sum assistance allowance.

Retirement Plan

Until 1986 retirement insurance programs in Japan were an amalgam of occupational plans and a national plan. In that year, all plans were combined into a single national plan. The national plan is supplemented by private plans, which unions often negotiate with very large firms. Although it has become common for retired workers to receive monthly retirement payments, many Japanese continue to prefer the traditional lump sum settlement on retirement.

The retirement insurance premium is 14.5 percent of standard monthly pay for males (16.3 percent for mine workers) and 14.3 percent for females. The premium is shared equally by employer and employee. In general, to receive retirement benefits, a person must have participated in the insurance plan for 25 years or more, be 65 years of age or older, and stop working.

LABOR RELATIONS

For the past twenty years, the relationship between labor and management in Japan has seldom degenerated into a major dispute. Employers and employees, managers and workers cooperate in a system that emphasizes consensus and seeks to minimize conflict. In fact, Japan seems to have tried to eliminate the clear distinction between workers and managers that is so visible in Europe and the United States. The tendency to stay with a single employer throughout one's career; the emphasis on promoting workers within a company; and the prevalence of enterprise unions that have close ties with their company help to promote harmony and continuity.

The incidence of labor disputes has declined considerably since the peak in 1974, when 9,662,945 worker days were lost from industrial disputes. For example, only 145,000 worker days were recorded as lost to labor disputes in 1990. Less than one-quarter of the work force now belongs to a labor union, but high dues mean that Japanese unions are well financed and maintain large staffs.

A recent reorganization created a new, national labor federation known as *Rengo*. It and other labor groups meet annually with well-established employer organizations to negotiate labor standards and renew contracts.

Unions

About 24 percent of the Japanese work force is unionized. Most Japanese unions are organized on an enterprise, rather than on a trade or professional, basis. As a result, unions in Japan are more closely tied to the success of their associated companies. The special bond between worker and company that results contrasts sharply with labor-management relationships in the West. Like the unions themselves, individual workers in Japan tend to identify more with a company than they do with a profession or occupation.

Enterprise unions, totaling 33,300, are both a product of and a means for many structural reforms, such as those bringing skilled workers and managers together, as well as equitable wage distribution and merit-based promotion within the company. Most important, the enterprise union brings all employees together in helping the company to deal with continuously changing technology and markets.

A major restructuring of organized labor occurred in 1989, when *Sohyo*, the General Council of Trade Unions of Japan, disbanded and its affiliated unions merged into *Rengo*, the Japanese Trade Union Confederation. This move was designed to increase the influence that organized labor could exert on national policy. *Rengo* now has some 7.6 million members, making it the most prominent labor organization in Japan.

In addition to their national activities, *Rengo* affiliates are heavily involved with the international trade secretariats, including the International Metalworkers Federation, the International Federation of Chemical, Energy, and General Workers Unions, and the Public Services International. *Rengo* is also an affiliate of the International Confederation of Free Trade Unions (ICFTU).

Before being joined by the public sector unions of *Sohyo*, *Rengo* represented unions in the private sector drawn from three rival federations: *Domei*, the Japanese Confederation of Labor; *Churitsuroren*, the Federation of Independent Unions of Japan; and *Shinsanbetsu*, the National Federation of Industrial Organizations.

Two other national labor organizations compete with *Rengo*, but they are much less influential than it. *Zenroren*, the National Confederation of Trade Unions, which was founded in November 1989, has a membership of 840,000. It is made up of public sector unions generally sympathetic to the Japanese Communist Party, with which *Rengo* refuses to affiliate. *Zenrokyo*, the National Trade Union Council, which has a membership of 299,000, is associated with a faction of the Japan Socialist Party (JSP). Although *Rengo* supports the JSP, among other parties, the *Zenrokyo* unions do not support *Rengo's* participation in the ICFTU.

Employer Organizations

There are four major employer organizations in Japan. *Keidanren*, the Federation of Economic Organizations, plays a major role in coordinating and guiding the interests of business and industry. *Keizai Doyukai*, the Japan Association of Corporate Executives, is an association that promotes the interests of leading Japanese corporate executives. *Nissho*, the Japan Chamber of Commerce and Industry, is a national organization of smaller firms.

Nikkeiren, the Japan Federation of Employers' Associations, is often referred to as the labor relations department of Japanese business. With 31,000 member corporations, *Nikkeiren* focuses on coordinating employers' policies toward unions and the government on all aspects of labor-management relations. The only sectors in which *Nikkeiren* does not represent employer's interests are agriculture, forestry, and the public corporations. Every year, it works out a strategy for employers' wage negotiations and issues its guidelines for the so-called spring labor offensive (*Shunto*). The basic operating principle is that any wage increases should be linked to increases in productivity. Other activities include conducting research and policy studies, maintaining communication between the government and trade unions, and operating training programs (including a management training center). It also is active in public relations and international affairs (including participation in the International Labor Organization).

Collective Bargaining

In the private sector, collective bargaining covers most aspects of labor-management relations. Every April labor and management reach a series of comprehensive labor agreements. To the Western reader it may seem ironic that these agreements do not cover wages, which are dealt with in separate annual negotiations held during the spring labor offensive.

Begun in 1956, the *Shunto* was developed by labor leaders specifically to form a common front for labor on wage bargaining. Spring was chosen because it is the traditional time for making financial settlements in Japan. It is also the time when new employees are hired and seniority pay increases are determined; firms calculate their profits and announce promotions; and the Diet (the national legislature), completes work on the budget for the new fiscal year, which in Japan begins on April 1. Wage negotiations are conducted by individual companies and their unions. Union positions are usually coordinated by industrial group. The negotiations take place between March and May. April sees the peak activity.

Business Law

INTRODUCTION

Japan is reforming its business laws, particularly as they relate to the activities of foreign businesses. Changes are frequent, and the trend is to improve the climate for foreign investment. In addition, many rules and regulations that significantly affect foreign businesses are in unpublished government advisories and internal policy statements, rather than in the statutes. You should investigate the status of the legal requirements that may affect your particular business activities. The information in this chapter is intended to emphasize the important issues in commercial law, but it should not replace legal advice or council. You should be certain to review your business activities with an attorney familiar with international transactions, the laws of Japan, and the laws of your own country. (Refer to "Important Addresses" for a list of attorneys in Japan.)

BASIS OF JAPAN'S LEGAL SYSTEM

Japan is a civil code country, which means its legal system is based on codified laws. Civil trials are nonjury, and judicial decisions are based directly on code provisions, not on case precedent.

Japan's legal system is a blend of Asian and Western traditions. Government reformers of the Meiji era (1868-1912) were strongly influenced by German legal theories, which still flavor Japan's legal system, even after constitutional reform in 1947. With modernization and industrialization, Japan has adapted Western law to its own domestic needs in such areas as copyright, antitrust, and unfair business practices.

STRUCTURE OF JAPAN'S GOVERNMENT AND LAWS

Japan's constitution, adopted in 1947, retains a monarch as a ceremonial figurehead (Constitution 4, 7). National legislative powers are placed in the popularly elected Diet, which consists of two houses: a House of Representatives and a House of Councillors (Constitution 41, 42). Japan's Prime Minister, who is selected from among Diet members, names and heads the Cabinet, all of whom must also be Diet members (Constitution 66-68). An independent judiciary, headed by the Supreme Court, has power of judicial review over legislative and executive acts (Constitution 76, 81). Japan's constitution also contains an elaborate bill of rights (Constitution 9-40).

The constitution is the country's supreme law and controls when in conflict with any of Japan's general codes or special statutes. In turn, special statutes will supersede conflicting provisions of the general codes. Finally, treaties ratified by Japan's national government generally prevail if in conflict with domestic law. Japan has ratified many international treaties and conventions, such as the Convention on Settlement of Investment Disputes Between States and Nationals of Other States, the Convention on Service Abroad of Judicial or Extrajudicial Documents, the Convention on Recognition and Enforcement of Foreign Arbitral Awards, the Patent Cooperation Treaty, and various international copyright agreements. Treaties or agreements related to commerce are in effect with approximately 50 other countries, and treaties concerning double taxation and tax evasion are in effect with about 40 other countries.

LAWS GOVERNING BUSINESS IN JAPAN

Foreign trade, both importing and exporting, is regulated by the Foreign Exchange and Foreign Trade Control Law. (*See* Foreign Trade Regulations.) Principal-agency relationships, contracts for business transactions, and contracts for sales of goods are generally governed by the Commercial Code and Civil

Introduction based on interviews with Alexander Calhoun, of Graham & James, in San Francisco, California; Roger Fleischman, of Fleischman & Fleischman, in San Francisco, California; and John Kakinuki of Baker & McKenzie, in San Francisco, California.

BUSINESS LAW
TABLE OF CONTENTS

Code, although additional or different requirements are sometimes provided in special statutes, such as the Usury Law, the International Carriage of Goods by Sea Act, and the National Accounting Law, which concerns government contracts. (*See* Principal and Agent; Contracts; and Sales.) Requirements for the financial aspects of a transaction are fixed by such laws as the Law of Bills and Notes and the Law of Checks. (*See* Bills and Notes.) Acknowledgment of documents must be made in accordance with the Commercial Code. (*See* Acknowledgments.)

Foreign entities that do business in Japan are subject to registration and other procedural requirements under general provisions of the Commercial Code and specific rules of the Commercial Registration Law. (*See* Records.) Formation and operation of business entities in Japan must be in compliance with Civil Code and Commercial Code provisions, as well as any applicable special acts of legislation, such as the Limited Corporation Law, or special legislative charters for public corporations. (*See* Corporations and Partnership.) Foreign investment, including the establishment of a branch in Japan, is governed by the Foreign Exchange and Foreign Trade Control Law. (*See* Foreign Exchange and Foreign Trade; and Foreign Investments.)

Protection of intellectual property and trademark rights is governed by the Copyright Law, Patent Law, and Trademark Law. (*See* Copyright; Patents; and Trademarks and Trade Names.) Labor relations are controlled by the Labor Standards Law, and dealings with labor unions are covered in the Labor Union Law. (*See* Labor Relations.) The Law Relating to Prohibition of Private Monopoly and Methods of Preserving Fair Trade prohibits monopolies, unfair business practices, and unreasonable restraints of trade. (*See* Monopolies and Restraint of Trade.)

GEOGRAPHICAL SCOPE OF JAPANESE LAWS

Laws digested in this section are in effect in all areas under the control of Japan's national government. The country is divided into 47 prefectures, which are subdivided into municipalities. Prefectures and municipalities have some powers of self-government, including taxing authority, as fixed by the Diet. A business owner may therefore need to comply with local regulations when doing business within a particular region.

PRACTICAL APPLICATION OF JAPANESE LAWS

Alteration of Contract Terms Although contracts are legally binding, the doctrine of changed circumstances is often cited to allow parties to alter contract terms informally. Under this doctrine, contracting parties have wide latitude to excuse non-performance and renegotiate contract terms. They may argue, for example, that performance is no longer possible because senior management has decided to reduce operations.

Dispute Resolution Legal disputes are better settled through informal negotiation than by lawsuit. Litigation of business disputes is rare because Japanese business owners tend to view a contract as one part of a long-term relationship, and lawsuits are deemed to disrupt social harmony. Parties tend to either forgive minor contract breaches or renegotiate terms. However, some Japanese business owners may be more amenable to suing foreigners than to suing another Japanese company.

If negotiation is impossible, parties may try to arbitrate. Arbitration is more common than litigation, but less common than informal negotiations. Arbitration is usually before the Japan Commercial Arbitration Association (JCAA). Such proceedings may be as lengthy and as expensive as a lawsuit. Most JCAA arbitrators are Japanese, and awards are written in Japanese. Foreigner businesses may prefer to seek arbitration outside Japan through, for example, the American Arbitration Association or, a more expensive alternative, the International Chamber of Commerce.

Even if a court action is brought, Japanese courts commonly require parties to compromise and settle contract disputes. (*See* Conciliation.) If an award is made, the courts often prefer to grant specific performance, at least to the extent that a party can perform, rather than damages. For example, if A contracts to make 100 widgets for B, but makes only 50, A is in breach of contract. If B sues, the court is likely to ascertain how many widgets A can in fact make and order A to do so. However, regardless of the court's decision, all parties recognize a tacit agreement that the breaching party will continue to perform until the original promise is fulfilled. That is, A will keep making widgets until 100 of them have been provided to B.

Use of Notaries Notaries, most of whom are retired judges or attorneys, prepare and authenticate instruments, including articles of incorporation and commercial documents. A notary must prepare instruments in the Japanese language and must keep copies of authenticated instruments for inspection by officials and parties in interest. (*See* Acknowledgments and Notaries Public.)

Intellectual Property Protection Intellectual property and trademark protection is more assured in Japan than in other Asian countries, but is still more difficult than in the United States. Two aspects of intellectual property and trademark protection are of particular importance to business operator—se-

curing rights and enforcing them.

No application is required to secure copyright protection in Japan. A copyright arises automatically on creation of a copyrightable item, and infringement is considered a violation of the author's moral rights, as well as a criminal offense. Copyright law thus emphasizes enforcement, as opposed to registration, for protection of copyrights. (*See* Copyright .)

Application and receipt of a patent in Japan is a long process, requiring months of government examination and public notice. Public objections to a patent application may further delay registration. A patent term is short, generally no longer than 20 years from the application date, and in complex cases nearly half that term may elapse before the patent is granted. An applicant may claim against an infringer only after public disclosure of the application, which may occur up to 18 months after the application is filed. Compensation for infringement is limited to an amount equal to royalties. (*See* Patents.)

Japan's trademark registration process is also slow, requiring almost three years. Trademarks are acquired on a "first in time, first in right" basis, meaning that whoever first applies to register a trademark, owns it, regardless of who is producing and marketing a product. Thus, as soon as a foreign company that might do business in Japan receives an exclusive trademark right in its own country, it should consider filing for registration in Japan. A foreign business operator should also negotiate contract terms to prohibit other contracting parties from using an established trademark. (*See* Trademark and Trade Names.)

Enforcement of intellectual property and trademark rights in Japan is difficult but not impossible. Courts are overburdened with cases, and trial procedures are fairly complex. Negotiation and arbitration should be considered as alternatives to resolve infringement disputes.

RELATED CHAPTERS

Refer to "Taxation" chapters for a discussion of tax issues, and to "Business Travel" chapter for details on immigration and visa requirements.

Foreign Corrupt Practices Act

United States business owners are subject to the Foreign Corrupt Practices Act (FCPA). The FCPA makes it unlawful for any United States citizen or firm (or any person who acts on behalf of a US citizen or firm) to use a means of US interstate commerce (examples: mail, telephone, telegram, or electronic mail) to offer, pay, transfer, promise to pay or transfer, or authorize a payment, transfer, or promise of money or anything of value to any foreign appointed or elected government official, foreign political party, or candidate for a foreign political office for a corrupt purpose (that is, to influence a discretionary act or decision of the official) and for the purpose of obtaining or retaining business.

It is also unlawful for a US business owner to make such an offer, promise, payment, or transfer to any person if the US business owner knows, or has reason to know, that the person will offer, give, or promise directly or indirectly all or any part of the payment to a foreign government official, political party, or candidate. For purposes of the FCPA, the term *knowledge* means *actual knowledge*—the business owner in fact knew that the offer, payment, or transfer was included in the transaction—and *implied knowledge* means the business owner should have known from the facts and circumstances of a transaction that the agent paid a bribe but failed to carry out a reasonable investigation into the transaction. A business owner should make a reasonable investigation into a transaction if, for example, the sales representative requests a higher commission on a particular sale for no apparent reason, the buyer is a foreign government, the product has a military use, or the buyer's country is one in which bribes are considered customary in business relationships.

The FCPA also contains provisions applicable to US publicly-held companies concerning financial record keeping and internal accounting controls.

Legal Payments

The provisions of the FCPA do not prohibit payments made to *facilitate* a routine government action. A facilitating payment is one made in connection with an action that a foreign official must perform as part of the job. In comparison, a corrupt payment is made to influence an official's discretionary decision. For example, payments are not generally considered corrupt if made to cover an official's overtime required to expedite the processing of export documentation for a legal shipment of merchandise or to cover the expense of additional crew to handle a shipment.

A person charged with violating FCPA provisions may assert as a defense that the payment was lawful under the written laws and regulations of the foreign country and therefore was not for a corrupt purpose. Alternatively, a person may contend that the payment was associated with demonstrating a product or performing a preexisting contractual obligation and therefore was not for obtaining or retaining business.

Enforcing Agencies and Penalties

Criminal Proceedings The Department of Justice prosecutes criminal proceedings for FCPA violations. Firms are subject to a fine of up to US$2 million. Officers, directors, employees, agents, and stockholders are subject to fines of up to US$100,000, imprisonment for up to five years, or both.

A US business owner may also be charged under other federal criminal laws, and on conviction may be liable for fines of up to US$250,000 or up to twice the amount of the gross gain or gross loss, provided the defendant derived pecuniary gain from the offense or caused pecuniary loss to another person.

Civil Proceedings Two agencies are responsible for enforcing civil provisions of the FCPA: the Department of Justice handles actions against domestic concerns, and the Securities and Exchange Commission (SEC) files actions against issuers. Civil fines of up to US$100,000 may be imposed on a firm; any officer, director, employee, or agent of a firm; or any stockholder acting for a firm. In addition, the appropriate government agency may seek an injunction against a person or firm that has violated or is about to violate FCPA provisions.

Conduct that constitutes a violation of FCPA provisions may also give rise to a cause of action under the federal Racketeer-Influenced and Corrupt Organizations Act, as well as under a similar state statute if enacted in the state with jurisdiction over the US business owner.

Administrative Penalties A person or firm that is held to have violated any FCPA provisions may be barred from doing business with the US government. Indictment alone may result in suspension of the right to do business with the government.

Department of Justice Opinion Procedure

Any person may request the Department of Justice to issue a statement of opinion on whether specific proposed business conduct would be considered a violation of the FCPA. The opinion procedure is detailed in 28 C.F.R. Part 77. If the Department of Justice issues an opinion stating that certain conduct conforms with current enforcement policy, conduct in accordance with that opinion is presumed to comply with FCPA provisions.

International Sales Contract Provisions

When dealing internationally, you must consider the business practices and legal requirements of the country where the buyer or seller is located. For a small, one-time sale, an invoice may be commonly accepted. For a more involved business transaction, a formal written contract may be preferable to define clearly the rights, responsibilities, and remedies of all parties. The laws of your country or the foreign country may require a written contract and may even specify all or some of the contract terms. Refer to Contracts and to Sales for specific laws on contracts and the sale of goods.

Parties generally have freedom to agree to any contract terms that they desire. Whether a contract term is valid in a particular country is of concern only if you have to seek enforcement. Thus, you have fairly broad flexibility in negotiating contract terms. However, you should always be certain to come to a definite understanding on four issues: the goods (quantity, type, quality); the time of delivery; the price; and the time of payment.

You need to consider the following clauses when you negotiate an international sales contract.

Contract date

State the date when the contract is signed. This date is particularly important if payment or delivery times are fixed in reference to it—for example, "shipment within 30 days of the contract date."

Identification of parties

Designate the names of the parties, and describe their relation to each other.

Goods

Description Describe the type and quality of the goods. You may simply indicate a model number, or you may have to attach detailed lists, plans, or drawings. This clause should be clear enough that both parties fully understand the specifications and have no discretion in interpreting them.

Quantity Specify the number of units, or other measure of quantity, of the goods. If the goods are measured by weight, you should specify net weight, dry weight, or drained weight. If the goods are prepack-

aged and are subject to weight restrictions in the end market, you may want to provide that the seller will ensure that the goods delivered will comply with those restrictions.

Price Indicate the price per unit or other measure, such as per pound or ton, and the extended price.

Packaging arrangements

Set forth packaging specifications, especially for goods that can be damaged in transit. At a minimum, this provision should require the seller to package the goods in such a way as to withstand transportation. If special packaging requirements are necessary to meet consumer and product liability standards in the end market, you should specify them also.

Transportation arrangements

Carrier Name a preferred carrier for transporting the goods. You should designate a particular carrier if, for example, a carrier offers you special pricing or is better able than others to transport the product.

Storage Specify any particular requirements for storage of the goods before or during shipment, such as security arrangements, special climate demands, and weather protection needs.

Notice provisions Require the seller to notify the buyer when the goods are ready for delivery or pickup, particularly if the goods are perishable or fluctuate in value. If your transaction is time-sensitive, you could even provide for several notices to allow the buyer to track the goods and take steps to minimize damages if delivery is delayed.

Shipping time State the exact date for shipping or provide for shipment within a reasonable time from the contract date. If this clause is included and the seller fails to ship on time, the buyer may claim a right to cancel the contract, even if the goods have been shipped, provided that the buyer has not yet accepted delivery.

Costs and charges

Specify which party is to pay the additional costs and charges related to the sale.

International Sales Contract Provisions (cont'd.)

IDuties and taxes Designate the party that will be responsible for import, export, and other fees and taxes and for obtaining all required licenses. For example, a party may be made responsible for paying the duties, taxes, and charges imposed by that party's own country, since that party is best situated to know the legal requirements of that country.

Insurance costs Identify the party that will pay costs of insuring the goods in transit. This is a critical provision because the party responsible bears the risk if the goods are lost during transit. A seller is typically responsible for insurance until title to the goods passes to the buyer, at which time the buyer becomes responsible for insurance or becomes the named beneficiary under the seller's insurance policy.

Handling and transport Specify the party that will pay shipping, handling, packaging, security, and any other costs related to transportation, which should be specified.

Terms defined Explain the meaning of all abbreviations—for example, FAS (free alongside ship), FOB (free on board), CIF (cost, insurance, and freight)—used in your contract to assign responsibility and costs for goods, transportation, and insurance. If you define your own terms, you can make the definitions specific to your own circumstances and needs. As an alternative, you may agree to adopt a particular standard, such as the Revised American Foreign Trade Definitions or Incoterms 1990. In either case, this clause should be clear enough that both parties understand when each is responsible for insuring the goods.

Insurance or risk of loss protection

Specify the insurance required, the beneficiary of the policy, the party who will obtain the insurance, and the date by which it will have been obtained.

Payment provisions

Provisions for payment vary with such factors as the length of the relationship between the contracting parties, the extent of trust between them, and the availability of certain forms of payment within a particular country. A seller will typically seek the most secure form of payment before committing to shipment, while a buyer wants the goods cleared through customs and delivered in satisfactory condition before remitting full payment.

Method of payment State the means by which payment will be tendered—for example, prepayment in cash, traveler's checks, or bank check; delivery of a documentary letter of credit or documents against payment; credit card, credit on open account, or credit for a specified number of days.

Medium of exchange Designate the currency to be use —for example, US currency, currency of the country of origin, currency of a third country.

Exchange rate Specify a fixed exchange rate for the price stated in the contract. You may use this clause to lock in a specific price and ensure against fluctuating currency values.

Import documentation

Require that the seller be responsible for presenting to customs all required documentation for the shipment.

Inspection rights

Provide that the buyer has a right to inspect goods before taking delivery to determine whether the goods meet the contract specifications. This clause should specify the person who will do the inspection—for example, the buyer, a third party, a licensed inspector; the location where the inspection will occur—for example at the seller's plant, the buyer's warehouse, a receiving dock; the time at which the inspection will occur; the need for a certified document of inspection; and any requirements related to the return of nonconforming goods, such as payment of return freight by the seller.

Warranty provisions

Limit or extend any implied warranties, and define any express warranties on property fitness and quality. The contract may, for example, state that the seller warrants that the goods are of merchantable quality, are fit for any purpose for which they would ordinarily be used, or are fit for a particular purpose requested by the buyer. The seller may also warrant that the goods will be of the same quality as any sample or model that the seller has furnished as representative of the goods. Finally, the seller may warrant that the goods will be packaged in a specific way or in a way that will adequately preserve and protect the goods.

Indemnity

Agree that one party will hold the other harmless from damages that arise from specific causes, such as the design or manufacture of a product.

Enforcement and Remedies

Time is of the essence Provide that timely performance of the contract is essential. The inclusion of this clause allows a party to claim breach merely because the other party fails to perform within the time prescribed in the contract. Common in United States contracts, a clause of this type is considered less important in other countries.

Modification Require the parties to make all changes to the contract in advance and in a signed written modification.

Cancellation State the reasons for which either party may cancel the contract and the notice required for cancellation.

Contingencies Specify any events that must occur before a party is obligated to perform the contract. For example, you may agree that the seller has no duty to ship goods until the buyer forwards documents that secure the payment for the goods.

Governing law Choose the law of a specific jurisdiction to control any interpretation of the contract terms. The law that you choose will usually affect where you can sue or enforce a judgment and what rules and procedures will be applied.

Choice of forum Identify the place where a dispute may be settled—for example, the country of origin of the goods, the country of destination, a third country that is convenient to both parties.

Arbitration provisions Agree to arbitration as an alternative to litigation for the resolution of any disputes that arise. You should agree to arbitrate only if you seriously intend to settle disputes in this way. If you agree to arbitrate but later file suit, the court is likely to uphold the arbitration clause and force you to settle your dispute as you agreed under the contract.

An arbitration clause should specify whether arbitration is binding or nonbinding on the parties; the place where arbitration will be conducted (which should be a country that has adopted a convention for enforcing arbitration awards, such as the United Nations Convention on Recognition and Enforcement of Foreign Awards); the procedure by which an arbitration award may be enforced; the rules governing the arbitration, such as the United Nations Commission on International Trade Law Model Rules; the institute that will administer the arbitration, such as the International Chamber of Commerce (Paris), the American Arbitration Association (New York), the Japan Commercial Arbitration Association, the United Nations Economic and Social Commission for Asia and the Pacific, the London Court of Arbitration, or the United Nations Commission International Trade Law; the law that will govern procedural issues or the merits of the dispute; any limitations on the selection of arbitrators (for example, a national of a disputing party may be excluded from being an arbitrator); the qualifications or expertise of the arbitrators; the language in which the arbitration will be conducted; and the availability of translations and translators if needed.

Severability Provide that individual clauses can be removed from the contract without affecting the validity of the contract as a whole. This clause is important because it provides that, if one clause is declared invalid and unenforceable for any reason, the rest of the contract remains in force.

Legal Glossary

Agent The person authorized to act on behalf of another person (the principal). Example: A sales representative is an agent of the seller.

Attachment The legal process for seizing property before a judgment to secure payment of damages if awarded. This process is also referred to as sequestration. Example: a party who claims damages for breach of contract may request a court to issue an order freezing all transfers of specific funds or property owned by the breaching party pending resolution of the dispute.

Authentication The act of conferring legal authenticity on a written document, typically made by a notary public who attests and certifies that the document is in proper legal form and that it is executed by a person identified as having authority to do so.

Bill of exchange A written instrument signed by a person (the drawer) and addressed to another person (the drawee), usually a bank, ordering the drawee to pay unconditionally a stated sum of money to yet another person (the payee) on demand or at a future time.

Composition with creditors An agreement between an insolvent debtor and one or more creditors under which the creditors consent to accept less than the total amount of their claims in order to secure immediate payment.

Crossed check A check that is stamped with the name of a specific bank to which the check must be presented.

Droit moral Moral right doctrine. A European legal theory that gives artists certain rights with respect to their works, including the right to create, disclose, and publish a work; to withdraw it from publication; to be identified as its creator; and to prevent its alteration without permission.

Emphyteusis A tenant's right to enjoy property owned by another individual or legal entity for a lengthy time and for rent as if the tenant owned it. The tenant may, and is usually expected to, improve the property. The tenant may also demise, assign, or otherwise transfer his or her interest in the property, but the tenant must preserve the property from destruction.

Execution The legal process for enforcing a judgment for damages, usually by seizure and sale of the debtor's personal property. Example: if a court awards damages in a breach of contract action and the breaching party has failed to remit the sum due, the party awarded damages may request the court to order seizure and sale of the breaching party's inventory to the extent necessary to satisfy the award.

Ex parte By one party or side only. Example: an application ex parte is a request that is made by only one of the parties involved in an action.

Force majeure A superior force. An event that is beyond the reasonable control of the parties to a contract, that adversely affects performance of the contract, and that therefore constitutes an excuse for breach. Example: a force majeure may be a natural disaster, labor strike, declaration of involuntary bankruptcy, or the failure of subcontractors to perform.

Inter absentee Among absent parties. Example: an inter absentee contract is made between parties who do not meet face to face.

Joint and several liability The liability of two or more persons who are responsible together and individually, allowing the person harmed to sue all or any of the wrongdoers.

Juridical person An individual or entity recognized under law as having legal rights and obligations. Example: companies, corporations, and partnerships are entities that are recognized as juridical persons.

Mala fide In bad faith.

Negotiable instrument A written document that can be transferred merely by endorsement or delivery. Example: a check or bill of exchange is a negotiable instrument.

Power of attorney A written document by which one person (the principal) authorizes another person (the agent) to perform stated acts on the principal's behalf. Example: a principal may execute a special power of attorney authorizing an agent to sign a specific contract or a general power of attorney authorizing the agent to sign all contracts for the principal.

Prima facie Presumption of fact as true unless contradicted by other evidence. Example: if a debtor stops paying the debts owed, that suspension constitutes prima facie evidence that the debtor cannot pay the debts and is bankrupt.

Principal A person who authorizes another party (the agent) to act on the principal's behalf.

Promoter of corporation The individual or entity that organizes a corporation.

Real rights Rights in real estate or in items attached to real estate.

Rescind A contracting party's right to cancel the contract. Example: a contract may give one party a right to rescind if the other party fails to perform within a reasonable time.

Rescission *See* Rescind.

Sequestration *See* Attachment.

Servitude A charge against or burden on property that benefits other property. Example: an owner of property may grant another person a right to travel over that property for a particular purpose, in which case the owner has created a servitude against the property.

Sight draft An instrument payable on demand. Example: a bill of exchange may be made payable at sight (that is, payable on demand) or after sight (that is, payable within a particular period after demand is made).

Statute of Frauds A law that requires designated documents to be in writing in order to be enforced by a court. Example: corporate instruments must be in writing to be recognized and upheld in court.

Superficies Rights to build on the surface of real property. Example: a landowner may transfer to a developer the right to build on the property in exchange for an annual rent, in which case the property becomes subject to superficies.

Vis major A major force or disturbance, usually a natural cause, that a person cannot prevent despite the exercise of due care.

LAW DIGEST

(Abbreviations used are: B.L. for Bankruptcy Law; C. for Constitution; C.C. for Civil Code; C.L. for Copyright Law; C.C.P. for Code of Civil Procedures; C.E.L. for Civil Execution Law; Com. C. for Commercial Code; C.P.E.L. for Civil Preliminary Execution Law; F.E.C.L. for Foreign Exchange and Foreign Trade Control Law; L.B.N. for Law of Bills and Notes; L.C. for Law of Checks; L.C.L. for Limited Corporation Law; P.L. for Patent Law; T.L. for Trademark Law.)

ABSENTEES

Subject to such restrictions as may be imposed under foreign exchange controls, nonresidents are permitted to own and utilize property to same degree as residents. Authority may be exercised by proper power of attorney.

Care of property, if not specifically entrusted by voluntary act of owner, can be directed by court order. (C.C. 25). Persons assuming control over property without legal duty are held responsible to strict standards of conduct. (C.C. 697).

Service of process may be made on agents in respect to matters within their scope of authority.

ACKNOWLEDGMENTS

Formality of acknowledgment is not, as a rule, essential to validity of an instrument. However, acknowledgment of notary authenticates the performance of a legal action and the identity of acting parties, and thereby affords to an otherwise private instrument a presumption of genuineness which is similar to that of an official document. Acknowledgment of original articles of incorporation in case of organization of joint stock corporations and limited corporations is made mandatory by statute. (Com. C. 167; L.C.L. 5). Frequently instruments to be recorded are both drafted and certified by notaries. *See* Notaries Public.

At present time, acknowledgments for use in US or by US citizens or corporations may be taken before American consular officials and certain designated Army officers. Acknowledgments for use in other countries usually may be taken by diplomatic representatives of those countries who are accredited to Japanese government. Japan is party to Convention Abolishing the Requirement of Legalization for Foreign Public Documents.

ALIENS

Supported by strong constitutional guarantees, an alien is now afforded virtually all rights of a Japanese except those of political nature. In general aliens are permitted to own property and to contract without governmental approvals but cannot practice professions of quasi-public character. Aliens must register at municipal offices having jurisdiction over their places of stay within 90 days from entry. (Alien Registration Law 3). Entrance into country is subject to governmental approval except for members of US Armed Forces, UN's agencies, diplomats, consuls and their dependents, and public officials of foreign governments and international organizations recognized by Japan. Alien has equal access to courts, but in case of certain kinds of tort actions against Japanese government, he is equally treated only if country of his nationality extends same right to Japanese nationals. (State Tort Claims Act 6).

Acquisitions of real estate or rights related thereto by nonresident aliens involve advance notification and possible issuance of recommendation of or order for alteration of contents or suspension of notified acquisition. In case of certain extraordinary circumstances such acquisition may be made subject to approval. (F.E.C.L. 20 through 23).

Corporations owned or controlled by aliens are regarded as "foreign investors" for purpose of inward direct investments including acquisition of shares. (F.E.C.L. 26). *See* Foreign Investments. *See also* Corporations, subhead Foreign Corporations.

ASSIGNMENTS

Assignment of property right, whether real or personal property, may be made by means of agreement between parties. (C.C. 176). However, in order for assignment to be effective against third persons, assignment of immovables must be recorded, and those of movables must be accompanied by delivery. (C.C. 177, 178). Obligations may be assigned if their character renders assignment possible, unless parties have expressed contrary intention. (C.C. 466). Specifically named obligee must give notice of assignment to obligor or secure his consent in order to assert assignment against either obligor or other third party. Notice of assignment or consent to assignment must be in writing and bear officially confirmed date in order to assert assignment against third party other than obligor. (C.C. 467).

ASSIGNMENTS FOR BENEFIT OF CREDITORS

See Bankruptcy.

ASSOCIATIONS

See Corporations.

ATTACHMENT AND INJUNCTIONS

Attachment is available before judgment (or even before institution of an action) upon proof (a) of existence of creditor's claim for money, and (b) that satisfaction of judgment will be impossible or extremely difficult unless attachment occurs. (C.P.E.L. 20). Attachment normally is issued ex parte without examination of or notice to debtor and as general rule requires posting by creditor of bond to secure debtor. (C.P.E.L.14). Attachment order may be attacked by debtor on ground that it was issued without any reason, that it has been rendered unnecessary by change in circumstances, and that action on principal claim was not instituted within proper and prescribed period of time. (C.P.E.L. 26). Attachment may be dissolved by deposit of prescribed amount in cash. (C.P.E.L. 32). Same general procedures apply to injunctions.

BANKRUPTCY

Term "insolvency" as used in Bankruptcy Law has restricted meaning of simply debtor's inability to make payments. (B.L. 126). Joint stock company's inability to pay its debts without resulting great difficulty in continuing its business also forms basis for institution of extensive reorganization processes under Company Reorganization Law. (Company Reorganization Law 30). Fear of insolvency on reasonable ground can be basis for still other reorganization procedures under Commercial Code. (Com. C. 381).

Petitions Bankruptcy proceedings are instituted through petition to district court having jurisdiction over principal place of business or legal residence of debtor who may be either natural person or juridical person. (B.L. 105). Petitions may be made by creditors or by debtor himself. (B.L. 132). In case of legal person its director or liquidator also may make petition. (B.L. 133). Ground for bankruptcy is debtor's inability to make payments, or (in case of legal person) excess of liabilities over assets. (B.L. 126, 127). Debtor's suspension of payments on debts is treated as prima facie evidence of inability to make payments.

Administration Upon adjudication of bankruptcy, court appoints a receiver, orders report of claims and requires assembly of creditors. (B.L. 142).

Assembly of creditors may appoint advisers to receiver, grant allowances to debtor, make decisions regarding continuation of business operations, and consent to important acts in liquidation of bankrupt estate. (B.L. 170, 194). As consequence of adjudication of bankruptcy, bankrupt person is immediately deprived of control over such of his property as is subject to legal attachment. (B.L. 6, 7).

Outstanding Obligations Obligations of bankrupt to third parties become due upon adjudication of bankruptcy. (B.L. 17). If performance of both parties to outstanding bilateral contract has not been completed, receiver may rescind such contract or demand performance by opposite party after performing bankrupt's obligation. (B.L. 59). Opposite party to bilateral contracts may call on receiver to make election regarding performance or rescission, and in event of failure of answer within reasonable period, rescission is presumed. (B.L. 59).

Powers of Receiver Power to administer and dispose of bankrupt estate belongs exclusively to receiver. (B.L. 7). Receiver represents bankrupt estate in litigation. (B.L. 162). Application may be made to him for restoration of property of third persons and also for payment of preferential claims against bankrupt estate in general or existing in regard to specific items of property included therein. He also may institute action to disapprove legal acts of debtor taken before issuance of adjudication of bankruptcy which were intended to prejudice creditors. (B.L. 72).

Preferential Payment Lien holders, mortgagees or pledgees on specific property included in bankrupt estate are entitled to be satisfied separately from such property outside receiver's control and to participate in bankruptcy proceedings only to extent of any deficiency. (B.L. 92 through 96). Persons whose own: property has come under receiver's control as bankrupt estate can regain such property from his control. (B.L. 87 through 91). Certain tax liabilities of bankrupt person can be paid by receiver outside of bankruptcy proceedings. (B.L. 47, 49). After these preferential treatments and payments are completed, lien holders on general property of bankrupt person receive distributions preferentially from bankrupt estate ahead of ordinary creditors. (B.L. 39). Receiver may deny and restore to bankruptcy estate repayments by bankrupt persons to creditors at certain time prior to occurrence of insolvency or application filed for bankruptcy or those simply prior to adjudication of bankruptcy if mala fide on part of repaid creditor is proven to affect adversely other creditors. (B.L. 72 et seq.).

Illegal Preferences *See* subheads Powers of Receiver and Preferential Payment, supra.

Termination Normally bankruptcy proceedings are terminated with distribution of assets to creditors. Distributions may be intermediate, final or supplemental. (B.L. 256 et seq.). However, decree in bankruptcy may be dissolved with consent of all creditors. (B.L. 347 et seq.). Bankruptcy proceedings also may be ended upon judicial finding that value of bankrupt estate is not sufficient to repay costs of liquidation. (B.L. 353, 145). When value of bankrupt estate is less than 1,000,000 yen a simplified form of procedure called "petty bankruptcy" may be followed in which court decisions replace many actions of assembly of creditors. (B L. 358 through 366).

Disabilities of Bankrupt Persons A person against whom an adjudication of bankruptcy is outstanding is subject to certain losses of rights, such as right to hold public office, and to practice law. However, these disabilities may be removed by court decree of rehabilitation in event of full payment of indebtedness, decision of discharge, or lapse of ten years without being punished for fraudulent bankruptcy. (B.L. 366-2l, 367).

Composition Compulsory composition is provided whereby debtors may apply to a court with alternative plan for continuation of business and thereby halt bankruptcy proceeding. (B.L. 290 et seq.). Decisions for compulsory composition made by majority of creditors present at assembly of creditors holding three-fourths of total obligations of debtor are binding upon other creditors. (B.L. 306, also see 332).

Reorganization A reorganization proceeding permits creditors and shareholders of joint stock corporations to present plan for reorganization of company to court for approval. Decisions made by majority (usually from one-half to four-fifths) of each class of creditors, shareholders or mortgagors are binding upon all persons within that class. (Company Reorganization Law, also see Com. C. 381 through 403).

Foreigners Bankruptcy procedures apply uniformly to Japanese and foreigners, provided that a Japanese is afforded reciprocal treatment by law of country of foreigner concerned. Effect of bankruptcy adjudications is limited to property found in Japan, both in cases of Japanese and foreigners. (B.L. 2, 3).

BILLS AND NOTES

In Japan bills (Tegata) are classified as bills of exchange (Kawase Tegata) and promissory notes (Yakusoku Tegata) and are distinguished from checks (Kogitte). Japanese law in regard to bills, notes and checks is in conformity with Geneva International Conventions on Uniform Law of 1930 and 1931.

Bills of Exchange

Essential provisions of a bill of exchange are: (1) Expression "bill of exchange" in body of instrument, (2) unconditional order for payment of fixed sum of money, (3) name of drawee, (4) designation of maturity, (5) designation of place for payment, (6) name of payee, (7) date and place where bill of exchange is drawn, and (8) signature of drawer. Lack of any of above-mentioned elements is fatal except that: (a) Payment is deemed to be at sight when no maturity is designated, (b) if no place of payment is designated but name of drawee is accompanied by place, such place is, unless otherwise indicated, deemed to be place of payment and residence of drawee, and (c) place of issue is deemed to be stated address of drawer. Bill of exchange may be payable to drawer, his order, or for account of third person. (L.B.N. 1 through 3).

Endorsements may be either in blank or contain a designation. They must be unconditional. Even though not drawn to order, every bill of exchange may be transferred by endorsement. Acceptance and payment is guaranteed by endorsement. (L.B.N. 11 through 13, 15).

Presentment for acceptance of bills payable at expiration of fixed period after sight must occur with one year after date of issuance. Presentment must be at residence of drawee and at a time prescribed by drawer or endorsers. (L.B.N. 21 through 23).

Acceptance may occur simply from signature of drawee on face of instrument. When bill is payable at expiration of fixed period after sight, acceptance must be dated. Acceptance may be for part of sum payable, but must be unconditional. Third party may guarantee payment of bill—act accomplished simply by his signature on face of instrument. (L.B.N. 25, 26, 30, 31).

Payment of bill of exchange may be: (1) At sight, (2) at expiration of fixed period after sight, (3) expiration of fixed period after issue date, and (4) at fixed date. (L.B.N. 33). Bill of exchange at sight is payable on presentment and presentment must occur within one year of date of issuance. (L.B.N. 34). Holder of bill of exchange payable on fixed date or at expiration of fixed period after issue date or sight must present for payment within two business days following due date. (L.B.N. 38). There are no days of grace. (L.B.N. 74). Unless specially provided payment is to be in currency of country where payment will occur, although rate of exchange and similar matters may be specified. (L.B.N. 41). Words prevail over figures in event of discrepancy as to amount, and as between more than one amount in either figures or words, smallest sum is deemed sum payable. (L.B.N. 6).

Recourse may be had by holder of bill of exchange against endorsers, drawer and other parties if payment has not been made at maturity. Holder has similar right before maturity: (1) If there has been total or partial refusal of acceptance, (2) if drawee has become bankrupt, or (3) if drawer (of nonacceptable bill) has become bankrupt. (L.B.N. 43). Default must be established through an officially authenticated instrument.

Except for bill of exchange payable at sight, protest for nonpayment must come within two business days after bill is payable. (L.B.N. 44). Holder must give notice of nonacceptance or nonpayment within four business days, and endorser must relay information to person from whom he received bill within two business days following date of notice. (L.B.N. 45).

Liability of persons signing bill is not affected by invalidity of one or more signatures of other persons thereon. (L.B.N.7). Person signing bill as agent is personally bound if lacking in authority. (L.B.N. 8). Both acceptance and payment are guaranteed by drawer, although by specific provision in bill the former responsibility may be escaped. (L.B.N. 9).

All drawers, acceptors, endorsers and guarantors are jointly and severally liable to holder who may proceed individually or collectively in any order. (L.B.N. 47). Holder's recovery includes amount of unpaid bill, interest at 6 percent per annum from maturity, and expenses. (L.B.N. 48, 49). Upon expiration of time limits set for presentment for protest or presentment for payment, holder loses rights of recourse against all parties other than acceptor. (L.B.N. 53). Presentment prevented by vis major or legal prohibition may be made at later date after termination of cause for delay. (L.B.N. 54).

Capacity of person to bind himself is determined by law of the country of his nationality, except that person lacking capacity nevertheless is bound if his signature is affixed in a country wherein he would have capacity. (L.B.N. 88). Acts performed by Japanese in foreign countries are valid as against other Japanese if in accordance with Japanese law. (L.B.N. 89). Laws of foreign country will govern in regard to obligations of acceptor as well as formalities for protest, when location of payment or act of protest is in that foreign country. (L.B.N. 90, 93).

Claims of holder arising out of bill of exchange expire three years from date of maturity as against acceptor, and one year from date of protest as against endorsers and drawer. Claims of endorser against other endorsers expire six months from date of payment or suit by endor.*See*. (L.B.N. 70).

Promissory Notes Essential provisions of a promissory note are: (1) Expression "promissory note" in body of instrument, (2) unconditional promise to pay fixed sum of money, (3) designation of maturity, (4) designation of place for payment, (5) name of payee, (6) date and place of issuance, (7) signature of maker. (L.B.N. 75). As in case of bills of exchange, lack of essential elements renders instrument invalid save in certain exceptional cases. (L.B.N. 76). Rules governing bills of exchange are made applicable by analogy to promissory notes. (L.B.N. 77).

Checks Essential provisions of a check are: (1) Expression "check" in body of instrument, (2) unconditional order to pay fixed sum of money,

(3) name of drawee, (4) designation of place of payment, (5) date and place where check is drawn, and (6) signature of drawer. (L.C. I). Lack of enumerated elements renders check invalid, except in instances similar to those governing bills of exchange. (L.C. 2). Check must be drawn on banker holding funds at disposal of drawer. (L.C. 3). Check is payable at sight. (L.C. 28). It must be presented for payment within ten days after issuance if in country of issuance, within 20 days if place of issue and payment are to same continent, and 70 days when places are in different continents. (L.C. 29). Crossed check may be paid by drawee only to banker or to customer of drawee. (L.C. 38).

Claims of holder against endorsers, drawer and other parties to check expire six months from last day of period in which presentment must be made, and claims of parties to check other than holder, such as endorsers, against other parties, such as other endorsers, expire six months from date of payment by or suit against such claimants. (L.C. 51). There is no acceptance. (L.C. 4). Subject to above-mentioned differences, provisions of law governing checks are similar to those pertaining to bills of exchange.

Special simplified civil procedures are provided for certain actions arising out of bills, notes and checks. (C.C.P. 444 through 463). Evidence in special procedures is exclusively documentary, except for testimony of parties regarding authenticity of instrument and fact of its presentation. In these procedures, defendant's cross-action is not allowed. Plaintiff may shift to ordinary procedures at any time during trial. No appeal is allowed from final judgment that issues under special procedures, but losing party has opportunity to have case retried under ordinary procedures. A monetary judgment on bill, note or check, whether issuing after ordinary or special procedures, always is accompanied by provisional execution order. (C.C.P. 196). Actions may be brought in court having geographical jurisdiction over place of payment designated on instrument, in addition to court of jurisdiction over place where obligor resides or has an office. (C.C.P. 2, 4, 6).

Revenue stamps must be affixed to bills and notes (but not checks) having face amount of 100,000 yen or more by drawer. Stamp tax rate varies with face amount. If amounts are stated in foreign currency, flat rate of 200 yen is applied. Failure to affix revenue stamps does not affect validity of documents, but does expose obligated party to criminal sanctions.

Choice of law rules are provided in Law of Bills and Notes and Law of Checks. (L.B.N. 88 through 94; L.C. 76 through 81). Form of any legal act in respect to bill and note is governed by law of place where instrument signed. (L.B.N. 89; L.C. 78). Validity of acceptance of bills of exchange or issuance of promissory notes is governed by law of place where instruments are payable. (L.B.N. 90). Validity of other acts in respect to bill or note, such as endorsement is governed by law of place of signature affixed. (L.B.N. 90; L.C. 79).

COMMERCIAL REGISTER

See Records.

CONCILIATION

Japanese jurisprudence possesses a highly developed system of conciliation whereby disputes are settled under court supervision but through nonjudicial methods. Parties may request application of conciliation procedures prior to institution of formal actions, and court also may order resort to conciliation at any time in course of formal proceedings, when it appears that such procedures might result in proper settlement. (Civil Conciliation Law 2, 20). Conciliation procedures are simple and relatively inexpensive. Conciliation panel consisting of judge and two or more individuals of good standing hears contentions of both sides and explores possibility of settlement. (Civil Conciliation Law 5 through 7). When agreement satisfactory to both parties is obtained, it has binding and enforceable effect which is similar to compromise accepted by court. (Civil Conciliation Law 16; C.C.P. 203). Conciliation is widely used.

CONTRACTS

A contract is a legal act which creates an obligation by agreement of two or more persons. Both natural and legal persons may be parties to contract. A number of standard forms of contracts, namely, gift, sale, exchange, loan for consumption, loan for use, lease, employment, contract for specific work, mandate, bailment, partnership, life annuity and compromise, are governed by special provisions of Civil Code. Number of standard forms of commercial transactions, namely, sale, account current, undisclosed association, brokerage, commission agency, forwarding agency, carriage, deposit and insurance, are governed by special provisions of Commercial Code. However, these provisions, may be modified by agreement of parties to contract.

Formation A contract arises through acceptance of an offer. An offer which recites a fixed time for acceptance cannot be withdrawn before termination of stated period. (C.C. 521). Dispatch of acceptance gives rise to contract, as also does occurrence of act which can be deemed declaration of intention to accept offer. (C.C. 526). Conditional acceptance of contract offer constitutes both refusal and counter-offer. (C.C. 528). Certain special provisions are applied to commercial transactions. (Com. C. 507 through 509).

Effect Either party to bilateral contract may refuse performance until other party tenders performance, except in situations where obligation to perform has not yet accrued. (C.C. 533). Once created, rights of third parties cannot be extinguished by actions taken by original parties to contract. (C.C. 538). In case of contract for establishment or transfer of real right in specified property, when property is lost or damaged for reasons or cannot be performed for intervening cause not attributable to assignor, loss falls on assignee. (C.C. 534).

Rescission Right of rescission may arise out of terms of contract, or by operation of law. Normally its exercise is preceded by a formal demand for performance made on delinquent party. (C.C. 541). Rescission serves to restore matters to state in which they were prior to formation of contract. (C.C. 545). Usually it is effected by declaration of intention to opposite party, although this formality is not required in all cases. (C.C. 540). Rescission does not preclude a demand for damages. (C.C. 545). Each of multiple persons who constitute a single party to a contract must join in notice of rescission and each must receive notice of rescission from opposite party. (C.C. 544).

Excuses for Nonperformance With exception of monetary obligation, nonperformance for reasons not attributable to responsibility of obligor, such as force majeure, can be invoked as a defense for nonperformance. (C.C. 415, 419). Unless specifically prohibited by law, such as that of contract for carriage by sea, parties can limit responsibility for nonperformance by special agreement. (C.C. 420; Com. C. 739; International Carriage of Goods by Sea Act 15).

Applicable Law Validity of contract is determined by law of place expressly or implicitly chosen by parties. In event of no choice governing law is that of place of act of creation of contractual relationship. (Horei 7).

Government Contracts In order to produce budgetary conformity, certain special statutory requirements exist for contracts to which government, either national or prefectural, is a party. These provisions generally take form of regulations of actions of government contracting officials, such as requiring competitive bidding, use of written contracts and inclusion therein of certain matters required by law, plus performance bonds of at least 5 percent of amount of contract, which they may waive under certain circumstances. (National Accounting Law 29 through 29-12).

COPYRIGHT

Creation Copyright is afforded automatically without application or grant from government upon creation of object in literary, scientific, artistic or musical field except for certain categories of materials whose free republication is in public interest (as for example, statutes, orders or ordinances of public authorities, official government publications, court decisions, etc.). (C.L. 2, 10, 13). Included are choreography, pantomimes, architectural works, maps, motion pictures, photographs and computer programs. Compilation and data base works can also be copyrighted. Similar to European concept of droit moral, moral rights are afforded to author to protect him from unauthorized use of his work not released to public. (C.L. 18). Moral rights also cover rights to identify author and rights against unauthorized alteration of copyrighted objects and their titles. (C.L. 19, 20). Copyright holder has rights to copy, perform in public, broadcast, recite in public, exhibit, screen, translate and adapt copyrighted objects. (C.L. 21 through 27). Transfer or pledge of copyright takes no effect against third persons unless registered at Ministry of Education or agent designated by Ministry of Education for computer program. (C.L. 77).

Neighboring rights are afforded to performers, phonographic record producers and broadcasters. Performer's rights include rights to record (both audio and video) or broadcast performance, to lease to public commercial phonographic records of performance which were first sold no more than one year before, to request payment for use of commercial phonographic records of performance for broadcast and to request payment for lease to public of commercial phonographic records of performance after one year of first sale. (C.L. 91 through 95-2). Phonographic record producer's rights include rights to reproduce phonographic records, to lease to public commercial phonographic records which he produced and which were first placed on sale no more than one year before, to request payment for use of commercial phonographic records for broadcast and to request payment for lease to public of commercial phonographic records after one year of first sale. (C.L. 96 through 97-2). Broadcaster's rights include rights to reproduce or rebroadcast programs, and to transmit or communicate television programs to public using facilities to enlarge images. (C.L. 98 through 100).

Duration Copyright projection continues for lifetime of author and for 50 years after his death, 50 years after publication if published under a nom de plume or 50 years after publication for works published as product of organization. Copyright protection for motion pictures and photographs lasts 50 years after publication. (C.L. 5l through 55). Moral rights are exercisable only by author. (C.L. 59). However, immediate family of deceased author may petition for injunction or for appropriate measures to recover honor of deceased against infringer of deceased author's moral rights. (C.L. 60, 116). Duration of neighboring rights is 30 years from Jan. 1 next following first performance, first phonographic recording or first broadcasting, as case may be. (C.L. 101). Periods of duration of copyright count from Jan. 1 next following death, creation or publication, as case may be. (C.L. 57).

Publication Copyright holder may create publication right, which is exclusive right to print and distribute original text. Unless otherwise agreed, holder of publication rights must publish within six months after receipt of manuscript and must keep in print if such would be normal in publishing business. (C.L. 81). If holder of publication rights fails to abide by these obligations, copyright holder may rescind publication rights. (C.L. 84). Unless otherwise provided, publication right expires after three years from first publication. (C.L. 83). Publication right is not effective against third persons unless registered at Ministry of Education. (C.L. 88).

Limited assignment of portions of general copyright is possible. (C.L. 61). Thus, all or each of attributes of general copyright such as reproduction rights, translation rights, performance rights, etc. may be assigned. (C.L. 21 through 28, 61, 63).

Infringement of copyright not only gives rise to rights to injunction and damages, but also, if infringement is of moral rights, rights to petition for appropriate measures for recovery of author's honor accrue. (C.L. 112, 115 through 118). Infringement also constitutes criminal offense. (C.L. 119, et seq.).

Copyright Treaties Japan is party to Berne Convention, UNESCO Treaty, Convention for Protection of Producers of Phonograms against Unauthorized Duplication of Their Phonograms and International Convention for the Protection of Performers, Producers of Phonograms and Broadcasting Organizations.

CORPORATIONS

Legal personality may be acquired by means of procedures outlined in Civil Code, Commercial Code, or special acts of legislation, as well as by means of special legislative charter. Although legal persons are classified in many ways such as private and public, or for profit and for public welfare, all are grouped together for convenience under title "corporations."

Legal Persons Under the Civil Code Civil Code recognizes two categories of legal persons (often termed juridical persons) which are organized in public interest—associations (Shadan) and foundations (Zaidan). Association is formed by a group of persons, and is governed by articles of association

prepared at time of its organization. (C.C. 37). Foundation is aggregation of property which has been set aside and dedicated to particular purpose through act of endowment. (C.C. 39). Both associations and foundations must be organized with approval of competent authorities in connection with religious worship, teaching, charity, art, or some similar public purpose. (C.C. 34). Operations of both are subject to supervision of competent authorities, and legal existence of both may be terminated upon completion of dissolution which may be caused upon occurrence of any event specified in articles of association or endowment, or bankruptcy or annulment of approval for incorporation or fulfillment of objective provided in articles of association or endowment or impossibility of such fulfillment. Associations may also be dissolved by resolution of general assembly of members or when no member remains. (C.C. 67, 68). Normally general assembly of members of an association elects directors while directorate of a foundation may either be self-perpetuating (if so provided in original act of endowment) or appointed by court. (C.C. 37, 40). Both associations and foundations can act only through legally authorized officials, and both are liable for damages for acts committed by officials in course of conduct of their duties. (C.C. 44, 53). If any damage has been done to other persons by act beyond scope of business, members and directors having supported resolution for such matter and directors and other representatives having carried it out shall be jointly and severally liable for damage compensation. (C.C. 44).

Business corporations are legal persons organized under Commercial Code and related acts.

Three classes of business corporations or companies are provided by Commercial Code—partnership corporations (Gomei Kaisha), limited partnership corporations (Goshi Kaisha) and joint stock corporations (Kabushiki Kaisha). A special act provides for a limited corporation (Yugen Kaisha) which closely resembles joint stock corporation. (L.C.L.). Each may be organized without special act of government approval through compliance with legal conditions of formation and subsequent registration. All business corporations must establish principal office and register that fact as well as subsequent creation of branch offices. All four varieties of business corporations are subject to judicial dissolution, and as legal persons, all may sue and be sued.

Partnership corporations (Gomei Kaisha) are fundamentally different from Anglo-American partnerships in that new and independent legal personality results from this form of commercial association. (Com. C. 53, 54). Partnership corporation is formed through articles of incorporation which state, among other items, value of contribution to be made by each member of corporation and are signed by each member. (Com. C. 63). Although one or more managers may be appointed through majority vote of members, each member (unless otherwise provided in articles of incorporation) has both right and duty to administer any of affairs of corporation. (Com. C. 70). All members must consent to alteration of articles of incorporation and to transfer of interest of any individual members. (Com. C. 72, 73). Individual members are prohibited from conducting business which competes with that of corporation or assuming official position in a competing concern unless with consent of other members of corporation. (Com. C. 74). All members are jointly and severally liable for obligations of firm in event of insufficiency of assets. (Com. C. 80). Admission to corporation is accompanied by liability for all obligations incurred prior thereto. (Com. C. 82). Members may withdraw at end of any business year with six-month prior notice from partnership corporation whose term is for indefinite period or for life, or from any partnership corporation at any time if unavoidable reasons exist. (Com. C. 84). Membership may be terminated upon consent of all members, or upon death, bankruptcy, adjudication of incompetency and expulsion of individual concerned. (Com. C. 85). Member's failure of contribution constitutes a reason for expulsion. Expulsion requires judicial process. (Com. C. 86). Withdrawing members are entitled to compensation for services rendered and contributions made to partnership corporation. (Com. C. 89). Partnership corporation itself may be dissolved upon expiration of term or happening of any other cause of dissolution provided in articles of incorporation, consent of all members, amalgamation, diminishing of membership to one, bankruptcy or court order. (Com. C. 94). Liquidation is accomplished through legally outlined procedures and under court supervision. (Com. C. 116 et seq.).

Limited Partnership Corporations (Goshi Kaisha) Limited partnership corporation resembles partnership corporation in most respects but differs in that members may have either unlimited or limited liability for corporate obligations. (Com. C. 146). Liability status of each member must be specified in articles of incorporation, and members with limited liability must make their contributions in form of money or property. (Com. C. 148, 150). Members with unlimited liability have rights and duties of representation similar to those of members of partnership corporation, while member with limited liability, although unable to act on behalf of corporation, is entitled to inspect and supervise. (Com. C. 151, 153). Termination of membership by all members of either category is ground for dissolution. (Com. C. 162).

Joint Stock Corporations (Kabushiki Kaisha) This form of corporate organization is most common in business circles and one which most closely resembles Anglo-American stock company or business corporation.

Incorporation requires formulation by one or more promoters of articles of incorporation which provide business object, trade name, number of shares authorized to be issued, number of shares to be issued at time of incorporation (not less than 1/4 of number of shares authorized to be issued) and number of these shares categorized by par value and nonpar value shares, par value per share of par value shares, seat of principal office, manner of giving corporation's public notices and name and residence of each promoter. (Com. C. 165, 166). Par value per share of par value shares and issue price per share of nonpar value shares to be issued at time of incorporation must be not less than 50,000 yen. (Com. C. 166, 168-3). Other matters, such as corporation's duration, special benefits to promoters, contribution in kind, property to be taken over upon incorporation, various classes of shares (preferred, common or deferred and voting or nonvoting), etc., are optional, but not effective unless stated in articles of incorporation. (Com. C. 94, 168, 222). Acknowledgment of articles of incorporation by notary public is mandatory. (Com. C. 167). Capitalization must be ten million yen or over. (Com. C. 168-4). Corporations incorporated prior to Apr. 1, 1991 whose capital amount is below ten million yen are required to meet this requirement by Apr. 1, 1996. Incorporation occurs upon registration which follows inaugural meeting of shareholders. (Com. C. 187). Liability of promoters resulting from acting as promoters in course of incorporation may continue after incorporation. (Com. C. 193). Only promoters are permitted to make payment for stock by property contributions subject to court confirmation of its delivery and valuation. However, if value of contribution is not more than one-fifth of capital and not more than five million yen, or if contribution is marketable securities or real estate evaluated by licensed real estate appraiser and certified by attorney, court confirmation is not required. (Com. C. 168, 172, 173, 181).

Shares may be par value or nonpar value shares, which may in general be exchanged with each other by resolution of board of directors, or upon request of stockholders unless prohibited by articles of incorporation. (Com. C. 199, 213). Shares must be nonbearer form. Unless otherwise provided by articles of incorporation, shareholders who do not wish to possess certificates may require corporation not to issue certificates for their shares. If in such case share certificates have already been issued, such certificates must be returned to corporation. (Com. C. 226-2). Shares are freely transferable, but articles of incorporation may make transfer of shares subject to board of directors' consent. When such consent is not given to specifically proposed transfer, transfer is consummated by procedures provided by Commercial Code. (Com. C. 204, 204-2 through 204-5). Transfer of shares may be effected simply by delivering share certificates, but cannot take effect against corporation unless registered in stockholders' registry. (Com. C. 205, 206). Corporation cannot acquire its own shares nor hold as pledgee its own shares representing more than 1/20 of all the then outstanding shares, and joint stock or limited corporation more than 50 percent of whose shares or contribution is directly or indirectly held by corporation cannot acquire shares of such parent corporation, other than in exceptional circumstances wherein corporation must dispose of them immediately or at proper time. (Com. C. 210, 211-2).

Holder of fractions of share constituting 1/100 of share or its multiples ("fractional share") is registered in fractional stockholders' registry unless he desires not to be so registered. Holder of fractional shares is entitled to certain limited rights as provided by Commercial Code or certain other limited rights if so provided in articles of incorporation. In no event can voting right at general assembly of stockholders be granted. (Com. C. 230-2 through 230-9). Fractional shares emerge in cases of issuance of new shares to shareholders, consolidation or split of shares by corporation of which par value per share of shares or net assets per share on latest balance is 50,000 yen or more.

New shares within number of shares authorized to be issued may be issued at any time by resolution of board of directors or, if articles of incorporation so provided, by stockholders. Issuance of new shares to nonstockholders at particularly favorable price is subject to special approval of stockholders. (Com. C. 280-2). Subscription rights to new shares may be made transferable if subscription warrants are issued. (Com. C. 280-2, 280-6-3).

Stockholder's Liability Once subscription price is paid, subscriber becomes stockholder, and, together with successors or assignees, is not personally liable for debts of corporation. (Com. C. 200).

General assembly of stockholders which is principal organ of corporation is held once each fiscal term in regular sessions and upon call in extraordinary sessions. (Com. C. 234, 235). At regular sessions this assembly approves balance sheet, income statement and disposition of profit and loss, except that in case of corporation having stated capital of 500,000,000 yen or more, or having total liabilities of 20,000,000,000 yen or more on latest balance sheet ("large size corporation"), balance sheet and income statement, when approved by board of directors, auditors and accountant auditor, are not required to be approved by general assembly of stockholders. (Com. C. 283; Law for Special Measures to Commercial Code in respect of Auditing, etc. of Joint Stock

Corporations 16). Each stockholder has one vote for each share. However, corporation is not entitled to vote in respect of its own shares, and neither joint stock corporation nor limited corporation more than 25 percent of whose outstanding shares or contribution is directly or indirectly held by another joint stock corporation is entitled to vote in respect of its shares in such other joint stock corporation. (Com. C. 241). Stockholders holding two or more shares on behalf of others may cast split votes by giving prior notice. (Com. C. 239-2).

Quorum for general assembly cannot be less than one-third of outstanding shares for election of directors or auditors. (Com. C. 256-2, 280). In case of amendment of articles of incorporation, capital decrease, issuance of new shares to nonstockholders at particularly favorable price, issuance of bonds convertible into stock on particularly favorable conversion terms to nonstockholders, merger, transfer of whole or important part of corporation's business or acquisition of whole of business of another corporation, and certain other major resolutions, quorum is more than one-half of outstanding shares in absence of stricter requirement in articles of incorporation. (Com. C. 375, 280-2, 341-2, 408, 245, 343). Quorum for other situations may be provided specially in articles of incorporation. In absence of special provisions in Commercial Code or articles of incorporation, quorum for resolutions is more than one-half of outstanding shares. Except for certain major resolutions which by statute require two-thirds majority vote, resolutions are adopted by simple majority of votes cast, in absence of special provision in articles of incorporation. (Com. C. 239).

Minority stockholders holding not less than 3 percent of outstanding shares for preceding six months are entitled to call general assembly of stockholders, with court permission. (Com. C. 237). Stockholders holding not less than 1 percent of outstanding shares or 300 shares for preceding six months may propose matters to be discussed at general assembly of stockholders. (Com. C. 232-2).

Board of directors takes charge of execution of business operation and supervises performance by individual director of his duties. (Com. C. 260).

Directors must be three or more in number, elected at stockholders' assembly, may hold office for term not in excess of two years (with certain exceptions), and must appoint one or more representative directors from among themselves to represent corporation. (Com. C. 255, 256, 261). Corporation is bound as against third persons acting in good faith for acts done by director with title of president, vice president, senior managing director or managing director even though he is not representative director. (Com. C. 262). Cumulative voting is available for election of two or more directors unless otherwise provided in articles of incorporation. (Com. C. 256-3).

Auditors (Kansayaku) who should not be confused with independent public accountants must be at least one in number, are elected at stockholders' assembly and hold office for term ending upon adjournment of regular assembly of stockholders for last settlement of accounts within two years after assumption of office. (Com. C. 273). Auditors of corporations (excluding those whose stated capital does not exceed 100,000,000 yen and total liabilities are less than 20,000,000,000 yen on latest balance sheet) are entitled to attend board of directors' meetings, have supervisory authority over performance of duties by directors and have duty to examine business and financial condition of corporation and its subsidiaries and financial statements and business report to be submitted to stockholders' assembly and also to report on them. (Com. C. 260-3, 274, 274-3, 275). Large size corporation must have two or more auditors at least one of whom must serve on full-time basis and, in addition, accountant auditor (Kaikei Kansanin), who must be independent certified public accountant and be elected at stockholders' assembly. (Law for Special Measures to Commercial Code in respect of Auditing, etc. of Joint Stock Corporations 2, 3, 18). Accountant auditors investigate financial statements of corporations and submit report thereon to directors and auditors. (Law for Special Measures to Commercial Code in respect of Auditing, etc. of Joint Stock Corporations 13.)

Bonds (straight, convertible or secured, or with warrants to subscribe for new shares) may be issued by, in principle, resolution of board of directors. (Com. C. 296). Amount of bonds cannot exceed lesser of: (i) Stated capital and statutory reserves or (ii) net assets set forth on latest balance sheet. (Com. C. 297). However, in case of straight bonds to be issued in foreign market, secured bonds or convertible bonds above ceiling is increased to two times lesser of (i) or (ii) above. (Provisional Measures Law for Bonds Issue Amount 1). Bonds with warrants to subscribe for new shares may be issued if issue price of shares to be issued upon exercise of such warrants does not exceed principal amount of such bonds. Such warrants may be transferred either with or separately from such bonds, according to their terms. (Com. C. 341-8). Assembly of bondholders may adopt resolutions, with court approval, on matters not provided by statute but which prejudice their interests. (Com. C. 319).

Statutory reserves consist of capital surplus reserve and earned surplus reserve. Capital surplus reserve includes portion of issue price not to be credited against stated capital. (Com. C. 288-2). Such portion is limited to excess over par value or (in case of issue of nonpar value shares at time of incorporation) excess over 50,000 yen and in no event can ex-

ceed one-half of issue price. (Com. C. 284-2). At least one-tenth of distributions paid from profits for each fiscal term and one-tenth of interim cash distribution must be set aside as statutory earned surplus until accumulated amount reaches one-fourth of stated capital. (Com. C. 288). Statutory reserves can be used only for replenishing of deficiencies in stated capital or for capital increase by transfer to stated capital. (Com. C. 289, 293-3).

Dividends for fiscal term can be declared only to extent of amount of net assets, less following: (i) Stated capital, (ii) statutory reserves (capital surplus reserve and earned surplus reserve), (iii) amount of earned surplus reserve required to be retained for fiscal term and (iv) excess, if any, of unamortized deferred accounts for business commencement or for research and development over aggregate of amounts referred to in (ii) and (iii). (Com. C. 290). In addition, corporation which closes its accounts only once a year may, if articles of incorporation so provide and certain other conditions are met, make interim cash distribution to stockholders by resolution of board of directors. In case of interim cash distribution, net assets are calculated by reference to latest balance sheet, but adjusted to reflect any subsequent dividend and earned surplus reserve set aside in respect thereof and in respect of proposed interim cash distribution, provided that interim cash distribution may not be made where risk exists that at end of that current fiscal term there might not be any excess of net assets over aggregate amount referred to in (i), (ii), (iii) and (iv) above. (Com. C. 293-5).

Amendment of articles or incorporation, except as hereinbelow mentioned, requires two-thirds majority vote of stockholders present at general assembly of stockholders. (Com. C. 343). If preferred stock is outstanding, special consent of general assembly of preferred stockholders also is required for amendments to articles of incorporation which are adverse to their preferred stockholder interests. (Com. C. 345). In order to amend articles of incorporation so as to require board of directors' consent to transfer of shares by stockholder, affirmative vote is required by majority of stockholders who hold not less than two-thirds of outstanding shares, either voting or nonvoting. (Com. C. 348).

Reorganization processes may occur under special legislation or under Commercial Code provisions. Under Commercial Code, reorganization may be ordered by court if there appears danger of insolvency. This order may be issued upon application of director or auditor of corporation or its major creditor or minority stockholder. (Com. C. 381). In course of reorganization court may intervene and impose restrictions. (Com. C. 386).

Dissolution may occur because of expiration of time provided in articles of incorporation, amalgamation, bankruptcy, court order of dissolution, and decision of general assembly of stockholders. (Com. C. 404). Except in case of amalgamation and bankruptcy, dissolution is followed by liquidation in which court may take special steps to protect interests of creditors and stockholders. (Com. C. 417 et seq.).

"Unit" Share System Listed corporation existing as of Oct. 1, 1982 is required to adopt "unit" share system if par value per share of its shares or its net assets per share on latest balance sheet is less than 50,000 yen. Number of unit shares is that obtained by dividing 50,000 yen by par value, or such other number as corporation may determined by its articles of incorporation as far as statutory requirement is met. Unlisted corporation existing as of Oct. 1, 1982 may adopt this system determining in its articles of incorporation number of unit shares in compliance with same requirement. Certificates for shares representing fractions of one unit ("unit fractional shares") are issued only in certain limited circumstances, wherein unit fractional shares are transferable. Holder of unit fractional shares may require corporation to purchase such shares and purchase is consummated by procedures provided by Supplementary Provisions to Law Partially Amending Commercial Code, etc. He is entitled to exercise certain limited rights which do not include voting rights. At date yet to be specified by law, one unit of shares will be consolidated into one share by operation of law. (Supplementary Provisions to Law Partially Amending Commercial Code, etc., 15, 16, 18, 19).

Limited corporations (Yugen Kaisha) resemble private companies or family corporations in English law. A limited corporation is created through execution of articles of incorporation which state object, trade name, capitalization, value of unit of contribution, name and residence of each member, number of units of contribution made by each member and principal office. Total number of members may not exceed 50. (L.C.L. 6, 8). Capitalization must be 3,000,000 yen or over. (L.C.L. 9). Corporations incorporated prior to Apr. 1, 1991 whose capital amount is below 3,000,000 yen are required to meet this requirement by Apr. 1, 1996. Each unit of contribution must be at least 50,000 yen, and transfer of unit by member to nonmember requires resolution of approval at general meeting. (L.C.L.10, 19). Directors are elected at general meeting, and represent corporation in business matters. Directors are prohibited from engaging in competitive business activity. (L.C.L. 11, 27, 29, 32; Com. C. 254). In most respects powers and pattern of organization of limited corporation are similar to that of joint stock corporation.

Other Legal Persons Certain acts of special legislation afford legal personality to associations and organizations as distinct from provisions of Civil or Commercial Codes. Trade associations and labor unions are examples. In addition, public law provides that many public agencies, such as municipalities, have legal entity. In a few instances Diet has enacted special charters for public corporations such as The Bank of Japan.

Subsidiaries of Foreign Corporation *See* Foreign Investments.

Foreign Corporations Except for treaty provisions, the only foreign bodies recognized as legal persons in Japan are states, administrative divisions of states, and commercial companies. (C.C. 36). However, a recognized foreign legal person enjoys same rights and capacities as similar legal person does under Japanese law, unless treaty or law provisions are to contrary. (C.C. 2, 36). At present time such treaty or law provisions are nonexistent.

Foreign corporation doing business in Japan upon a continuing basis must register its place of business, name and address of its legal representative, law under which it has been established and various related facts following procedures similar to those used by Japanese corporations in registering branch offices. (Com. C. 479). Until such registration has been accomplished, foreign corporation is not authorized to engage in business, and any person violating such provisions is jointly liable with corporation. (Com. C. 481). Failure to engage in business within one year, engaging in business for illegal purpose and continuing violations of criminal laws in defiance of warnings issued by Minister of Justice are grounds for issuance of court order for termination and liquidation of business office. (Com. C. 484). Fines not to exceed 1,000,000 yen are provided for various infractions of registration requirements. (Com. C. 498).

Establishment of branch in Japan or substantial change in kind or business purpose of branch in Japan by foreign corporation (excluding financial and public utility corporation) is categorized as inward direct investment under Foreign Exchange and Foreign Trade Control Law and prior notification must be filed. Subsequent procedures are similar to those applicable to inward direct investment type of share acquisition. Once such notification is cleared, remittances to and from branch office can be made freely unless special method of payment is involved and subject to possible restriction under extraordinary circumstances. *See* Foreign Exchange and Foreign Trade; and Foreign Investments.

EXCHANGE CONTROL
See Foreign Exchange and Foreign Trade.

EXECUTIONS

Execution follows from judgment of court, from settlement made in court or through conciliation procedures, from court order of payment or decree for provisional execution or from certain categories of contracts which provide for payment of fixed amount of money or securities and which are executed before notary public. (C.E.L. 22). (*See* Notaries Public, subhead Officially Authenticated Instrument). In all of above cases, however, execution certificate which certifies as to existence and maturity of obligation, must be obtained either from clerk of court issuing order or notary public certifying as to contract. (C.E.L. 25 through 27). Execution is conducted by bailiff or court, according to nature of claim or property. (C.E.L. 2, 3, 44, 113, 122, 143, 167).

Claim of a monetary nature may be satisfied through seizure of cash, seizure and sale at auction of property in debtor's hands, or through court order for assumption of management of real property. (C.E.L. 43, 112, 134). Obligations calling for surrender of particular item of property may be satisfied by seizure and transfer to creditor and obligations requiring merely legal action may be ordered by court. (C.E.L. 168, 169, 173). Specific performance is not available for obligations which can be performed only by debtor or through his inaction. *See* Garnishment.

Creditors entitled to execute their monetary claims by themselves and certain other specified creditors may apply for share in distribution of sales proceeds of real property, vessels and airplanes during period specified by court. (C.E.L. 49, 51, 121 and Civil Execution Rules 84).

Holders of preferential rights and pledgees may apply for share in distribution before seizure of cash or before receipt by bailiff of sales proceeds of movables. (C.E.L. 133, 140).

See also Preferential Rights.

Exemptions from Execution *See* Exemptions.

EXEMPTIONS

Exemptions from execution are following: clothing and household equipment needed by debtor; food and fuel for debtor and his family for two month period; cash not exceeding 210,000 yen; implements and tools of technicians, laborers, farmers, and other varieties of professional men; three-fourths (in principle) of income derived from pensions and remuneration of workmen; seals, decorations and awards, genealogical materials and objects of worship; unpublished manuscripts or unrevealed inventions; and school books. (C.E.L. 131, 152 and Civil Execution Enforcement Ordinance 1).

In addition court is empowered to provide additional exemptions when necessary to afford debtor proper means with which to recoup himself. (C.E.L. 132, 153).

FOREIGN EXCHANGE AND FOREIGN TRADE

Foreign Exchange and Foreign Trade Control Law is major act of legislation and by its amendment which became effective on Dec. 1, 1980, its coverage has been broadened so that it covers transactions theretofore covered by Foreign Investment Law. Wide areas are regulated by Law such as: (1) Payments directed abroad, payments to or receipts of payment from "exchange nonresident," and settlements of account between "exchange resident" and "exchange nonresident"; (2) transactions between "exchange resident" and "exchange nonresident" concerning creation, modification or liquidation of claimable assets arising from deposit, trust or monetary loan or guaranty or contract providing for purchase of foreign means of payment or claimable assets; and transactions between "exchange resident" and another `"exchange resident" concerning creation, modification or liquidation of claimable assets payable in foreign currency arising from such contracts; (3) acquisition by "exchange resident" of foreign securities from "exchange nonresident"; acquisition by "exchange nonresident" of securities from "exchange resident"; issuance or flotation by "exchange resident" of securities in foreign country or of foreign securities in Japan; issuance or flotation by "exchange nonresident" in Japan of securities, and in foreign country securities expressed or payable in Japanese currency; (4) acquisition by "exchange resident" of immovables in foreign country or rights related thereto or acquisition by "exchange nonresident" of immovables in Japan or rights related thereto; (5) receipt and payment of funds between office in Japan of corporation and its office outside Japan; (6) certain service contracts between "exchange resident" and "exchange nonresident"; (7) acquisition of shares of Japanese corporation by "foreign investor" and its consent to substantial change in business purpose of Japanese corporation in which it has lot less than one-third of issued shares; (8) establishment of branch, etc., in Japan or substantial change in its kind or business purpose; (9) conclusion of technology introduction contract between "exchange resident" and "exchange nonresident"; and (10) export and import trade, including export and import of means of payment, securities, and precious metals. (F.E.C.L. 16 through 55). "Exchange residents" mean all natural persons who have their permanent place of abode or who customarily live in Japan, and also juridical persons (corporate bodies, enterprises) having their seat or place of administration in Japan. Branches, local offices and other offices in Japan of exchange nonresidents are considered to be exchange residents irrespective of whether or not they have legal authority to represent "exchange nonresidents" and even if their headquarters are located abroad. "Exchange nonresidents" mean all persons, natural or juridical, other than "exchange residents." (F.E.C.L. 6). By virtue of various rules and regulations issued thereunder, general rules prescribed by Foreign Exchange and Foreign Trade Control Law and many restrictions have been eased, and by above-mentioned amendment to Law restrictions have been eased further.

See Foreign Investments.

FOREIGN INVESTMENTS

By amendment of Foreign Exchange and Foreign Trade Control Law which became effective on Dec. 1, 1980, Foreign Investment Law which theretofore regulated investments by foreign investors, including acquisition of shares and conclusion of technology introduction contracts with durations exceeding one year, has come under purview of Foreign Exchange and Foreign Trade Control Law. Under said Law as so amended, these transactions are regulated as set forth below.

Acquisition of Shares For regulatory purposes manner of share acquisition is divided into two types: (a) Inward direct investment and (b) portfolio investment.

Inward direct investment type of share acquisition by foreign investors involves advance notification and possible issuance of recommendation of or order for alteration of contents or suspension of notified share acquisition. Foreign investor is defined by Law to include exchange nonresident individual, foreign corporation, any corporation one-half or more of whose issued shares are directly or indirectly held by exchange nonresident individuals or foreign corporations, and any juridical person majority of whose directors or of whose officers having authority to represent it are nonresident individuals. Foreign investor desiring to acquire shares of Japanese corporation must in principle file notification in advance with Minister of Finance and ministers having authority over business concerned (collectively "competent ministers") and withhold share acquisition for 30-day period, which is normally shortened to two weeks. In case shares to be acquired are listed on stock exchange or are designated by government as similar to listed shares, this advance notification is not required, if ratio of holding by single foreign investor of shares (including both presently held and to be newly acquired) is less than 10 percent and if, in ease of issuing companies designated by competent ministers (presently 11 companies), ratio of holding by foreign investors as group (including both

presently held and to be newly acquired) is less than 25 percent or such higher percentages (presently ranging up to 50 percent) is fixed by competent ministers as being applicable to respective designated companies. Competent ministers may extend above 30-day period to as much as four months if they deem it necessary to consider whether, if shares were acquired as notified: (a) Safety of Japan would be impaired, maintenance of public order would be disturbed or public safety would be hindered or (b) smooth operation of Japanese economy, including activities of business in Japan similar to business which is subject of share acquisition concerned, would be very harmfully influenced, or whether it is deemed necessary to alter contents of share acquisition or suspend it: (a) in order to treat notified share acquisition on substantially equal basis with treatment of Japanese investors in country to which foreign investor belongs and with which Japan has not concluded treaty concerning direct investment or (b) because whole or part of notified share acquisition is found to fall into category of capital transactions for which approval must be obtained in view of use of funds and other factors. If competent ministers are convinced that there are grounds for apprehension, they may within above four-month period (or five-month period if extended in case of necessity) recommend that foreign investor alter contents of or suspend notified share acquisition. Foreign investor who has accepted recommendation within ten days after its receipt may acquire shares in compliance with recommendation before elapse of above waiting period. If recommendation is not accepted or no acceptance reply is given, competent ministers may, but only within above four- or five-month period, order alteration of contents or suspension of notified share acquisition. (F.E.C.L. 26, 27, Supplemental Provisions of F.E.C.L. 2, 3).

Portfolio investment type of share acquisition also involves advance notification but not recommendation of or order for alteration or suspension. However, in case of certain extraordinary circumstances portfolio investment may be made subject to approval. In particular, exchange nonresident (including foreign corporation) desiring to acquire shares from exchange residents must in principle file notification in advance with Minister of Finance. This notification is not required if share acquisition is made from or through Japanese or foreign securities company designated by Minister of Finance acting as intermediary, commission broker or agent. Alteration of contents or suspension of notified portfolio investment cannot be recommended or ordered. However, Minister of Finance may impose obligation to obtain approval but only if and when he deems that: (a) Maintenance of balance of international payments of Japan would become difficult, (b) foreign exchange rate of Japanese currency might suddenly change or (c) movement of substantial funds to and from Japan would threaten Japanese financial market and/or capital market, and that it would become difficult to attain purpose of Law if portfolio investment were without restriction. (F.E.C.L. 20 through 22).

Technology Introduction Contracts Any exchange nonresident (including branch, etc., in Japan of exchange nonresident) and exchange resident desiring to conclude, renew or alter terms of contract under which nonresident transfers industrial property rights or other rights concerning technology, establishes rights to use these rights or advises on technology concerning operation of business ("conclusion, etc. of contract") must file notification in advance with Minister of Finance and ministers concerned (collectively "competent ministers") and withhold notified conclusion, etc. of contract for 30 days (or shortened period). Such notification is not required if branch, etc., in Japan of exchange nonresident concludes, renews or alters contract covering technology developed independently by branch, etc. Competent ministers may extend above 30-day period to as much as four months if they deem it necessary to consider whether, if notified conclusion, etc. of contract were carried out: (a) Safety of Japan would be impaired, maintenance of public order would be disturbed or public safety would be hindered, or (b) smooth operation of Japanese economy, including activities of business in Japan similar to business which is subject of contract, would be very harmfully influenced. If competent ministers are convinced that grounds for apprehension exist, they may recommend that parties alter whole or part of terms of contract or suspend conclusion, etc. of contract. Such recommendation can be made only within above four-month period (or five-month period if extended in case of necessity). Time and manner of carrying out conclusion, etc. of contract by parties having accepted recommendation and of issuance of order of alteration or suspension against parties not having accepted recommendation are same as stated in inward direct investment type of share acquisition above. (F.E.C.L. 29, 30).

Repatriation Right Validation granted under abolished Foreign Investment Law for acquisition of shares and conclusion of technology introduction contract carries right to withdraw profits and repatriate investment subject to such conditions as may be imposed therein or as provided in Law. Under Foreign Exchange and Foreign Trade Control Law, which makes overseas payment generally free from any regulation, such right is not specifically provided. However, obligation to obtain approval for payment of dividends on and repatriation of investment in shares and royalties under technology introduction contracts may be imposed if it is deemed necessary for faithful performance of treaties or other international agreements concluded by Japan. (F.E.C.L. 16).

In addition, in cases of sudden and substantial changes in international economy, if emergency exists, competent ministers can suspend such payments, delaying them for period specified by Cabinet Order. (F.E.C.L. 9).

FOREIGN TRADE REGULATIONS

Foreign trade is regulated by Foreign Exchange and Foreign Trade Control Law. Export of goods is permitted with minimum of restrictions, insofar as it is consistent with objective of Law. (F.E.C.L. 47). Export of goods of certain type, or to certain destination, or under certain method of transaction or settlement may be subject to approval from Minister of International Trade and Industry. (F.E.C.L. 48). When Minister of International Trade and Industry deems it urgently necessary, he may place embargo by specifying type or destination of goods for period not exceeding one month. (F.E.C.L. 51). Import of goods may be subject to approval in certain circumstances for purpose of sound development of foreign trade and national economy. (F.E.C.L. 52).

See Foreign Exchange and Foreign Trade; Foreign Investments.

FRAUDS, STATUTE OF

Although Japan has 110 specific statute of frauds, certain forms of expression of intention, such as . . . corporate instruments, must be in writing or executed before notaries. (C.C. 969, 970, 972; Com. C. 167).

GARNISHMENT

Outstanding claim of debtor may be attached by his creditor through court order of garnishment which prohibits garnishee from discharging his obligation to original debtor, and also forbids debtor to dispose of or accept payment for obligation. (C.E.L. 145). Payment in violation of this court order cannot be set up against garnisher.

Exemptions from garnishment are as stated under topic Exemptions.

IMMIGRATION

Alien's authorized period of stay varies with his immigration status and is renewable with some exceptions and limitations. Three-year commercial visa may be given to aliens who engage in business in Japan. Instructors at educational institutions, aliens who are sent by foreign religious organization to engage in religious activities in Japan, foreign news reporters and aliens who are invited by a public or private Japanese organization for provision of advanced or specialized industrial technologies may also be given three-year period of stay. Student researchers and skilled laborers normally are admitted on year by year basis. Tourists and other aliens who intend to stay for short period may be given 90 day visa. Minister of Justice has discretionary powers to authorize other statuses and periods of stay up to three years.

Entry-check, procedures for status change or renewal, and deportation process are provided in Immigration Control and Refugee Recognition Law. For registration requirements, *see* Aliens.

Japan is party to Convention Relating to Status of Refugees of July 28, 1951.

INJUNCTIONS

See Attachment and Injunctions.

INSOLVENCY

See Bankruptcy.

INTEREST

Loan interest rates may not exceed 20 percent per annum if principal is less than 100,000 yen, 18 percent if 100,000 yen or over and less than 1,000,000 yen, and 15 percent if 1,000,000 yen or over. If not specified, rate is 5 percent per annum on civil transactions and 6 percent on commercial transactions. (C.C. 404, Com. C. 514; Usury Law 1).

According to court precedents, if interest has been paid voluntarily at rates over above maximum rates, excess is deemed to have been applied toward principal repayment.

If interest for one year or more is not paid despite payment request, it may be added to principal of obligation and compound interest may be charged. (C.C. 405).

Contract for or actual receipt of interest at rates exceeding limits prescribed in Law Concerning Control on Acceptance of Contributions, Deposits and Interest Rates, Etc. is punishable. (Law Concerning Control on Acceptance of Contributions, Deposits and Interest Rates, Etc. 5).

Under this Law, maximum permissible interest rate to be charged by money-lending traders is 0.2 percent per day for three years from Nov. 1, 1983, 0.15 percent per day thereafter until date after Nov. 1, 1988 yet to be fixed by law and 0.1096 percent per day thereafter.

Subject to certain requirements, interest paid voluntarily to money-lending traders at rates over maximum rates under Usury Law but not exceeding maximum permissible rates under Law Concerning Control on Acceptance of Contributions, Deposits and Interest Rates, Etc. is deemed to be valid interest notwithstanding provisions of Usury Law. (Law of Restrictions, Etc. on Money-Lending Business 43).

LABOR RELATIONS

Rules of employment must be established by every employer of ten or more workers in compliance with minimum standards of law. (Labor Standards Law 89). Establishment of such rules requires first a presentation to representative employees and then filing with Prefectural Labor Standards Supervising Office. Such rules must deal with wage programs and scales, working hours, time off, holidays, paid vacations, discharge, and to extent that these are customary in line of business concerned, with retirement allowances, safety, sanitation, accident compensation, etc. (Labor Standards Law 89, 90).

Labor agreements are made between company and lawfully organized union. When labor agreements become applicable to at least three-fourths of regular workers of plant, their terms then become applicable to all workers. (Labor Union Law 17). Normally content of labor agreements resembles that of rules of employment. Labor agreements do not require government approval. Injunctions and suits for civil damages are available for breaches of agreements. Labor agreements may be for three years or less and, unless term is provided therein, may be terminated by at least 90 days notice. (Labor Union Law 14, 15, 17).

Labor practices in Japan make the provisions of retirement allowances and substantial bonuses a virtual necessity. Employers also normally provide a wide range of benefits including medical and housing facilities. Employers are prohibited from setting off wages against advances to employees or requiring employees to deposit funds with employers. At least 30 days notice or pay in lieu of notice is necessary for discharge. (Labor Standards Law 17, 18, 20).

See also Infancy.

LICENSES

See Patents. Licensing of industrial know-how cannot be registered but is regulated as element of foreign investment. *See also* Foreign Exchange and Foreign Trade; and Foreign Investments.

LIENS

Lien is right of retention of object (movable or immovable), which is security for obligation created in relationship to that object. (C.C. 295). It affords lien holder initially right to deprive owner of possession until obligation is performed and right to apply for auction sale of property concerned to collect his claim, although he has no priority in distribution of sales proceeds. Provisions concerning auction sale for enforcement of preferential rights are applied to auction sale applied for by holder of lien. (C.E.L. 195). *See* Preferential Rights. Holder of lien arising out of commercial transactions is entitled to priority over general creditors in event of bankruptcy of debtor. (Com. C. 51, 521, 557, 562, 589, 753; B.L. 93). Retention of possession is essential for most types of liens. In case of immovables possession under lien is valid by virtue of possession alone and therefore constitutes exception to usual requirement for registration of real rights. In commercial transactions, scope of lien is extended to give possessor power of detention pending satisfaction of any commercial claims. (Com. C. 521). Lien holder is entitled to apply fruits of retained object toward satisfaction of outstanding indebtedness in priority to other creditors, and to repayment for sum of necessary expenses or improvements. (C.C. 297, 299). However, he may not use, lease, pledge or encumber object without consent of owner. (C.C. 298). Lien may be extinguished through offer of reasonable security in substitution thereof. (C.C. 301).

LIMITATION OF ACTIONS

Statutes that establish time limitations on institution of litigation operate automatically, and such time limitations cannot be extended even upon consent of both parties. Such limitations differ from extinctive prescription (*See* Prescription) whereunder assertion must be made in litigation in order to be effective; also effect is retroactive. (C.C. 145, 144). Rights to damages, reduction of purchase price and cancellation of sales contract for seller's warranty are subject to one year limitation of actions. (C.C. 564 through 566).

LIMITED PARTNERSHIP

See Corporations.

MONOPOLIES AND RESTRAINT OF TRADE

Private monopolization, unreasonable restraint of trade and unfair business practices are prohibited under Law Relating to Prohibition of Private Monopoly and Methods of Preserving Fair Trade ("Anti-Monopoly Law"). However, many types of activities are exempted by special statutes, particularly in regard to rationalization of medium and small domestic enterprises. Extent of these exemptions narrows actual scope of Anti-Monopoly Law, but these exemptions have been reduced since 1965. Fair Trade Commission of five members enforces provisions of this Law. Its findings are subject to review by Tokyo High Court. Commission checks business transfers, mergers, shareholding status (including that of foreign firms) and international agreements, all of which are subject to certain restrictions. International agreements for period of one year or more and certain types of continuous sales or export and import agreements must be reported by Japanese party to Commission which screens them in order to confirm their compliance with its standards.

NOTARIES PUBLIC

Notaries are officials whose principal functions are preparation and authentication of instruments.

Notaries may act only in localities for which they are licensed, and are liable for damages which result from intentional or negligent acts performed in course of duty.

Instruments which notary prepares must be in Japanese language and must not provide for void or illegal act. Notary may act only on behalf of parties personally known to him or those whose identity is proved by official certificate as to seal or officially issued certificate of identification, such as passport or alien registration in case of foreigner, or those whose identity can be established by two persons with whom notary is personally acquainted.

Officially authenticated instrument is document either prepared or authenticated by notary in course of his official duties. Officially authenticated instrument has two qualities which distinguish it from private documents. As result of formalities under which it was executed, it carries strong presumption of validity which resembles that accompanying official record or official document. Also, when purport of instrument is a claim for delivery of a fungible or payment of a fixed sum of money or transfer of fixed amount of negotiable securities, instrument itself is sufficient to obtain an immediate execution against obligor if statement is made therein that obligor, at time of preparation of instrument, agrees to execution in event of default. (C.E.L. 22). Officially authenticated instrument prepared in one locality has force and effect in other parts of Japan, but similar instruments prepared in other countries may not form basis for execution.

Copies of officially authenticated instruments are preserved by notaries and may be inspected by officials or parties of interest.

PARTNERSHIP

Anglo-American institution of partnership is not known to Japan. Two categories of associations, namely, partnership corporations (*See* Corporations) and informal associations (Kumiai) as provided in Civil Code, have many features similar to partnership.

An informal association is created when several parties contract to contribute to common undertaking. (C.C. 667). One or more managers may be designated, and thereafter managers who are also members may not resign or be removed without cause. (C.C. 672). Association acts through majority vote of its members or managers but every member or manager is empowered to transact ordinary affairs on behalf of association, unless objections are raised by other members or managers. (C.C. 670). Profits and losses are shared in proportion to respective contributions of members unless otherwise provided in partnership contract, although creditor may exercise rights equally against each member if he has no knowledge of actual ratio of assumption of loss. (C.C. 674, 675). Claims of association against third party cannot be offset by latter's claims against individual members. (C.C. 677). When duration of association is not fixed, or is fixed to last during lifetime of member, any member may withdraw at any time, except when this withdrawal would prejudice association. (C.C. 678). Membership also expires by death, bankruptcy, incompetency, and expulsion. (C.C. 679). Upon termination of membership, accounting must be made between association and withdrawing member. Dissolution of association occurs when object of its creation has been accomplished, or becomes impossible of attainment. (C.C. 682). Upon dissolution, affairs of association are liquidated and assets distributed. (C.C. 685 through 688).

PATENTS

Patent rights come into existence by registration with Patent Office. (P.L. 66). Foreigner residing or doing business in Japan applies for patents on same footing as Japanese, while right of application of foreigner living abroad is governed by reciprocity principle or by treaty, and "one year rule" of International Convention applies. Nonresidents applying for patents or taking formal actions relating to patent rights must be locally represented. (P.L. 8). Both licensed attorneys and patent agents may perform this representation.

Patentability is afforded to new "high grade" inventions of articles or of processes of an industrial nature (i.e., relating to productive industry in the broad sense), subject to the following exceptions: (1) material to be manufactured by process of transformation of atomic nucleus and (2) things potentially injurious to public order, morals or health. (P.L. 32). With certain exceptions, inventions publicly used or known in Japan, inventions described in publication distributed in Japan or any foreign country before application for patent or inventions described in prior patent application are not regarded as new. (P.L. 29, 29-2, 30). If several applications are made on different days on same invention, first application is entitled to patent. If multiple applications are made on same day, no applicant is entitled to patent on invention unless agreement is reached among applicants as to who is entitled to patent on invention. (P.L. 39).

Applications for patents are made to Patent Office. On request by patent applicant or other interested parties, patent application is examined by examiners of that office. (P.L. 48-2). Request for examination must be made within seven years following patent application. (P. L 48-3). Examiners pass on substantial questions of patentability. Should examiner find no ground for objection, publication of patent application in Patent Gazette follows. (P.L. 51). For two months following publication, patent application is open for public inspection, during which period objection may be filed by any person. (P.L. 51, 55). Unless sooner published or issuance of patent denied, patent application is disclosed to public in Patent Gazette upon elapse of 18 months from patent application in any case. (P.L. 65-2). Public disclosure entitles patent applicant to claim compensation equivalent to normal royalty from any infringer, this claim being exercisable only after publication following examination. (P.L. 65-3). After publication following examination, patent applicant has virtually equal rights as patent holder, with certain limitations. (P.L. 52).

Patent Office jurisdiction covers decisions in respect to: (1) Appeals from decisions of examiners who refuse issuance of patents, (2) invalidity of patents, (3) amendments of specification or drawings involved in application for which patent was granted. (P.L. 121, 123, 126). Actions contesting such decisions may be instituted in Tokyo High Court. (P.L. 178).

Scope of patent is determined on basis of description of scope in application. Interested person may apply for Patent Office's opinion as to scope of patent, which opinion is advisory and not binding on court. (P.L. 71).

Term of patent rights is 15 years from date of publication of application therefor but not to exceed 20 years as from date of application. Term of patent may be extended for maximum period of five years, by application, where patented invention cannot be used for two years or more for reasons of development of data for government registration required under Agricultural Chemicals Control Law or Pharmaceutical Affairs Law. (P.L. 67). As property rights, patents are subject to transfer, inheritance, pledge, etc., but all such acts except inheritance cannot take effect unless registered. (P.L. 98). Consent of all other co-owners is necessary for co-owner of patent to license patent or to assign or transfer co-ownership. (P.L. 73). Transfer of right to apply for patents is recognized. (P.L. 33). Once acquired, patents may be terminated through various processes such as invalidation by Patent Office or abandonment.

Patent licenses consist of "exclusive licenses" and "ordinary licenses." Exclusive license arises only from contract and requires Patent Office registration. (P.L. 77, 98). Exclusive license affords exclusive rights of use even as against patent owner; also licensee can seek injunctive relief and civil damages for injury to his own interest. (P.L. 77, 100, 106). Ordinary license may arise from contract, from compulsory order of Director General of Patent Office or Minister of International Trade and Industry, or from operation of law (such as employer's right to use his employee's invention under certain circumstances). (P.L. 35, 78 through 83, 92, 93). Ordinary licensee cannot act to enjoin infringement but may probably sue for damages. Registration of ordinary license although not required affords certain benefits, primary being firm confirmation of licensee rights. Without such registration, holder of ordinary license arising from contract has no rights against third party who is recorded assignee of patent. (P.L. 99).

Compulsory license may be granted by Director General of Patent Office in case patented invention has not been appropriately worked more than three consecutive years in Japan or by Minister of International Trade and Industry in case it relates to public interest. (P.L. 83, 93). Owner of improvement patent may also request a license to patent on which his own patent is based. (P.L. 92).

Employee rights are protected by Patent Law which renders void assignments or exclusive license commitments made in advance of invention, in case where invention is not an "in service" invention. An "in service" invention is defined as one which belongs to scope of employer's business and is related to employee's performance of his past or present duty. Employee is entitled to reasonable consideration in case of a subsequent exclusive license or assignment to employer of an "in service" invention. (P.L. 35).

Utility model rights are related to patents but are governed by separate statute. (Utility Models Law). A new invention, which is not required to be as "high grade" as that subject to patent but has a practical utility in regard to form, composition or assembly of goods, can be registered, and owner afforded protection similar to that held by patent holder. Utility model rights last for ten years from date of publication thereof but not to exceed 15 years from date of application. (Utility Models Law 15). Registration is preceded by an examination by officials of Patent Office and public disclosure and/or publication procedures in regard to application. When utilization of patent requires concurrent use of utility model, license may be required of holder of utility model right.

Designs also are afforded legal protection through process of registration similar to that followed with utility models and patents. (Design Law). Design to be recorded must be of new variety and of industrial nature, and must relate to form, pattern, coloring or combination thereof of goods. Designs are distinguished from utility models and patents in that they may concern ornaments instead of objects having a practical use. Unlike patents and utility model rights, however, design is registered without publication although preceded by an examination both of merits and of formal regularity before registration. Registration of design may be challenged on ground of lack of statutory requirements. Design rights are valid for 15 years following registration. (Design Law 21).

Patent Treaty Japan is party to Patent Cooperation Treaty done at Washington, June 19, 1970.

PLEDGES

Pledge is a real right (i.e., a right in a thing) created by contract and is form of encumbrance on property on which creditor obtains possession of right or object as security for an indebtedness and thereby gains preferential position over general creditors in regard to proceeds which can be realized from sale of property by auction. (C.C. 342). In general, any item of property, movable, immovable, or obligation, may be pledged, although specific statutory prohibitions exist in respect to certain specific rights or objects. (C.C. 343; Com. C. 850; Agricultural Land Law 3, 5, etc.). Except in case of pledges arising out of commercial transactions, pledgor may not contract before maturity of obligation for acquisition of ownership by pledgee or for disposition of ownership by means other than those provided by law. (C.C. 349; Com. C. 515). A thing once pledged may be re-pledged or, in case of immovable, may be used by pledgee for his own benefit. (C.C. 348, 356). In return, pledgee must answer for all changes in object and in case of an immovable, may not demand repayment of sum of management expenses nor demand interest for claim secured. (C.C. 348, 357, 358; however, see 299). Pledges of movables require a continuation of possession by pledgee in order to be set up against third party. (C.C. 352). Pledges of immovables are limited to ten years, subject to another ten years renewal. (C.C. 360). When claim is subject of pledge, notice must be given to obligor or his consent obtained in order for pledge to be set up against obligor or third party except in cases of shares of stock. (C.C. 364). Pledgee may collect a pledged claim directly. (C.C. 367). When object pledged is warehouse receipt, holder of instrument for pledge must protest according to procedures applicable to bills of exchange. (Com. C.

609). After one week from day of protest, holder may demand sale by auction of goods deposited in warehouse. (Com. C. 610). If sale is insufficient, satisfaction may be obtained from endorsers or debtor. (Com. C. 613). Recourse against endorsers may be made if application for sale of goods is made within two weeks from protest. (Com. C. 614).

Enforcement of pledges requires auction sale of property concerned (C.E.L. 181, 189, 190) in same manner as enforcement of preferential rights. (*See* Preferential Rights.)

PREFERENTIAL RIGHTS

Preferential right is a real right (i.e., a right in a thing) which affords its holder a position superior to other creditors in respect to satisfaction of obligation from either entire property of debtor or from some particular item of his property. (C.C. 303). It arises by operation of law rather than by agreement. All preferential rights are specifically provided by statute. (C.C. 306 through 328). Their enforcement requires auction sale of property concerned. (C.E.L. 181, 189, 190). Provisions concerning auction sale for execution of judgment of court (*See* Executions) are generally applicable in enforcement of preferential rights. (C.E.L. 188, 189, 192).

General preferential rights are those which attach to all of property of debtor. Those provided by Civil Code arise in regard to: (a) Expenses incurred for common benefit of all creditors in connection with preservation, liquidation or distribution of debtor's property, (b) last six months of wages for servants, (c) funeral expenses of debtor or of relatives for whose support he is liable, and (d) last six months' supply of comestibles, and firewood, charcoal and oil necessary for debtor, his servants, and his relatives living with him and to whom he owes a duty of support. (C.C. 306 through 310). Order of priority of above-mentioned preferential rights is that given. However, as between these rights and special preferential rights, latter prevail. (C.C. 329). Order of recourse to property of debtor in enforcement of general preferential rights is (1) movables, and (2) immovables which are not subject of special security. (C.C. 335).

Special preferential rights differ in respect to movables and immovables. Preferential rights may exist in respect to following categories of movables: (1) Movables which belong to or are attached by lessee to land or buildings (i.e., fixtures), movables employed in use of land, and fruits of land which remain in possession of lessee, (2) baggage in possession of hotel, in respect to bill of guest, servants and animals, (3) luggage in possession of carrier, in regard to fare of traveler, cost of transportation of luggage and other miscellaneous expenses, (4) bonds deposited by public official, in respect to obligations arising as result of negligence in performance of his duty, (5) movables in respect to costs of their preservation, (6) movables in respect to purchase price for which they were acquired, (7) fruits derived from land for period of one year, in respect to seeds, seedlings and fertilizer supplied for use on land, and similar right to silk products in case of supply of silkworms or mulberry leaves, and (8) fruits or manufactured articles which are product of labor, in respect to agricultural wages for one year, and for industrial wages for three months. (C.C. 311 through 324). Priorities between special preferential rights pertaining to same movables are set by statute, although in certain instances knowledge of prior right serves to disqualify holders of all otherwise superior right which was created later. (C.C. 330).

Special preferential rights pertaining to immovables are ranked as follows: (1) Money necessary for their preservation or for enforcement of rights required for their preservation, when registered immediately; (2) work done by artisans, engineers, or contractors, in regard to increase in value effected thereby when registered in advance of performance; and (3) sale price with interest, if registered at time of a contract for sale. (C.C. 326, 337, 327, 338, 328, 340). *See* Shipping.

PRESCRIPTION

Japanese concepts distinguish extinctive prescription, acquisitive prescription and limitation of actions. Prescription must be asserted to obtain court recognition and its benefits cannot be waived in advance. (C.C. 145, 146).

Period for extinctive prescription is ten years in case of obligations in general, five years for obligations arising from commercial transactions, and 20 years for all other rights excluding ownership. (C.C. 167; Com. C. 522). However, following special terms are provided: (1) Five years for obligation to deliver money or other things which will become due periodically once a year or at shorter intervals, or monetary claim of or against government; (2) three years for obligations in favor of doctors, construction engineers, contractors, etc.; (3) three years for tort liability after awareness of damage and identity of tortfeasor; (4) two years for obligations in favor of lawyers, notaries and bailiffs when arising out of their duties (dated from completion of services) or five years in regard to performance of any particular service by such persons; (5) two years for obligations in favor of producers, wholesalers, retailers, masters and teachers, etc.; (6) one year for obligations for wages of workers by month or lesser period and professional entertainers, freight charges, for rooms and lodgings, rent of movables; (7) one year for claims arising from general average or from collision between ships, etc.; and (8) six months, one year and three years for various liabilities arising out of bills, notes and checks. (C.C. 167 through 174, 724; Com. C. 798; L.B.N. 70, 77; L.C. 51). *See* Bills and Notes.

Interruption of prescriptive period results from: (1) Demand, such as occurs through judicial action which is not dismissed or withdrawn, participation in bankruptcy, or formal demand notice if followed within six months by institution of action; (2) seizure, attachment or injunction; and (3) acknowledgment. (C.C. 147 through 156). Prescription which has been interrupted commences to run anew from time when cause of such interruption was concluded. (C.C. 157).

Suspension of effects of prescription may also occur for six months following recovery of capacity or appointment of guardian, if minor or incompetent had no legal representative during six months preceding end of prescriptive period. (C.C. 158, 159). Likewise actions between husband and wife may be brought within six month period following divorce. (C.C. 159-2). Prescription also is suspended in respect to inherited property until six months after confirmation of successor, selections of administrator for property, or adjudication of bankruptcy. (C.C. 160). When natural calamity has prevented interruption of prescription, prescriptive period does not mature until two weeks following removal of the impediment. (C.C. 161).

Acquisitive prescription, such as affords ownership, has 20-year term in respect to possession of property in general, and ten-year period when possession initially was acquired in good faith. (C.C. 162, 163). *See* Limitation of Actions.

PRINCIPAL AND AGENT

Valid declaration of intention by agent, made within scope of his authority and with showing that he acts for a principal, binds or accrues to benefit of principal. (C.C. 99). Similar declaration of intention made in absence of revelation of principal, as a general rule, binds only agent unless opposite party knows or should have known of principal's relationship. In commercial transactions, principal is bound but opposite party may demand performance of contract from agent if he does not know of principal's relationship. (C.C. 100; Com. C. 504). In noncommercial transactions, contract made as agent by one without authority is not valid against principal unless ratified. (C.C. 113). Opposite party may request ratification within reasonable time and has right of cancellation until ratified. (C.C. 114, 115). When authority cannot be provided or ratification obtained, agent is bound at option of opposite party either to perform or to pay damages. (C.C. 117).

Role of agent may be assumed by person who has no legal capacity. (C.C. 102). Unless specified, powers of agent are limited to performance of acts of preservation, utilization or improvement which do not change fundamental nature of object of agency. (C.C. 103). Creation of a subagency is not permitted except with permission of principal or where unavoidable reason exists. (C.C. 104). No agent may act for both parties unless so authorized, or unless in discharge of obligation. (C.C. 108). Person who has represented to third parties creation of agency relationship is responsible for acts done by ostensible agent within ostensible scope of authority. (C.C. 109). If agent acts beyond his authority and opposite party has reasonable grounds to believe agent is acting within his authority, principal is responsible for such act by agent. (C.C. 110). Agency ceases with: (1) Death of principal (except when principal dies in case of commercial agency), (2) bankruptcy, death or adjudication of incompetency of agent, and (3) upon completion of term provided by contract. (C.C. 111; Com. C. 506).

RECORDS

Registration offices under Ministry of Justice are located in all parts of Japan and maintain records relating to property and commercial matters. Family register records, although also under general supervision of Ministry of Justice, are maintained separately at every municipal office and are in custody of local officials. Registers of patents, trademarks, designs and utility models are kept by Patent Office in Tokyo.

Real rights in immovables subject to registration include ownership, superficies, emphyteusis, lease, and reversion. Certain forms of encumbrances on immovables, such as pledge, mortgage, and preferential right, may also be placed on record. (Real Property Registration Law 1). Although unrecorded real rights are actionable as between parties to their creation, they must be placed on record to be set up against third persons. (C.C. 177). Same is true of rights of ownership in vessels. (Com. C. 687). A peculiar feature of Japanese law permits a separation of ownership of buildings from land on which erected and can result in maintenance of separate records regarding buildings. (C.C. 86). A provisional registration system affords protection against subsequent transfers of property to third parties through recording of contractual arrangements or incomplete assignments. (Real Property Registration Law 2, 6, 7).

Commercial matters upon which registration is required are: business name, seals, business activities by minors, guardianship, managerial positions and details relating to incorporated concerns. (Commercial Registration Law). Provisional corporate name system affords protection against use of name by other person during interim period of moving principal office, incorporation procedures, and change of trade name or business purpose. (Commercial Registration Law 35, 35-2). Registration must be made both at principal and branch offices. (Com. C. 10). Foreign corporation is prohibited from doing business on continuous basis prior to registration of first business place in Japan. (Com. C. 479, 481). Valid registration of designated facts normally provides defense against third parties. (Com. C. 12).

Injunctions prohibiting disposition of registered rights and attachments of registered property as well as adjudications of bankruptcy and commencement of reorganization procedures are also recorded. (C.E.L. 48, 175, 180; B.L. 119 et seq.).

SALES

Nature Sale is form of contract created when one person agrees to transfer property right to another party and other party agrees to pay price for it. (C.C. 555). Where option contract does not provide option period, option grantor may urge option grantee to exercise option by giving reasonable option period. (C.C. 556). When neither party has yet begun to perform contract of sale in which bargain money (Tetsuke) has been given, purchaser may rescind contract of sale by forfeiting that sum and conversely vendor may rescind by refunding double amount of bargain money. In both cases, further claims for damages are barred. (C.C. 557).

Warranties Following warranties exist in respect to sales, and even express provision for freedom therefrom will not release vendor if his liability arises out of facts of which he had knowledge but did not reveal to purchaser or if breach results from creation or assignment of rights by vendor to third persons: (1) Vendor has an obligation to acquire and transfer to purchaser right of third person which has been made subject of sale. (C.C. 560, 572). Failure on part of vendor to perform entitles purchaser to rescind contract, and to receive damages if he had no knowledge, at time of contract, that the particular right did not belong to vendor. Vendor has similar right to rescind, upon payment of damages, if he lacked knowledge, at time of contract, of fact that he did not possess that right. (C.C. 561, 562). (2) Purchaser may demand reduction in price if thing sold is deficient in stipulated quantity, or if vendor is unable to transfer full right because part thereof belongs to another person. Or, if purchaser having acted in good faith would not have bought remaining part alone, he may rescind contract. A reduction in price or rescission still leaves vendor liable for damages to purchaser acting in good faith. (C.C. 563, 565). All rights to obtain reduction, to rescind, or to damages, must be exercised within one year of purchaser's

knowledge of fact, if he acted in good faith or one year from day of contract if he acted in bad faith. (C.C. 564). (3) If object of sale is subject to a superficies, emphyteusis, servitude, lien or pledge, or contains latent defect of which purchaser had no knowledge at time of contract, purchaser may rescind contract, providing encumbrance or defect prevents attainment of objective for which contract was made; otherwise purchaser has right for damages alone. Both recovery of damages and rescission are barred one year after purchaser obtains knowledge of fact. (C.C. 566, 570). (4) If purchaser loses ownership of an immovable as result of exercise of preferential right or mortgage covering the property, he may rescind and claim damages as well. (C.C. 567).

Price Expenses in connection with sales must be borne equally by both parties. (C.C. 558). Date fixed for delivery of object of sale is presumed to be date of payment. (C.C. 573). Fruits of a thing sold but not delivered belong to vendor. Purchaser is liable for interest on purchase price from date of delivery, unless another date for payment has been provided. (C.C. 575). If right is asserted by third party in respect to subject of a sale, purchaser may refuse to pay whole or part of purchase price unless vendor furnishes suitable security. (C.C. 576). If preferential right exists or a right of pledge or mortgage is registered in respect to immovable which is subject of sale, purchaser may refuse to pay purchase price until encumbrance is removed. (C.C. 577).

Repurchase This is type of security device in which vendor of immovable may, by special provision in sale agreement, be provided with right of repurchase, through exercise of which he may rescind sale through repayment of purchase price plus expenses. Unless contrary provision is made, fruits of an immovable and interest on purchase price are deemed to offset one another in event of repurchase. (C.C. 579). Term in which repurchase is possible cannot exceed ten years, and in absence of a specifically provided term, repurchase must occur within five years. (C.C. 580). When creditor of vendor seeks to exercise vendor's right of repurchase, purchaser may retain ownership of property by discharging vendor's obligation out of excess value of property over and beyond purchaser's price plus expenses and returning any remaining excess to vendor. (C.C. 582). If one co-owner has sold his share in an immovable with provision for repurchase, and immovable later is partitioned, former co-owner (vendor) may repurchase that part of the property received by purchaser in division. (C.C. 584). If purchaser received payment upon later auction of co-owned immovable, vendor (former co-owner) may assert a claim to extent of proceeds less purchase price. (C.C. 584).

Resale In case of a sale between merchants, if purchaser refuses or is unable to accept delivery of subject of sale, vendor may deposit it or may sell it at public auction after notifying buyer to accept it within reasonable time. Perishable goods may be sold without notification. Vendor has right to appropriate whole or part of proceeds of sale to satisfaction of purchase price but must deposit remainder with government deposit office. (Com. C. 524). If, according to nature of sale or any declared intention of parties, object for which contract was made cannot be attained unless performed at fixed time or within a fixed period, and such time has elapsed, other party is deemed to have rescinded contract unless he demands performance immediately. (Com. C. 525).

Inspection and Rescission As between merchants, purchaser must examine object of a sale without delay upon taking delivery, and must notify seller of any defect or shortage in quantity. Failure to take action provided above prevents purchaser from rescinding contract or demanding reduction in price or damages. Immediate notification also must be given in situations where hidden defects are discovered within six months, if purchaser is to preserve similar rights. Bad faith on part of vendor, however, removes purchaser's obligation to give immediate notification in cases mentioned above. (Com. C. 526). When purchaser rescinds, custody of object of sale is at expense of vendor. When there is danger of loss or deterioration of object of sale following rescission, purchaser must obtain order of court and sell goods at auction; proceeds of sale shall be placed in public deposit or kept in purchaser's custody and vendor given immediate notice of auction sale, if he does not reside or do business in same area as purchaser. (Com. C. 527). Similar rules apply when delivered goods differ from those ordered or are delivered in excessive amount. (Com. C. 528).

Notices Required No written notice is required for claim of nonconformity against seller after delivery.

Applicable Law Choice of law rules follow those of contracts in general (*See* Contracts) but with regard to passage of title, law of location of property governs. (Horei 7, 10).

SEALS

Extensive use is made of seals in Japan, and most petty transactions are consummated through seals rather than signatures. Certain categories of important seals may be registered at municipal office of possessor or at registry office of corporate representative. Once registered, municipal office or registry office will issue certificate of seal. Which may be used to identify person attaching seal to instrument. Although some form of consular verification often is required for special transactions, foreigners may substitute signatures for seals.

SEQUESTRATION

Court may issue ancillary attachment order for purpose of preservation of enforcement of monetary claims or restraining order for purpose of preservation of rights which are liable to change and adversely affect interests of litigant. (C.C.P. 737 through 747, 755 through 763-2).

SHIPPING

Principal features of shipping and maritime law are contained in Book IV of Commercial Code, Law of Ships, Ship Registration Rules, Marine Collisions Prevention Act, Ship Employees Act, Ship's Tonnage Act, Maritime Transportation Act, International Carriage of Goods by Sea Act, Act relating to Limitation of Liability of Owners, etc. of Ships, and other ordinances and regulations issued incidental thereto.

Ships have Japanese nationality if they belong to Japanese government, to Japanese citizens or commercial companies whose principal offices are in Japan and whose directors are Japanese or to legal persons whose principal office is in Japan and whose legal representatives are Japanese. (Law of Ships 1). A roster of ships at Maritime Office contains information regarding type, name, port of registry, construction and tonnage of all Japanese ships, except those of less than 20 tons gross and sailing boats. (Com. C. 686; Law of Ships 4, 20). In addition, records relating to ownership and rights in vessels of 20 tons gross or over are to be found at registration office having jurisdiction over home port of ship. Registration of ships produces results similar to registration of immovables. *See* Records.

Matters relating to use of ship are decided by majority of votes based on value of interest of each co-owner. (Com. C. 693). Any owner dissenting to extensive repairs or a new voyage may require co-owners to purchase his interest. (Com. C. 695). Any owner, except ship's husband, may transfer his interest without consent of co-owners, but should transfer of interest or loss of nationality by co-owner result in loss of Japanese nationality by ship, other co-owners may either purchase interest at reasonable price or have interest sold at auction. (Com. C. 698, 702). Profits and loss are apportioned at end of each voyage. (Com. C. 697). Sale in course of voyage transfers profits and losses to purchaser unless otherwise specified. (Com. C. 688).

Ship's husband may represent owners on all matters except: (1) Transfer, (2) lease or mortgage, (3) insurance, (4) new voyages, (5) extensive repairs, and (6) borrowing money. (Com. C. 700). Ship's master has authority to do all acts necessary for voyage (subject to certain limitations while ship is in home port), but may not, except in order to defray expenses necessary for continuance of voyage; (1)

Mortgage ship, (2) borrow money or (3) sell or pledge whole or part of cargo (subject to certain exceptions when done in interest of cargo owner). If ship becomes unrepairable in course of voyage, master may sell it by auction. Limitations on master's authority will not bind third persons acting in good faith. (Com. C. 712 through 715, 717). Shipowner has no liability for damages to money, negotiable instruments and other valuables unless these are declared by consignor. Successive participants in carriage are jointly and severally liable for damage to cargo. (Com. C. 578, 579, 766).

Act relating to Limitation of Liability of Owners, etc. of Ships adopts system of limiting amount of damages arising during voyage which must be paid by liable shipowners, etc., structured to conform with Convention on Limitation of Liability for Maritime Claims, 1976. Limits of total liability of shipowner or his employees are: (a) Where claims are for loss of life or personal injury to passengers of ship, amount of 46,666 Units of Account (Special Drawing Rights as defined by International Monetary Fund) multiplied by authorized number of passengers or 25,000,000 Units of Account, whichever is less; and (b) where all claims are for property damage, 167,000 Units of Account plus, where applicable, 167, 125 and 83 Units of Account for each ton from 501 to 30,000 tons, from 30,001 to 70,000 tons and in excess of 70,000 tons, respectively. In other cases limits of liability are provided in patterns similar to (b), but amounts are approximately three times those in (b). Salvors and their employees are now eligible for limitation of liabilities. Certain claims are excepted from limitation and certain kinds of conduct bar limitation.

Liability of consignee for freight and other expenses arises upon receipt of cargo. Failure to accept cargo empowers shipowner to deposit. (Com. C. 753, 754). Also shipowner may, in event of failure of payment of charges, and with approval of court, sell cargo at auction for two-week period following date of delivery, as long as no third person has acquired possession. (Com. C. 757). Full charterer may rescind carriage contract before commencement of voyage, upon payment of one-half of freight. (Com. C. 745). Part charterer who rescinds independently before commencement of voyage must pay full amount of freight, less freight earnings from other sources. (Com. C. 748). Damages or expenses occurring from disposition by master to save ship or cargo from a common danger are shared by all persons of interest in accordance with stated rules of general average. (Com C. 789). Liability of contribution in case of general average is limited by value remaining at time of arrival of ship or delivery of cargo. (Com C. 790, 791). Salvage is recognized, amount being determined by court on basis of circumstances. (Com. C. 800, 801).

Preferential right exists against ship, her appurtenances and unpaid freight for voyage for: (1) Expenses of a sale of ship and her appurtenances at public auction and expenses of preservation after commencement of proceedings for public sale; (2) expenses of preservation of ship and its appurtenances at last port; (3) fees and dues payable for ship in respect to voyage; (4) pilotage and towage; (5) expenses for assistance in distress and salvage and for ship's portion of any general average; (6) obligations which have arisen from necessity of continuing voyage; (7) obligations in favor of master or other mariners arising out of contract of hiring; and (8) obligations arising from sale or building and outfitting of ship effected prior to commencement of voyage, and for outfitting, supplies and fuel for her last voyage (Com. C. 842); and (9) claims for compensation of damage arising during voyage subject to possible limitation under Act relating to Limitation of Owners, etc. of Ships (Act relating to Limitation of Owners, etc. of Ships 95). Priority exists in order given, except that in cases (4), (5), and (6), later claims take precedence over earlier claims and later voyages over earlier voyages. (Com. C. 844). Assignee of ship must, after registering assignment, call on holders of preferential rights for notification within one month. Preferential rights take precedence over mortgages and last for one year following creation. (Com. C. 846 through 849).

Under Japanese International Carriage of Goods by Sea Act, preferential right against ship and her equipment is given to person who has right to claim compensation for damages to cargo arising within scope of master's duties when contract of carriage has been made with reference to whole or part of a ship and charterer in turn makes a contract of carriage with third person. Priority given to this preferential right is in same order as (9) above. (International Carriage of Goods by Sea Act 19).

Oil Pollution Damage Compensation Law implements International Convention on Civil Liability for Oil Pollution Damage, 1969 and its supplementary Convention to which Japan is party.

TRADEMARKS AND TRADE NAMES

Trademarks are any written characters, designs, signs or combinations thereof or any combinations of these and colors which are used to distinguish merchandise as being manufactured, worked upon, certified or dealt with by a person. (T.L. 2). However, only trademarks registered through a process of application to Patent Office are entitled to be protected as trademark rights under Trademark Law. Registration is not permitted of trademarks which are not distinctive, which resemble marks of international organizations, governmental insignia, red cross mark, which are apt to be injurious to public morals, or which resemble registered or widely known trademarks for same or similar goods. (T.L. 4). Service mark is made registrable starting Apr. 1, 1992.

Trademark rights registration continue for ten years commencing on date of registration, with subsequent ten-year renewals possible. (T.L. 19). Trademark rights can be transferred independently from transfer of business. Trademark licenses are authorized. In case trademark designates more than two categories of goods, trademark right may be transferred separately for each of designated goods. Transfer of trademark right, which must be preceded by public notice in daily newspaper, cannot take effect without registration. (T.L. 24, 35). Consent of all other co-owners is necessary for co-owner to assign or transfer co-ownership or to license trademark.

In case registered trademark conflicts with previously registered design or previously created copyright, such trademark cannot be used without consent of owner of design or copyright. (T.L. 29). Infringement of a trademark exposes party to injunction, action for damages and criminal prosecution. (T.L. 36 through 38, 78). Any person may file application with Patent Office for invalidation of registration of trademark which fails to satisfy requisites for registration. (T.L. 46). Also application for cancellation of a trademark can be filed for reason of improper use either by its owner or by licensee and for nonuse of more than three years. (T.L. 50, 51). A foreign trademark may be registered in Japan.

Trade Names Recording of trade name at registration office affords registrant protection against use of same or similar name by third persons in municipal area for same business. (Com. C. 19). Temporary recording of trade name is available to business corporation in advance of change of its seat of principal office, trade name or business object, or in advance of its incorporation. Infringement may be enjoined and damages recovered. (Com. C. 20). Trade name of business corporation must indicate category of corporation. (Com. C. 17). Trade name of individual may be transferred or inherited in connection with business, but no transfer can be set up against third persons unless recorded. (Com. C. 24). Trade name continues on record until canceled, upon showing of two year period in which name has not been used. (Com. C. 30, 31).

Financial Institutions

The Japanese financial sector is highly developed and diversified, offering virtually any financial service that can be found anywhere else in the world. Various kinds of financial institutions ranging from giant banks to highly specialized entities can take care of almost any financial requirements that foreign businesses might have. Investment and capital markets in money market instruments, equities, bonds, foreign exchange, futures, and commodities are all highly developed and offer companies many ways to raise, invest, and manage funds.

After several decades of rapid development, Japan's economy is now essentially mature. As the second-largest economy in the world and by far the wealthiest country in Asia, Japan is a major power in the global financial community. It is the largest creditor nation in the world, has the world's third largest export economy, and boasts financial institutions that are truly international in scope. Because of the size and complexity of the Japanese economy, the variations on financing and the financial system are virtually impossible to summarize in any detail. What follows is a basic outline of the Japanese financial system. Those interested in operating within it are encouraged to consult practitioners concerning details on specific arrangements and current circumstances.

In theory, very few official limits on the financial activities of foreigners exist in Japan, especially given the push toward internationalization and deregulation in recent years. However, the country's financial system possesses many characteristics that are uniquely and idiosyncratically Japanese and that make it difficult for outsiders to function freely. Foreign entities wishing to do business in Japan must be aware of these differences in order to operate successfully.

In Japan, financial institutions tend to be specialized, concentrating in a few narrow areas of business, so that customers must go to separate institutions for different services that are obtainable from a single source in most other developed financial systems. Unlike banks in most of the rest of the world, banks in Japan are generally permitted to invest in, own, and operate nonbank-related companies. Japanese financial institutions tend to have extremely close relationships with their clients, often exercising a degree of influence that in other places would be viewed as interference in the business decisions of an independent firm. Companies are usually allied with a specific bank and never even investigate the services and rates of, much less do business with, another bank. However, despite this close linkage, companies often raise capital from a variety of nonbank financial institutions such as insurance companies and trading houses that are considered to be specialists in this area, as well as directly from capital markets worldwide. In the first half of the fiscal year that ended September 30, 1993, Japanese companies raised US$23.1 billion directly in capital markets both in Japan and abroad, double the amount raised during the same period a year earlier. Large Japanese companies have already shifted the bulk of their borrowing from banks to the capital markets, but smaller companies are also beginning to take advantage of such funding. This trend is worrisome to Japanese banks that derive about 85 percent of their revenues from lending.

Overshadowing all the rest of the financial sphere in Japan stands the government, which plays a very active role in the economy through pointedly directive policy formulation, investment and regulation in support of its policies, and the use of moral suasion and arm-twisting to direct economic activity into approved channels. More than half of the government's fall 1993 ¥6 trillion (about US$54 billion) stimulus package is designated for subsidized loans for housing and small businesses. Lending by government financial institutions was ¥1.65 trillion (about US$15 billion) in the 12 months ending August 1993, up 11 percent from the previous 12 month period. Bank lending was up only 1.3 percent during the same period, and some bankers are beginning to speak of government efforts to jump-start the economy through below market lending as heralding the nationalization of the financial system.

A final critical point about the Japanese ethos that extends to its financial system: despite its highly competitive and often contentious system, Japan functions through consensus. This practice is worth remembering because it goes a long way toward placing in context, if not actually accounting for, some ways of doing business that outsiders find bemusing.

THE BANKING SYSTEM

Japanese banks are a powerful international force. The six largest banks in the world as determined by assets at the close of 1992 were Japanese institutions, as were eight of the top 10 and 29 of the top 100 banks. The Japanese banking system can be divided into four sectors: the Bank of Japan (BOJ), the central bank that manages the Japanese financial system; private commercial banking institutions, including the branches of foreign banks operating within Japan; various government financial institutions; and private nonbank financial institutions. Japan's 151 private banks account for 75 percent of all lending funds in Japan. (Refer to "Important Addresses" chapter for a listing of banks and financial institutions in Japan.)

Each category of bank was designed in the years following World War II to serve a specific niche. Japanese financial institutions traditionally do not compete across category lines but rather offer complementary services. This structure has slowly begun to change to adapt to new demands. For instance, mutual savings banks have fallen by the wayside, either converting to local banks or closing down now that the need for deposit gathering by such medium-scale localized operations has been filled by other institutions. Both the extinction of such savings banks and the lessening in importance of credit associations and credit cooperatives are by-products of Japan's financial growth. These institutions were all designed to collect individual deposits and funnel them to the cash-starved larger banks that dealt with businesses, and this need is no longer paramount in a Japanese financial system that can command ample funding through its international trading desks.

The Bank of Japan

The Bank of Japan (BOJ), or *Nippon Ginko*, was established in 1882 as the nation's central bank. Along with the Ministry of Finance (MOF), from which it is legally separate, and in consultation with the Ministry of International Trade and Industry (MITI), it assumes overall control of the banking sector and of monetary and financial affairs. The BOJ is the sole issuer of bank notes (currency). It also functions as the government's bank by receiving government deposits, extending loans to the government, and subscribing to and underwriting government bonds. As

the agency responsible for the implementation of government fiscal and monetary policy, the BOJ uses four main techniques to carry out its mandate.

The BOJ establishes and implements discount policy, primarily by setting discount rates for lending to the government through the sale of government securities, as well as by setting interest rates on discount window and reserve position lending to other financial institutions. In late 1993 the discount rate was dropped to an all-time low of 1.75 percent in an effort to stimulate Japan's ailing economy. The BOJ also buys and sells securities and bills in open market operations to stabilize and fine-tune the economy. And the BOJ sets reserve policy, requiring financial institutions to maintain interest-free amounts with it that represent a specified percentage of their deposits. According to the financial situation, the BOJ raises or lowers these reserve requirements in order to ease or tighten the money supply. Finally, the BOJ uses informal methods of controlling private financial institutions by urging banks to operate within specified fiscal and policy guidelines. While not legally binding upon banks, these "consultations" are usually quite effective in directing bank lending policies and investment strategies so that they serve the policy needs of the economy as a whole.

Private Banking Institutions

A variety of private banking institutions operate in Japan. The most prominent of these are the so-called city banks. There are 11 city banks, most of which are headquartered in the main business centers of Tokyo and Osaka: Sanwa, Sumitomo, Mitsubishi, Sakura, Fuji, Dai-Ichi Kangyo, Bank of Tokyo, Tokai, Asahi, Daiwa, and Hokkaido Takushoku. Collectively, these city banks hold ¥3.85 trillion (about US$34.5 billion) in assets. The credit and deposit business of these banks accounts for about one-fifth of all bank activity in Japan. Three-quarters of their business is with large- and medium-sized corporations, but in recent years they have been trying to broaden their client base by reaching out to offer services to smaller entities as well.

City banks are authorized to engage in most international business-related banking operations such as trade financing and foreign exchange. Many city banks have overseas branches that commonly assist in trade and business operations with Japanese entities doing business abroad. These banks also have correspondent relations with world-class banks in other countries and can easily provide international banking services.

City banks are often closely allied to the nation's *keiretsu*, or corporate conglomerates, giving them a key position in the Japanese economy. These banks provide the financial underpinnings for the *keiretsu*, and foreign enterprises working with subsidiaries of these conglomerates are usually expected to channel financial dealings through the *keiretsu*-affiliated house bank.

Local Banks

There are 132 local or regional banks—67 of them were mutual savings banks until that category was reorganized out of existence in 1989—catering primarily to the needs of small- and medium-sized enterprises. The local banking sector accounts for about one-eighth of all deposits and lending. Some of these banks may engage directly in foreign exchange operations, but most rely on correspondent relations with city banks for this type of service. Local banks typically maintain close relations with local governments, which can be important for foreign businesses seeking permits and incentives.

Long-term Credit Banks

Although long-term financing is not extensive in Japan, three Japanese banks specialize in long-term lending to industry: Long-Term Credit Bank of Japan, Industrial Bank of Japan, and Nippon Credit Bank. Their loans are usually extended to larger enterprises for the acquisition of land, capital equipment, and other fixed assets. Funds are raised primarily through the sale of long-term bank debentures rather than from deposits or in the interbank market. In late 1993 the long-term credit banks were authorized to expand their securities operations.

Trust Banks

Seven trust banks in Japan are authorized to extend long-term credits as well as provide normal bank services such as deposit-taking: Mitsubishi Trust & Banking, Sumitomo Trust & Banking, Mitsui Trust & Banking, Yasuda Trust & Banking, Toyo Trust & Banking, Chuo Trust & Banking, and Daiwa Bank. In addition to these domestic institutions, several branches of foreign banks also operate as trust banks.

In late 1993 as part of its financial liberalization Japan authorized the Bank of Tokyo and several local banks to engage in the trust business. In a reciprocal gesture, the trust banks were allowed to broaden their securities operations.

Cooperatives

Each prefecture has its own array of cooperative financial institutions. More than 400 private credit cooperatives and 445 private credit associations, or *Shinkin* banks exist. These organizations are usually owned jointly by a number of small enterprises in the same industry. These enterprises also provide the primary customer base both for deposits and loans from the cooperatives. Many cooperatives cater specifically to agricultural or fishery concerns. Norinchukin Bank, the central financial institution that provides service to almost 8,000 agricultural, forestry, and fishery cooperatives, was for a long time the world's largest bank in terms of customer deposits and still ranks as the eighth-largest bank in the world.

Foreign Banks

Some 87 foreign commercial banks, operating more than 100 branches, do business in Japan. In addition, 120 other foreign banks maintain representative offices in Japan; although these cannot carry on normal banking business, they serve important liaison functions with local businesses and correspondents. In short, most major world banks consider Japan to be such an important market that they feel obligated to maintain a presence there. Banks headquartered in the United States represent almost one-quarter of all foreign banks in Japan. Permission to open a foreign bank branch is subject to approval from the MOF, which restricts such approval to large, highly ranked foreign institutions. Banks from some countries are not permitted to do business in Japan because a lack of reciprocity arrangements prevents Japanese banks from operating in the applicant's home territories.

Despite the large number of foreign banks, they are responsible for only a small percentage of overall banking activity in Japan. They generally service international clients with operations in Japan and provide links between their headquarters and Japanese clients, most of whom have offices in the foreign banks' home countries.

Among their other activities, foreign banks provide foreign currency loans to domestic and foreign businesses in Japan, as well as letters of credit, foreign exchange (forex) trading, and interbank foreign currency deposit operations. In recent years foreign banks have also moved into yen-denominated lending.

Types of Lending and Sources of Credit

The vast majority of loans made in Japan are short-term credits that are often refinanced through rollovers of 90- or 120-day promissory notes. Loans are usually secured by compensating time deposits, current or fixed assets, or guarantees. Notes receivable are often pledged as collateral on short-term lending, and short-term overdraft financing, which was only recently authorized, is becoming common. Formal compensating balances of at least 10 to 15 percent of the loan used to be standard practice, but such balances are usually no longer required. It is still common for companies to channel other business through the lending bank. Banks have usually expected new

---

clients to sign a standard contract, stating that they plan to establish a long-term and basically exclusive relationship with the bank. Companies have often borrowed more than they needed to promote the relationship, expecting the bank to be there for them during periods of tight credit, and banks and customers often hold each other's shares as investments. Banks commonly expect to be asked to advise companies on business issues, especially those involving finance. With hard times, this relationship approach is becoming less common and less strong.

Medium- and long-term loans are not as common in Japanese business practice as they are in that of many Western nations. Such lending has often been arranged through 90-day notes that are rolled over indefinitely, although the bank can usually cancel the facility anytime it comes up for renewal. Many foreign and domestic firms used to go abroad for longer-term loans, known as impact loans, but the need for such loans has diminished as Japan has become a net exporter of capital. Where longer-term lending is undertaken, government financial institutions are often asked to participate in the financing.

Foreign corporations in Japan have often raised funds through issues of equity or debt to supplement their short-term bank loans. Lending to foreign entities is not discriminatory and large foreign businesses can usually obtain loans under the same terms as domestic companies and at rates that are competitive by international standards. Such loans are usually secured by tangible collateral or parent company guarantees.

Although large foreign companies can readily find domestic financing sources in Japan, small- and medium-sized companies complain that it is often nearly impossible to secure the financing they need to import and distribute goods or support other operations. Many have been forced to rely on funding from foreign banks operating in Japan or from offshore sources. Knowledgeable businesspeople note that teaming up with Japanese firms in joint ventures has helped them to obtain loans from Japanese banks through an introduction to the house bank of their Japanese partners.

In recent years many foreign corporations have turned more and more to Japanese stock and bond markets to obtain financing. Not because these markets are performing well—they are not—but because banks are still paralyzed and overly cautious about new lending, even on the most favorable and secure terms they can think of.

Trade Financing

Despite the cutback in many banking activities, trade financing is still generally available in Japan. The term "usance" is often used in reference to trade financing arrangements. Such financing often ex-

tends to preshipment financing for the production of the goods ordered. Trade credit terms can be extended through the use of noninterest-bearing promissory notes, usually for terms ranging from 60- to 150-days. Open account arrangements are also common. The nature of instruments used can stretch out the period of cash collection, and many operations choose to allow banks to discount their notes. When credit is tight, the management of such receivables and payables becomes critical because even a technical default on an individual instrument is enough to trigger bankruptcy proceedings.

Five major public finance organizations make low-interest loans to encourage international trade: the Export-Import Bank of Japan, the Japan Development Bank, the Small Business Finance Corporation, the People's Finance Corporation, and the Japan Small Business Corporation. Foreign companies can be eligible for lending from these institutions under certain circumstances. Some ¥220 billion (about US$2 billion) is currently earmarked for such trade finance purposes.

Types of Deposit Accounts

Deposits in Japanese and foreign banks are held by both individuals and businesses. Such accounts can provide a stable source of interest income paid on balances held. The main types of deposits used by both domestic and foreign businesses include current, ordinary, notice, tax payment, time, and foreign currency deposits.

Current deposits allow the customer to deposit and withdraw funds on demand. Transactions can be made using checks, automatic teller machines (ATMs), or bankbooks. Companies often use current deposits as settlement and transaction accounts, making their payments by check. Current deposits do not earn interest.

Ordinary deposits offer nearly the same flexibility as current deposits; however, transactions are conducted exclusively by the presentation of a bankbook or by using an ATM card. Such accounts do not offer checking, so the physical presence of the authorized person and the book or card is required for withdrawals, making the accounts inconvenient and somewhat illiquid. However, ordinary accounts can be used to make regular direct transfer payments, such as pensions, dividends, insurance premiums, or other regular and fixed operating expenses. Interest is paid semiannually based on the basis of units of ¥100 (about US$0.90) and is added to the account balance.

Notice deposits must be left in the account for a minimum of seven days after deposit, and can only be withdrawn after two days' advance notice. Companies often use notice accounts to park excess funds temporarily because the interest paid is slightly higher than that paid on ordinary accounts and withdrawals are somewhat less cumbersome.

Tax payment deposits are left on account as a reserve fund until tax payments are due. The interest paid on such accounts is higher than that paid for notice deposits and accrues tax-free.

Time deposits are the most common form of savings deposits used in Japan. The term of the deposit is fixed and funds are not accessible before the end of the stated period. Deposit terms are usually standard, and three-, six-, 12- or 24-month terms are most common. Interest is paid in a lump sum at maturity. A variety of time deposit accounts are offered in Japan, many of which bear interest rates linked to long- or medium-term government bond rates. Recently, government bonds have attracted considerable interest because of their safety, and time deposit accounts linked to such bonds are seen as a way for investors to capitalize on this safety without having to invest directly in the securities themselves.

In addition to such yen-denominated accounts, foreign exchange banks can also offer deposit accounts denominated in foreign currency. These can be configured in the same fashion as the yen accounts normally available. To hedge against foreign exchange fluctuations, depositors often simultaneously purchase a forward exchange contract to match the term of maturity of the deposits kept in time accounts, and many banks offer this service.

At present, interest rates are low, and depositors are looking for better yields than are available through bank accounts. While such accounts remain a relatively secure and convenient repository for operating funds, foreign companies with excess funds may well be able to get better rates in their home countries through banks or by purchasing government bonds, the added cost of transferring the funds in and out of Japan being more than offset by the additional interest earned. In addition, Japanese deposit insurance covers a maximum of ¥10 million (about US$90,000) in deposits. There have been no recent defaults by financial institutions to test the Japanese deposit insurance system. So far the Japanese government seems determined to prop up its ailing banks, but depositors could still find themselves left holding the bag in case of a default.

The Japan Offshore Financial Market

The revision of the Foreign Exchange and Foreign Trade Control Law (FEFTCL) in 1986 authorized the creation of what is known as the Japan Offshore Financial Market. This mechanism deals with international funding and other transactions occurring in markets outside Japan but administered within the country involving authorized foreign exchange banks,

foreign companies, foreign governments, and international agencies. The main transactions in the market entail the raising of funds from foreign entities for use by other foreign entities. The offshore financial market is regulated by the MOF, and applicants to operate in it must be foreign exchange-authorized banks. Conditions of operation are strictly controlled, and, because the market is designed primarily to serve entities operating offshore, activities are carefully monitored to prevent spillover into domestic markets.

Because of their offshore nature such activities are exempt from reporting requirements. Offshore accounts are further exempt from reserve requirements, interest rate caps, and various other regulatory limitations. Offshore accounts held by companies incorporated elsewhere are not subject to tax withholding, although Japanese branches of a foreign company do not qualify because incorporation in Japan makes them resident entities. Earnings on accounts that are deemed to be funded from sources not attributable to any operations within Japan are not subject to corporate taxes.

Deregulation and Internationalization

The increasingly global nature of financial markets and Japan's rising role in world economic affairs have led to several shifts in policy designed to keep pace with these developments. During the late 1980s Japanese regulators began to ease controls to allow the development of instruments to support more active trading in the money markets. It is now easier for banks to issue negotiable certificates of deposit (CDs), and companies are now allowed to issue commercial paper both in domestic and foreign markets. A whole new category of instrument—the money market certificate—has also appeared. Interest rate caps on deposits greater than ¥10 million (about US$90,000) have been phased out. Foreign exchange controls have been relaxed to allow for greater ease of trading, and controls that protected the yen have been eased, so that the international use of the yen—the so-called Euroyen market—is growing.

The government and Japanese banks have agreed to meet the capital reserve guidelines of 4 percent in hard liquid assets and 8 percent in primary capital set by the Bank for International Settlements (BIS) to retain Japan's preeminent financial position. Because of the setbacks experienced by Japanese banks in recent years, it has been difficult to meet the capital requirements established by these guidelines, and some observers argue that the required levels have been reached as much by accounting tricks as by accumulation of actual reserves. A side effect of the scramble to meet these requirements has been the

---

Refer to "Important Addresses" chapter for names and addresses of financial institutions in Japan.

acceleration of the retreat of Japanese banks from lending, especially in overseas markets, in order to retain funds and reduce the assets on which the reserves are calculated.

As part of the trend toward internationalization, the trading of government bonds and the trust banking investment business have been opened up to foreign participation. Foreign firms have also been granted licenses to operate in the securities business. Barriers between commercial and investment banking that were established after World War II based on United States practice are being made more permeable with more types of financial institutions, both foreign and domestic, being allowed to operate in areas of securities trading and underwriting. Previously, banks had been restricted from investment operations except for limited trust, transfer, and custody businesses. As noted, local banks have been allowed into the trust business, and the long-term credit and trust banks have been allowed into the securities business, while commercial banks can offer investment trusts—mutual funds—for the first time. Liberalization was authorized in 1991, but regulators only began issuing licenses in late 1993.

Recent Developments and Trends

The 1980s were years of record growth and profits for Japanese banks. Through a combination of aggressive lending and huge investments in stocks and bonds, Japanese banks reported profit increases during this period unparalleled in the history of banking anywhere in the world.

However, during the past five years Japan's banking establishment has suffered tremendous setbacks. The city banks reported that net profits for the fiscal year ending March 31, 1993, fell 43 percent from the previous year, marking the fourth consecutive year that profits have fallen. In fact, since the late 1980s, city banks have scarcely turned a profit on normal banking operations. Instead, the bulk of reported profits have come from ancillary securities trading, operations that are also threatened by the continued precipitate drop in the securities markets.

Local banks have also suffered, mainly due to overinvestment in the real estate market. Many of these banks are rumored to be facing insolvency. As a result, corporations have been withdrawing their deposits, and private sources have denied requests for funds to shore up the more-troubled banks. In the past city banks have been eager to absorb troubled local banks in order to expand by acquiring their branch networks. Now that the city banks are facing their own financial woes, they have been unwilling to buy up unprofitable smaller banks, removing the safety net from under these more-limited institutions.

The primary reasons for the banking sector's re-

cent dismal performance can be attributed to poor lending practices in the 1980s, a collapse in real estate prices both in Japan and abroad, and a four-year decline in stock prices. During the 1980s economic boom, Japanese banks were extremely aggressive in their lending practices both at home and overseas. Gaining local and worldwide market share seemed to be more important than actually turning a profit, and international competitors in Europe and America were often frozen out, unable to compete with the Japanese banks' razor-thin interest margins. As a result, Japanese banks took a 46 percent share of new international lending in 1989.

These practices returned to haunt Japanese banks in the 1990s. Japanese sources report that in late 1993 bad loans at the 20 largest Japanese banks totaled at least ¥15 trillion (about US$134 billion), with such loans exceeding ¥1 trillion (about US$9 billion) at each of the four largest city banks—Sakura, Fuji, Sumitomo, and Dai-Ichi Kangyo. In March 1993 the cumulative nonperforming loans—those that have not paid interest in six months—of the 11 city banks had risen to more than US$75 billion. Some observers argue that the total bad dept of the 11 city banks is closer to US$268 billion than the acknowledged US$134 billion, nearly equal to the conservative US$285 billion estimate given for the entire banking system, which is likely to be proportionally higher still. At the end of 1993 the 11 Japanese city banks announced an unprecedented 10,000 layoffs in response to their dismal situation. These layoffs, to be accomplished over three years primarily through attrition, are expected to help the banks reduce their overblown cost structure.

Bankruptcies declined slightly to just over 14,000 in 1993, the first such decline in three years. However, a record 61 percent were due to the financial pressures of the recession and larger firms are now involved. In October 1993 US$5.5 billion Muramoto Construction failed, leaving several Japanese banks on the hook. This default surpassed that of Itoman & Co., a high-flying real estate investment and development firm which had previously held the record with US$1.9 billion as the largest business failure in Japan. The brunt of this default fell on Sumitomo Bank, Itoman's house bank. Companies that failed in 1993 had total liabilities of about US$60.5 billion. Such announcements are expected to continue because Japanese firms tend to delay as long as possible before admitting problems.

The problem with bad loans is closely related to the worldwide declines in the real estate market, in which banks invested heavily during the 1980s. Real estate prices, which had risen to unsustainable levels in major markets worldwide but especially in Japan, have fallen by as much as 50 percent in prime Japanese markets since their peak in 1989, and analysts expect prices to drop even further before they stabilize. Loan defaults have transferred ownership of a great deal of property to banks. Current market values are far below their original assessed value as collateral, resulting in huge write-downs for the banks. Although Japanese banking rules force banks to write down such assets to a greater degree that many other countries require, there is still a lag as the problem works its way through the system. Moreover, the inability of banks to resell these assets at virtually any price has tied up huge amounts of capital, lessening the banks' ability to lend.

The unprecedented collapse of the Japanese securities market has nearly doomed many of Japan's leading banks. Unlike banks in Europe and the United States, Japanese banks are permitted to purchase shares in nonfinancial institutions for investment purposes. During the 1980s, when no end was in sight to the fabulous profits to be made in equities, banks invested heavily in shares. Virtually assured of profits from their stock portfolios, banks had plenty of cheap money to lend and were able to offer generous loans at extremely low interest rates.

A vicious cycle ensued in which companies issued stock at virtually no cost because share prices rose so steeply and regularly that they could borrow against their stock to invest in other assets, including stock in other companies and real estate. In fact, during the late 1980s many of Japan's most prominent firms derived the vast majority of their earnings from such financial manipulations rather than from the operation of the businesses they were set up to engage in. Banks were willing to lend—and to invest for their own accounts—based on inflated paper valuations. Japanese firms spread out to gain beachheads worldwide, offering premium prices for everything from Van Gogh paintings to Rockefeller Center, paying with a strong yen fed by home financial successes—and excesses. No matter how expensive it was overseas, it was still cheaper than at home and the almighty yen could handle it.

The stock market collapsed from a high of nearly 40,000, as measured by the Nikkei 225 Average Stock Index at the end of 1989, to just above 14,000 points in August 1992—a drop of almost two-thirds—virtually destroying the value of the banks' stock portfolios. What had been a sure thing quickly turned into sheer disaster. The institutions were simultaneously saddled with bad debts put on the books at wildly inflated prices that suddenly bore no relation to actual market values. In 1991 the Japanese share of new international lending fell to just 5 percent from 43 percent just three years before, and some large banks report not having made a major new loan in more

than two years.

Faced with the near-destruction of its domestic banking establishment, the government acted in 1992 to prevent further decline. The MOF allowed banks to place their reserves in special tax-free accounts, and the BOJ has offered troubled banks extensive discount privileges at rapidly plummeting rates. In an effort to free up bank assets, the government established a land bank to buy ¥3 trillion (about US$28 billion) of real estate that banks had acquired through foreclosing on bad loans, although actual acquisitions have been few. Various authorities have recently floated proposals for additional entities that would buy out bad real estate, relieving the banks of their mistakes and holding the property until it could be sold off at a later date. These entities would be funded by the lenders and the government. Previous proposals for such bail-outs fell victim to disapproval from the public and the Ministry of Finance which seems reluctant to spend funds to shore up the dicey real estate market.

For too long Japanese banks operated in an artificial environment maintained by protective regulators. The environment was also one in which growth disguised mistakes. Between these two factors that insulated them from the outside, the banks lost or failed to develop their competitive edge. Observers tell horror stories such as that of the merger of Mitsui Bank and Taiyo Kobe Bank to form Sakura Bank and how three years later the bank still has three separate personnel departments, one from each of the preexisting banks and one for the new institution that has not yet been able to incorporate the holdover organizations.

Japanese banks are expected to struggle for a few years before they regain their financial strength. They are beginning to demand repayment from accounts that they would have carried in the past, forcing more and larger companies into bankruptcy. And they have adopted a more cautious approach to lending, paying more attention to creditworthiness than to relationships. New lending is expected grow by less than 0.5 percent during 1993, a postwar low and down from 6 percent in 1991 and 2 percent in 1992. Banks are likely to remain overly cautious in their approach to the securities and real estate markets, restricting their activities to more traditional but less profitable banking services.

As a cost-cutting measure, they will continue their trend of closing unprofitable bank branches at home and abroad, especially in the United States, where by most estimates they are heavily overrepresented and where they own an estimated US$315 billion in assets. It is only in growing Asian markets such as China and Southeast Asia that Japanese banks are expected to expand operations over the intermediate term.

Refer to "Important Addresses" chapter for names and addresses of financial institutions in Japan.

NONBANK FINANCIAL INSTITUTIONS

Government Financial Institutions

In addition to the Bank of Japan, the government also operates several other financial institutions designed to further specific economic policies or contribute to maintaining and stabilizing the economy in general. The degree of government influence in the financial sector is far beyond that found in other developed nations, leading some observers to classify Japan's economic system as a form of managed capitalism, a characterization that the Japanese hotly deny. And as they face tough times and the exodus of customers, private bankers are beginning to complain about the unfair competition offered by government sponsored and subsidized institutions.

The Postal Savings System The postal savings system, which provides the model for similar systems in other Asian countries, allows citizens to maintain savings accounts through 24,000 local post offices. Postal accounts, including savings, annuities, and insurance policies, remain one of the prime repositories for household savings in Japan. Although these accounts lost their tax-free status in 1988, making them somewhat less attractive, they still pay interest rates higher than those available from banks and other private consumer financial institutions. In 1993 the postal savings system held accounts valued at ¥1.65 trillion (about US$14.75 billion), up 7 percent from the previous year.

Money from these and other government sponsored accounts is managed by the BOJ, which channels it back into the economy through other financial institutions. The Government General Account, a fund dedicated to backing the operations of government-owned financial institutions, is another source of funds. Investments in various government-managed life insurance programs are also used, and the government can call on pension funds as well to inject money into the system as needed.

The Japan Development Bank The Japan Development Bank (JDB) supplies long-term funding to industries determined to be important to the nation's overall economy. Loans have been directed mainly to the capital-intensive power, shipping, and mining industries, but the JDB is beginning to extend financing to foreign firms for import-related operations and for direct capital investment in Japan. The JDB's Loan Program for the Promotion of Foreign Direct Investment can cover up to 40 percent of new construction of foreign plants in designated less-developed areas.

The Export-Import Bank The Export-Import Bank of Japan provides subsidies to private financial institutions that offer export, import, and overseas investment financing to approved clients. Large projects that are considered to be particularly desirable by the government and that involve foreigners are potentially eligible for financing from this bank. The government has recently broadened its criteria for borrowers and imports eligible for reduced-rate financing that covers up to 70 percent of the value of the transaction.

The Overseas Economic Cooperation Fund The Overseas Economic Cooperation Fund (OECF) provides grants and loans to foreign governments and international aid projects. The OECF is the conduit for Japan's foreign aid and operates as an important tool in achieving Japan's foreign policy objectives, especially in the lesser-developed countries toward which it is primarily aimed. Foreign critics have complained that the aid invariably requires the recipients to spend the funds with Japanese firms, so that it restrains trade and amounts to an overseas publicly funded subsidy for Japanese industry.

Public Finance Corporations In addition, Japan operates nine public financing corporations and several government-managed business financing organizations, including the National Financing Public Corporation; the Medium and Small Enterprise Financing Public Corporation; the Commercial and Industrial Association Central Bank; the Environment Sanitation Business Financing Public Corporation; and the Agriculture, Forestry, and Fishing Business Financing Public Corporation. Unlike the more prominent JDB and Export-Import Bank of Japan, which deal chiefly with large corporations, these organizations are designed to serve the needs of small- and medium-sized enterprises. Financing is usually offered on the basis of specific project incentives. As indicated by the names of the agencies, funding is directed at specific industries and includes such arrangements as credit insurance for the acquisition of machinery, lease financing, loans for equipment upgrades, and construction loans, all for small businesses.

Nonbank Private Financial Institutions

Nonbank private institutions also play a large role in Japan's complex lending and investment system. Insurance companies, trading houses, and leasing agencies provide businesses with short-, medium-, and long-term financing for a variety of projects.

Insurance Companies

Japan's insurance industry provides an often-tapped source of private investment funds. At the end of 1992 five of the 10 largest insurance companies in the world were Japanese, including the largest, Nippon Life, which in the late 1980s was reportedly the single largest holder of US Treasury securities in the world. The country's 25 life insurance companies hold assets of about ¥146 trillion (about

US$1.35 trillion), and its 27 general, or property and casualty, insurers hold assets of about ¥27 trillion (about US$240 billion). Premiums paid to these institutions during fiscal 1991 totaled about US$390 billion. Insurers tend to invest heavily in the securities markets and extend loans through private placements, usually to companies with which they have close business relationships.

Japanese consumers are very insurance conscious and the market is somewhat saturated. More than 90 percent of the population has life insurance, and the amount per person is 50 percent higher than in the United States.

Japanese insurance companies had lost some of their financial strength as they headed into the 1990s because of overcommitment to the sagging securities market and bad loans, particularly in real estate. Since 1990 profits generated from equities market activities have dropped by more than 80 percent. To prop up the financial markets, which could collapse if cash-strapped property and casualty insurers were to dump their eroding stock portfolios, the MOF has allowed such companies to refinance their holdings through bank borrowing. This is only the second time that insurers have been allowed to do so since 1949. Rules have also been eased to allow life insurers to pay policyholders out of capital gains earnings as well as of out of current operating income, from which such payments had to come in the past.

Foreign participation in Japan's insurance sector has been hampered by tight government controls and corporate allegiances that have excluded foreigners from such business as they were allowed to conduct. Foreign insurers underwrite 5 percent of property and casualty policies and only 1.9 percent of life policies in the Japanese market. Overseas insurers complain that they are effectively barred from doing business with major corporations because *keiretsu* affiliates do business only with insurance companies in which they have an interest. MOF oversight has also kept tight controls over pricing—particularly as regards cuts and discounts—and the introduction of innovative products that could help foreign companies establish a toehold in the market.

Regulators are considering a major revamping of insurance rules. Observers suggest that insurers will be allowed to sell both life and property and casualty policies, a mix of businesses that has been banned in the past. This reform should serve to increase competition and give consumers a larger variety of products to choose from and an opportunity for new insurers to bid on the accounts. Another reform concerns the partial deregulation of premiums, which have been set collusively by agreement among insurers under the supervision of the MOF.

An additional proposal would allow insurance companies to deal directly in securities for their own accounts, saving them tremendous amounts in commissions that currently must be paid to brokers.

The Export-Import Insurance Division of MITI provides special insurance for repayment of export credits to banks, encouraging them to lend to approved clients and projects. It also offers trade insurance to resident and nonresident exporters, importers, and investors.

Trading Houses

The nine large Japanese trading houses—C. Itoh, Marubeni, Sumitomo, Mitsui, Nissho Iwai, Mitsubishi, Nichimen, Tomen, and Kanematsu, also known as the *sogo shosha*—are huge operations providing services far beyond the scope of what are normally considered trade operations elsewhere. They market and distribute goods, finance trade, provide shipping, and gather commercial information, services that in other countries would be offered by import-export companies, freight forwarders, banks, law firms, and business consultants. This one-stop consolidation of services, including financing, makes Japanese traders among the most competitive in the world. Close ties to a trading house can be a make-or-break factor for foreign businesses doing business in Japan, especially those introducing a new product to Japanese consumers, as well as a source of trade financing.

Leasing Agencies

Leasing agencies are often among the best sources of long-term financing for capital equipment and other fixed assets. Usually, such financing covers items such as machine tools and medical equipment that fall within the US$50,000 to US$250,000 range, a niche that is often incompletely served by other institutions. Leasing companies offer financing to either the end user or the manufacturer. In about 80 percent of transactions, the user buys the equipment at the end of the lease term. Most leasing agencies are affiliates of banks or trading houses. Some securitize their leases for sale in financial markets.

Underground Financial Operations

Financing and services have generally been relatively easy to obtain in Japan, although credit has been growing tighter in recent years as banks pull back from lending and the securities markets offer fewer advantages for companies. The status of the yen as an international currency makes the exchange controls surrounding it more of an inconvenience than an actual obstacle or a reason for circumvention, removing an area of manipulation that exists elsewhere.

Because of the size of its financial markets, Japan is a target of those with funds to launder, although the government is a signatory to the G-7 accords regarding money laundering. Japanese organized criminals, the *yakuza*, are engaged in illicit activities that generate large volumes of funds that need to be redeployed, and both licit and illicit businesses have traditionally used so-called black money to buy influence with politicians. In general, however, there is little in the way of an underground financial market in Japan.

FINANCIAL MARKETS

Securities Markets

Stock Exchanges Eight separate stock exchanges operate in Japan in Tokyo, Osaka, Nagoya, and five smaller cities. The Tokyo market is by far the largest, listing more than 80 percent of all stocks and handling more than 90 percent of all transactions in Japan. The Tokyo Stock Exchange (TSE) is second in the world only to the New York Stock Exchange (NYSE) in capitalization, volume, and value of shares traded. As it approached its height in 1988 the Tokyo Exchange surpassed the NYSE to become the largest in the world based on its total market capitalization, while the relatively small Osaka Exchange ranked third. However, while the Japanese exchanges weathered the crash of 1987 the localized but more violent crash in 1989 dropped these exchanges well below the NYSE in market capitalization as well as by most other measures. In 1991 the total value of shares traded on the TSE was US$774 million, about half the level of turnover on the NYSE. At the close of 1991 there were 332 billion shares on the TSE valued at ¥378 trillion (about US$2.9 trillion).

The rise of Japanese stock markets occurred in tandem with the international development of the Japanese economy but was due primarily to the shift among large companies during the mid-1980s away from bank financing to the direct issuance of debt and equity. At the height of the market in 1989 listed companies raised ¥8.85 trillion (about US$61.6 billion) in new capital on the Tokyo exchange alone. This fell by more than 40 percent, to ¥3.8 trillion (about US$28.4 billion) in 1990. In 1991 the government placed a ban on new listings, although existing firms were allowed to float new shares. Volume fell to a low of ¥420 million (about US$3.4 million) in 1992 before rebounding somewhat in 1993.

These issues provided a huge new stock of securities, fueling broader and more active investment and trading. The other development boosting the exchanges was the admission of foreign brokerage houses in 1986, internationalizing the markets and bringing in outside investors.

Stocks on the Exchanges There are roughly 2,100 listed Japanese stocks. Stocks are divided into first and second section shares, with first section shares representing companies with more shareholders and greater trading volume, usually larger, more seasoned companies. Second section shares make up the bulk of listed shares. Shares of smaller, newer, more speculative companies are traded in a separate over-the-counter (OTC) market.

The Nikkei-225 Average Stock Index, a composite index of 225 major companies traded on the eight exchanges, is the prime measure of Japanese stock market performance. A value-weighted index that focuses on the shares of larger supposedly representative listed companies, it is modeled after the Dow-Jones Industrial Average on the NYSE and plays much the same role in Japanese equity markets as the Dow plays in tracking the performance of US stock markets. Additional stock market indicators include the fledgling Nikkei-300, which was instituted in October 1993 to provide a somewhat broader and more accurate measure of market activity, and the even broader Tokyo Stock Price Index, or Topix, that includes all first section shares traded on the TSE. But the Nikkei remains the most prominent index both nationally and internationally.

As measured by the Nikkei, Japanese stocks rose by 338 percent from 1985 through mid-1993 in US dollar terms. In yen terms, their rise was a much less exciting 83 percent. The second figure reflects the steady appreciation of the yen and the disastrous drops that the market experienced in this period during which it gave up more than half its total value. By comparison, the US market rose by 198 percent in US dollar terms during the same period. The Nikkei rose from 6,850 in 1982 to a high of 39,915.87 in 1989, falling to a low of 14,309 in 1992. As of November 30, 1993, the Nikkei stood at 16,078, a new low for the year, some 20 percent below where it stood at the beginning of November and well below what was previously considered a critical support level of 17,000. The Nikkei ended 1993 with a weak rebound to 17,417.24.

Japanese stock markets have become increasingly volatile. Between May 1992 and November 1993 the Nikkei average moved by more than 3 percent of its total value on 24 separate days, whereas moves of 1 percent are considered outsized and infrequent in developed Western markets. At the end of January 1994 the Nikkei surged 7.8 percent in one session after the Hosokawa government was finally able to pass its compromise reform bill. This volatility is becoming ingrained in the Japanese markets, where investors move in concert to an even greater degree than elsewhere in the world. Waning volume exacerbates the problem. At the high point of market activity in 1989, annual turnover was 218.4 billion shares; in 1992 it fell to 65.4 billion, a drop of 70 percent.

Volume recovered somewhat during 1993, but was still only a third of what it was at its high point.

Market Trends Following the 1989 crash, more firms began switching from equity to debt issues, halting the growth of the securities available to trade. This change worsened the float problem caused by cross-shareholdings, or *mochiai*, in which firms hold each others' shares on a more or less permanent basis. *Mochiai* cements relationships but also reduces shares available for trading, meaning that managerial status quo is maintained, greater potential for market manipulation exists, and price movement among the remaining shares is more volatile. In 1950 70 percent of stocks were held by individuals. By the early 1990s individuals held only 20 percent of Japanese stocks, with perhaps 50 percent being tied up in corporate dead storage.

As the recession enters its fourth year, cracks are beginning to appear in Japan's imposing financial edifice. Companies are beginning to unload stock positions to raise cash, unwinding long-held positions and making available more float. However, this selling puts pressure on prices and removes the floor that permanent holdings had provided under the market. Bank stocks have been among the hardest hit because virtually all borrowers used to hold shares in their lenders. Now that lending is no longer based on relationships to the extent that it was in the past, clients are dumping their bank stock holdings. And banks are in no position to complain because they are doing the same thing, and they know that their clients need the proceeds to pay off their loans and keep their operations going. Since the beginning of 1993, firms have sold an estimated US$9 billion of *mochiai* holdings. Observers, however, note that at current rates it would take nearly four years for companies to liquidate all such holdings. The liquidation of all *mochiai* holdings would put such pressure on prices that the market would collapse long before all such shares could be redistributed.

Government Management of Markets An additional problem has been the government's rather inept attempts at managing securities markets, including privatization. In recent years the government has arranged the sale of portions of two huge monopolies, Nippon Telegraph & Telephone (NTT) and East Japan Railway Company (JR East). In both cases restrictions on purchases were designed to give domestic individual investors the inside track on the issues. However, the issues were pricey, and initial positive response was taken as a cue for promoters to throw more shares into the market, causing prices to drop, scaring away the individuals the offering was designed to attract, and wreaking havoc in the broader markets as well.

Although it generally denies doing so, the government has traditionally stepped in to support stock prices, urging deep pockets investors such as banks and insurance companies to hold the securities they already own and buy more while funneling pension monies and other government controlled assets into the market. The MOF has also suggested to companies that they extend their stock market investment horizon to five years, which would allow them to keep stocks in their portfolios. Following the market drop in 1992 the government injected massive amounts of funds into the exchanges, pouring at least US$28 billion into the markets between July 1992 and October 1993. In late November 1993 expressions of concern about the falling stock market by the Hosokawa government—in the past a signal that the government was preparing to support prices—were enough to cause the market to recover briefly. However, within a few days prices resumed their downward trend after investors determined that the government had failed to take concrete action.

Elements Affecting Market Operations Trading on the TSE is in units of ¥50,000 (about US$450) based on par value, usually 1,000 ¥50 par value shares. In actuality the price of a minimum lot can be extremely high because the lot that can be traded is determined by the par value, not the market value, which can be 10 or 100 times higher. This practice serves to discourage many individual investors.

The availability of accounting information continues to be an issue for overseas investors. For the most part Japanese financial statements are not comparable with those produced according to the accounting norms of most Western nations, leading to difficulties in evaluating securities. Japanese stocks trade at what is a high price-to-earnings (P/E) multiple by Western standards—about 50 on the TSE as opposed to around 20 on the NYSE—an indication of greater risk. Japanese stocks traditionally have also paid very low dividends and limited shareholder participation and input.

Participation on the Japanese stock markets is theoretically open to Japanese and foreigners alike, and foreign entities often make portfolio and speculative investments in the Japanese securities markets. Regulations establish effective limits on foreign holdings, and technical procedural requirements can make direct investment cumbersome. Foreign investors must file a request for approval with the MOF for all acquisitions of shares in a Japanese-incorporated firm. This request is usually a formality, but it takes time and effort and holds the possibility that acquisitions may be denied at some point. Mutual funds available in the United States and Europe provide foreigners with indirect vehicles for investing in Japanese securities. Foreign net purchases of Japanese stocks were US$45.3 billion in 1991 but fell by over 80 percent to US$8.5 billion in 1992 due to the poor performance of the market.

However, foreign purchases rose dramatically in late 1993 and early 1994 as the market began to seem much cheaper by many measures. One reason for recent foreign interest is that because the market had performed so poorly and been seen as so overpriced in recent years, foreign investors had bailed out to a large extent, leaving them underweighted in Japanese stocks. Prices began to look better at the end of 1993.

In principle, foreigners can buy up to 100 percent of a listed Japanese company. In practice, such acquisitions are not allowed. While not legally prohibited, takeovers, especially by foreign interests, are not condoned as being against the Japanese ethic calling for consensus and harmony. All acquisitions must be reported to the MOF, which can intervene for policy reasons, although approval is routinely granted. Foreigners can acquire up to 10 percent of the equity in a nonfinancial public company or 5 percent in a financial firm without official approval. Any additional purchases require prior official approval. Theoretically, 10 foreign firms could each acquire 10 percent of a listed company, but the authorities would most likely intervene to prevent such an occurrence.

Regulation The Japanese markets are administered by the MOF and the board of the particular exchange. Listing applications must be approved by the MOF but constitute a contractual arrangement between the exchange and the listing company. The MOF and the separate boards governed operations on the exchanges until 1992 when the Securities Exchange Surveillance Commission (SESC) was created to ensure compliance with legal requirements in the midst of the stock market's free fall. Many observers have wondered why it took so long to institute a special market watchdog agency.

The need has long been apparent. Several leading brokerage houses have admitted to illegal trading practices, the reimbursement of large clients for market losses, and unsavory dealings with politicians and organized-crime figures. These revelations came on top of the Recruit scandal, involving securities manipulation and payoffs to officials, that brought down the government in the late 1980s. Leading brokerage managers were fired, and several groups of investors that were operating unseemly, if not actually illegal, speculative schemes were disbanded.

Insider trading and market manipulation have been considered relatively common. Although the growth in the size and internationalization of the market has made it more difficult for operators to pull off raids, insider trading has remained rampant.

The SESC is considered woefully understaffed, and many doubt the organization's ability to effectively police stock trading. It has a staff of 200 compared to the 2,600 members of the United States' Securities Exchange Commission on which it is modeled. In addition, the SESC is dominated by MOF officials with links to the industry. Retiring regulators are often offered lucrative positions at brokerage houses, and the public perception is that officials will be less than zealous in pursuing investigations of wrongdoing by cronies and potential employers.

Organizational and Listing Requirements Securities offered to the public are regulated under the Securities and Exchange Law and the Ministerial Ordinance Concerning Public Offerings of Securities. All offerings involving 50 or more subscribers are subject to regulation, and those valued at ¥500 million or more (about US$4.5 million) are required to go through the process of submitting a prospectus, registration statement, and security report to the MOF, all of which become public record. Smaller offerings require a slightly less arduous procedure, with a security notification being substituted for the more rigorous registration statement. Certain types of limited offerings can be made without registration. These include offerings of national and local government bonds, bonds of specially incorporated entities (usually foundations), capital subscriptions of special legal entities (akin to private placements), beneficiary certificates of investment trusts and similar organizations, and securities with a total subscription value of less than ¥1 million (about US$9,000).

Public offerings can be made by prospectus 15 days after the registration statement of a newly incorporated company has been accepted by the MOF. The prospectus requires a great deal of detailed disclosure, and many firms try to qualify for a lesser issuance permit under which securities are issued over a two-year period to avoid having to prepare the document. Foreign invested companies must meet additional disclosure requirements related to their home country operations in order to list shares.

Disclosure is relatively limited compared to that required in developed Western countries, although Securities and Exchange statements are more detailed than those generally required of unlisted companies. In general, Japanese companies will openly discuss a great deal of operational information but balk at disclosing financial data. Parent firms must prepare comprehensive financial statements consolidating the operations of any subsidiaries of which they own more than 50 percent. Small subsidiaries can be excluded from consolidated statements if their operations are not material to the company as a whole, but their results must be provided in full as addenda to the main report. Statements must also include holdings of between 20 to 50 percent in another company, with balances and transactions with such entities detailed separately. Companies must provide shareholders with semiannual reports.

Each stock exchange has somewhat different listing requirements and listing is by contract with the exchange in question. The TSE is the only Japanese exchange that lists shares of foreign companies, currently listing about 125 such issues. A foreign company wishing to list on the Tokyo Exchange must be listed on an exchange in its country of origin; have been in continuous operation for at least five years; be liquid in its home market, having adequate float and turnover; and testify to the probability that there will be at least 1,000 Japanese holders of its securities as of the date of issue. A foreign company must also have shareholders' equity in the year preceding listing of at least ¥10 billion (about US$90 million); have recorded pretax profits of at least ¥2 billion (about US$18 million) in each of the preceding three years; have paid dividends in each of the last three years and plan to be able to pay dividends in the future; present testimony from CPAs that its financial reporting is adequate and that its statements are unqualified; and must not have had any reorganization, merger, acquisition, divestiture, or other material event within six months prior to listing.

At the end of 1993, regulators agreed to lift the three year ban on new listings, suggesting some criteria for any new applicants. Applicants are expected to have return on equity (ROE) of at least 10 percent (the average for Japanese firms is currently around 3 percent). Observers estimate that perhaps 30 Japanese firms might meet this requirement. Firms are also expected to pledge to boost dividends by a cumulative 20 percent over a period to be specified and observe a 10 percent cap on bonds convertible to equity relative to outstanding equity. Regulators have also eased restrictions on the sale of warrant bonds—those with equity kickers—in foreign markets. Another issue involves investment trusts, as mutual funds are known in Japan. Fund operators currently do not have to disclose information about investment policy, holdings, portfolio managers, or past performance. The MOF set up an advisory committee to study the matter in the summer of 1993, an indication that new regulations are to follow at some point.

Brokerage Houses There are more than 250 brokerage houses operating in Japan. They offer a variety of investment services and strategies. The so-called Big Four—Nomura, Nikko, Daiwa, and Yamaichi—are among the 10 largest such outfits in the world and handle the bulk of trading and other securities-related activity. To capture the business of international investors, these brokerages have established offices in major financial centers throughout the world. Their presence in New York and London during the 1980s led to the rise of the TSE as a global force. Nomura Securities, the largest brokerage outfit in the world, has capital 50 percent greater than that of the next largest firm, Merrill Lynch. It has a strong presence in the European and US markets as well as in Japan.

The largest Japanese firms began by specializing in basic transactions, branching out into more operations as they gained heft and expertise. Although aggressive, they have not been considered to be particularly innovative. Recently, Japanese firms have begun to deal in more sophisticated derivative products, but their entry into such areas has not been an unqualified success. Attempts to deal in mortgage-backed securities, a specialized and volatile area, have resulted in large losses and reimbursements to retail customers to whom such deals were deemed to have been inappropriately sold. Brokerages have also been left holding the bag in defaults by customers on transactions and loans, especially on credits extended for operations in speculative markets.

Following the four largest Japanese firms are 10 smaller second-tier firms, five of which are still large enough to be ranked among the 25 largest brokerage houses in the world. These medium-sized firms are prominent mostly in Japan, although they operate in international markets as well. The remaining third-tier small securities firms are usually specialized subsidiaries of the larger brokers or of banks. Most of the world's leading foreign brokerage houses operate in Japan as well, although they were not allowed to operate in the country until 1986 and did not play a significant role until the late 1980s.

Debt Markets

Japanese bond markets have taken some time to reach prominence, but the economic boom in the 1980s and the shift from equity to debt financing following the stock market crash in 1989, encouraged the market for all varieties of debt to grow to be second only to that found in the United States in terms of the value of issues traded. In 1991 total turnover in all bond markets was ¥2,808 trillion (about US$21.75 trillion). Nearly 98 percent of this activity took place in the Tokyo OTC market; trading in corporate bonds listed on the TSE made up the majority of the remainder. Repurchase agreements accounted for nearly 40 percent of trading activity. Foreign net purchases of Japanese debt securities hit an all-time high of US$21.3 billion in 1991 but fell to a net sales position of US$8.2 billion in 1992 as foreign investors dumped Japanese securities.

Money Markets The short-term money markets

---

include trading in the interbank and open markets. Interbank markets, which are open only to financial institutions, involve the call market, bill market, and Tokyo dollar call market. Open markets, which are available to a wider range of participants, deal in repurchase agreements, negotiable CDs, commercial paper, treasury bills, and finance bills, as well as other instruments such as banker's acceptances and Euroyen paper.

The interbank market accounts for about 50 percent of all balances in the money market. In the open market, negotiable CDs account for the largest portion of money market balances, about 17 percent of the total money market, followed closely by commercial paper—the fastest-growing category—which runs a close second at about 16 percent. Repurchase agreements account for about 11 percent and treasury and finance bills for the remaining 6 percent. Commercial paper was introduced in 1987 and its use has grown rapidly since then as companies have sought to reduce their costs of borrowing and their dependency on bank funding.

The money market nearly doubled in size in terms of the value of instruments issued between 1986 and 1990, from ¥46.6 trillion (about US$288 billion) in 1986 to ¥88.8 trillion (about US$663 billion) in 1990. Growth leveled off following the crash of the financial markets in 1989. However, with the continued turmoil in the securities markets and the drop in interest rates, more companies are looking to shorter financing, and the money market has experienced renewed growth over the last three years.

Government Debt The Japanese government issues long-term (10 and 20 year) and medium-term (five- to 10-year) bonds, five-year discount notes, and short-term (less than 365-day) discounted treasury and finance bills. In 1992 total turnover in government securities in the OTC market was ¥28.6 trillion (about US$230 billion). On average about two-thirds of activity represents trading in short-term instruments: 46 percent of trading was in treasury bills and 19 percent was in finance bills. Long-term bonds accounted for about one-third, with five-year and intermediate bonds accounting for a minuscule 0.3 percent of the value of all transactions in the market.

Corporate Debt Corporate bonds, once scarcely used in Japan, are becoming increasingly attractive to corporations and investors alike. Corporations have more than ¥17 trillion (about US$152 billion) in bonds outstanding. In the first quarter of calendar 1993 companies issued a record ¥1.2 trillion (about US$9.7 billion) in bonds, an increase of 118 percent over the same period a year earlier. In 1992 foreign corporations issued a total of US$9.1 billion in bonds in Japan. Most debt issues consist of straight bonds. Convertibles and warrant bonds are also issued, but these instruments have lost popularity since the

stock market crash in 1989, and the issuance of new warrant bonds has been restricted until recently.

The bond market is still small compared to bank loans outstanding—more than ¥230 trillion (about US$2.1 trillion)—however, the proportion of bonds to loans is expected to increase. With banks still struggling to overcome losses from previously incurred bad debts, companies are finding it more difficult to obtain new loans, and the MOF has only recently eased its moratorium on new stock issues to allow a very few firms to list new shares. With such traditional sources of capital severely curtailed companies have had no alternative but to sell more bonds. In response to this need the MOF has lifted a 17-year ban on issuing bonds in Europe. It has also removed the prohibition on the issuance of bonds beyond a company's net capital, paving the way for companies to seek financing by issuing junk bonds.

Futures Markets

Futures trading is conducted on the TSE and the Osaka Stock Exchange. Such trading began with the establishment of the Japanese government bond (JGB) futures market by the TSE in 1985. The Osaka Exchange began trading a futures contract based on its own stock index in 1987, followed by the TSE, which began offering a contract based on the Topix index in 1988. In 1988 Osaka began offering a Nikkei-225 futures contract. The Tokyo International Financial Futures Exchange opened in 1989, offering a variety of contracts in interest rates and currencies.

Commodity Exchanges

Japan has 16 separate formal commodities exchanges, many dating back centuries and specializing in somewhat arcane products. Exchanges offer trading in commodities including raw silk and dried silkworm cocoons, intermediate products such as textiles and yarn, precious metals—gold, silver, and platinum—and more standard products such as grain, sugar, and rubber. Trading is active and involves hedging, arbitrage, and speculative activity.

FURTHER READING

This discussion is provided as a basic guide to finances, financial institutions, and financial markets in Japan. Those interested in current developments may wish to consult the *Wall Street Journal*, the *Far Eastern Economic Review*, or *Asia Money*, all of which frequently cover economic and financial developments in Japan.

Currency & Foreign Exchange

INTERNATIONAL PAYMENT INSTRUMENTS

Japan is a major international trader and as such its financial and business institutions are well versed in the use of internationally recognized payment instruments. Open accounts, letters of credit (L/Cs), and documentary collections—documents against acceptance (D/A) and documents against collection (D/C)—are the most common arrangements, although domestic and foreign banks can usually arrange other methods to accommodate special circumstances. (Refer to "International Payments" chapter.)

CURRENCY

The currency in use is the yen (¥). The Bank of Japan—the BOJ or *Nippon Ginko* in Japanese—issues coins in denominations of ¥1, ¥5, ¥10, ¥50, ¥100, and ¥500 and bank notes of ¥1,000, ¥5,000, and ¥10,000. The ¥100 coin is worth about US$0.90 and the ¥5,000 note is worth about US$45. At year-end 1993, the yen was 111.68 to the US dollar. The Japanese currency, among the strongest in the world due to the size and influence of Japan's economy, is backed by the faith and credit of the government.

REMITTANCE AND EXCHANGE CONTROLS

Japanese laws prohibit most direct foreign exchange transactions between individuals and businesses. Foreign exchange operations are carried out by authorized foreign exchange banks. These include city banks, foreign branch banks, and some smaller local banks. The BOJ oversees foreign exchange in the country. One city bank, the Bank of Tokyo, specializes exclusively in foreign exchange transactions of one variety or another, a holdover from its role during the 1950s and 1960s as the exclusive agent for external operations. Unlimited amounts of foreign currency can be brought into the country as long as it is declared to customs on entry. Visitors

can reconvert yen into foreign exchange when leaving the country up to any amount they have converted while in the country as demonstrated by presentation of the receipts showing the initial conversion. Residents can take up to ¥5 million (about US$45,000) out of the country.

Exchange controls are mainly theoretical rather than practical barriers, designed to delay rather than shut off convertibility if a core meltdown in the financial system occurs. These rules have never been invoked. No black market in currency exists because both the yen and foreign exchange are readily available. Businesses will almost always operate through a bank and may be able to negotiate wholesale rates, although the reduction in the spread will be marginal.

For smaller transactions foreign exchange banks, all of the larger institutions and many of the smaller ones, are the primary outlet, and rates are generally uniform no matter which bank is used. Money can be changed with licensed money changers, at the airport, and in most of the larger hotels. All outlets require the presentation of a passport. Foreign currency is not accepted in Japan as it is in some other Asian countries. Traveler's checks are readily negotiable and usually get a slightly better exchange rate as well. Most retail outlets, except for the smallest, will accept yen-denominated traveler's checks. Personal checks are not generally used, even those drawn in yen on a Japanese bank. Major credit cards have gained wide acceptance, mostly within the past five years, in larger outlets in urban areas. Usually no cash discount is offered in preference to a credit card, but merchants may balk at accepting a card in payment for a small transaction. In general, people in Japan use cash for most purposes, including some that in most other countries would call for some other form of payment.

Foreigners can get money from home by using automated teller machines (ATMs), most of which provide cash advances on major credit cards and some of which will take foreign ATM or debit cards. Users will need to know which systems their bank is affiliated with, their personal identification number (PIN), and the Japanese characters for basic instructions. The ease of using these procedures is offset by the costs—interest and transfer fees—although the institutions issuing the cards commonly offer decent exchange rates on such transactions. Money transfers are usually available from most large banks; branch-to-branch transfers within the same bank are quickest and easiest, but transfers can also be arranged via correspondent banks.

FOREIGN EXCHANGE OPERATIONS

The exchange control system is operated jointly by the Ministry of Finance, the Ministry of International Trade and Industry, and the Bank of Japan, to which the implementation of policy is delegated. In practice, the BOJ delegates foreign exchange operations to authorized foreign exchange banks. There are no taxes on foreign exchange transactions.

Foreign exchange markets operate in Tokyo and Osaka with authorized foreign exchange banks, licensed foreign exchange (forex) brokers, and the BOJ as the only participants. Yen-US dollar transactions account for about 80 percent of all activity on the primary Tokyo market. Volume has been falling in recent years with average daily turnover dropping from US$18.9 billion in 1991 to US$16.2 billion in 1992, about one-third of that in Hong Kong and one-quarter of that in Singapore. Trading is about two-thirds in forward contracts and one-third in spot contracts, a proportion that has remained fairly stable in recent years.

The Foreign Exchange and Foreign Trade Control Law (FEFTCL), amended in 1980, opened up payments except in the following cases, which require advance approval: payments made via credits or debits to current accounts, payments made over a longer period than the standard one specified by the MOF, and payments made by exceptional methods as determined by the MOF.

Because of its size, importance in the world economy, general financial sophistication, and geographic location between financial centers in Europe and the United States, Japan is an important foreign exchange market. However, the controls that it maintains on foreign exchange operations have allowed it to be outstripped by both Singapore and Hong Kong in this critical and free wheeling area of international financial operations.

Foreign exchange markets are often used by international businesses to hedge against foreign exchange fluctuations from the time of an agreement on a transaction to the time of the actual sale of goods or services. Businesses agree to purchase foreign currency in the future at a predetermined rate of exchange, a relatively standard process in repatriating profits from Japan.

RATES OF EXCHANGE

Japan allows the yen to float freely, although the BOJ undertakes open-market operations in attempts to support the currency within what it considers to be acceptable limits as dictated by policy. The size and internationalization of the market has rendered such operations less effective in recent years. Since Japan's rise as a world economic power began in the late 1960s the yen has steadily appreciated against the US dollar, climbing from a low of 358.0 in January 1971 to 111.7 at the end of 1993. During summer

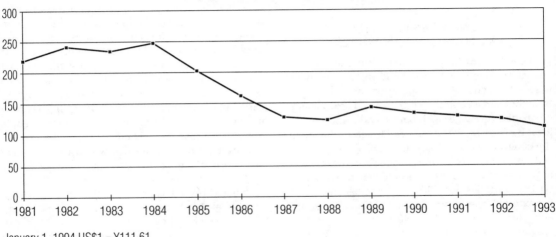

Japan's Foreign Exchange Rates - Year End Actual
Yen (¥) to United States Dollar (US$)

January 1, 1994 US$1 = ¥111.61

1993 the yen briefly flirted with the 100 level before recovering to remain on the three-digit side of that important psychological barrier. Japan's stubbornly strong balance of trade surplus is likely to keep the yen stronger than Japan would like for the foreseeable future, unless the Japanese economy weakens enough to require the authorities to draw heavily on the government's reserves to keep it going.

FOREIGN RESERVES

As of May 1993 Japan's foreign reserves stood at US$82.5 billion, the highest in the world except for those of Taiwan, which held an anomalously high US$84.9 billion in international reserves. Despite efforts to reduce its balance of trade surpluses, Japan's 1993 reserve position was up 16 percent in US dollar terms from US$71 billion a year earlier. Much of this change could be attributed to the depreciation of the dollar against the yen, but the trade surpluses feeding the growth of international reserves continue to grow. To date the rise in the yen has made Japanese goods less affordable, cutting Japan's exports somewhat, although the higher prices it gets for what it does sell abroad have more than offset the drop in

dollar terms. The slowdown at home has kept imports from rising significantly, especially because Japan pays for its primary import—oil—with relatively cheap dollars.

Japan is the world's largest creditor nation, its foreign interest income serving to offset its own public debt. Although the government issues large volumes of public debt, this has been primarily used in recent years to manage interest and foreign exchange rates and to provide liquidity to the system. This situation is expected to change as Japan gets set to make massive infrastructure investments and care for its rapidly aging population. Policymakers are also considering a substantial cut in income tax rates to stimulate consumption, which could lead to more debt issuance to make up the shortfall.

FURTHER READING

This discussion is provided as a basic guide to money and financial markets in Japan. Those interested in current developments may wish to consult the *Wall Street Journal*, the *Far Eastern Economic Review*, or *Asia Money*, all of which frequently cover economic and financial developments in Japan.

Exchange Rates—¥/US$

	Jan	Feb	Mar	Apr	May	Jun	Jul	Aug	Sep	Oct	Nov	Dec
1981	202.4	205.7	208.8	215.0	220.6	224.2	232.3	233.3	229.5	231.5	223.1	218.9
1982	224.8	235.3	241.2	244.1	237.0	251.2	255.0	259.0	263.3	271.6	264.1	241.9
1983	232.7	236.1	238.2	237.7	234.7	240.0	240.5	244.5	242.3	232.9	235.0	234.5
1984	233.8	233.6	225.3	225.2	230.5	233.6	243.1	242.3	245.4	246.7	243.6	248.0
1985	254.2	260.5	257.9	251.8	251.7	248.8	241.1	237.5	236.5	214.7	204.1	202.8
1986	199.9	184.8	178.7	175.1	167.0	167.5	158.6	154.2	154.7	156.5	162.8	162.0
1987	154.8	153.4	151.4	142.9	140.5	144.5	150.3	147.3	143.3	143.3	135.4	128.2
1988	128.8	129.2	127.1	124.9	124.8	127.5	133.0	133.8	134.3	128.7	123.2	123.6
1989	127.4	127.7	130.5	132.0	137.9	144.0	140.4	141.5	145.1	142.2	143.5	143.7
1990	145.0	145.7	153.7	158.4	154.0	153.7	149.0	147.5	138.4	129.6	129.2	133.9
1991	133.7	130.5	137.4	137.1	138.2	139.7	137.8	136.8	134.3	130.8	129.6	129.0
1992	125.5	127.7	132.9	133.5	130.8	126.8	125.9	126.2	122.6	121.2	123.9	124.2
1993	125.0	120.7	117.0	112.4	110.3	107.4	107.7	103.8	105.6	105.9	108.9	111.7

International Payments

International transactions add an additional layer of risk for buyers and sellers that are familiar only with doing business domestically. Currency regulations, foreign exchange risk, political, economic, or social upheaval in the buyer's or seller's country, and different business customs may all contribute to uncertainty. Ultimately, however, the seller wants to make sure he gets paid and the buyer wants to get what he pays for. Choosing the right payment method can be the key to the transaction's feasibility and profitability.

There are four common methods of international payment, each providing the buyer and the seller with varying degrees of protection for getting paid and for guaranteeing shipment. Ranked in order of most security for the supplier to most security for the buyer, they are: Cash in Advance, Documentary Letters of Credit (L/C), Documentary Collections (D/P and D/A Terms), and Open Account (O/A).

Cash in Advance

In cash in advance terms the buyer simply prepays the supplier prior to shipment of goods. Cash in advance terms are generally used in new relationships where transactions are small and the buyer has no choice but to pre-pay. These terms give maximum security to the seller but leave the buyer at great risk. Since the buyer has no guarantee that the goods will be shipped, he must have a high degree of trust in the seller's ability and willingness to follow through. The buyer must also consider the economic, political and social stability of the seller's country, as these conditions may make it impossible for the seller to ship as promised.

Documentary Letters of Credit

A letter of credit is a bank's promise to pay a supplier on behalf of the buyer so long as the supplier meets the terms and conditions stated in the credit. Documents are the key issue in letter of credit transactions. Banks act as intermediaries, and have nothing to do with the goods themselves.

Letters of credit are the most common form of international payment because they provide a high degree of protection for both the seller and the buyer. The buyer specifies the documentation that he requires from the seller before the bank is to make payment, and the seller is given assurance that he will receive payment after shipping his goods so long as the documentation is in order.

Documentary Collections

A documentary collection is like an international cash on delivery (COD), but with a few twists. The exporter ships goods to the importer, but forwards shipping documents (including title document) to his bank for transmission to the buyer's bank. The buyer's bank is instructed not to transfer the documents to the buyer until payment is made (Documents against Payment, D/P) or upon guarantee that payment will be made within a specified period of time (Documents against Acceptance, D/A). Once the buyer has the documentation for the shipment he is able to take possession of the goods.

D/P and D/A terms are commonly used in ongoing business relationships and provide a measure of protection for both parties. The buyer and seller, however, both assume risk in the transaction, ranging from refusal on the part of the buyer to pay for the documents, to the seller's shipping of unacceptable goods.

Open Account

This is an agreement by the buyer to pay for goods within a designated time after their shipment, usually in 30, 60, or 90 days. Open account terms give maximum security to the buyer and greatest risk to the seller. This form of payment is used only when the seller has significant trust and faith in the buyer's ability and willingness to pay once the goods have been shipped. The seller must also consider the economic, political and social stability of the buyer's country as these conditions may make it impossible for the buyer to pay as promised.

DOCUMENTARY COLLECTIONS (D/P, D/A)

Documentary collections focus on the transfer of documents such as bills of lading for the transfer of ownership of goods rather than on the goods themselves. They are easier to use than letters of credit and bank service charges are generally lower.

This form of payment is excellent for buyers who wish to purchase goods without risking prepayment and without having to go through the more cumbersome letter of credit process.

Documentary collection procedures, however, entail risk for the supplier, because payment is not made until after goods are shipped. In addition, the supplier assumes the risk while the goods are in transit and storage until payment/acceptance take place. Banks involved in the transaction do not guarantee payments. A supplier should therefore only agree to a documentary collection procedure if the transaction includes the following characteristics:

- The supplier does not doubt the buyer's ability and willingness to pay for the goods;
- The buyer's country is politically, economically, and legally stable;
- There are no foreign exchange restrictions in the buyer's home country, or unless all necessary licenses for foreign exchange have already been obtained;
- The goods to be shipped are easily marketable.

Types of Collections

The three types of documentary collections are:
1. Documents against Payment (D/P)
2. Documents against Acceptance (D/A)
3. Collection with Acceptance (Acceptance D/P)

All of these collection procedures follow the same general step-by-step process of exchanging documents proving title to goods for either cash or a contracted promise to pay at a later time. The documents are transferred from the supplier (called the remitter) to the buyer (called the drawee) via intermediary banks. When the supplier ships goods, he presents documents such as the bill of lading, invoices, and certificate of origin to his representative bank (the remitting bank), which then forwards them to the buyer's bank (the collecting bank). According to the type of documentary collection, the buyer may then do one of the following:

- With Documents against Payment (D/P), the buyer may only receive the title and other documents after paying for the goods;
- With Documents against Acceptance (D/A), the buyer may receive the title and other documents after signing a time draft promising to pay at a later date;

- With Acceptance Documents against Payment, the buyer signs a time draft for payment at a later date. However, he may only obtain the documents after the time draft reaches maturity. In essence, the goods remain in escrow until payment has been made.

In all cases the buyer may take possession of the goods only by presenting the bill of lading to customs or shipping authorities.

In the event that the prospective buyer cannot or will not pay for the goods shipped, they remain in legal possession of the supplier, but he may be stuck with them in an unfavorable situation. Also, the supplier has no legal basis to file claim against the prospective buyer. At this point the supplier may:

- Have the goods returned and sell them on his domestic market; or
- Sell the goods to another buyer near where the goods are currently held.

If the supplier takes no action the goods will be auctioned or otherwise disposed of by customs.

Documentary Collection Procedure

The documentary collection process has been standardized by a set of rules published by the International Chamber of Commerce (ICC). These rules are called the Uniform Rules for Collections (URC) and are contained in ICC Publication No. 322. (See the last page of this section for ICC addresses and list of available publications.)

The following is the basic set of steps used in a documentary collection. Refer to the illustration on the following page for a graphic representation of the procedure.

(1) The seller (remitter, exporter) ships the goods.
(2) and (3) The seller forwards the agreed upon documents to his bank, the remitting bank, which in turn forwards them to the collecting bank (buyer's bank).
(4) The collecting bank notifies the buyer (drawee, importer) and informs him of the conditions under which he can take possession of the documents.
(5) To take possession of the documents, the buyer makes payment or signs a time deposit.
(6) and (7) If the buyer draws the documents against payment, the collecting bank transfers payment to the remitting bank for credit to the supplier's account. If the buyer draws the documents against acceptance, the collecting bank sends the acceptance to the remitting bank or retains it up to maturity. On maturity, the collecting bank collects the bill and transfers it to the remitting bank for payment to the supplier.

Documentary Collection Procedure

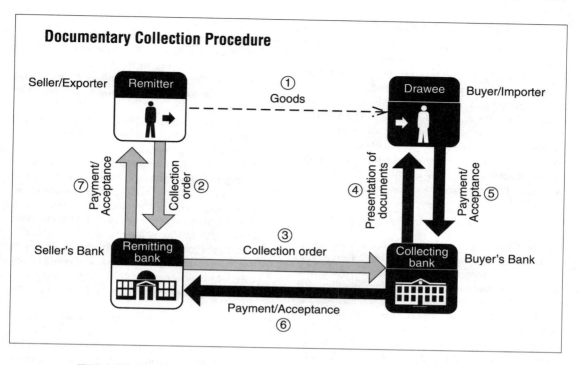

Seller/Exporter — Remitter

① Goods

Drawee — Buyer/Importer

⑦ Payment/Acceptance

② Collection order

④ Presentation of documents

⑤ Payment/Acceptance

Seller's Bank — Remitting bank

③ Collection order

Collecting bank — Buyer's Bank

Payment/Acceptance ⑥

TIPS FOR BUYERS

1. The buyer is generally in a secure position because he does not assume ownership or responsibility for goods until he has paid for the documents or signed a time draft.
2. The buyer may not sample or inspect the goods before accepting and paying for the documents without authorization from the seller. However, the buyer may in advance specify a certificate of inspection as part of the required documentation package.
3. As a special favor, the collecting bank can allow the buyer to inspect the documents before payment. The collecting bank assumes responsibility for the documents until their redemption.
4. In the above case, the buyer should immediately return the entire set of documents to the collecting bank if he cannot meet the agreed payment procedure.
5. The buyer assumes no liability for goods if he refuses to take possession of the documents.
6. Partial payment in exchange for the documents is not allowed unless authorized in the collection order.
7. With documents against acceptance, the buyer may receive the goods and resell them for profit before the time draft matures, thereby using the proceeds of the sale to pay for the goods. The buyer remains responsible for payment, however, even if he cannot sell the goods.

TIPS FOR SUPPLIERS

1. The supplier assumes risk because he ships goods before receiving payment. The buyer is under no legal obligation to pay for or to accept the goods.
2. Before agreeing to a documentary collection, the supplier should check on the buyer's creditworthiness and business reputation.
3. The supplier should make sure the buyer's country is politically and financially stable.
4. The supplier should find out what documents are required for customs clearance in the buyer's country. Consulates may be of help.
5. The supplier should assemble the documents carefully and make sure they are in the required form and endorsed as necessary.
6. As a rule, the remitting bank will not review the documents before forwarding them to the collecting bank. This is the responsibility of the seller.
7. The goods travel and are stored at the risk of the supplier until payment or acceptance.
8. If the buyer refuses acceptance or payment for the documents, the supplier retains ownership. The supplier may have the goods shipped back or try to sell them to another buyer in the region.
9. If the buyer takes no action, customs authorities may seize the goods and auction them off or otherwise dispose of them.
10. Because goods may be refused, the supplier should only ship goods which are readily marketable to other sources.

LETTERS OF CREDIT (L/C)

A letter of credit is a document issued by a bank stating its commitment to pay someone (supplier/exporter/seller) a stated amount of money on behalf of a buyer (importer) so long as the seller meets very specific terms and conditions. Letters of credit are often called documentary letters of credit because the banks handling the transaction deal in documents as opposed to goods. Letters of credit are the most common method of making international payments, because the risks of the transaction are shared by both the buyer and the supplier.

STEPS IN USING AN L/C

The letter of credit process has been standardized by a set of rules published by the International Chamber of Commerce (ICC). These rules are called the Uniform Customs and Practice for Documentary Credits (UCP) and are contained in ICC Publication No. 400. (See the last page of this section for ICC addresses and list of available publications.) The following is the basic set of steps used in a letter of credit transaction. Specific letter of credit transactions follow somewhat different procedures.

- After the buyer and supplier agree on the terms of a sale, the buyer arranges for his bank to open a letter of credit in favor of the supplier.
- The buyer's bank (the issuing bank), prepares the letter of credit, including all of the buyer's instructions to the seller concerning shipment and required documentation.
- The buyer's bank sends the letter of credit to a correspondent bank (the advising bank), in the seller's country. The seller may request that a particular bank be the advising bank, or the domestic bank may select one of its correspondent banks in the seller's country.
- The advising bank forwards the letter of credit to the supplier.
- The supplier carefully reviews all conditions the buyer has stipulated in the letter of credit. If the supplier cannot comply with one or more of the provisions he immediately notifies the buyer and asks that an amendment be made to the letter of credit.
- After final terms are agreed upon, the supplier prepares the goods and arranges for their shipment to the appropriate port.
- The supplier ships the goods, and obtains a bill of lading and other documents as required by the buyer in the letter of credit. Some of these documents may need to be obtained prior to shipment.
- The supplier presents the required documents to the advising bank, indicating full compliance with the terms of the letter of credit. Required documents usually include a bill of lading, commercial invoice, certificate of origin, and possibly an inspection certificate if required by the buyer.
- The advising bank reviews the documents. If they are in order, the documents are forwarded to the issuing bank. If it is an irrevocable, confirmed letter of credit the supplier is guaranteed payment and may be paid immediately by the advising bank.
- Once the issuing bank receives the documents it notifies the buyer who then reviews the documents himself. If the documents are in order the buyer signs off, taking possession of the documents, including the bill of lading, which he uses to take possession of the shipment.
- The issuing bank initiates payment to the advising bank, which pays the supplier.

The transfer of funds from the buyer to his bank, from the buyer's bank to the supplier's bank, and from the supplier's bank to the supplier may be handled at the same time as the exchange of documents, or under terms agreed upon in advance.

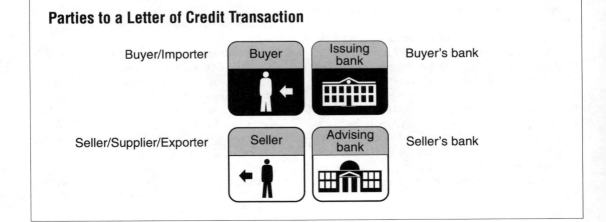

Parties to a Letter of Credit Transaction

| Buyer/Importer | Buyer | Issuing bank | Buyer's bank |
| Seller/Supplier/Exporter | Seller | Advising bank | Seller's bank |

Issuance

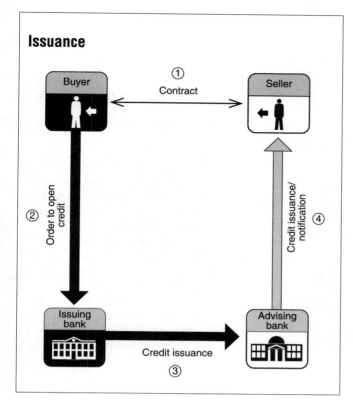

Issuance of a Letter of Credit

① Buyer and seller agree on purchase contract.
② Buyer applies for and opens a letter of credit with issuing ("buyer's") bank.
③ Issuing bank issues the letter of credit, forwarding it to advising ("seller's") bank.
④ Advising bank notifies seller of letter of credit.

Amendment

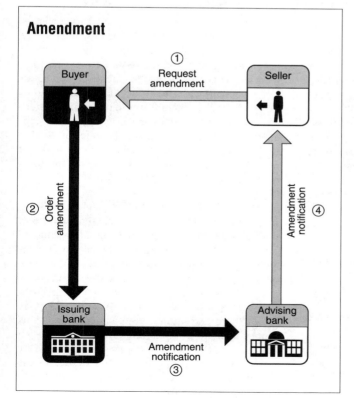

Amendment of a Letter of Credit

① Seller requests (of the buyer) a modification (amendment) of the terms of the letter of credit. Once the terms are agreed upon:
② Buyer issues order to issuing ("buyer's") bank to make an amendment to the terms of the letter of credit.
③ Issuing bank notifies advising ("seller's") bank of amendment.
④ Advising bank notifies seller of amendment.

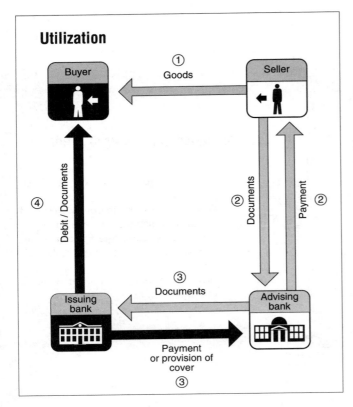

Utilization

1 Goods

Buyer

Seller

2 Documents

2 Payment

4 Debit / Documents

3 Documents

Issuing bank

Advising bank

Payment or provision of cover

3

Utilization of a Letter of Credit

(irrevocable, confirmed credit)

① Seller ships goods to buyer.
② Seller forwards all documents (as stipulated in the letter of credit) to advising bank. Once documents are reviewed and accepted, advising bank pays seller for the goods.
③ Advising bank forwards documents to issuing bank. Once documents are reviewed and accepted, issuing bank pays advising bank.
④ Issuing bank forwards documents to buyer. Seller's letter of credit, or account, is debited.

COMMON PROBLEMS IN LETTER OF CREDIT TRANSACTIONS

Most problems with letter of credit transactions have to do with the ability of the supplier to fulfill obligations the buyer establishes in the original letter of credit. The supplier may find the terms of the credit difficult or impossible to fulfill and either tries to do so and fails, or asks the buyer for an amendment to the letter of credit. Observers note that over half of all letters of credit involving parties in East Asia are amended or renegotiated entirely. Since most letters of credit are irrevocable, amendments to the original letter of credit can only be made after further negotiations and agreements between the buyer and the supplier. Suppliers may have one or more of the following problems:

- Shipment schedule stipulated in the letter of credit cannot be met.
- Stipulations concerning freight cost are deemed unacceptable.
- Price is insufficient due to changes in exchange rates.
- Quantity of product ordered is not the expected amount.
- Description of product to be shipped is either insufficient or too detailed.
- Documents stipulated in the letter of credit are difficult or impossible to obtain.

Even when suppliers accept the terms of a letter of credit, problems often arise at the stage where banks review, or negotiate, the documents provided by the supplier against the requirements specified in the letter of credit. If the documents are found not to be in accord with those specified in the letter of credit, the bank's commitment to pay is invalidated. In some cases the supplier can correct the documents and present them within the time specified in the letter of credit. Or, the advising bank may ask the issuing bank for authorization to accept the documents despite the discrepancies found.

Limits on Legal Obligations of Banks

It is important to note once again that banks *deal in documents and not in goods.* Only the wording of the credit is binding on the bank. Banks are not responsible for verifying the authenticity of the documents, nor for the quality or quantity of the goods being shipped. As long as the *documents* comply with the specified terms of the letter of credit, banks may accept them and initiate the payment process as stipulated in the letter of credit. Banks are free from liability for delays in sending messages caused by another party, consequences of Acts of God, or the acts of third parties whom they have instructed to carry out transactions.

TYPES OF LETTERS OF CREDIT

Basic Letters of Credit

There are two basic forms of letters of credit: the Revocable Credit and the Irrevocable Credit. There are also two types of irrevocable credit: the Irrevocable Credit not Confirmed, and the Irrevocable Confirmed Credit. Each type of credit has advantages and disadvantages for the buyer and for the seller. Also note that the more the banks assume risk by guaranteeing payment, the more they will charge for providing the service.

1. Revocable credit This credit can be changed or canceled by the buyer without prior notice to the supplier. Because it offers little security to the seller revocable credits are generally unacceptable to the seller and are rarely used.

2. Irrevocable credit The irrevocable credit is one which the issuing bank commits itself irrevocably to honor, provided the beneficiary complies with all stipulated conditions. This credit cannot be changed or canceled without the consent of both the buyer and the seller. As a result, this type of credit is the most widely used in international trade. Irrevocable credits are more expensive because of the issuing bank's added liability in guaranteeing the credit. There are two types of irrevocable credits:

a. The Irrevocable Credit not Confirmed by the Advising Bank (Unconfirmed Credit) This means that the buyer's bank which issues the credit is the only party responsible for payment to the supplier, and the supplier's bank is obliged to pay the supplier only after receiving payment from the buyer's bank. The supplier's bank merely acts on behalf of the issuing bank and therefore incurs no risk.

b. The Irrevocable, Confirmed Credit In a confirmed credit, the advising bank adds its guarantee to pay the supplier to that of the issuing bank. If the issuing bank fails to make payment the advising bank will pay. If a supplier is unfamiliar with the buyer's bank which issues the letter of credit, he may insist on an irrevocable confirmed credit. These credits may be used when trade is conducted in a high risk area where there are fears of outbreak of war or social, political, or financial instability. Confirmed credits may also be used by the supplier to enlist the aid of a local bank to extend financing to enable him to fill the order. A confirmed credit costs more because the bank has added liability.

Special Letters of Credit

There are numerous special letters of credit designed to meet specific needs of buyers, suppliers, and intermediaries. Special letters of credit usually involve increased participation by banks, so financing and service charges are higher than those for basic letters of credit. The following is a brief description of some special letters of credit.

1. Standby Letter of Credit This credit is primarily a payment or performance guarantee. It is used primarily in the United States because US banks are prevented by law from giving certain guarantees. Standby credits are often called non-performing letters of credit because they are only used as a backup payment method if the collection on a primary payment method is past due.

Standby letters of credit can be used, for example, to guarantee the following types of payment and performance:

- repayment of loans;
- fulfillment by subcontractors;
- securing the payment for goods delivered by third parties.

The beneficiary to a standby letter of credit can draw from it on demand, so the buyer assumes added risk.

2. Revolving Letter of Credit This credit is a commitment on the part of the issuing bank to restore the credit to the original amount after it has been used or drawn down. The number of times it can be utilized and the period of validity is stated in the credit. The credit can be cumulative or noncumulative. Cumulative means that unutilized sums can be added to the next installment whereas noncumulative means that partial amounts not utilized in time expire.

3. Deferred Payment Letter of Credit In this credit the buyer takes delivery of the shipped goods by accepting the documents and agreeing to pay his bank after a fixed period of time. This credit gives the buyer a grace period, and ensures that the seller gets payment on the due date.

4. Red Clause Letter of Credit This is used to provide the supplier with some funds prior to shipment to finance production of the goods. The credit may be advanced in part or in full, and the buyer's bank finances the advance payment. The buyer, in essence, extends financing to the seller and incurs ultimate risk for all advanced credits.

5. Transferable Letter of Credit This allows the supplier to transfer all or part of the proceeds of the letter of credit to a second beneficiary, usually the ultimate producer of the goods. This is a common financing tactic for middlemen and is used extensively in the Far East.

6. Back-to-Back Letter of Credit This is a new credit opened on the basis of an already existing, nontransferable credit. It is used by traders to make payment to the ultimate supplier. A trader receives a letter of credit from the buyer and then opens another letter of credit in favor of the supplier. The first letter of credit is used as collateral for the second credit. The second credit makes price adjustments from which come the trader's profit.

OPENING A LETTER OF CREDIT

The wording in a letter of credit should be simple but specific. The more detailed an L/C is, the more likely the supplier will reject it as too difficult to fulfill. At the same time, the buyer will wish to define in detail what he is paying for.

Although the L/C process is designed to ensure the satisfaction of all parties to the transaction, it cannot be considered a substitute for face-to-face agreements on doing business in good faith. It should therefore contain only those stipulations required from the banks involved in the documentary process.

L/Cs used in trade with East Asia are usually either irrevocable unconfirmed credits or irrevocable confirmed credits. In choosing the type of L/C to open in favor of the supplier, the buyer should take into consideration generally accepted payment processes in the supplier's country, the value and demand for the goods to be shipped, and the reputation of the supplier.

In specifying documents necessary from the supplier, it is very important to demand documents that are required for customs clearance and those that reflect the agreement reached between the buyer and the supplier. Required documents usually include the bill of lading, a commercial and/or consular invoice, the bill of exchange, the certificate of origin, and the insurance document. Other documents required may be copies of a cable sent to the buyer with shipping information, a confirmation from the shipping company of the state of its ship, and a confirmation from the forwarder that the goods are accompanied by a certificate of origin. Prices should be stated in the currency of the L/C, and documents should be supplied in the language of the L/C.

THE APPLICATION

The following information should be included on an application form for opening an L/C.

(1) **Beneficiary** The seller's company name and address should be written completely and correctly. Incomplete or incorrect information results in delays and unnecessary additional cost.

(2) **Amount** Is the figure a maximum amount or an approximate amount? If words like "circa," "ca.," "about," etc., are used in connection with the amount of the credit, it means that a difference as high as 10 percent upwards or downwards is permitted. In such a case, the same word should also be used in connection with the quantity.

(3) **Validity Period** The validity and period for presentation of the documents following shipment of the goods should be sufficiently long to allow the exporter time to prepare his documents and ship them to the bank. Under place of validity, state the domicile of either the advising bank or the issuing bank.

(4) **Beneficiary's Bank** If no bank is named, the issuing bank is free to select the correspondent bank.

(5) **Type of Payment Availability** Sight drafts, time drafts, or deferred payment may be used, as previously agreed to by the supplier and buyer.

(6) **Desired Documents** Here the buyer specifies precisely which documents he requires. To obtain effective protection against the supply of poor quality goods, for instance, he can demand the submission of analysis or quality certificates. These are generally issued by specialized inspection companies or laboratories.

(7) **Notify Address** An address is given for notification of the imminent arrival of goods at the port or airport of destination. Damage of goods in shipment is also cause for notification. An agent representing the buyer may be used.

(8) **Description of Goods** Here a short, precise description of the goods is given, along with quantity. If the credit amount carries the notation "ca.," the same notation should appear with the quantity.

(9) **Confirmation Order** It may happen that the foreign beneficiary insists on having the credit confirmed by the bank in his country.

Sample Letter of Credit Application

Sender	Instructions to open a Documentary Credit
M ü l l e r Ltd. Tellstrasse 26 4053 Basel Our reference AB/02	Basel, 30th September 19.. Place / Date

Please open the following

[X] irrevocable   [ ] revocable documentary credit

Swiss Bank Corporation
Documentary Credits
P.O. Box
4002 Basel

Beneficiary	Beneficiary's bank (if known)
① Adilma Trading Corporation 27, Nihonbashi, Chiyoda-ku Tokyo 125 / Japan	④ Japanese Commercial Bank Ginza Branch Tokyo 37 / Japan

Amount
② US$ 70'200.--

Please advise this bank
[ ] by letter
[X] by letter, cabling main details in advance
[ ] by telex / telegram with full text of credit

Date and place of expiry
③ 25th November 19.. in Basel

Partial shipments	Transhipment	Terms of shipment (FOB, C & F, CIF)
[X] allowed [ ] not allowed	[ ] allowed [X] not allowed	CIF Rotterdam

Despatch from / Taking in charge at	For transportation to	Latest date of shipment	Documents must be presented not later than
Japan	Rotterdam	10th Nov. 19..	③ 15 days after date of despatch

Beneficiary may dispose of the credit amount as follows

[X] at sight upon presentation of documents   ⑤

[ ] after .... days, calculated from date of ....

[ ] by a draft due ....

drawn on   [ ] you   [ ] your correspondents

which you / your correspondents will please accept

against surrender of the following documents ⑥

[X] invoice   (....3....copies)

Shipping document
[X] sea: bill of lading, to order, endorsed in blank
[ ] rail: dublicate waybill
[ ] air: air consignment note
[ ]

[X] insurance policy, certificte   (................ copies)
covering the following risks:
"all risks" including war up to
[ ] Additional documents final destination in
Switzerland
[X] Confirmation of the carrier that the
ship is not more than 15 years old
[X] packing list (3 copies)

Notify address on bill of lading / goods addressed to

Müller AG, Tellstrasse 26, ⑦
4053 Basel

Goods insured by	[ ] us	[X] seller

Goods ⑧

1'000 "Record players ANC 83 as per proforma invoice
no. 74/1853 dd 10th September 19.."

at US$ 70.20 per item

Your correspondents to advise beneficiary [ ] adding their confirmation [X] without adding their confirmation ⑨

Payments to be debited to our... Swiss Francs .... account no 10-326'791.0

NB. The applicable text is marked by [X]

E 6801 N 1/2 3.81 5000

MÜLLER   AG   BASEL

Signature _____

For mailing please see overleaf

This credit is subject to the «Uniform customs and practice for documentary credits» fixed by the International Chamber of Commerce. It is understood that you do not assume any responsibility neither for the correctness, validity or genuineness of the documents which will be remitted to you nor for the description, quality, quantity and weight of the goods thereby represented.

TIPS FOR PARTIES TO A LETTER OF CREDIT

Buyer

1. Before opening a letter of credit, the buyer should reach agreement with the supplier on all particulars of payment procedures, schedules of shipment, type of goods to be sent, and documents to be supplied by the supplier.
2. When choosing the type of L/C to be used, the buyer should take into account standard payment methods in the country with which he is doing business.
3. When opening a letter of credit, the buyer should keep the details of the purchase short and concise.
4. The buyer should be prepared to amend or renegotiate terms of the L/C with the supplier. This is a common procedure in international trade. On irrevocable L/Cs, the most common type, amendments may be made only if all parties involved in the L/C agree.
5. The buyer can eliminate exchange risk involved with import credits in foreign currencies by purchasing foreign exchange on the forward markets.
6. The buyer should use a bank experienced in foreign trade as the L/C issuing bank.
7. The validation time stated on the L/C should give the supplier ample time to produce the goods or to pull them out of stock.
8. The buyer should be aware that an L/C is not failsafe. Banks are only responsible for the documents exchanged and not the goods shipped. Documents in conformity with L/C specifications cannot be rejected on grounds that the goods were not delivered as specified in the contract. The goods shipped may not in fact be the goods ordered and paid for.
9. Purchase contracts and other agreements pertaining to the sale between the buyer and supplier are not the concern of the issuing bank. Only the terms of the L/C are binding on the bank.
10. Documents specified in the L/C should include those the buyer requires for customs clearance.

Supplier

1. Before signing a contract, the supplier should make inquiries about the buyer's creditworthiness and business practices. The supplier's bank will generally assist in this investigation.
2. The supplier should confirm the good standing of the buyer's bank if the credit is unconfirmed.
3. For confirmed credit, the supplier should determine that his local bank is willing to confirm credits from the buyer and his bank.
4. The supplier should carefully review the L/C to make sure he can meet the specified schedules of shipment, type of goods to be sent, packaging, and documentation. All aspects of the L/C must be in conformance with the terms agreed upon, including the supplier's address, the amount to be paid, and the prescribed transport route.
5. The supplier must comply with every detail of the L/C specifications, otherwise the security given by the credit is lost.
6. The supplier should ensure that the L/C is irrevocable.
7. If conditions of the credit have to be modified, the supplier should contact the buyer immediately so that he can instruct the issuing bank to make the necessary amendments.
8. The supplier should confirm with his insurance company that it can provide the coverage specified in the credit, and that insurance charges in the L/C are correct. Insurance coverage often is for CIF (cost, insurance, freight) value of the goods plus 10 percent.
9. The supplier must ensure that the details of goods being sent comply with the description in the L/C, and that the description on the invoice matches that on the L/C.
10. The supplier should be familiar with foreign exchange limitations in the buyer's country which may hinder payment procedures.

GLOSSARY OF DOCUMENTS IN INTERNATIONAL TRADE

The following is a list and description of some of the more common documents importers and exporters encounter in the course of international trade. For the importer/buyer this serves as a checklist of documents he may require of the seller/exporter in a letter of credit or documents against payment method.

Bill of Lading A document issued by a transportation company (such as a shipping line) to the shipper which serves as a receipt for goods shipped, a contract for delivery, and may serve as a title document. The major types are:

Straight (non-negotiable) Bill of Lading Indicates that the shipper will deliver the goods to the consignee. The document itself does not give title to the goods. The consignee need only identify himself to claim the goods. A straight bill of lading is often used when the goods have been paid for in advance.

Order (negotiable or "shippers order") Bill of Lading This is a title document which must be in the possession of the consignee (buyer/importer) in order for him to take possession of the shipped goods. Because this bill of lading is negotiable, it is usually made out "to the order of" the consignor (seller/exporter).

Air Waybill A bill of lading issued for air shipment of goods, which is always made out in straight non-negotiable form. It serves as a receipt for the shipper and needs to be made out to someone who can take possession of the goods upon arrival—without waiting for other documents to arrive.

Overland/Inland Bill of Lading Similar to an Air Waybill, except that it covers ground or water transport.

Certificate of Origin A document which certifies the country of origin of the goods. Because a certificate of origin is often required by customs for entry, a buyer will often stipulate in his letter of credit that a certificate of origin is a required document.

Insurance Document A document certifying that goods are insured for shipment.

Invoice/Commercial Invoice A document identifying the seller and buyer of goods or services, identifying numbers such as invoice number, date, shipping date, mode of transport, delivery and payment terms, and a complete listing and description of the goods or services being sold including prices, discounts, and quantities. The commercial invoice is usually used by customs to determine the true cost of goods when assessing duty.

Certificate of manufacture A document in which the producer of goods certifies that production has been completed and that the goods are at the disposal of the buyer.

Consular Invoice An invoice prepared on a special form supplied by the consul of an importing country, in the language of the importing country, and certified by a consular official of the foreign country.

Dock Receipt A document/receipt issued by an ocean carrier when the seller/exporter is not responsible for moving the goods to their final destination, but only to a dock in the exporting country. The document/receipt indicates that the goods were, in fact, delivered and received at the specified dock.

Export License A document, issued by a government agency, giving authorization to export certain commodities to specified countries.

Import License A document, issued by a government agency, giving authorization to import certain commodities.

Inspection Certificate An affidavit signed by the seller/exporter or an independent inspection firm (as required by the buyer/importer), confirming that merchandise meets certain specifications.

Packing List A document listing the merchandise contained in a particular box, crate, or container, plus type, dimensions, and weight of the container.

Phytosanitary (plant health) Inspection Certificate A document certifying that an export shipment has been inspected and is free from pests and plant diseases considered harmful by the importing country.

Shipper's Export Declaration A form prepared by a shipper/exporter indicating the value, weight, destination, and other information about an export shipment.

GLOSSARY OF TERMS OF SALE

The following is a basic glossary of common terms of sale in international trade. Note that issues regarding responsibility for loss and insurance are complex and beyond the scope of this publication. The international standard of trade terms of sale are "Incoterms," published by the International Chamber of Commerce (ICC), 38, Cours Albert Ier, F-75008 Paris, France. Other offices of the ICC are British National Committee of the ICC, Centre Point, 103 New Oxford Street, London WC1A 1QB, England and US Council of the ICC, 1212 Avenue of the Americas, New York, NY 10010 USA.

C&F (Cost and Freight) Named Point of Destination The seller's price includes the cost of the goods and transportation up to a named port of destination, but does not cover insurance. Under these terms insurance is the responsibility of the buyer/importer.

CIF (Cost, Insurance, and Freight) Named Point of Destination The seller's price includes the cost of the goods, insurance, and transportation up to a named port of destination.

Ex Point of Origin ("Ex Works" "Ex Warehouse" etc.) The seller's price includes the cost of the goods and packing, but without any transport. The seller agrees to place the goods at the disposal of the buyer at a specified point of origin, on a specified date, and within a fixed period of time. The buyer is under obligation to take delivery of the goods at the agreed place and bear all costs of freight, transport and insurance.

FAS (Free Alongside Ship) The seller's price includes the cost of the goods and transportation up to the port of shipment alongside the vessel or on a designated dock. Insurance under these terms is usually the responsibility of the buyer.

FOB (Free On Board) The seller's price includes the cost of the goods , transportation to the port of shipment, and loading charges on a vessel. This might be on a ship, railway car, or truck at an inland point of departure. Loss or damage to the shipment is borne by the seller until loaded at the point named and by the buyer after loading at that point.

Ex Dock—Named Port of Importation The seller's price includes the cost of the goods, and all additional charges necessary to put them on the dock at the named port of importation with import duty paid. The seller is obligated to pay for insurance and freight charges.

GLOSSARY OF INTERNATIONAL PAYMENT TERMS

Advice The forwarding of a letter of credit or an amendment to a letter of credit to the seller, or beneficiary of the letter of credit, by the advising bank (seller's bank).

Advising bank The bank (usually the seller's bank) which receives a letter of credit from the issuing bank (the buyer's bank) and handles the transaction from the seller's side. This includes: validating the letter of credit, reviewing it for internal consistency, forwarding it to the seller, forwarding seller's documentation back to the issuing bank, and, in the case of a confirmed letter of credit, guaranteeing payment to the seller if his documents are in order and the terms of the credit are met.

Amendment A change in the terms and conditions of a letter of credit, usually to meet the needs of the seller. The seller requests an amendment of the buyer who, if he agrees, instructs his bank (the issuing bank) to issue the amendment. The issuing bank informs the seller's bank (the advising bank) who then notifies the seller of the amendment. In the case of irrevocable letters of credit, amendments may only be made with the agreement of all parties to the transaction.

Back-to-Back Letter of Credit A new letter of credit opened in favor of another beneficiary on the basis of an already existing, nontransferable letter of credit.

Beneficiary The entity to whom credits and payments are made, usually the seller/supplier of goods.

Bill of Exchange A written order from one person to another to pay a specified sum of money to a designated person. The following two versions are the most common:

Draft A financial/legal document where one individual (the drawer) instructs another individual (the drawee) to pay a certain amount of money to a named person, usually in payment for the transfer of goods or services. Sight Drafts are payable when presented. Time Drafts (also called usance drafts) are payable at a future fixed (specific) date or determinable (30, 60, 90 days etc.) date. Time drafts are used as a financing tool (as with Documents against Acceptance D/P terms) to give the buyer time to pay for his purchase.

Promissory Note A financial/legal document wherein one individual (the issuer) promises to pay another individual a certain amount.

Collecting Bank (also called the presenting bank) In a Documentary Collection, the bank (usually the buyer's bank) that collects payment or a time draft from the buyer to be forwarded to the remitting bank (usually the seller's bank) in exchange for shipping and other documents which enable the buyer to take possession of the goods.

Confirmed Letter of Credit A letter of credit which contains a guarantee on the part of both the issuing and advising bank of payment to the seller so long as the seller's documentation is in order and terms of the credit are met.

Deferred Payment Letter of Credit A letter of credit where the buyer takes possession of the title documents and the goods by agreeing to pay the issuing bank at a fixed time in the future.

Discrepancy The noncompliance with the terms and conditions of a letter of credit. A discrepancy may be as small as a misspelling, an inconsistency in dates or amounts, or a missing document. Some discrepancies can easily be fixed; others may lead to the eventual invalidation of the letter of credit.

D/A Abbreviation for "Documents against Acceptance."

D/P Abbreviation for "Documents against Payment."

Documents against Acceptance (D/A) *See* Documentary Collection

Documents against Payment (D/P) *See* Documentary Collection

Documentary Collection A method of effecting payment for goods whereby the seller/exporter instructs his bank to collect a certain sum from the buyer/importer in exchange for the transfer of shipping and other documentation enabling the buyer/importer to take possession of the goods. The two main types of Documentary Collection are:

Documents against Payment (D/P) Where the bank releases the documents to the buyer/importer only against a cash payment in a prescribed currency; and

Documents against Acceptance (D/A) Where the bank releases the documents to the buyer/importer against acceptance of a bill of exchange guaranteeing payment at a later date.

Draft *See* Bill of exchange.

Drawee The buyer in a documentary collection.

Forward Foreign Exchange An agreement to purchase foreign exchange (currency) at a future date at a predetermined rate of exchange. Forward foreign exchange contracts are often purchased by buyers of merchandise who wish to hedge against foreign exchange fluctuations between the time the contract is negotiated and the time payment is made.

Irrevocable Credit A letter of credit which cannot be revoked or amended without prior mutual consent of the supplier, the buyer, and all intermediaries.

Issuance The act of the issuing bank (buyer's bank) establishing a letter of credit based on the buyer's application.

Issuing Bank The buyer's bank which establishes a letter of credit in favor of the supplier, or beneficiary.

Letter of Credit A document stating commitment on the part of a bank to place an agreed upon sum of money at the disposal of a seller on behalf of a buyer under precisely defined conditions.

Negotiation In a letter of credit transaction, the examination of seller's documentation by the (negotiating) bank to determine if they comply with the terms and conditions of the letter of credit.

Open Account The shipping of goods by the supplier to the buyer prior to payment for the goods. The supplier will usually specify expected payment terms of 30, 60, or 90 days from date of shipment.

Red Clause Letter of Credit A letter of credit which makes funds available to the seller prior to shipment in order to provide him with funds for production of the goods.

Remitter In a documentary collection, an alternate name given to the seller who forwards documents to the buyer through banks.

Remitting Bank In a documentary collection, a bank which acts as an intermediary, forwarding the remitter's documents to, and payments from the collecting bank.

Sight Draft *See* Bill of Exchange.

Standby Letter of Credit A letter of credit used as a secondary payment method in the event that the primary payment method cannot be fulfilled.

Time Draft *See* Bill of Exchange.

Validity The time period for which a letter of credit is valid. After receiving notice of a letter of credit opened on his behalf, the seller/exporter must meet all the requirements of the letter of credit within the period of validity.

Revocable Letter of Credit A letter of credit which may be revoked or amended by the issuer (buyer) without prior notice to other parties in the letter of credit process. It is rarely used.

Revolving Letter of Credit A letter of credit which is automatically restored to its full amount after the completion of each documentary exchange. It is used when there are several shipments to be made over a specified period of time.

FURTHER READING

For more detailed information on international trade payments, refer to the following publications of the International Chamber of Commerce (ICC), Paris, France.

Uniform Rules for Collections This publication describes the conditions governing collections, including those for presentation, payment and acceptance terms. The Articles also specify the responsibility of the bank regarding protest, case of need and actions to protect the merchandise. An indispensable aid to everyday banking operations. (A revised, updated edition will be published in 1995.) ICC Publication No. 322.

Documentary Credits: UCP 500 and 400 Compared This publication was developed to train managers, supervisors, and practitioners of international trade in critical areas of the new UCP 500 Rules. It pays particular attention to those Articles that have been the source of litigation. ICC Publication No. 511.

The New ICC Standard Documentary Credit Forms Standard Documentary Credit Forms are a series of forms designed for bankers, attorneys, importers/exporters, and anyone involved in documentary credit transactions around the world. This comprehensive new edition, prepared by Charles del Busto, Chairman of the ICC Banking Commission, reflects the major changes instituted by the new "UCP 500." ICC Publication No. 516.

The New ICC Guide to Documentary Credit Operations This new Guide is a fully revised and expanded edition of the "Guide to Documentary Credits" (ICC publication No. 415, published in conjunction with the UCP No. 400). The new Guide uses a unique combination of graphs, charts, and sample documents to illustrate the Documentary Credit process. An indispensable tool for import/export traders, bankers, training services, and anyone involved in day-to-day Credit operations. ICC Publication No. 515.

Guide to Incoterms 1990 A companion to "Incoterms," the ICC "Guide to Incoterms 1990" gives detailed comments on the changes to the 1980 edition and indicates why it may be in the interest of a buyer or seller to use one or another trade term. This guide is indispensable for exporters/importers, bankers, insurers, and transporters. ICC Publication No. 461/90.

These and other relevant ICC publications may be obtained from the following sources:

ICC Publishing S.A.
International Chamber of Commerce
38, Cours Albert Ier
75008 Paris, France
Tel: [33] (1) 49-53-28-28 Fax: [33] (1) 49-53-28-62
Telex: 650770

International Chamber of Commerce
Borsenstrasse 26
P.O. Box 4138
8022 Zurich, Switzerland

British National Committee of the ICC
Centre Point, New Oxford Street
London WC1A QB, UK

ICC Publishing, Inc.
US Council of the ICC
156 Fifth Avenue, Suite 820
New York, NY 10010, USA
Tel: [1] (212) 206-1150 Fax: [1] (212) 633-6025

Corporate Taxation

AT A GLANCE

Corporate Income Tax Rate (%)	37.5 (a)
Capital Gains Tax Rate (%)	37.5 (a)
Branch Tax Rate (%)	37.5 (a)
Withholding Tax (%) (b)	
Dividends	20
Interest	20 (c)
Royalties from Patents, Know-how, etc.	20
Branch Remittance Tax	0
Net Operating Losses (Years)	
Carryback	1 (d)
Carryforward	5

(a) Excluding temporary surcharge of 2.5 percent (see Taxes on Corporate Income and Gains).
(b) Except for the withholding tax on royalties, these withholding taxes are imposed on both residents and nonresidents. For nonresidents, these are final taxes, unless the income is effectively connected with a permanent establishment in Japan. Royalties paid to residents are not subject to withholding.
(c) For residents, this tax consists of a national tax of 15 percent and a local tax of 5 percent.
(d) The loss carryback is temporarily suspended (see Determination of Trading Income).

TAXES ON CORPORATE INCOME AND GAINS

Corporate Tax

Japanese domestic companies are subject to tax on their worldwide income, while nonresident companies pay taxes only on Japanese-source income. If a company is incorporated or has a head office in Japan, its worldwide income is subject to Japanese taxes; Japan does not use the "central management and control" criteria for assessing the residence of a company.

Rates of Corporation Tax

For fiscal years beginning after April 1,1990, the basic rate of national corporation tax is 37.5 percent. For corporations capitalized at ¥100 million or less, however, the rate is 28 percent when the taxable income is less than ¥8 million.

As a temporary measure to raise revenue, a 2.5 percent surtax is levied on corporate income tax of Japanese and nonresident companies for fiscal years ending from April 1, 1992, through March 31, 1994. The surtax applies to corporate tax after deducting applicable credits and a deduction of ¥4 million.

Capital Gains

In general, for Japanese corporate tax purposes, capital gains are not taxed separately. Such gains are treated as ordinary income to which normal tax rates apply.

Administration

A corporation must file a tax return within two months of the end of its fiscal period, paying the tax at that time. Except for newly established corporations, if the fiscal year is longer than six months, the corporation must file an interim return within two months of the end of the first six months and pay a liability on account at that time.

Dividends Received/Paid

Dividends received from another domestic corporation, net of any related interest expense incurred for acquisition of the shares, are generally excluded from gross income. However, if the recipient corporation owns not more than 25 percent of the domestic corporation distributing the dividends, then 20 percent of the net dividend income is includible in gross income. Dividends distributed from a domestic corporation are subject to 20 percent withholding tax unless a tax treaty modifies the rate.

Foreign Tax Credit

A Japanese company may be entitled to claim a foreign tax credit against both Japanese corporation tax and local inhabitant tax (*see* Other Significant Taxes). Creditable foreign income taxes for a Japanese company include foreign income taxes paid directly by a Japanese company and its foreign branches (direct tax credit) and foreign income taxes paid by an affiliated foreign company (indirect tax credit). Also, a tax-sparing credit is available to domestic companies with a branch or subsidiary in a developing country.

DETERMINATION OF TRADING INCOME

General

The tax law prescribes which adjustments to accounting income are required in computing taxable income. Expenditures incurred in the conduct of the business, except as otherwise provided by the law, are allowed as deductions from gross income.

Bonuses to directors are considered a distribution of income and are not deductible by the corporation. The deductibility of entertainment expenses incurred by a corporation is restricted according to the size of the corporation. Donations, except for those to national or local governments or similar organizations, are not normally deductible expenses.

Inventories

A corporation may select one of the following methods for valuing stock:

- cost method including actual cost, FIFO, LIFO, weighted average, moving average, straight average, most recent purchase and retail; or
- lower of cost or market value, with notification to the tax office.

In the absence of such notification, the recent purchase price method is deemed to have been adopted by the corporation.

Depreciation

Tangible property is depreciated over a fixed period under statutory depreciation methods (such as straight-line and declining balance). Depreciation for tax purposes must conform in amount to the depreciation used for accounting purposes. Depreciation rules for intangible assets differ from those for tangible assets, in terms of statutory salvage value and limit of depreciation.

Investment Tax Credit

A corporation that acquired or produced certain qualifying machinery or equipment before March 31, 1993 (for use in its business within one year of acquisition) may receive a credit against its corporate tax liability. The credit equals 7 percent of the cost or 20 percent of the corporation tax, whichever is smaller, and acts as a substitute for additional depreciation. In addition, a corporation may claim a credit equal to the lower of 20 percent of certain incremental research and development expenditures or 10 percent of the corporation tax before the credit.

Net Operating Losses

Legislation provides that the net operating loss of certain corporations may be carried forward five years and back one year. However, the loss carryback is suspended for fiscal years ending from April 1, 1992 through March 31, 1994. For certain Japanese branches and subsidiaries of foreign companies, net operating losses incurred during the fiscal years that end within the first three years of the company's existence may be carried forward seven years.

OTHER SIGNIFICANT TAXES

This table summarizes other significant taxes.

Nature of Tax	Rate (%)
Consumption tax, on a broad range of goods and services	3
Enterprise tax, on taxable income (deductible from taxable income on a cash basis); rate depends on business location	6 to 12.6
Local inhabitant tax, based on the company's capitalization and the number of employees; computed as a percentage of national income tax (annual assessments range from ¥50,000 to ¥3,750,000)	17.3 to 20.7
Social insurance contributions, on monthly standard remuneration, paid by both employer and employee in equal amounts	
Rate paid by each for male employees	14.5
Rate paid by each for female employees	14.3

MISCELLANEOUS MATTERS

Foreign Exchange Controls

The Bank of Japan controls inbound and outbound investments and transfers of money.

Transfer Pricing Legislation

The transfer pricing law stipulates that pricing between internationally affiliated entities should be at an arm's length rate. Internationally affiliated entities means that there is a relationship by way of holding 50 percent or more of the shares either directly or indirectly. The legislation stipulates that the burden of proof as to the reasonableness of the pricing is passed to the taxpayer, and, if the taxpayer fails to provide proof or disclose pertinent information to the tax authorities, taxable income will be increased at the discretion of the tax authorities.

Tax Haven Legislation

Japanese tax law has tax haven rules. If a Japanese domestic company owns 5 percent or more of the issued shares of a tax haven subsidiary of which more than 50 percent is owned directly or indirectly by Japanese domestic companies, the undistributed income of the subsidiary must be included in the Japanese parent company's taxable income in proportion to the equity held. This rule will also apply to the undistributed income of a subsidiary not incorporated in a tax haven if its foreign branch income is exempt from income tax and it operates a foreign branch in a tax haven country. Losses of a foreign affiliate cannot offset the taxable income of the Japanese parent company.

Debt-to-Equity Rules

Thin capitalization rules, which were introduced in 1992, limit the deduction for interest expense for companies with foreign related-party debt if the debt-to-equity ratio exceeds 3:1.

TREATY WITHHOLDING TAX RATES

For treaty countries (as of January, 1993): the rates reflect the lower of the treaty rate and the rate under domestic tax laws on outbound payments.

	Dividends %	Interest %	Royalties %
Australia	15	10	10
Austria	10/20 (a)	10	10
Bangladesh	10/15	10 (c)	10
Belgium	10/15 (c)	15	10
Brazil	12.5	12.5 (c)	12.5/15/20 (f)
Bulgaria	10/15	10 (c)	10
Canada	10/15 (a)	10 (c)	10
China	10	10 (c)	10
Czechoslovakia	10/15 (a)	10 (c)	0/10 (i)
Denmark	10/15 (a)	10	10
Egypt	15	20	15
Finland	10/15 (a)	10	10
France	10/15 (a)	10 (c)	10

	Dividends %	Interest %	Royalties %
Germany	10/15 (a)	10 (c)	10
Hungary	10	10 (c)	0/10 (i)
India	15	10/15 (c) (j)	20
Indonesia	10/15 (a)	10 (c)	10
Ireland	10/15 (a)	10	10
Italy	10/15 (a)	10	10
Korea	12	12 (c)	12
Luxembourg	5/15 (a)	10 (c)	10
Malaysia	10/15 (a)	10 (c)	10
Netherlands	5/15 (a)	10 (c)	10
New Zealand	15	20	20
Norway	5/15 (a)	10 (c)	10
Pakistan	15/20 (a)	0/20	0
Philippines	10/20 (a)	10/15 (c)	15/20 (g)
Poland	10	10 (c)	0/10 (i)
Romania	10	10 (c)	10/15 (i)
Singapore	10/15 (a)	15 (c) (d)	10
Spain	10/15 (a)	10	10
Sri Lanka	20	20 (c)	0/10 (h)
Sweden	10/15 (a)	10	10
Switzerland	10/15 (a)	10 (e)	10
Thailand	15/20 (a)	10/20 (c) (d)	15
USSR (k)	15	10 (c)	0/10 (i)
United Kingdom	10/15 (a)	10	10
United States	10/15 (b)	10 (c)	10
Zambia	0	10 (c)	10
Nontreaty countries	20	20	20

(a) The treaty withholding rate is increased to 15 percent or 20 percent if the recipient is not a corporation owning at least 25 percent (France—15 percent; Pakistan—33 percent; Austria—50 percent) of the distributing corporation.

(b) The rate is 15 percent unless the recipient is a corporation which owned at least 10 percent of the voting shares of the payer since the beginning of the prior taxable year, and not more than 25 percent of the payer's gross income for the prior year was from dividends and interest (other than from a subsidiary or financial institution).

(c) Interest paid to a contracting state, subdivision or certain financial institutions is exempt.

(d) Interest paid to a contracting state pursuant to loans made to the other contracting state, for use in an industrial undertaking, is exempt (Thailand—10 percent).

(e) Interest paid to a Swiss resident pursuant to debt claims guaranteed or insured by Switzerland is exempt.

(f) The withholding rate for trademark royalties is 20 percent, for motion picture films and videotapes the rate is 15 percent.

(g) The withholding rate for motion picture films is 15 percent.

(h) The withholding rate for motion picture films is 0 percent and for patented royalties is 10 percent.

(i) The withholding tax on cultural royalties is exempt (Romania— 10 percent) and on industrial royalties is 10 percent (Romania—15 percent).

(j) The rate is generally 15 percent, except it is reduced to 10 percent for interest paid to banks.

(k) The USSR treaty applies only to the Russian Federation.

Personal Taxation

AT A GLANCE—MAXIMUM RATES

Income Tax Rate (%)	65
Capital Gains Tax Rate (%)	65 (a)
Net Worth Tax Rate (%)	0
Inheritance and Gift Tax Rates (%)	70 (b)

(a) Capital gains rates vary according to the type of property. See Capital Gains and Losses.
(b) A 20 percent surtax is Imposed on transfers to heirs who are not family members. See Inheritance and Gift Taxes.

INCOME TAXES—EMPLOYMENT

Who Is Liable

For Japanese tax purposes, the tax liability of individuals is determined by residency status. Individual taxpayers are classified into three categories:

- A permanent resident is an individual who has a permanent domicile in Japan or who has resided continuously in Japan for more than five years.
- A nonpermanent resident is an individual who does not intend to reside permanently in Japan and who has not resided in Japan more than five years.
- A nonresident is an individual who has not established a domicile in Japan and who has resided in Japan for less than one year.

Foreign nationals arriving in Japan will be considered to have established residency in Japan unless employment contracts or other documents clearly indicate that they will stay in Japan less than one year. Permanent residents are subject to income tax on their worldwide income regardless of source; nonpermanent residents are taxed on their Japanese-source income and foreign-source income that is paid in or remitted to Japan. Nonresidents are subject to tax on only their Japanese-source income.

Taxable Income and Deductions

Individuals who have employment income are liable for income tax. Employment income includes salaries, wages, bonuses and other compensation of a similar nature. Benefits in kind (such as company housing) provided by the employer are included in employment income.

Taxable employment income is gross receipts minus an employment income deduction, computed as indicated in the following table.

Gross Compensation Exceeding (¥)	Gross Compensation Not Exceeding (¥)	Employment Income Deduction
0	1,650,000	Gross receipts x 40% (minimum ¥650,000)
1,650,000	3,300,000	¥660,000 + [(Gross receipts − ¥1,650,000) x 30%]
3,300,000	6,000,000	¥1,155,000 + [(Gross receipts − ¥3,300,000) x 20%]
6,000,000	10,000,000	¥1,695,000 + [(Gross receipts − ¥6,000,000) x 10%]
10,000,000	—	¥2,095,000 + [(Gross receipts − ¥10,000,000) x 5%]

If the aggregate amount of specific employment-related expenditures incurred during a year exceeds the amount of the employment income deduction, the excess may be deducted in addition to the employment income deduction. Specific expenditures include commuting expenses, moving expenses on transfer and training expenses in gaining technology

Note: This section is courtesy of and © Ernst & Young from their Worldwide Personal Tax Guide, 1993 Edition. This material should not be regarded as offering a complete explanation of the taxation matters referred to. Ernst & Young is a leading international professional services firm with offices in 100 countries, including Japan. Refer to "Important Addresses" chapter for addresses and phone numbers of the Ernst & Young offices in Japan.

or knowledge directly required in performing duties. Expenditures must be documented and certified by the employer. The deduction of specific expenditures may be claimed only by filing a tax return.

Other allowable deductions include the following:

Casualty losses Deductible amount = The greater of (amount of loss, including expenditures incurred in relation to the casualty) – (insurance reimbursement – (10 percent of adjusted total income) or (expenditures incurred in relation to the casualty – ¥50,000).

Medical expenses Deductible amount = (Medical expenses) – (insurance reimbursement) – (the lesser of 5 percent of adjusted total income and ¥100,000). Maximum deduction is ¥2 million.

Insurance Premiums Social insurance premiums are fully deductible. Life insurance premiums are deductible up to a maximum of ¥50,000. Individual pension premiums are deductible up to ¥50,000. For casualty Insurance premiums, the deductible amount is ¥3,000 for short-term insurance (less than 10 years) and ¥15,000 for long-term insurance. The deductible amount of combined short-term and long-term insurance premiums may not exceed ¥15,000.

Contributions Contributions to the government or local authorities, to institutions for educational, scientific or other public purposes as designated by the Minister of Finance and to institutions for scientific study or research specifically provided for in tax law are deductible. The deductible amount is the lesser of the amount of the contribution or 25 percent of adjusted total income, minus ¥10,000.

Income Tax Rates

Individual income taxes consist of national income tax and local inhabitant tax. National income tax rates are progressive. For 1993 the rates range from 10 percent on taxable income of up to ¥3 million to 50 percent on a taxable income, exceeding ¥20 million.

Local Inhabitant Tax Rates (Prefectural and Municipal) Local inhabitant taxes, both prefectural and municipal, consist of per capita and income levies.

Individuals are also subject to a local enterprise tax on income from businesses or professions at rates ranging from 3 to 5 percent.

1993 Tax Rate for Per Capita Levy

Population	Municipal Inhabitant Tax Standard (¥)	Municipal Inhabitant Tax Maximum (¥)	Prefectural Inhabitant Tax (¥)
500,000 or more	2,500	3,200	700
From 50,000 to 499,999	2,000	2,600	700
Up to 49,999	1,500	2,000	700

1993 Tax Rate for Income Levy

Municipal Tax

Taxable Income Exceeding (¥)	Not Exceeding (¥)	Tax on Lower Amount (¥)	Rate (%)
0	1,600,000	0	3
1,600,000	5,500,000	48,000	8
5,500,000	—	360,000	11

Prefectural Tax

Taxable Income Exceeding (¥)	Not Exceeding (¥)	Tax on Lower Amount (¥)	Rate (%)
0	5,500,000	0	2
5,500,000	—	110,000	4

National Individual Income Tax Rates

Taxable Income Exceeding ¥	Not Exceeding ¥	Tax on Lower Amount ¥	Rate on Excess %
0	3,000,000	0	10
3,000,000	6,000,000	300,000	20
6,000,000	10,000,000	900,000	30
10,000,000	20,000,000	2,100,000	40
20,000,000	—	6,100,000	50

Personal Deductions and Allowances

The following personal deductions are available for purposes of income tax.

	(¥)
Physically handicapped person	270,000
Seriously physically handicapped person	350,000
Seriously physically handicapped dependent, living with the taxpayer	650,000
Aged person (taxpayer who is 65 years of age or older with total income not exceeding ¥10 million)	500,000
Widow (or divorcee), widower, or working student	270,000
Spouse	350,000
Aged spouse (70 years of age or older)	450,000
Dependent	350,000
Aged dependent (70 years of age or older)	450,000

Aged dependent who is a parent
of the taxpayer and living with
him or her 550,000
Basic deduction 350,000
Special deduction for spouse,
applicable only if the taxpayer's
total income does not exceed
¥10 million:
Spouse having no income 350,000
If spouse has income, the deductible
amount is reduced according to a
prescribed formula.

For eligible dependents from age 16 to 22, an additional deduction of ¥100,000 is allowed for education.
Personal deductions for purposes of inhabitant
tax are lower than those for purposes of income tax.

INCOME TAXES—
SELF-EMPLOYMENT/
BUSINESS INCOME

Individuals who derive income from business and
professional activities are liable for income taxes.
Taxable income consists of gross receipts minus reasonable and necessary expenses incurred in connection with the business. Certain advantages are available to individual taxpayers filing a "blue form" tax
return (*see* Administration) provided they meet the
necessary bookkeeping requirements.

DIRECTORS' FEES

Directors' fees are considered employment income and are taxed accordingly.

INVESTMENT INCOME

Dividends Dividend income includes dividends
and distributions of profits from corporations and
distributions of earnings of security investment
trusts (except for public and corporate debenture
investment trusts). It also includes constructive dividends realized as distributions of remaining assets
on the liquidation of a company or as distributions
on the reduction of capital or on the retirement of
shares. Interest on borrowings for the acquisition of
the shares on which the dividend was paid may be
deducted from the gross amount of dividends.

Dividends from domestic corporations are subject
to a 20 percent withholding tax at source. Dividend
credits may be applied against the taxpayer's total
income tax liability for the year. A taxpayer may elect
to have dividend income excluded from ordinary income and taxed separately at the source at the rate
of 35 percent withholding tax if the taxpayer owns
less than 5 percent of the shares of the company pay-

ing the dividends or if the amount of each dividend is
less than ¥500,000 in a calendar year (¥250,000 if the
company's fiscal period is less than one year). If a dividend received from one domestic corporation does
not exceed ¥50,000 (¥100,000 if the paying
corporation's fiscal period is one year or more), the
dividend need not be included in dividend income, in
which case a tax credit would not be applicable.

Dividends on security investment trusts are taxed
separately at the source at a rate of 15 percent withholding tax (plus a 5 percent local tax), and a tax
credit is not allowed.

Interest Interest income includes interest on
public bonds and corporate debentures, deposits
and postal savings as well as interest on distributions of earnings of joint operation trusts or public
bonds and debenture investment trusts. No deductions are allowed for expenses. Interest is separately
taxed from other income and subject to a final 15
percent withholding income tax (plus a 5 percent final local withholding tax) at source. Interest on public bonds and debentures issued overseas is subject
to a 15 percent final withholding tax when received
through a paying dealer in Japan.

Interest up to certain amounts on postal savings
and deposits, public bonds and security investment
trusts received by qualified taxpayers is exempt from
income tax. Qualified taxpayers include persons 65
years of age or older, spouses qualifying for
survivor's annuities or widow's annuities and handicapped persons. The following interest is exempt:

- interest on postal savings, up to a maximum
  principal amount of ¥3 million;
- interest on time deposits, public bonds,
  debentures, security investment trusts and so
  forth, up to a maximum principal amount of ¥3
  million; and
- interest on national bonds, up to a maximum
  principal amount of ¥3 million.
  Interest on employees' savings for pensions
  and acquisitions of housing is exempt up to a
  maximum principal amount of ¥5 million under
  the workers' savings program for assets
  accumulation.

Rental Income Income from the rental of real
property is taxed as ordinary income.

RELIEF FOR LOSSES

Only losses from rental, business and forestry
activities and from capital transactions may be used
to offset other categories of income. The portion of
a rental loss equal to the ratio of interest expense on
loans to acquire the land to total rental expenses may
not offset other income.

The net loss remaining after all available losses

have been used to reduce income may be carried forward for three years by a taxpayer filing a blue return. A taxpayer who does not file a blue return (*see* Administration) is allowed a carryforward of three years for certain losses, such as the loss of business assets due to a natural disaster.

CAPITAL GAINS AND LOSSES

Capital gains from the sale of assets other than securities, land and buildings are divided into short-term and long-term gains, included in ordinary income and subject to normal income tax rates. If the property has been held longer than five years, the gains are long-term, and one-half is taxable. A ¥500,000 deduction is available from the total of short-term and long-term gains.

The following rates apply to the 1993 tax year.

For capital gains from the sale of stocks and bonds, taxpayers may either elect to pay a 20 percent income tax plus a 6 percent inhabitant tax on net gains when they file their income tax return or have 1 percent of the sales value (0.5 percent for bonds) withheld at the time of sale as a final tax.

Capital gains from the sale of land and buildings are taxed separately from other income and at different rates. Gains from the sale of land and buildings held for no longer than five years are considered short-term, and gains from those held more than five years are treated as long-term gains. Long-term gains are taxed at a flat rate of 30 percent, plus a 9 percent inhabitant tax. A special deduction of at least ¥1 million is allowed for long-term gains.

Gains on the sale of residential property held for more than 10 years are taxed at a 10 percent rate (plus a 4 percent inhabitant tax) on taxable gains up to ¥60 million and 15 percent plus 5 percent inhabitant tax on gains in excess of ¥60 million. A special deduction of ¥30 million is available on gains from the sale of residential property if specified conditions are met. The tax amount on short-term gains is the higher of 40 percent of taxable gains plus 12 percent inhabitant tax or 110 percent of the tax amount computed under the aggregate taxation method.

INHERITANCE AND GIFT TAXES

Inheritance tax is levied on heirs and legatees who acquire property by inheritance or bequest. An individual domiciled in Japan is subject to tax on all property regardless of location. An individual not domiciled in Japan is taxed only on the property located in Japan at the time of the decedent's death.

Gifts made within three years of death are treated as inherited property and included in taxable property. Certain exemptions and allowances are permitted in the computation of total net taxable property.

A basic exemption of ¥48 million plus ¥9.5 million times the number of statutory heirs is deductible from taxable properties. The inheritance tax is calculated separately for each statutory heir. The aggregate of the calculated tax is then prorated to those who actually receive the property.

In 1993 inheritance tax rates range from 10 percent to 70 percent, with a 20 percent surtax on transfers to heirs who are not family members (those other than parents and children of the decedent).

Inheritance Tax

Taxable Income Exceeding ¥	Taxable Income Not Exceeding ¥	Tax on Lower Amount ¥	Rate on Excess %
0	7,000,000		10
7,000,000	14,000,000	700,000	15
14,000,000	25,000,000	1,750,000	20
25,000,000	40,000,000	3,950,000	25
40,000,000	65,000,000	7,700,000	30
65,000,000	100,000,000	15,200,000	35
100,000,000	150,000,000	27,450,000	40
150,000,000	200,000,000	47,450,000	45
200,000,000	270,000,000	69,950,000	50
270,000,000	350,000,000	104,950,000	55
350,000,000	450,000,000	148,950,000	60
450,000,000	1,000,000,000	208,950,000	65
1,000,000,000		566,450,000	70

Tax credits are allowed for a surviving spouse, minors, gift taxes and foreign estate and inheritance taxes paid on property located outside Japan. The credit for a spouse is the amount of inheritance tax on the spouse's statutory share of the estate or an estate of ¥80 million, whichever is larger.

Gift Tax

Taxable Income Exceeding ¥	Taxable Income Not Exceeding ¥	Tax on Lower Amount ¥	Rate on Excess %
0	1,500,000	—	10
1,500,000	2,000,000	150,000	15
2,000,000	2,500,000	225,000	20
2,500,000	3,500,000	325,000	25
3,500,000	4,500,000	575,000	30
4,500,000	6,000,000	875,000	35
6,000,000	8,000,000	1,400,000	40
8,000,000	10,000,000	2,200,000	45
10,000,000	15,000,000	3,100,000	50
15,000,000	25,000,000	5,600,000	55
25,000,000	40,000,000	11,100,000	60
40,000,000	100,000,000	20,100,000	65
100,000,000	—	59,100,000	70

Gift tax is levied on an individual receiving a gift from another individual. A donee domiciled in Japan is taxable on all gifts of property regardless of their location. A donee not domiciled in Japan is taxable only on gifts of property located in Japan at the time of the gift. There is an annual exemption of ¥600,000. Spouses are entitled to a one-time exemption of up to ¥20 million on a gift of a residential house or land, provided the period of marriage was 20 years or longer.

In 1993 gift tax rates ranged from 10 to 70 percent.

SOCIAL SECURITY TAXES

Social security programs include health insurance, welfare pension insurance, unemployment insurance and workmen's accident compensation insurance. For 1993 the premium for health insurance is 8.2 percent of monthly remuneration up to a maximum of ¥80,360. For welfare pensions, the premium is 14.5 percent for male employees (up to a maximum of ¥76,850) and 14.3 percent for female employees (up to a maximum of ¥75,790). Costs are borne equally by employers and employees. The premium for unemployment insurance is 1.45 percent, of which 0.9 percent is borne by the employer and 0.55 percent by the employee. The premium for workmen's accident compensation insurance, 0.5 percent of total compensation paid to employees, is borne entirely by the employer.

ADMINISTRATION

Individual income taxation in Japan is based on the principle of self-assessment. Taxpayers must file a tax return to declare income and deductions and pay the tax due. National income tax liability of individuals compensated in yen at gross annual amounts not exceeding ¥15 million, however, is settled through employer withholding if income other than employment income does not exceed ¥200,000.

Income tax returns must be filed and the final tax paid during the period from February 16 to March 15 for income accrued during the previous calendar year. For those taxpayers who filed a final tax return for the preceding year and had a tax liability of ¥150,000 or more after deduction of withholding tax, prepayment of income tax for the current year is due on July 31 and November 30. Each pre-payment is normally one-third of the previous year's tax liability, less amounts withheld at the source. To the extent prepaid or withheld payments exceed the total tax due, they are refundable if a final return is filed. Tax returns need not be filed if tax liability is settled through withholding.

Under the blue form tax return system, a taxpayer is required to keep a set of books that clearly reflect all transactions affecting assets, liabilities and capital in accordance with the principle of double-entry bookkeeping and to settle accounts on the basis of those books. Financial statements must be attached to the tax return.

Blue form taxpayers receive certain benefits. A net operating loss for any taxable year in which a taxpayer filed a blue return may be carried forward for three years. Reassessments are made based on the results of an actual tax examination if a mistake was made in computing taxable income, deductible reserves or the additional depreciation deduction for the taxable year (the authorities may not make arbitrary adjustments).

NONRESIDENTS

A nonresident is an individual who has not established a domicile in Japan and has resided in Japan for less than one year. Nonresidents are subject to Japanese income tax on income from sources within Japan. Normally, a 20 percent withholding tax is levied with no deductions available to the taxpayer, but, depending on the type of income, the tax may be levied at progressive rates through self-assessment. If taxes are withheld from payments to nonresidents and the amount withheld satisfies the Japanese tax liability, the individual need not file an income tax return.

Dividends paid by Japanese companies, interest income and salaries paid by Japanese companies, plus annuities, prizes and so forth, are subject to a 20 percent withholding tax when paid to nonresidents. Directors' fees paid by a Japanese corporation for services as a director are considered Japanese-source income and are subject to tax in Japan, even when the services are performed outside Japan.

Proceeds on the sale of land and buildings held by nonresidents are subject to 10 percent withholding tax unless the property has been purchased by individuals for residential use and the sales value is no more than ¥100 million.

If a nonresident is a resident of a country with which Japan has concluded a tax treaty, income may be either exempt or subject to a lower rate of tax. A nonresident is not subject to local inhabitant tax.

DOUBLE TAX RELIEF/ DOUBLE TAX TREATIES

A foreign tax credit is allowed within limitations for income taxes paid by a resident taxpayer to foreign governments if the income is taxed by both Japan and the other country. The credit is generally limited to the lesser of foreign income tax paid or the Japanese tax on foreign-source income. If the foreign tax paid exceeds the limitation, the excess may be carried forward for three years. A taxpayer may elect to deduct foreign tax from taxable income.

As of January, 1993, Japan had concluded treaties to avoid double taxation with the following countries:

Australia	Germany	Phillipines
Austria	Hungary	Poland
Bangladesh	India	Romania
Belgium	Indonesia	Singapore
Brazil	Ireland	Spain
Bulgaria	Italy	Sri Lanka
Canada	Korea	Sweden
China	Luxembourg	Switzerland
Czechoslovakia	Malaysia	Thailand
Denmark	Netherlands	USSR*
Egypt	New Zealand	United Kingdom
Finland	Norway	United States
France	Pakistan	Zambia

*Japan honors the treaty of the former USSR with only the Russian Federation.

Most treaties reduce the tax rates on Japanese-source interest, dividends royalties and similar income, and also provide relief from double taxation through tax credits.

Ports & Airports

The late 1980s and early 1990s have seen a major increase in the amount of air and shipping traffic passing through East Asia. Planners saw this coming some years back, and have been scrambling to expand and improve facilities at ports and airports throughout the region; many are currently at or over capacity. Air cargo traffic has been growing faster in Asia than anywhere else in the world, and passenger traffic has increased by leaps and bounds. However, with all the new facilities opening in the near future, there are estimates that by 1997 airport capacity will actually exceed demand. This may mean that airlines and cargo carriers will schedule more frequent service with smaller aircraft, something which is not currently possible, largely because of the small number of slots available at airport terminals and the many major airports operating with only one runway. Long a major center for shipping, Asia is fast becoming the leader in container port traffic. The largest increases in container traffic worldwide have been at the Asian hub ports, and four of the world's five leading countries in container traffic are located on the western side of the Pacific Rim: Japan, Singapore, Hong Kong and Taiwan are ranked two through five, respectively, with the USA at number one.

AIRPORTS

There are over 65 commercial airports throughout Japan, with 14 of these handling international traffic. Japanese travelers fly more international passenger miles in a year than any other travelers, save American and the British, and Japan also ranks third in the number of domestic passengers handled annually. Despite this, or perhaps because of this, Japan's airports are notoriously congested, expensive and often inefficient. Narita International Airport, which serves Tokyo, actually handled fewer metric tons of air cargo in 1992 than in the previous year, dropping to the number three position worldwide, while other major Asian airports gained from 6 percent to 14 percent. With the spurt in airport

construction throughout Asia, it is believed that the region's airport capacity may even exceed demand in coming years, drawing business away from Narita in particular and Japanese airports in general, and possibly forcing rates down.

Japan, too, is caught up in a large drive to build or refurbish airports, spending US$24.5 billion over five years. Plans include improvements at New Tokyo Narita International Airport and Tokyo Haneda and entirely new airports in Osaka and six other cities. Such construction is far more difficult and expensive in Japan than in many other Asian countries, in large part because of active, and sometimes violent, anti-land expropriation and anti-noise lobbies.

Tokyo

New Japan Narita International Airport, located an inconvenient 66 km (41 miles) from the city, is Tokyo's international gateway, and Japan's largest and most important airport. It has been plagued by logistical problems almost from opening day in 1978, reaching capacity almost immediately. It was built to handle 5.4 million passengers a year, reconstructed for a capacity of 13 million, and hit 20 million by 1989. Virtually all of Narita's traffic is international, with Tokyo's domestic traffic routed through Haneda Airport, 80 km (50 miles) southeast of Narita. Since its conception, local residents and national lobbies have protested Narita's construction and every phase of its expansion. Problems at the airport have become so onerous that the government has been looking at expanding service at other local airports throughout the country or even building a third Tokyo area airport.

A new terminal finally opened at Narita in 1992, but it was delayed for so long and the crowding problems are so severe that it has not done much to alleviate congestion. Work has progressed on a second runway, but as of this writing, it had not been completed because the owners of a small portion of the land needed had so far refused to move. Further limitations come from the curfew at Narita, which prevents flights from taking off or landing between 11 pm and 6 am every day, and the restriction to only 360 movements a day.

Despite all the problems at Narita described here, it remains, at least for now, the most important facility in Japan to international air cargo. 50 carriers with regularly scheduled flights serve Narita from virtually every corner of the globe. In 1992, it ranked third in the world and number one in Asia in the amount of cargo handled, with 1,336 metric tons passing through Narita that year. The Japanese carriers flying out of Narita are Japan Asia Airways, Japan Air System, Japan Air Lines, Nippon Cargo Airlines, and All Nippon Airways. North American lines American, Canadian, Delta, Northwest, and United serve Narita, along with all-cargo carriers Federal Express and United Parcel Service, while the flagship airlines of most major European and Asian countries also land at Narita. For telephone information, refer to the Transportation section of "Important Addresses" chapter.

Because most of Tokyo's domestic air traffic goes through Haneda, the domestic/international connections need improvement, although they are working on expanding domestic trunk service from Narita. An additional air cargo terminal is to be built at the airport, but most non-perishable freight will continue to go through the Tokyo Air Cargo City Terminal, 50 km (31 miles) from Narita, which increased its capacity by 50 percent in 1992.

The address for the airport administration is:

New Tokyo International Narita Airport
1-2 Goryobokujyo Sanrizuka
Narita City, Chiba Pref., Japan
Tel: [81] (476) 639-6126

Osaka

Osaka Itami International Airport is due to be demoted to a purely domestic facility when the brand-new, and long-delayed Osaka Kansai International Airport opens in September 1994. Itami has been the second largest international airport in Japan, but because of its location only 16 km (10 miles) from the city, as well as other factors, it has been subject to a particularly strict curfew and small number of movements allowed per day.

Japan is holding its breath over the opening of the US$14 billion Kansai Airport, which is opening 18 months later than the date originally planned. Most of the delays are due to the fact that the airport is constructed on a 511 hectare (1,300 acre) man-made island which has already shown signs of sinking into Osaka Bay. Despite this, the offshore location will have a major payoff because the airport will be able to operate 24 hours a day and will not be subject to many noise restrictions. The planned capacity is 160,000 flights a year, which translates into

an average of 438 flights a day, more than twice the number of daily movements allowed at Itami for more than 20 years. The new terminal will have 41 gates serving a mixture of domestic and international flights. One aspect of the planning which has surprised many is that the government opted, once again, for a single runway—something which they may come to regret.

Kansai Airport may significantly alter the traffic patterns within Japan, largely because it will serve both domestic and international flights in the same terminal, making transfers from one to another far easier at Kansai than at Narita. (Most Narita passengers making transfers have to travel 80 km (50 miles) to Haneda Airport by bus.) Those making other kinds of domestic connections will find Kansai easier to deal with as well, since a major highway and rail link are under construction and a high-speed boat link will connect Kansai with the Kobe City Air Terminal. These considerations, plus the air cargo terminals at three Osaka city locations and the 24-hour cargo operation at the airport itself, will make Kansai an important center for freight as well. The major downside to all this is that Kansai will be even more expensive than Narita, with the highest rents, landing fees and food prices in the world. Landing fees alone could be as much as four times those charged at New York's Kennedy International.

Osaka Itami Airport is currently served by 20 regular cargo carriers, although this number will undoubtedly increase at Kansai. Air Nippon and all Japanese lines which also serve Narita land at Kansai, while foreign carriers include Air France, British Airways, Cathay Pacific Airways, China Eastern Airlines, Federal Express, Korean Air, Lufthansa, Northwest Airlines, SAS, Singapore Airlines, and Thai Airways. For telephone information, refer to the Transportation section of "Important Addresses" chapter.

Nagoya

Nagoya Komaki Airport is Japan's third busiest for international traffic, although it ranks far lower for domestic passengers and cargo. A new international arrivals area and 6000-square-meter freight terminal were completed recently. It currently serves 26 air cargo carriers. Many of these also serve Osaka (see list above), but Continental, Canadian Airlines, Delta, Garuda Indonesia, Malaysia Airlines, Air New Zealand, Asiana, Qantas, and Varig all land at Nagoya as well. For telephone information, refer to the Transportation section of "Important Addresses" chapter.

Fukuoka

The third busiest domestic and fourth busiest international airport in Japan is at Fukuoka. A third domestic terminal opened in 1993, while the international terminal is being expanded for an annual

National Transportation

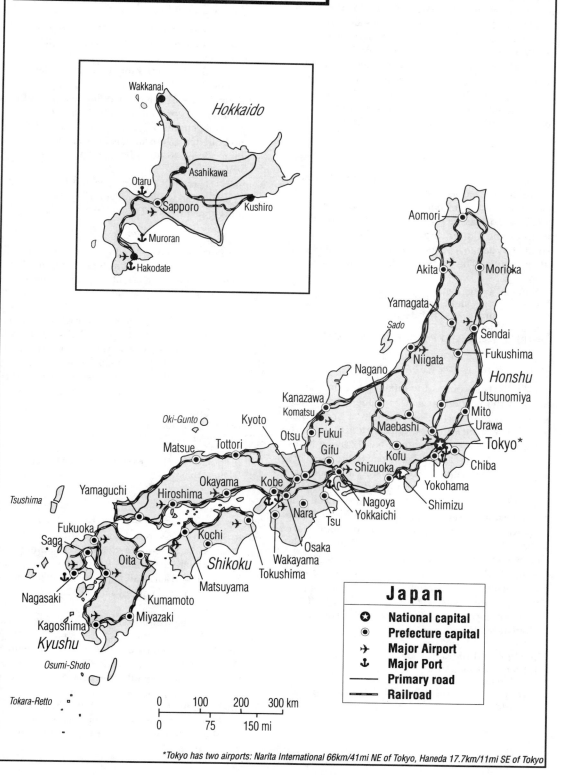

Hokkaido

Wakkanai

Asahikawa

Otaru

Sapporo

Kushiro

Muroran

Hakodate

Aomori

Akita

Morioka

Yamagata

Sendai

Sado

Fukushima

Niigata

Nagano

Honshu

Kanazawa

Utsunomiya

Komatsu

Mito

Oki-Gunto

Kyoto

Otsu

Fukui

Maebashi

Urawa

Matsue

Tottori

Gifu

Kofu

Tokyo*

Tsushima

Yamaguchi

Hiroshima

Okayama

Kobe

Shizuoka

Chiba

Yokohama

Shimizu

Nara

Nagoya

Shimizu

Fukuoka

Saga

Oita

Kochi

Shikoku

Tsu

Yokkaichi

Nagasaki

Kumamoto

Matsuyama

Wakayama

Tokushima

Osaka

Kagoshima

Miyazaki

Kyushu

Osumi-Shoto

Tokara-Retto

Japan	
✪	**National capital**
◉	**Prefecture capital**
✈	**Major Airport**
⚓	**Major Port**
——	**Primary road**
══	**Railroad**

0	100	200	300 km
0	75	150 mi	

*Tokyo has two airports: Narita International 66km/41mi NE of Tokyo, Haneda 17.7km/11mi SE of Tokyo

capacity of 2.4 million passengers by 1996 and 3.4 million by 2001. Also under construction is a new cargo building, which will be able to handle 58,000 metric tons of international freight and five times that amount of domestic freight. 20 air cargo carriers serve Fukuoka, including all major Japanese carriers, Continental, Northwest, and a number of Asian lines, including several which do not serve any other international airports in Japan: Taiwan's China Airlines, Cargolux, Phillipine Airlines, and Airlanka. For telephone information, refer to the Transportation section of "Important Addresses" chapter.

PORTS

Japan has over 1,000 ports and harbors, of which 19 are designated as major ports for foreign trade and 11 are container handling ports. Japan's ports handle almost as much international cargo as the ports of the United States, and the total cargo handled by Japan's ports is greater than that of any other country. The ports are administered by:

Ministry of Transport
Bureau of Ports and Harbors
2-1-3, Kasumigaseki, Chiyoda-ku
Tokyo 100, Japan
Tel: [81] (3) 3580-3111 Fax: [81] (3) 3593-0846.

Kobe

The Port of Kobe is the number one port in Japan and the second largest container port in the world. It has 37 berths, of which 28 are container berths. There are four separate districts in the port. Shinko Piers, for general cargo, has 12 piers. Maya Piers, built in the late 1960s, consists of four piers and handles a combination of general cargo and container cargo. Rokko Island and Port Island are the other two districts, both of which are newer. The inner harbor can accommodate ships up to 70,000 dwt, while the outer harbor can accommodate 100,000 dwt vessels. Reclamation work at Rokko Island is going on to create space for new berths to handle Ro-Ro and containers. Port Island is constructing new container berths which will accommodate 60,000 dwt vessels, plus six berths for general cargo. Completion is expected by 1997. The port is administered by:

Kobe Port and Harbour Bureau
5-1, Kano-cho, 6-chome
Kobe, Japan
Tel: [81] (78) 331-8181 Fax: [81] (78) 322-6120
Tlx: 78548

Port facilities:

Transportation Service—Truck, rail and barge.
Cargo Storage—Covered, 1,627,890 square meters. Open, 143,617 square meters. Refrigerated, 698,953 cubic meters.
Special Cranes—Heavy lift capacity is 4100 metric tons. Container, several to 40 metric tons maximum.
Air Cargo—Osaka International Airport, 30 km from port.
Cargo Handling—Extensive handling equipment is available for containerized, bulk (liquid and dry) and general cargo. Ore and bulk, tanker and liquefied gas terminals handle special commodities. Ro-Ro off-loading points are available.
Weather—Heavy rains fall in June and July. Annual accumulation is 120 cm. Typhoons threaten from August to October.

Nagoya

The Port of Nagoya handles only half as much domestic cargo as Kobe, but a similar amount of foreign cargo. Its location, about halfway between Tokyo and Osaka has made the port, along with the airport, attractive for international shipment. Ships up to 250,000 dwt can be accommodated at the outer harbor, while the inner harbor has berths for 100,000 dwt vessels. Two container berths are due to be completed in January 1995, and six more are opening between 1993 and the end of the decade. The port is administered by:

Nagoya Port Authority
8-21, Irifune, 1-chome, Minato-ku
Nagoya 455-91, Japan
Tel: [81] (52) 661-4111 Fax: [81] (52) 661-0155
Tlx: 0446 3816 NPA J

Port facilities:

Transportation Service—Truck, rail and barge.
Cargo Storage—Covered, 1,630,624 square meters. Open, 2,096,535 square meters. Refrigerated, 50,667 square meters.
Special Cranes—Heavy lift capacity is 150 metric tons. Container, nine with up to 47.7 ton capacity.
Air Cargo—Komaki Airport, located 30 km from port.
Cargo Handling—All normal cargo can be adequately handled by existing port equipment. Ore and bulk, tanker, liquefied gas and container terminals handle specialized goods. Ro-Ro off-loading points are available.
Weather—Temperatures range from -4°C to 35°C. Typhoon season extends from August to October although heaviest rainfall occurs in June and July.

Construction—The construction of the commercial port area at Kinjo Pier is progressing well.

Osaka

The Port of Osaka is the third largest port in Japan. It has 65 wharves and piers. A recently completed Bay Bridge links the port with downtown Osaka. Special storage is available for dangerous cargo, bulk liquids, inflammable and combustible materials. The port is operated by:

Osaka Port & Harbor Bureau
8-24, Chikko, 2-chome, Minato-ku
Osaka 552, Japan
Tel: [81] (6) 572-5121 Fax: [81] (6) 572-0554
Tlx: 5356320

Port facilities:
Transportation Service—Truck, rail and barge.
Cargo Storage—Covered, 1,662,907 square meters. Open area is available. Refrigerated, 1,215,274 cubic meters.
Special Cranes—Heavy lift capacity is 3,000 metric tons with advance notice. Container, numerous 40 metric ton units.
Air Cargo—Osaka International Airport, located 15 km from the harbor.
Cargo Handling—Containerized, bulk and general cargo can all be adequately handled by existing port equipment. Iron ore, coal, steel and metal products are among Osaka's chief imports. Container, Ro-Ro, ore and bulk, tanker and liquefied gas terminals are available.
Weather—Temperatures range from -2˚C to 35˚C. Typhoon season is August through October.
Construction—One new container berth is now under construction and several berths in Sukemater Region are planned.

Yokohama

The Port of Yokohama is 29 km (18 miles) from Tokyo, in southwestern Tokyo Bay, and is the largest port serving the Tokyo metropolitan area. Yokohama has the largest grain silo capacity in Japan and a number of specialized cargo terminals and berths, including ones for petroleum, steel, automobiles, chemicals and 11 container berths amongst its 100 public piers and 38 terminals. Construction has just begun on the Yokohama Port International Distribution Center, scheduled for completion June. 1996. The port is administered by:

Yokohama Port & Harbour Bureau
5th Fl., Sango Boeki Center Building
2, Yamashita-ch, Naka-ku
Yokohama City 231, Japan
Tel: [81] (45) 671-2888 Fax: [81] (45) 671-7158

Port facilities:
Transportation Service—Truck and barge.
Cargo Storage—Covered, 1,038,197 square meters. Open, 140,284 square meters.
Special Cranes—Heavy lift with 650 metric ton capacity. Container, 12 with 30.5 metric ton capacity.
Cargo Handling—Containerized, liquid bulk and general cargo tonnage can be adequately processed by existing port equipment. For specialized cargo handling, tanker, container and Ro-Ro terminals are available.
Weather—Temperatures range from -3.7˚C to 33.5˚C with 155 cm annual rainfall.
Construction—Land reclamation and updating of facilities continues.

Tokyo

The Port of Tokyo is at the innermost portion of the Bay of Tokyo. Several terminals can accommodate ships to up 25,000 dwt or 35,000 dwt. A new berth at Aomi Container Terminal was completed in 1992. The port is administered by:

Port and Harbor Bureau of Tokyo
Metropolitan Government
8-1, Nishi-Shinkuku 2-chome, Shinkuku-ku
Tokyo, Japan
Tel: [81] (3) 3212-5111 Fax: [81] (3) 3212-3539

Port facilities:
Transportation Service—Truck and barge.
Cargo Storage—Covered, 139,747 square meters. Open, 549,038 square meters.
Special Cranes—Heavy lift capacity is 49 metric tons. Container, 4 with 30.5 metric ton capacity.
Air Cargo—New Tokyo International Airport (Narita), 66 km from port, is a world class facility.
Cargo Handling—Tokyo's port equipment adequately handles most normal throughput. Container and Ro-Ro terminals handle these special cargo.
Weather—Temperatures range from -3.5˚C to 33.9˚C with annual rainfall at 146 cm.

Business Dictionary

VOWELS

The following vowels are short and pure, and should be pronounced as individual vowel sounds (e.g., "**ai**" is ah-ee, not "eye").

JAPANESE VOWEL	SOUND IN ENGLISH	EXAMPLE	
a	as in **fa**ther	*akai*	ah-kah-ee
e	as in m**e**n	*ebi*	eh-bee
i	as in s**ee**	*imi*	ee-mee
o	as in b**oa**t	*otoko*	oh-toh-koh
u	as in f**oo**d	*uma*	oo-mah

The following vowels are like the ones above, but held longer.

JAPANESE VOWEL	SOUND IN ENGLISH	EXAMPLE	
aa	as in **fa**ther, but lengthened	*bataa*	bah-tah
ei	as in m**e**n, but lengthened	*eigo*	eh-goh
ii	as in s**ee**, but lengthened	*iiharu*	ee-hah-roo
oo	as in b**oa**t, but lengthened	*oosama*	oh-sah-mah
uu	as in f**oo**d, but lengthened	*yuubin*	yoo-been

CONSONANTS

The letter "**g**" in the Pronunciation column represents the sound heard in the word "**g**um," not that in "**G**eor**g**e."

Some English words in the fourth column have been used where the pronunciation is almost exactly the same as a Japanese sound, e.g., "gain," "pine," "boots"; otherwise, we have used the "pure" vowel symbols above. In this case an "**h**" indicates a long vowel.

English	Japanese	Transliteration	Pronunciation

GREETINGS AND POLITE EXPRESSIONS

English	Japanese	Transliteration	Pronunciation
Hello.			
(morning)	おはよう ございます。	ohayoo- gozaimasu.	o-hayoh- go-zigh-mass.
(daytime)	こんにちは。	konnichiwa.	kong-ni-chi-wa.
(evening)	こんばんわ。	konbanwa.	kong-bung-wa.
Good-bye.	さようなら。	sayoonara.	sa-yoh-nara.
Please.	どうぞ／お願い します。	doozo/ onegai shimasu.	dough-zo/ o-ne-guy she-mass.
Pleased to meet you.	はじめまして。	hajimemashite.	ha-jee-meh-mash-te.
Please excuse me.	すみません／ ごめんなさい。	sumimasen/ gomen nasai.	su-mi-ma seng/ go-men na-sigh.
Excuse me for a moment (when leaving a meeting)	失礼します。	shitsurei shimasu.	sh't su-reigh she-mass.
Congratulations.	おめでとうござい ます。	omedetoo gozai- masu.	o-me-de-toh go-zuy- mass.
Thank you.	どうもありがとう。	doomo arigato.	dough-mo ah-ri-gah- toh.
Thank you very much.	どうもありがとう ございます。	doomo arigatoo gozaimasu.	dough-mo ah-ri- gah-toh go-zuy-mass.
Thank you for the gift.	贈物をありがとう ございます。	okurimono o ari- gatoo gozaimasu.	o-ku-ri mono o ah-ri -ga-toh go-zuy-mass.
I am sorry. I don't understand Japanese.	すみません。 日本語は、わか りません。	sumimasen. Nihongo wa, wakarimasen.	su-mi ma-seng. Ni-hong-go wa, wa-ka-ri ma-seng.
Do you speak English?	英語を 話しますか？	Eigo o hanashimasu ka?	Eigh go o hanna-she mass-ka?
My name is...	私の名前は...です。	watashi no namae wa, ...desu.	wa-ta-she no na-ma -eigh wa, ...dess.
Is Mr./Ms. ... there? (on the telephone)	...さんを、お願い します。	...san o, onegai shimasu.	...sang o, o-ne-guy she-mass.

English	Japanese	Transliteration	Pronunciation
Can we meet (tomorrow)?	（明日）お会いできますか？	(ashita) oai deki masu ka?	(ash-tah) o eye de-key mass-ka?
Would you like to have dinner together?	夕食をご一緒にいかがですか？	yuushoku o goissho ni ikaga desu ka?	you-shock o go-ish-show ni i-ka-ga dess-ka?
Yes	はい／ええ。	hai/ ee.	hi/ eigh.
No	いいえ。	iie.	i-eigh.

DAY/TIME OF DAY

morning	朝／午前	asa/ gozen	a-sa/ go-zeng
noon	正午	shoogo	show-go
afternoon	昼／午後	hiru/ gogo	hi-lu/ go-go
evening	夕方	yuugata	you-gatta
night	夜／晩	yoru/ ban	yo-lu/ bang
today	今日	kyoo	k'yoh
yesterday	昨日	kinoo	key-know
tomorrow	明日	ashita/ asu	ash-ta/ ass
Monday	月曜日	Getsuyoobi	Get-su-yoh-be
Tuesday	火曜日	Kayoobi	Kah-yoh-be
Wednesday	水曜日	Suiyoobi	Swee-yoh-be
Thursday	木曜日	mokuyoobi	mock-yoh-be
Friday	金曜日	Kinyoobi	King-yoh-be
Saturday	土曜日	Doyoobi	Do-yoh-be
Sunday	日曜日	Nichiyoobi	Ni-chi-yoh-be
holiday	休日	kyuu jitsu	q-jeet-su
New Year's Day	元旦／正月	gantan/ shoogatsu	gun-tongue/ show-gut-su
time	時間	jikan	ji-kung

NUMBERS

one	一	ichi	itchy
two	二	ni	ni
three	三	san	sun
four	四	shi	she
five	五	go	go
six	六	roku	ro-ku
seven	七	nana/ shichi	nana/ she-chi

English	Japanese	Transliteration	Pronunciation
eight	八	hachi	ha-chi
nine	九	kyuu/ ku	q/ ku
ten	十	jyuu	jew
eleven	十一	jyuu ichi	jew-itchy
fifteen	十五	jyuu go	jew-go
twenty	二十	ni jyuu	ni-jew
twenty-one	二十一	nijyuu ichi	ni-jew itchy
thirty	三十	san jyuu	sun-jew
thirty-one	三十一	sanjyuu ichi	sun-jew itchy
fifty	五十	go jyuu	go-jew
one hundred	百	hyaku	h'yuck
one hundred one	百一	hyaku ichi	h'yuck ichy
one thousand	千	sen	seng
one million	百万	hyaku man	h'yuck-mung
first	一番	ichi ban	itchy-bun
second	二番	ni ban	ni-bun
third	三番	san ban	sum-bun

GETTING AROUND TOWN

English	Japanese	Transliteration	Pronunciation
Where is...?	…はどこですか？	...wa doko desu ka?	...wa do-ko dess ka?
Does this train go to ...?	この電車は…に行きますか？	kono densha wa ... ni ikimasu ka?	ko-no den-sha wa ... ni i-key mass ka?
Please take me to (location).	（　）へ連れて行って下さい。	（　）e tsurete itte kudasai.	（　）et-su-ray -tay-eat -tay-ku-dah-sigh.
Where am I?	ここは何処ですか？	koko wa doko desu ka?	koko-wa do-ko dess ka?
airplane	飛行機	hikooki	hi-koh-key
airport	空港／飛行場	kuukoo/ hikoo jyoo	kuh-koh/ hi-koh-joh
bus (public)	バス	basu	bass
taxi	タクシー	takushii	tuck-she
train	電車／汽車	densha/ kisha	den-sha/ key-sha
train station	駅	eki	e-key
ticket	切符／券	kippu/ ken	kip-pu/ keng
one-way (single) ticket	片道切符	katamichi kippu	ka-ta-mi-chi kip-pu
round trip (return)ticket	往復切符	oohuku kippu	oh-fu-ku kip-pu

English	Japanese	Transliteration	Pronunciation

PLACES

English	Japanese	Transliteration	Pronunciation
airport	空港	kuukoo	kuh-koh
bank	銀行	ginkoo	gin-koh
barber shop	床屋	tokoya	to-ko-ya
beauty parlor	美容院	biyooin	bi-yoh-in
business district	商業地域	shoogyoo chiiki	showg-yoh cheeky
chamber of commerce	商工会議所	shookoo kaigisho	show-koh-kigh gi-show
clothes store	衣料品店	iryoohin ten	ear-yoh-hin ten
exhibition	展示場	tenji jyoo	ten-ji-joh
factory	工場	koujyoo	koh-joh
hotel	ホテル	hoteru	ho-teh-du
hospital	病院	byooin	b'-yoh-in
market	市場	ichiba	itchy-ba
post office	郵便局	yuubin kyoku	you-bink-yock
restaurant	レストラン	resutoran	rest-run
rest room/toilet (W.C.):	トイレ／お手洗い	toire/ otearai	toy-re/ oh-teh-ah-lie
sea port	港	minato	mi-na-to
train station	駅	eki	e-key

At the bank

English	Japanese	Transliteration	Pronunciation
What is the exchange rate?	両替レートは いくらですか？	ryoogae reeto wa ikura desuka?	r'yoh-guy ray-to wah i-ku-ra dess-ka?
I want to exchange...	...を両替したい のですが。	...o ryoogae shitai nodesuga.	...oh r'yoh-guy she-tie no dess ga.
Australian dollar	オーストラリア・ ドル	Oosutoraria doru	Oh-su-to-raly-ah do-lu
British pound	英国ポンド	Eikoku pondo	Eigh-kock pond
Chinese yuan (PRC)	中国・元	Chuugoku gen	Chew-gock-gain
French franc	フランス・フラン	Furansu furan	Flan-su flan
German mark	ドイツ・マルク	Doitsu maruku	Do-it-su ma-lu-ku
Hong Kong dollar	ホンコン・ドル	Honkon doru	Hong-kong do-lu
Indonesia rupiah	インドネシア・ ルピア	Indoneshia rupia	In-do-neh-sheer rupiah
Japanese yen	日本円	Nihon en	Ni-hong eng
Korean won	韓国・ウォン	Kankoku won	Kan-koku won
Malaysia ringgit	マレーシア・ リンギット	Mareeshia ringitto	Malay-sheer ring-git-to
Philippines peso	フィリピン・ペソ	Firipin peso	Philip-pin peso

English	Japanese	Transliteration	Pronunciation
Singapore dollar	シンガポール・ドル	Shingapooru doru	Shinga-pole do-lu
New Taiwan dollar (ROC)	新台湾ドル	Shin taiwan doru	Shing-taiwan do-lu
Thailand baht	タイ・バーツ	Tai batsu	Tie Baht-su
U.S. dollar	アメリカ・ドル	Amerika doru	Ameri-ka do-lu
Can you cash a personal check?	個人小切手を換金できますか？	kojin kogitte o kankin deki masu ka?	ko-jin ko-git-te o kang-king decky mass ka?
Where should I sign?	どこにサインをすればよろしいですか？	doko ni sain o sureba yoroshi desu ka?	do-ko ni sign o su-lay-bah yoh-ro she dess ka?
traveler's check	トラベラーズチェック	toraberaazu-chekku	tra-beller-zu check-ku
bank draft	銀行手形	ginkoo tegata	gin-koh teh-gutta

At the hotel

English	Japanese	Transliteration	Pronunciation
I have a reservation.	予約をしてあります。	yoyaku o shite ari masu.	yo-yuck osh-teh ah-ri-mass.
Could you give me a single/ double room?	シングル／ダブルルームをお願いします。	shinguru/ daburu ruumu o onegai shimasu.	shingle/ dub-u-lu luh-mu o o-ne-guy she-mass.
Is there...?	...はありますか？	...wa arimasu ka?	...wa ah-ri-mass ka?
air-conditioning	冷房／エアコン	reiboo/ eakon	rey-boh/ air-kong
heating	暖房	danboo	dum-boh
private toilet	個人用トイレ	kojinyoo toire	ko-jin-yoh to-i-ray
hot water	お湯	oyu	o-you
May I see the room?	部屋を見せてもらえますか？	heya o misete morae masu ka?	hey-a o mi-set-teh mo-ra-eigh mass ka?
Would you mail this for me please?	この手紙を出してもらえますか？	kono tegami o dashite morae masu ka?	ko-no teh-gummy o dash-teh mo-ra-eigh mass ka?
Do you have any stamps?	切手はありますか？	kitte wa arimasuka?	kit-teh wa ah-ri masska?

English	Japanese	Transliteration	Pronunciation
May I have my bill?	清算をお願い します。	seisan o onegai shimasu.	say-sun o o-ne-guy she-mass.

At the store

Do you sell...?	…を売って いますか？	...o utte imasu ka?	...o ut-teh i-mass ka?
Do you have anything less expensive?	もっと安いものは ありますか？	motto yasuimono wa arimasu ka?	mot-to yah-su-i mono- wa ah-ri-mass ka?
I would like (quantity).	（　　）ください。	（　）kudasai.	（　）ku-da-sigh.
I'll take it.	これを買います。	kore o kaimasu.	ko-ray-o kigh-mass.
I want this one.	これをください。	kore o kudasai.	ko-ray-o ku-da-sigh.
When does it open/ close?	開店／閉店は 何時ですか？	kaiten/ heiten wa nanji desu ka?	kigh-ten/ hey-ten wa nan-ji dess ka?

COUNTRIES

English	Japanese	Transliteration	Pronunciation
America (USA)	アメリカ （アメリカ合衆国）	Amerika (Amerika gasshuu koku)	Ameri-ka (Ameri-ka gash-shoe ko-ku)
Australia	オーストラリア	Oosutoraria	Aust-o-ra-ri-ah
China (PRC)	中国 （中華人民共和国）	Chuu goku (Chuka jinmin kyoowakoku)	Chew-go-ku (Chew-ka jim-mink yoh wa-ko-ku)
France	フランス	Furansu	Flan-su
Germany	ドイツ	Doitsu	Do-it-su
Hong Kong	香港	Honkon	Hong-kong
Indonesia	インドネシア	Indoneshia	In-do-neh-sheer
Japan	日本	Nihon	Ni-hong
Korea	韓国	Kankoku	Kang-koku
Malaysia	マレーシア	Mareeshia	Marey-sheer
Philippines	フィリピン	Firipin	Philip-pin
Singapore	シンガポール	Shingapooru	Shinga-pole
Taiwan (ROC)	台湾（中華民国）	Taiwan (Chuka minkoku)	Tie-won (Chew-kah min-koku)
Thailand	タイ	Tai	Tie
United Kingdom	イギリス	Igirisu	Iggy-liss

English	Japanese	Transliteration	Pronunciation

EXPRESSIONS IN BUSINESS

1) General business-related terms

English	Japanese	Transliteration	Pronunciation
accounting	会計／決算	kaikei/ kessan	kigh-kay/ kess-sung
additional charge	追加料金	tsuika ryookin	tsu-e-kah r'yoh-king
advertise	宣伝する	senden suru	sen-den su-lu
advertisement	広告	kookoku	koh koku
bankrupt	倒産	toosan	toh-sun
brand name	商品名	shoohin mei	show-hin may
business	ビジネス／経営	bijinesu/ keiei	bi-ji-ness/ keigh eigh
buyer	買い手	kaite	kigh-teh
capital (money)	資本	shihon	she-hong
cash	現金	genkin	gain-king
charge	料金	ryookin	r'yoh king
check	小切手	kogitte	ko-git-tay
claim	請求する(v)	seikyuu suru (v)	say-q su-lu
collect	収集する(v)	shuushuu suru (v)	shoe-shoe su-lu
commission			
(fee)	手数料	tesuu ryoo	tay-suh-r'yoh
(agency)	取次	toritsugi	toritt-su-gi
company	会社	kaisha	kigh-sha
copyright	著作権	chosaku ken	cho-suck keng
corporation	社団法人／	shadan hoojin/	shuddan hoh-jin/
	株式会社	kabushiki gaisha	kub-she-key guy-sha
cost (expense)	原価／費用	genka/ hiyoo	gain-ka/ he-yoh
currency	通貨	tsuuka	tsuh-ka
customer	顧客	kokyaku	ko-k'yuck
D/A (documents	手形引受書類渡し	tegata hikiuke	teh-gatta hicky-u-ke
against acceptance)		shorui watashi	sho-lui wah-tah-she
D/P (documents	手形支払書類渡し	tegata shiharai	teh-gatta she-ha-righ
against payment)		shorui watashi	sho-lui wah-tah-she
deferred payment	延べ払い	nobe barai	no-bey ba-lie
deposit	預金	yokin	yo-king
design	デザイン	dezain	design
discount	割引(n)	waribiki (n)	worry-be-key
distribution	分配／流通	bunpai/ ryuu tsuu	boom-pie/ r'you tsu
dividends	配当	haitoo	high-toh
documents	書類	shorui	sho-lui
due date	期日	kijitsu	key-jitt-su

English	Japanese	Transliteration	Pronunciation
exhibit	展示（会）	tenji (kai)	ten-ji (kigh)
ex works	工場渡し	koojyoo watashi	koh-joh wa-ta-she
facsimile (fax)	ファクシミリ／（ファックス）	fakushimiri/ (fakkusu)	fac-she-milli/ (fac-su)
finance	金融	kinyu	king-you
foreign businessman	外国人ビジネスマン	gaikokujin bijinesu man	guy-koku jin be-ji-ness mung
foreign capital	海外資本	kaigai shihon	kigh-guy she-hong
foreign currency	外国通貨	gaikoku tsuuka	guy-koku tsuh-ka
foreign trade	対外貿易	taigai booeki	tie-guy boh-ecky
government	政府	seifu	say-who
industry	産業	sangyoo	sung-g'yoh
inspection	視察	shisatsu	she-sats
insurance	保険	hoken	ho-keng
interest	利子	rishi	ri-she
international	国際的	kokusaiteki	koku-sigh-te-key
joint venture	ジョイントベンチャー／合弁	jyointo benchaa/ gooben	joint-beng-char/ goh-beng
label	ラベル／標示	raberu/ hyooji	la-be-du/ h'-yoh-ji
letter of credit	信用状	shinyoo jyo	shin-yoh-joh
license	ライセンス	raisensu	lie-seng-su
loan	ローン	roon	loan
model (of a product)	モデル／型	moderu/ kata	mo-de-lu/ ka-ta
monopoly	独占	dokusen	doc-seng
office	オフィス／事務所	ofisu/ jimusho	o-fis-su/ jim-show
patent	特許	tokkyo	tock-k'yo
pay	支払う	shiharau	she-ha-<u>lou</u> (as in "loud")
payment for goods	商品の支払い	shoohin no shiharai	show-hin no she-ha-lie
payment by installment	分割払い	bunkatsu barai	boon-cut-su bar-eye
permit	許可	kyoka	k'yocka
principal:			
(financial)	元金	gankin	gun-king
(legal)	本人	hon nin	hon-nin
private	私有の	shiyuu no	she-you-no
(not government)			
product	製品	seihin	say-hin
profit margin	利ざや	rizaya	li-za-ya
registration	登録	tooroku	toh-rock
report	レポート	repooto	le-port

English	Japanese	Transliteration	Pronunciation
research and development (R&D)	研究開発	kenkyuu kaihatsu	ken-k'you kigh-hat-su
return (on investment)	（投資）利益率	(tooshi) riekiritsu	(toh-she) re-ecky-rit-su
sample	サンプル／見本	sanpuru/ mihon	sum-pu-lu/ mi-hon
seller	売主	urinushi	u-ri-nu-she
settle accounts	決算を行なう	kessan o okonau	kes-sun o o-ko-now
service charge	サービス料金	saabisu ryookin	sah-biss r'yoh-king
sight draft	一覧払為替手形	ichiran barai- kawase tegata	ichy-run ba-lie- ka-wa-say te-gatta
tax	税金	zeikin	zey-king
telephone	電話	denwa	den-wah
telex	テレックス	terekkusu	teleck-su
trademark	トレードマーク／ 商標	toreedo maaku/ shoohyoo	to-ray-do mark/ show-h'yoh
visa	ビザ／査証	biza/ sashoo	be-za/ sa-show

2) Labor

English	Japanese	Transliteration	Pronunciation
compensation (salary)	給料	kyuu ryoo	q-r'yoh
employee	従業員	jyuu gyoo in	jew-g'yoh-inn
employer	雇用者	koyoosha	ko-yoh-sha
fire, dismiss	解雇する	kaiko suru	kigh-ko su-lu
foreign worker	外国人労働者	gaikokujin roodoosha	guy-koku-jin law-dough -sha
hire	雇う	yatou	ya-tow
immigration	移民	imin	E-min
interview	面接	mensetsu	men-set-su
laborer:	労働者	roodoosha	law-dough-sha
skilled	熟練	jyukuren	jew-ku-len
unskilled	未熟練	mi jyukuren	mi Jew-ku-len
labor force	労働力	roodoo ryoku	law-dough r'yock
labor shortage	労働力不足	roodoo ryoku busoku	law-dough r'yock bu-sock
labor stoppage	労働停止	roodoo teishi	law-dough tey-she
labor surplus	労働力過剰	roodoo ryoku kajyoo	law-dough r'yock ka-joh
minimum wage	最低賃金	saitei chingin	sigh-tey chin-ging
profession/ occupation	専門職／職業	senmon shoku/ shokugyoo	seng-mong shock/ shock-g'yoh

English	Japanese	Transliteration	Pronunciation
salary (annual)	年棒	nennbou	nem-boh
strike	ストライキ／スト	sutoraiki/ suto	stow-lie-key/ sto
training	トレーニング／ 研修	yoreeningu/ kenshuu	yo-re-eh-ning/ ken-shoe
union	組合	kumiai	ku-mi-eye
wage	賃金	chingin	chin-gin

3) Negotiations (Buying/Selling)

English	Japanese	Transliteration	Pronunciation
agreement	合意	gooi	goh-i
arbitrate	調節する	choosetsu suru	choh-set-su su-lu
brochure, pamphlet	パンフレット	panfuretto	pan-phlet-to
buy	買い	kai	kigh
confirm	確認	kakunin	ka-ku-nin
contract	契約	keiyaku	keigh-yack
cooperate	協力する	kyoo ryoku suru	k'yoh r'yock su-lu
cost	原価	genka	gain-ka
counteroffer	反対申込	hantai mooshi- komi	hang-tie mow-she- ko-mi
countersign	副署	fukusho	fu-ku sho
deadline	最終期限	saishuu kigen	sigh-shoe key-gain
demand	需要	jyuyoo	ju-yoh
estimate	見積り	mitsumori	mitt-su-mo-ri
guarantee	保証	hoshoo	ho-show
label	ラベル	raberu	la-beh-du
license	ライセンス	raisensu	lie-sence
market	市場	shijyoo	she-joh
market price	市場価格	shijyoo kakaku	she-joh ka-ka-ku
minimum quantity	注文引受可能 最小量	chuumon hikiuke kanoo saishoo- ryo	chew-mong hicky-u- kay ka-know sigh- show-r'yoh
negotiate	交渉する	koosho suru	koh-show su-lu
negotiate payment	支払い交渉	shiharai koosho	she-ha-righ koh-show
order	注文	chuumon	chew-mong
packaging	包装	hoosoo	hoh-saw
place an order	発注する	hacchu suru	hat-chew su-lu
price	価格	kakaku	ka-ka-ku
price list	価格表	kakaku hyoo	ka-ka-ku h'yoh
product features	製品特徴	seihin tokuchoo	say-hin to-ku-choh
product line	製品種目	seihin shumoku	say-hin shoe-mock

English	Japanese	Transliteration	Pronunciation
quality	品質	hinshitsu	hin-she-tsu
quantity	数量	suuryo	suh-r'yoh
quota	割当て額	wariate gaku	worry-a-tay guck
quote (offer)	相場をつける	sooba o tsukeru	soh-ba ot su-ke-lu
sale	販売	hanbai	hum-buy
sales confirmation	販売確認	hanbai kakunin	hum-buy ka-ku-nin
sell	売る	uru	u-lu
sign	サイン(n)／	sain (n)/	sign/
	署名する(v)	shomei suru (v)	sho-may su-lu
signature	署名	shomei	sho-may
specifications	明記	meiki	may-key
standard (quality)	標準	hyoojyun	h'yoh-jun
superior (quality)	上級	jyookyuu	joh-q
trade	貿易	booeki	boh-ecky
unit price	単価	tanka	tongue-ka
value	価値	kachi	ka-chey
value added	付加価値	huka kachi	fu-ka ka-chey
warranty	保証	hoshoo	ho-show
(and services)	（とサービス）	(to saabisu)	(to sah-biss)
The price is too high.	それは高すぎます。	sore wa takasugi masu.	so-rey-wa ta-ka-suggy-mass.
We need a faster delivery.	もっと早く受取りたい。	motto hayaku uke-toritai.	mot-to high-a-ku u-kay-to-ri-tie.
We need it by...	...までに必要です。	...madeni hitsuyoo desu.	... ma-day-ni hit-su-yoh-dess.
We need a better quality.	もっと品質の良いものを下さい。	motto hinshitsu no yoi mono o kudasai.	mot-to hing-sh't-su no yoy mono o ku-da-sigh.
We need it to these specifications.	ここに明記されている通りにして下さい。	koko ni meiki sareteiru toorini-shite kudasai.	koko-ni may-key sa-ray-te i-lu toh-ri nish-teh-ku-da-sigh.
I want to pay less.	もっと安くして下さい。	motto yasuku shite kudasai.	mot-to yass-kush-teh ku-da-sigh.
I want the price to include...	...を価格に入れて下さい。	...o kakaku ni irete kudasai.	... o ka-ka-ku ni i-ray-te ku-da-sigh.

English	Japanese	Transliteration	Pronunciation
Can you guarantee delivery?	引渡しの保証はありますか？	hikiwatashi no ho-shoo wa arimasuka?	hi-key-wa-ta-she no ho-show wa ah-ri-mass ka?

4) Products/Industries

English	Japanese	Transliteration	Pronunciation
aluminum	アルミニウム	aruminiumu	ah-lu-mi-new-mu
automobile	自動車	jidoosha	ji-dough-sha
automotive accessories	自動車付属品	jidoosha-huzokuhin	ji-dough-sha fu-zock-hin
biotechnology	バイオテクノロジー	baio tekunorojii	bio-teck-no-lo-ji
camera	カメラ	kamera	ka-me-ra
carpets	カーペット	kaapetto	kah-pet-to
cement	セメント	semento	cement-to
ceramics	セラミック	seramikku	cera-mick
chemicals	化学製品	kagaku seihin	ka-gack say-hing
clothing:	衣類	irui	i-rui
for women	女性用	jyosei yoo	jo-say yoh
for men	男性用	dansei yoo	dan-say yoh
for children	子供用	kodomo yoo	ko-do-mo yoh
coal	石炭	sekitan	se-key-tongue
computer	コンピューター	konpyuutaa	compuh-ta
computer hardware	コンピューター・ハードウエアー	konpyuutaa-haadoueaa	compuh-ta hah-do we-ah
computer software	コンピューター・ソフトウエアー	konpyuutaa-sofutoueaa	compuh-ta sof-toe we-ah
construction	建設	kensetsu	ken-set-su
electrical equipment	電気装置	denki soochi	den-key soh-chi
electronics	エレクトロニクス	erekutoro nikusu	elec-to-ro nik-su
engineering	エンジニアリング	enji nia ringu	engineer-ringg
fireworks	花火	hanabi	hana-be
fishery products	漁業製品	gyogyoo seihin	g'yog-yoh-say-hing
food products	食品	shoku hin	shock-ku-hing
footwear	はきもの	hakimono	hockey-mono
forestry products	林業製品	ringyoo seihin	ring-yoh say-hing
fuel	燃料	nen ryoo	nen-r'yoh
furniture	家具	kagu	ka-gu
games	ゲーム	geemu	gay-mu
gas	ガス	gasu	gus
gemstone	宝石用原石	hooseki yoo gen seki	hoh-seckey-yoh gain-secky

English	Japanese	Transliteration	Pronunciation
glass	ガラス	garasu	galass
gold	金／ゴールド	kin/ goorudo	king/ goh-lu-do
hardware	金属製品	kinzoku seihin	king-zock say-hing
iron	鉄	tetsu	tet-su
jewelry	宝石	hooseki	hoh-secky
lighting fixtures	照明装置	shoomei soochi	show-may soh-chi
leather goods	革製品	kawa seihin	ka-wah say-hing
machinery	機械	kikai	key-kigh
minerals	ミネラル	mineraru	minera-du
musical instruments	楽器	gakki	gack-key
paper	紙	kami	ka-mi
petroleum	石油	sekiyu	secky-you
pharmaceuticals	薬物	yaku butsu	yuck-boots
plastics	プラスチック	purasuchikku	plus-chic
pottery	陶器	tooki	toh-key
rubber	ゴム	gomu	go-mu
silk	きぬ／シルク	kinu/ shiruku	key-nu/ she-lu-ku
silver	銀／シルバー	gin/ shirubaa	gin/ she-lu-bah
spare parts	予備部品	yobi buhin	yo-bi bu-hing
sporting goods	スポーツ用品	supootsu yoohin	sports yo-hing
steel	スチール	suchiiru	su-cheal
telecommunications equipment	テレコミュニケーション装置	tere komyuni keeshon soochi	te-reh-communica-shong soh-chi
television	テレビ	terebi	te-re-bi
textiles	繊維	sen i	seng-i
tobacco	タバコ	tabako	tah-bako
tools:	道具	doogu	dough-gu
hand	手工具	shukoogu	shoe-koh-gu
power	動力機械	douryoku kikai	dough-r'yock key-kigh
tourism	観光業	kankoo gyoo	kang-koh-g'yoh
toys	おもちゃ	omocha	o-mo-cha
watches /clocks	時計	tokei	to-kay
wood	木材	mokuzai	mock-zigh

5) Services

accounting service	会計サービス	kaikei saabisu	kigh-keigh sah-biss
advertising agency	広告代理店	kookoku dairi ten	koh-koku die-ri-teng
agent	代理店	dairi ten	die-ri-teng

English	Japanese	Transliteration	Pronunciation
customs broker	税関貨物取扱人	zeikan kamotsu tori atsukai nin	zay-kang ka-mot-su tory at-su-kigh ning
distributor	配送業者	haisou gyoo sha	high-soh-g'yoh sha
employment agency	職業安定所	shokugyoo antei jyo	shock-g'yoh an-tay-joh
exporter	輸出業者	yu shutsu gyoo sha	you-shut-su g'yoh-sha
freight forwarder	小口運送業者	koguchi unsoo gyoo sha	ko-Gucci un-soh-g'yoh -sha
importer	輸入業者	yu nyuu gyoo sha	you-new-g'yoh-sha
manufacturer	製造業者	seizoo gyoo sha	say-zohg'yoh-sha
packing service	包装サービス	hoosoo saabisu	hoh-soh sah-biss
printing company	印刷会社	insatsu gaisha	inn-sat-su guy-sha
retailer	小売業者	kouri gyoo sha	ko-uli g'yoh-sha
service(s)	サービス	saabisu	sah-biss
supplier	供給者	kyookyuu sha	k'yoh-q-sha
translation services	翻訳業	honyaku gyoo	hon-yuck g'yoh
wholesaler	卸売業者	oroshi uri gyoo sha	o-rosh-uli g'yoh-sha

6) Shipping/Transportation

English	Japanese	Transliteration	Pronunciation
bill of lading	船荷証券	funani shooken	fu-nanny show-ken
cost, insurance, freight (CIF)	運賃保険料込み値段	unchin hokenryoo komi nedan	ung-chin ho-ken-r'yoh ko-mi ne-dan
customs	税関	zeikan	zeigh-kan
customs duty	関税	kanzei	kang-zeigh
date of delivery	配達日／出荷日／納品日	haitatsu bi/ shukka-bi/ noohin bi	hi-tat-su be/ shuk-ka be / no-hin be
deliver (delivery)	配達／出荷／納品	haitatsu/ shukka / noohin	hi-tat-su/ shuk-ka / no-hing
export	輸出する(v)	yu shutsu suru (v)	you-shut-su sue-lu
first class mail	第一種郵便	dai isshu yuubin	die ish-shoe you-bin
free on board (F.O.B.)	本船渡し	honsen watashi	hon-sen wah-tah-she
freight (goods)	貨物	kamotsu	ka-mott-su
import	輸入する(v)	yu nyu suru (v)	you-new su-lu
in bulk	ばら荷	bara ni	bala ni
mail (post)	郵送する(v)	yuuso suru (v)	you-soh su-lu
country of origin	原産国	gensan koku	gain-sun ko-ku
packing	包装	hoosoo	hoh-soh
packing list	包装リスト	hoosoo risuto	hoh-soh lis-to
port	港	minato	mi-na-to

English	Japanese	Transliteration	Pronunciation
ship (to send):	輸送する	yusoo suru	yu-soh su-lu
by air	航空便	kookuu bin	koh-kuh bin
by sea	船積み送り	hunazumi okuri	fu-na-zu-mi o-ku-ri
by train	汽車積み送り	kishazumi okuri	ki-sha-zu-mi o-ku-ri
by truck	トラック積み送り	torakkuzumi okuri	truck-ku-zu-mi o-ku-ri

WEIGHTS, MEASURES, AMOUNTS

English	Japanese	Transliteration	Pronunciation
barrel	バレル	bareru	ba-deh-du
bushel	ブッシェル	bussheru	boosh-shed-u
centimeter	センチメートル	senchi meetoru	sent-chi meh-toh-du
dozen	ダース	daasu	dah-su
foot	フィート	fiito	fi-to
gallon	ガロン	garon	ga-dong
gram	グラム	guramu	gra-mu
gross (144 pieces)	グロス	gurosu	gros-su
gross weight	総重量	soo jyuuryoo	soh-jew-r'yoh
hectare	ヘクタール	hekutaaru	heck tah-lu
hundred (100)	百	hyaku	h'yuck
inch	インチ	inchi	in-chi
kilogram	キログラム	kiro guramu	kilogra-mu
kilometer	キロメートル	kiro meetoru	kilo-may-to-lu
meter	メートル	meetoru	may-to-lu
net weight	正味重量	shoomi jyuuryoo	show-mi jew-r'yoh
mile (English)	マイル	mairu	my-lu
liter	リットル	rittoru	litt-to-lu
ounce	オンス	onsu	on-su
pint	パイント	painto	pine-to
pound (weight measure avoirdupois)	ポンド（重量）	pondo (jyuuryoo)	pon-do (jew-r'yoh)
quart (avoirdupois)	クォート（重量）	kuoto (jyuuryoo)	quaw-to (jew-r'yoh)
square meter	平方メートル	heihoo meetoru	hey-hoh may-to-lu
square yard	平方ヤード	heihoo yaado	hey-hoh yah-do
size	サイズ	saizu	sigh-zu
ton	トン	ton	tong
yard	ヤード	yaado	yah-do

English	Japanese	Transliteration	Pronunciation

JAPAN-SPECIFIC ORGANIZATIONAL TITLES

English	Japanese	Transliteration	Pronunciation
board of directors	取締役会	torishimariyaku kai	torish-mary-yuck-kigh
chairman	会長	kaichoo	kigh-choh
manager	部長／マネージャー	buchoo/ Maneejaa	bu-choh/ money-jar
(assistant manager)	（副部長／ アシスタント マネージャー）	(fuku buchoo/ ashisutanto- maneejyaa)	(hook bu-choh/ a-she-su-tan-to money-jar)
president	社長	shachoo	sha-choh
(vice president)	（副社長）	fuku shachoo	hook sha-choh
Salaried office worker	サラリーマン	sarariiman	sa-ra-li-mung

JAPAN-SPECIFIC EXPRESSIONS AND TERMS

English	Japanese	Transliteration	Pronunciation
(Form of thanks after asking a favor.)	よろしくお願い します。	yoroshiku onegai shimasu.	yolo-shick o-ne-guy she-mass.
(Used when seeking attention.)	すみませんが。	sumimasenga.	su-mi-ma-seng gah.
(Before a meal.)	いただきます。	itadakimasu.	i-ta-da-key-mass.
(After a meal.)	ごちそうさま でした。	gochisou sama deshita.	go-chi-soh summa desh-tah.
Hello (on the phone)	もしもし。	moshimoshi.	moshy-moshy.
See you later.	それでは後ほど。	soredewa- nochihodo.	sorry-day-wa notchy-ho-do.
Coffee:	コーヒー	koohii	koh-hi
Tea:	紅茶	koocha	koh-cha
Japanese tea:	お茶	ocha	o-cha
McDonald's:	マクドナルド	Makudonarudo	Ma-ku-do naru-do

COMMON SIGNS

English	Japanese	Transliteration	Pronunciation
Enter	入口	iri guchi	irri Gucci
Exit	出口	de guchi	day Gucci
Man	男性	dansei	dan-say
Woman	女性	jyosei	jo-say
Up	上	ue	u-eigh
Down	下	shita	sh'tah

Important Addresses

IMPORTANT ADDRESSES
TABLE OF CONTENTS

GOVERNMENT

GOVERNMENT AGENCIES

Administrative Management Agency
1-1, Kasumigaseki 3-chome, Chiyoda-ku
Tokyo 100
Tel: (3) 3581-6361

Agency of Natural Resources and Energy
3-1, Kasumigaseki 1-chome, Chiyoda-ku
Tokyo 100
Tel: (3) 3501-1511

Center for Development of Power Supply Regions
107 Ark Mori Building
1-12-32 Akasaka, Minato-ku
Tokyo
Tel: (3) 5562-9711 Fax: (3) 5562-9802

Defense Agency
7-45, Akasaka 9-chome, Minato-ku
Tokyo 107
Tel: (3) 3408-5211

Economic Planning Agency
1-1, Kasumigaseki 3-chome, Chiyoda-ku
Tokyo 100
Tel: (3) 3581-0261

Environmental Agency
1-2-2, Kasumigaseki, Chiyoda-ku
Tokyo 100
Tel: (3) 3581-3351
Global Environment Department
Tel: (3) 3580-4982 Fax: (3) 3504-1634

Food Agency
2-1, Kasumigaseki 1-chome, Chiyoda-ku
Tokyo 100
Tel: (3) 3502-8111

Hokkaido Development Agency
1-1, Kasumigaseki 3-chome, Chiyoda-ku
Tokyo 100
Tel: (3) 3581-9111

Japan Fair Trade Commission
International Affairs Division
2-2-1 Kasumigaseki, Chiyoda-ku
Tokyo 100
Tel: (3) 3581-5481 x574/5

Kobe Port and Harbor Bureau
5-1, Kano-cho, 6-chome
Kobe
Tel: (78) 331-8181 Tlx: 78548

Management and Coordination Agency
3-1-1 Kasumigaseki, Chiyoda-ku
Tokyo 100
Tel: (3) 3582-6361, 3508-8321

Ministry of Agriculture, Forestry and Fisheries
1-2-1, Kasumigaseki 1-chome, Chiyoda-ku
Tokyo 100
Tel: (3) 3502-8111

Ministry of Construction
1-3, Kasumigaseki 2-chome, Chiyoda-ku
Tokyo 100
Tel: (3) 3580-4311

Ministry of Education
2-2, Kasumigaseki 3-chome, Chiyoda-ku
Tokyo 100
Tel: (3) 3581-4211

Ministry of Finance
3-1-1 Kasumigaseki, Chiyoda-ku
Tokyo 100
Tel: (3) 3581-4111 Fax: (3) 3508-7324

Ministry of Finance
Customs & Tariff Bureau
1-1 Kasumigaseki 3-chome, Chiyoda-ku
Tokyo 100
Tel: (3) 3581-2852 Fax: (3) 3593-1223, 3581-0460
Tlx: 24980 MOFJ

Ministry of Foreign Affairs
2-1, Kasumigaseki 2-chome, Chiyoda-ku
Tokyo 100
Tel: (3) 3580-3111, 3508-7118, 3508-3311

Ministry of Health & Welfare
2-1, Kasumigaseki 1-chome, Chiyoda-ku
Tokyo 100
Tel: (3) 3502-7111, 3503-1711, 3508-7527
Water Supply and Environmental Sanitation
Department
Tel: (3) 3501-0040 Fax: (3) 3502-6879

Ministry of Home Affairs
1-2, Kasumigaseki 2-chome, Chiyoda-ku
Tokyo 100
Tel: (3) 3581-5311

Ministry of International Trade & Industry
3-1, Kasumigaseki 1-chome, Chiyoda-ku
Tokyo 100
Tel: (3) 3501-1511
Industrial Location Guidance
Tel: (3) 3501-0645
International Business Affairs Division
Tel: (3) 3501-6623
Industrial Location & Environmental Protection
Bureau
Tel: (3) 3501-1679 Fax: (3) 3580-6379

Ministry of Justice
1-1, Kasumigaseki 1-chome, Chiyoda-ku
Tokyo 100
Tel: (3) 3580-4111

Ministry of Justice, Immigration Office
1-1, Kasumigaseki 1-chome, Chiyoda-ku
Tokyo 100
Tel: (3) 3213-8111

Ministry of Labor
1-2-2 Kasumigaseki, 1-chome, Chiyoda-ku
Tokyo 100
Tel: (3) 3593-1211, 3508-7505

Ministry of Posts & Telecommunications
3-2, Kasumigaseki 1-chome, Chiyoda-ku
Tokyo 100
Tel: (3) 3504-4411 Fax: (3) 3592-9157

Ministry of Transport
1-3, Kasumigaseki 2-chome, Chiyoda-ku
Tokyo 100
Tel: (3) 3580-3111

Nagoya Port Authority
8-21, Irifune, 1-chome, Minato-ku
Nagoya 455-91
Tel: (52) 661-4111 Fax: (52) 661-0155
Tlx: 0446 3816 NPA J

Osaka Port Authority
8-24, Chikko, 2-chome, Minato-ku
Osaka
Tel: (6) 572-2121 Tlx: 5356320

Patent Office
4-3, Kasumigaseki 3-chome, Chiyoda-ku
Tokyo 100
Tel: (3) 3581-1101

Prime Minister's Office
6-1, Nagatacho 1-chome, Chiyoda-ku
Tokyo 100
Tel: (3) 3581-2361

Science & Technology Agency
2-1, Kasumigaseki 2-chome, Chiyoda-ku
Tokyo 100
Tel: (3) 3581-5271

Sendai Port Authority
Miyagi Prefectural Government
8-1, Honcho, 3-chome
Sendai
Tel: (22) 221-3211 Fax: (22) 211-3296

Small and Medium Enterprises Agency
1-3-1 Kasumigaseki, Chiyoda-ku
Tokyo 100
Tel: (3) 3501-1511

Tokyo Metropolitan Government
Bureau of Port and Harbor
8-1, Nishi-shinjuku, 2-chome, Shinjuku-ku
Tokyo 163-01
Tel: (3) 5320-5547 Fax: (3) 5388-1576

Yokohama Port & Harbor Bureau
5th Fl., Sangul Boeki Center Building
2, Yamachia-cho, Naka-ku
Yokohama City
Tel: (45) 671-2880

OVERSEAS DIPLOMATIC MISSIONS OF JAPAN

Algeria
Embassy of Japan
1, Chemin, Macklay (AL Bakri)
Ben-Aknoun, Algiers, Algeria
Postal address: B.P. 80, El-Biar, Algiers
Tel: [213] 78-63-41 Fax: [213] 79-22-93

Argentina
Embassy of Japan
Avenida Paseo Colón 275, 9 Piso
Buenos Aires, Argentina
Tel: [54] (1) 343-2561 Fax: [54] (1) 334-5203

Australia
Embassy of Japan
112 Empire Circuit, Yarralumla
Canberra, ACT 2600, Australia
Tel: [61] (62) 273-3244 Fax: [61] (62) 273-1848
Tlx: 62034

Consulate General of Japan (Brisbane)
17th Fl., Comalco Place
12 Creek Street
Brisbane, Qld. 4000, Australia
Tel: [61] (7) 221-5188 Fax: [61] (7) 229-0878

Consulate General of Japan (Melbourne)
3rd Fl., Holland House
492 St. Kilda Road
Melbourne, Vic. 3004, Australia
Tel: [61] (3) 867-3244 Fax: [61] (3) 867-2871

Consulate General of Japan (Perth)
21st Fl., The Forrest Center
221 St. George's Terrace
Perth, W.A. 6000, Australia
Postal address: PO Box 7347
Cloisters Square, Perth WA 6000, Australia
Tel: [61] (9) 321-7816 Fax: [61] (9) 321-2030

Consulate General of Japan (Sydney)
Level 34, State Bank Centre
52 Martin Place
Sydney, NSW 2000, Australia
Postal address: GPO Box 4125
Sydney 2001
Tel: [61] (2) 231-3455 Fax: [61] (2) 221-6157

Austria
Embassy of Japan
Argentinierstrasse 21
1040 Wien, Austria
Tel: [43] (1) 501710 Fax: [43] (1) 5054537

Belgium
Embassy of Japan
Avenue des Arts 58
1040 Brussels, Belgium
Tel: [32] (2) 513-2340 Fax: [32] (2) 513-1556

Brazil
Embassy of Japan
Avenida das Nações, Lote 39
70425, Brasilia, D.F. Brazil
Tel: [55] (61) 242-6866 Fax: [55] (61) 242-0738

Canada
Embassy of Japan
255 Sussex Drive
Ottawa, ON K1N 9E6, Canada
Tel: [1] (613) 236-8541 Fax: [1] (613) 563-9047

Consulate General of Japan (Edmonton)
2480 ManuLife Place, 10180-101 Street
Edmonton, AB T5J 3S4, Canada
Tel: [1] (403) 422-3752 Fax: [1] (403) 424-1635

Consulate General of Japan (Montreal)
600, rue de la Gauchetièrée ouest
Suite 1785
Montreal, PQ H3B 4L8, Canada
Tel: [1] (514) 866-3429 Fax: [1] (514) 395-6000

Consulate General of Japan (Toronto)
Suite 2702, Toronto Dominion Bank Tower
Toronto, ON M5K 1A1, Canada
Tel: [1] (416) 363-7038 Fax: [1] (416) 367-9392

Consulate General of Japan (Vancouver)
900-1177 West Hastings Street
Vancouver, BC V6E 2K9, Canada
Tel: [1] (604) 684-5868 Fax: [1] (604) 684-6939

Consulate General of Japan (Winnipeg)
730-215 Garry St., Credit Union Central Plaza
Winnipeg, MB R3C 3P3, Canada
Tel: [1] (204) 943-5554 Fax: [1] (204) 957-0374

Chile
Embassy of Japan
Av. Providencia 2653
19 Piso, Casilla 2877
Santiago, Chile
Tel: [56] (2) 2321807 Fax: [56] (2) 2321812

China
Embassy of Japan
7 Ri Tan Road
Jian Guo Men Wai
Beijing, PRC
Tel: [86] (1) 5322361 Fax: [86] (1) 5324625

Consulate General of Japan (Guangzhou)
Garden Tower
368 Huanshi Dong Lu
Guangzhou, PRC
Tel: [86] (20) 3338999 Fax: [86] (20) 3338972

Consulate General of Japan (Shenyang)
50 Shisi Wei Lu, He Ping Qu
Shenyang, Liaoning, PRC
Tel: [86] (24) 220340 Fax: [86] (24) 720727

Consulate General of Japan (Shanghai)
1517 Huai Hai Road Central
Shanghai, PRC
Tel: [86] (21) 4336639 Fax: [86] (21) 4331008

Colombia
Embassy of Japan
Carrera 9A No. 99-02 (Piso 6)
Edificio Seguros del Comercio
Santa fe de Bogotá, Colombia
Tel: [57] (1) 618-2800/7 Fax: [57] (1) 618-2828

All addresses and telephone numbers are in Japan unless otherwise noted. The country code for Japan is [81].

Costa Rica
Embassy of Japan
Barrio Rohrmoser
Sabana oeste de la primera entrada
500 mts. oeste y 100 mts. norte
San José, Costa Rica
Tel: [506] 32-1255 Fax: [506] 31-3140

Denmark
Embassy of Japan
Pilestraede 61
1112 Copenhagen K, Denmark
Tel: [45] 33-11-33-44 Fax: [45] 33-11-33-77

Dominican Republic
Embassy of Japan
Tore BHD 8 Piso, av. Winston Churchill
Esquina Luis F. Thomen
Santo Domingo, República Dominicana
Postal address: PO Box 1236, Santo Domingo
Tel: [1] (809) 566-8023, 567-3365
Fax: [1] (809) 566-8013

Ecuador
Embassy of Japan
Calle Juan León Mera No. 130 y av. Patria
Edificio de la Corp. Financiera Nacional, 7-Piso
Quito, Ecuador
Postal address: PO Box 1721-01518, Quito
Tel: [593] (2) 561-899 Fax: [593] (2) 503-670

Egypt
Embassy of Japan
3rd Fl. Cairo Center Building
2, Abdel Kader Hamza Street
Garden City, Cairo, Arab Rep. of Egypt
Postal address: PO Box 281, Cairo
Tel: [20] (2) 3553962 Fax: [20] (2) 3563540/7

Finland
Embassy of Japan
Eteläranta 8
00130 Helsinki, Finland
Tel: [358] (0) 633011 Fax: [358] (0) 633012

France
Embassy of Japan
7, avenue Hoche
75008 Paris, France
Tel: [33] (1) 47-66-02-22
Fax: [33] (1) 42-27-50-81

Consulate General of Japan (Strasbourg)
"Tour Europe" 20, Place des Halles
67000 Strasbourg, France
Tel: [33] (88) 75-98-00 Fax: [33] (88) 22-62-39

Consulate General of Japan (Marseilles)
70, avenue de Hambourg
13008 Marseilles, France
Tel: [33] (91) 73-45-55 Fax: [33] (91) 72-55-45

Germany
Embassy of Japan
Godesberger Alice 102-104
5300 Bonn 2, Germany
Tel: [49] (228) 81910 Fax: [49] (228) 379399

Consulate General of Japan (Berlin)
Wachtelstr. 8
1000 Berlin 33, Germany
Tel: [49] (30) 832-7026 Fax: [49] (30) 832-6967

Consulate General of Japan (Düsseldorf)
c/o Deutsch-Japanisches Center
Germany Immermannstr., 45
4000 Düsseldorf 1, Germany
Tel: [49] (211) 35-33-11 Fax: [49] (211) 35-76-50

Consulate General of Japan (Frankfurt)
Hamburger Allee 2-10
6000 Frankfurt am Main 90, Germany
Tel: [49] (69) 77-03-51 Fax: [49] (69) 77-38-73

Consulate General of Japan (Hamburg)
Rathausmarkt 5
2000 Hamburg 1, Germany
Tel: [49] (40) 33-30-170 Fax: [49] (40) 32-67-96

Consulate General of Japan (Munich)
Prinzregentenplatz 10
8000 München 80, Germany
Tel: [49] (89) 47-10-43 Fax: [49] (89) 47-05-710

Greece
Embassy of Japan
2-4, Messoghion Avenue
Athens Tower Building, 21st Fl.
Athens, Greece
[30] (1) 775-8101 Fax: [30] (1) 770-5964

Hong Kong
Consulate General of Japan
25th Fl., Bank of America Tower
12 Harcourt Road
Central, Hong Kong
Tel: [852] 5221184 Fax: [852] 8680156

Hungary
Embassy of Japan
1024 II, Rómer Flóris Utca 56-58
H-1525 Budapest, Hungary
Postal address: PO Box 78, Budapest
Tel: [36] (1) 1564-533 Fax: [36] (1) 1754-777

India
Embassy of Japan
50-G Shanti Path, Chanakyapuri
New Delhi 110 021, India
Tel: [91] (11) 6876564 Fax: [91] (11) 6885587

Indonesia
Embassy of Japan
Jalan M.H. Thamrin 24
Jakarta, Indonesia
Tel: [62] (21) 324308, 2694244 Fax: [62] (21) 325460

Ireland
Embassy of Japan
Nutley Building, Merrion Centre
Dublin 4, Ireland
Tel: [353] (1) 269-4033 Fax: [353] (1) 283-8726

Israel
Embassy of Japan
Asia House, 4, Weizman Street
64239 Tel Aviv, Israel
Tel: [974] (3) 695-7292 Fax: [972] (3) 691-0516

Italy
Embassy of Japan
via Quintino Sella 60
00187 Rome, Italy
Tel: [39] (6) 481-7151 Fax: [39] (6) 487-3316

Consulate General of Japan (Milan)
via F. Turati 16/18
20121 Milan, Italy
Tel: [39] (2) 2900-2316 Fax: [39] (2) 6597201

Jamaica
Embassy of Japan
32 Trafalgar Road, 3rd Fl.
Atrium Building
Kingston 10, Jamaica, West Indies
Postal address: PO Box 8104, CSO Jamaica
Tel: [1] (809) 929-3338 Fax: [1] (809) 968-1373

Jordan
Embassy of Japan
Between 4th and 5th Circles, Al-Aqsa Street
Jabal Amman, Amman, Jordan
Postal address: PO Box 2835, Amman
Tel: [962] (6) 672486 Fax: [962] (6) 672006

Kenya
Embassy of Japan
16th Fl., ICEA Building
Kenyatta Avenue
Nairobi, Kenya
Postal address: PO Box 60202, Nairobi
Tel: [254] (2) 332955 Fax: [254] (2) 216530

Korea (South)
Embassy of Japan
18-11 Chunghak-dong, Chongno-ku
Seoul, South Korea
Tel: [82] (2) 733-5626 Fax: [82] (2) 734-4528

Consulate General of Japan (Pusan)
No. 1147-11, Choryang-dong, Dong-ku
Pusan, Korea
Tel: [82] (51) 465-5101 Fax: [82] (51) 464-1630

Kuwait
Embassy of Japan
Block 9, Plot No 496, Jabriya
Kuwait City, Kuwait
Postal address: PO Box 2304, Safat
Tel: [965] 5312870 Fax: [965] 5326168

Luxembourg
Embassy of Japan
17, rue Beaumont
L-1219 Luxembourg
Tel: [352] 464151, 464176 Fax: [352] 464176

Malaysia
Embassy of Japan
No. 11, Pesiaran Stonor
Off Jalan Tun Razak
50450 Kuala Lumpur, Malaysia
Tel: [60] (3) 242-7044 Fax: [60] (3) 242-6570

Mexico
Embassy of Japan
Paseo de la Reforma 396, Col. Cuauhtémoc
06500 México City, D.F., México
Postal address: PO Box 5-101, México City
Tel: [52] (5) 211-0028 Fax: [52] (5) 207-7743

Morocco
Embassy of Japan
70, Avenue des Nations Unies
Agdal, Rabat, Morocco
Tel: [212] (7) 67-41-63 Fax: [212] (7) 67-22-74

Netherlands
Embassy of Japan
Tobias Asserlaan 2
2517 KC The Hague, Netherlands
Tel: [31] (70) 3469544 Fax: [31] (70) 3106341

New Zealand
Embassy of Japan
7th Fl., Norwich Insurance House
3-11 Hunter Street
Wellington 1, New Zealand
Postal address: PO Box 6340, Wellington
Tel: [64] (4) 473-1540 Fax: [64] (4) 471-2951

Consulate General of Japan (Auckland)
6th Fl., National Mutual Centre Building
37-45, Shortland Street
Auckland 1, New Zealand
Postal address: PO Box 3959, Auckland
Tel: [64] (9) 303-4106 Fax: [64] (9) 377-7784

Consular Office of Japan (Christchurch)
Level 5, R.J.I. House
764 Colombo St.
Christchurch 1, New Zealand
Postal address: PO Box 1469, Christchurch
Tel: [64] (3) 366-5680 Fax: [64] (3) 365-3173

Nigeria
Embassy of Japan
Plot 24-25 Apese Street
Victoria Island, Lagos, Nigeria
Postal address: PO Box 2111, Lagos
Tel: [234] (1) 61-37-97 Fax: [234] (1) 61-40-35

Norway
Embassy of Japan
Parkvem 33-B
0244 Oslo 2, Norway
Tel: [47] 22-55-10-11

Pakistan
Embassy of Japan
Plot No. 53-70, Ramna 5/4
Diplomatic Enclave 1
Islamabad, Pakistan
Tel: [92] (51) 820181 Fax: [92] (51) 821009

Panama
Embassy of Japan
Calle 50 y 60E, Obarrio
Apartado No. 1411
Panamá City 1, Rep. of Panamá
Tel: [507] 63-6155 Fax: [507] 63-6019

Paraguay
Embassy of Japan
Av. Mariscal López No. 2364
Casilla de Correo No. 1957
Asunción, Paraguay
Tel: [595] (21) 604-616 Fax: [595] (21) 606-901

All addresses and telephone numbers are in Japan unless otherwise noted. The country code for Japan is [81].

Peru
Embassy of Japan
Avenida San Felipe 356, Jesús Maria
Lima, Perú
Postal address: Apdo. 3708, Lima
Tel: [51] (14) 63-0000, 61-4041
Fax: [51] (14) 63-0302

Philippines
Embassy of Japan
375 Senator Gil J. Puyat Avenue
Makati, Metro Manila, Philippines
Postal address: PO Box 891, Makati
Tel: [63] (2) 818-9011 Fax: [63] (2) 817-6562

Poland
Embassy of Japan
ul. Willowa 7
00-790 Warsaw, Poland
Tel: [48] (22) 49-87-81 Fax: [48] (22) 3912-0497

Portugal
Embassy of Japan
Rua Mouzinho da Silveira, 11
1200 Lisbon, Portugal
Tel: [351] (1) 3523485 Fax: [351] (1) 534802, 537600

Russia
Embassy of Japan
Kalashny Perenlok 12
Moscow, Russia
Tel: [7] (095) 291-8500 Fax: [7] (095) 200-1240

Consulate General of Japan (St. Petersburg)
Nab. Reki Noiki 29
St. Petersburg 191065, Russia
Tel: [7] (812) 314-1434 Fax: [7] (812) 311-4891

Saudi Arabia
Embassy of Japan
A-11 Diplomatic Quarter
Riyadh, Saudi Arabia
Postal address: PO Box 4095, Riyadh
Tel: [966] (1) 488-1100 Fax: [966] (1) 488-0189

Singapore
Embassy of Japan
16, Nassim Road
Singapore 1025
Tel: [65] 2358855 Fax: [65] 7320781

South Africa
Embassy of Japan
2nd Fl., Sanlam Building
353 Festival St.
Hatfield, Pretoria 0083, South Africa
Postal address: PO Box 11434
Brooklyn 0011, Pretoria
Tel: [27] (12) 342-2100 Fax: [27] (12) 43-3922

Office of Consul of Japan (Cape Town)
654 Main Tower, Standard Bank Centre
Heerengrachat
Cape Town 8001, South Africa
Tel: [27] (21) 25-1695 Fax: [27] (21) 418-2116

Spain
Embassy of Japan
Calle de Joaquín Costa, 29
28002 Madrid, Spain
Tel: [34] (1) 262-5546 Fax: [34] (1) 262-7868

Consulate General of Japan (Barcelona)
Edificio Banca Catalana
Planta 3, avda. Diagonal 662-664
08034 Barcelona, Spain
Tel: [34] (3) 280-3433 Fax: [34] (3) 280-4496

Sweden
Embassy of Japan
Gärdesgatan 10
115 27 Stockholm, Sweden
Tel: [46] (8) 663-0440 Fax: [46] (8) 661-8820

Switzerland
Embassy of Japan
43, Engerstrasse
3012 Berne, Switzerland
[41] (31) 24-08-11 Fax: [41] (31) 23-53-25

Consulate General of Japan (Geneva)
3, Chemin des Fins
1218 Genève, Switzerland
Tel: [41] (22) 717-31-11 Fax: [41] (22) 788-38-11

Syria
Embassy of Japan
No. 18 Mihdi Bin Baraka St.
Damascus, Syria
Postal address: PO Box 3366, Damascus
Tel: [963] (11) 338273 Fax: [963] (11) 335314

Thailand
Embassy of Japan
1674, New Phetchburi Road
Bangkok 10310, Thailand
Tel: [66] (2) 252-6151 Fax: [66] (2) 253-4153

Turkey
Embassy of Japan
Resit Galip Caddesi 81
Gaziosmanpasa
Ankara, Turkey
Postal address: PlK. 31-Kayaklidere, Ankara
Tel: [90] (4) 446-0500 Fax: [90] (4) 437-1812

United Arab Emirates
Embassy of Japan
PO Box 2430
Abu Dhabi, UAE
Tel: [971] (2) 344696 Fax: [971] (2) 333219

United Kingdom
Embassy of Japan
101-104 Piccadilly
London W1V 9FN, UK
Tel: [44] (71) 465-6500 Fax: [44] (71) 491-9348

Consulate General of Japan (Edinburgh)
2 Melvile Crescent
Edinburgh EH3 7HW, UK
Tel: [44] (31) 225-4777 Fax: [44] (31) 225-4828

United States of America
Embassy of Japan
2520 Massachusetts Ave., NW
Washington, DC 20008-2869, USA
Tel: [1] (202) 939-6700 Fax: [1] (202) 328-2187

Consulate General of Japan (Atlanta)
100 Colony Square Building, Suite 2000
1175 Peachtree Street, NE
Atlanta, GA 30361, USA
Tel: [1] (404) 892-2700 Fax: [1] (404) 881-6321

Consulate General of Japan (Boston)
Federal Reserve Plaza, 14th Fl.
600 Atlantic Avenue
Boston, MA 02210, USA
Tel: [1] (617) 973-9772 Fax: [1] (617) 542-1329

Consulate General of Japan (Chicago)
Olympia Centre, Suite 1100
737 North Michigan Avenue
Chicago, IL 60611, USA
Tel: [1] (312) 280-0400 Fax: [1] (312) 280-9568

Consulate General of Japan (Honolulu)
1742 Nuuanu Avenue
Honolulu, HI 96817-3294, USA
Tel: [1] (808) 536-2226 Fax: [1] (808) 537-3276

Consulate General of Japan (Houston)
First Interstate Bank Plaza, Suite 5300
1000 Louisiana Street
Houston, TX 77002, USA
Tel: [1] (713) 652-2977 Fax: [1] (713) 651-7822

Consulate General of Japan (Kansas City)
2519 Commerce Tower
911 Main Street
Kansas City, MO 64105-2076, USA
Tel: [1] (816) 471-0111 Fax: [1] (816) 472-4248

Consulate General of Japan (Los Angeles)
250 East First Street, Suite 1507
Los Angeles, CA 90012, USA
Tel: [1] (213) 624-8305 Fax: [1] (213) 625-2231

Consulate General of Japan (Miami)
World Trade Center Building, Suite 3200
80 SW 8th St.
Miami, FL 33130, USA
Tel: [1] (305) 530-9090 Fax: [1] (305) 530-0950

Consulate General of Japan (New York)
299 Park Avenue
New York, NY 10171, USA
Tel: [1] (212) 371-8222 Fax: [1] (212) 319-6357

Consulate General of Japan (New Orleans)
One Poydras Plaza, Suite 2050
639 Loyola Avenue
New Orleans, LA 70113, USA
Tel: [1] (504) 529-2101 Fax: [1] (504) 568-9847

Consulate General of Japan (Portland)
First Interstate Tower, Suite 2400
1300 SW Fifth Avenue
Portland, OR 97201, USA
Tel: [1] (503) 221-1811 Fax: [1] (503) 224-8936

Consulate General of Japan (San Francisco)
50 Fremont Street, Suite 2300
San Francisco, CA 94105, USA
Tel: [1] (415) 777-3533 Fax: [1] (415) 974-3660

Consulate General of Japan (Seattle)
601 Union Street, Suite 500
Seattle, WA 98101, USA
Tel: [1] (206) 682-9107 Fax: [1] (206) 624-9097

Uruguay
Embassy of Japan
Bulevar Artigas 953
Montevideo, Uruguay
Postal address: PO Box 1273, Montevideo
Tel: [598] (2) 48-7645 Fax: [598] (2) 48-7980

Venezuela
Embassy of Japan
Quinta Sakura, Avenida San Juan Bosco
Entre 8a y 9a, Transversal, Altamira
Caracas D.F., Venezuela
Tel: [58] (2) 261-8333 Fax: [58] (2) 261-6780

FOREIGN DIPLOMATIC MISSIONS IN JAPAN

Algeria
Embassy
10-67, Mita 2-chome, Meguro-ku
Tokyo 153
Tel: (3) 3711-2661 Fax: (3) 3710-6534 Tlx: 23260

Argentina
Embassy
Chiyoda House, 2nd-3rd Fl.
17-8, Nagata-cho 2-chome, Chiyoda-ku
Tokyo 100
Tel: (3) 3592-0321 Fax: (3) 3506-8469 Tlx: 22489
Economic & Commercial Office
Tel: (3) 3593-1280 Fax: (3) 3593-1282

Australia
Embassy
2-1-14, Mita, Minato-ku
Tokyo 108
Tel: (3) 5232-4111 Fax: (3) 5232-4149
Austrade
Sankatdo Building 7th Fl.
9-13, Akasaka 1-chome, Minato-ku
Tokyo 107
Tel: (3) 3582-7231 Fax: (3) 3582-7239

Australia-Japan Foundation
Cultural Relations Section
Aoyama Eric Building, 5th Fl.
5-1-2 Minami Aoyama, Minato-ku
Tokyo
Tel: (3) 3498-4141 Fax: (3) 3498-0794

Consulate General (Osaka)
Kojusai Building, 23rd Fl.
3-13 Azuchimachi 2-chome, Chuo-ku
Osaka 541
Tel: (6) 271-7071 Fax: (6) 271-7070 Tlx: 5225334

Austria
Embassy
1-20, Moto Azabu 1-chome, Minato-ku
Tokyo 106
Tel: (3) 3451-8281 Fax: (3) 3451-8283 Tlx: 26361

All addresses and telephone numbers are in Japan unless otherwise noted. The country code for Japan is [81].

Trade Commission
13-3, Moto Azabu 3-chome, Minato-ku
Tokyo 106
Tel: (3) 3403-1777 Fax: (3) 3403-3407 Tlx: 28203

Belgium
Embassy
5, Niban-cho, Chiyoda-ku
Tokyo 102
Tel: (3) 3262-0191 Fax: (3) 3262-0651 Tlx: 24979

Brazil
Embassy
11-12, Kita Aoyama 2-chome, Minato-ku
Tokyo 107
Tel: (3) 3403-5211 Fax: (3) 3405-5846 Tlx: 22590

Canada
Embassy
3-38, Akasaka 7-chome, Minato-ku
Tokyo 107
Tel: (3) 3408-2101 Fax: (3) 3479-5320 Tlx: 22218
Consular and Information Sections
Fax: (3) 3470-7278
Science and Technology Section
Fax: (3) 3470-7280
Customs and Excise Section
Fax: (3) 3408-6933
Visa Section
Tel: (3) 3403-9176 Fax: (3) 3470-7278

Consulate General (Osaka)
Daisan Shoho Building, 12th Fl.
2-3, Nishi Shinsaibashi, 2-chome, Chuo-ku
Osaka 542
Postal address: PO Box 150, Osaka 542-91
Tel: (6) 212-4910 Fax: (6) 212-4914

Chile
Embassy
Nihon Seimei Akabanebashi Bldg., 8th Fl.
3-1-14, Shiba, Minato-ku
Tokyo 105
Tel: (3) 3452-7561 Fax: (3) 3769-4156 Tlx: 24585

China
Embassy
3-4-33, Moto Azabu, Minato-ku
Tokyo 106
Tel: (3) 3403-3380 Fax: (3) 3403-3345 Tlx: 28705

Consular Section
5-30, Minami Azabu 4-chome, Minato-ku
Tokyo 106
Tel: (3) 3473-7825

Commercial Section
8-16, Minami Azabu 5-chome, Minato-ku
Tokyo 106
Tel: (3) 3440-2011

Office of Economic Counselor
5-30, Minami Azabu 4-chome, Minato-ku
Tokyo 106
Tel: (3) 3442-2325

Education Section
2-8, Hirano 2-chome, Koto-ku
Tokyo 135
Tel: (3) 3643-0305

Colombia
Embassy
10-23, Kami Osaki 3-chome, Shinagawa-ku
Tokyo 141
Tel: (3) 3440-6451 Fax: (3) 3440-6724

Government Trade Bureau
Rm. 805, No. 38, Kowa Building
12-24, Nishi Azabu 4-chome, Minato-ku
Tokyo 106
Tel: (3) 3499-0440

Office of Commercial Counselor (Coffee Affairs)
10-54, Kami Osaki 3-chome, Shinagawa-ku
Tokyo 141
Tel: (3) 3440-6041 Fax: (3) 3440-6043

Costa Rica
Embassy
Kowa Building, No. 38, Rm. 901
12-24, Nishi Azabu 4-chome, Minato-ku
Tokyo 106
Tel: (3) 3486-1812 Fax: (3) 3486-1813

Denmark
Embassy
29-6, Sarugaku-cho, Shibuya-ku
Tokyo 150
Tel: (3) 3496-3001 Fax: (3) 3496-3440
Tlx: 24417

Consulate
10 Toyo Kaiji Building
31-7 Nishi-Shinbashi 2-chome, Minato-ku
Tokyo 105
Postal address: PO Box 432, Tokyo 100-91
Tel: (3) 459-9230 Fax: (3) 459-8238
Tlx: 242-4224

Dominican Republic
Embassy
Kowa Building, No. 38, Rm. 904
12-24, Nishi Azabu 4-chome, Minato-ku
Tokyo 106
Tel: (3) 3499-6020 Fax: (3) 3499-6010
Tlx: 33701

Ecuador
Embassy
Kowa Building, No. 38, Rm. 806
12-24, Nishi Azabu 4-chome, Minato-ku
Tokyo 106
Tel: (3) 3498-3974, 3499-2800
Fax: (3) 3499-4400 Tlx: 25880
Consular Affairs Tel: (3) 3499-2866
Commercial Section Tel (3) 3498-3974

Consulate General
TOC Building, 2nd Fl.
7-22-7 Nishi Gotanda, Shinagawa-ku
Tokyo
Tel: (3) 3494-2130

Egypt
Embassy
5-4, Aobadai 1-chome, Meguro-ku
Tokyo 153
Tel: (3) 3770-8022 Fax: (3) 3770-8021
Tlx: 23240

Commercial Section
Kowa Building, No. 38, Rm. 808
12-24, Nishi Azabu 4-chome, Minato-ku
Tokyo 106
Tel: (3) 3409-3361, 3770-8401

Cultural Promotion Section
Annex Building, 2nd Fl.
19-8, Akasaka 2-chome, Minato-ku
Tokyo 107
Tel: (3) 3589-0653

Finland
Embassy
3-5-39, Minami Azabu, Minato-ku
Tokyo 106
Tel: (3) 3442-2231 Fax: (3) 3442-2175
Tlx: 26277
Commercial Section Fax: (3) 3440-6013
Scientific Section Fax: (3) 3442-2336

France
Embassy
11-44, Minami Azabu 4-chime, Minato-ku
Tokyo 106
Tel: (3) 3473-0171 Fax: (3) 3442-9755

Office of Financial Counselor
French Bank Building
1-2, Akasaka 1-chome, Minato-ku
Tokyo 107
Tel: (3) 3583-9895 Fax: (3) 3582-0490

Office of Commercial Counselor
Tameike Tokyu Building
1-1-14, Akasaka, Minato-ku
Tokyo 107
Tel: (3) 3584-8333 Tlx: 22652

Consulate General (Osaka)
Ohbayashi Building, 24th Fl.
4-33, Kitahama-Higashi, Chuo-ku
Osaka 540
Tel: (6) 946-6181 Fax: (6) 949-1887

Germany
Embassy
5-10, Minami Azabu 4-chome, Minato-ku
Tokyo 106
Postal address: PO Box 955, Tokyo 100-91
Tel: (3) 3473-0151 Fax: (3) 3473-4243
Tlx: 22292

Consulate (Fukuoka)
c/o Saibu Gas Kabushiki Kaisha
17-1, Chigo 1-chome, Hakata-ku
Fukuoka-shi 812-91
Tel: (92) 633-2211 Fax: (92) 633-2291

Consulate (Nagoya)
c/o Chubu Denryoku KK
Toshin-cho 1, Higashi-ku
Nagoya-shi 461
Tel: (52) 951-8211 Tlx: 44405

Greece
Embassy
16-30, Nishi Azabu 3-chome, Minato-ku
Tokyo 106
Tel: (3) 3403-0871 Fax: (3) 3402-4642

Guatemala
Embassy
38 Kowa Building, Rm. 905
4-12-24, Nishi Azabu, Minato-ku
Tokyo 106
Tel: (3) 3400-1830 Fax: (3) 3400-1820

Hungary
Embassy
2-17-14, Mita, Minato-ku
Tokyo 108
Tel: (3) 3476-6061, 3798-8801
Fax: (3) 3798-8812 Tlx: 22688

Commercial Office
Mori Building, No. 28
16-13, Nishi-Azabu 4-chome, Minato-ku
Tokyo 106
Tel: (3) 3499-4951 Fax: (3) 3499-4918

India
Embassy
2-11, Kudan Minami 2-chome, Chiyoda-ku
Tokyo 102
Tel: (3) 3262-2391 Fax: (3) 3234-4866
Information Section Tel: (3) 3239-2485
Consular Section Tel: (3) 3239-2449

Indonesia
Embassy
2-9, Higashi Gotanda 5-chome, Shinagawa-ku
Tokyo 141
Tel: (3) 3441-4201 Fax: (3) 3447-1697
Tlx: 22920

Ireland
Embassy
Kowa Building, No. 25
8-7 Sanban-cho, Chiyoda-ku
Tokyo 102
Tel: (3) 3262-0695 Fax: (3) 3265-2275
Tlx: 23926

Consulate
c/o Mitsui & Co. Ltd.
1-2-1 Otemachi, Chiyoda-ku
Tokyo 100-91
Tel: (3) 3285-7723 Fax: (3) 3546-9161
Tlx: 22967

Israel
Embassy
3, Niban-cho, Chiyoda-ku
Tokyo 102
Tel: (3) 3264-0911 Fax: (3) 3261-1138
Tlx: 22636

Italy
Embassy
5-4, Mita 2-chome, Minato-ku
Tokyo 108
Tel: (3) 3453-5291 Fax: (3) 3456-2319
Tlx: 22433

Jordan
Embassy
4A-B, Chiyoda House, 4th Fl.
17-8, Nagata-cho 2-chome, Chiyoda-ku
Tokyo 100
Tel: (3) 3580-5856 Fax: (3) 3593-9385

All addresses and telephone numbers are in Japan unless otherwise noted. The country code for Japan is [81].

Korea (South)
Embassy
2-5, Minami Azabu 1-chome, Minato-ku
Tokyo 106
Tel: (3) 3452-7611 Fax: (3) 3452-2696
Tlx: 22045

Consular Section
7-32, Minami Azabu 1-chome, Minato-ku
Tokyo 106
Tel: (3) 3455-2601

Cultural Section
Sunshine 60, 5th Fl.
1-1, Higashi Ikebukuro 3-chome, Toshima-ku
Tokyo 170
Tel: (3) 3988-9271

Kuwait
Embassy
13-12, Mita 4-chome, Minato-ku
Tokyo 108
Tel: (3) 3455-0361 Fax: (3) 3456-6290
Tlx: 25501

Lebanon
Embassy
Chiyoda House, 5th Fl.
17-8, Nagata-cho 2-chome, Chiyoda-ku
Tokyo 100
Tel: (3) 3580-1206, 3580-1227
Fax: (3) 3580-2281 Tlx: 25356

Luxembourg
Embassy
TS Building, 4th Fl.
2-1, Niban-cho, Chiyoda-ku
Tokyo 102
Tel: (3) 3265-9621 Fax: (3) 3265-9624
Tlx: 28822

Malaysia
Embassy
1-11, Minami Azabu 2-chome, Minato-ku
Tokyo 106
Tel: (3) 3280-7601 Fax: (3) 3280-7606
Tlx: 24221

Mexico
Embassy
15-1, Nagata-cho 2-chome, Chiyoda-ku
Tokyo 100
Tel: (3) 3581-1131 Fax: (3) 3581-4058
Tlx: 26875
Commercial Counselor
Tel: (3) 3580-0811 Fax: (3) 3580-9204
Consular Section Tel: (3) 3580-2961
Cultural Attaché Tel: (3) 3581-2150
Tourism Section Tel: (3) 3581-2110
Press & Information Tel: (3) 3581-0845

Morocco
Embassy
Silva Kingdom Building, 5th-6th Fl.
16-3, Sendagaya 3-chome, Shibuya-ku
Tokyo 151
Tel: (3) 3478-3271 Fax: (3) 3402-0898
Tlx: 23451

Netherlands
Embassy
6-3, Shiba Koen 3-chome, Minato-ku
Tokyo 105
Tel: (3) 3431-5126 Fax: (3) 3432-7560
Tlx: 22855

Agricultural Office
Amerex Building, 7th Fl.
5-7, Azabudai 3-chome, Minato-ku
Tokyo 106
Tel: (3) 3582-2500 Fax: (3) 3505-6360

Industrial and Scientific Offices
Denmark House
17-35, Minami Aoyama 4-chome, Minato-ku
Tokyo 107
Tel: (3) 3403-4261 Fax: (3) 3403-4230

New Zealand
Embassy
20-40, Kamiyama-cho, Shibuya-ku
Tokyo 150
Tel: (3) 3467-2271 Fax: (3) 3467-2285

Consulate (Fukuoka)
2-12-1 Diamyo-cho, Chuo-ku
Fukuoka 810
Tel: (92) 751-4429 Fax: (92) 751-4626

Consulate (Nagoya)
Rinmai Corporation
2-26, Fukuzumi-cho, Nakagawa-ku
Nagoya 454
Tel: (52) 361-8211 Fax: (52) 3653-9554

Consulate (Osaka)
Yamanishi Fukushi Kinen Kaikan
11-12, Kamiyama-cho, Kita-ku
Osaka 530
Tel: (6) 315-1868 Fax: (6) 316-1094

Nigeria
Embassy
2-19-7, Uehara, Shibuya-ku
Tokyo 151
Tel: (3) 3468-5531 Tlx: 24397

Norway
Embassy
12-2, Minami Azabu 5-chome, Minato-ku
Tokyo 106
Tel: (3) 3440-2611 Fax: (3) 3440-2689
Tlx: 26440

Pakistan
Embassy
14-9, Moto Azabu 2-chome, Minato-ku
Tokyo 106
Tel: (3) 3454-4861 Fax: (3) 3454-4863

Panama
Embassy
Kowa Building, No. 38, Rm. 902
12-24, Nishi Azabu 4-chome, Minato-ku
Tokyo 106
Tel: (3) 3499-3741 Fax: (3) 5485-3548
Tlx: 22157

Paraguay
Embassy
Asahi Kami Osaki Building, 5th Fl.
5-8, Kami Osaki 3-chome, Shinagawa-ku
Tokyo 141
Tel: (3) 3447-7496 Fax: (3) 3447-6184
Tlx: 27496

Peru
Embassy
4-27, Higashi 4-chome, Shibuya-ku
Tokyo 150
Tel: (3) 3406-4240 Fax: (3) 3409-7589
Tlx: 26435

Commercial Office
Estate MB
19-3, Tsurumaki 5-chome, Setagaya-ku
Tokyo 154
Tel: (3) 3439-0261

Philippines
Embassy
11-24, Nampeidai-machi, Shibuya-ku
Tokyo 150
Tel: (3) 3496-2731 Tlx: 22694

Poland
Embassy
13-5, Mita 2-chome, Meguro-ku
Tokyo 153
Tel: (3) 3711-5224 Fax: (3) 3760-3100
Tlx: 23314

Portugal
Embassy
Olympia Annex, Apt. 304-306
31-21, Jingumae 6-chome, Shibuya-ku
Tokyo 105
Tel: (3) 3400-7907 Fax: (3) 3400-7909
Tlx: 24826

Romania
Embassy
16-19, Nishi-Azabu 3-chome, Minato-ku
Tokyo 106
Tel: (3) 3479-0311 Fax: (3) 3479-0312
Tlx: 22664

Russia
Embassy
2-1-1, Azabudai, Minato-ku
Tokyo 106
Tel: (3) 3583-0408, 3583-4224
Fax: (3) 3505-0593 Tlx: 24231

Press Section
9-13, Higashi Gotanda 3-chome, Shinagawa-ku
Tokyo 141
Tel: (3) 3447-3536

Office of Trade Representative
6-9, Takanawa 4-chome, Minato-ku
Tokyo 108
Tel: (3) 3447-3291

Saudi Arabia
Embassy
1-53, Azabu Nagasaka-cho, Minato-ku
Tokyo 106
Tel: (3) 3589-5241 Tlx: 25731

Singapore
Embassy
12-3 Roppongi 5-chome, Minato-ku
Tokyo 106
Tel: (3) 3586-9111 Fax: (3) 3582-1085
Tlx: 22404
Commercial Section
Tel: (3) 3584-6032 Fax: (3) 3584-6135
Tlx: 26354

Industry Section
Imperial Tower, 8th Fl.
1-1-1 Uchisaiwai-cho, Chiyoda-ku
Tokyo 100
Tel: (3) 3501-6041 Fax: (3) 3501-6060

Consulate General (Osaka)
14th Fl., Osaka Kokusai Building
3-13 Azuchimachi, 2-chome, Chuo-ku
Osaka 541
Tel: (6) 261-5131/2, 262-2662
Fax: (6) 261-0338 Tlx: 64596

South Africa
Consulate General
414 Zenkyoten Building
7-9, Hirakawa-cho 2-chome, Chiyoda-ku
Tokyo 102
Tel: (3) 3265-3366 Fax: (3) 3237-6458
Tlx: 26208

Spain
Embassy
3-29 Roppongi 1-chome, Minato-ku
Tokyo 106
Tel: (3) 3583-8531 Fax: (3) 3582-8627

Sweden
Embassy
10-3, Roppongi 1-chome, Minato-ku
Tokyo 106
Tel: (3) 5562-5350 Fax: (3) 5562-9095
Office of Science & Technology
Tel: (3) 3470-4181 Fax: (3) 3470-4185
Commercial Section
Tel: (3) 3403-9241 Fax: (3) 3408-2086
Tlx: 24586

Switzerland
Embassy
9-12, Minami Asabu 5-chome, Minato-ku
Tokyo 106-91
Tel: (3) 3473-0121 Fax: (3) 3473-6090

Consulate General (Osaka)
Dokito-Daibiru Building, 7th Fl.
2-5, Dojima 1-chome, Kita-ku
Osaka 530
Tel: (6) 344-7671 Fax: (6) 344-7678

Syria
Embassy
Hornat Jade
19-45, Akasaka 6-chome, Minato-ku
Tokyo 107
Tel: (3) 3586-8977/9 Tlx: 29405

All addresses and telephone numbers are in Japan unless otherwise noted. The country code for Japan is [81].

Thailand
Embassy
14-6, Kami Osaki 3-chome, Shinagawa-ku
Tokyo 141
Tel: (3) 3441-1386, 3441-7352
Fax: (3) 3442-6750

Office of the Commercial Counselor
Shuwa Kioicho TBR Building, Rm. 401
7, Kojimachi 5-chome, Chiyoda-ku
Tokyo 102
Tel: (3) 3221-9482 Fax: (3) 3221-9484

Office of the Economic Counselor
Akasaka Brighton Building, 3rd Fl.
5-2, Akasaka 1-chome, Minato-ku
Tokyo 107
Tel: (3) 3582-0976 Fax: (3) 3589-5176

Turkey
Embassy
33-6, Jinguamae 2-chome, Shibuya-ku
Tokyo 150
Tel: (3) 3470-5131 Fax: (3) 3470-5136

United Arab Emirates
Embassy
Kotsu Ansen Kyiku Centre Bldg., 7th Fl.
24-20, Nishi Azabu 3-chome, Minato-ku
Tokyo 106
Tel: (3) 3478-0650 Tlx: 23522

United Kingdom
Embassy
1, Ichiban-cho, Chiyoda-ku
Tokyo 102
Tel: (3) 3265-5511 Fax: (3) 5275-3164
Tlx: 22755
Commercial, Information, Science, Technology
and Atomic Energy Sections
Tel: (3) 3265-6340 Fax: (3) 3265-5580
Consular Section
Tel: (3) 3265-6340 Fax: (3) 5275-0346
Visa Section
Tel: (3) 3265-4001 Fax: (3) 5275-0346

Office of the Commercial Counselor
c/o The British Council
2, Kagurazaka 1-chome, Shinjuku-ku
Tokyo 162
Tel: (3) 3235-8031 Tlx: 27761

Consulate (Hiroshima)
c/o Hiroshima Bank Ltd.
3-8, 1-chome, Kamiyacho, Naka-ku
Hiroshima
Tel: (82) 247-5151 Fax: (82) 247-3664

Consulate General (Osaka)
Hongkong and Shanghai Bank Building
6-1, 3-chome, Awaji-machi, Chuo-ku
Osaka
Tel: (6) 231-3355 Fax: (6) 202-4312

Consulate (Nagoya)
c/o Tokai Bank Ltd.
21-24, 3-chome, Nishi, Naka-ku
Nagoya
Tel: (52) 211-1111 Fax: (52) 211-0920

United States of America
Embassy
10-1, Akasaka 1-chome, Minato-ku
Tokyo 107
Tel: (3) 3224-5000 Fax: (3) 3581-0496
Tlx: 22118

Export Development Office
7th Fl., World Import Mart
1-3, Higashi Ikebukuro 3-chome, Toshima-ku
Tokyo 170
Tel: (3) 3987-2441 Fax: (3) 3987-2447

Consulate General (Okinawa)
2564 Nishihara
Urasoe City, Okinawa 90121
Tel: (98) 876-4211 Fax: (98) 876-4243

Consulate General (Fukuoka)
5-26, Ohori 2-chome, Chuo-ku
Fukuoka 810
Fax: (92) 713-9222

Consulate General (Osaka)
11-5, Nishitenma 2-chome, Kita-ku
Osaka 530
Tel: (6) 315-5900 Fax: (6) 361-5397

Consulate General (Sapporo)
Kita 1-Jo, Nishi 28-chome, Chuo-ku
Sapporo 064
Tel: (11) 641-1115 Fax: (11) 643-1283

Uruguay
Embassy
Kowa Building, No. 38, Rm. 908
12-24, Nishi Azabu 4-chome, Minato-ku
Tokyo 106
Tel: (3) 3486-1888 Fax: (3) 3486-9872

Venezuela
Embassy
Kowa Building, No. 38, Rm. 703
12-24, Nishi Azabu 4-chome, Minato-ku
Tokyo 106
Tel: (3) 3409-1501 Fax: (3) 3409-1505

TRADE PROMOTION ORGANIZATIONS

WORLD TRADE CENTERS

World Trade Center of Japan
37th Fl., World Trade Center Building
4-1, Hammamatsu-cho 2-chome, Minato-ku
Tokyo 105
Tel: (3) 3435-5651/7 Fax: (3) 3436-4368

World Trade Center Osaka
1-3-20, Nakanoshima, Kita-ku
Osaka 530
Tel: (6) 208-8960 Fax: (6) 202-6966

GENERAL TRADE ASSOCIATIONS

Center for Inducement for Industry to Rural Areas,
Operation Division
1-11-35, Nagatcho, Chiyoda-ku
Tokyo 100
Tel: (3) 3580-1668

Center for Small Business Development in Asia
Osaka Chamber of Commerce and Industry
Building
58-7, Uchihommachi Hashizzumecho
Higashi-ku
Osaka 540
Tel: (6) 944-6215

Federation of Economic Organizations
Keidanren Kaikan
9-4, Ote-machi 1-chome, Chiyoda-ku
Tokyo 100
Tel: (3) 3279-1411 Fax: (3) 5255-6250

Federation of Japan Wholesalers' Association
Zenra Kaikan
6-1, Yushima 3-chome, Bunkyo-ku
Tokyo 113
Tel: (3) 3832-4291

Industry Club of Japan
4-6, Marunouchi 1-chome, Chiyoda-ku
Tokyo 100
Tel: (3) 3281-1711 Fax: (3) 3281-1797

International Management Association of Japan
No. 10 Mori Building
18-1, Toranomon 1-chome, Minato-ku
Tokyo 105
Tel: (3) 3502-3051

Japan Association of Corporate Executives
Kogyo Club Building
1-4-6, Marunouchi, Chiyoda-ku
Tokyo 100
Tel: (3) 3211-1271 Fax: (3) 3213-2946
Tlx: 32531

Japan Committee for Economic Development
4-6, Marunouchi 1-chome, Chiyoda-ku
Tokyo 100
Tel: (3) 3211-1271

Japanese BIAC to the OECD
Keidanren Kaikan
9-4, Otemachi 1-chome, Chiyoda-ku
Tokyo 100
Tel: (3) 3279-1411

Japan Federation of Employers' Association
(Nikkeiren)
4-6, Marunouchi 1-chome, Chiyoda-ku
Tokyo 100
Tel: (3) 3213-4463, 3213-4451 Tlx: 23244

Japan Federation of Smaller Enterprise
Organizations (JFSEO)
2-8-4, Nihonbashi, Kayaba-cho, Chuo-ku
Tokyo 103
Tel: (3) 3668-2481

Japan Industrial Location Center
Operation Division
1-4-2, Toranomon, Minato-ku
Tokyo 105
Tel: (3) 3502-2361

Japan Productivity Center
1-1, Shibuya 3-chome, Shibuya-ku
Tokyo 150
Tel: (3) 3409-1111 Fax: (3) 3409-1986
Tlx: 23296

Japan Regional Development Corporation
3-8-1, Kasumigaseki, Chiyoda-ku
Tokyo 100
Tel: (3) 3501-5211

Japan Small Business Corporation
No. 37, Mori Building
5-1, Toranomon 3-chome, Minato-ku
Tokyo 105
Tel: (3) 3433-8811 Fax: (3) 5470-1506

Japanese Standards Association
1-24, Akasaka 4-chome, Minato-ku
Tokyo 107
Tel: (3) 3583-8001/3 Fax: (3) 3586-2029

Japan Technomart Foundation
3rd Fl., Ringo Building
2-13, Gobancho, Chiyoda-ku
Tokyo 102
Tel: (3) 3288-6901

National Federation of Small Business Associations
Jitensha Kaikan
9-3, Akasaka 1-chome, Minato-ku
Tokyo 107
Tel: (3) 3586-5071 x2628

Overseas Economic Cooperation Fund
Iino Building
1-1, Uchisaiwaicho 2-chome, Chiyoda-ku
Tokyo 100
Tel: (3) 3501-2156

Small Business Promotion Corp.
Sankaido Building
9-13, Akasaka 1-chome, Minato-ku
Tokyo 107
Tel: (3) 3584-0351

All addresses and telephone numbers are in Japan unless otherwise noted. The country code for Japan is [81].

JAPANESE CHAMBERS OF COMMERCE

Central Federation of Societies of Commerce and
Industry Japan
New Shimbashi Building
16-1, Shimbashi 2-chome, Minato-ku
Tokyo 105
Tel: (3) 3503-1251 Fax: (3) 3580-6577

Japan Chamber of Commerce and Industry (JCCI)
2-2, Marunouchi 3-chome, Chiyoda-ku
Tokyo 100
Tel: (3) 3283-7660, 3283-7500 Fax: (3) 3216-6497

Japan Junior Chamber of Commerce
14-3, Hirakawa-cho 2-chome, Chiyoda-ku
Tokyo 100
Tel: (3) 3234-5601

Japanese National Committee of the International
Chamber of Commerce
Tosho Building
2-2, Marunouchi 3-chome, Chiyoda-ku
Tokyo 100
Tel: (3) 3213-8585 Fax: (3) 3213-8589

Kawasaki Chamber of Commerce and Industry
11-2, Ekimaehoncho, Kawasaki-ku
Kawasaki 210
Tel: (44) 211-4111

Kitakyushu Chamber of Commerce and Industry
1-35, Furusemba, Kokurakita-ku
Kitakyushu 802
Tel: (93) 541-0181

Kobe Chamber of Commerce and Industry
6-1, Minatojima Naka-machi, Chuo-ku
Kobe 650
Tel: (78) 303-5801

Kyoto Chamber of Commerce and Industry
Ebisugawa-agaru, Karasumadori, Nakagyo-ku
Kyoto 604
Tel: (75) 231-0181 Fax: (75) 255-1985

Nagoya Chamber of Commerce and Industry
10-19, Sakae 2-chome, Naka-ku
Nagoya 460
Tel: (52) 221-7211

Osaka Chamber of Commerce and Industry
2-8, Honmachi-bashi, Chuo-ku
Osaka 540
Tel: (6) 944-6215

Sapporo Chamber of Commerce and Industry
2-1, Kitaichijo Nishi 2-chome, Chuo-ku
Sapporo 060
Tel: (11) 231-1122

Tokyo Chamber of Commerce and Industry
2-2, Marunouchi 3-chome, Chiyoda-ku
Tokyo 100
Tel: (3) 3283-7823

Yokohama Chamber of Commerce and Industry
2, Yamashitacho, Naka-ku
Yokohama 231
Tel: (45) 671-7411

JAPAN CHAMBER OF COMMERCE AND INDUSTRY (JCCI) OVERSEAS OFFICES

Argentina
Libertad 836, 2° Piso, Of. 38
Buenos Aires, Argentina
Tel: [54] (1) 398-2104

Australia
Level 29, 1 Market St.
Sydney, NSW 2000, Australia
Tel: [61] (2) 267-3377 Fax: [61] (2) 267-4670

Brazil
Av. Paulista, 475 13° and CEP 01311
São Paulo, Brazil
Tel: [55] (11) 287-6233 Fax: [55] (11) 284-9424

Canada
130 Adelaide St. W, Suite 3301
Toronto, ON M5H 3P5, Canada
Tel: [1] (416) 360-0236

France
1 av. de Friedland
75008 Paris, France
Tel: [33] (1) 45-63-27-42 Fax: [33] (1) 45-61-08-62

Germany
c/o Bank of Tokyo AG
Wiesenhüttenstr. 10
6000 Frankfurt/Main, Germany
Tel: [49] (69) 25760 Fax: [49] (69) 2576280

Italy
c/o JETRO Milan
I.N.A. Building
via Agnello 6/1
20121 Milan, Italy
Tel: [39] (2) 866343, 865546
Fax: [39] (2) 72023072

Mexico
Calle Sevilla No. 9-2°, Col. Juar ez
06600 Mexico City, D.F., Mexico
Tel: [52] (5) 514-3410 Fax: [52] (5) 207-7116

Netherlands
World Trade Center Amsterdam
Tower B, 9th Fl.
Strawinskylaan 935
1077 XX Amsterdam, Netherlands
Tel: [31] (20) 6621457 Fax: [31] (20) 6649781

United Kingdom
2nd Fl., Salisbury House
29 Finsbury Circus
London EC2M 5QQ, UK
Tel: [44] (71) 628-0069 Fax: [44] (71) 628-0248

United States of America
401 N. Michigan Ave., Suite 602
Chicago, IL 60611, USA
Tel: [1] (312) 332-6199 Fax: [1] (312) 822-9773

244 San Pedro St., Suite 504
Los Angeles, CA 90012, USA
Tel: [1] (213) 626-3067 Fax: [1] (213) 246-8002

145 West 57th St., 6th Fl.
New York, NY 10019, USA
Tel: [1] (212) 246-8001 Fax: [1] (212) 246-8002

685 Market St., Suite 280
San Francisco, CA 94105, USA
Tel: [1] (415) 543-8522 Fax: [1] (415) 543-8799

FOREIGN BUSINESS
ORGANIZATIONS IN JAPAN

American Chamber of Commerce
No. 2 Fukide Building
1-21, Toranomon 4-chome, Minato-ku
Tokyo 105
Tel: (3) 3433-5381 Fax: (3) 3436-1446

ASEAN Promotion Center on Trade, Investment
and Tourism
Central Building
10-3, Ginza 4-chome, Chuo-ku
Tokyo 104
Tel: (3) 3546-1221 Fax: (3) 3546-9050

Australian Chamber of Commerce
PO Box 1096
Chuo Post Office, Shiyoda-ku
Tokyo 100-91
Tel: (3) 3212-8787

Belgium-Luxembourg Chamber of Commerce
Rm. 802, Ichiban-cho Central Building
22-1, Ichiban-cho, Chiyoda-ku
Tokyo 102
Tel: (3) 3237-9281 Fax: (3) 3237-9282

British Chamber of Commerce
No. 16, Kowa Building
9-20, Akasaka 1-chome, Minato-ku
Tokyo 107
Tel: (3) 3505-1734 Fax: (3) 3505-2680

Canadian Chamber of Commerce
PO Box 79, Akasaka, 107-91
Tokyo
Tel: (3) 3408-4311 Fax: (3) 3408-4190

Danish Chamber of Commerce
20th Fl., Kobe CIT Center Building
1-14, Hamabedori 5-chome, Chuo-ku
Kobe 651
Tel: (78) 232-1333 Fax: (78) 232-1334

Europe Fashion Center
1-10, Toranomon 3-chome, Minato-ku
Tokyo 105
Tel: (3) 3431-9732 Fax: (3) 3434-3820

Far East Trade Service Center (Taiwan)
12-19, Shibuya 2-chome, Shibuya-ku
Tokyo 150
Tel: (3) 3407-9711 Fax: (3) 3407-9715

French Chamber of Commerce
Hanzomon MK Building
8-1, Koji-machi 1-chome, Chiyoda-ku
Tokyo 102
Tel: (3) 3288-9621, 3590-6415
Fax: (3) 3288-9558

German Agricultural Marketing Board
8th Fl., Akasaka Tokyu Building
14-2, Nagata-cho 2-chome, Chiyoda-ku
Tokyo 100
Tel: (3) 3580-0169 Fax: (3) 3580-0458

German Chamber of Commerce & Industry
7th Fl., Akasaka Tokyu Building
14-3, Nagata-cho 2-chome, Chiyoda-ku
Tokyo 100
Tel: (3) 3581-9881 Fax: (2) 3593-1350

Hong Kong Trade Development Council
4th Fl., Toho Twin Tower Building
5-2, Yuraku-cho 1-chome, Chiyoda-ku
Tokyo 100
Tel: (3) 3502-3251 Fax: (3) 3591-6484

Italian Chamber of Commerce
c/o Montecatini K.K.
21st Fl., 25 Mori Building
4-30, Roppongi 1-chome, Minato-ku
Tokyo 106
Tel: (3) 3224-7238 Fax: (3) 3588-8524

Italian Trade Commission Tokyo Office
Shin-Aoyama West Building
1-1, Minami-Aoyama 1-chome, Minato-ku
Tokyo 107
Tel: (3) 3475-1401 Fax: (3) 3475-1440

Japan and Republic of China Economy Association
2-6, Shiroganedai 4-chome, Minato-ku
Tokyo 108
Tel: (3) 3446-5008

Japan Association for Trade with Russia and
Central-Eastern Europe
Kanayama Building
2-12, Shinkawa 1-chome, Chuo-ku
Tokyo 104
Tel: (3) 3551-6215 Fax: (3) 3555-1052

Japan-China Association on Economy and Trade
Aoyama Building
2-3, Kita-Aoyama 1-chome, Minato-ku
Tokyo 107
Tel: (3) 3402-1981 Fax: (3) 3423-2938

Japan-Korea Economic Association
Kanda Amerex Building
1-6, Misakicho 3-chome, Chiyoda-ku
Tokyo 101
Tel: (3) 3222-0622 Fax: (3) 3222-0559

Japan-Korea Trade Association
Yoshietsu Building
17-4, Nihonbashi Ohdenmacho, Chuo-ku
Tokyo 103
Tel: (3) 3662-1810 Fax: (3) 3662-1015

Japan-Russia Trade Association
4th Fl., Sanko Building
4-3, Koujimachi 1-chome, Chiyoda-ku
Tokyo 102
Tel: (3) 3262-8401 Fax: (3) 3262-8403

Korea Trade Center, Tokyo
2nd Fl., Yurakucho Building
10-1, Yuraku-cho 1-chome, Chiyoda-ku
Tokyo 100
Tel: (3) 3214-6951 Fax: (3) 3214-6950

All addresses and telephone numbers are in Japan unless otherwise noted. The country code for Japan is [81].

Korean Chamber of Commerce
Kankoku Chuo Kaikan
7-32, Minami Azabu 1-chome, Minato-ku
Tokyo 106
Tel: (3) 3456-1190 Fax: (3) 3456-3176

Netherlands Chamber of Commerce
CPO Box 1296
Tokyo 100-91
Tel: (3) 5210-0300 Fax: (3) 5210-0431

Philippine Chamber of Commerce & Industry
11-24, Nanpeidai-machi, Shibuya-ku
Tokyo 150
Tel: (3) 3464-4177 Fax: (3) 3462-2678

Swiss Chamber of Commerce & Industry
CS Tower
11-30, Akasaka 1-chome, Minato-ku
Tokyo 107
Tel: (3) 3587-1122 Fax: (3) 3587-2266

Taipei Economic and Cultural Rep. Office
20-2, Shiroganedai 5-chome, Minato-ku
Tokyo 108
Tel: (3) 3280-7880/3 Fax: (3) 3280-7928

US Trade Center
7th Fl., World Import Mart
103, Higashi-Ikebukuro 3-chome, Toshima-ku
Tokyo 170
Tel: (3) 3987-2441 Fax: (3) 3987-2447

JAPAN EXTERNAL TRADE ORGANIZATION (JETRO) OFFICES IN JAPAN

Tokyo (JETRO Head office)
2-5, Toranomon 2-chome, Minato-ku
Tokyo 105
Tel: (3) 3582-5570 Fax: (3) 3505-6248
Investment Promotion Division
Tel: (3) 3582-5571

Tokyo (MIPRO office)
World Import Mart Bldg.
1-3, Higashi-Ikebukuro 3-chome, Toshima-ku
Tokyo 170
Tel: (3) 3984-5960 Fax: (3) 3984-4205

Fukuoka
Sunlight Bldg., 8th Fl.
23-8, Watanabedori 5-chome, Chuo-ku
Fukuoka City 810
Tel: (92) 741-9122 Fax: (92) 714-0709

Kobe
Kobe Shoko Boeki Center Bldg., 6th Fl.
1-14, Hamabedori 5-chome, Chuo-ku
Kobe 651
Tel: (78) 231-3081 Fax: (78) 232-3439

Kyoto
Kyoto-fu Chusho Kigyo Sogo Center Bldg.
17, Chudoji Minami-machi, Shimogyo-ku
Kyoto City 600
Tel: (75) 315-2811 Fax: (75) 315-1551

Nagasaki
Nagasaki Shoko Kaikan Bldg., 9th Fl.
4-1, Sakura-machi
Nagasaki City 850
Tel: (958) 23-7704 Fax: (958) 28-0037

Osaka
Bingo-cho Nomura Bldg., 4th Fl.
1-8, Bingo-cho 2-chome, Chuo-ku
Osaka 541
Tel: (6) 203-3601/3 Fax: (6) 222-5675

Sendai
Sendai Chamber of Commerce & Industry Building,
8th Fl.
16-12, Honcho 2-chome, Aoba-ku
Sendai City, Miyagi Pref. 980
Tel: (22) 213-5022 Fax: (22) 262-6230

Yokohama
Silk Center
Kokusai Boeki Kanko Kaikan Bldg., 2nd Fl.
1, Yamashita-cho, Naka-ku
Yokohama 231
Tel: (45) 641-4990 Fax: (45) 641-9097

JAPAN EXTERNAL TRADE ORGANIZATION (JETRO) OFFICES OVERSEAS

Algeria
30, Rue Djenen el Malik Hydra
Algiers, Algeria
Postal address: B.P. 277, PTT Hydra, Algiers
Tel:[213] (2) 59-1558 Fax: [213] (2) 59-2173
Tlx: 66605

Argentina
Tte. Gral. Juan D. Peron 955-7
1038 Buenos Aires, Argentina
Tel: [54] (1) 35-9399, 35-9699
Fax: [54] (1) 11-2790 Tlx: 33-18757

Australia
4th Fl., Standard Chartered House
30 Collins St.
Melbourne, Vic. 3000, Australia
Tel: [61] (3) 654-4949 Fax: [61] (3) 654-2962

8th Fl., St. George's Court Building
16 St. George's Terrace
Perth, W.A. 6000, Australia
Tel: [61] (9) 325-2809, 325-9707
Fax: [61] (9) 325-2472

Level 19, Gateway 1, Macquarie Place
Sydney, NSW 2000, Australia
Tel: [61] (2) 241-1181 Fax: [61] (2) 251-7631

Austria
Mariahilferstrasse 41-43/3, Stock
1060 Wien, Austria
Tel: [43] (1) 587-5628/9 Fax: [43] (1) 586-2293
Tlx: 11-41-89

Belgium
Rue d'Arlon 69-71, Boite 2
B-1040 Bruxelles, Belgium
Tel: [32] (2) 230-4858 Fax: [32] (2) 230-0703

Brazil

Centro Empresarial-Rio Praia de Botafogo
228 Sector B-8°, Botofogo
CEP 22250 Rio de Janeiro, Brazil
Tel: [55] (21) 551-8144 Fax: [55] (21) 552-1196
Tlx: 2134809

Avenida Paulista, 1274-16
CEP 01310 São Paulo, Brazil
Tel: [55] (11) 287-2855, 287-2100
Fax: [55] (11) 288-5731 Tlx: 1121972

Bulgaria

World Trade Center, Rm. 818
36 Dragon Tsankov Blvd.
1057 Sofía, Bulgaria
Tel: [359] (2) 70-60-18, 70-82-18
Fax: [359] (2) 70-51-27

Canada

Place Montreal Trust Tower, Suite 2902
1800 McGill College Ave.
Montreal, PQ H3A 3J6, Canada
Tel: [1] (514) 849-5911 Fax: [1] (514) 849-5061

Suite 700, Britannica House
151 Bloor St. West
Toronto, ON M5S 1T7, Canada
Tel: [1] (416) 962-5050 Fax: [1] (416) 962-1124

World Trade Center, Suite 660
999 Canada Place
Vancouver, BC V6C 3E1, Canada
Tel: [1] (604) 684-4174 Fax: [1] (604) 684-6877

Chile

Catedral 1009, 4 Piso, Oficina 407
Santiago, Chile
Tel: [56] (2) 6726978 Fax: [56] (2) 6987191
Tlx: 645143 ATT JETRO

China

303 Chang Fu Gong Office Building
Jia-26, Jian Guo Men Wai St.
Beijing 100022, PRC
Tel: [86] (1) 513-7075/8 Fax: [86] (1) 513-7079

Rm. 412, West Tower, Shanghai Centre
1376 West Nanjing Rd.
Shanghai, PRC
Tel: [86] (21) 2798090 Fax: [86] (21) 2798092

Colombia

Carrera 16A, No. 78-65, Piso 4
Edificio Carlos Alberto
Bogotá, Colombia
Postal address: Apdo Aereo 89154
Bogotá 8, Colombia
Tel: [57] (1) 256-4418, 611-1092, 256-1974
Fax: [57] (1) 611-1985

Costa Rica

Local 2-13, Edificio Centro Colon Piso 2
San José, Costa Rica
Postal address: PO Box 7680-1000, San Jose
Tel: [506] 55-1222 Fax: [506] 55-1536

Denmark

Vesterbrogade Ic, 1st Fl.
1620 Copenhagen V, Denmark
Tel: [45] 33-14-73-12 Fax: [45] 33-11-01-36

Egypt

7th Fl., World Trade Center Cairo
1191 Corniche El Nil
Cairo, Egypt
Postal address: PO Box 1885, Cairo
Tel: [20] (2) 574-1111 Fax: [20] (2) 756966
Tlx: 91-93136

France

151 bis, rue Saint-Honoré
75001 Paris, France
Postal Address: 2, place du Palais Royal
75044 Paris, Cedex 01 France
Tel: [33] (1) 42-61-27-27
Fax: [33] (1) 42-61-19-46 Tlx: 212015

Germany

Internationales Handelszentrum Berlin
Fach 39, Friedrichstrasse 95
0-1086 Berlin, Germany
Tel: [49] (30) 2643-3162/3
Fax: [49] (30) 2643-3165

Königsallee 58
4000 Düsseldorf, Germany
Tel: [49] (211) 13-60-20
Fax: [49] (211) 32-64-11 Tlx: 41-8587449

Rossmarkt 17
6 Frankfurt 1, Germany
Tel: [49] (69) 28-32-15, 28-42-21
Fax: [49] (69) 28-33-59

Colonnaden 72
2000 Hamburg 36, Germany
Tel: [49] (40) 35-600800 Fax: [49] (40) 346837
Tlx: 214328

Prielmayerstrasse 3/IV, Elisenhof
8000 Munich 2, Germany
Tel: [49] (89) 59-34-59, 59-44-11
Fax: [49] (89) 59-20-14

Greece

4 Kubari St., Kolonaki
Athens, Greece
Tel: [30] (1) 3630820 Fax: [30] (1) 3621231
Tlx: 601-222091

Hong Kong

1910-1915 Hutchinson House
10 Harcourt Rd.
Central, Hong Kong
Tel: [852] 5264067, 5264070, 5227795
Fax: [852] 8681455

Hungary

1012 Budapest
Logodi u. 22-23
Hungary
Tel: [36] (1) 201-4799, 201-4389, 201-6589
Fax: [36] (1) 201-5189

All addresses and telephone numbers are in Japan unless otherwise noted. The country code for Japan is [81].

India
Flat No. 501-505, World Trade Centre
Barakhamba Lane
New Delhi 110 001, India
Tel: [91] (11) 3312194, 3712268, 3713369
Fax: [91] (11) 3313453

Indonesia
Summitmas Tower, 6th Fl.
Jln. Jend. Sudirman Kav 61-62
Jakarta, Indonesia
Tel: [62] (21) 5200264, 5200266, 5205097
Fax: [62] (21) 5200261 Tlx: 60740

Ireland
1 Setanta Place
Dublin 2, Ireland
Tel: [353] (1) 714003, 714156
Fax: [353] (1) 714302

Italy
I.N.A. Building
via Agnello 6/1
20121 Milan, Italy
Tel: [39] (2) 866343, 865546
Fax: [39] (2) 72023072

Via San Filippo Martire, 1/B
00197 Rome, Italy
Tel: [39] (6) 8084752, 8088155
Fax: [39] (6) 8075230 Tlx: 680244

Kenya
International House, 4th Fl.
Mama Ngina St.
Nairobi, Kenya
Mailing Address: PO Box 59739, Nairobi
Tel: [254] (2) 337622, 226741, 338678
Fax: [254] (2) 334842 Tlx: 22590

Korea
7th Fl., The Korea Press Center Building
25, 1-ka, Taepyung-ro, Chung-ku
Seoul, South Korea
Mailing Address: CPO Box 8499, Seoul
Tel: [82] (2) 739-8657, 739-4503
Fax: [82] (2) 739-4658

Malaysia
23rd Fl., Menara tun Ruzak
(Mail Box 16 & 17)
Jalan Raja Laut
50350 Kuala Lumpur, Malaysia
Tel: [60] (3) 2930244, 2930259
Fax: [60] (3) 2930132 Tlx: 31372

Mexico
Paseo de las Plamas, No. 239-3° Piso
Col. Lomas de Chapultepec
Deleg Miguel Hildalgo C.P.
11000 Mexico City, D.F., Mexico
Tel: [52] (5) 202-7132, 202-7900, 202-0454
Fax: [52] (5) 202-8003

Netherlands
World Trade Center, Amsterdam
Tower C, 4th Fl.
Strawinskylaan 447
1077 XX Amsterdam, Netherlands
Tel: [31] (20) 6765075 Fax: [31] (20) 6647597

Groothandelsgebouw, B-3 Weena 695
3013 AM Rotterdam, Netherlands
Tel: [31] (10) 4113360 Fax: [31] (10) 4129930

New Zealand
Rm. 301, Dilworth Building
Customs St. East
Auckland, New Zealand
Mailing Address: PO Box 2123, Auckland, C1
Tel: [64] (9) 379-7427, 379-7428
Fax: [64] (9) 309-5046

Nigeria
Flat No. 1, No. 4A, Kofo Abayomi St.
Victoria Island
Lagos, Nigeria
Mailing Address: PO Box 3189, Lagos
Tel: [234] (1) 613751, 615777
Fax: [234] (1) 618482 Tlx: 23493

Norway
Parkveien 55
0256 Oslo 2, Norway
Tel: [47] (2) 558611 Fax: [47] (2) 558610

Peru
Av. Paseo de La Republica 3587, Of. 702
Edificio el Sol San Isidro
Lima, Peru
Postal address: Apdo 2062, Lima 100
Tel: [51] (14) 41-5175 Fax: [51] (14) 40-0527

Philippines
23rd Fl., Pacific Star Building
Sen. Gil J. Puyat Ave., Extension cor.
Makati Ave., Makati
Metro Manila, Philippines
Tel: [63] (2) 88-4373, 88-4359, 88-4376
Fax: [63] (2) 818-7490 Tlx: 23312 RHP

Poland
ul. Szpitalna 6M21
00-031, Warsaw, Poland
Tel: [48] (22) 27-84-21 Fax: [48] (22) 27-95-42
Tlx: 63-812432

Portugal
Empreendimento Das Amoreiras
Av. Eng. Duarte Pacheco, Torre 2
11° Andar, Sala 1
1000 Lisbon, Portugal
Tel: [351] (1) 659381, 692718, 3876274
Fax: [351] (1) 691818

Romania
Hotel Bucures ti, Strada Luterana
Compound D, Entrance C2, 4th Fl., Apt. 14
Bucharest, Romania
Tel: [40] (1) 6148876, 3122739
Fax: [40] (1) 3120432 Tlx: 65-92541

Russia
123610 Moscow
Krasnopresnenska-ja, Nab. 12
Hotel Mezhdunarodna-ja-2, Rm. 1129
Russia
Tel: [7] (095) 253-1129 Fax: [7] (095) 253-9516

Singapore
Hong Leong Building
15 Raffles Quay #38-05
Singapore 0104
Tel: [65] 2218174 Fax: [65] 2241169
Tlx: 60740

South Africa
1813 Sanlam Center, Jeppe St.
Johannesburg, South Africa
Postal address: PO Box 2811
2000 Johannesburg
Tel: [27] (11) 29-8231, 333-7036
Fax: [27] (11) 333-3700

Spain
Plaza de Colòn, 2
Torres de Colòn, 1, 7°
28046 Madrid, Spain
Tel: [34] (1) 319-5564, 319-5852, 319-8247
Fax: [34] (1) 310-3659

Sweden
Kungsgatan 48, 4th Fl.
11135 Stockholm, Sweden
Tel: [46] (8) 118173 Fax: [46] (8) 111888

Switzerland
82 rue de Lausanne
1202 Geneva, Switzerland
Tel: [41] (22) 732-1304 Fax: [41] (22) 732-0772

Stampfenbachstrasse 38
8023 Zürich, Switzerland
Tel: [41] (1) 362-2323, 362-2387
Fax: [41] (1) 362-7056

Thailand
JETRO Building
159 Rajadamri Rd.
Bangkok, Thailand
Tel: [66] (2) 253-6441/5, 253-6447
Fax: [66] (2) 253-2020 Tlx: 87319

Turkey
Sakir Kesebir Caddesi
Balmumcu Plaza 4, No. 36/12
80700 Balmumuc/Istanbul, Turkey
Tel: [90] (1) 275-5180, 274-5702, 274-0389
Fax: [90] (1) 288-0739

United Arab Emirates
No. 438 Al Ghurair Centre
Dubai, UAE
Postal address: PO Box 2272, Dubai
Tel: [971] (4) 232093 Fax: [971] (4) 214372
Tlx: 893-48339

United Kingdom
6th Fl., Leconfield House
Curzon St.
London W1Y 7FB, UK
Tel: [44] (71) 493-7226 Fax: [44] (71) 491-7570
Tlx: 51-265011

United States of America
245 Peachtree Center Ave., Suite 2208
Marquis One Tower
Atlanta, GA 30303, USA
Tel: [1] (404) 681-0600 Fax: [1] (404) 681-0713

401 North Michigan Ave., Suite 660
Chicago, IL 60611, USA
Tel: [1] (312) 527-9000, 527-9117/9
Fax: [1] (312) 670-1223

World Trade Center, Suite 152-1
2050 Stemmons Freeway
Dallas, TX 75258-0234, USA
Postal address: PO Box 58234
Dallas, TX 75258-0234
Tel: [1] (214) 651-0859 Fax: [1] (214) 651-1831

1200 17th St., Suite 1110
Denver, CO 80202, USA
Tel: [1] (303) 629-0404 Fax: [1] (303) 893-9522

One Houston Center, Suite 2360
1221 McKinney St.
Houston, TX 77010, USA
Tel: [1] (713) 759-9595 Fax: [1] (713) 759-9210

725 S. Figueroa St., Suite 1890
Los Angeles, CA 90017, USA
Tel: [1] (213) 624-8855 Fax: [1] (213) 629-8127

McGraw-Hill Building, 44th Fl.
1221 Avenue of the Americas
New York, NY 10020-1060, USA
Tel: [1] (212) 997-0400
Fax: [1] (212) 997-0464, 302-1581

235 Pine St., Suite 1700
San Francisco, CA 94104, USA
Tel: [1] (415) 392-1333 Fax: [1] (415) 788-6927

Venezuela
Multicentro Empresarial del Este
Edificio Libertadore Nucleo A
Piso 8, Oficina A-81
Av. Libertador, Chacao
Caracas, Venezuela
Tel: [58] (2) 32-5284 Fax: [58] (2) 2613705

GENERAL FOREIGN TRADE ASSOCIATIONS

All Japan International Traders Federation
Sinko Building
6-7, Kotobuki 1-chome, Taito-ku
Tokyo 111
Tel: (3) 3841-6163 Fax: (3) 3847-1880

Asia Trade Association
Osaka Chamber of Commerce and Industry
Building, 5th Fl.
2-8, Hommachi-bashi, Chuo-ku
Osaka 540
Tel: (6) 944-6150 Fax: (6) 944-6151

Association for the Promotion of International
Trade, Japan
Nihon Building
6-2, Ohtemachi 2-chome, Chiyoda-ku
Tokyo 100
Tel: (3) 3245-1561

Council of All Japan Exporters' Association
Kikai Shinko Kaikan
5-8, Shibakoen 3-chome, Minato-ku
Tokyo 105
Tel: (3) 3431-9507 Fax: (3) 3436-6455

Fukuoka Foreign Trade Association
9-28, Hakata-Ekimai 2-chome, Hakata-ku
Fukuoka 812
Tel: (92) 441-2866 Fax: (92) 414-0141

International Business Organization of Osaka, Inc.
My Dome Osaka Building
2-5, Honmachi-bashi, Chuo-ku
Osaka 540
Tel: (6) 942-2674 Fax: (6) 942-2258

Japan External Trade Organization (JETRO)
2-5, Toranomon 2-chome, Minato-ku
Tokyo 105
Tel: (3) 3582-5511 Fax: (3) 3587-0219

Japan Federation of Importers' Organizations
19-14, Toranomon 1-chome, Minato-ku
Tokyo 105
Tel: (3) 3581-9251 Fax: (3) 3581-9217

Japan Foreign Trade Council, Inc.
World Trade Center Building
4-1, Hamamatsu-cho 2-chome, Minato-ku
Tokyo 105
Tel: (3) 3435-5952 Fax: (3) 3435-5969

Japan Institute for Social and Economic Affairs
(Keizai Koho Center)
Otemachi Bldg.
6-1, Otemachi 1-chome, Chiyoda-ku
Tokyo 100
Tel: (3) 3201-1411 Fax: (3) 3201-1418

Japan Overseas Development Corporation
Kyoei Seimei Akasaka Building
11-1, Akasaka 6-chome, Minato-ku
Tokyo 107
Tel: (3) 3505-5981 Fax: (3) 3505-5980

Kobe Foreign Trade Association
Kobe Shoko Boeki Center Building
1-14, Hamabedori 5-chome, Chuo-ku
Kobe 651
Tel: (78) 251-3341 Fax: (78) 251-3345

Kyoto Foreign Trade Association
Kyoto Sangyo-Kaikan Building
Shijo-muromachi-kado, Shimogyo-ku
Kyoto 600
Tel: (75) 211-4396

Manufactured Imports Promotion Organization
(MIPRO)
1-3, Higashi Ikebukuro 3-chome, Toshima-ku
Tokyo 170
Tel: (3) 3988-2791 Fax: (3) 3988-1629

Nagoya Foreign Trade Association
10-19, Sakae 2-chome, Naka-ku
Nagoya 460
Tel: (52) 221-6331 Fax: (52) 221-6332

Osaka Exporters & Importers Association
c/o Trade & Tourist Department, Osaka Municipal
Government
3-20, Nakanoshima 1-chome, Kita-ku
Osaka 530
Tel: (6) 202-8587 Fax: (6) 232-2749

Osaka Foreign Trade Association
My Dome Osaka Building
2-5, Honmachi-bashi, Chuo-ku
Osaka 540
Tel: (6) 942-2701/4 Fax: (6) 942-2258

Tokyo Foreign Trade Association
c/o Tokyo Trade Center
7-8, Kaigan 1-chome, Minato-ku
Tokyo 105
Tel: (3) 3438-2026/7 Fax: (3) 3433-7164

Tokyo International Trade Fair Commission
7-24, Harumi 4-chome, Chuo-ku
Tokyo 104
Tel: (3) 3541-3371 Fax: (3) 3581-1344

Yokohama Foreign Trade Association
1, Kaigan-dori 1-chome, Naka-ku
Yokohama 231
Tel: (45) 211-0282 Fax: (45) 211-0285

INDUSTRY-SPECIFIC IMPORT/EXPORT ORGANIZATIONS

Agricultural Products Exporters' Association
[Japan]
Arai Building
10-7, Shimbashi 2-chome, Minato-ku
Tokyo 105
Tel: (3) 3591-8323 Fax: (3) 3508-2335

Antimony Wares for Export
[Industrial Association of]
3-1, Kuramae 4-chome, Taito-ku
Tokyo 111
Tel: (3) 3851-7133 Fax: (3) 3851-7134

Aromatics Traders' Association of Japan
[International]
c/o Tanemura & Co. Ltd.
Toranomon Jitugyo Kaikan
1-20, Toranomon 1-chome, Minato-ku
Tokyo 105
Tel: (3) 3503-3911 Fax: (3) 3503-3917

Automobile Importers' Association [Japan]
7th Fl., Akiyama Building
5-3, Kojimachi, Chiyoda-ku
Tokyo 102
Tel: (3) 3222-5421 Fax: (3) 3222-1730

Banana Importers Association [The Japan]
5th Fl., Zenkyoren Building
7-9, Hirakawa-cho 2-chome, Chiyoda-ku
Tokyo 102
Tel: (3) 3263-0461 Fax: (3) 3263-0463

Bicycle Exporters' Association [Japan]
25, Karakiyo-cho 8-chome, Tennoji-ku
Osaka 543
Tel: (6) 762-7371 Fax: (6) 762-4102

Book Importers Association [Japan]
Chiyoda Kaikan
21-4, Nihombashi 1-chome, Chuo-ku
Tokyo 103
Tel: (3) 3271-6901 Fax: (3) 3271-6920

Canned Foods Exporters' Association [Japan]
Fuji Building, 6 Fl.
5-3, Yaesu 1-chome, Chuo-ku
Tokyo 103
Tel: (3) 3281-5341 Fax: (3) 3281-5344

Cement Exporters Association [Japan]
Hattori Building
1, Kyobashi 1-chome, Chuo-ku
Tokyo 104
Tel: (3) 3561-1030

Chemical Exporters' Association [Japan]
Nihon Shuzo Kaikan
1-21, Nishi Shimbashi 1-chome, Minato-ku
Tokyo 105
Tel: (3) 3504-1801 Fax: (3) 3595-3344

Chemical Importers' Association [Japan]
Nihon Shuzo Kaikan
1-21, Nishi Shimbashi 1-chome, Minato-ku
Tokyo 105
Tel: (3) 3501-1304 Fax: (3) 3595-3344

Citrus Fruits Importers Association [Japan]
Kinoshita Building
8-10, Kyobashi 2-chome, Chuo-ku
Tokyo 104
Tel: (3) 3561-1366 Fax: (3) 3535-6620

Clothing Manufacturers Association [Japan Export]
Osaka YM Building
15-26, Fukushima 7-chome, Fukushima-ku
Osaka 553
Tel: (6) 453-9221 Fax: (6) 453-9220

Coffee Importers' Association of Japan
c/o Marubeni Corp.
4-2, Ote-machi 1-chome, Chiyoda-ku
Tokyo 100-88
Tel: (3) 3282-4775 Fax: (3) 3282-7372

Confectionery Importers Association [Japan]
c/o Meidiya Co. Ltd.
2-8, Kyobashi 2-chome, Chuo-ku
Tokyo 104
Tel: (3) 3271-9518 Fax: (3) 3274-4890

Cosmetics Importers Association, Inc. [Japan]
Azabu Town House 107
2-40, Nishiazabu 3-chome, Minato-ku
Tokyo 106
Tel: (3) 3408-7541 Fax: (3) 3408-7541

Cotton Textile Exporters Association [Japan]
The Textile Exporters House
4-9, Bingo-machi 3-chome, Chuo-ku
Osaka 541
Tel: (6) 201-0261 Fax: (6) 203-7738

Cotton Traders' Association
7th Fl., Ebisu Building
2-9, Awajimachi 3-chome, Chuo-ku
Osaka 541
Tel: (6) 201-2215 Fax: (6) 231-5122

Cotton Waste & General Fiber Exporters Association [Japan]
c/o Kansai Orimono Oroshi Shogyo Kyodo Kumiai
3-15, Kawara-machi 1-chome, Chuo-ku
Osaka 541
Tel: (6) 231-3853 Fax: (6) 231-3854

Cotton Yarn Trade Association [Japan]
16, Uchiawajimachi 1-chome, Higashi-ku
Osaka 540
Tel: (6) 942-5151

Diamonds & Precious Stones Importers' Association [All Japan]
Tokyo Biho Kaikan
1-24, Akashi-cho, Chuo-ku
Tokyo 104
Tel: (3) 3542-5023 Fax: (3) 3542-5023

Dried Fruits Importers Association [Japan]
c/o Shoei Foods Corp.
7, Akihabara 5-chome, Taito-ku
Tokyo 110
Tel: (3) 3253-1231 Fax: (3) 5256-1914

Dyestuff Exporters' Association [Japan]
Senryo Kaikan
18-17, Roppongi 5-chome, Minato-ku
Tokyo 106
Tel: (3) 3585-3372 Fax: (3) 3589-4236

Eel Importers Association [Japan]
Shuhosha Building
6, Nihombashi Muromachi 1-chome, Chuo-ku
Tokyo 103
Tel: (3) 3279-2501 Fax: (3) 3279-2516

Electric Wire & Cable Exporters' Association [Japan]
Konwa Building
12-22, Tsukiji 1-chome, Chuo-ku
Tokyo 104
Tel: (3) 3542-7531 Fax: (3) 3542-7533

Electronic Products Importers' Association
1-13, Shinjuku 1-chome, Shinjuku-ku
Tokyo 160
Tel: (3) 3225-8910 Fax: (3) 3225-9001

Feed Trade Association [Japan]
Koizumi Building
3-13, Ginza 4-chome, Chuo-ku
Tokyo 104
Tel: (3) 3563-6441 Fax: (3) 3567-2297

Fertilizer Traders Association
Hoei Nishikicho Building
1-13, Kanda Nishiki-cho, Chiyoda-ku
Tokyo 101
Tel: (3) 3293-5471 Fax: (3) 3293-5471

Frozen Foods Exporters' Association [Japan]
Rm. 206, Chuo Mansion
1-5, Arai 1-chome, Nakano-ku
Tokyo 165
Tel: (3) 3386-4116 Fax: (3) 3386-4234

Frozen Marine Products Association [Japan Export]
Rm. 206, Chuo Mansion
1-5, Arai 1-chome, Nakano-ku
Tokyo 165
Tel: (3) 3386-4358 Fax: (3) 3386-4234

Galvanized Iron Sheet Exporters' Association [Japan]
Tekko Kaikan
2-10, Nihombashi Kayaba-cho 3-chome
Chuo-ku
Tokyo 103
Tel: (3) 3669-5331 Fax: (3) 3669-6685

General Merchandise Exporters' Association [Japan]
Sekai Boeki Center Building
4-1, Hamamatsu-cho 2-chome, Minato-ku
Tokyo 105
Tel: (3) 3435-3471 Fax: (3) 3434-6739

General Merchandise Importers Association [Japan]
World Trade Center Building
4-1, Hamamatsu-cho 2-chome, Minato-ku
Tokyo 105
Tel: (3) 3435-3477 Fax: (3) 3434-6739

Grain Importers Association [The]
1-16, Nihombashi 2-chome, Chuo-ku
Tokyo 103
Tel: (3) 3274-0172 Fax: (3) 3274-0177

Graphic Arts Machines and Materials [Importers Association for]
c/o Printing Machine Trading Co. Ltd.
21-4, Minami Oi 3-chome, Shinagawa-ku
Tokyo 140
Tel: (3) 3763-4141 Fax: (3) 3766-0120

Hardwood Exporters' Association [Japan]
Matsuda Building
1-9-1, Ironai, Otaru
Hokkaido 047
Tel: (134) 23-8411 Fax: (134) 22-7150
Tlx: 95270

Imitation Pearl & Glass Beads Exporters' Association [Japan]
6, Tai-cho
Tzumi-shi, Osaka Pref. 594
Tel: (725) 41-2133 Fax: (725) 41-2135

Iron & Steel Exporters' Association [Japan]
Tekko Kaikan
2-10, Nihombashi Kayaba-cho 3-chome
Chuo-ku
Tokyo 103
Tel: (3) 3669-4811 Fax: (3) 3667-0245

Iron & Steel Scrap Importers Association [Japan]
Fuji Building
5-3, Yaesu 1-chome, Chuo-ku
Tokyo 103
Tel: (3) 3201-7906 Fax: (3) 3281-3674

Livestock Traders Association [Japan]
6th Fl., Osakaya Building
1-9, Mita 3-chome, Minato-ku
Tokyo 108
Tel: (3) 3454-1435 Fax: (3) 3453-7095

Luggage Export & Import Association [Japan]
16-3, Kuramae 4-chome, Taito-ku
Tokyo 111
Tel: (3) 3861-9857 Fax: (3) 3862-3520

Lumber Importers' Association [Japan]
Yushi Kogyo Kaikan
13-11, Nihombashi 3-chome, Chuo-ku
Tokyo 103
Tel: (3) 3271-0926 Fax: (3) 3271-0928

Machine Tool Importers Association of Japan
Toranomon Kogyo Building
2-18, Toranomon 1-chome, Minato-ku
Tokyo 105
Tel: (3) 3501-5030 Fax: (3) 3501-5040

Machinery Exporters' Association [Japan]
Kikai Shinko Kaikan
5-8, Shiba-koen 3-chome, Minato-ku
Tokyo 105
Tel: (3) 3431-9507 Fax: (3) 3436-6455

Machinery Importers' Association [Japan]
Koyo Building
2-11, Toranomon 1-chome, Minato-ku
Tokyo 105
Tel: (3) 3503-9736 Fax: (3) 3503-9779

Marine Products Importers Association [Japan]
Yurakucho Building
10-1, Yuraku-cho 1-chome, Chiyoda-ku
Tokyo 100
Tel: (3) 3214-3407 Fax: (3) 3214-3408

Medical Instruments Traders' Association [Tokyo]
39-15, Hongo 3-chome, Bunkyo-ku
Tokyo 113
Tel: (3) 3811-6761 Fax: (3) 3818-4144

Medical Products International Trade Association [Japan]
Ninjin Building
7-1, Nihombashi Honcho 4-chome, Chuo-ku
Tokyo 103
Tel: (3) 3241-2106 Fax: (3) 3241-2109

Molasses Conference [Import]
Toranomon Jitsugyo Kaikan
1-20, Toranomon 1-chome, Minato-ku
Tokyo 105
Tel: (3) 3591-8729 Fax: (3) 3591-8729

Non-Ferrous Metal Exporters' Association [Japan]
c/o Nihon Shindo Kyokai
Konwa Building
12-22, Tsukiji 1-chome, Chuo-ku
Tokyo 104
Tel: (3) 3542-6551 Fax: (3) 3542-6556

Oil & Fat Importers & Exporters Association
[The Japan]
Kyodo Building (Shin Horidome)
10-12, Nihonbashi, Horidome-cho 1-chome
Chuo-ku
Tokyo 103
Tel: (3) 3662-9821 Fax: (3) 3667-7867

Oil Meal & Vitamin Exporters' Association [Japan]
Kyodo Building (Shin Horidome)
10-12, Nihombashi, Horidome-cho 1-chome
Chuo-ku
Tokyo 103
Tel: (3) 3662-9823 Fax: (3) 3667-7867

Paper Exporters' Association [Japan]
Kami Parupu Kaikan
5-6, Nihonbashi Hisamatsu-cho, Chuo-ku
Tokyo 103
Tel: (3) 3249-4831 Fax: (3) 3246-1686

Paper Importers' Association [Japan]
Kami Parupu Kaikan
5-6, Nihonbashi Hisamatsu-cho, Chuo-ku
Tokyo 103
Tel: (3) 3249-4832 Fax: (3) 3249-4834

Paper-Products Exporters' Association [Japan]
2-6, Kotobuki 4-chome, Taito-ku
Tokyo 111
Tel: (3) 3844-4434 Fax: (3) 3844-4434

Pearl Export & Processing Cooperative Association
[Japan]
Shinju Kaikan
6-15, Kyobashi 3-chome, Chuo-ku
Tokyo 104
Tel: (3) 3562-5011

Pearl Exporters' Association [Japan]
Nihon Shinju Kaikan
122, Higashi-machi, Chuo-ku
Kobe 650
Tel: (78) 331-4031 Fax: (78) 331-4345

Pottery Exporters' Association [Japan]
Nihon Tojiki Center
39-18, Daikan-cho, Higashi-ku
Nagoya 461
Tel: (52) 935-7232 Fax: (52) 936-8424

Raw Silk Exporters' Association [Japan]
Silk Center Building
1, Yamashita-cho, Naka-ku
Yokohama 231
Tel: (45) 641-1953 Fax: (45) 641-1955

Raw Silk Importers' Association [Japan]
Sanshi Kaikan
9-4, Yuraku-cho 1-chome, Chiyoda-ku
Tokyo 100
Tel: (3) 3214-1526 Fax: (3) 3214-1529

Rayon Yarn Traders' Association [Japan]
Yagi Building
10, Minamikyutaro 2-chome, Higashi-ku
Osaka 541
Tel: (6) 261-9201

Rolling Stock Exporters' Association [Japan]
Tekko Building
8-2, Marunouchi 1-chome, Chiyoda-ku
Tokyo 100
Tel: (3) 3201-3145 Fax: (3) 3214-4717

Rubber Importers Association [The Japan]
Tosen Building
10-8, Nihonbashi, Horidome-cho 1-chome
Chuo-ku
Tokyo 103
Tel: (3) 3666-1460 Fax: (3) 3668-8462

Scarf Makers' Industry Association [Japan Export]
2, Sumiyoshi-cho 1-chome, Naka-ku
Yokohama 231
Tel: (45) 681-3261 Fax: (45) 681-3264

Sewing Machine Exporters' Association [Japan]
Ota Building
11, Sumiyoshi-cho 2-chome, Shinjuku-ku
Tokyo 162
Tel: (3) 3353-8471 Fax: (3) 3341-7919

Sheep Casing Importers Association [The Japan]
Yoshinoya Building
32-6, Nishi Gotanda 1-chome, Shinagawa-ku
Tokyo 141
Tel: (3) 3493-6301 Fax: (3) 3491-1772

Ship Exporters' Association [Japan]
Senpaku-Shinko Building
15-16, Toranomon 1-chome, Minato-ku
Tokyo 105
Tel: (3) 3502-2094 Fax: (3) 3508-2058

Silk & Synthetic Textiles Exporters' Association
[Japan]
The Textile Exporters House
4-9, Bingo-machi 3-chome, Chuo-ku
Osaka 541
Tel: (6) 201-1812 Fax: (6) 201-1819

Sporting Goods Importers' Association of Japan
c/o Tyrolia Japan K.K.
3-19, Kanda-Jimbocho, Chiyoda-ku
Tokyo 101
Tel: (3) 3265-0901 Fax: (3) 3265-0805

Sprouting Bean Importers Association [The Japan]
Dai-ichi Suzumaru Building
39-8, Nishishimbashi 2-chome, Minato-ku
Tokyo 105
Tel: (3) 3431-3895 Fax: (3) 3431-3882

Stainless Steel Exporters' Association [Japan]
Tekko Kaikan
16, Nihombashi Kayabacho 3-chome
Chiyoda-ku
Tokyo 103
Tel: (3) 3669-0871, 3669-4431

Steel Exporters' Association [Japan Special]
2-10, Nihonbashi Kayaba-cho 3-chome
Chuo-ku
Tokyo 103
Tel: (3) 3669-2631 Fax: (3) 3668-1540

Sugar Import & Export Council [The Japan]
Ginza Gas Hall
9-15, Ginza 7-chome, Chuo-ku
Tokyo 104
Tel: (3) 3571-2362 Fax: (3) 3571-2363

Suisan Kanzume Packers Association [Japan]
Echizenya Building
1-6, Kyobashi 1-chome, Chuo-ku
Tokyo 104
Tel: (3) 3281-7446 Fax: (3) 3281-6854

Tea Exporters' Association [Japan]
81, Kitaban-cho
Shizuoka, Shizuoka Pref. 420
Tel: (54) 271-3428 Fax: (54) 252-0331
Tlx: 20331

Textile Products Exporters' Association [Japan]
The Textile Exporters House
4-9, Bingo-machi 3-chome, Chuo-ku
Osaka 541
Tel: (6) 201-1712 Fax: (6) 201-1719

Textiles Importers Association [The Japan]
Nihombashi Daiwa Building
9-4, Nihombashi Hon-cho 1-chome, Chuo-ku
Tokyo 103
Tel: (3) 3270-0791 Fax: (3) 3243-1088

Textiles Importers Association [The Japan]
Yushutsu Sen-i Kaikan
4-9, Bingo-machi 3-chome, Chuo-ku
Osaka 541
Tel: (6) 202-5575 Fax: (6) 202-5585

Toy Registration Association [Japan Export]
22-4, Higashikomagata 4-chome, Sumida-ku
Tokyo 130
Tel: (3) 3829-2518 Fax: (3) 3829-2549

Watch and Jewelry Wholesalers Association [Japan Import]
Sakata Higashi Ueno Building
19-6, Higashi Ueno 1-chome, Taito-ku
Tokyo 110
Tel: (3) 3832-7567 Fax: (3) 3834-4040

Watch Importers Association [Japan]
Chuokoron Building
8-7, Kyobashi 2-chome, Chuo-ku
Tokyo 104
Tel: (3) 3563-5901 Fax: (3) 3563-1360

Wine and Spirits Importers' Association [Japan]
Dai-ichi Tentoku Building
13-5, Toranomon 1-chome, Minato-ku
Tokyo 105
Tel: (3) 3503-6505 Fax: (3) 3503-6504

Wire Products Exporters' Association [Japan]
Tekko Kaikan
2-10, Nihombashi Kayaba-cho 3-chome
Chuo-ku
Tokyo 103
Tel: (3) 3669-5311 Fax: (3) 3666-6835

Wood Screw Export Association [Japan]
16-5, Higashi Nippori 6-chome, Arakawa-ku
Tokyo 116
Tel: (3) 3807-9651 Fax: (3) 3897-9653

Wool Importers' Association [The Japan]
Mengyo Kaikan
5-8, Bingo-machi 2-chome, Chuo-ku
Osaka 541
Tel: (6) 231-6201 Fax: (6) 231-6276

Wool Importers' Federation [The Nippon]
Takisada Building
3-6, Bingo-machi 2-chome, Chuo-ku
Osaka 541
Tel: (6) 222-9612 Fax: (6) 232-3625

Woolen & Linen Textiles Exporters Association [Japan]
The Textile Exporters House
4-9, Bingo-machi 3-chome, Chuo-ku
Osaka 541
Tel: (6) 201-4741 Fax: (6) 231-1045

Woolen Yarn Traders Association [Japan]
Osaka Keori Kaikan
38, Awajicho 3-chome, Higashi-ku
Osaka 541
Tel: (6) 231-5787

INDUSTRY-SPECIFIC TRADE ORGANIZATIONS

Abrasive Cloth and Paper Association
Kikai Shinko Kaikan
5-8, Shibakoen 3-chome, Minato-ku
Tokyo 105
Tel: (3) 3431-0949

Aerospace Companies, Inc. [The Society of Japan]
Hibiya Park Building
8-1, Yuraku-cho 1-chome, Chiyoda-ku
Tokyo 100
Tel: (3) 3211-5678 Fax: (3) 3211-5018

Agricultural Chemical Industry [Society of]
Nihombashi Club Kaikan
5-8, Nihombashi Muro-machi, 1-chome
Chuo-ku
Tokyo 103
Tel: (3) 3241-0215 Fax: (3) 3241-3149

Agricultural Chemical Wholesalers Union [National]
Zen-Noyaku Building
3-4, Uchikanda 3-chome, Chiyoda-ku
Tokyo 101
Tel: (3) 3254-4171

Aluminum Federation [Japan]
Nihombashi Asahi Seimei-kan
1-3, Nihombashi 2-chome, Chuo-ku
Tokyo 103
Tel: (3) 3274-4551 Fax: (3) 3274-3179

Aluminum Products Association
13-13, Akasaka 2-chome, Minato-ku
Tokyo 107
Tel: (3) 3583-7971 Fax: (3) 3589-4574

Aromatic Industry Association [The Japan]
5-2, Nihombashi Kayaba-cho 3-chome
Chuo-ku
Tokyo 103
Tel: (3) 3666-5341 Fax: (3) 3666-5375

Artificial Abrasive Industrial Association
2-6, Kasumigaseki 3-chome, Chiyoda-ku
Tokyo 100
Tel: (3) 3580-0866 Fax: (3) 3580-0867

Asbestos Cement Products Association
Takahashi Building
10-8-7, Ginza, Chuo-ku
Tokyo
Tel: (3) 3571-1359

Asbestos Products Industrial Association [Japan]
Tomono Honsha Building
12-4, Ginza 7-chome, Chuo-ku
Tokyo 104
Tel: (3) 3541-4584 Fax: (3) 3541-4958

Asphalt Association [The Japan]
6-7, Toranomon 2-chome, Minato-ku
Tokyo 105
Tel: (3) 3502-3956 Fax: (3) 3502-3376

Atomic Energy Commission
2-1, Kasumigaseki 2-chome, Chiyoda-ku
Tokyo 100
Tel: (3) 3581-2585

Auto Body Industries Association Inc. [Japan]
Kishimoto Building
2-1, Marunouchi 2-chome, Chiyoda-ku
Tokyo 100
Tel: (3) 3213-2031 Fax: (3) 3213-2034

Auto Parts Industries Association [Japan]
Jidosha Buhin Kaikan
16-15, Takanawa 1-chome, Minato-ku
Tokyo 108
Tel: (3) 3445-4211 Fax: (3) 3447-5372
Tlx: 2829

Automobile Dealers Association [Japan]
7-27, Minami-Aoyama 5-chome, Minato-ku
Tokyo 107
Tel: (3) 3400-8404

Automobile Manufacturers' Association, Inc.
[Japan]
Otemachi Building
6-1, Otemachi 1-chome, Chiyoda-ku
Tokyo 100
Tel: (3) 3216-5771 Fax: (3) 3287-2072

Automobile Tire Manufacturers' Association
[Japan]
Toranomon Building
1-23, Toranomon 1-chome, Minato-ku
Tokyo 105
Tel: (3) 3503-0191, 3216-5778
Fax: (3) 3287-2072, 3503-0199

Automotive Machinery and Tool Manufacturers'
Association [Japan]
Kikai Shinko Kaikan
5-8, Shiba Koen 3-chome, Minato-ku
Tokyo 105
Tel: (3) 3431-3773 Fax: (3) 3431-5880

Bankers' Associations of Japan [Federation of]
3-1, Marunouchi 1-chome, Chiyoda-ku
Tokyo 100
Tel: (3) 3216-3761 Fax: (3) 3201-5608

Bar Associations [Japan Federation of]
1-1-1 Kasumigaseki, Chiyoda-ku
Tokyo 100
Tel: (3) 3580-9841 Fax: (3) 3580-2866

Battery and Appliance Industries Association
[Japan]
No. 9 Mori Building
2-2, Atago 1-chome, Minato-ku
Tokyo 105
Tel: (3) 3436-2471 Fax: (3) 3436-2617

Beer Breweries Foundation of Japan
Showa Building
8-18, Kyobashi 2-chome, Chuo-ku
Tokyo 104
Tel: (3) 3561-8386

Bench Machine Tool Builders Association [Japan]
Kikai Shinko Kaikan
5-8, Shibakoen 3-chome, Minato-ku
Tokyo 105
Tel: (3) 3431-5054 Fax: (3) 3434-6955

Bicycle Manufacturers' Association [Japan]
9-3, Akasaka 1-chome, Minato-ku
Tokyo 107
Tel: (3) 3583-3123 Fax: (3) 3589-3125

Bioindustry Association [Japan]
Dowa Building
10-5, Shimbashi 5-chome, Minato-ku
Tokyo 105
Tel: (3) 3433-3545 Fax: (3) 3459-1440

Boiler Association [Japan]
Meiji-Seimei Mita Building
14-10, Mita 3-chome, Minato-ku
Tokyo 108
Tel: (3) 3453-0103 Fax: (3) 3798-0630

Brass Makers' Association [Japan]
12-22, Tsukiji 1-chome, Chuo-ku
Tokyo
Tel: (3) 3542-6551 Fax: (3) 3542-6556

Brewing Machinery Industry Association [Japan]
Todoroki Kanda Building
21, Kanda Nishiki-cho 1-chome, Chiyoda-ku
Tokyo 101
Tel: (3) 3291-9383 Fax: (3) 3291-9383

Brewing Society of Japan [The]
6-30, Takinogawa 2-chome, Kita-ku
Tokyo 114
Tel: (3) 3910-3853 Fax: (3) 3910-3748

All addresses and telephone numbers are in Japan unless otherwise noted. The country code for Japan is [81].

Brush Manufacturers Association [Japan]
10-6, Ebisu Nishi 3-chome, Naniwa-ku
Osaka 556
Tel: (6) 643-1887 Fax: (6) 643-1888

Business Machine Makers Association [Japan]
Dai-Ichi Mori Building
12-1, Nishi-Shombashi 1-chome, Minato-ku
Tokyo 105
Tel: (3) 3503-9821 Fax: (3) 3591-3646

Camera Industry Association [Japan]
JCII Building
25, Ichiban-cho, Chiyoda-ku
Tokyo 102
Tel: (3) 5276-3891 Fax: (3) 5276-3893

Canners' Association [Japan]
Marunouchi Building
4-1, Marunouchi 2-chome, Chiyoda-ku
Tokyo
Tel: (3) 3213-4751

Carbon Association [Japan]
Tokyo Kaijo Building
Shinkan, 2-1, Marunouchi 1-chome
Chiyoda-ku
Tokyo 100
Tel: (3) 3213-3488 Fax: (3) 3212-4490

Cast Iron Foundry Association [Nippon]
Kikai Shinko Kaikan
5-8, Shiba Koen 3-chome, Minato-ku
Tokyo 105
Tel: (3) 3432-2991

Cement Association [Japan]
Hattori Building
10-3, Kyobashi 1-chome, Chuo-ku
Tokyo 104
Tel: (3) 3561-8632 Fax: (3) 3567-8570

Ceramic Society of Japan
22-17, Hyakunincho 2-chome, Shinjuku-ku
Tokyo 160
Tel: (3) 3362-5231

Ceramic Tile Manufacturers' Association [Japan]
39-18, Daikan-cho, Higashi-ku
Nagoya 461
Tel: (52) 935-7235 Fax: (52) 935-4072

Certified Public Accountants [Japanese Institute of]
5-18-3 Hongo, Bunkyo-ku
Tokyo
Tel: (3) 3818-5551 Fax: (3) 3815-5756

Certified Public Accountants Associations [Japan Federation of]
Toshiba Building
1-1-1 Shibaura, Minato-ku
Tokyo 105
Tel: (3) 3798-0031 Fax: (3) 3798-0037

Chain Stores Association [Japan]
No. 11 Mori Building
6-4, Toranomon 2-chome, Minato-ku
Tokyo 105
Tel: (3) 3503-2826

Chemical Engineers [Japan Society of]
Kyoritsu Kaikan
6-19, Kohinata 4-chome, Bunkyo-ku
Tokyo 112
Tel: (3) 3943-3527

Chemical Fibers Association [Japan]
Seni Kaikan, 6 Fl.
1-11, Nihonbashi Honcho 3-chome, Chuo-ku
Tokyo 103
Tel: (3) 3241-2311 Fax: (3) 3246-0823

Chemical Industry Association [Japan]
Tokyo Club Building
2-6, Kasumigaseki 3-chome, Chiyoda-ku
Tokyo 100
Tel: (3) 3580-0751 Fax: (3) 3580-0764

Clock and Watch Association [Japan]
Kudan TS Building
9-16, Kudankita 1-chome, Chiyoda-ku
Tokyo 102
Tel: (3) 5276-3411 Fax: (3) 5276-3414

Cloth Industry Association
Sunshine 60
1-1, Higashi Ikebukuro 3-chome, Toshima-ku
Tokyo 170
Tel: (3) 3986-3503 Fax: (3) 3986-3497

Coal Association [Japan]
Hibiya Park Building
18-1, Yuraku-cho, Chiyoda-ku
Tokyo 100
Tel: (3) 3214-0581

Coffee Association [All Japan]
5th Fl., Kitamura Building
17-15, Nishi Shimbashi 1-chome, Minato-ku
Tokyo 105
Tel: (3) 3580-9870 Fax: (3) 3580-1516

Coke Association [Japan]
15-12, Toranomon 1-chome, Minato-ku
Tokyo 105
Tel: (3) 3502-0581 Fax: (3) 3502-0584

Commercial Arbitration Association [The Japan]
6th Fl., Tokyo Kotsu Kaikan
10-1, Yuraku-cho, Chiyoda-ku
Tokyo 100
Tel: (3) 3214-0641/3 Fax: (3) 3201-1336

Commodity Exchanges Association [Japan]
Tokyo Commodity Exchange Building
12-5, Nihombashi Kakigaracho 1-chome
Chiyoda-ku
Tokyo 103
Tel: (3) 3664-5731

Communications Industry Association
of Japan (CIA-J)
Sankei Building Annex
1-7-2, Otemachi, Chiyoda-ku
Tokyo 100
Tel: (3) 3231-3156 Fax: (3) 3246-0495

Construction Material Industries
[Japan Federation of]
Nihonbashi MI Building
4-3, Nihonbashi Horidome-cho 1-chome
Chuo-ku
Tokyo 103
Tel: (3) 5640-0901 Fax: (3) 5640-0905

Convenience Foods Industry Association [Japan]
Kimura Building
5-5, Alakusabashi 5-chome, Taito-ku
Tokyo 111
Tel: (3) 3865-0811 Fax: (3) 3865-0815

Copper Development Association [Japan]
Konwa Building
12-22, Tsukiji 1-chome, Chuo-ku
Tokyo 104
Tel: (3) 3542-6631

Cosmetic Industry Association [Japan]
Hatsumei Kaikan
9-14, Toranomon 2-chome, Minato-ku
Tokyo 105
Tel: (3) 3502-0576, 3502-0892 Fax: (3) 3502-0892

Cotton and Staple Fibre Weavers' Association
[Japan]
8-7, Nishi-Azabu 1-chome, Minato-ku
Tokyo
Tel: (3) 3403-9671

Dairy Association [National]
Nyugyo Kaikan
3, Kioicho, Chiyoda-ku
Tokyo 102
Tel: (3) 3264-4131

Dairy Products Association [Japan]
6th Fl., Komodo Kudan Building
14-19, Kudan-Kita 1-chome, Chiyoda-ku
Tokyo 102
Tel: (3) 3264-4131 Fax: (3) 3264-4139

Defense Industries [Japan Association of]
2nd Fl., Le Dond Building
21-3, Akasaka 2-chome, Minato-ku
Tokyo 107
Tel: (3) 3584-6755 Fax: (3) 3584-7363

Dental Machine Manufacturers' Association
[Japan]
16-14, Kojima 2-chome, Taito-ku
Tokyo 111
Tel: (3) 3851-6123 Fax: (3) 3851-6124

Dental Materials Manufacturers Association
[Japan]
5th Fl., Kyodo Building
18-7, Higashiueno 2-chome, Taito-ku
Tokyo 110
Tel: (3) 3831-3974 Fax: (3) 3831-3983

Department Stores Association [Japan]
Yanagiya Building
1-10, Nihombashi 2-chome, Chuo-ku
Tokyo 103
Tel: (3) 3272-1666

Die Casting Association [Japan]
Kikai Shinko Kaikan
5-8, Shiba-koen 3-chome, Minato-ku
Tokyo 105
Tel: (3) 3434-1885 Fax: (3) 3434-8829

Direct Marketing Association [Japan] (JDMA)
Mori Building, No. 32
3-4-30 Shibakoean, Minato-ku
Tokyo 105
Tel: (3) 3434-4700 Fax: (3) 3434-4518

Electrical Manufacturers' Association [Japan]
4-15, Nagatacho 2-chome, Chiyoda-ku
Tokyo 100
Tel: (3) 3581-0391, 3581-4841/4 Fax: (3) 3593-3198

Electric Association [Japan]
7-1, Yurakucho 1-chome, Chiyoda-ku
Tokyo 100
Tel: (3) 3216-0551 Fax: (3) 3214-6005

Electric Measuring Instruments Manufacturers'
Association [Japan]
9-10, Toranomon 1-chome, Minato-ku
Tokyo 105
Tel: (3) 3502-0601 Fax: (3) 3502-0600

Electric Power Companies [The Federation of]
Keidaren Kaikan
9-4, Otemachi 1-chome, Chiyoda-ku
Tokyo 100
Tel: (3) 3279-3741

Electric Wire & Cable Makers' Association [The
Japanese]
12-22, Tsukiji 1-chome, Chuo-ku
Tokyo 104
Tel: (3) 3542-6031 Fax: (3) 3542-6037

Electro Plating Industry Association, Japan
[Federation of]
Kikai Shinko Kaikan
5-8, Shibakoen 3-chome, Minato-ku
Tokyo 105
Tel: (3) 3433-3855 Fax: (3) 3433-3915

Electronic Industries Association of Japan
Tosho Building
2-2, Marunouchi 3-chome, Chiyoda-ku
Tokyo 100
Tel: (3) 3211-2765, 3213-1073 Fax: (3) 3287-1712

Electronic Industry Development Association
[Japan]
Kikai Shinko Kaikan
5-8, Shibakoen 3-chome, Minato-ku
Tokyo 105
Tel: (3) 3433-6296 Fax: (3) 3433-6350

Electronic Materials Manufacturers
Association of Japan
Toranomon Kotohirakaikan Building
2-8, Toranomon 1-chome, Minato-ku
Tokyo 105
Tel: (3) 3504-0351 Fax: (3) 3591-8130

Energy Association [Japan]
Shinbashi SY Building
14-2, Nishishinbashi 1-chome, Minato-ku
Tokyo 105
Tel: (3) 3501-3988 Fax: (3) 3501-2428

Explosives Industry Association [Japan]
Gumma Building
3-21, Nihombashi 2-chome, Chuo-ku
Tokyo 103
Tel: (3) 3271-6715 Fax: (3) 3271-7592

Export Insurance Association
New Toranomon Building
11-8, Toranomon 1-chome, Minato-ku
Tokyo 105
Tel: (3) 3502-2731

Fasteners Institute of Japan
Kikai Shinko Kaikan
5-8, Shiba-koen 3-chome, Minato-ku
Tokyo 105
Tel: (3) 3434-5831 Fax: (3) 3434-0546

Felt Association [Japan]
11-6, Yaesu 2-chome, Chuo-ku
Tokyo 104
Tel: (3) 3281-1906 Fax: (3) 3281-8415

Fisheries Association [Japan]
Sankaido Building
9-13, Akasaka 1-chome, Minato-ku
Tokyo 107
Tel: (3) 3587-2551, 3585-6681/3
Fax: (3) 3582-2337

Flat Glass Association of Japan
Shin Tokyo Building
3-1, Marunouchi 3-chome, Chiyoda-ku
Tokyo 100
Tel: (3) 3212-8631 Fax: (3) 3216-3726

Flour Millers Association
15-6, Nihombashi Kabuto-cho, Chuo-ku
Tokyo 103
Tel: (3) 3667-1011 Fax: (3) 3667-1673

Food and Nutrition Association
Sin Kokusai Building
4-1, Marunouchi 3-chome, Chiyoda-ku
Tokyo 100
Tel: (3) 3211-5628 Fax: (3) 3211-5629

Food Machinery Manufacturers' Association [The
Japan]
Window Building, 2nd Fl.
4-8, Roppongi 7-chome, Minato-ku
Tokyo 106
Tel: (3) 3796-0981 Fax: (3) 3796-1655

Foodstuff Association [The Japan]
c/o Nihon Nogyo Kenhyusho
3, Kioicho, Chiyoda-ku
Tokyo 102
Tel: (3) 3265-4917

Forging Industry Association [Japan]
1-13, Nihombashi Hon-cho 3-chome, Chuo-ku
Tokyo 103
Tel: (3) 3241-7661, 3242-8102
Fax: (3) 3241-7663

Fur Association [Japan]
Ginza-Toshin Building
3-11-15, Ginza, Chuo-ku
Tokyo
Tel: (3) 3541-6987 Fax: (3) 3546-2772

Furniture Association [Federation of All Japan]
24-13, Yushima 3-chome, Bunkyo-ku
Tokyo 113
Tel: (3) 3834-1581 Fax: (3) 3834-1583

Gas Association [Japan]
15-12, Toranomon 1-chome, Minato-ku
Tokyo 105
Tel: (3) 3502-0111/6
Fax: (3) 3502-0013, 3502-3676

Glass Bottle Association [Japan]
Nihon Garas Kogyo Center, 6th Fl.
1-9, Shimbashi 3-chome, Minato-ku
Tokyo 105
Tel: (3) 3591-3698 Fax: (3) 3592-1259

Glass Fiber Association of Japan
Kawada Building
5-8, Nishishimbashi 1-chome, Minato-ku
Tokyo 105
Tel: (3) 3591-5406

Golf Goods Association [Japan]
4th Fl., Kobayashi Building
6-11-11 Soto-Kanda, Chiyoda-ku
Tokyo 101
Tel: (3) 3832-8589 Fax: (3) 3832-8594

Housing Equipment & System Association [Japan]
23 Mori Building
23-7, Toranomon 1-chome, Minato-ku
Tokyo 105
Tel: (3) 3503-4546 Fax: (3) 3503-4540

Industrial Machinery Manufacturers [The Japan
Society of]
Kikai Shinko Kaikan
5-8, Shiba Koen 3-chome, Minato-ku
Tokyo 105
Tel: (3) 3434-6821 Fax: (3) 3433-4767

Industrial Vehicles Association [Japan]
Tobu Building
5-26, Motoakasaka 1-chome, Minato-ku
Tokyo 107
Tel: (3) 3403-5556

Information Service Industry Association [Japan]
Yusei Gojokai Kotohiro Building
14-1, Toranomon 1-chome, Minato-ku
Tokyo 105
Tel: (3) 3595-4051 Fax: (3) 3595-4055

Inorganic Chemical Industry Association [Japan]
6th Fl., Haiji Nihonbashi Building
9-9, Nihonbashi Kodenma-cho, Chuo-ku
Tokyo 103
Tel: (3) 5640-1648 Fax: (3) 5640-2368

Instrumentation Control Association [Japan]
Nihon Keiryo Kaikan
25-1, Nandocho, Shinjuku-ku
Tokyo 162
Tel: (3) 3260-2419

Insurance Association of Japan [Marine & Fire
Insurance]
Sonpo Kaikan
9, Kanda Awaji-cho 2-chome, Chiyoda-ku
Tokyo 101
Tel: (3) 3255-1211 x2621 Fax: (3) 32255-5376

Iron and Steel Federation [The Japan]
Keidanren Kaikan
9-4, Otemachi 1-chome, Chiyoda-ku
Tokyo 100
Tel: (3) 3279-3611 Fax: (3) 3245-0144

Iron and Steel Wholesalers' Association [Japan]
Tekko Kaikan
16, Nihombashi Kayabacho 3-chome
Chiyoda-ku
Tokyo 103
Tel: (3) 3669-5861

Knitting Industry Association [Japan]
3rd Fl., TKF Kaikan
37-2, Ryogoku 4-chome, Sumida-ku
Tokyo 130
Tel: (3) 5600-2100 Fax: (3) 5600-2101

Kozai Club [The]
c/o Tekko Kaikan
3-2-10, Nihonbashi Kayaba-cho, Chuo-ku
Tokyo 103
Tel: (3) 3669-4811 Fax: (3) 3667-0245

Lacquer Ware Cooperative Association [Japan]
6th Fl., Inagaki Building
5-24, Asakusabashi 1-chome, Taito-ku
Tokyo 111
Tel: (3) 3866-8632 Fax: (3) 3866-8678

Leather & Leather Goods Industries Association
[Japan]
2nd Fl., Meiyu Building
4-9, Kaminarimon 2-chome, Taito-ku
Tokyo 111
Tel: (3) 3847-1451 Fax: (3) 3847-1510

Leather Association [All Japan]
Toyo Shinyo-Kumiai Honten Building
1-13, Asakusa 6-chome, Taito-ku
Tokyo 111
Tel: (3) 3874-8791

Light Metal Association [Japan]
Nihombashi Asahi Seimei Building
1-3, Nihombashi 2-chome, Chuo-ku
Tokyo 103
Tel: (3) 3273-3041 Fax: (3) 3213-2918

Livestock Dealers Association [Japan]
Baji Chikusan Kaikan
2, Kanda Surugadai 1-chome, Chiyoda-ku
Tokyo 101
Tel: (3) 3291-9394 Fax: (3) 3291-0126

Livestock Industry [Central Association of]
Zenkoku Choson Kaikan
11-35, Nagata-cho 1-chome, Chiyoda-ku
Tokyo 100
Tel: (3) 3581-6676 Fax: (3) 5511-8205

LP-Gas Associations [Federation of Japan]
Sogo No. 6 Building
4-12, Hirakawacho 1-chome, Chiyoda-ku
Tokyo 102
Tel: (3) 3264-3457

Luggage Association [Japan]
16-3, Kuramae 4-chome, Taito-ku
Tokyo 111
Tel: (3) 3861-9857 Fax: (3) 3862-3520

Lumber Association [All Japan Federation of]
Nagatacho Building
4-3, Nagatacho 2-chome, Chiyoda-ku
Tokyo 100
Tel: (3) 3580-3215

Lumber Conference [Japan American]
Yushi Kogyo Kaikan
13-11, Nihombashi 3-chome, Chuo-ku
Tokyo 103
Tel: (3) 3271-0929

Machine Tool Builders' Association [Japan]
Kikai Shinko Kaikan
5-8, Shiba Koen 3-chome, Minato-ku
Tokyo 105
Tel: (3) 3434-3961 Fax: (3) 3434-3763

Machinist Hand Tool Manufacturers' Association
[All Japan]
Kikai Shinko Kaikan
5-8, Shibakoen 3-chome, Minato-ku
Tokyo 105
Tel: (3) 3432-2007 Fax: (3) 3437-6783

Marine Equipment Association [Japanese]
Bansui Building
5-16, Toranomon 1-chome, Minato-ku
Tokyo 105
Tel: (3) 3504-0391, 3502-2041
Fax: (3) 3504-0397, 3591-2206

Measuring Instruments Federation [Japan]
25-1, Nando-cho, Shinjuku-ku
Tokyo 162
Tel: (3) 3268-2121 Fax: (3) 3268-2167

Medical Trading & Manufacturing Association
[Japan Federation]
Ika Kikai Kaikan
39-15, Hongo 3-chome, Bunkyo-ku
Tokyo 113
Tel: (3) 3811-6761

Medium Trawlers [National Federation of]
Toranomon Chuo Building
1-16, Toranomon 1, Minato-ku
Tokyo
Tel: (3) 3508-0361 Tlx: 25404

Microscope Manufacturers' Association [Japan]
c/o Olympus Optical Co. Ltd.
43-2, Hatagaya 2-chome, Shibuya-ku
Tokyo 151
Tel: (3) 3377-2139 Fax: (3) 3377-2139

Mining Industry Association [Japan]
Shin Hibiya Building
3-6, Uchisaiwaicho 1-chome, Chiyoda-ku
Tokyo 100
Tel: (3) 3502-7451 Fax: (3) 3591-9841

Motion Picture Equipment Industrial Association
[Japan]
Kikai Shinko Building
5-8, Shiba Koen 3-chome, Minato-ku
Tokyo 105
Tel: (3) 3434-3911 Fax: (3) 3434-3912

Motion Picture Producers' Association of Japan
Senkei Building
7-2, 1-chome, Otemachi, Chiyoda-ku
Tokyo 100
Tel: (3) 3231-6417 Fax: (3) 3231-6420

Natural Gas Association [Japan]
No. 5 Mori Building
17-1, Toranomon 1-chome, Minato-ku
Tokyo 105
Tel: (3) 3501-1396 Fax: (3) 3501-1398

Optical and Precision Instruments Manufacturers'
Association [Japan]
Kikai Shinko Kaikan
5-8, Shiba Koen 3-chome, Minato-ku
Tokyo 105
Tel: (3) 3431-7073

Optical Industry Association [Japan]
Kikai Shinko Building
5-8, Shiba Koen 3-chome, Minato-ku
Tokyo 105
Tel: (3) 3431-7073

Optical Measuring Instruments Manufacturers'
Association [Japan]
Kikai Shinko Kaikan
5-8, Shiba Koen 3-chome, Minato-ku
Tokyo 105
Tel: (3) 3431-7073

P.V.C. Association [Japan]
Iino Building
1-1, Uchisaiwai-cho 2-chome, Chiyoda-ku
Tokyo 100
Tel: (3) 3506-5481 Fax: (3) 3506-5487

Packaging Machinery Manufacturers
Association [Japan]
7th Fl., Kimura Building
5-5, Asakusabashi 5-chome
Tokyo 111
Tel: (3) 3865-2815 Fax: (3) 3865-2850

Paint Manufacturers Association [Japan]
Tobu Building
5-26, Moto Akasaka 1-chome, Minato-ku
Tokyo 107
Tel: (3) 3478-3451 Fax: (3) 3405-5565

Paper Products Manufacturers'
Association [Japan]
2-6, Kotobuki 4-chome, Taito-ku
Tokyo
Tel: (3) 3543-2411 Fax: (3) 3844-4434

Paper Trade Association [Japan]
Kami Parupu Kaikan
9-11, Ginza 3-chome, Chuo-ku
Tokyo 104
Tel: (3) 3541-7139, 3543-2411

Pearl Export & Processing Cooperative
Association [Japan]
Shinju Kaikan
7, Kyobashi 3-chome, Chiyoda-ku
Tokyo 104
Tel: (3) 3562-5011

Perfumery and Flavoring Association [Japan]
Nitta Building
2-1, Ginza 8-chome, Chuo-ku
Tokyo 104
Tel: (3) 3571-3855 Fax: (3) 3571-3855

Petrochemical Industries [The Association of]
Iino Building
1-1, Uchisaiwaicho 2-chome, Chiyoda-ku
Tokyo 100
Tel: (3) 3501-2151

Petroleum Association of Japan
Keidanren Kaikan
9-4, Otemachi 1-chome, Chiyoda-ku
Tokyo 100
Tel: (3) 3279-3811

Petroleum Dealers Association [National]
Sekiyu Kaikan
17-14, Nagata-cho 2-chome, Chiyoda-ku
Tokyo 100
Tel: (3) 3593-5771 Fax: (3) 3597-1712

Petroleum Development Association [Japan}
Keidanren Kaikan
9-4, Otemachi 1-chome, Chiyoda-ku
Tokyo 100
Tel: (3) 3279-5841 Fax: (3) 3279-5844 Tlx: 29400

Petroleum Producers' Association of Japan
Keidanren Kaikan
9-4, Otemachi 1-chome, Chiyoda-ku
Tokyo 100
Tel: (3) 3279-5841

Pharmaceutical Manufacturers' Association of
Japan [The Federation of]
Tokyo Yakugyo Kaikan
9, Nihonbashi Honcho 2-chome, Chuo-ku
Tokyo 103
Tel: (3) 3270-0581 Fax: (3) 3241-2090

Photo-Sensitized Materials Manufacturers'
Association
JCCI Building
25, Ichiban-cho, Chiyoda-ku
Tokyo 102
Tel: (3) 5276-3561 Fax: (3) 5276-3563

Plasticizer Industry [Association of]
Shin Nisseki Building
4-2, Marunouchi 3-chome, Chiyoda-ku
Tokyo 100
Tel: (3) 3213-5725 Fax: (3) 3213-5726

Plastics Industry Federation [The Japan]
Tokyo Club Building
2-6, Kasumigaseki 3-chome, Chiyoda-ku
Tokyo 100
Tel: (3) 3580-0771 Fax: (3) 3580-0775

Plastic Toy Manufacturers' Association [Japan]
22-13, Yanagibashi 2-chome, Taito-ku
Tokyo 111
Tel: (3) 3863-4075 Fax: (3) 3864-9726

Plywood Manufacturers' Association [Japan]
Meisan Building
18-17, 1-chome, Nishi-Shimbashi, Minato-ku
Tokyo
Tel: (3) 3591-9246 Fax: (3) 3591-9240

Polyethylene Products Industry Association
[Japan]
Kyoei Building
15-17, Nihombashi Kofune-cho, Chuo-ku
Tokyo 103
Tel: (3) 3661-3834 Fax: (3) 3661-3849

Pottery Manufacturers' Federation [Japan]
Toto Building
1-28, Toranomon 1-chome, Minato-ku
Tokyo
Tel: (3) 3503-6761

Pouch Association [Tokyo]
16-14, Yanagibashi 2-chome, Taito-ku
Tokyo 111
Tel: (3) 3851-5278 Fax: (3) 3851-7725

Precision Measuring Instruments Association
[Japan]
Kiuchi Building
7-4, Toranomon 3-chome, Minato-ku
Tokyo 105
Tel: (3) 3434-9557 Fax: (3) 3434-1695

Precision Tool Makers Association [Tokyo]
Parasto Kamata 304
45-6, Kamata 5-chome, Ota-ku
Tokyo 144
Tel: (3) 3730-8585 Fax: (3) 3730-8118

Printing Industries [Japan Federation of]
1-16-8, Shintomi, Chuo-ku
Tokyo 104
Tel: (3) 3553-6051 Fax: (3) 3553-6079

Printing Machinery Manufacturers Association
[Japan]
Kikai Shinko Kaikan
5-8, Shibakoen 3-chome, Minato-ku
Tokyo 105
Tel: (3) 3434-4661 Fax: (3) 3434-0301

Pyrotechnics Association [Japan]
4th Fl., Furuyama Building
7-9, Nihonbashi 3-chome, Chuo-ku
Tokyo 103
Tel: (3) 3281-9871 Fax: (3) 3274-5200

Raw Silk Association of Japan [Central]
7, 1-chome, Yuraku-cho, Chiyoda-ku
Tokyo
Tel: (3) 3214-5777 Fax: (3) 3214-5778

Raw Silk Reelers' Association [Japan]
Sanshi Kaikan
9-4, Yuraku-cho 1-chome, Chiyoda-ku
Tokyo 100
Tel: (3) 3214-1431 Fax: (3) 3201-6685

Refractories Association [The Japan]
3-13, Ginza 7-chome, Chuo-ku
Tokyo 104
Tel: (3) 3571-3300 Fax: (3) 3572-4831

Refrigeration and Air-Conditioning Industry
Association [The Japan]
Kikai Shinko Kaikan
5-8, Shibakoen 3-chome, Minato-ku
Tokyo 105
Tel: (3) 3432-1671 Fax: (3) 3438-0308

Rolling Stock Industries [Japan Association of]
Daiichi Tekko Building
8-2, Marunouchi 1-chome, Chiyoda-ku
Tokyo 100
Tel: (3) 3201-1911 Fax: (3) 3201-3053

Rubber Footwear Manufacturers' Association
[Japan]
Tobu Building
5-26, Moto-Akasaka 1-chome, Minato-ku
Tokyo 107
Tel: (3) 3478-0174 Fax: (3) 3478-0227

Rubber Manufacturers' Association [The Japan]
Tobu Building
5-26, Moto-Akasaka 1-chome, Minato-ku
Tokyo 107
Tel: (3) 3408-7101 Fax: (3) 3408-7106

Sake Brewers Association [Japan]
1-21, Nishi Shimbashi 1-chome, Minato-ku
Tokyo 105
Tel: (3) 3501-0101 Fax: (03) 3501-6018

Sanitary Equipment Industry Association [Japan]
39-18, Daikan-cho, Higashi-ku
Nagoya 461
Tel: (52) 935-7235 Fax: (52) 935-4072

Scientific Instrument Associations [Japan
Federation of]
No. 2 Tomihisa Building
9-7, Nihombashi Hon-cho 3-chome, Chuo-ku
Tokyo 103
Tel: (3) 3661-5131 Fax: (3) 3668-0324

Securities Dealers' Association [The Japan]
Tokyo Shoken Kaikan
5-8, Nihombashi Kayabacho 1-chome
Chiyoda-ku
Tokyo 103
Tel: (3) 3667-8451

All addresses and telephone numbers are in Japan unless otherwise noted. The country code for Japan is [81].

Sewing Machinery Manufacturers Association
[Japan]
Ota Building
2-11, Sumiyoshi-cho, Shinjuki-ku
Tokyo 162
Tel: (3) 3341-7615 Fax: (3) 3341-7919

Shipbuilders' [The Cooperative Association of
Japan]
Sempaku Shinko Building
15-16, Toranomon 1-chome, Minato-ku
Tokyo 105
Tel: (3) 3502-2061 Fax: (3) 3502-1479

Shipowners' Association [Japanese]
Kaiun Building
6-4, Hirakawa-cho 2-chome, Chiyoda-ku
Tokyo
Tel: (3) 3264-7171 Fax: (3) 3262-4760 Tlx: 22148

Shoe Manufacturers' Association [Japan]
Kume Building
3-9, Nihombashi Ningyo-cho 3-chome, Chuo-ku
Tokyo 103
Tel: (3) 3661-4672 Fax: (3) 3661-3972

Silk & Rayon Weavers' Association [Japan]
15-12, Kudankita 1-chome, Chiyoda-ku
Tokyo 102
Tel: (3) 3262-4101 Fax: (3) 3262-4270

Silk Spinners' Association [Japan]
4-5, Nihombashi Horidome-cho 2-chome
Chuo-ku
Tokyo 103
Tel: (3) 3661-0235 Fax: (3) 3661-0596

Small Tool Makers' Association [The Japan]
Kikai Shinko Kaikan
5-8, Shibakoen 3-chome, Minato-ku
Tokyo 105
Tel: (3) 3433-6891 Fax: (3) 3432-6947

Soap and Detergent Association [Japan]
13-11, Nihombashi 3-chome, Chuo-ku
Tokyo 103
Tel: (3) 3271-4301 Fax: (3) 3281-1870

Socks & Stockings Association [The Japan]
27-4, Higashi Nihombashi 2-chome, Chuo-ku
Tokyo 103
Tel: (3) 3851-4848 Fax: (3) 3851-5374

Soft Drinks Bottlers Association [Japan]
4-17, Koishikawa 2-chome, Bunkyo-ku
Tokyo 112
Tel: (3) 3814-0666

Spinners' Association [Japan]
Mengyo Kaikan
8, Bingocho 3-chome, Higashi-ku
Osaka 541
Tel: (6) 231-8431 Fax: (6) 229-1590

Spirits & Liquors Makers Association [Japan]
Koura Dai 1 Building
1-6, Nihombashi Kayaba-cho 1-chome
Chuo-ku
Tokyo 103
Tel: (3) 3668-4621 Fax: (3) 3668-7077

Steel Castings & Forgings Association of Japan
Tekko Building
8-2, Marunouchi 1-chome, Chiyoda-ku
Tokyo 100
Tel: (3) 3201-0461 Fax: (3) 3211-6903

Steel Constructors Association [Japan]
2-18, Ginza 2-chome, Chuo-ku
Tokyo 104
Tel: (3) 3535-5078 Fax: (3) 3562-4657

Sugar Refiners' Association [Japan]
5-7, Sambancho, Chiyoda-ku
Tokyo 102
Tel: (3) 3262-0176, 3288-1511 Fax: (3) 3288-3399

Surveying Instruments Manufacturers'
Association [Japan]
Kikai Shinko Kaikan
5-8, Shibakoen 3-chome, Minato-ku
Tokyo 105
Tel: (3) 3431-1629

Synthetic Organic Chemistry, Japan
[The Society of]
Kagaku Kaikan
5, Kanda Surugadai 1-chome, Chiyoda-ku
Tokyo 101
Tel: (3) 3292-7621 Fax: (3) 3294-7622

Tea Association [Japan]
2-9-12, Higashi Shinbashi, Minato-ku
Tokyo 105
Tel: (3) 3431-6711 Fax: (3) 3431-6711

Telescope Manufacturers' Association [Japan]
Kikai Shinko Kaikan
5-8, Shibakoen 3-chome, Minato-ku
Tokyo 105
Tel: (3) 3431-7708

Testing Machinery Association of Japan
Nihon Keiryo Kaikan Building
25-1, Nando-cho, Shinjuku-ku
Tokyo 162
Tel: (3) 3268-4849 Fax: (3) 3268-4840

Textile Council [Japan]
Seni Kaikan
9, Nihombashi Honcho 3-chome, Chuo-ku
Tokyo 103
Tel: (3) 3241-7801

Textile Machinery Association [Japan]
Kikai Shinko Building
5-8, Shiba Koen 3-chome, Minato-ku
Tokyo 105
Tel: (3) 3434-3821 Fax: (3) 3434-3043

Towel Industries Association [Japan]
4-5, Nihonbashi Ningyoucho 3-chome, Chuo-ku
Tokyo 103
Tel: (3) 3663-1087 Fax: (3) 3662-5398

Toy Association [The Japan]
22-4, Higashi-Komagata 4-chome, Sumida-ku
Tokyo 130
Tel: (3) 3829-2513 Fax: (3) 3829-2549

Toy Manufacturers' Association [Tokyo]
4-16-3, Higashi-Komagata, Sumida-ku
Tokyo 130
Tel: (3) 3624-0461 Fax: (3) 3623-0891

Tuna Packers' Association of Japan
3rd Fl., N.P. One Building
5-6, Ueno 3-chome, Taito-ku
Tokyo 110
Tel: (3) 3832-3150 Fax: (3) 3832-3165

Valve Manufacturers' Association [The Japan]
Kikai Shinko Kaikan
5-8, Shibakoen 3-chome, Minato-ku
Tokyo 105
Tel: (3) 3434-1881 Fax: (3) 3436-4335

Vinyl Goods Manufacturers' Association [Japan]
Tobu Building
5-26, Moto Akasaka 1-chome, Minato-ku
Tokyo 107
Tel: (3) 3408-7201 Fax: (3) 3401-9351

Wire Products Association
Tekko Kaikan
16, Nihombashi Kayabacho 3-chome, Chuo-ku
Tokyo 103
Tel: (3) 3669-5311

Wire Rope Association [Japan]
Mako Building
2-22, Minami-Senba 3-chome, Chuo-ku
Osaka 542
Tel: (6) 252-7477 Fax: (6) 252-7479

Wood Technological Association of Japan
Dai 1 Maki Building
2-16, Shiba-Koen 1-chome, Minato-ku
Tokyo 105
Tel: (3) 3432-3053 Fax: (3) 3431-5075

Woodworking Machinery Association [The Japan]
Kikai Shinko Kaikan
5-8, Shibakoen 3-chome, Minato-ku
Tokyo 105
Tel: (3) 3433-6511 Fax: (3) 3433-6513

Wool Dyers' & Finishers' Association [Japan]
Ueno DK Building
15-4, Ueno 1-chome, Taito-ku
Tokyo 110
Tel: (3) 3837-2877

Wool Spinners' Association [Japan]
Ueno DK Building
15-4 Ueno 1-chome, Taito-ku
Tokyo
Tel: (3) 3837-7916 Fax: (3) 3837-7918

Yarn Twisters Association
5th Fl., Towa Sotokanda Building
10-3, Sotokanda 3-chome, Chiyoda-ku
Tokyo 101
Tel: (3) 3255-0351 Fax: (3) 3255-0380

FINANCIAL INSTITUTIONS

BANKS

Federation of Bankers' Associations of Japan
3-1, Marunouchi 1-chome, Chiyoda-ku
Tokyo 100
Tel: (3) 3216-3761 Fax: (3) 3201-5608 Tlx: 26830

Central Bank

Bank of Japan (Nihon Ginko)
1-1, Hongoku-cho 2-chome, Nihonbashi
Chuo-ku
Tokyo 103
Tel: (3) 3279-1111 Fax: (3) 3245-0358 Tlx: 22763

Commercial & Domestic Banks

Bank of Tokyo Ltd.
3-2, Nihonbashi, Hongoku-cho 1-chome
Chuo-ku
Tokyo 103
Tel: (3) 3245-1111 Fax: (3) 3279-3926 Tlx: 22220

Central Cooperative Bank for Agriculture, Forestry
& Fisheries (Norinchukin Bank)
8-3, Otemachi 1-chome, Chiyoda-ku
Tokyo 100
Tel: (3) 3279-0111 Fax: (3) 3245-0564 Tlx: 23918

Dai-Ichi Kangyo Bank Ltd.
1-5, Uchisaiwai-cho 1-chome, Chiyoda-ku
Tokyo 100
Tel: (3) 3596-1111 Tlx: 22315

Export-Import Bank of Japan
4-1, Otemachi 1-chome, Chiyoda-ku
Tokyo 100
Tel: (3) 3287-1221 Fax: (3) 3287-9540 Tlx: 23728

Fuji Bank Ltd.
5-5, Otemachi 1-chome, Chiyoda-ku
Tokyo 100
Tel: (3) 3216-2211 Tlx: 22367

Industrial Bank of Japan Ltd. (Nippon Kogyo
Ginko)
3-3, Marunouchi 1-chome, Chiyoda-ku
Tokyo 100
Tel: (3) 3214-1111 Tlx: 22325

Japan Development Bank (JDB)
9-1, Otemachi 1-chome, Chiyoda-ku
Tokyo 100
Tel: (3) 3244-1770 Fax: (3) 3245-1938 Tlx: 24343

Long-Term Credit Bank of Japan Ltd.
2-4, Otemachi 1-chome, Chiyoda-ku
Tokyo 100
Tel: (3) 3211-5111 Tlx: 24308

Nippon Credit Bank Ltd.
13-10, Kudan-kita 1-chome, Chiyoda-ku
Tokyo 102
Tel: (3) 3263-1111 Tlx: 26291

Overseas Economic Co-operation Fund
Takebashi Godo Building
4-1, Otemachi 1-chome, Chiyoda-ku
Tokyo 100
Tel: (3) 3215-1311 Fax: (3) 3215-2897 Tlx: 28430

Sanwa Bank Ltd.
3-5-6, Fushimi-machi, Chuo-ku
Osaka 541
Tel: (6) 206-8111 Tlx: 63234

Shoko Chukin Bank
10-17, Yaesu 2-chome, Chuo-ku
Tokyo 104
Tel: (3) 3272-6111 Tlx: 25388

Sumitomo Bank Ltd.
4-6-5, Kitahama, Chuo-ku
Osaka 541
Tel: (6) 227-2111 Tlx: 63266

Foreign Banks

ABN Amro Bank NV (Netherlands)
South Tower, Yurakucho Denki Building
7-1, Yuraku-cho 1-chome, Chiyoda-ku
Tokyo 100
Tel: (3) 3217-8795 Fax: (3) 3214-1409

Bank of America NT & SA (USA)
ARK Mori Building
12-32, Akasaka 1-chome, Minato-ku
Tokyo 107
Tel: (3) 3587-3111 Fax: (3) 3587-3373 Tlx: 22272

Banque Nationale de Paris (France)
Usen Building
3-2, Marunouchi 2-chome, Chiyoda-ku
Tokyo 100
Tel: (3) 3214-2882 Tlx: 24825

Citibank NA (USA)
1-1-3 Marunouchi, Chiyoda-ku
Tokyo 100
Tel: (3) 3214-6660

Deutsche Bank AG (Germany)
ARK Mori Building
12-32, Akasaka 1-chome, Minato-ku
Tokyo 107
Tel: (3) 3582-3188 Fax: (3) 3582-8446 Tlx: 24814

First National Bank of Chicago (USA)
Hibaya Central Building
2-9, Nishi Shimbashi 1-chome, Minato-ku
Tokyo 105
Tel: (3) 3596-8700 Fax: (3) 3596-8744 Tlx: 24977

Hongkong and Shanghai Banking Corporation
(Hong Kong)
1-2, Marunouchi 2-chome, Chiyoda-ku
Tokyo 100
Tel: (3) 3216-0110 Tlx: 22372

Korea Exchange Bank
Shin Kikusai Building
4-1, Marunouchi 3-chome, Chiyoda-ku
Tel: (3) 3216-3561 Fax: (3) 3214-4491 Tlx: 24243

Lloyds Bank (UK)
Ohte Center Building
1-3, Ohtemachi 1-chome, Chiyoda-ku
Tokyo 100
Tel: (3) 3214-6771

Oversea-Chinese Banking Corporation Ltd.
(Singapore)
Shin Tokyo Building
3-1, Marunouchi 3-chome, Chiyoda-ku
Tokyo 100
Tel: (3) 3214-2841 Fax: (3) 3214-4007
Tlx: 26186

Standard Chartered Bank (UK)
Fuji Building
2-3, Marunouchi 3-chome
Tokyo 100
Tel: (3) 3213-6541 Tlx: 22484

Swiss Bank Corporation
Swiss Bank House
1-8, Toranomon 4-chome, Minato-ku
Tokyo 105
Tel: (3) 5473-5000 Fax: (3) 5473-5175
Tlx: 24842

INSURANCE COMPANIES

Export Insurance Association
New Toranomon Building
11-8, Toranomon 1-chome, Minato-ku
Tokyo 105
Tel: (3) 3502-2731

Fire and Marine Insurance Rating Association of
Japan
7, Kanda Mitoshiro-cho, Chiyoda-ku
Tokyo 101
Tel: (3) 5259-0819 Fax: (3) 5259-0874
Tlx: 24829

Marine & Fire Insurance Association of Japan
Sonpo Kaikan
9, Kanda Awaji-cho 2-chome, Chiyoda-ku
Tokyo 101
Tel: (3) 3255-1211 x2621 Fax: (3) 3255-5376

Ministry of International Trade & Industry
Export-Import Insurance Division (EID/MITI)
1-3-1 Kasumigaseki, Chiyoda-ku
Tokyo 100
Tel: (3 3501-1511

Asahi Fire and Marine Insurance Co. Ltd.
6-2, Kaji-cho 2-chome, Chiyoda-ku
Tokyo 101
Tel: (3) 3254-2211 Tlx: 26974

Chiyoda Fire and Marine Insurance Co. Ltd.
Kyobashi Chiyoda Building
1-9, Kyobashi 2-chome, Chuo-ku
Tokyo 104
Tel: (3) 3281-3311 Fax: (3) 3273-1375
Tlx: 24975

Dai-Tokyo Fire and Marine Insurance Co. Ltd.
1-6, Nihonbashi 3-chome, Chuo-ku
Tokyo 103
Tel: (3) 3272-8811 Fax: (3) 3271-4156
Tlx: 26968

Daiichi Mutual Fire & Marine Insurance Co.
5-1, Niban-cho, Chiyoda-ku
Tokyo 102
Tel: (3) 3239 -0011 Fax: (3) 5275-5858

John Swire & Sons (Japan) Ltd.
Swire House
14, Ichiban-cho, Chiyoda-ku
Tokyo 102
Tel: (3) 3230-9100 Fax: (3) 3230-9288
Tlx: J22248 SWIRE A

Mitsui Marine & Fire Insurance Co. Ltd.
9, Kanda Surugadai 3-chome, Chiyoda-ku
Tokyo 101-11
Tel: (3) 3259-3111 Fax: (3) 3291-5466
Tlx: J24670 KALMSEA

Nippon Express Co. Ltd.
12-9, Sitokanda 3-chome, Chiyoda-ku
Tokyo 101
Tel: (3) 5294-5801 Fax: (3) 5294-5809

Nippon Fire and Marine Insurance Co. Ltd.
2-10, Nihombashi 2-chome, Chuo-ku
Tokyo
Tel: (3) 3272-8111 Fax: (3) 3281-1788

Nissin Corp.
Keihin Building
84, Onoe-cho 6-chome, Naka-ku
Yokohama 231
Tel: (45) 671-6112 Fax: (45) 671-6118
Tlx: 3822137 NISSIN J

Sumitomo Marine and Fire Insurance Co. Ltd.
27-2, Shinkawa 2-chome, Chuo-ku
Tokyo 104
Tel: (3) 3297-1111 Fax: (3) 3297-6895
Tlx: 23051

Suzuyo & Co. Ltd.
11-1, Irifune-cho, Shimizu
Shizuoka 424
Tel: (543) 54-3271 Fax: (543) 52-2397

Taisei Fire and Marine Insurance Co. Ltd.
2-1, 4-chome, Kudan-kita, Chiyoda-ku
Tokyo 102
Tel: (3)3234-3111 Fax: (3) 3234-4073
Tlx: 8351

Yasuda Fire and Marine Insurance Co. Ltd.
26-1, Nishi-Shinjuku 1-chome, Shinjuku-ku
Tokyo 160
Tel: (3) 3349-3111 Fax: (3) 3348-3041
Tlx: 22790

STOCK AND COMMODITY EXCHANGES

Japan Commodity Exchanges Association
Tokyo Commodity Exchange Building
12-5, Nihombashi Kakigaracho 1-chome
Chiyoda-ku
Tokyo 103
Tel: (3) 3664-5731

Japan Securities Dealer's Association Japan
Tokyo Shoken Kaikan
5-8, Nihombashi Kayabacho 1-chome
Chiyoda-ku
Tokyo 103
Tel: (3) 3667-8451

All addresses and telephone numbers are in Japan unless otherwise noted. The country code for Japan is [81].

Fukuoka Stock Exchange
2-14-2, Tenjin, Chuo-ku
Fukuoka 810

Hiroshima Stock Exchange
14-18, Kanayama-cho
Hiroshima 730

Hokkaido Grain Exchange
3, Ordori Nishi 5-chome, Chuo-ku
Sapporo, Hokkaido
Tel: (11) 221-9131

Kobe Rubber Exchange
49, Harima-cho, Chuo-ku
Kobe 650
Tel: (78) 331-4211/4

Maebashi Dried Cocoon Exchange
1-49-1, Furuichi-Machi
Maebashi City, Gunma Pref. 371
Tel: (272) 521-401 Fax: (272) 521305

Nagoya Stock Exchange (NSE)
3-17, Sakae, 3-chome, Naka-ku
Nagoya 460
Tel: (52) 262-3171/2, 241-1521 Fax: (52) 241-1527

Osaka Grain Exchange
1-10-14, Awaza, Nishi-ku
Osaka 550
Tel: (6) 531-7931

Osaka Securities Exchange (OSE)
8-16, Kitahama, 1-chome, Chuo-ku
Osaka 541
Tel: (6) 229-8643 Fax: (6) 231-2639

Osaka Stock Exchange
1, Kitahama, 2-chome, Higashi-ku
Osaka 541
Tel: (6) 226-0058

Osaka Textile Exchange
3-32-1, Kitakyutaro-Machi, Higashi-ku
Osaka 541
Tel: (6) 253-0031

Sapporo Stock Exchange
5-14-1, Nishi, Minami Ichijo, Chuo-ku
Sapporo, Hokkaido

Tokyo Commodity Exchange (TCE)
10-8, Nihonbashi Horidomecho, 1-chome, Chuo-ku
Tokyo 103
Tel: (3) 3661-9191 Fax: (3) 3661-7568

Tokyo Commodity Exchange for Industry
Tosen Building
10-8, Horidome, 1-chome, Nihonbashi
Chuo-ku
Tokyo
Tel: (3) 3661-9191

Tokyo Grain Exchange
1-12-5, Kakigara-cho, Chuo-ku
Tokyo 103
Tel: (3) 3668-9311

Tokyo International Financial Futures Exchange (TIFFE)
NTT Data Otemachi Building
2-2-2, Otemachi, Chiyoda-ku
Tokyo 100
Tel: (3) 3275-2400 Fax: (3) 3275-2862

Tokyo Stock Exchange (TSE)
2-1, Nihombashi Kabuto-cho, Chuo-ku
Tokyo 103
Tel: (3) 3666-0141 Fax: (3) 3666-0625 Tlx: 22759

Toyohashi Dried Cocoon Exchange
52-2 Ekimae-odori
Toyohashi City, Aichi pref. 440
Tel: (532) 52-6231

SERVICES

ACCOUNTING FIRMS

Japan Federation of Certified Public Accountants
Associations
Toshiba Building
1-1-1 Shibaura, Minato-ku
Tokyo 105
Tel: (3) 3798-0031 Fax: (3) 3798-0037

Japanese Institute of Certified Public Accountants
5-18-3 Hongo, Bunkyo-ku
Tokyo
Tel: (3) 3818-5551 Fax: (3) 3815-5756

Century Audit Corporation (Peat Marwick)
Umeshin Daiichi-Seimei Building Nishikan
4-5, Sonezaki 2-chome, Kita-ku
Osaka 530
Tel: (6) 365-3135 Fax: (6) 365-3167

Coopers & Lybrand
Kasumigaseki Building, 32nd Fl.
2-5, Kasumigaseki 3-chome, Chiyoda-ku
Tokyo 100
Tel: (3) 3581-6281/7535 Fax: (3) 3580-1868
Tlx: 2226771

Inoe Saito Eiwa Audit Corporation
(Arthur Andersen & Co.)
Nihom Seimei Akasaka Building
8-1-19, Akasaka, Minato-ku
Tokyo 107
Tel: (3) 3403-4211 Fax: (3) 3470-2313

K.K. Peat Marwick
Century Audit Corporation
Japan Red Cross Building
1-3, Shiba Daimon 1-chome, Minato-ku
Tokyo 105
Tel: (3) 3578-1910 Fax: (3) 3434-2122
International Tax Division
Tel: (3) 5400-7300 Fax: (3) 5400-7373

K.K. Peat Marwick, International Tax
SKF Building
9-1, Shiba Daimon 1-chome, Minato-ku
Tokyo 105
Tel: (3) 5462-2800 Fax: (3) 5462-2820

Price Waterhouse
Aoyama Building, 7th Fl.
2-3 Kita-Aoyama 1-chome, Minato-ku
Tokyo 107
Tel: (3) 3404-9351 Fax: (3) 3404-8610

Price Waterhouse
Takanawa Court Building
13-1 Takanawa 3-chome, Minato-ku
Tokyo 108
Tel: (3) 3280-8011 Fax: (3) 3280-8097/8/9

Price Waterhouse
FT Building, 4th Fl.
8-28 Watanabedori 4-chome, Chuo-ku
Fukuoka 810
Tel: (92) 715-6001 Fax: (92) 715-6060

Price Waterhouse
Mainichi Building, 5th Fl.
7-35 Meieki 4-chome, Nakamura-ku
Nagoya 450
Tel: (52) 571-6271 Fax: (52) 571-6273

Price Waterhouse Osaka
Osaka Center Building, 10th Fl.
1-3, Kyutaro-machi 4-chome, Chuo-ku
Osaka 541
Tel: (6) 252-6791 Fax: (6) 252-6798

Showa Ota & Co.
(Ernst & Young International)
Hibiya Kokusai Building
2-2-3, Uchisaiwai-cho, Chiyoda-ku
Tokyo 100
Postal address: CPO Box 1196, Tokyo 100-91
Tel: (3) 3503-1191 Fax: (3) 3503-1277

Showa Ota & Co.
(Ernst & Young International)
Fukuoka Tokai Building
1-12-1, Tenjin, Chuo-ku
Fukuoka 810
Tel: (92) 761-7231

Showa Ota & Co.
(Ernst & Young International)
Nagoya Tokyo Kaijo Building
2-20-19, Marunouchi, Naka-ku
Nagoya City, Aichi 460
Tel: (52) 211-3202

Showa Ota & Co.
(Ernst & Young International)
Osaka Kodusai Building
2-3-13, Asuchi-cho, Chuo-ku
Osaka 541
Tel: (6) 263-5171 Fax: (6) 263-5170

Tohmatsu & Co.
M.S. Shibaura Building
13-23, Shibaura 4-chome, Minato-ku
Tokyo 108
Tel: (3) 3457-7321 Fax: (3) 3457-1695

Uno Tax Accountant Office
(Arthur Andersen)
Chuo Building
2-17 Kagurazaka, Shinjuko-ku
Tokyo 162
Tel: (3) 5228-1600 Fax: (3) 5228-1650

ADVERTISING AGENCIES

Asatsu/BBDO
1-9-6, Shimbashi, Minato-ku
Tokyo 105
Tel: (3) 3575-3171 Fax: (3) 3575-1470 Tlx: 29217

Bozell Meitsu
No. 5, Toyokaiji Building
3-2-5, Shinbashi, Minato-ku
Tokyo 105
Tel: (3) 3503-7411 Fax: (3) 3503-7410
Tlx: 2223173 MKETYO J

All addresses and telephone numbers are in Japan unless otherwise noted. The country code for Japan is [81].

BSB Japan Ltd.
Shibaura Square Building
4-9-25, Shibaura, Minato-ku
Tokyo 108
Tel: (3) 3455-4123 Fax: (3) 3453-9633
Tlx: 781-2223644

Daiko Advertising, Inc. (Main office)
3-39, Miyahara 4-chome, Yodogawa-ku
Osaka 532
Tel: (6) 3928111 Fax: (6) 3928004

Daiko Advertising, Inc. (Tokyo)
Shuwa Shiba Park Building, B-8
2-4-1, Shiba-koen, Minato-ku
Tokyo 105
Tel: (3) 3437-8086, 3437-8111 Fax: (3) 3437-8477

Daiko Advertising, Inc. (Nagoya)
Nagoya Kokusai Center Building, 13th Fl.
47-1, Nagono 1-chome, Nakamura-ku
Nagoya 450
Tel: (52) 581-7161

DDB Needham Japan Ltd.
Royal Building, 2nd Fl.
12-18 Nibancho, Chiyoda-ku
Tokyo 102
Tel: (3) 3288-7551 Fax: (3) 3288-7555

Dentsu Inc.
1-11, Tsukiji, Chuo-ku
Tokyo 104
Tel: (3) 3544-5111 Fax: (3) 3545-1764
Tlx: Dentsu J26223

Dentsu Inc. Chubu
4-16-36, Sakae, Naka-ku
Nagoya 460
Tel: (52) 263-8111

Dentsu Inc. Kansai
2-4-5, Dojima, Kita-ku
Osaka 530
Tel: (6) 342-3111

Dentsu Inc. Kyushu
4-1-2, Tenjin, Chuo-ku
Fukuoka 810
Tel: (92) 713-2555

Dentsu, Young & Rubicam
Kyobashi K-1 Building
2-7-12, Yaesu, Chuo-ku
Tokyo 104
Tel: (3) 3278-4811 Fax: (3) 3278-4809 Tlx: 761-2738

Hakuhodo Inc. (Osaka)
12th Fl., Shin-Asahi Building
2-3-18, Nakanoshima, Kita-ku
Osaka 530
Tel: (6) 228-3905 Fax: (6) 228-3999 Tlx: 5224878

Hakuhodo Inc. (Nagoya)
7th Fl., Chunichi Building
4-1-1, Safae, Naka-ku
Nagoya 460
Tel: (52) 251-2125 Fax: (52) 242-1492

Hakuhodo Inc. (Fukuoka)
Matsushita Watanabe Building, 9th Fl.
4-10-10, Watanabe-dori, Chuo-ku
Fukuoka 810
Tel: (92) 781-7531 Fax: (92) 781-7538

Hakuhodo Inc. (Tokyo)
3-22, Kanda-Nishikicho, Chiyoda-ku
Tokyo 101
Tel: (3) 3233-6161

Hakuhodo Lintas
Tokyo Building
7-3, Marunouchi, 2-chome, Chiyoda-ku
Tokyo 100
Tel: (3) 3240-7640 Fax: (3) 3240-7697
Tlx: 2225457 haklin J

Inter-Image Inc.
No. 28 Mori Building
4-16-13, Nishi Azabu, Minato-ku
Tokyo 106
Tel: (3) 3407-8691 Fax: (3) 3486-0867

J. Walter Thompson Japan Ltd.
1-4-10, Takanawa, Minato-ku
Tokyo 108
Tel: (3) 3449-2511 Fax: (3) 3440-4858

JDAC
303 Yotsuya Mansion
1-22, Arakicho, Shinjuku-ku
Tokyo 160
Tel: (3) 3358-2441 Fax: (3) 3358-2866

Leo Burnett Kyodo Co. Ltd.
Akasaka Twin Tower
17-22, Akasake 2-chome, Minato-ku
Tel: (3) 3584-2331 Fax: (3) 3584-2330

McCann-Erickson Hakuhodo Inc.
Koncho Tosabori Building, 7th Fl.
4-11, Tosabori 1-chome, Nishi-ku
Osaka 550
Tel: (6) 342-6800

McCann-Erickson Hakuhodo Inc.
Shin Aoyama Building, E
1-1, Minami-Aoyama 1-chome, Minato-ku
Tokyo 107
Tel: (3) 3746-8111 Fax: (3) 3746-8017
Tlx: 2426611

Medicus Intercon K.K.
Daiko Building, 3rd Fl.
2-5, Nishitenma 2-chome, Kita-ku
Osaka 530
Tel: (6) 362-0330 Fax: (6) 362-0338

Nippon Inc.
272 Chome, 17-2, Ginza, Chuo-ku
Tokyo 104
Tel: (3) 3545-7800 Fax: (3) 3544-0347

Saatchi & Saatchi Advertising
Akasaka Nine Park Building
9-2-16, Akasaka, Minato-ku
Tokyo 107
Tel: (3) 5410-8600 Fax: (3) 5410-8610

SEP (Soft, Event & Promotion) Planning, Inc.
Kinseisha Building
3-15, Kanda-Nishikicho, Chiyoda-ku
Tokyo 101
Tel: (3) 3233-6400

Tokyu Agency International Inc. DMB&B
Akasaka Dai-ichi Building
4-9-17, Akasaka, Minato-ku
Tokyo 107
Tel: (3) 3404-4411 Fax: (3) 3423-6047

LAW FIRMS

Japan Commercial Arbitration Association
6th Fl., Tokyo Kotsu Kaikan
10-1, Yuraku-cho, Chiyoda-ku
Tokyo 100
Tel: (3) 3214-0641/3 Fax: (3) 3201-1336

Japan Federation of Bar Associations
1-1-1 Kasumigaseki, Chiyoda-ku
Tokyo 100
Tel: (3) 3580-9841 Fax: (3) 3580-2866

Adachi, Henderson, Miyatake & Fujita (USA)
10th Fl., Time & Life Building
3-6, Otemachi 2-chome, Chiyoda-ku
Tokyo 100
Tel: (3) 3270-7461/5 Fax: (3) 3245-1534
Tlx: J28314

Aoki, Christensen & Nomoto
Suite 729, New Tokyo Building
3-1, Marunouchi 3-chome, Chiyoda-ku
CPO Box 2107
Tokyo
Tel: (3) 2118-8713 Fax: (3) 3213-2365 Tlx: J24809

Blakemore & Mitsuki
912 Iino Building
1-1, Uchisaiwaicho 2-chome, Chiyoda-ku
Tokyo
Tel: (3) 3503-5571 Fax: (3) 3503-4707
Tlx: J25296

Clifford Chance (UK)
6th Fl., South Hill Nagatacho Building
11-30, Nagatacho 1-chome, Chiyoda-ku
Tokyo 100
Tel: (3) 3581-4311 Fax: (3) 3593-0651
Tlx: 2425512 LEGIS J

Coudert Brothers (USA)
1355 West Tower, Aoyama Twin Towers
1-1-1, Minami-Aoyama, Minato-ku
Tokyo 107
Tel: (3) 423-0337 Fax: (3) 423-3550, 423-0929
Tlx: 02425523 CBLAW J

Denton, Hall, Burgin & Warrens
2nd Fl., Ichibancho 27 Building
Chiyoda-ku
Tokyo 102
Tel: (3) 3222-5977 Fax: (3) 3222-5980

Lovell, White, Durrant
Shin-Kasumigaseki Building, 20th Fl.
3-3-2 Kasumigaseki, Chiyoda-ku
Tokyo 100
Tel: (3) 3503-2571 Fax: (3) 3503-0699

McKenna & Co. (UK)
Toya Kaiji Building, No. 3, 7th Fl.
2-23-1, Nishi-shinbashi, Minato-ku
Tokyo 105
Tel: (3) 3578-0955 Fax: (3) 3578-0958 Tlx: J32589

Mitsui, Yasuda, Wani & Maeda
Nissei Ichibancho Building
23, Ichibancho, Chiyoda-ku
Tokyo 102
Tel: (3) 3221-7760 Fax: (3) 3221-7344
Tlx: J33276 MYWMTYO

Nishimura & Sanada
ARK Mori Building, 29th Fl.
12-32, Akasaka 1-chome, Minato-ku
Tokyo 107
Tel: (3) 5562-8500 Fax: (3) 5561-9711/4
Tlx: J27691 JURISTS

Oh-Ebashi Law Office
Suite 803, Umedashinmichi Building
1-5, Dojima 1-chome, Kita-ku
Osaka 530
Tel: (6) 341-0461 Fax: (6) 347-0688, 347-0698

Ohara & Kano
#902 City Coop
2-7, Minami-Morimachi, 2-chome, Kita-ku
Oskaka 530
Tel: (6) 313-1208 Fax: (6) 313-1209
Tlx: OKLOSAKA J64133

Richards Butler
Sunbridge Ogawamachi Building
2-2, Kanda-Ogawamachi, Chiyoda-ku
Tokyo 101
Tel: (3) 3292-2500 Fax: (3) 3292-2506
Tlx: J33232 RBLAW

Tokyo Aoyama Law Office (Baker & McKenzie)
410 Aoyama Building
2-3, Kita Aoyama 1-chome
Tokyo 107
Mailing Address: CPO Box 1576, Tokyo 100-91
Tel: (3) 3403-5281 Fax: (3) 3470-3152 Tlx: 28249

White & Case (USA)
American International Building
20-5, Ichibancho, Chiyoda-ku
Tokyo 102
Tel: (3) 3239-2350, 3239-2385 Fax: (3) 239-2385

TRANSLATORS & INTERPRETERS

AELS, Inc.
Shandorie Building, 3rd Fl.
5-25, Kitakawara-machi 1-chome
Sakai City, Osaka Pref. 590
Tel: (755) 21-3400 Fax: (755) 22-6953

Alpha Corporation
5-7, Hirakawacho 2-chome, Chiyoda-ku
Tokyo 102
Tel: (3) 3230-0090 Fax: (3) 3234-5336

Berlitz Translation Service (Tokyo)
Kowa Building 2BI
1-11-39 Akasaka, Minato-ku
Tokyo 107
Tel: (3) 3505-3356 Fax: (3) 3582-7393

All addresses and telephone numbers are in Japan unless otherwise noted. The country code for Japan is [81].

Berlitz Translation Service (Osaka)
Sakurabashi Niko Building 4th Fl.
4-7 Umeda, 2-chome, Kita-ku
Osaka
Tel: (6) 348-9531 Fax: (6) 348-9621

Best International, Inc.
Rm. 402, L'inmeuble Nogizaka
6-30, Akasaka 9-chome, Minato-ku
Tokyo 107
Tel: (3) 3423-4800 Fax: (3) 3423-4818

Business Associates, Inc.
1-2-9 Shinjuku, Shinjuku-ku
Tokyo
Tel: (3) 3225-1931 Fax: (3) 3294-0657

Convention Promoters Ltd.
3rd Fl., Imai Building
15-10, Nishi Nippori 5-chome, Arakawa-ku
Tokyo 116
Tel: (3) 3891-1541 Fax: (3) 3891-1543

Four C's Ltd.
6th Fl., 3-3-5, Kameari, Katsushika-ku
Tokyo 125
Tel: (3) 5680-2581 Fax: (3) 5680-2582

Idea Institute, Inc.
1-19-15, Ebisu, Shibuya-ku
Tokyo 150
Tel: (3) 3446-8660 Fax: (3) 3446-3134

IIJ Interpreting Translating Center
2nd Fl., Belair Gardens Building
2-11, Jingumae 4-chome, Shibuya-ku
Tokyo 150
Tel: (3) 3405-0754 Fax: (3) 3405-1082

International Transaction Center Ltd.
Kyobashi Y'sus Building
6-12, Kyobashi 1-chome, Chuo-ku
Tokyo 104
Tel: (3) 3561-7401 Fax: (3) 3561-7406

Japan Convention Services, Inc.
Nihon Press Center Building
2-1, Uchisaiwai-cho 2-chome, Chiyoda-ku
Tokyo 100
Tel: (3) 3508-1215 Fax: (3) 3508-0820

Japan Guide Assn.
Shin Kokusai Building
4-1, Marunouchi 3-chome, Chiyoda-ku
Tokyo 100
Tel: (3) 3213-2706

Japan Interpreters' Assn.
Chiyoda Seimei Building
5-20, Takadanobaba 1-chome, Shinjuku-ku
Tokyo 169
Tel: (3) 3209-4741 Fax: (3) 3209-0968

Japan Technical System Co. Ltd.
JTS Building
36-12, Eitai 2-chome, Koto-ku
Tokyo 135
Tel: (3) 3642-9911 Fax: (3) 3642-9920

Japan Translation Center Ltd.
1-21, Kanda Nishiki-cho, Chiyoda-ku
Tokyo 101
Tel: (3) 3291-0655 Fax: (3) 3294-0657

Kojima International Patent Office
Ikebukuro White-House Building, 4th Fl.
1-20-2, Higashi-Ikebukuro, Toshima-ku
Tokyo 170
Tel: (3) 3982-6881 Fax: (3) 3982-9802

Linguapower Service Division
Shibuya Kyowa Building
20-11, Shibuya 2-chome, Shibuya-ku
Tokyo 150
Tel: (3) 3498-5181

Management & Communications Consultancy
Keio Plaza
2-1, Nishi Shinjuku 2-chome, Shinjuku-ku
Tokyo 160
Tel: (3) 3349-1976 Fax: (3) 3349-8185

Manpower Japan Co. Ltd. (Osaka)
Midosuji Mitsui Building
1-3, Bingo-machi 4-chome, Chuo-ku
Osaka 541
Tel: (6) 222-6300

Manpower Japan Co. Ltd. (Fukuoka)
Hinode Tokyo Kaijo Building
12-20, Tenjin 1-chome, Chuo-ku
Fukuoka 810
Tel: (92) 741-9531

Manpower Japan Co. Ltd. (Nagoya)
Meiji Seimei Nagoya Building
1, Shin Sakae-machi 1-chome, Naka-ku
Nagoya 460
Tel: (52) 962-7771

NS International Inc.
Ichibankan Building, 7th Fl.
6-19, Ichibancho 1-chome, Aoba-ku
Sendai 980
Tel: (22) 261-3234 Fax: (22) 261-3235

Simul International, Inc.
Kowa Building, No. 9
8-10, Akasaka 1-chome, Minato-ku
Tokyo 107
Tel: (3) 3586-5641 Fax: (3) 3583-8336

Sinohara Corporation
No. 1-2-6-903, Ikeburkuro, Toshima-ku
Tokyo 170
Tel: (3) 3989-9891 Fax: (3) 3989-9510

Transtec, Inc.
20th Fl., Nagoya International Center Building
47-1, Nagono 1-chome, Nakamura-ku
Nagoya 450
Tel: (52) 571-5611 Fax: (52) 563-8669

TRANSPORTATION

AIRLINES

Aeroflot
Tokyo Tel: (3) 3434-9681

Air China
Tokyo Tel: (3) 3505-2021
Fukuoka Tel: (92) 472-6642
Osaka Tel: (6) 946-1702

Air France
Tokyo Tel: (3) 3475-1511
Nagoya Tel: (52) 551-4141
Osaka Tel: (6) 201-5161

Air India
Tokyo Tel: (3) 3214-7639
Osaka Tel: (6) 264-5911

Airlanka
Tokyo Tel: (3) 3573-4261
Fukuoka Tel: (92) 451-2855

Air New Zealand
Tokyo Tel: (120) 30-0747 (toll-free)
Nagoya Tel: (120) 30-0747 (toll-free)

Air Nippon
Tokyo Tel: (3) 3552-6311
Fukuoka Tel: (92) 411-2211

Air Pacific
Tokyo Tel: (3) 3593-7030

Alitalia
Tokyo Tel: (3) 3580-2181

All Nippon
Tokyo Tel: (3) 3272-1212
Fukuoka Tel: (92) 474-1212
Nagoya Tel: (52) 971-5588
Osaka Tel: (6) 372-1212

American
Tokyo Tel: (3) 3248-2011

AOM French Airlines
Tokyo Tel: (3) 3503-0751

Asiana Airlines
Tokyo Tel: (3) 5472-6600
Fukuoka Tel: (92) 411-8800
Nagoya Tel: (52) 937-3731

Austrian
Tokyo Tel: (3) 3582-2231

British Airways
Tokyo Tel: (3) 3593-8811
Fukuoka Tel: (92) 751-3830
Nagoya Tel: (52) 582-0631
Osaka Tel: (6) 347-0762

Canadian Airlines
Tokyo Tel: (3) 3281-7426
Nagoya Tel: (120) 04-8048 (toll-free)

Cathay Pacific
Tokyo Tel: (3) 3504-1531
Fukuoka Tel: (92) 441-1811
Nagoya Tel: (52) 962-6931
Osaka Tel: (6) 245-6731

China Airlines
Tokyo Tel: (3) 3436-1661
Fukuoka Tel: (92) 471-7788

China Eastern
Tokyo Tel: (3) 3505-2021
Fukuoka Tel: (92) 472-6642
Osaka Tel: (6) 946-1702

Continental
Tokyo Tel: (3) 3592-1631
Fukuoka Tel: (120) 24-2414 (toll-free)
Nagoya Tel: (120) 24-2414 (toll-free)

Delta
Tokyo Tel: (3) 5275-7000
Nagoya Tel: (120) 33-3742 (toll-free)

Egyptair
Tokyo Tel: (3) 3211-4521

Finnair
Tokyo Tel: (3) 3222-6801

Garuda Indonesia
Tokyo Tel: (3) 3593-1181
Fukuoka Tel: (92) 475-3577
Nagoya Tel: (52) 561-0901

Hawaiian Airlines
Fukuoka Tel: (120) 15-8012 (toll-free)

Iberia
Tokyo Tel: (3) 3582-3831

Iran Air
Tokyo Tel: (3) 3586-2101

Japan Airlines
Tokyo Tel: (3) 5489-1111
Fukuoka Tel: (92) 733-3111
Nagoya Tel: (52) 265-4141
Osaka Tel: (6) 203-1212

Japan Air System
Tokyo Tel: (3) 3432-6111
Fukuoka Tel: (92) 271-5111
Nagoya Tel: (52) 201-8111
Osaka Tel: (6) 243-8111

Japan Asia
Tokyo Tel: (3) 3455-7511
Osaka Tel: (6) 223-2222

KLM
Tokyo Tel: (3) 3216-0771

Korean Air
Tokyo Tel: (3) 3211-3311
Fukuoka Tel: (92) 441-3311
Nagoya Tel: (52) 586-3311
Osaka Tel: (6) 264-3311

All addresses and telephone numbers are in Japan unless otherwise noted. The country code for Japan is [81].

Lufthansa
Tokyo Tel: (3) 3580-2111
Nagoya Tel: (52) 561-2428
Osaka Tel: (6) 345-0231

Malaysia Airlines
Tokyo Tel: (3) 350-5961
Fukuoka Tel: (92) 733-6006
Nagoya Tel: (52) 561-3636

Northwest
Tokyo Tel: (3) 3533-6000
Fukuoka Tel: (92) 262-2772
Nagoya Tel: (52) 562-0867
Osaka Tel: (6) 228-0747

Olympic
Tokyo Tel: (3) 3201-0611

Pakistan International Airlines
Tokyo Tel: (3) 3216-6511

Philippine Airlines
Tokyo Tel: (3) 3580-1571

Qantas
Tokyo Tel: (3) 3593-7000
Fukuoka Tel: (120) 20-7020 (toll-free)
Nagoya Tel: (120) 20-7020 (toll-free)

Sabena Belgian World
Tokyo Tel: (3) 3585-6151

SAS
Tokyo Tel: (3) 3503-8101

Singapore Airlines
Tokyo Tel: (3) 3213-3431
Fukuoka Tel: (92) 481-7007
Nagoya Tel: (52) 252-8282
Osaka Tel: (6) 364-0881

Swissair
Tokyo Tel: (3) 3212-1016

Thai Airways
Tokyo Tel: (3) 3503-3311
Nagoya Tel: (52) 963-8585
Osaka Tel: (6) 202-5161

Turk Hava Yollari
Tokyo Tel: (3) 5251-1551

United
Tokyo Tel: (3) 3817-4411
Osaka Tel: (6) 271-5951

UTA
Tokyo Tel: (3) 3475-1511

Varig
Tokyo Tel: (3) 3211-6751
Nagoya Tel: (52) 565-1641

Virgin Atlantic
Tokyo Tel: (3) 3435-8330
Nagoya Tel: (52) 565-1641

TRANSPORTATION & CUSTOMS BROKERAGE FIRMS

Companies may offer more services in addition to those listed here. Service information is provided as a guideline and is not intended to be comprehensive.

All Nippon Airways
Yanmar Tokyo Building
2-1-1, Yaesu, Chuo-ku
Tokyo 104
Tel: (3) 3281-2158
Air cargo

Daiichi Chuo K.K.
Dowa Building
5-15, Nihonbashi 3-chome, Chuo-ku
Tokyo 103
Tel: (3) 3278-6800
Shipping

Dodwell-Kamigumi Aircargo Co. Ltd.
Takahashi Building
2-1-7, Nihonbashi Kayaba-cho, Chuo-ku
Tokyo 103
Tel: (3) 3667-2181
Air cargo

Evergreen International Corporation
Hakutsuru Building
5-12-5, Ginza, Chuo-ku
Tokyo 104
Tel: (3) 3546-6601 Fax: (3) 3546-6640
Shipping

Federal Express Japan K.K.
3-6, Honden 3-chome, Nishi-ku
Osaka 550
Tel: (6) 584-6565 Fax: (6) 584-6464
Air cargo, courier

Federal Express Japan K.K.
11-8, Hanhata 1-chome, Adachi-ku
Tokyo 121
Tel: (3) 3884-8281 Fax: (3) 3858-1646
Air cargo, courier

Federal Express Japan K.K.
3-1, Marunouchi 3-chome, Chiyoda-ku
Tokyo 100
Tel: (3) 3201-4320
Air cargo, courier

Federal Express Japan K.K.
3-10, Tatsumi, Koto-ku
Tokyo 135
Tel: (3) 3521-4300 Fax: (3) 3521-4941
Air cargo, courier

Hanjin Shipping Co. Ltd.
KAL Building
3-1-9 Honmachi, Chuo-ku
Osaka 541
Tel: (6) 263-2232 Fax: (6) 263-2230
Shipping

Japan Air Lines Co. Ltd.
Tokyo Building
2-7-3, Marunouchi, Chiyoda-ku
Tokyo 100
Tel: (3) 2842039 Fax: (3) 2843100
Air cargo

JAS Forwarding Co. Ltd.
Kayabacho K1 Building
3-14, Nihonbashi, Koami-cho, Chuo-ku
Tokyo 103
Tel: (3) 3661-5856 Fax: (3) 3667-3137
Freight forwarder

Kansai K.K.
Osaka Building
6-32, 3-chome, Nakanoshima, Kita-ku
Osaka 552
Tel: (6) 574-9171
Shipping

Maersk K.K.
4th Fl., Palace Building
1-1, Marunouchi 1-chome, Chiyoda-ku
Tokyo 100
Tel: (3) 3211-6359 Fax: (3) 3287-2478
Shipping, worldwide shipping agent

Maruzen Air Express International Ltd.
6-2-13 Akasaka, Minato-ku
Tokyo 107
Tel: (3) 3278-6611 Fax: (3) 3582-3041
Air cargo, freight forwarder

Mitsubishi Warehouse & Transportation Co. Ltd.
19-1, Nihombashi 1-chome, Chuo-ku
Tokyo 103
Tel: (3) 3278-6611 Fax: (3) 3278-6694
Customs broker, forwarding, transportation, warehousing

Mitsui-Soko Co. Ltd.
13-12, Nihombashi Kayaba-cho 1-chome
Chuo-ku
Tokyo 103
Tel: (3) 3667-5333 Fax: (3) 3699-5051
Air cargo agents customs broker, forwarding, shipping agent, transportation, warehousing

Nedlloyd Lines K.K.
12th Fl., Akasaka Twin Tower East Building
17-22, Akasaka 2-chome, Minato-ku
Tokyo 107
Tel: (3) 5563-0271 Fax: (3) 5563-0289
General agents for Nedlloyd Line and other Nedlloyd Group Companies

Nippon Cargo Airlines Corp.
Kasumigaseki Building
3-2-5 Kasumigaseki, Chiyoda-ku
Tel: (3) 3593-5000 Fax: (3) 3593-2629
Air cargo

Nippon Express Co. Ltd.
12-9, Sotokanda 3-chome, Chiyoda-ku
Tokyo 101
Tel: (3) 5294-5801 Fax: (3) 5294-5809
Air freight, marine and surface forwarding, customs broker, packing, shipping agency, warehousing

Nippon Yusen K.K.
3-2, Marunouchi 2-chome, Chiyoda-ku
Tokyo 100
Tel: (3) 3284-5151 Fax: (3) 3284-6371
Air, marine and surface transportation, freight forwarding, warehousing

Nissin Corp.
Keihin Building
84, Onoe-cho 6-chome, Naka-ku
Yokohama 231
Tel: (45) 671-6112 Fax: (45) 671-6118
Air cargo agency, customs broker, freight forwarding, marine transportation, packing, shipping

NYK Line
3-2, Marunouchi 3-chome, Chiyoda-ku
Tokyo 100
Tel: (3) 3284-5151
Shipping

Panalpina World Transport Ltd.
Sunshine Building, 8th Fl.
5-31-10 Shiba, Minato-ku
Tokyo 108
Tel: (3) 3451-7511 Fax: (3) 3453-6757
Freight forwarder

Purcei International Forwarding Japan Ltd.
Hamacho Ochiai Building
3-7-1, Nihonbashi, Hama-cho, Chuo-ku
Tel: (3) 3666-2161 Fax: (3) 3667-1027
Freight forwarding

Rinko Corp.
11-30, Bandai 5-chome, Niigata
Niigata 950
Tel: (25) 245-4113 Fax: (25) 245-1744
Customs broker, forwarding agent, land and marine transportation

Sagawa World Express Inc.
Kohnan Hirose Building
5-16, Kohnan 3-chome, Minato-ku
Tokyo 108
Tel: (3) 3470-4331 Fax: (3) 3740-4349
Customs agent, freight forwarder, international air cargo agent

Shibusawa Warehouse Co. Ltd.
13-16, Nihombashi Kayaba-cho 1-chome, Chuo-ku
Tokyo 103
Tel: (3) 3660-4040 Fax: (3) 3639-2176
Air freight service, customs broker, freight forwarding, land and sea transportation, warehousing

Showa Line Ltd.
Hibiya Kokusai Building
2-2-3, Uchisaiwai-cho, Chiyoda-ku
Tokyo 100
Tel: (3) 3581-8353 Fax: (3) 3581-8538
Shipping

Tatsumi Shokai Co. Ltd.
1-1, Chikko 4-chome, Minato-ku
Osaka 552
Tel: (6) 576-1821 Fax: (6) 576-1846
Air freight forwarder, customs broker, forwarding agents, harbor and land transportation, shipping agency, warehousing

---

All addresses and telephone numbers are in Japan unless otherwise noted. The country code for Japan is [81].

TNT Express Worldwide (Japan) Inc.
1-515, Tokugawa, Higashi-ku
Nagoya 461
Tel: (52) 937-4831 Fax: (52) 937-4796
Tlx: 2425506 TNTTYOJ
Air cargo, courier

TNT Express Worldwide (Japan) Inc.
PO Box 1090, New Tokyo Int'l Airport
No. 2 Cargo Agent Building, 1st Fl.
2091 Dainota, Aza, Komanin
Narita City, Chiba 282
Tel: (476) 32-6593 Fax: (476) 32-6340
Tlx: 2425506 TNTTYO J
Air cargo, courier

TNT Express Worldwide (Japan) Inc.
2-6-2, Hotarugaike-Nishimachi
Toyanaka City, Osaka 560
Tel: (6) 843-7562 Fax: (6) 843-5043
Tlx: 2425506 TNTTYO J
Air cargo, courier

TNT Express Worldwide (Japan) Inc.
Nagasaka Building
7-21, Higashi-Nihonbashi 1-chome, Chuo-ku
Tokyo 103
Tel: (3) 5821-3291 Fax: (3) 5821-3296
Tlx: 2425506 TNTTYP J
Air cargo, courier

TNT Express Worldwide (Japan) Inc. (Head Office)
No. 7, Koike Building, 4th Fl.
3-6, Minami-Shinagawa 2-chome
Shinagawa-ku
Tokyo 140
Tel: (3) 3740-4300 Fax: (3) 3740-4306
Tlx: 2425506 TNTTYOJ
Air cargo, courier

Unistar Air Cargo (UPS Yamato Co. Ltd.)
Customer Service Department
717-74 Futamata
Ichikawa City, Chiba
Tel: (473) 27-1040 Fax: (473) 28-3120
Air cargo, courier

Yamato Transport Co. Ltd.
16-10, Ginza 2-chome, Chuo-ku
Tokyo 104
Tel: (3) 3541-3411 Fax: (3) 3541-7579
*Air and sea freight forwarding, customs broker, land
transport, packaging, warehousing*

Yusen Air & Sea Service Co. Ltd.
30-1, Nihonbashi Hakozaki-cho, Chuo-ku
Tokyo 103
Tel: (3) 3669-4381 Fax: (3) 3669-8540
Air and sea freight forwarder, customs broker

MEDIA & INFORMATION SOURCES

All publications are in English unless otherwise noted.

DIRECTORIES & YEARBOOKS

Asia Pacific Leather Directory
(Annual)
Asia Pacific Leather Yearbook
(Annual)
Asia Pacific Directories Ltd.
6th Fl., Wah Hen Commercial Centre
381 Hennessy Rd.
Hong Kong
Tel: [852] 8936377 Fax: [852] 8935752

Asian Computer Directory
(Monthly)
Washington Plaza
1st Fl., 230 Wanchai Rd.
Wanchai, Hong Kong
Tel: [852] 8327123 Fax: [852] 8329208

Asian Printing Directory
(Annual)
Travel & Trade Publishing (Asia)
16th Fl., Capitol Centre
5-19 Jardines Bazaar
Causeway Bay, Hong Kong
Tel: [852] 8903067 Fax: [852] 8952378

Bankers Handbook For Asia
(Annual)
Dataline Asia Pacific Inc.
3rd Fl., Hollywood Center
233 Hollywood Road
Hong Kong
Tel: [852] 8155221 Fax: [852] 8542794

Diamond's Japan Business Directory
(Annual)
Diamond Lead Company Ltd.
4-2 Kasumigaseki 1-chome Chiyoda-ku
Tokyo 100
Tel: (3) 3504-6791 Fax: (3) 3504-6798

Directory of the Japanese Publishing Industry
(Biennial)
Publishers Association for Cultural Exchange
2-1, Saragaku-cho 1-chome, Chiyoda-ku
Tokyo 101
Tel: (3) 3233-3645

Guide to the Motor Industry of Japan
(Annual)
Japan Motor Industrial Federation Inc.
Otemachi Building
6-1 Otemachi, Chiyoda-ku
Tokyo 100
Tel: (3) 3216-5771

International Tax and Duty Free Buyers Index
(Annual)
Pearl & Dean Publishing Ltd.
9th Fl. Chung Nam Building
1 Lockhart Rd.
Hong Kong
Tel: [852] 8660395 Fax: [852] 2999810

Japan Aviation Directory
(Annual)
Wings Aviation Press Inc.
Kanda Kitamura Building
1302 Kanda Higashi Konya-cho
Tokyo 101
Tel: (3) 3258-0880 Fax: (3) 3258-5004

Japan Chemical Annual
(Annual)
Chemical Daily Company Ltd.
3-16-8, Nihonbashi Hama-cho, Chuo-ku
Tokyo 103
Tel: (3) 3663-7932 Fax: (3) 3663-2530

Japan Chemical Directory
(Annual)
Chemical Daily Company Ltd.
3-16-8, Nihonbashi Hama-cho, Chuo-ku
Tokyo 103
Tel: (3) 3663-7932 Fax: (3) 3663-2530

Japan Company Datafile
(Annual)
Toyo Keizai Inc.
1-2-1, Nihombashi Hongoku-cho, Chuo-ku
Tokyo 103
Tel: (3) 3246-5621 Fax: (3) 3241-5543

Japan Company Handbook
(Quarterly)
Toyo Keizai Inc.
1-2-1, Nihombashi Hongoku-cho, Chuo-ku
Tokyo 103
Tel: (3) 3246-5621 Fax: (3) 3241-5543

Japan Directory: Business & Society
(Annual)
Japan Press Ltd.
CPO Box 6
Tokyo 100-91
Tel: (03) 3404-5161 Fax: (3) 3423-2358

Japan Electronic Buyers' Guide
(Annual)
Dempa Publications Inc.
11-15, Higashi Gotanda 1-chome
Shinagawa-ku
Tokyo 141
Tel: (3) 3445-6111 Fax: (3) 3445-6101

Japanese Press
(Annual)
Nihon Shinbun Kyokai
Press Center Building, 7th Fl.
2-1, Uchisaiwai-cho 2-chome, Chiyoda-ku
Tokyo 100
Tel: (3) 3591-4401 Fax: (3) 3591-6149

Japan Graphic Arts
(Annual)
Intercontinental Marketing Corp.
PO Box 5056
Tokyo 100-31
Tel: (3) 3661-7458 Fax: (3) 3667-9646

All addresses and telephone numbers are in Japan unless otherwise noted. The country code for Japan is [81].

Japan Plastics Industry Annual
(Annual)
Plastics Age Company Ltd.
10-6, Kajicho 1-chome, Chiyoda-ku
Tokyo 101

Japan Trade Directory (Nihon Boeki Shinkokai)
(Annual)
JETRO Publication Department
2-5, Toranomon 2-chome, Minato-ku
Tokyo 105
Fax: (3) 3587-2485-

Statistical Yearbook of Ministry of Agriculture,
Forestry and Fisheries (Norin Suisansho Tokeihyo)
(Annual)
Norin Tokei Kyokai
c/o Otori Building
11-14, Meguro 2-chome, Meguro-ku
Tokyo 153
Tel: (3) 3492-2942

Textile Asia Index
(Annual)
Business Press Ltd.
30-32 d'Aguilar Street
Tak Yan Commercial Building, 11th Fl.
GPO 185
Central Hong Kong
Tel: [852] 5247441 Tlx: 60275 TEXIA HX

World Jewelogue
(Annual)
Headway International Publications Co.
907 Great Eagle Center
23 Harbour Rd.
Hong Kong
Tel: [852] 8275121 Fax: [852] 8277064

NEWSPAPERS

Asahi Evening News
8-5, Tsukiji 7-chome, Chuo-ku
Tokyo 104
Tel: (3) 3546-7181 Fax: (3) 3543-1660

Asahi Shimbun
(Japanese)
3-2, Tsukiji 5-chome, Chuo-ku
Tokyo 104-11
Tel: (3) 3545-0131 Fax: (3) 3545-0358

Asian Wall Street Journal
Dow Jones Publishing Co. (Asia)
2nd Fl. AIA Building
1 Stubbs Rd.
GPO Box 9825
Hong Kong
Tel: [852] 5737121 Fax: [852] 8345291

Daily Summary of Japanese Press
US Embassy Tokyo
Office of Translation Services
10-1, Akasaka 1-chome, Minato-ku
Tokyo 107
Tel: (3) 3224-5000 Fax: (3) 3581-0496
Tlx: 22118
*Translations and summaries of significant articles
appearing in leading Japanese newspapers.*

Daily Yomiuri
1-7-1, Ohtemachi, Chiyoda-ku
Tokyo 100-55
Tel: (3) 3242-1111

Industrial Daily News (Nikkan Kogyo Shimbun)
8-10, Kudan-kita 1-chome, Chiyoda-ku
Tokyo 102
Tel: (3) 3222-7111 Fax: (3) 3262-6031

International Herald Tribune
7th Fl. Malaysia Building
50 Gloucester Rd.
Wanchai, Hong Kong
Tel: [852] 8610616 Fax: [852] 8613073

Japan Maritime Daily (Nihon Kaiji Shimbun)
5-13-4, Shimbashi, Minato-ku
Tokyo 105
Tel: (3) 3436-3221

Japan Times
4-5-4, Shibaura, Minato-ku
Tokyo 108
Tel: (3) 3453-5312

Mainichi Daily News
1-1-1, Hitotsubashi, Chiyoda-ku
Tokyo 100
Tel: (3) 3212-0321

Nihon Keizai Shimbun
(Japanese)
1-9-5, Ohtemachi, Chiyoda-ku
Tokyo 100-66
Tel: (3) 3270-0251
*Leading financial daily. Weekly English-languange
version is Nikkei Weekly.*

Nihon Kogyo Shimbun
(Japanese)
1-7-2, Ohtemachi, Chiyoda-ku
Tokyo 100
Tel: (3) 3231-7111
A financial daily.

Nikkei Weekly
(Weekly)
Nihon Keizai Shimbun
1-9-5, Ohtemachi, Chiyoda-ku
Tokyo 100-66
Tel: (3) 3270-0251
English language edition of Nihon Keizai Shimbun

Sankei Shimbun
(Japanese)
1-7-2, Ohtemachi, Chiyoda-ku
Tokyo 100-77
Tel: (3) 3231-7111

Shipping and Trade News
Tokyo News Service Ltd.
Tsukiji Hamarikyu Building
3-3, Tsukiji 5-chome, Chuo-ku
Tokyo 104
Tel: (3) 3542-8521 Fax: (3) 3542-5086

Yomiuri Shimbun
(Japanese)
1-7-1, Ohtemachi, Chiyoda-ku
Tokyo 100-55
Tel: (3) 3242-1111 Fax: (3) 3246-0455

GENERAL BUSINESS AND
TRADE PERIODICALS

Asian Business
(Monthly)
Far East Trade Press Ltd.
2nd Fl., Kai Tak Commercial Building
317 Des Voeux Rd.
Central, Hong Kong
Tel: [852] 5457200 Fax: [852] 5446979

Asian Finance
(Monthly)
3rd Fl., Hollywood Center
233 Hollywood Rd.
Hong Kong
Tel: [852] 8155221 Fax: [852] 8504437

Asian Monetary Monitor
(Bimonthly)
GPO Box 12964
Hong Kong
Tel: [852] 8427200

Asiaweek
(Weekly)
Asiaweek Ltd.
199 Des Voeux Rd.
Central, Hong Kong
Tel: [852] 8155662 Fax: [852] 8155903

Business Week, Asia Edition
(Weekly)
2405 Dominion Centre
43-59 Queens Rd. East
Hong Kong
Tel: [852] 3361160 Fax: [852] 5294046

The Economist, Asia Edition
(Weekly)
The Economist Newspaper Ltd.
1329 Chater Rd.
Hong Kong
Tel: [852] 8681425

Far Eastern Economic Review
(Weekly)
Review Publishing Company Ltd.
6-7th Fl., 181-185 Gloucester Rd.
Hong Kong
Tel: [852] 8328381 Fax: [852] 8345571

Japan 21st
(Monthly)
Nihon Kogyo Shimbun
1-7-2, Ohtemachi, Chiyoda-ku
Tokyo 100
Tel: (3) 3231-7111 Fax: (3) 3295-3991

Japan Economic Institute (JEI) Report
(Weekly)
Japan Economic Institute of America
1000 Connecticut Ave NW, Suite 211
Washington, DC 20036, USA
Tel: [1] (202) 296-5633 Fax: [1] (202) 296-8333

Japanese Finance and Industry
(Quarterly)
Industrial Bank of Japan Ltd. (Nippon Kogyo
Ginko)
3-3, Marunouchi 1-chome, Chiyoda-ku
Tokyo 100
Tel: (3) 3214-1111 Tlx: 22325

Japan Journal
(Monthly)
Cross Cultural Communications, Inc.
MSD 15 Building, 3rd Fl.
3-7-4, Sendagaya, Shibuya-ku
Tokyo 151
International edition of Tokyo Journal

Japan Labor Bulletin
(Monthly)
Japan Institute of Labor
Chutaikin Building
7-6, Shibakoen 1-chome, Minato-ku
Tokyo

Japan Quarterly
(Quarterly)
Asahi Shimbun Publishing Co.
5-3-2, Tsukiji, Chuo-ku
Tokyo 103
Tel: (3) 3245-0131 Fax: (3) 3544-1428

Journal of Japanese Trade & Industry
(Bimonthly)
Maruzen Company Ltd.
3-10, Nihombashi, 2-chome, Chuo-ku
Tokyo 103
Tel: (3) 3272-7211 Fax: (3) 3274-3238

Journal of the American Chamber of Commerce
in Japan
(Monthly)
American Chamber of Commerce
No. 2 Fukide Building
1-21, Toranomon 4-chome, Minato-ku
Tokyo 105
Tel: (3) 3433-5381 Fax: (3) 3436-1446

Management Japan
(Semiannual)
International Management Association of Japan
No. 10 Mori Building
18-1, Toranomon 1-chome, Minato-ku
Tokyo 105
Tel: (3) 3502-3051

MERI's Circular
(Monthly)
Mitsubishi Economic Research Institute
3-3-1 Marunouchi Chiyoda-ku
Tokyo 100 Japan
Tel: (3) 3214-4416 Fax: (3) 3292-0410

Money Japan
(Monthly)
S.S. Communications, Inc.
Cosmo Hirakawacho Building
3-14, Hirakawa-cho 1-chome, Chiyoda-ku
Tokyo 102
Tel: (3) 5276-2140 Fax: (3) 5276-2149

All addresses and telephone numbers are in Japan unless otherwise noted. The country code for Japan is [81].

Newsweek International, Asia Edition
(Weekly)
Newsweek, Inc.
47th Fl., Bank of China Tower
1 Garden Road
Central, Hong Kong
Tel: [852] 8104555

Nikkei Business
(Weekly; Japanese)
Nikkei Business Publications, Inc.
2-7-6, Hirakawa-cho, Chiyoda-ku
Tokyo 101
Tel: (3) 5210-8502 Fax: (3) 5210-8119

Statistics Monthly
(Monthly)
Toyo Keizai Inc.
1-2-1, Nihonbashi Hongoku-cho, Chuo-ku
Tokyo 103
Tel: (3) 3246-5621 Fax: (3) 3241-5543

Time, Asia Edition
(Weekly)
Time, Inc.
31st Fl., East Tower, Bond Centre
89 Queensway
Hong Kong
Tel: [852] 8446660 Fax: [852] 5108799

Tokyo Business Today
(Monthly)
Toyo Kezai, Inc.
1-2-1 Nihonbashi Hongokucho, Chuo-ku
Tokyo 103
Tel: (3) 3246-5740 Fax: (3) 3241-5543

World Executives Digest
(Monthly)
3rd Fl. Garden Square Building
Greenbelt Drive Cor.
Legaspi Makati
Metro Manila, Phillipines
Tel: [63] (2) 8179126

INDUSTRY-SPECIFIC PERIODICALS

AEU: Journal of Asia Electronics Union
(Bimonthly)
Dempa Publications
1-11-15, Higashi Gotanda, Shinagawa-ku
Tokyo 141
Tel: (3) 3445-6111

AIDEA (Graphic Arts)
(Bimonthly)
Seibundo Shinkosha Publishing Company
1-13-7, Yayoi-cho, Nakano-ku
Tokyo
Tel: (3) 3373-7243 Fax: (3) 3373-7303

Asia Computer Weekly
(Bimonthly)
Asian Business Press Pte. Ltd.
100 Beach Rd., #26-00 Shaw Towers
Singapore 0718
Tel: [65] 2943366 Fax: [65] 2985534

Asia Labour Monitor
(Bimonthly)
Asia Monitor Resource Center
444-446 Nathan Road, 8th Fl., Flat B
Kowloon, Hong Kong
Tel: [852] 3321346

Asia Pacific Broadcasting & Telecommunications
(Monthly)
Asian Business Press Pte. Ltd.
100 Beach Rd.
#26-00 Shaw Towers
Singapore 0718
Tel: [65] 2943366 Fax: [65] 2985534

Asia-Pacific Dental News
(Quarterly)
Adrienne Yo Publishing Ltd.
4th Fl., Vogue Building
67 Wyndham Street
Central, Hong Kong
Tel: [852] 5253133 Fax: [852] 8106512

Asia Pacific Food Industry
(Monthly)
Asia Pacific Food Industry Publications
24 Peck Sea St., #03-00 Nehsons Building
Singapore 0207
Tel: [65] 2223422 Fax: [65] 2225587

Asia Pacific Food Industry Business Report
(Monthly)
Asia Pacific Food Industry Publications
24 Peck Sea St., #03-00 Nehsons Building
Singapore 0207
Tel: [65] 2223422 Fax: [65] 2225587

Asia Travel Guide
(Monthly)
Interasia Publications Ltd.
190 Middle Road, #11-01 Fortune Center
Singapore 0718
Tel: [65] 3397622 Fax: [65] 3398521

Asiamac Journal: The Machine-Building and Metal Working Journal for the Asia Pacific Region
(Quarterly)
Adsale Publishing Company
21st Fl., Tung Wai Commercial Building
109-111 Gloucester Road
Hong Kong
Tel: [852] 8920511 Fax: [852] 8384119, 8345014
Tlx: 63109 ADSAP HX

Asian Architect And Contractor
(Monthly)
Thomson Press Hong Kong Ltd.
Tai Sang Commercial Building, 19th Fl.
24-34 Hennessy Road
Hong Kong
Tel: [852] 5283351 Fax: [852] 8650825

Asian Aviation
(Monthly)
Asian Aviation Publications
2 Leng Kee Rd., #04-01 Thye Hong Centre
Singapore 0315
Tel: [65] 4747088 Fax: [65] 4796668

Asian Computer Monthly
(Monthly)
Computer Publications Ltd.
Washington Plaza, 1st Fl.
230 Wanchai Road
Wanchai, Hong Kong
Tel: [852] 9327123 Fax: [852] 8329208

Asian Defence Journal
(Monthly)
Syed Hussain Publications (Sdn)
61 A&B Jelan Dato, Haji Eusoff
Damai Complex
PO Box 10836
50726 Kuala Lumpur, Malaysia
Tel: [60] (3) 4420852 Fax: [60] (3) 4427840

Asian Electricity
(11 per year)
Reed Business Publishing Ltd.
5001 Beach Rd., #06-12 Golden Mile Complex
Singapore 0719
Tel: [65] 2913188 Fax: [65] 2913180

Asian Electronics Engineer
(Monthly)
Trade Media Ltd.
29 Wong Chuck Hang Road
Hong Kong
Tel: [852] 5554777 Fax: [852] 8700816

Asian Hospital
(Quarterly)
Techni-Press Asia Ltd.
PO Box 20494
Hennessy Road
Hong Kong
Tel: [852] 5278682 Fax: [852] 5278399

Asian Hotel & Catering Times
(Bimonthly)
Thomson Press (HK)
19th Fl., Tai Sang Commercial Building
23-34 Hennessy Rd.
Hong Kong
Tel: [852] 5283351 Fax: [852] 8650825

Asian Manufacturing
Far East Trade Press Ltd.
2nd Fl., Kai Tak Commercial Building
317 Des Voeux Road
Central, Hong Kong
Tel: [852] 5453028 Fax: [852] 5446979

Asian Medical News
(Bimonthly)
MediMedia Pacific Ltd.
Unit 1216, Seaview Estate
2-8 Watson Rd.
North Point, Hong Kong
Tel: [852] 5700708 Fax: [852] 5705076

Asian Meetings & Incentives
(Monthly)
Travel & Trade Publishing (Asia)
16th Fl., Capitol Centre
5-19 Jardines Bazaar
Causeway Bay, Hong Kong
Tel: [852] 8903067 Fax: [852] 8952378

Asian Oil & Gas
(Monthly)
Intercontinental Marketing Corp.
PO Box 5056
Tokyo 100-31
Fax: (3) 3667-9646

Asian Plastic News
(Quarterly)
Reed Asian Publishing Pte. Ltd.
5001 Beach Rd.
#06-12 Golden Mile Complex
Singapore 0719
Tel: [65] 2913188 Fax: [65] 2913180

Asian Printing: The Magazine for the Graphic Arts
Industry
(Monthly)
Travel & Trade Publishing (Asia)
16th Fl., Capitol Centre
5-19 Jardines Bazaar
Causeway Bay, Hong Kong
Tel: [852] 8903067 Fax: [852] 8952378

Asian Security & Safety Journal
(Bimonthly)
Elgin Consultants Ltd.
Tungnam Building
Suite 5D, 475 Hennessy Rd.
Causeway Bay, Hong Kong
Tel: [852] 5724427 Fax: [852] 5725731

Asian Shipping
(Monthly)
Asia Trade Journals Ltd.
7th Fl., Sincere Insurance Building
4 Hennessy Road
Wanchai, Hong Kong
Tel: [852] 5278532 Fax: [852] 5278753

Asian Sources: Computer Products
Asian Sources: Electronic Components
Asian Sources: Gifts & Home Products
Asian Sources: Hardware
Asian Sources: Timepieces
(Monthly)
Asian Sources Media Group
22nd Fl., Vita Tower
29 Wong Chuk Hang Road
Wong Chuk Hang, Hong Kong
Tel: [852] 5554777 Fax: [852] 8730488

Asian Water & Sewage
(Quarterly)
Techni-Press Asia Ltd.
PO Box 20494, Hennessy Rd.
Hong Kong
Fax: [852] 5278399

Asiatechnology
(Monthly)
Review Publishing Company Ltd.
6-7th Fl., 181-185 Gloucester Rd.
GPO Box 160
Hong Kong
Tel: [852] 8328381 Fax: [852] 8345571

ATA Journal: Journal for Asia on Textile & Apparel
(Bimonthly)
Adsale Publishing Company
Tung Wai Commercial Building, 21st Fl.
109-111 Gloucester Rd.
Wanchai, Hong Kong
Tel: [852] 8920511 Fax: [852] 8384119

Building & Construction News
(Weekly)
Al Hilal Publishing (FE) Ltd.
50 Jalan Sultan, #20-06, Jalan Sultan Centre
Singapore 0719
Tel: [65] 2939233 Fax: [65] 2970862

Business Traveller Asia-Pacific
(Monthly)
Interasia Publications
200 Lockhart Rd., 13th Fl.
Wanchai, Hong Kong
Tel: [852] 5749317 Fax: [852] 5726846

Cargo Clan
(Quarterly)
Emphais (HK) Ltd.
10th Fl., Wilson House
19-27 Wyndham St.
Central, Hong Kong
Tel: [852] 5215392 Fax: [852] 8106738

Cargonews Asia
(Bimonthly)
Far East Trade Press Ltd.
2nd Fl., Kai Tak Commercial Building
317 Des Voeux Road
Central, Hong Kong
Tel: [852] 5453028 Fax: [852] 5446979

Catering & Hotel News, International
(Biweekly)
Al Hilal Publishing (FE) Ltd.
50 Jalan Sultan, #20-26, Jalan Sultan Centre
Singapore 0719
Tel: [852] 2939233 Fax: [852] 2970862

Chemical Industry
(Monthly)
Maruzen Company Ltd.
3-10, Nihonbashi 2-chome, Chuo-ku
Tokyo 103
Tel: (3) 3272-7211 Fax: (3) 3274-3238

Electronic Business Asia
(Monthly)
Cahners Publishing Company
275 Washington St.
Newton, MA 02158, USA
Tel: [1] (617) 964-3030 Fax: [1] (617) 558-4506

Energy Asia
(Monthly)
Petroleum News Southeast Asia Ltd.
6th Fl., 146 Prince Edward Road W
Kowloon, Hong Kong
Tel: [852] 3805294 Fax: [852] 3970959

Far East Health
(10 per year)
Update-Siebert Publications
Reed Asian Publishing Pte
5001 Beach Rd.
#06-12 Golden Mile Complex
Singapore 0719
Tel: [65] 2913188 Fax: [65] 2913180

Farming Japan
(Bimonthly)
Maruzen Company Ltd.
3-10, Nihonbashi 2-chome, Chuo-ku
Tokyo 103
Tel: (3) 3272-7211 Fax: (3) 3274-3238

Fashion Accessories
(Monthly)
Asian Sources Media Group
22nd Fl., Vita Tower
29 Wong Chuk Hang Road
Wong Chuk Hang, Hong Kong
Tel: [852] 5554777 Fax: [852] 8730488

Food Industry (Shokuhin Kogyo)
(Semimonthly; Japanese)
Korin Publishing Co.
PO Box 41, Shitaya
Tokyo 110-91

Gateux/Gatou
(Monthly; Japanese)
Federation of Japan Confectionery Associations
10-26, Ebisu 1-chome, Shibuya-ku
Tokyo 150
Tel: (3) 3444-8711 Fax: (3) 3444-8935

International Construction
(Monthly)
Reed Business Publishing Ltd.
Reed Asian Publishing Pte.
5001 Beach Rd.
#06-12 Golden Mile Complex
Singapore 0719
Tel: [65] 2913188 Fax: [65] 2913180

Japan Chemical Week
(Weekly)
Chemical Daily Company Ltd.
3-16-8, Nihonbashi, Hama-cho, Chuo-ku
Tokyo 103
Tel: (3) 3663-7932 Fax: (3) 3663-2530

Japan Petroleum & Energy Trends
(Biweekly)
Japan Petroleum & Energy Consultants Ltd.
CPO Box 1185
Tokyo 100-91
Tel: (4) 7573-1931 Fax: (4) 7573-1934

Japan Plastics Age
(Monthly)
Plastics Age Company Ltd.
10-6, Kajicho 1-chome, Chiyoda-ku
Tokyo 101

All publications are in English unless otherwise noted.

Japan Spinners' Association Monthly Report
(Nihon Boseki Geppo) (Monthly; Japanese)
Japan Institute of Cotton Textile Technology
and Economy
Mengyo Kaikan
5-8, 2-chome, Bingo-machi, Chuo-ku
Osaka
Tel: (6) 203-5161 Fax: (6) 229-1590

JEI, Journal Of The Electronics Industry
(Monthly)
Dempa Publications, Inc.
1-11-15, Higashi Gotanda, Shinagawa-ku
Tokyo 141
Tel: (3) 3445-6111

Jewellery News Asia
(Monthly)
Jewellery News Asia Ltd.
Rooms 601-603, Guardian House
32 Oi Kwan Road
Wanchai, Hong Kong
Tel: [852] 8322011 Fax: [852] 8329208

Journal of Electronic Engineering
Dempa Publications, Inc.
1-11-15, Higashi Gotanda, Shinagawa-ku
Tokyo 141
Tel: (3) 3445-6111

Journal of the Fuel Society of Japan (Nenryo
Kyokaishi)
(Monthly; Japanese, summaries in English)
Maruzen Company Ltd.
3-10, Nihonbashi 2-chome, Chuo-ku
Tokyo 103
Tel: (3) 3272-7211 Fax: (3) 3274-3238

Journal of the Marine Engineering Society in Japan
(Nihon Hakuyo Kikan Gakkai Shi)
(Monthly; Japanese, summaries in English)
Nihon Hakuyo Kikan Gakkai
c/o Osaoa Building
2-Gokan Chiyoda-ku, 2-2 Uchisaiwaicho 1
Tokyo
Tel: (3) 3503-5518

Journal of the Mining and Metallurgical
Institute of Japan
(Monthly; Japanese, summaries in English)
Maruzen Company Ltd.
3-10, Nihonbashi 2-chome, Chuo-ku
Tokyo 103
Tel: (3) 3272-7211 Fax: (3) 3274-3238

Journal of the Textile Machinery Society of Japan
(Monthly)
Textile Machinery Society of Japan
Osaka Science & Technology Building
Utsubo Koen
8-4, Utsubo Hon-machi 1-chome, Nishi-ku
Osaka 550
Tel: (6) 443-4691

JSAE Review
(Quarterly)
Society of Automotive Engineers of Japan
10-2, Goban-cho, Chiyoda-ku
Tokyo 102
Tel: (3) 3262-8211 Fax: (3) 3261-2204

JSN International (Textiles)
(Monthly)
JSN International Inc.
4-9 Lidabashi 4-chome, Chiyoda-ku
Tokyo 102
Tel: (3) 3265-6488 Fax: (3) 3263-9078

Law in Japan
(Annual)
University of Tokyo Press
7-3-1, Hongo, Bunkyo-ku
Tokyo 131
Tel: (3) 3811-0964 Fax: (3) 3812-6958

Lloyd's Maritime Asia
(Monthly)
Lloyd's of London Press (FE)
Rm. 1101 Hollywood Centre
233 Hollywood Road
Hong Kong
Tel: [852] 8543222 Fax: [852] 8541538

Media: Asia's Media and Marketing Newspaper
(Biweekly)
Media & Marketing Ltd.
1002 McDonald's Building
46-54 Yee Wo St.
Causeway Bay, Hong Kong
Tel: [852] 5772628 Fax: [852] 5769171

Medicine Digest Asia
(Monthly)
Rm. 1903, Tung Sun Commercial Centre
194-200 Lockhart Rd.
Wanchai, Hong Kong
Tel: [852] 8939303 Fax: [852] 8912591

Metalworking Engineering and Marketing
(Bimonthly)
News Digest Publishing Company Ltd.
Editorial and Business Office
3-5-3 Uchiyama, Chikusa-ku
Nagoya 464

OEP: Office Equipment & Products
(Monthly)
Dempa Publications
1-11-15, Higashi Gotanda, Shinagawa-ku
Tokyo 141
Tel: (3) 3445-6111

Oil & Gas News
(Weekly)
Al Hilal Publishing (FE) Ltd.
50 Jalan Sultan, #20-06, Jalan Sultan Centre
Singapore 0719
Tel: [65] 2939233 Fax: [65] 2970862

Packaging Japan
(Bimonthly)
Nippo Company Ltd
3-1-5 Misaki-cho, Chiyoda-ku
Tokyo 101
Fax: (3) 3263-2560

Petroleum News, Asia's Energy Journal
(Monthly)
Petroleum News Southeast Asia Ltd.
6th Fl., 146 Prince Edward Road West
Kowloon, Hong Kong
Tel: [852] 3805294 Fax: [852] 3970959

Science & Technology in Japan
(Quarterly)
Three "I" Publications
Yamaguchi Building
5-16, Uchikanda 1-chome, Chiyoda-ku
Tokyo 101
Tel: (3) 3291-3161 Fax: (3) 3291-3764

Shipping & Transport News
(Monthly)
Al Hilal Publishing (FE) Ltd.
50 Jalan Sultan, #20-06, Jalan Sultan Centre
Singapore 0719
Tel: [65] 2939233 Fax: [65] 2970862

Telecom Asia
(Bimonthly)
CCI Asia-Pacific (HK)
Suite 905, Guardian House
32 Oi Kwan Road
Wanchai, Hong Kong
Tel: [852] 8332181 Fax: [852] 8345620

Textile Asia: The Asian Textile and Apparel
Monthly
(Monthly)
Business Press Ltd.
11th Fl., California Tower
30-32 d'Aguilar Street
Central, Hong Kong
Tel: [852] 5247467 Fax: [852] 8106966

Travel News Asia
(Bimonthly)
Far East Trade Press Ltd.
2nd Fl. Kai Tak Commercial Building
317 Des Voeux Road
Central, Hong Kong
Tel: [852] 5453028 Fax: [852] 5446979

What's New in Computing
(Monthly)
Asian Business Press Pte. Ltd.
100 Beach Rd., #26-00 Shaw Towers
Singapore 0718
Tel: [65] 2943366 Fax: [65] 2985534

RADIO & TELEVISION STATIONS

Asahi National Broadcasting Co. Ltd.
1-1, Roppongi 1-chome, Minato-ku
Tokyo 106
Tel: (3) 3587-5111 Fax: (3) 3505-3539

Fuji Television Network
3-1, Kawada-cho, Shinjuku-ku
Tokyo 162-88
Tel: (3) 3353-1111 Fax: (3) 3358-8038

Japan Broadcasting Corp. (NHK)
2-1, Jinnan 2-chome, Shibuya-ku
Tokyo 150
Tel: (3) 3465-1111 Fax: (3) 3481-1576

National Association of Commercial Broadcasters
3-23, Kioi-cho, Chiyoda-ku
Tokyo 102
Tel: (3) 3265-7481 Fax: (3) 3261-2860

Yomuri Telecasting Corp.
2-33, Shiromi 2-chome, Chuo-ku
Osaka 540-10
Tel: (6) 947-2298

LIBRARIES

Japanese Standards Association Library
4-1-24 Akasaka, Minato-ku
Tokyo 107
Tel: (3) 3583-8001

Kyushu University Library
(Kyushu Daigaku Toshokan)
6-10-1 Hakozaki Higashi-ku
Fukuoka 812
Tel: (92) 641-1101

Ministry of International Trade and Industry
Library
1-3-1, Kasumigaseki, Chiyoda-ku
Tokyo 100
Tel: (3) 3501-1511

National Diet Library
(Kokuritsu Kokkai Toshokan)
1-1-10, Nagatacho, Chiyoda-ku
Tokyo 100
Tel: (3) 3581-2331

Osaka University Library
(Osaka Daigaku Toshokan)
1-1, Machikaneyama-cho, Toyonaka
Osaka 560
Tel: (6) 844-1151

University of Tokyo Library
(Tokyo Daigaku Toshokan)
7-3-1, Hongo, Bunkyo-ku
Tokyo 113
Tel: (3) 3812-2111

Waseda University Library
(Waseda Daigaku Toshokan)
1-6-1, Nishi-Waseda, Shinjuku-ku
Tokyo 160
Tel: (3) 3203-4141

All publications are in English unless otherwise noted.

Index

F

I

M

T

Y